Family, Community, & Disability

Series Editors:
George H.S. Singer
Ann P. Turnbull
H. Rutherford Turnbull, III
Larry K. Irvin
Laurie E. Powers

Redefining Family Support

Also available in the Family,
Community, & Disability series:

Children with Acquired Brain Injury:
Educating and Supporting Families
edited by George H.S. Singer, Ph.D.,
Ann Glang, Ph.D., and Janet M. Williams, Ph.D.

Family,
Community,
&Disability

Redefining
Family Support

Innovations in Public–Private Partnerships

Edited by

George H.S. Singer, Ph.D.
Hood Center for Family Support
Dartmouth Medical School
Lebanon, New Hampshire

Laurie E. Powers, Ph.D.
Hood Center for Family Support
Dartmouth Medical School
Lebanon, New Hampshire

and

Ardis L. Olson, M.D.
Dartmouth Medical School
Lebanon, New Hampshire

·P A U L·H·
BROOKES
PUBLISHING C°

Baltimore • London • Toronto • Sydney

Paul H. Brookes Publishing Co.
Post Office Box 10624
Baltimore, Maryland 21285-0624

Copyright © 1996 by Paul H. Brookes Publishing Co., Inc.
All rights reserved.

Typeset by PRO-Image Corporation, Techna-Type Division, York, Pennsylvania.
Manufactured in the United States of America by
Vail-Ballou Press, Binghamton, New York.

The case studies and examples used in the text are based on real individuals with disabilities. Identifying information has been changed to protect confidentiality; in some cases, individual stories have been combined or slightly altered to produce a stronger illustration.

Permission to reprint the information on the following pages is gratefully acknowledged:
Page 119
Numbered list from S. Kagan, D. Powell, B. Weissbourd, & E. Zigler (Eds.), *America's family support programs.* New Haven, CT: Yale University Press; copyright © 1987. Reprinted by permission.
Page 298
Numbered list from Stroul, B.A., & Friedman, R.M. (1986). *A system of care for severely emotionally disturbed children and youth.* Washington, DC: CASSP Technical Assistance Center, Center for Child Health and Mental Health Policy, Georgetown University Child Development Center; reprinted by permission.

Library of Congress Cataloging-in-Publication Data

Redefining family support : innovations in public–private partnerships
edited by George H.S. Singer, Laurie E. Powers, and Ardis L. Olson.
p.   cm.—(Family, community, and disability ; v. 1)
Includes bibliographical references and index.
ISBN 1-55766-217-7
1. Handicapped—Home care—United States.   2. Handicapped—United States—Family relationships.   3. Caregivers—United States—Psychology.   I. Singer, George H.S.   II. Powers, Laurie E.
III. Olson, Ardis L.   IV. Series.
HV1553.R43   1996
362.4'048—dc20   95-13026
                                                  CIP

British Library Cataloguing-in-Publication data are available from the British Library.

Contents

Series Preface

The purpose of the *Family, Community, & Disability* series is to provide a forum for contemporary work on the challenges and issues that families face, as well as effective ways of supporting families as they fulfill their roles in the lives of people with disabilities. The authors for each volume strive to create a vehicle for making state-of-the-art theory, research, and practice readily accessible to a diverse audience.

In the United States, the institution of the family has undergone revolutionary changes during the last half of the 20th century. Fundamental changes have taken place, increasing the rates of women's employment outside of the home, the prevalence of divorce and remarriage, and the numbers of single and never-married mothers, as well as in the traditional roles of men and women in homes and geographic mobility. Demographic changes, including the rapid growth of non-European ethnic populations and the burgeoning numbers of older adults, also contribute to the transformation of U.S. families. At the same time as these trends are evident, the percentage of people with long-term disabilities has grown dramatically—a trend that will continue during the first quarter of the 21st century. Families are the primary source of day-to-day assistance for people with disabilities. They are crucial to the quality of life for people with developmental disabilities, chronic illnesses, mental illnesses, and disabilities associated with aging.

Much progress has been made in recognizing the key roles of families in early intervention, education, transitions to adulthood, and supported living for people with disabilities. However, the knowledge base about practical ways to strengthen and support families in their multiple roles is still in a nascent stage. Theories of family change, adaptation, and life-span development need to be tested against the phenomena of modern family life. Ethical and social policy issues need to be articulated and analyzed. And, perhaps most important, effective ways of supporting families need to be tested and disseminated. We will endeavor to address these topics in this series.

No single discipline has a primary claim to the field of family and disability studies and much is to be gained by the cross-fertilization of ideas from many traditions, including psychology, history, anthropology, education, sociology, economics, medicine, law, and philosophy. It is also essential that the voices of family members and people with disabilities be heard in this forum.

We hope to address a number of essential topics in this series, including social support, the changing roles of fathers and mothers, the training of family support workers, the demonstration and evaluation of family support models, the roles of various community institutions in assisting families, the implications of ethnic diversity for family policy and practices, the role of self-help and advocacy, and the prevention and treatment of family dysfunction, to name but a few.

An inherent goal of this series is to enhance the long-term development of the field of family and disability studies in such a way that families will benefit from new programs and practices that are informed by an emerging body of knowledge.

Editorial Advisory Board

Foreword

R*edefining Family Support* brings together a range of topics and experiences that focus on supports to families of children with disabilities and other special needs. The family support movement has been gathering strength as state after state has developed policies that acknowledge the lifelong role of the family in caring for members with disabilities and other special needs. National disability policy has also been moving slowly but steadily toward a more family-centered and family-guided approach in the design and implementation of supports to individuals with special needs.

I believe that the notion of having policy and services directed by and supportive of the needs of participating families is an especially powerful one. It provides us with a core concept on which we can structure and guide new ways of providing and coordinating services and supports that are responsive, flexible, and effective. Policy is beginning to underscore and acknowledge what parents have been telling us for years—that they are at the center of a child's network of supports and the focal point for the coordination of services. It is my hope that by building ways of directly supporting families in a range of policy, legislative, and programmatic initiatives, we may increasingly move the United States toward strengthening families' natural resources.

In the 103rd Congress we enunciated a series of principles for family support efforts that we hope will help guide future national, state, and local efforts. The Families of Children with Disabilities Support Act of 1994, which I sponsored, adds a new part to the Individuals with Disabilities Education Act. Its principles will help move services for families with a member with a disability toward a new partnership that builds on families' strengths and incorporates their dreams and preferences for support.

The overarching principles embodied in the legislation state the following:

- Family support for families of children with disabilities must focus on the needs of the entire family.
- Families should be supported in determining their own needs and in making decisions concerning necessary, desirable, and appropriate services.
- Families should play decision-making roles in policies and programs that affect their lives.
- Family needs change over time, and family support for families of children with disabilities must be flexible and respond to the unique needs, strengths, and cultural values of the family.
- Family support for families of children with disabilities is proactive, not solely in response to a crisis.
- Families should be supported in promoting the integration and inclusion of their children with disabilities into the community.

- Family support for families of children with disabilities should promote the use of existing social networks, strengthen natural resources of support, and help build connections to existing community resources.
- Services and support must be provided in a manner that demonstrates respect for individual dignity, personal responsibility, self-determination, personal preferences, and cultural differences.

Policy and practice that are guided by these principles will help transform current systems—many of which now foster dependence, separation, and paternalism—into systems that foster inclusion, independence, and empowerment for families who provide care to relatives challenged by a disability. These principles can also serve as an effective vehicle for strengthening overall efforts to meet the needs of all children in the United States and set forth a template for providing needed services to families in a manner that treats them with dignity and respect.

I believe that this book can significantly further the work initiated by scores of parents, providers, agency administrators, and law makers across the United States. It can help deepen the understanding of family support principles and expand discussions of application and implementation. I am also particularly pleased by the breadth of chapters contained in the book. They provide a careful and extensive discussion of family support practices, the contexts in which they can be implemented, and the results that can be expected. This type of scholarship can clearly help to move policy closer to recognizing and addressing the needs of families who have a member with disabilities or other special needs and help to structure practice so that it is more family centered and family directed. I applaud the authors for their timely analysis of such an important aspect of human services policy and look forward to the continuing dialogue that I know their work will energize.

Tom Harkin
U.S. Senator
Washington, D.C.
October 1995

Contributors

Reva I. Allen, M.A., ACSW
Beach Center on Families and Disability and
 School of Social Welfare
University of Kansas
Lawrence, Kansas 66045

Tanya Baker-McCue
Parents Reaching Out
1000 A Main Street
Los Lunas, New Mexico 87031

Patricia A. Barber, Ph.D.
Research Associate
Schiefelbusch Institute for Life Span Studies
1052 Dole Human Development Center
University of Kansas
Lawrence, Kansas 66045

Deborah Bass, M.S.W.
President
Deborah Bass Associates
7092 Kings Arm Drive
Manassas, Virginia 22111

Allan I. Bergman
Deputy Director, Community Services Division
Director, State–Federal Relations
United Cerebral Palsy Associations, Inc.
1660 L Street, NW
Suite 700
Washington, D.C. 20036-5602

Bruce Blaney, M.A.
Senior Research Assistant
Human Services Research Institute
2336 Massachusetts Avenue
Cambridge, Massachusetts 02140

Valerie J. Bradley
President
Human Services Research Institute
2336 Massachusetts Avenue
Cambridge, Massachusetts 02140

Robert W. Chamberlin, M.D., M.P.H.
Adjunct Professor
Department of Pediatrics
Dartmouth Medical School
Adjunct Professor
School of Health and Human Services
University of New Hampshire
Canterbury, New Hampshire 03224

Chris C. Clatterbuck, M.S.Ed.
Beach Center on Families and Disability
University of Kansas
Lawrence, Kansas 66045

W. Carl Cooley, M.D.
Assistant Professor of Pediatrics
Dartmouth Center for Genetics and Child
 Development
Dartmouth Medical School
One Medical Center Drive
Lebanon, New Hampshire 03756

Barbara J. Friesen, Ph.D.
Director
Research and Training Center on Family
 Support and Children's Mental Health
Graduate School of Social Work
Portland State University
Portland, Oregon 97207-0751

Janet A. Garlow
2415 Harvard Road
Lawrence, Kansas 66049

Theresa M. Jones
Beach Center on Families and Disability
Bureau of Child Research
4138 Haworth Hall
University of Kansas
Lawrence, Kansas 66045

Steve Kairys, M.D.
Dartmouth-Hitchcock Medical Center
One Medical Center Drive
Lebanon, New Hampshire 03756-0001

Naomi Karp
Consulting Services
2823 North Yucatan Street
Arlington, Virginia 22213

Jeannie Kleinhammer-Tramill, Ph.D.
University Affiliated Program
1052 Dole Human Development Center
University of Kansas
Lawrence, Kansas 66045

James A. Knoll, Ph.D.
Department of Elementary, Reading, and
  Special Education
401 Ginger Hall
Morehead State University
Morehead, Kentucky 40351

M. Powell Lawton, Ph.D.
Senior Research Scientist
Polisher Research Institute
Philadelphia Geriatric Center
5301 Old York Road
Philadelphia, Pennsylvania 19141

Bruce L. Mallory, Ph.D.
Department of Education
University of New Hampshire
Durham, New Hampshire 03824

Brenda K. Oas, M.Ed.
Department of Public Instruction
600 East Boulevard
Bismarck, North Dakota 58505-0440

Ardis L. Olson, M.D.
Associate Professor of Pediatrics
Dartmouth Medical School
One Medical Center Drive
Lebanon, New Hampshire 03756

Christopher G. Petr, M.S.W., Ph.D.
School of Social Welfare and Beach Center on
  Families and Disability
University of Kansas
Lawrence, Kansas 66045

Laurie E. Powers, Ph.D.
Associate Director
Hood Center for Family Support
Dartmouth-Hitchcock Medical Center
Assistant Professor of Pediatrics and
  Adolescent Medicine
Dartmouth Medical School
One Medical Center Drive
Lebanon, New Hampshire 03756-0001

Wayne Sailor, Ph.D.
Director
Lawrence Campus
University Affiliated Program
1052 Dole Human Development Center
University of Kansas
Lawrence, Kansas 66045

George H.S. Singer, Ph.D.
Director
Hood Center for Family Support
Dartmouth-Hitchcock Medical Center
Associate Professor of Pediatrics
Dartmouth Medical School
One Medical Center Drive
Lebanon, New Hampshire 03756-0001

Thomas Skrtic, Ph.D.
Department of Special Education
3001 Dole Human Development Center
University of Kansas
Lawrence, Kansas 66045

H. Rutherford Turnbull, III, LL.B., LL.M.
Beach Center on Families and Disability
Life Span Institute
3111 Haworth Hall
University of Kansas
Lawrence, Kansas 66045

Janet M. Williams, M.S.W.
Research and Training Center on
  Independent Living
4089 Dole Human Development Center
University of Kansas
Lawrence, Kansas 66045

Karen Witkin
Parent to Parent of Vermont
58 West Street
Essex Junction, Vermont 05452

Susan Yuan, Ph.D.
University Affiliated Program of Vermont
499C Waterman Building
University of Vermont
Burlington, Vermont 05405

Volume Preface

Now thinking has begun to influence social policy regarding families in the United States. As the strains of contemporary family life have grown, many concerned people have begun to argue that our society needs to create new social institutions to support the family. Families most vulnerable to these stresses are those whose members require extra assistance to live typical lives in the community. They include young children, people with disabilities and ongoing health conditions, and frail older adults. When given sufficient community support, most families can take care of their own members who require assistance or accommodations. However, without this support, the strains of family home caregiving can overload even families with the most advantages.

It is clear that our traditional approaches to helping families are both inadequate and inappropriate to meet the needs of family home caregivers. In the past, most family services have been created as part of our frayed safety net for the poor and have often been excessively bureaucratic or oriented toward family pathology. If we are truly to tackle the task of bolstering families so that they can care for their vulnerable members, we need a very different approach.

Some of the principles underlying a new approach to family support are already being tested in model programs around the United States. When taken together, these new—and often disparate—efforts are thought to have a common values base and similar approaches to families. These commonalities run through the chapters in this volume, unifying the many different types of family support approaches discussed herein thematically. In brief, the commonalities are as follows:

1. Most families have the desire and capability to take care of their own members. They often possess many strengths and are the best long-term allies for vulnerable people.
2. All families need support from their community at some time, including formal assistance such as homemaker services or home nursing as well as informal help provided by friends, neighbors, church groups, and other voluntary associations.
3. A primary function of the community is to support families.
4. State and national governments should provide communities with the resources, both human and fiscal, to allow them to assist families effectively.
5. The autonomy and self-determination of the vulnerable family member must be respected.
6. Families should define their own needs and determine the type and form of supports they need from the community.
7. Support services should strengthen and build upon informal supports, not supplant them.
8. Help should be given in a way that provides family members with new skills and strengthens their ability to help themselves.

9. Family members should be full partners with professionals in designing, implementing, and evaluating family supports. Family members should be in control of
   policy that affects them. When needed, training should be provided to family members to permit them to participate meaningfully in policy making.

These common principles emerged during a national conference on family caregiving—sponsored jointly by the Hood Center for Family Support at the Dartmouth Medical
School, the Beach Center on Families and Disability, the Human Services Research Institute,
and the United Cerebral Palsy Associations, Inc.—to bring together family researchers, scholars, advocates, and policy makers focusing on different populations of people
with disabilities and their families. The conference was held in Hanover, New Hampshire, in June of 1993, promoting conversation among people working in several parallel,
but usually nonconversant, fields.

The purpose of this volume is to explore the ways that communities can enhance
the capacity of families to support people with disabilities in valued lifestyles. Designed
to point out the commonalities and differences among these families' needs, the authors
speak eloquently and provide us reason to hope that new approaches to bolstering family
life will enrich our communities and strengthen the safety net for everyone. We hope
that this volume will contribute to efforts to build coalitions across disability groups and
promote the growth of new family support programs and practices in the United States.

To all of the families, self-advocates, and committed professionals who are catalyzing a historic change in public policy

and

to the Trustees of the Charles H. Hood Foundation for their generosity and vision

I

THE CONCEPT OF FAMILY SUPPORT FOR FAMILIES OF PEOPLE WITH SPECIAL NEEDS

1

Introduction: Trends Affecting Home and Community Care for People with Chronic Conditions in the United States

George H.S. Singer

The purpose of this book is to bring together current recommended practices in public–private partnerships to assist families in their many roles that support people with disabilities and special health care needs. By public–private partnerships, we mean new social arrangements whereby the larger community assists families to carry out their roles as the primary long-term support system for people with disabilities. It is an equal relationship that links formal and informal social support. Contemporary political and scholarly work on family support has tended to focus on specific disabilities, social classes, or illness groups. Consequently, there are books, journal articles, advocacy groups, and publicly funded programs that concentrate on specific groups, such as families of people with Alzheimer's disease, families of people with mental illnesses, families of people with developmental disabilities, and families who are economically disadvantaged. However, there has been relatively little scholarly or public discussion of the commonalities among caregiving families (for a groundbreaking exception to this trend, see Moroney, 1986).

It is the premise of this book that many of the functional needs of caregiving families are similar, regardless of the specific illness or disability.

Although unique challenges accompany specific conditions, there are also many underlying similarities. At the level of public policy and political advocacy, it makes sense to examine the needs of caregiving families as a whole (Moroney, 1986). This chapter presents a case for looking at these similarities among caregiving families and the policy implications of such an examination. The first national legislation aimed at creating support programs for caregiving families, the Families of Children with Disabilities Support Act, PL 103-382, was passed in late 1994. Unfortunately, no funds were authorized to enact it and, at the time of publication in the fall of 1995, this initiative is stalled. However, given the trends described herein, eventual government action will be necessary. The information contained in this volume is intended to provide policy makers and citizens with the relevant background information for implementing new family support policies, such as state legislation to support caregivers and initiatives in public school and child welfare systems.

The United States has entered a historically unprecedented, advanced industrial era. As a result of medical advances and changes in societal values, home communities now include unprecedented numbers of citizens with disabilities or long-term health care problems. Since the United States was founded, the family has been the primary source of support for people with ongoing needs for assistance in daily living. However, the nature of family life has undergone a revolution at the same time that the number of people who rely on families for assistance has multiplied. Contemporary family life is characterized by smaller, more mobile, and less stable groupings. Traditionally, caregiving has been carried out by women, usually mothers, older sisters, or grandmothers, in their homes. Many women no longer accept caregiving as an unquestioned obligation, and many who do wish to assist their relatives are now working outside the home and need help to carry out caregiving tasks. Thus, at a time when the need for family support to people who require long-term accommodations is increasing, the number of family members and hours available for providing care has decreased.

One response to this collision of opposing trends is the family support movement, which has been percolating in the United States since the 1980s. It aims to create new social institutions and new allocations of public resources to assist families in their roles as providers of daily assistance to vulnerable people. These new approaches to assisting families represent a considerable divergence from traditional social welfare practices in the United States. An overview of family support necessarily involves a discussion of values and principles, as well as facts and figures, because the family support movement represents a substantial change in the idea of society's relationship to families. The movement also requires some essential changes in the way that community institutions do their jobs; these include schools, workplaces, hospitals, clinics, and recreational facilities.

THE GROWING NUMBER OF PEOPLE WITH DISABILITIES

Biomedical and Technological Advances

Advances in medical science and technology are bringing to pass an unprecedented change in the makeup of the human population in the United States and other advanced industrial countries. Since the 1940s, medical science has greatly reduced mortality from acute illness, lengthened the life span of people with chronic illnesses, and increased the longevity of older adults. The result of these advances has been improvement of the overall health of the population and a significant increase in the numbers of people with long-term chronic conditions.

At every phase of the life span, people whose conditions would have caused death now live with the help of new technologies and treatments. A paradigmatic example of this trend is the recent revolution in care for babies with extremely low birth weights. Infants as small as 600 grams now have an 80% survival rate in the most advanced neonatal intensive care units (NICUs) (Edwards, 1994). The benefits and social challenges posed by new medical technologies are well illustrated in regard to this population. These common themes include the following:

1. Medical technology has improved survival rates but increased chronicity.
2. The main location of care has moved out of hospitals and into homes.
3. The community is seen as the preferred place of residence and care; thus, other societal institutions (e.g., local.hospitals, public schools, workplaces) must respond to the long-term needs of the new population.
4. Pressures to cut costs have led to increased reliance on unpaid family help to care for vulnerable people.

In all cases, family members become integral to long-term care provision. As recently as the 1980s, infants with extremely low birth weights were considered hopeless cases. Survival data from one NICU are presented in Figure 1. Although these very premature babies now have dramatically improved odds of survival, they are also at high risk for long-term conditions. Because human lung tissue is underdeveloped in very premature babies, they often require oxygen to stay alive. The levels of oxygen that the infants require frequently cause damage to the lungs, necessitating the temporary use of mechanical respirators to facilitate breathing. Respirators are now portable and many of these infants go home attached to life-sustaining machines. On average, infants outgrow the problem after 9 months, but it is not uncommon for children to require respirators for 2 years or more. Recent development of new medications is rapidly reducing the need for long-term respirator support.

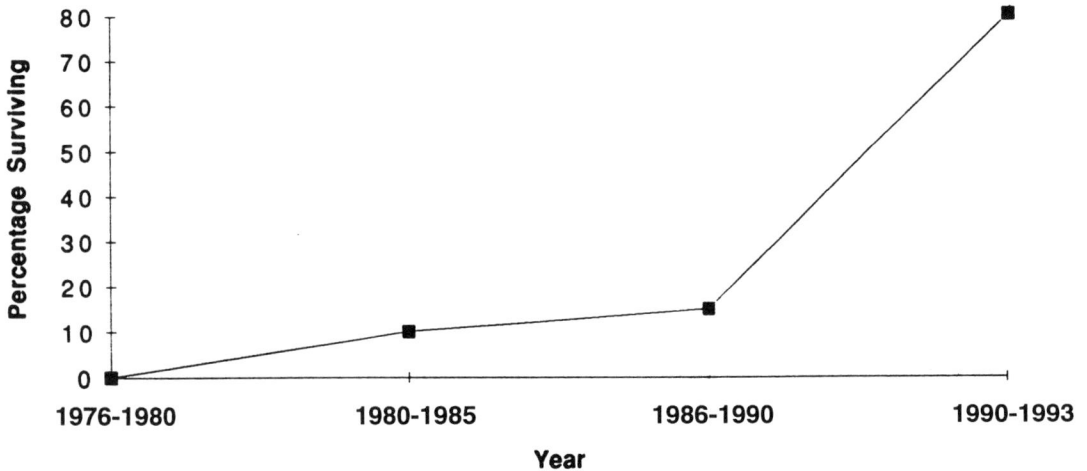

Figure 1. One neonatal intensive care unit's longitudinal data on the survival rates of infants with extremely low birth weights.

While on the respirators, the infants require intensive care and often must be monitored around the clock. Thus, the home lives of their parents are transformed into a hybrid of a home and a high-technology medical facility. Over the long term approximately half of these infants encounter learning problems in public school and require remedial assistance, which in some cases is also needed in work settings later. Approximately 15% of these infants develop neuromotor problems that affect their mobility.

Historical trends regarding children with severe brain injury follow a similar pattern. Beginning in the 1970s, innovations in emergency room treatment and emergency transport of people with brain injury resulted in improvements in survival rates. Physicians in emergency rooms began to use steroids to reduce brain swelling, and ambulance attendants began to stabilize the head and neck of people with brain injuries. Many of the new survivors were children who probably would have died without these innovations. Statistics reported by the May Institute in 1993 estimate that approximately 30,000 children a year acquire permanent disabilities from brain injuries. Children with the most severe injuries require a variety of long-term accommodations. Many of these long-term supports are provided by families with the help of education programs in public schools and rehabilitation programs. In the best of circumstances, the many mediating institutions that make up a community are also partners in supporting a family member with disability; these institutions may include churches, youth groups, employers, self-help organizations, neighborhood associations, and informal groups of friends and acquaintances.

Childhood chronic illness follows a historical pattern similar to that of infants with extremely low birth weights. Figure 2 presents historical data from the National Health Survey. It shows the number of children with major activity limitations resulting from chronic illness. Increases in the percentage of children with such limitations again reflect medical and technological advances. There is evidence from Denmark regarding the numbers of children with chronic conditions who survive to age 21. Between 1945 and 1973, there was a twofold or greater increase in survival rates for children with spina bifida, leukemia, and congenital heart disease. There was a sevenfold increase for children with cystic fibrosis (Gortmaker, 1985). Improvements in treatment for all of these conditions have continued to increase survival rates since the mid-1970s. Children with these conditions require frequent medical, educational, and social accommodations to allow them to participate in typical home and community life.

In turning to adult-onset illnesses, similar patterns emerge. Conditions previously considered acute and fatal are now often considered chronic and entail some disability. Figure 3 presents the 5-year survival rate for cancer. Between 1930 and 1989, survival rates have more than doubled. For almost half of all people with cancer, the disease involves a number of years of

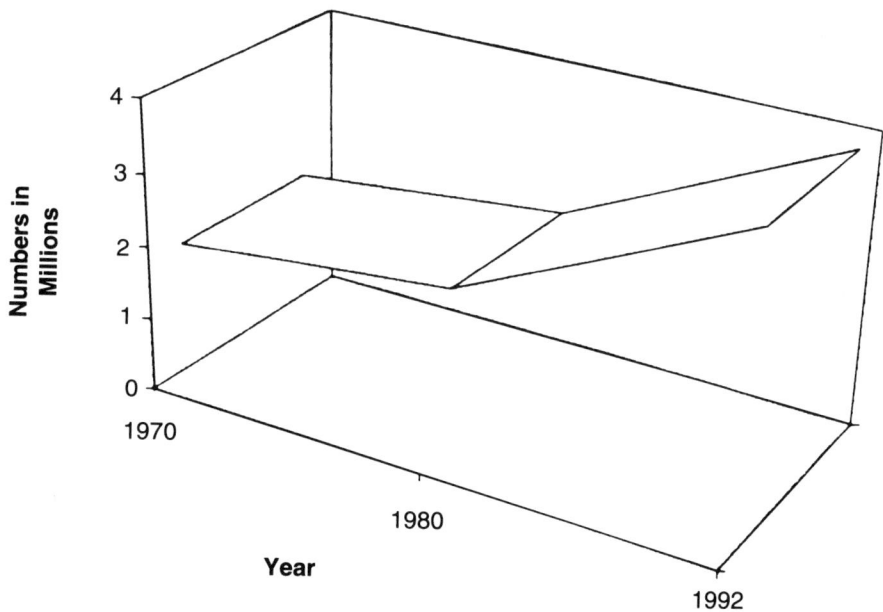

Figure 2.   Historical data illustrating the increasing number of children with activity limitations resulting from chronic conditions.

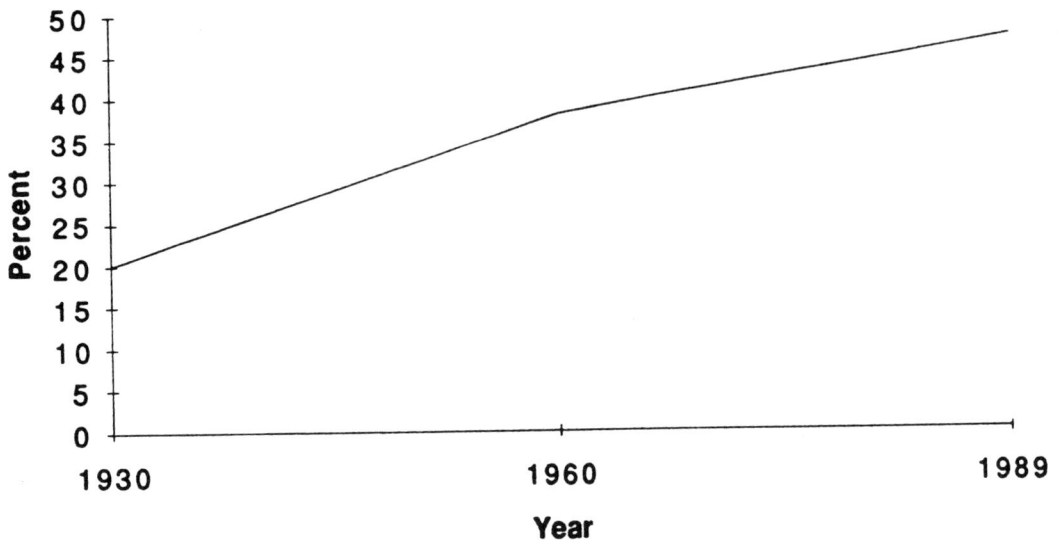

Figure 3.   The 5-year cancer survival rate from 1930 to 1989.

treatment with fluctuations in the amount of assistance needed to live at home, work, and play. During this period of long-term treatment, many people with cancer require a range of supports to help them cope with the illness and its often harsh treatments. Spouses and children of people with cancer provide many different kinds of assistance, ranging from emotional support to transportation and reminders to take medications. Many cancer survivors seek assistance from self-help organizations and, less commonly, from counselors to help them deal with the emotional challenges of living with the disease.

Changes in Social Policy: Deinstitutionalization

As important as medical trends have been, they represent only a part of the picture of the number of people requiring care in the United States. Equally important are changes in social policy, beliefs about the proper social role for people with chronic conditions, and demographic and economic trends.

Nowhere have medical advances and changes in social policies had such a marked impact as on the long-term care for people with mental illness. At the end of World War II, treatments for severe mental illness varied little from previous centuries. People with mental illness were confined in out-of-the-way places and subjected to a variety of strange and often extremely harsh treatments, including lobotomy, induced diabetic coma, and induced fevers. The introduction of administrative reforms and the discovery of psychoactive medications led to unprecedented changes in the duration, nature, and location of treatment for mental illness. In 1950, the average length of stay in psychiatric hospitals for a person with psychosis was 20 years and for a person with neurosis, 9 years. By 1977, the average length of stay in a mental hospital was 210 days (Kiesler & Simpkins, 1993). The number of episodes of mental illness (residents plus admissions) treated in state psychiatric hospitals dropped from 818,000 in 1955 to 445,181 in 1985–1986. Figure 4 illustrates this trend. Downsizing of psychiatric hospitals was spurred by civil libertarians who won restrictions on involuntary commitment, and by psychiatric hospitals as a result of advances in social treatment and psychopharmacology. Unfortunately, deinstitutionalization of care for people with mental illness was not matched by an equal commitment of resources to community care. For hundreds of thousands of people with mental illness, their families became key providers of long-term support without the benefit of adequate community mental health services. McFarlane (1983) reported that in New York between 1980 and 1981, 51% of all discharges from state psychiatric hospitals returned patients to relatives' homes. Presently, the majority of people with mental illness are treated in community general hospitals, which release approximately 75% of patients to families (Goldman, 1982; Kiesler & Simpkins, 1993). Active partnerships between family care providers and professionals

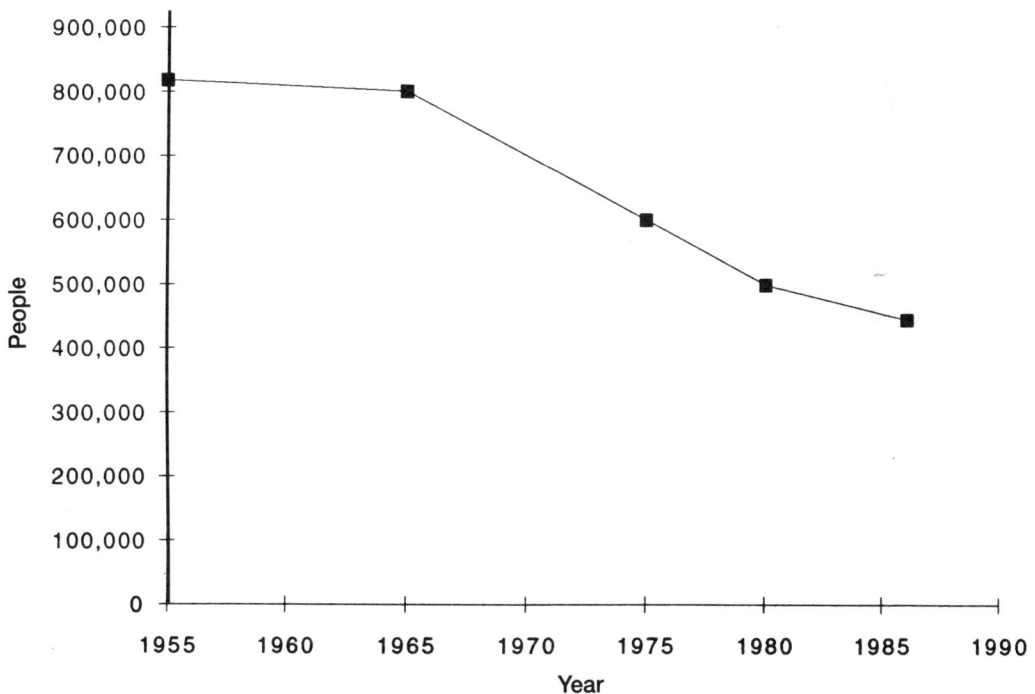

Figure 4.   The number of people treated in state psychiatric hospitals over a 35-year period.

can considerably improve the outcomes for people with mental illness. Recent studies have demonstrated that when family members are provided with adequate support and training, they can reduce rehospitalization rates substantially (Goldstein & Kopeiken, 1981; Leff, Kuipers, Berkowitz, Eberbein-Vries, & Sturgeon, 1982; McFarlane, 1983). When left on their own to cope with mental illness, family members can also undergo severe stress and prolonged strain (see Chapter 12). Stress is particularly pronounced among families of children with emotional and behavior problems. As discussed in Chapter 12, few community-based services exist for children with mental illness and their families.

In summary, social changes have had a profound impact on the prevalence of people with disabilities who live in family homes and participate in community life. The long-overdue extension of civil rights to all citizens and the belief that communities should be open to all people regardless of the physical or emotional challenges they face have resulted in a shift in social policy. As a result the populations of large congregate care institutions for people with mental retardation and mental illness have decreased. Similarly, the number of frail older adults living in their own or family homes has increased as a result of the belief that removal of older people from familiar surroundings should be an intervention of last resort.

Changes in social policy have also had a marked impact on other groups of people with chronic conditions. For example, the independent living movement has insisted that people with physical disabilities should be allowed to live in their own homes, work in typical workplaces, and pursue their own dreams. People with mental retardation and other disabilities commonly live in their home communities. The number of people with mental retardation who reside in large institutions began to decline in 1975, a trend that continues in 1995. Several large institutions have closed and state governments have begun to create programs aimed at helping families to care for their children with mental retardation at home. State and national initiatives in the 1990s have aimed to open up typical community jobs to adults with mental retardation.

Demographic and Economic Trends

The demographic change that accounts for the largest increase in the numbers of people with chronic conditions is the aging of the U.S. population. Figure 5 presents a graphic display of the expansion of the population of older adults in the United States. It documents a 50% increase in longevity since 1900. As aging occurs, the risk of experiencing a chronic illness increases. Among people 85 and older, illness-related restrictions in daily activities are the norm. This group is the most likely to need intensive supports to continue living in the community. The percentage of people age 85 and older has doubled since 1970 and is expected to double again by 2015. Figure 6 illustrates the relationship between age and disability.

THE ELDERLY POPULATION BOOM

AGE

80 to 84

75 to 79

65 to 74

PROJECTED

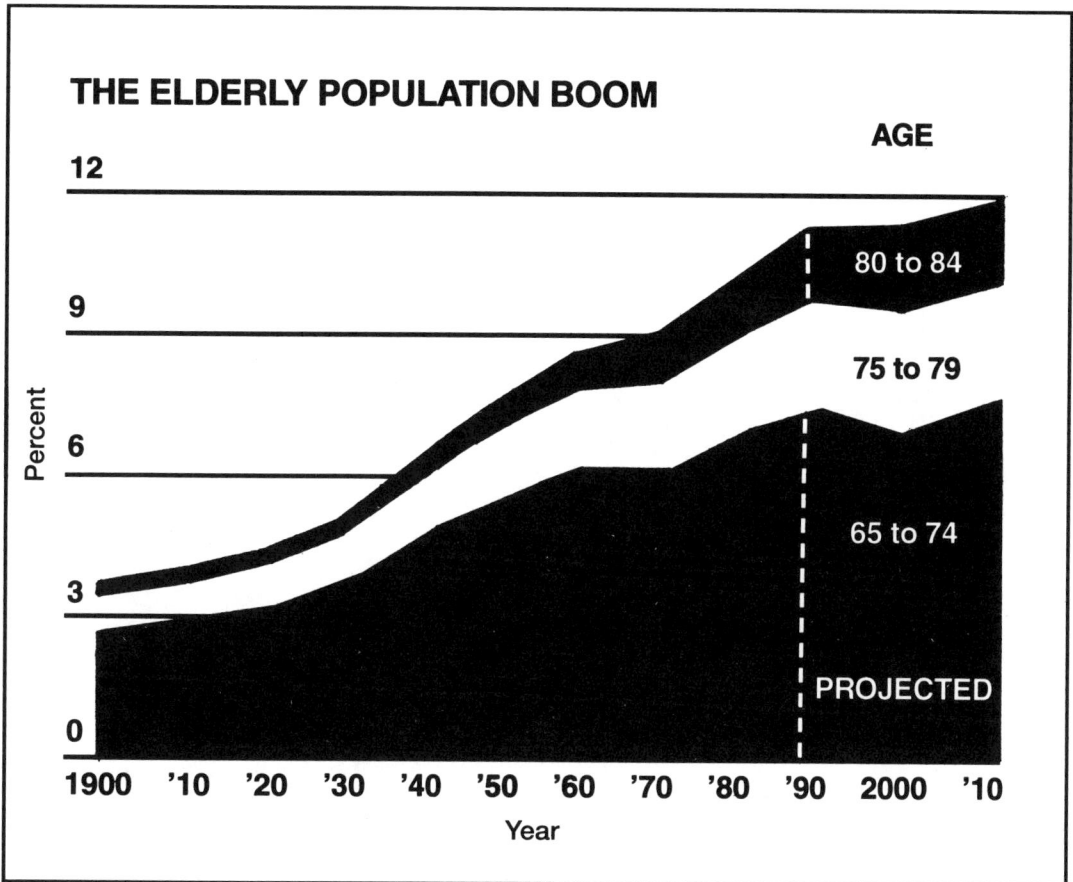

Figure 5.　Since 1900, the U.S. population of older adults has increased by 50%.

Families play a crucial role in sustaining community life for older citizens. One way to highlight this family role is to look at the population of older adults who live in nursing facilities. The great majority (88%) of people in nursing facilities are not married, roughly half are childless, and those with children have fewer children, children who are older, or children who live far away (Brody, 1989).

Severity of disability is a weaker predictor of institutionalization than involvement of relatives. For example, although a majority of people in nursing facilities have dementia, an equal number of people with Alzheimer's disease live in the community and are cared for by relatives (Brody, 1989).

Further major demographic and economic changes are affecting the need for family support services. Poverty affects family caregiving in a

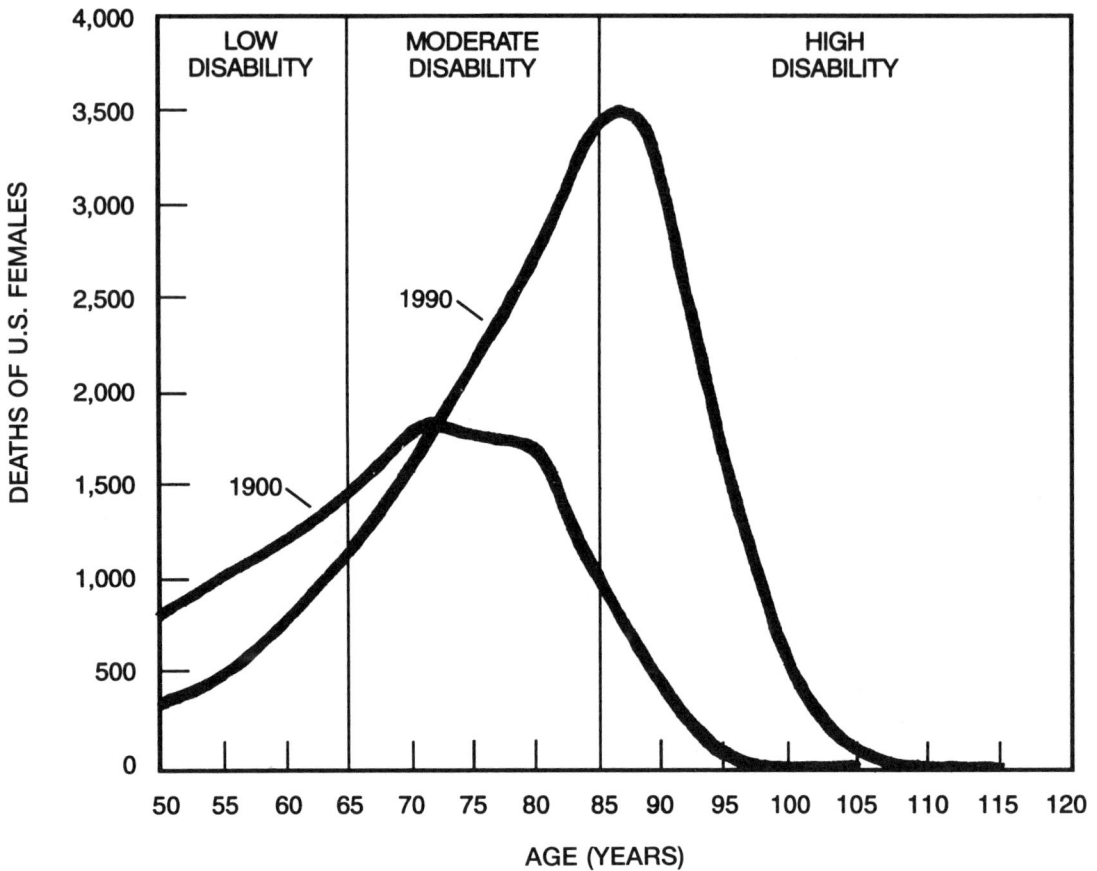

Figure 6.   The proportion and severity of disabilities in female adults increases with age in the United States (*Source:* Social Security Administration, 1993).

number of ways. First, poor people are at higher risk than the rest of the population for experiencing chronic illness and disability. For example, children whose families earn wages below the poverty line are much more likely to have disabilities than those living above it (Perrin & MacLean, 1988). The percentage of children who live in poverty has increased in the United States since 1980 so that as of 1995, 20% of all children are poor. Along with the increase in child poverty, the number of children living with single parents has skyrocketed since 1970. A trend that has raised great concern among child advocates has been the explosive growth in teenage single-parenthood since the mid-1980s (Blankenhorn, 1990). From 1970 to 1985 the percentage of children living with only one parent climbed from 11.9% to 23.4% (Laosa, 1988). Problems of single and teenage parenthood and poverty require new supports to young families. When disability or chronic illness is also present in these families, the typical problems of home caregiving are compounded and exacerbated. For example, a child with chronic illness in a two-parent, middle-class family has a risk of 1.5 times the typical risk for severe emotional problems. A child with the same illness who is born to a poor unmarried teenage mother is at 14 times the risk (Cadman, Boyle, & Orford, 1988). Thus, family support policies for the broad population of caregivers must make special provisions for the growing number of families that face multiple challenges.

A final demographic trend that must have a major impact on effective family support efforts is the changing racial and ethnic makeup of the population. Projections of birth rates suggest that in the 45 years between 1985 and 2030, the proportion of children from nonwhite, non-Anglo groups will rise from 28% to 41% (Lynch & Hanson, 1992). Cultural diversity brings with it different conceptions of family, illness, disability, relationships with the outside community, help giving and receiving, and quality of life. Virtually every social transaction that makes up support for families is shaped by culture. Creating family support policies and practices that respond to the changing face of the United States will be a major challenge.

In summary, the number of Americans who need unusual levels of assistance in order to carry on the typical activities of daily living is growing dramatically. Medical advances have transformed many conditions from short-term terminal illnesses into long-lasting chronic illnesses. There is widespread agreement that people with disabilities should live and participate in typical community life. Families sustain the social infrastructure that maintains a decent life for most citizens with disabilities whether from extreme old age, chronic illness, mental illness, or developmental disability.

THE ROLE OF WOMEN AS SOURCES OF SUPPORT FOR VULNERABLE PEOPLE

Family caregiving for older adults usually falls to adult daughters. Currently, a woman can expect to spend more years caring for a parent than looking after dependent children (Brody, 1989). It is increasingly common for women to fill dual caregiving roles involving young children or children with disabilities and older family members. At the same time, a majority of these daughters and mothers work outside the home and must juggle work, family, and dual caregiving roles. There is cause for concern about the impact of multiple role demands. A recent large-scale study of employed women found that women with multiple caregiving roles experienced the most work-related stress, absenteeism, and work days lost due to health problems (Neal, Chapman, Ingersoll-Dayton, & Emlen, 1993).

Current efforts to establish new ways to support the caregiving of families can be understood only in light of the dramatic contemporary revision of traditional gender roles. A look back at the history of home caregiving illuminates the origin of current dilemmas. Traditionally, women have been responsible for the care of young children, sick family members, and frail older adults. This gender role was prevalent in colonial times when most men and women worked in or near their homes to maintain farms or shops. Although both men and women worked the farm, women were solely responsible for two areas of domestic life: the care of young children and the care of the sick (Risse, Numbers, & Leavitt, 1977). Women, usually mothers and older daughters, carried out nursing tasks, such as sitting at bedsides, swabbing foreheads, changing bandages, handling bedpans, preparing medications, and cooking for the ill (Cowan, 1987).

Diseases that are now controlled by vaccine and antibiotics were commonplace. Medical self-help books were popular because physicians did not possess many effective treatments and many families were isolated. The relative isolation of families in the face of medical emergencies was commonplace well into the 19th century. "During much of the nineteenth century it was difficult for many rural families to get a doctor. They lived, often, in isolation, roads were poor, travel slow, sickness prevalent, emergencies many" (Blake, 1977, p. 26).

Writing in the 1850s, the New England physician William A. Alcott complained about the traditional ways that mothers doctored their own children. He blamed a high infant mortality rate on "maternal dosing and drugging." In his experience, "the vast majority of mothers . . . doctor their own children . . . [with] a vast amount of elixirs, cordials, etc." (Cassedy, 1977, p. 34).

With the advent of industrialization, men's and women's work roles and places of work diverged. As men began to work away from the homestead in factories and offices, a new ideology about the home emerged, termed by historians *the doctrine of separate spheres* (Cowan, 1987). According to this view, men were to do daily battle in the virulent, masculine world of the marketplace, while women were to provide a sanctuary for rest and nourishment in the home. Women were to be nurturers, upholders of the family, and representatives of the gentle side of human nature. They were discouraged from competing with men in the outside world and were not to enter the professions or the marketplace. Thus, women's traditional role of nurturing the sick and caring for young children was continued during the industrialization of the United States and most of their work at home was still not rewarded with market income. However, unlike their role in colonial times, women no longer worked side by side with men and their labor was not so visibly essential for survival. Women's roles as homemakers were detached from the income-earning and goods-producing sectors of society. It was assumed that women's work at home was done voluntarily, without pay, and without a significant impact on the marketplace. This tradition continues today—for example, in the way that economists calculate the gross national product. The billions of hours that women work in their own homes are not accounted for when the wealth of a nation is calculated (Waring, 1988). This can lead to problems when homemaking and caregiving services need to be purchased in the marketplace.

While men in the 19th and early 20th centuries were the wage earners, women were responsible for most of the labor that turns wages into sustenance—cooking, homemaking, laundering clothes, and so forth (Cowan, 1987). This labor was particularly essential in assisting people with disabilities to maintain their health and involvement in community life. However, most of this work has been hidden from public view and accepted as a cultural norm, resulting in a kind of default that surrounds the care of the rapidly expanding number of people with disabilities and chronic illnesses: *Let women provide the care.*

However, at the same time that modern medicine has increased the numbers of people with special ongoing health care needs, there have been enormous changes in this notion about family life. These revolutions include the employment of married women in the market economy, increased divorce rates, greater geographic mobility, and increases in the number of single parents. Since World War II, job roles in the marketplace have undergone an upheaval. By 1994 more than 60% of married women worked outside of the home. The economic basis of the doctrine of separate spheres has eroded.

However, changes in work roles inside the home have not kept pace with the gender revolution in employment. Because they are now working outside of the home, women have fewer hours available for work inside the home. Thus, from 1967 to 1987 the average number of hours that women spent on housework declined (Schor, 1992). Men have not, however, taken up the chores. As illustrated in Figure 7, recent surveys show that 70% of working women still perform all or most of the work at home (Schor, 1992). Even though they are now spending far fewer hours in the home, women are still the main domestic workers. Homemaking still requires cooking, cleaning, laundering, transporting children, and caring for family members with illnesses and disabilities.

Even though a majority of women have entered the paid labor force, little has changed concerning women's role as caregivers. Two large studies of caregiving for older people have found that women are their predominant caregivers (American Association of Retired Persons [AARP], 1988; Stone, Cafferata, & Sangl, 1987). One third of the caregivers were spouses, one fourth were adult female children, and the remainder were other relatives, usually women. Over three quarters of the sample provided care 7 days a week, for an average of 3 hours per day. In another study examining the way men and women allocate caregiving tasks in families of children with developmental disabilities, Gallagher, Cross, and Scharfman (1981) found that mothers performed the bulk of typical daily tasks, in addition to the work created by the child's condition. This includes taking the child to medical appointments, attending school meetings, and arranging child care. When mothers take care of children who have developmental disabilities, they devote considerably more time to maternal tasks than mothers of children without disabilities. Harris and McHale (1989) compared time

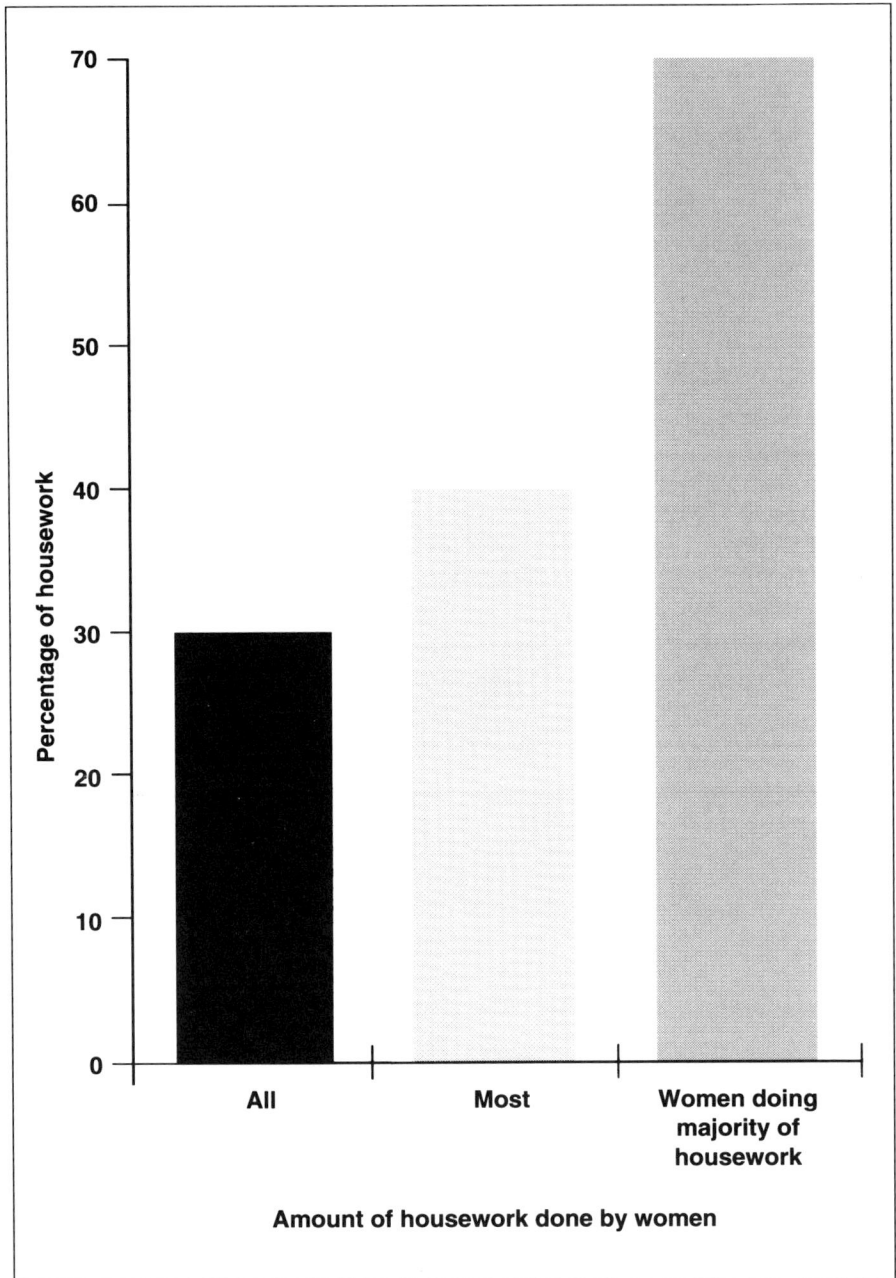

Figure 7. Survey data showing that, even today, working women still perform a majority of household chores (■ All housework done by woman of the house; ▦ Most housework done by woman of the house; ▨ Women doing majority of housework).

allocation between mothers of young children with mental retardation and mothers of children without mental retardation. Figure 8 presents their findings. It shows that, on average, time spent in joint activities with children increases by 40% when caring for a young child with mental retardation; these increased time demands correlate with family problems. At a time when the work load for the traditional home caregiving system is expand-

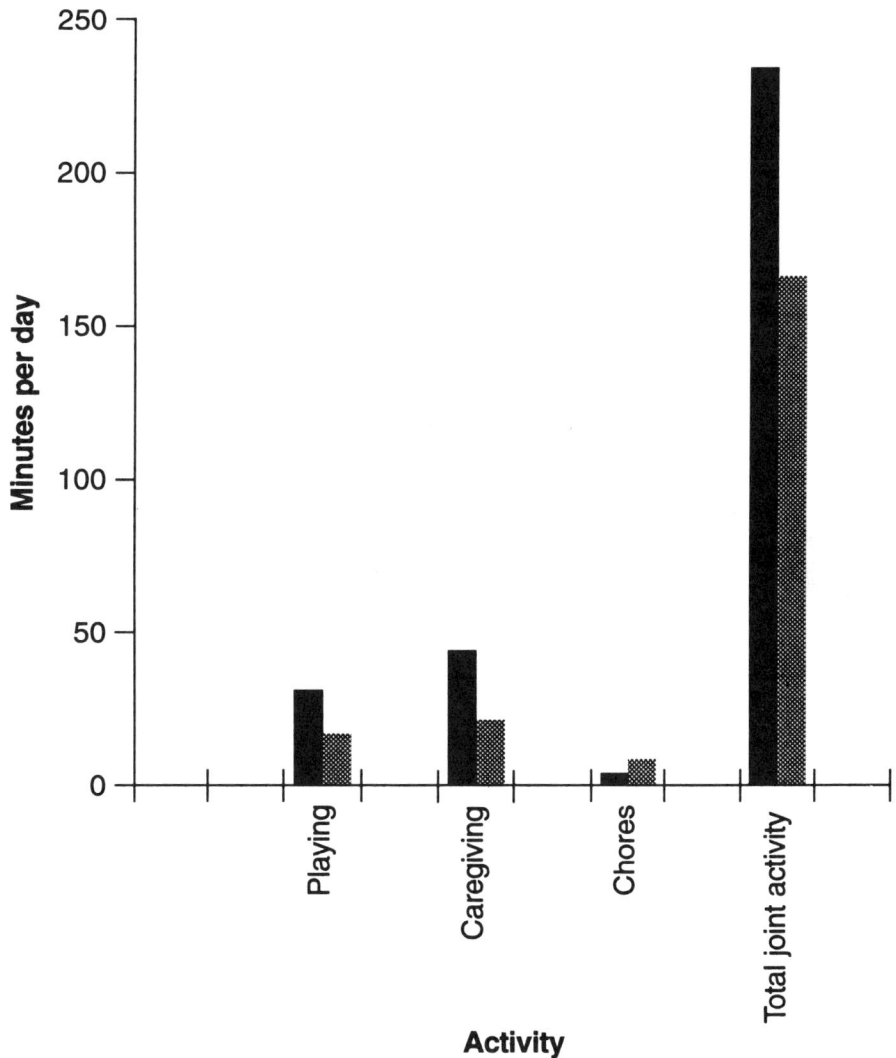

Figure 8.   The increased amount of time mothers of children with mental retardation must devote to these children each day (■ Mothers of children with mental retardation; ▓ mothers of typically developing children).

ing dramatically as a result of biomedical advances, and changes in social policy and demographics, the capacity of the system to meet this demand is declining. The decline in the system's capacity results from women's increased labor force participation and men's apparent reluctance to assume more caregiving responsibilities.

Other trends also contribute to the family's diminishing ability to care for its members with disabilities. These trends include the increasing divorce rate, the aging of the general population, the increasing number of single adults, and the mobility of the U.S. population. The divorce rate for new marriages is hovering around 50% and may reach 60% by the year 2000 (Demo & Ganong, 1994). Divorced women often experience economic hardship and, at the same time, are predominantly responsible for the post-divorce care of children (Demo, 1992). Little is known about the way divorce affects mothers of children with disabilities or women who care for older people, but it is likely that high divorce rates contribute to caregiver stress. Popenoe (1990) has marshaled evidence to support his assertion that the family is in decline in the United States. Since 1970, the percentage of nonfamily homes has increased from 15% to 28% of all households. Approximately 85% of these households consist of a person living alone. Some of the new family support services that have been established in several states for families of people with disabilities report that calls for crisis intervention services are frequently prompted by a divorce or family break-up.

CAREGIVING BENEFITS

Because family caregiving is becoming such a pervasive part of society and is increasingly preferred by families and people with special care needs alike, its positive benefits should be considerable. Benefits may be evaluated in terms of the positive contributions that home caregiving gives to the general society, and the positive effects on people with long-term care needs and caregivers.

The benefits of home caregiving to the larger society are usually stated in terms of the cost savings that the informal support system yields. The 1982 Long-Term Care Survey showed that less than 15% of all "helper days" for people needing assistance with activities of daily living were provided by nonfamily workers (Brody, 1989). Furthermore, only 4% of older people who receive daily care have it paid for by the government (Brody, 1989). Thus, the day-to-day care that families provide represents an enormous amount of unpaid work that otherwise would have to be paid with public funds. If paid for as a commodity, home care for vulnerable citizens would cost billions of dollars annually.

The fact that home care can save taxpayers' money has not been overlooked by politicians and administrators. In acute care medicine, the average length of hospital stays has been reduced dramatically in the name of cost-saving measures. Surgeries that used to involve a 3- to 5-day stay in the hospital are routinely performed as same-day procedures with patients sent home to the care of their family as soon as the anesthetic wears off. In the realm of long-term care, similar transfers of patients from expensive hospitals into homes have become common in an array of situations, from premature infants who require life-sustaining technology to home-based hospice care for older people with terminal illnesses. A recent study of the financial impact of home oxygen therapy for premature infants serves as an example. McAleese, Knapp, and Rhodes (1993) studied 59 infants with bronchopulmonary dysplasia (BPD), a condition caused by underdeveloped lungs in premature infants. The median cost for children in the intensive care nursery was $173,160 each. The children then moved home with portable breathing equipment for an average of 92 days at a median cost of $5,195 each. If the same children were provided this therapy in the hospital, the cost would have been another $46,920 each. The parents of these children saved $2.76 million dollars—most of it public funds. There is general agreement that premature infants have the best developmental outcomes when they bond with their family as early as possible, and home care can contribute to this social-emotional integration into the family. Thus, there are cost savings from reduced hospital usage and less familial damage as a result of increased parent–infant contact.

The cost benefits of informal caregiving are not the only example of its positive impact on the general society. The commitments that bind families, friends, and neighbors together in looking after vulnerable persons are fundamental human links that serve as a foundation for the larger community. It is hard to imagine a civil society in which parents do not take care of young children, adult children do not aid older adults, communities do not take care of people with mental illnesses, and colleagues do not assist co-workers with illnesses or disabilities. The day-to-day life of any community requires innumerable acts of decency, kindness, and mutual care, ranging from parents feeding their children to drivers letting others cut into traffic ahead of them (Wilson, 1993). Informal caregiving is not, of course, merely a matter of labor freely given. In the best of caregiving relationships, families offer love and concern and embed day-to-day activities in a familiar context. Writing about aging adults and their families, Brody (1989) describes a system that applies equally to many different disability groups.

> Families perform many services that are not usually counted in surveys. They respond in emergencies, provide intermittent acute care, and implement professional recommendations for rehabilitation procedures. Most importantly, they give emotional support (concern, affection, socialization, and a sense of having someone to rely on), the most universal and the one most wanted by the old. (Brody, 1989, p. 4)

These kinds of affective supports should also be considered part of the national wealth of a society.

Family Benefits of Caregiving

At the family level, the tasks of taking care of a valued member of the family can provide a shared purpose and focus for cooperation among family members. Of the small body of research that examines the positive impacts of caregiving on the family, most assumes that families that are predisposed to communicating well, assigning roles flexibly, and working together cooperatively are better able to perform caregiving without detrimental effects. The possibility that the direction of causality works in reverse must also be considered; that is, it is also very likely that the need to provide care itself can be a catalyst for positive family interactions. The demands of caregiving may require families to develop cooperation skills. Although families may experience painful crises related to the disability, many family members suggest that they learn from these experiences and are strengthened by them (Turnbull, Guess, & Turnbull, 1988). Research on family care providers for older adults has also revealed benefits. Colerick and George (1986) found caregivers to have positive feelings of self-satisfaction and accomplishment. Similarly, Hooyman, Gonyea, and Montgomery (1985) reported increased life satisfaction in caregivers.

Recent studies using a new self-report measure designed to examine the positive impacts of disability in the family also support this view. Behr, Murphy, and Summers (1992) developed the Kansas Inventory of Parental Perceptions (KIPP) to measure the way that parents of people with disabilities adapt cognitively. A majority of the 1,262 parents of people with disabilities surveyed agreed with these statements:

> I consider my child (with a disability) to be what gives our family a sense of continuity—a sense of history.
> I consider my child to be what makes me realize the importance of planning for my child's future.
> The presence of my child makes us more in charge of ourselves as a family.
> Because of my child, my family is more understanding about special problems.
> Because of our child, our family has become closer. (Behr et al., 1992, pp. 26–27)

Upon nationwide standardization of the KIPP, the majority of parents of people with disabilities answered these questions affirmatively, as well. The differences between parents of people without disabilities and the sample of parents of people with disabilities were nonsignificant.

Similarly, in a study focusing on strengths in families of people with disabilities, Schwab (1989) found that a majority of the people in her sample (59.1%) reported that the best thing about their family was the love, concern, and caring found in relationships with the family members with disabilities. Schwab surveyed 224 individuals of all ages from families with family members with disabilities. Patterson and Leonard (1994), reporting on a longitudinal study of families whose children require technology assistance living at home, found roughly equal numbers of positive and negative responses. Their study interviewed couples about the impact of caring for a child with complex health care needs at home. Among the positive responses received, most emphasized the way that caregiving had brought them closer together as a couple, created a stronger bond, and built a stronger sense of family (Patterson & Leonard, 1994).

Individual Benefits

Just as families of people with disabilities can benefit from caregiving, individuals who provide care may also benefit by learning new skills and perceptions, acquiring a sense of purpose and self-efficacy, and gaining emotional closeness and faith. A majority of respondents to the KIPP (Behr et al., 1992) agreed with the following statements about being the parent of a child with a disability:

> The presence of my child is very uplifting.
> Because of my child, I have many unexpected pleasures.
> My child is the reason I am a more responsible person.
> My child is the reason my life has better structure. (p. 26)

Benefits to People with Special Caregiving Needs

Finally, evidence from a variety of sources shows that family caregiving can have a salutary effect on people with disabilities and chronic illnesses. The following examples illustrate this point:

1. Preterm babies treated at home
2. Children with mental retardation living with their own families
3. Children with cystic fibrosis and diabetes
4. Adults with chronic mental illness living at home

In regard to preterm infants, the medical literature generally agrees that an adequate home is a far preferable environment to a hospital for facilitating the infant's psychological and social adjustment (McAleese et al., 1993). Nurses and physicians in intensive care nurseries must give first priority to their medical duties, and the crucial face-to-face interactions between adults and infants that characterize the first year of typical childhood development often fall by the wayside. Home treatment is a way to create more opportunities for typical child rearing.

For children with mental retardation, there is some evidence from correlational studies that family environments have a strong effect on the development of independence and community living skills in these children. Mink, Nihira, and Meyers (1983) studied the families of school-age children with mental retardation. They correlated measures of family climate with school adjustment and children's independent living skills. The children who were doing the best in school and who had the most independent living skills came from homes in which the families were cohesive and valued independence. Similarly, McCubbin (1983) studied the family as a predictor of the health status of children with cystic fibrosis. He looked at children's weight gain over a year as an indicator of child health. Rationalizing that the two were interrelated, he found that family cohesion predicted the children's weight gain.

There is ample evidence that adults with chronic mental illness living with relatives benefit when the relatives receive support and skills training (Goldstein & Kopeiken, 1981; Leff et al., 1982; McFarlane et al., 1993). When cared for by their family, adults with mental illness are less likely to become homeless; and when their families receive training and join ongoing support groups, they are much less likely to be returned to inpatient hospitals. McFarlane et al., (1993) found that, specifically, regular multifamily support groups with skills training reduced hospital recidivism, an effect equal to what is typically reported when people with chronic mental illness are medicated. Families that are able to identify symptoms of relapse early, communicate clearly, manage stress, and coach the family member with chronic mental illness are able to significantly reduce the number of hospitalization episodes experienced by people with chronic mental illness.

In summary, home care for people with disabilities and / or chronic illness is indeed beneficial for our society, families, and individuals. The benefits include immense public fiscal savings and general enhancement of the social bonds that serve as a foundation to civil society. Benefits also include strengthened families, increased tolerance and understanding of diversity, and personal growth. There is also evidence for improved medical and social outcomes for people with disabilities or chronic illnesses when they are supported by their families.

CAREGIVING COSTS

Providing day-to-day support for a vulnerable relative also entails costs to the general society, family members, and people who require long-term assistance. With a clearer understanding of these costs, public policies and practices can be drafted to reduce stress associated with caregiving and maximize the conditions that promote benefits.

Social costs of family care are usually discussed in economic terms. As the number of employees who are caregivers has expanded, employers have grown increasingly interested in the effects of informal home care on their businesses and industries. Two groups of employees have been studied: parents of young children and relatives of frail older adults. Emlen (1993) found that employees with very young children experienced more physical ailments and fatigue than other workers. But, a survey of business executives indicates that employers view caregiving for older people as having undesirable effects on work. A 1989 survey of Fortune 500 company executives found that executives reported increased absenteeism, increased employee stress, and lateness for work or early departure from work ("Corporate and employee response to caring for the elderly," 1989).

As a result, employers have begun to adopt policies to assist workers with caregiving challenges. Galinsky, Friedman, Hernandez, and Axel

(1991) interviewed 71 human resources directors and vice presidents from Fortune 500 companies. The interviewees gave the following reasons for their companies' commitment to work and family issues: to improve recruitment and retention, to improve morale, to reduce stress that might lower productivity and service quality, and to keep up with their competition.

Family caregiving can have negative impacts on families also. Some studies suggest that rates of divorce are unusually high among parents of children with disabilities. Breslau and Davis (1986) reported that over a 5-year period, mothers of children with developmental disabilities or chronic illnesses reported a divorce rate double to that of a population-based sample comparison group. However, other studies with smaller samples have not confirmed this finding and it remains controversial. When marital discord occurs in families of children with disabilities, it is likely that disagreements arise over housework, emotional support, and maternal demoralization (Bristol, Gallagher, & Schopler, 1988; Singer et al., 1993). In their study of children with complex health care needs living at home with life-sustaining technology, Patterson and Leonard (1994) found that couples reported several negative impacts of home caregiving on their marriages, including exhaustion, tension, irritability, and little time together.

Still, the clearest body of evidence regarding caregiver costs points to increased psychological distress in women who are caregivers of children with chronic illnesses, children with developmental disabilities, and adults with Alzheimer's disease. There is also evidence that mothers of children with severe emotional disturbances (SED) live with high levels of stress. Another considerable body of evidence (Singer & Irvin, 1991; Singer et al., 1993) indicates that mothers of children with developmental disabilities experience elevated levels of depressive symptoms, such as sleeplessness, hopelessness, worry, low self-esteem, and guilt. Several studies compare groups of mothers of children with disabilities with mothers of children without disabilities. When analyzed together using meta-analytic methodology, these studies show that, on average, mothers of children with disabilities have substantially higher levels of depressive symptoms (Singer & Yovanoff, 1994).

Care of children with chronic illnesses has also been linked to maternal depressive symptoms. In a study of 600 parents of children with chronic illness, Perrin (1993) found that 60% of his sample had elevated scores on a commonly used measure of depressive symptoms, the Center for Epidemiological Studies Depression Measure (CES–D) (Radloff, 1977), scoring over the cutoff that indicates depression. Comparative studies find that, roughly, only 15% of mothers of children without disabilities score over this cutoff on the CES–D. The emotional challenges of caring for a child who is seriously ill over a long period of time have also been documented in families of technology assistance users. Patterson and Leonard (1994) tracked a group of 48 families with children requiring technology assistance for 2.5

years; and unlike most studies, they reported on the emotional well-being of both fathers and mothers. On a measure of psychological distress, they found that over half of the parents were seriously distressed, a condition that continued over time. This group included half the fathers, even though they did not have the primary responsibility as caregivers. The fathers labeled the financial crisis of meeting catastrophic expenses, the limited time with their spouses, and the need to take over more caregiving for other children in the family as their main stressors.

When considering this information in light of the benefits of home care for infants who require technology assistance, it becomes apparent that in roughly half of the affected families, the savings in dollars and the developmental progress of the infants are gained at high cost to parental well-being. Family support services and interventions aim to reduce some of this burden.

Evidence from families who care for members with severe emotional disturbances or Alzheimer's disease also indicates that caregiving often, but not always, takes a toll on the primary care providers. In a larger-scale survey of parents of children with severe emotional disturbances, Friesen (1989) found that 44% of her respondents reported that they had been physically threatened by their children with SED. Although her study did not directly measure the psychological well-being of the parents, it is virtually certain that people who face ongoing fear of attack in their own homes also experience higher than usual levels of psychological distress. In regard to parents of adults with mental illnesses, a recent study by Spaniol, Jung, Zipple, and Fitzgerald (1987) surveyed a sample of the National Association for the Mentally Ill (NAMI) members and found that a majority of parents reported stress-related difficulties, including anxiety, worry, frustration, and a sense of burden. Of 140 parents, 48% reported difficulties with depression.

It is important to note that these studies measure *depressive symptoms,* not clinical depression. The instruments used in these studies measure self-reported moods, but they cannot determine the presence of full clinical depression, a mental illness. When Breslau and Davis (1986) examined the rates of clinical depression in mothers of children with special health care needs, they found no significant differences in the percentage of mothers with diagnosed mental illness (clinical depression) compared to a large sample of mothers of children without disabilities; that is, higher levels of depressive symptoms did not predict higher levels of clinically diagnosed mental illness. These results show that although many of the people in these studies are struggling with low morale, they are not necessarily dysfunctional, and most carry on typical work and family roles in addition to their caregiving tasks.

Given that depressive symptoms are elevated among these women, what specific factors contribute to psychological distress? Several studies have examined correlates of depression in this population. Among the largest and best designed of these studies is the work of Pahl and Quine (1987), who identified a set of variables that are most predictive of distress in mothers of children with severe disabilities. These conditions include the following:

1. Regular loss of sleep because of caregiving demands at night
2. The child's severe medical problems
3. The child's severe behavior problems
4. The child's unusual appearance
5. Adversity in the family combined with caregiving responsibilities

Gallimore, Weisner, Kaufman, and Bernheimer (1989) have further clarified the nature of caregiver stress by conducting in-depth interviews with 101 parents of children with mild to moderate disabilities regarding their routine home activities. From these data, they concluded that families develop accommodations in daily routines as a way of coping with a child's disability. For example, a parent might decide to awaken her child with a physical disability earlier in order to allow for more time in dressing for school. Waking early is one of these accommodations. Gallimore et al. (1989) concluded that accommodations should be evaluated for *sustainability,* their ability to be maintained over time. Although waking up 20 minutes early to prepare a child for school seems to be an accommodation that a parent could implement over a long period of time, some mothers of children with disabilities report that they regularly miss sleep to take care of their child. One would expect that major sleep deprivation would not be sustainable over a long period of time without a high cost in the mother's emotional or physical health. The sustainability of everyday accommodations may very likely prove to be one of the best predictors of depressive symptoms in caregivers. The practical focus of this concept lends itself to the design of interventions. Family support interventions can be viewed as one way to create accommodations for disabilities and make those ongoing accommodations sustainable.

A similar, but more extreme, picture emerges from the literature on home care provided for older people with Alzheimer's disease or other severe chronic illnesses. Alzheimer's-type dementia is a progressive, degenerative disease that brings with it severe aberrant behavior, loss of memory, and eventually loss of the ability to recognize familiar people. Caregivers are often older themselves, usually spouses. Several studies have found elevated levels of major and minor depression in caregivers. However, there is evidence that older adults (usually women) who provide home care for elders with *any* severe chronic illnesses are also at risk. For example, Gallagher et al. (1981) compared caregivers of older adults with dementia and severe chronic illnesses that do not involve cognitive disabilities with normative data on depression in older people. They reported that 46% of the caregivers of older adults with cognitive impairments experienced depressive disorders, compared to 47% of caregivers of older adults with chronic illness. Compared with depression rates of 2%–5% for the general population of older people (age 65 and older) (Gallagher et al., 1981), it appears that taking care of a person with a severe chronic illness, whether or not it includes dementia, is difficult for many older people.

In summary, it is important to remember that home caregiving exacts a cost. Families can experience internal conflict as a result of the demands and stresses of caregiving. Individuals, particularly women who provide the majority of caregiving, can experience social and emotional problems, the best documented of these problems being depression. Studies of depressive symptoms in caregivers suggest that from 30% to 50% of primary caregivers experience at least mild levels of depression. Caregivers also face serious financial costs resulting from high medical bills and related expenses, interrupted employment, and the purchase of assistance (Birenbaum, Guyot, & Cohen, 1990). There are hidden economic costs in the form of lost hours, missed work, and withdrawal from the labor force.

REDUCING THE SOCIAL-EMOTIONAL STRESS IN CAREGIVERS AND PROMOTING POSITIVE ADAPTATION

Researchers have produced evidence that shows that the stresses of home caregiving can be reduced through a combination of social and psychological interventions. Table 1 presents a selective review of the literature on treatment of caregiver stress across the following populations: adults with chronic illnesses, adults with dementia, children with mental retardation, children with other developmental disabilities, children with chronic illnesses, and adults with mental illnesses. This review is not meant to be exhaustive, but to illustrate major findings. It shows that model demonstration and research projects have emphasized the following common set of interventions for caregivers:

1. Service coordination to link families to services and provide information
2. Psychoeducational support groups to generate social support and increase coping skills
3. Respite care to give caregivers time for themselves and the other members of their families
4. Financial assistance to reduce fiscal costs
5. Behavior training in managing problematic behavior at home

It also shows that the quality of the evidence for efficacy is varied, ranging from well-designed controlled research to less rigorous evaluation studies. These and other studies suggest that society has the knowledge to greatly reduce the personal and familial costs of home caregiving.

Public Programs to Support Home Care

The notion that contemporary families require assistance to carry out their traditional roles has gained widespread recognition and support across the

Table 1. Treatment studies of caregiver stress across disability groups

Caregivers	Authors	Design	Intervention	Subjects	Findings
Parents of children with developmental disabilities	Nixon & Singer (1993)	Two-group random assignment: treatment[a] versus waiting list[b]	Five 2-hour structured discussion groups focused on attributions of blame and responsibility	Parents of children with severe disabilities, selected for high initial levels of self-blame	Significant reductions in depressive symptoms and self-blame
	Singer, Glang, Powers, Cooley, Nixon, Kerns, & Williams (1994)	Two-group random assignment: stress management skills training group versus informational/emotional support group	Stress management skills training class in groups—eight 2-hour meetings	Parents of children with acquired brain injury	Significant reductions in depressive symptoms and anxiety
	Singer, Irvin, Irvine, Hawkins, & Cooley (1989)	Two-group random assignment: intensive services group versus less intensive services group	Intensive group received 16 weeks of stress management and behavioral parent training, service coordination, and respite; comparison group received service coordination only	Parents of children with severe disabilities	Significant reductions in depressive symptoms and anxiety; reduced symptoms maintained at 1-year follow-up
Caregivers of frail older adults living at home	Lovett & Gallagher (1988)	Three-group random assignment: problem solving versus depression management training versus waiting list control	Problem-solving group received ten 2-hour group classes on problem-solving skills; depression group received ten 2-hour group classes on mood control	Older caregivers of people who were frail and older living at home	Significant reductions in depression, increases in morale
Spouse caregivers of people with terminal cancer	Theorell, Haggmark, & Eneroth (1987)	Two-group random assignment	Counseling, medical care, information, and psychosocial support	Spouses of people who died of cancer	At 2 months after death, treatment group spouses had significantly lower mental exhaustion scores

(continued)

Table 1. (continued)

Caregivers	Authors	Design	Intervention	Subjects	Findings
Relatives of people with chronic mental illnesses	McFarlane, Dunne, Lukens, & Newmark (1993)	Two-group comparison: single-family psychoeducational versus multifamily psychoeducational treatment	Multifamily format consisted of group meetings with several families to learn and practice family stress management and illness management skills; same treatment for single families	People with schizophrenia living at home and their caregiving relatives	Multifamily group members had significantly lower risk of relapse than single-family treatment group members
	Singer, Irvin, & Hawkins (1988)	Two-group random assignment: treatment versus waiting list control	Stress management skills training class received eight 2-hour meetings in groups	Parents of children with severe disabilities	Significant reductions in depressive symptoms and anxiety
Relatives of people with Alzheimer's disease	Mittelman, Ferris, Steinberg, Shulman, Mackell, Ambinder, & Cohen (1993)	Two group random assignment: treatment versus waiting list control	Individual counseling sessions followed by weekly support group meetings and service coordination	Relatives of people with Alzheimer's disease living at home	Significant reductions in nursing facility placements and caregiver depression

[a]N = 21.
[b]N = 19.

political spectrum. Public programs have grown in a piecemeal fashion at both the state and federal levels with policies often tailored to specific populations. There are eight major strands in national family support initiatives.

1. Prevention programs to assist families in poverty
2. Early intervention programs for infants at high risk and those with disabilities
3. School-based services
4. Employment-based policies and services
5. Programs for families of people with developmental disabilities
6. Programs for people with mental illnesses
7. Programs for frail older people
8. Child protective–family preservation programs

The Values Base for Family Support

All of the approaches to family support discussed in this chapter share a general set of values that differentiates them from traditional "safety net" programs, such as Aid to Families with Dependent Children and traditional child protective services. Moroney (1986) has characterized traditional governmental interventions for families as "residualist." Residualist programs draw their name from their emphasis on serving a small residual group of families, only after these families have failed. Residualist programs provide a level of assistance that is below the minimal amount needed to ensure safety and basic comfort in order to minimize dependency. Residualist programs take great pains to sort out worthy recipients from unworthy freeloaders and are generally administered by professionals who must operate under rigid regulations. The process of obtaining services is often complicated and punitive, and parents have little say in the design or delivery of them.

Most of the new family support programs developed during the 1970s and 1980s have consciously repudiated this residualist tradition. Rather than serving families after they have failed, these newer approaches emphasize prevention and promotion. They de-emphasize the social control function of program workers, opting instead to stress the need for partnerships between professionals and parents. These newer approaches aim to develop flexible, individualized forms of assistance. Rather than viewing their recipients as social failures, they focus on a family's strengths and their ability to learn new coping skills. Many of these newer programs also reflect a communitarian set of values that stresses familial responsibility in regard to caregiving. At the same time, they recognize the duty of the wider community to assist individuals and families in meeting these responsibilities. In this schema, the role of the national government is to enhance the capacity of local communities to support families as care providers. Table 2 presents a set of communitarian principles of social justice, an outlook

Table 2. Communitarian values

- People have a responsibility to help themselves as best they can.
- A second line of responsibility lies with those closest to the person.
- Communities should support the capacity of people to assist each other.
- State and national resources should be used to build and enhance the capacity of local communities.

Adapted from Etzioni (1993).

implicit in many of the family support approaches documented in this volume.

Communitarian concepts of social justice are corollaries of a social-ecological model of families and communities. Bronfenbrenner (1979) developed the social-ecological model to describe the interrelationships between child development and interconnecting social groups, but the model is applicable to caregivers (Kazak & Christakis, 1994). It is often illustrated by showing the target person nested in a series of concentric circles, with each larger circle encompassing all of the smaller ones. For parsimony, Bronfenbrenner limited this model to four concentric circles surrounding the target person, in this case a family member with a disability or chronic illness. Figure 9 illustrates this, highlighting the fact that the social environment that surrounds families is critical to their success. In contrast with interpsychic theories (e.g., personality theories) or more limited contextual theories (e.g., most versions of applied behavior analysis), the social-ecological model points to the crucial importance of the *interrelationships* between key persons and larger social units or institutions in maintaining vital social functions, such as family home caregiving.

In terms of ecological levels, caregivers are directly affected by the *microsystem*, which consists of "activities, roles, and interpersonal relationships experienced by the [caregiver]" (Bronfenbrenner, 1979, p. 29). This includes the family member with a chronic illness and the many other people who come into direct contact with the caregiver, such as other family members, medical personnel, friends, neighbors, insurance adjustors, counselors, co-workers, and church members. To keep the model manageable, it is necessary to limit the microsystem's universe to those people who are most relevant to caregiving. The extent to which these roles are supportive of caregiving has a powerful impact on the sustainability of home care. Because the extent to which the caregiver's activity patterns (i.e., the day-to-day behavioral patterns that make up caregiving) are stressful, meaningful, enjoyable, aversive, or controllable has a major impact on caregiver morale, most of the research on the treatment of caregiver stress has focused on the microsystem; interventions have included support groups, service coordination, psychoeducational interventions, counseling, respite care, and behavior modification. However, this volume is primarily concerned with the outer circles of Bronfenbrenner's model.

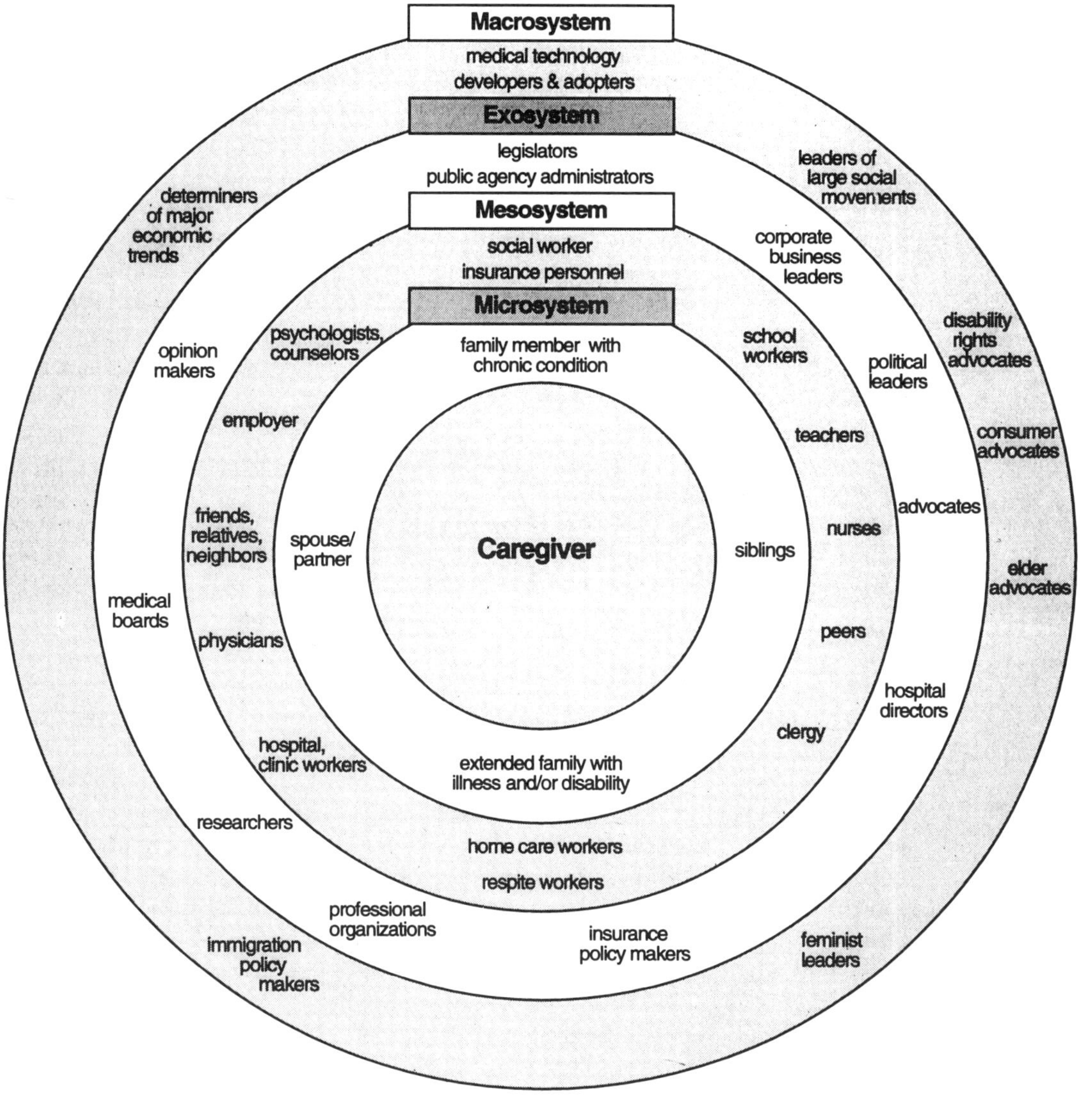

Figure 9.   Bronfenbrenner's (1979) social-ecological model highlighting the critical interrelationships caregivers rely upon to carry out their daily tasks.

The next concentric circle in the social-ecological model is the *mesosystem* representing "the interrelationships of two or more settings in which the developing person actively participates" (Bronfenbrenner, 1979, p. 25). For example, the interrelationship between a caregiver's place of employment and an ill child's school is likely to have a profound impact on the caregiver (Neal et al., 1993). For instance, imagine the difference between a place of employment that disapproves of telephone messages and emergency requests from the child's school compared to a work setting that encourages contact and allows emergency absences. Similarly, the interconnections between a primary care physician and a medical specialist have an impact on the consistency of medical information provided to the caregiver. In most cases, the mesosystem for family home caregivers is poorly developed. Two of the primary complaints caregivers express are the complexity of obtaining help and the poor quality of communication among providers. Most of the new family support programs emphasize the role of a coordinator variously named *service coordinators, family support coordinators,* or *family workers.* In both the fields of developmental disabilities and treatment for substance abuse, innovative programs have introduced ways of assembling key microsystem people into cooperative groups (H.R. Turnbull, personal communication, June 1994). Efforts to organize the mesosystem in a fashion that supports caregivers are a hallmark of the contemporary family support movement.

Bronfenbrenner (1979) defines the *exosystem* as "one or more settings that do not involve the developing person as an active participant, but in which events occur that affect, or are affected by, what happens in the setting containing the [caregiver]" (p. 25). Examples of settings in the exosystem for family caregivers are hospital boardrooms, insurance offices, school board meetings, state and federal legislative buildings, church meeting halls, and so forth. Work at this level involves community building and has been the province of political activists, community organizers, and advocates who have focused on policy, the enactment of policy, organizational structures, and the interrelationships among these organizations. At this level, it is often necessary to obtain agreement about basic values and goals, because when working with these large social units, global visions about the purpose and goals of the organization are often more salient than microsocial behavioral changes. Thus, much of the discussion about social change at this level concerns values and principles of organizational purpose and design. Of course, to be effective these global visions must be translated into practical behavior at the street level. In this volume, many of the contributors discuss the importance of a change in values in major social institutions.

The outermost ring in Bronfenbrenner's (1979) model is the *macrosystem,* defined as "consistencies in the form and content of lower-order systems that exist, or could exist, at the level of the subculture or the culture as a whole, along with any belief systems or ideology underlying such consistencies" (p. 26). This includes such underlying factors as biomedical and demographic change, traditional gender roles, traditional economic devaluation of caregiving, and the residualist tradition. These broad societal forces and cultural beliefs provide the backdrop for the interventions and policy changes that aim to strengthen the role of the informal system of care for millions of citizens and future citizens.

Chapter Review

CHALLENGES

- The number of people with disabilities is increasing in the United States, as a result of biomedical advances and the general aging of the population.
- Changes in social policy and medical treatment have moved most people with disabilities into typical communities.
- Family members provide a large proportion of the supports that people with disabilities require to live in the community.
- Women are the primary caregivers in home settings.
- There is heightened strain on families as a result of increases in work hours, employment outside of the home, high divorce rates, and a growth in the percentage of lower-income families.

CHARACTERISTICS OF HELPFUL PROGRAMS

- New programs aim to enhance the capacity of families to care for their members with disabilities.
- New programs are designed to be flexible and highly responsive to the self-defined concerns of families.
- New programs emphasize family strengths, resources, and priorities.
- New programs build connections between caregiving families and sources of support, both formal and informal.
- New programs aim to empower families, by giving them key roles in the design and governance of programs.

POLICY IMPLICATIONS

- Policy makers should identify the common concerns of families of people with many different disabilities.
- Policies should aim to prevent family stress and promote family well-being so that families can continue their traditional caregiving roles in a rapidly changing society.
- Workplaces must become more flexible in providing employees with assistance in their caregiving responsibilities.
- A variety of social innovations will be needed to support families as demands for caregiving at home increase; these include financial subsidies, service coordination, respite care, home visiting, home nursing,

counseling, linkage to informal social supports, in-home behavioral interventions, and connections to other caregivers.

- The system of support for people with disabilities needs to overcome its strong institutional bias and redirect efforts and funds to preventive support for caregiving families.

References

American Association of Retired Persons (AARP). (1988, October). *National survey of caregivers: Summary of findings.* Washington, DC: Author.

Behr, S.K., Murphy, D.L., & Summers, J.A. (1992). *User's manual: Kansas Inventory of Parental Perceptions (KIPP).* Lawrence: University of Kansas, Beach Center on Families and Disability.

Birenbaum, A., Guyot, D., & Cohen, H.J. (1990). *Health care financing for severe developmental disabilities.* Washington, DC: American Association on Mental Retardation.

Blake, J.B. (1977). From Buchan to Fishbein: The literature of domestic medicine. In G.B. Risse, R.L. Numbers, & J.W. Leavitt (Eds.), *Medicine without doctors* (pp. 11–30). New York: Science History.

Blankenhorn, D. (1990). American family dilemmas. In D. Blankenhorn, S. Bayme, & J.B. Elshtain (Eds.), *Rebuilding the nest: A new commitment to the American family* (pp. 3–26). Milwaukee, WI: Family Service America.

Breslau, N., & Davis, G.C. (1986). Chronic stress and major depression. *Archives of General Psychiatry, 43,* 309–314.

Bristol, M.M., Gallagher, J.J., & Schopler, E. (1988). Mothers and fathers of young developmentally disabled and nondisabled boys: Adaptation and spousal support. *Developmental Psychology, 24,* 441–451.

Brody, E.M. (1989). The family at risk. In E. Light & B. Lebowitz (Eds.), *Alzheimer's disease treatment and family stress: Directions for research* (pp. 2–49). Rockville: National Institute of Mental Health.

Bronfenbrenner, U. (1979). *The ecology of human development.* Cambridge, MA: Harvard University Press.

Cadman, D., Boyle, M., & Orford, D.R. (1988). The Ontario child health study: Social adjustment and mental health of siblings of children with chronic health problems. *Developmental and Behavioral Pediatrics, 9*(3), 117–121.

Cassedy, J.H. (1977). Why self-help? Americans alone with their diseases 1800–1850. In G.B. Risse, R.L. Numbers, & J.W. Leavitt (Eds.), *Medicine without doctors* (pp. 31–48). New York: Science History.

Colerick, E.J., & George, L.K. (1986). Predictors of institutionalization among caregivers of patients with Alzheimer's disease. *Journal of the American Geriatrics Society, 34,* 493–498.

Corporate and employee response to caring for the elderly: A national survey of U.S. companies and the workforce. (1989). New York: Time Magazine Company & John Hancock Financial Services.

Cowan, R.S. (1987). Women's work, housework, and history: The historical roots of inequality in work-force participation. In N. Gerstel & H.E. Gross (Eds.), *Families and work* (pp. 164–177). Philadelphia: Temple University Press.

Demo, D.H. (1992). Parent–child relations: Assessing recent changes. *Journal of Marriage and the Family,* 104–117.

Demo, D.H., & Ganong, L.H. (1994). Divorce. In P.C. McKenry & S.J. Price (Eds.), *Families and change: Coping with stressful events* (pp. 197–218). Beverly Hills: Sage Publications.

Edwards, W. (1994). *Survival data from the Dartmouth-Hitchcock neonatal intensive care nursery 1980–1993.* Unpublished manuscript, Department of Pediatrics, Dartmouth Medical School, Lebanon, NH.

Emlen, A.C. (1993). Child care, work, and family. In M.B. Neal, N.J. Chapman, B. Ingersoll-Dayton, & A.C. Emlen (Eds.), *Balancing work and caregiving for children, adults, and elders* (p. 75). Beverly Hills: Sage Publications.

Etzioni, A. (1993). *The spirit of community: Rights, responsibilities, and the communitarian agenda.* New York: Crown Publications.

Families of Children with Disabilities Support Act of 1994, PL 103-382. (October 20, 1994). Title 20, U.S.C. 1491 et seq: *U.S. Statutes at Large, 108,* 3937.

Friesen, B.J. (1989). National study of parents whose children have serious emotional disorders: Preliminary findings. In *Children's mental health services and policy: Building a research base* (pp. 29–44). Tampa: Research and Training Center for Children's Mental Health, University of South Florida.

Galinsky, E., Friedman, D., Hernandez, C.A., & Axel, H. (1991). *Corporate reference guide to work–family programs.* New York: Families and Work Institute.

Gallagher, J., Cross, A., & Scharfman, W. (1981). Parental adaptation to a young handicapped child: The father's role. *Journal of the Division for Early Childhood, 3,* 3–14.

Gallimore, R., Weisner, T.S., Kaufman, S.Z., & Bernheimer, L.P. (1989). The social construction of ecocultural niches: Family accommodation of developmentally delayed children. *American Journal on Mental Retardation, 94,* 216–230.

Goldman, H.H. (1982). Mental illness and family burden: A public health perspective. *Hospital and Community Psychiatry, 33,* 557–560.

Goldstein, M.J., & Kopeiken, H.S. (1981). Short- and long-term effects of combining drug and family therapy. In M.J. Goldstein (Ed.), *New developments in interventions with families of schizophrenics (New Directions for Mental Health Services, 12,* 5–26.). San Francisco: Jossey-Bass.

Gortmaker, S.L. (1985). Demography of chronic childhood diseases. In N. Hobbs & J.M. Perrin (Eds.), *Issues in the care of children with chronic illness* (pp. 135–154). San Francisco: Jossey-Bass.

Harris, V.S., & McHale, S.M. (1989). Family life problems, daily caregiving activities, and the psychological well-being of mothers of mentally retarded children. Special issue: Research on families. *American Journal on Mental Retardation, 94*(3), 231–239.

Hooyman, N., Gonyea, J.G., & Montgomery, R.J.V. (1985). The impact of in-home service termination on family caregivers. *The Gerontologist, 25,* 141–145.

Kazak, A.E., & Christakis, D.A. (1994). Caregiving and children. In E. Kahana, D. Biegel, & M. Wykle (Eds.), *Family caregiving across the lifespan* (pp. 331–355). Beverly Hills: Sage Publications.

Kiesler, C.A., & Simpkins, C.G. (1993). *The unnoticed majority in psychiatric inpatient care.* New York: Plenum.

Laosa, L.M. (1988). Ethnicity and single parenting in the United States. In E.M. Hetherington & J.D. Arastesh (Eds.), *Impact of divorce, single parenting, and step parenting on children.* Hillsdale, NJ: Lawrence Earlbaum Associates.

Leff, J., Kuipers, L., Berkowitz, R., Eberbein-Vries, R., & Sturgeon, D. (1982). A controlled trial of social intervention in the families of schizophrenic patients. *British Journal of Psychiatry, 141,* 121–134.

Lovett, S., & Gallagher, D. (1988). Psychoeducational interventions for family caregivers: Preliminary efficacy data. *Behavior Therapy, 19,* 321–330.

Lynch, E.W., & Hanson, M.J. (Eds.). (1992). *Developing cross-cultural competence: A guide for working with young children and their families.* Baltimore: Paul H. Brookes Publishing Co.

May Institute. (1993). *Information on pediatric brain injury.* Brochure, Research and Training Center on Rehabilitation and Childhood Trauma, New England Medical Center, Boston, MA.

McAleese, K.A., Knapp, M.A., & Rhodes, T.T. (1993). Financial and emotional cost of bronchopulmonary dysplasia. *Clinical Pediatrics, 32*(7), 393–400.

McCubbin, H.I. (1983). The impact of family life events and changes on the health of a chronically ill child. *Family Relations Journal of Applied Family and Child Studies, 32*(2), 255–264.

McFarlane, W.R. (1983). Introduction. In W.R. McFarlane (Ed.), *Family therapy in schizophrenia.* New York: Guilford Press.

McFarlane, W.R., Dunne, E., Lukens, E., & Newmark, M. (1993). From research to clinical practice: Dissemination of New York state's family psychoeducation project. *Hospital and Community Psychiatry, 44*(3), 265–270.

McFarlane, W.R., Dunne, E., Lukens, E., Newmark, M., McLaughlin-Toran, J., Deakins, S., & Horen, B. (1993). From research to clinical practice: Dissemination of New York state's family psychoeducation project. *Hospital and Community Psychiatry, 44*(3), 265–270.

Mink, I.T., Nihira, K., & Meyers, C.E. (1983). Taxonomy of family life styles: I. Homes with TMR children. *American Journal on Mental Deficiency, 87*(5), 484–497.

Mittelman, M.S., Ferris, S.H., Steinberg, G., Shuman, E., Mackell, J.A., Ambinder, A., & Cohen, J. (1993). An intervention that delays institutionalization of Alzheimer's disease patients: Treatment of spouse-caregivers. *The Gerontologist, 33*(6) 730–740.

Moroney, R.M. (1986). *Shared responsibility: Families and social policy.* Chicago: Aldine.

Neal, M.B., Chapman, N.J., Ingersoll-Dayton, B., & Emlen, A.C. (Eds.). (1993). *Balancing work and caregiving for children, adults, and elders.* Beverly Hills: Sage Publications.

Nixon, C., & Singer, G.H.S. (1993). A group cognitive-behavioral treatment for excessive parental self-blame and guilt. *American Journal of Mental Retardation, 97*(6), 665–672.

Pahl, J., & Quine, L. (1987). Families with mentally handicapped children. In J. Orford (Ed.), *Treating the disorder, treating the family* (pp. 39–61). Baltimore: The Johns Hopkins University Press.

Patterson, J.M., & Leonard, B.J. (1994). Caregiving and children. In E. Kahana, D. Biegel, & M. Wykle (Eds.), *Family caregiving across the lifespan* (pp. 133–158). Beverly Hills: Sage Publications.

Perrin, J.M., & MacLean, W.E. (1988). Children with chronic illness: The prevention of dysfunction. *Pediatric Clinics of North America, 35*(6), 1325–1337.

Popenoe, D. (1990). Family decline in America. In D. Blankenhorn, S. Bayme, & J.B. Elshtain (Eds.), *Rebuilding the nest: A new commitment to the American family* (pp. 39–52). Milwaukee, WI: Family Service America.

Radloff, L.S. (1977). The CES–D Scale: A self-report depression scale for research in the general population. *Applied Psychological Measurement, 1,* 385–401.

Risse, G.B., Numbers, R.L., & Leavitt, J.W. (Eds.). (1977). *Medicine without doctors.* New York: Science History.

Schor, J.B. (1992). *The overworked American: The unexpected decline of leisure.* New York: Harper Collins.

Schwab, L.O. (1989). Strengths of families having a member with a disability. *Journal of the Multihandicapped Person, 2,* 105–117.

Singer, G.H.S., Glang, A., Powers, L., Cooley, E., Nixon, C., Kerns, K., & Williams, D. (1994). A comparison of two psychosocial interventions for parents of children with acquired brain injury: An exploratory study. *Journal of Head Trauma Rehabilitation, 9,* 38–49.

Singer, G.H.S., & Irvin, L.K. (1991). Supporting families of persons with severe disabilities: Emerging findings, practices, and questions. In L.H. Meyer, C.A. Peck, & L. Brown (Eds.), *Critical issues in the lives of persons with severe disabilities* (pp. 271–312). Baltimore: Paul H. Brookes Publishing Co.

Singer, G.H.S., Irvin, L.K., & Hawkins, N.E. (1988). Stress management training for parents of severely handicapped children. *Mental Retardation, 26*(5), 269–277.

Singer, G.H.S., Irvin, L.K., Irvine, B., Hawkins, N.E., & Cooley, E. (1989). Evaluation of communities-based support services for families of persons with developmental disabilities. *Journal of The Association for Persons with Severe Handicaps, 14*(4), 312–323.

Singer, G.H.S., Irvin, L.K., Irvine, B., Hawkins, N.E., Hegreness, J., & Jackson, R. (1993). Helping families adapt positively to disability. In G.H.S. Singer & L.E. Powers (Eds.), *Families, disability, and empowerment: Active coping skills and strategies for family interventions* (pp. 67–83). Baltimore: Paul H. Brookes Publishing Co.

Singer, G.H.S., & Yovanoff, P. (1994). *Depressive symptoms in parents of children with disability and chronic illness: A meta analysis.* Dartmouth Medical School, Lebanon, NH.

Social Security Administration. (1993). *Quarterly report on SSI disabled workers and work incentive programs: June 1993.* Baltimore: Office of Supplemental Security Income, Division of Property Management and Analysis.

Spaniol, L., Jung, H., Zipple, A.M., & Fitzgerald, S. (1987). Families as a resource in the rehabilitation of the severely psychiatrically disabled. In A.B. Hatfield & H.P. Lefley (Eds.), *Families of the mentally ill: Coping and adaptation* (pp. 167–190). New York: Guilford Press.

Stone, R., Cafferata, G.L., & Sangl, J. (1987). Caregivers of the frail elderly: A national profile. *The Gerontologist, 27,* 616–626.

Theorell, T., Haggmark, C., & Eneroth, P. (1987). Psycho-endocrinological reactions in female relatives of cancer patients: Effects of an activation programme. *Acta Oncologia (Sweden), 26*(6), 419–424.

Turnbull, H.R., III, Guess, D., & Turnbull, A.P. (1988). Vox Populi and Baby Doe. *Mental Retardation, 26*(3), 127–132.

Waring, M. (1988). *If women counted.* San Francisco: Harper & Row.

Wilson, J.Q. (1993). *The moral sense.* New York: Free Press.

2

Family Support Across Programs and Populations

Deborah Bass

Since the 1980s, politicians and professionals have discussed how best to support families. Those who work on welfare issues worry about providing supports that strengthen families in order to break the cycles of dependency, especially among low-income families through programs such as Head Start. They believe that programs should examine a family's economic, health, and social services needs and help the family develop a plan of action. Family systems professionals emphasize the need to help families in crisis develop ways to cope with a wide variety of stressors. Programs such as Family Preservation and Support Services, subpart #2 of Title IV-B of the Social Security Act created by the Omnibus Budget Reconciliation Act of 1993, PL 103-66, help families at high risk of abusing or neglecting their children to learn coping skills and obtain needed resources. Professionals who work on issues affecting children and older people with disabilities or impairments have developed services for both the person with disabilities and the family members assisting that person. Professionals concerned about people with mental health problems try to involve families in plan development and goal setting when they are expected to help provide care.

An immense number of people need help or receive some help from family support programs. Between 10% and 15% of children under age 18, or 6,360,443–9,540,665 children according to the 1990 Census (Annie E. Casey Foundation, 1992), have chronic illnesses. Currently 80% of people over 65 years of age, which is more than 23 million people, have at least one chronic health problem (Eisdorfer, Kessler, & Spector, 1989). In 1991, an average of 11,439,000 people per month received Aid to Families with Dependent Children (AFDC) maintenance payments. In 1992, 621,078 children were enrolled in Head Start, and over 13% of them had disabilities. More than 29 million Americans with mental health problems live in their own homes or communities. Life-saving medical technologies and drug therapies continue to increase the life span of infants and children with severe illnesses or disabilities, older people, and those who have been severely injured. In the future, it seems that the number of families in need of support will continue to grow.

Although the medical and therapeutic needs of different groups of people may not be similar, they and their families share similar needs for supportive services. This chapter examines whether the available services are likely to meet their needs.

DEFINING THE FAMILY AND ITS PRIMARY FUNCTIONS

What constitutes "family" is expressed in a variety of ways. Some medical literature defines family as the most important force in shaping individuality, personality, and the expression of physical illness (Eisenberg, Sutkin, & Jansen, 1984). Family systems literature defines the family as greater than the sum of its members and suggests that programs need to be concerned about supporting family development, not just child development (Weiss & Jacobs, 1988).

The common concern about family support expressed in all literature, however, assumes that there is a family or a caregiving structure. The definition used in this chapter, developed by the Commission on Families of the National Association of Social Workers, is "two or more people who consider themselves family and assume obligations, functions, and responsibilities generally essential to healthy family life" (National Association of Social Workers, 1991).

What are these obligations, functions, and responsibilities? Aside from the obvious needs for food, shelter, and clothing, families provide for the economic security of all members. They provide health care, including emotional support during crises. Even more important, family members help each other through each developmental phase of life so they can achieve their maximum potential.

Income Support

Because economic security is a basic family function, when the family is not able to provide that security it often becomes dysfunctional in other ways. Medical, therapeutic, and social services can be quite costly. Many families whose family members have disabilities or chronic illnesses are unable to meet these costs; consequently, their income becomes inadequate.

Although families receiving AFDC income may appear to be different from families in which someone has an illness or disability, their economic needs are often similar and can benefit from similar programs. For instance, are low-income families who cannot meet their daily requirements less in need of support than families with a member who is ill or has a disability? Are they less in need of routine health care and support when one of their members has a serious illness or disability? If they lack the necessary skills to acquire and maintain a job or an independent household, they too need support and training until they can reach that level of independence.

There are programs that serve low-income families and families on welfare who need job training, child care, and transportation and also serve families in which someone has a disability or chronic illness, particularly when the disability or illness has drained the family's resources. The AFDC program provides cash payments to low-income families with dependent children throughout the United States, including those in which a parent cannot provide support due to death, continued absence, or incapacity. It also provides cash payments to low-income older adults, people who are blind, and people who meet the requirements of "permanently and totally disabled" criteria in Guam, Puerto Rico, and the Virgin Islands. People in these groups who reside in the other parts of the United States are eligible for Supplemental Security Income (SSI), which provides cash assistance for those individuals or couples who are living independently. States may also offer supplemental cash assistance, with State Supplemental Payments (SSP).

Health and Long-Term Care

Medicaid is a joint federal–state program that pays for medical services for certain groups of low-income people, with each state developing its own entitlement program within federal guidelines. Although states must provide payments for certain services (e.g., in- and outpatient hospital services, rural health clinic services, nursing facility services, home health services for people over age 21, family or pediatric nurse practitioner services) to specific groups of people (i.e., cash assistance recipients, children, pregnant women, older people who meet income and resource requirements), the states may choose to cover other groups and provide additional services.

Families who are categorically eligible for AFDC and SSI automatically qualify for Medicaid to cover health care costs. Single adults and couples without children cannot qualify for Medicaid regardless of their income or medical condition. In a two-parent family with one parent working full time, only the children receive Medicaid coverage. The mother is eligible for Medicaid coverage only during pregnancy (Congressional Research Service, 1993).

In simple terms, these eligibility rules mean that in the United States, single people and couples without children who have income-depleting illnesses or short-term, activity-limiting disabilities are not considered family members deserving of income support or health care. Unfortunately, it also means that they do not qualify for other types of support. Efforts since the 1980s to identify categories of people who "deserve" family support have backfired and now only those who meet political definitions of family may receive that support.

Older people have generally been considered deserving of help. Consequently, not only is the SSI program available to them, but also the Medicare program. Medicare is a health insurance program for older people and certain people with disabilities—most Americans ages 65 or older are eligible for it. People under 65 who have been entitled to Social Security disability benefits for at least 24 months or to railroad benefits based on disability hospital insurance benefits for 29 consecutive months are also eligible. Most people who have chronic kidney disease and require dialysis or transplant are eligible. For eligible individuals, Medicare provides hospital insurance benefits for participating hospitals, emergency hospitals, skilled nursing facilities, home health agencies, and hospices for prospective payment or for a reasonable cost of medically necessary services.

Yet, even for Medicare, there has been concern about restricting coverage to deserving older people and people with disabilities. For example, Medicare covers intermittent home health care for people who need skilled nursing care, physical therapy, or speech-language therapy—but only if they are "homebound" (Committee on Ways and Means, 1991).

There has been tremendous controversy over the term *homebound*, though, because the home health benefit is one of the fastest growing portions of the Medicare program. Without homebound clearly defined, policy makers have virtually no way to limit its boundaries. Conservatives have interpreted it to mean that the person cannot physically walk out of the house. More liberal political leaders believe that the term should be decided by the attending physician on an individual basis. As it is, Medicare requires the largest federal expenditure of any of the key programs supporting income assistance or health care. Congress and the Executive Branch continue to try to limit expenditures under the program because expenditures are growing faster than money is coming into the Medicare trust fund (Committee on Ways and Means, 1991).

Despite efforts to limit help to "deserving" families, an increasingly tremendous amount of resources is spent routinely on family support, as shown in Table 1.

Medicaid, the program requiring the second largest expenditure of federal funds out of the programs discussed here, spent all but 7% of its resources (almost $50 billion) legitimately, according to its mandate, on low-income recipients. Although viewed primarily as a program for low-income people, 42% of Medicaid's recipients were also in need of long-term care. Of the payments made for services, 26.9% were to nursing homes, 10% were for Intermediate Care Facilities for People with Mental Retardation (ICF/MR), and 5.3% were for home health care (Congressional Research Service, 1993).

In 1991, the 28.3 million Medicaid beneficiaries included the following groups:

Table 1.   Resources spent on family support through a few key programs

Program	1991 dollars spent	1994 dollars spent	Differences in spending (in dollars)	Percentage increase
Aid to Families with Dependent Children	12,666,768,000	15,541,966,000	2,875,198,000	23
Job Opportunities and Basic Skills Training Program	684,113,000	900,000,000	215,887,000	32
Medicaid	53,393,353,000	87,155,929,000	33,762,576,000	63
Medicare Hospital Insurance	68,486,313,000	101,450,000,000	32,963,687,000	48
Medicare Supplemental	45,456,110,000	56,752,000,000	11,295,890,000	25
Supplemental Security Income	15,277,188,000	24,319,000,000	9,041,812,000	59

Source: Executive Office of the President and the U.S. General Services Administration (1991).

- 45% AFDC recipients
- 18% low-income non–AFDC-receiving families, pregnant women, and children
- 16% SSI recipients
- 12% medically needy recipients (people who do not meet the eligibility requirements for income support programs but whose income and resources are low enough to meet state standards)
- 7% non–SSI-receiving older adults, people who are blind, and people with disabilities
- 2% unknown

Medicaid continued to serve low-income people according to its mandate in 1993, with approximately 83% of the recipients falling into the categorically needy (e.g., AFDC, SSI) and medically needy (e.g., low income) categories (Health Care Financing Administration, 1994). The Medicaid program also continued to pay a large proportion of its resources for long-term care, including 25.7% to nursing facilities, 9.3% for ICF/MR care, and 5.3% for home health care.

Emotional Support Through Crises and Developmental Assistance

Many professionals who work with older adults or individuals who have disabilities assess family competence during times of crises. Some believe that a family history naming which member carries out adaptational tasks is important to developing a plan of action to help the family through a current crisis (Power, Orto, & Gibbons, 1988). Assessments conducted through most programs, however, focus on immediate family needs, not on family members' strengths and abilities. Programs do not routinely encourage an assessment of family roles and responsibilities to determine whether they are based on each member's particular strengths, skills, and/or interests and whether the roles and responsibilities change during times of crisis. These programs also fail to accommodate family change.

All human services professionals acknowledge that individuals move through developmental stages throughout their lives; some believe that most families progress through predictable stages as a group. Each family member must adjust to the family's progression to another stage, which, intrinsically, changes the needs of the family (Hutton & Dippel, 1989). Yet, no program assesses these changes or considers how they affect the family's need for supports.

In the case of mental health programs, although most deal primarily with the mental health issues of individuals, there has been some interest in other family members. Unfortunately, these programs have focused on changing the family, not on understanding family dynamics and how these dynamics affect the family's need for assistance (Hatfield & Lefley, 1987). In addition, mental health programs generally receive smaller amounts of resources than the programs described above. For example, in 1991, Congress obligated $1,205,237,000 for the Alcohol and Drug Abuse and Mental Health Services Block Grant, as opposed to Medicaid's almost $50 billion budget.

Lack of a Family Focus
Despite such enormous expenditures, these programs are still failing to meet the needs of both individuals with disabilities and their families because most programs, beyond the mental health programs, are not designed to help all family members or to help the family learn to meet all of its obligations, functions, and responsibilities. A closer examination of several government-funded programs illustrates this point.

Aid to Families with Dependent Children AFDC's policies concentrate only on the needs of the head of the household, not the family as a unit. AFDC recipients must participate in the Job Opportunities and Basic Skills (JOBS) Training Program, created by the Family Support Act of 1988, PL 100-485. This program is designed to help AFDC recipients obtain remedial education, job training, and work experience. All AFDC recipients must participate unless they are one of the following:

- Incapacitated
- Needed in the home to care for another family member
- Caring for a young child
- Employed 30 hours or more per week
- Pregnant
- Residing in an area where the program is not available

Thus, when AFDC recipients have severe problems that limit their ability to work, they do not have to work; they also are not eligible for the family supports that those who can work receive. When AFDC recipients can participate in JOBS, they are supposed to receive an assessment of the following:

- Their education, child care, and supportive services needs
- Their work experience and employment skills
- Their individual family circumstances

Based on this assessment, they are supposed to receive an employability plan. Whereas there are some programs that have done this well and developed plans that support the parent and child(ren), the primary emphasis remains on the person who "should" be working, rather than on the family as a whole.

Supplemental Security Income   The SSI program is strictly a cash transfer program that makes no effort to assess any other needs that people who are older or who have disabilities may have, except for the safety of their living conditions. Many people on SSI live in board- and care-homes as a result of the deinstitutionalization of those considered to have mental illness and the shortage of nursing facility beds and other long-term care services. Therefore, Congress enacted the Keys Amendment [Section 1616(e) of the Social Security Act] in 1976, which requires states to set standards for these facilities. A 1990 study by the Inspector General of the U.S. Department of Health and Human Services revealed that state standards address personal care services, fire safety, physical structure, sanitation, and licensing. According to the report, state standards do not adequately address the residents' level of care needs; how to deal with unlicensed facilities; how to respond to complaints; and coordination among agencies, providers, and consumers (Office of Evaluation and Inspections, 1990). And not all states have established standards or licensed facilities. A General Accounting Office (GAO) study of six states revealed that four states believed they had licensed most board- and care-homes, while the other two made very limited efforts to regulate their homes (U.S. General Accounting Office, 1989).

In addition, SSI has done little to resolve the following questions: Are these SSI recipients truly without family? Or has little or no effort been made to find and work with family members so they do not feel overwhelmed by assuming some caregiving functions? If no family members exist, why has no one assessed how a family-like structure or environment might be created that, together with family supports besides the cash assistance, could meet the SSI recipients' needs?

Medicaid   The Medicaid program is not considered a family support program, yet it helps individuals and families meet one of their obligations—the provision of health care to family members. A 1990 study (Knoll et al., 1990) showed that 11 states regarded Medicaid as one mechanism for supporting families, while another 10 saw Medicaid as a major source of support for families. However, most states did not yet view Medicaid as a source of family support. Medicaid does provide one important support service to families—service coordination. This service, however, is limited and focuses primarily on meeting the individual's and/or family's medical and long-term needs.

Medicare   Again, Medicare was designed as a health insurance program, not as a family support program. Its focus has been on cost-cutting. It does little to help family members determine how to identify the best options for meeting health care needs, which, in the long term, would produce cost savings. Only if someone has been hospitalized and is fortunate enough to have a good discharge planner is it likely that the person's overall medical and long-term care needs have been addressed. Discharge planners conduct assessments, provide counseling services for the patient, and help to arrange services necessary for a patient leaving the hospital. They are usually familiar with the types of services Medicare will pay for following hospitalization (Ross, 1995).

Toward a Family Focus

To assess the impact of providing family support, the U.S. Department of Health and Human Services funded special projects. One of these efforts, through the National Long-Term Care Demonstration (Channeling) projects, assessed the impact of service coordination and family support—specifically on cost savings. It concentrated on questions that assessed cost-benefits, such as the following:

- Did formal services such as service coordination decrease the help provided by family and friends and increase the use of formal (and more costly) services?
- Did formal community services decrease (i.e., replace) the help provided by family and friends?
- Did community services reduce the use of costly nursing home care?
- Did community services reduce the use of costly hospitals?
- Did community services improve the quality of life for both clients and caregivers?

The study found that the use of services such as personal care, home-making, home-delivered meals, transportation, and child care as well as the use of special equipment increased; while the use of informal care from neighbors and friends decreased slightly. However, the increased use of these services did not prevent the use of more costly services in hospitals and nursing homes. The study also found that client and caregiver satisfaction with life improved somewhat (Kemper et al., 1988). It would be useful to have a family-focused demonstration project, however, to assess the ability of the family and each of its members to meet their obligations, functions, and responsibilities. Any cost savings would have to be assessed, for example, in terms of the entire family's ability to provide food, shelter, and clothing, and its contribution to the overall economy through employment and spending over the long term.

MODEL PROGRAMS

Home-Visiting Program

Some prevention programs do focus on family needs and anticipated needs. A recent evaluation of a nurse home-visiting program showed that teen mothers at high risk who received services had an abuse rate one fifth that of teen mothers who did not receive the services (U.S. General Accounting Office, 1992). Services included educating parents on fetal and infant development; discussing issues relating to the mother's decision to return to or find work and have additional children; involving other family members and friends in the pregnancy, birth, and care of the child and support for the mother; and helping family members acquire other health and human services. Other outcomes identified by the evaluation include the following:

- Poor and unmarried women who received home visits were employed 82% longer and had 43% fewer subsequent pregnancies during 4 years after the delivery of the child.
- Children required less emergency medical care during the first 2 years of life.
- Of the home visiting program's cost, 96% was recovered within 2 years after the program ended.
- For the first 2 years after the program ended, the estimated savings to the government were $1,502 per family for the entire sample and $1,999 per family for low-income families; for the first 4 years after the program ended, estimated savings were $1,709 per family for the entire sample and $3,013 per family for low-income families.

Job Opportunities and Basic Skills Training Program

Some JOBS programs are beginning to build agendas that take into consideration the needs of all family members. The Hawaii JOBS program conducts team assessments for all of its new enrollments. The team consists of a public health nurse, a social worker, an employment counselor, and a general service coordinator—all of whom help the family deal with crisis situations first, then with ongoing problems such as domestic violence or substance abuse and ongoing issues such as family planning. They encourage use of the Early and Periodic Screening, Diagnosis, and Treatment (EPSDT) program to assess the children's health care needs. Service coordination is ongoing and includes home visits by the professional who deals with an identified problem. For instance, a social worker would conduct home visits to help with problems of family conflict; whereas, a nurse would conduct home visits to help the family learn how to provide care to a child with a chronic illness. The JOBS staff is also responsible for finding and developing services for JOBS participants (Smith, Blank, & Collins, 1992).

Head Start Program

The Head Start program, a human services program considered successful across the political spectrum, uses a family-focused approach to provide assistance to low-income children and their families. It offers developmental, educational, social, medical, dental, nutritional, and mental health services. This social services component is designed to help families identify their own strengths and weaknesses so that they can decide when they need help and how to get it, which empowers families to make their own decisions. Within the Head Start program, a needs assessment is conducted for each family in order to identify their needs, because most families need help not only with financial assistance, but also with many other problems such as employment, education/training, housing, transportation, health/nutrition, mental health, family interrelationships, and/or parenting. Once staff members complete the needs assessment, they must provide counseling, referrals to appropriate community services, and/or help securing needed services.

Some Head Start programs improved their programs conceptually by developing links with the JOBS program. In Lexington, Kentucky, the JOBS program and two Head Start programs have established formal agreements.

One of the Head Start programs in Kentucky, a Comprehensive Child Development Program (CCDP), targets low-income families with children under age 1 and pregnant women and serves them for 5 years, emphasizing long-term career goals. The CCDP provides service coordination to help families acquire child and parent health care, education and training, and developmental child care. Staff members meet with families twice each week, including at least one home visit, to review the parent's progress toward achieving his or her personal and parenting goals and to gauge improvements in the parent's problem-solving abilities. Staff members are able to provide such intensive services because each one has a caseload of only 20 families.

Eighty-five percent of the participants are also JOBS participants. Through the agreement, the JOBS program helps pay for services such as transportation and child care when the CCDP does not have sufficient funds to cover these costs. JOBS tracks the parent's progress through CCDP reports to determine whether she is meeting JOBS requirements (Smith et al., 1992).

This emphasis on setting and achieving goals makes Head Start unique, because most family support programs merely help families get through crises. Although some programs help families establish goals in specific areas, such as goals for meeting the long-term care needs of an ill member or a family member with a disability, few help individuals or families with developmental planning as they move through different stages or respond to a variety of stressors or problems. *Developmental planning* means learning to expect and plan for changes as individuals and as a family unit. It may mean revising previously planned directions and goals based upon new needs, skills, and available supports (Bass, 1990). Thus, employment goals, for example, would be based upon both the person's skills and training and the availability of training programs and specific types of jobs within a given community. If a person's abilities changed due to disability, illness, or family needs, then his or her goals would be adjusted, as would the goals of the family as a whole. Figure 1 shows a developmental approach to family coping with disability and illness, but it can easily be adapted to generic family coping.

Any type of stress or problem can lead to family dysfunction, which results in an inability to meet obligations, functions, and responsibilities. Any change in individual roles and responsibilities can lead to a longing to fulfill goals that are no longer possible due to personal limitations or family problems; yet every family must adjust if it is to be functional and

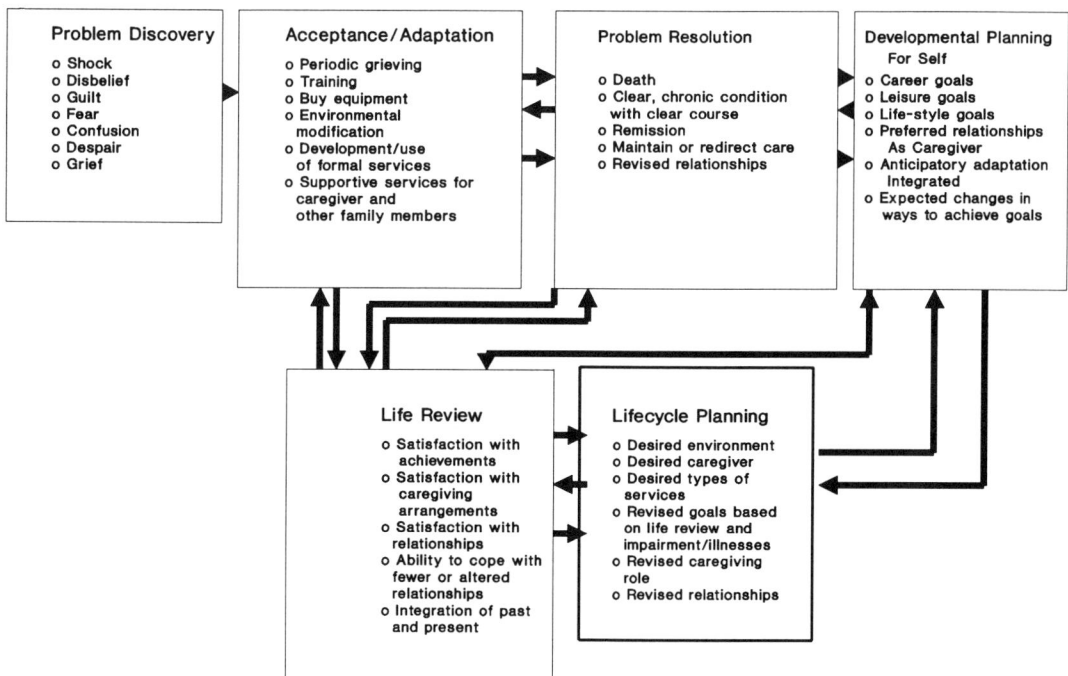

Problem Discovery	Acceptance/Adaptation	Problem Resolution	Developmental Planning For Self
o Shock o Disbelief o Guilt o Fear o Confusion o Despair o Grief	o Periodic grieving o Training o Buy equipment o Environmental modification o Development/use of formal services o Supportive services for caregiver and other family members	o Death o Clear, chronic condition with clear course o Remission o Maintain or redirect care o Revised relationships	o Career goals o Leisure goals o Life-style goals o Preferred relationships As Caregiver o Anticipatory adaptation Integrated o Expected changes in ways to achieve goals

Life Review	Lifecycle Planning
o Satisfaction with achievements o Satisfaction with caregiving arrangements o Satisfaction with relationships o Ability to cope with fewer or altered relationships o Integration of past and present	o Desired environment o Desired caregiver o Desired types of services o Revised goals based on life review and impairment/illnesses o Revised caregiving role o Revised relationships

Figure 1. A flow chart outlining steps a family with a member who has a disability or illness must undertake in order to effectively use developmental planning when faced with a problem or change. (From Bass, D. Copyright 1990, National Association of Social Workers, Inc., *Caring Families: Supporting and Interventions*; reprinted by permission.)

meet the needs of its members. Figure 2 shows how Figure 1 might be adapted to any situation.

IMPLICATIONS FOR SOCIAL POLICY

Programs Must Meet the Needs of the Entire Extended Family

In order for social policy to succeed, it must always place the focus of programs and administrative structures on the entire family—including older people and siblings who may not be living in the same household; family members of people who are older and / or have disabilities provide support even when they do not live in the same household, just as families on welfare use extended family members for child care and emotional support. These supports may include financial assistance, transportation to medical or other appointments, housecleaning, grocery shopping, and emotional support.

However, recommending improved policies and administrative structures does not mean that government should make decisions for families; rather, these changes should help families make decisions that will allow

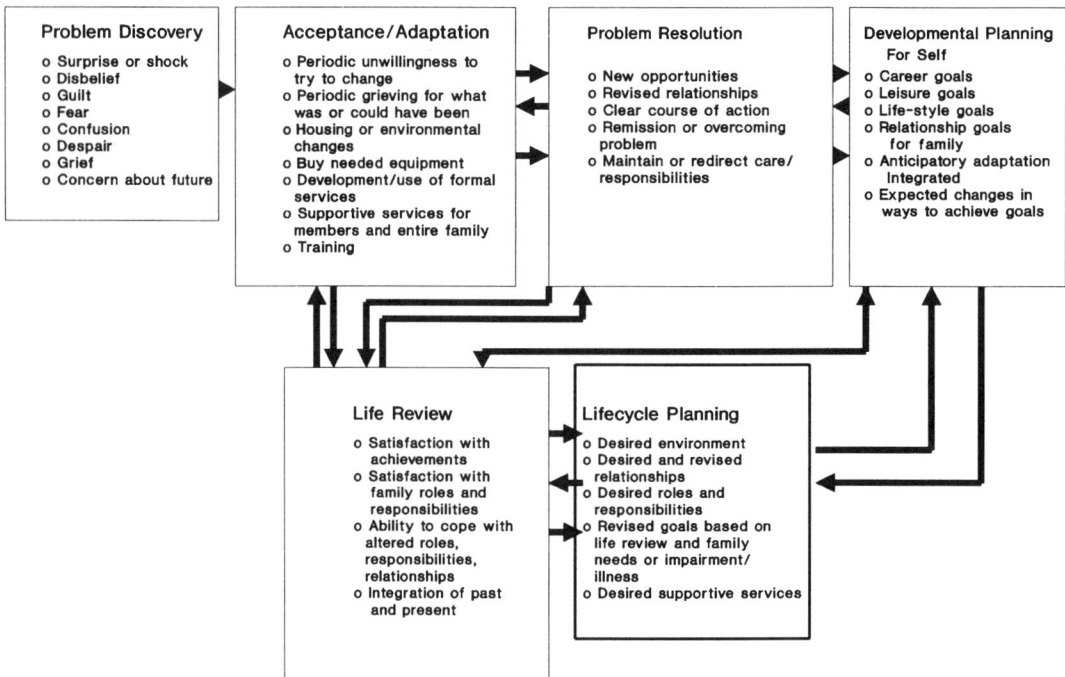

Problem Discovery	Acceptance/Adaptation	Problem Resolution	Developmental Planning For Self
o Surprise or shock o Disbelief o Guilt o Fear o Confusion o Despair o Grief o Concern about future	o Periodic unwillingness to try to change o Periodic grieving for what was or could have been o Housing or environmental changes o Buy needed equipment o Development/use of formal services o Supportive services for members and entire family o Training	o New opportunities o Revised relationships o Clear course of action o Remission or overcoming problem o Maintain or redirect care/ responsibilities	o Career goals o Leisure goals o Life-style goals o Relationship goals for family o Anticipatory adaptation Integrated o Expected changes in ways to achieve goals

Life Review	Lifecycle Planning
o Satisfaction with achievements o Satisfaction with family roles and responsibilities o Ability to cope with altered roles, responsibilities, relationships o Integration of past and present	o Desired environment o Desired and revised relationships o Desired roles and responsibilities o Revised goals based on life review and family needs or impairment/ illness o Desired supportive services

Figure 2. A flow chart outlining the general steps any family would undertake when faced with a problem or change. (Adapted from Bass, 1990.)

them to meet their obligations, functions, and responsibilities, in light of their culture and community.

Family Supports Must Be Comprehensive

The Department of Health and Human Services' programs that provide supportive services to children and their families and programs for people with disabilities have been submerged under programs that provide welfare benefits and job training (e.g., AFDC, JOBS). Although conceptually it is sound to integrate all programs that provide family support, in reality these programs emphasize income support, not family support. Yet, they fail to take into account that every family's needs may differ. Some may require more income support than others; while some do not need any income support but require other extensive support services.

If Congress and the Clinton administration succeed in limiting the maximum time that a family may receive welfare benefits as part of an overhaul of welfare programs, supportive services will become even more important. Because over 42% of the people receiving Medicaid, many of them on welfare, do require long-term assistance, many issues, such as the following, must be of concern:

- How will those requiring long-term assistance, who have qualified for Medicaid because they were welfare recipients, still qualify for Medicaid once their welfare status is revoked?
- Research has shown that most families on welfare do not remain in the program over the long term but return in times of crisis when they can no longer meet their obligations. What would happen to these families if that support was no longer available? Would such a family continue to function or would it begin to crumble, placing children in foster care, people with disabilities in special programs, and so on, thereby costing the federal government more?

Programs Must Be Flexible and Permit Individualized Responses to Family Needs

The current system for allocating support services seems to pose problems for all involved. Families find it difficult to understand the complicated eligibility requirements that allow them to receive some supports but not others. Program managers are frustrated when they assess the needs of a family but can only authorize resources to meet a need that qualifies under their program.

However, there are several solutions. Instead of having a number of program managers assess individual and family needs, each helping the family to obtain some supports, program policies need to be flexible enough to allow one program to assess needs and authorize resources. Another option is to allow state and local entities to develop teams staffed with assessors and program managers from several programs to serve one family. Guidelines could still specify when each program would assume primary responsibility and how each would assume a share of the costs. A third option, which would be more difficult to achieve politically, is to develop a single financing mechanism for each family in need of assistance that could then be used for whatever types of supports the family needed. This option would place one person responsible for working with that family.

IMPLICATIONS FOR RESEARCH

As it stands, family support programs' most important goal is to develop new measures for evaluating programmatic success. Evaluations based solely on the help a program provides to one or two family members are useless, as are concrete measures of programmatic success that relate only to a program's intended impact. Measures of change in individual and total family functioning must be developed in order to identify changes in all aspects of family obligations, functions, and responsibilities. Family support should enable a family to provide economic support, health care, and social and emotional support for all its members. However, measures cannot be unique to the type of support. For example, adequate social and emotional support may result in improved emotional well-being, as well as in an improved ability to provide economic support if a person is able to get and maintain a job after receiving those social and emotional supports. Measures also need to be developed to assess family members' progress toward and achievement of the goals they establish for themselves and the entire family. Unless measures for evaluating the success of family support efforts are developed, programmatic funding decisions will continue to be based only on political views.

Chapter Review

CHALLENGES

- A large number of people affected by various challenges require family support.
- Family support needs tend to be consistent across populations of families with different disabilities or challenges.
- When families are unable to meet the basic security needs of their members, they are likely to experience strain and have difficulty addressing other family needs.
- Eligibility requirements for income support and health care programs utilize constricted definitions of family; they often fail to provide for single people and couples without children who have income-depleting illnesses or short-term disabilities.
- Programs typically respond to immediate needs rather than promote long-term family strengths and abilities.
- Programs typically focus on individual needs and goals, instead of those of the family.

CHARACTERISTICS OF HELPFUL PROGRAMS

- Successful home visiting supports for teen mothers at high risk have included education; discussion of mother's educational, child-bearing, and vocational goals; involvement of the mother's natural support network; assistance to gain access to other services; and ongoing support for the mother and child.
- Successful job programs provide team-based assessments and interventions to assist families to address employment and other family challenges.
- Successful early child education programs offer developmental, educational, social, medical, nutritional, and mental health services based on family goals.

POLICY IMPLICATIONS

- Programs must meet the needs of the entire extended family.
- Policies and programs must assist families to make and implement decisions that will allow them to meet their obligations, functions, and responsibilities.
- Supports must be comprehensive, coordinated, and flexible, and they must respond to individual and family needs.
- Policies must be informed by outcome data that clearly document program success across multiple dimensions of family needs.

References

Annie E. Casey Foundation. (1992). *Kids count data book: State profiles of child well-being*. Greenwich, CT: Author.

Bass, D. (1990). *Caring families: Supports and interventions*. Silver Spring, MD: NASW Press.

Committee on Ways and Means, U.S. House of Representatives. (1991). *Overview of entitlement programs 1991 green book*. Washington, DC: U.S. Government Printing Office.

Congressional Research Service. (1993). *Medicaid source book: Background data and analysis (A 1993 update)*. Washington, DC: U.S. Government Printing Office.

Eisdorfer, C., Kessler, D., & Spector, A. (1989). *Caring for the elderly: Reshaping health policy*. Baltimore: The Johns Hopkins University Press.

Eisenberg, M.G., Sutkin, L.C., & Jansen, M.A. (1984). *Chronic illness and disability through the life span: Effects on self and family*. New York: Springer-Verlag.

Executive Office of the President and the U.S. General Services Administration. (1991). *1991 catalog of federal domestic assistance*. Washington, DC: U.S. Government Printing Office.

Executive Office of the President and the U.S. General Services Administration. (1994). *Update to the 1994 catalog of federal domestic assistance*. Washington, DC: U.S. Government Printing Office.

Family Support Act of 1988, PL 100-485. Title 42, U.S.C. 1305 et seq: *U.S. Statutes at Large, 92*, 2292–2296.

Hatfield, A.B., & Lefley, H.P. (1987). *Families of the mentally ill: Coping and adaptation*. New York: Guilford Press.

Health Care Financing Administration. (1994). *Medicaid statistics program and financial statistics, fiscal year 1993*. Washington, DC: U.S. Department of Health and Human Services.

Hutton, T.H., & Dippel, R.L. (1989). *Caring for the Parkinson patient*. New York: Prometheus Books.

Kemper, P., Brown, R.S., Carcagno, G.J., Applebaum, R.A., Christianson, J.B., Corson, W., Dunstan, S.M., Grannemann, T., Harrigan, M., Holden, N., Phillips, B.R., Schore, J., Thornton, C., Wooldridge, J., & Skidmore, F. (1988). The evaluation of the national long-term care demonstration. *Health Services Research, 23*(1).

Knoll, J.A., Bradley, V.J., Covert, S., Osuch, R., O'Connor, S., Agosta, J., & Blaney, B. (1990). *Family support services in the United States: An end of decade status report*. Cambridge, MA: Human Services Research Institute.

National Association of Social Workers. (1991). *Social work speaks: NASW policy statements* (2nd ed.). Silver Spring, MD: Author.

Office of Evaluation and Inspections, Office of the Inspector General. (1990). *Board and care*. Washington, DC: U.S. Department of Health and Human Services.

Omnibus Budget Reconciliation Act of 1993, PL 103-66. (August 10, 1993). *U.S. Statutes at Large, 107*, 312.

Power, P., Orto, A., & Gibbons, M. (1988). *Family interventions throughout chronic illness and disability*. New York: Springer-Verlag.

Ross, J.W. (1995). Hospital social work. In *19th Encyclopedia of social work* (pp. 1365–1375). Washington, DC: National Association of Social Workers.

Smith, S., Blank, S., & Collins, R. (1992) *Pathways to self-sufficiency for two generations*. New York: Foundation for Child Development.

U.S. General Accounting Office. (1989). *Board and care: Insufficient assurances that residents' needs are identified and met.* Washington, DC: Author.

U.S. General Accounting Office. (1992). *Child abuse: Prevention programs need greater emphasis.* Washington, DC: Author.

Weiss, H., & Jacobs, F. (1988). *Evaluating family programs.* New York: Aldine De Gruyter.

3

Toward Developing Standards and Measurements for Family-Centered Practice in Family Support Programs

Reva I. Allen and Christopher G. Petr

At our best level of existence, we are parts of a family, and at our highest level of achievement, we work to keep the family alive.

Maya Angelou

Families, in all their rich and confusing complexity, hold within themselves the greatest possibilities of nourishing each member.

Albert Gore

The term *family-centered* has been used to describe the nature of certain forms of service delivery to families with children since at least the 1950s (Birt, 1956; Scherz, 1953). The term now is used in a range of disciplines, including social work (Bribitzer & Verdieck, 1988; Dedmon, 1990; Frankel, 1988; Hartman & Laird, 1983; Marcenko & Smith, 1992), education (Bailey, Buysse, Smith, & Elam, 1992; Burton, Hains, Hanline, McLean, & McCormick, 1992; Dunst, Johanson, Trivette, & Hamby, 1991; Murphy & Lee, 1991; Roush, Harrison, & Palsha, 1991a, b), health care (Brown, Pearl, & Carrasco, 1991; Brucker & MacMullen, 1985; Fagin, 1970; Krehbiel, Munsick-Bruno, & Lowe, 1991; Larimore, 1993; Weiner & Starfield, 1983), psychology (Roberts

& Magrab, 1991), sociology (Sung, 1991), occupational therapy (Bazyk, 1989; Pierce & Frank, 1992), and communication disorders (Donahue-Kilburg, 1992).

Despite its broad use, the term *family-centered* still causes confusion because it is used by authors in different ways and because a variety of terms are used to refer to similar service delivery characteristics (Dunst et al., 1991; Lee, 1993; Nelson, Landsman, & Deutelbaum, 1990; Rushton, 1990). Confusion also surrounds the concept of *recommended practice standards* for family-centered service delivery, because these standards have never been developed into a single collection that could be used to guide practice across disciplines and settings.

Because the family-centered service delivery approach exemplifies recommended professional practice for families with dependent children, clarification and elaboration of the basic concept are essential. In short, family-centered practice is considered a hallmark of family support programs, an essential component of family support. With a clear definition of the term, the concept could be interpreted into specific standards for professional behavior. In this way, family support programs could be evaluated in terms of their degree of family centeredness and improvements made as needed. This also would allow researchers to determine if higher levels of family-centered practice lead to more effective outcomes.

This chapter reviews the literature on the development of the concept of family-centered service delivery in several disciplines, notably social work, education, and health care, culminating in a definition of family-centered practice for families with dependent children that captures the thinking in these fields as of 1995. This definition is critiqued, and some clarification of ill-defined aspects of the concept are offered. An alternative model for conceptualizing family-centered service delivery across disciplines is presented, along with examples of its application for practice and research.

REVIEW OF THE LITERATURE

The central, common element of family-centered practice is *the family as the unit of attention*. This section analyzes broad historical trends in service delivery that have bolstered this family focus and reviews family-centered developments in the fields of education, health care, and social work.

Historical Trends

There are several historical trends, common across disciplines, that have supported the development of family-centered service delivery philosophies—parental advocacy for change, criticisms of the medical model, the deinstitutionalization movement, the elaboration of social systems theory, and an increase in the willingness of politicians to consider the adoption of family-oriented policies.

Parents have served as more of an impetus for change in family-centered practice for families with dependent children than have professionals (Collins & Collins, 1990; Friesen & Koroloff, 1990; Leviton, Mueller, & Kauffman, 1992; Petr & Spano, 1990; Turnbull & Summers, 1987; Turnbull & Turnbull, 1990). Historically, service providers across disciplines have tended to focus solely upon the child, resulting in what has been termed *child-centered service delivery*. If the family was considered at all, it was viewed as the source of the problems, as an obstacle to the person's growth, or as irrelevant to the intervention process. Families have resented and disputed this approach and have pushed for changes in service delivery systems (Collins & Collins, 1990; Cournoyer & Johnson, 1991; Cunningham & Davis, 1985; Turnbull & Summers, 1987).

Ambivalence by today's professionals about whether to focus on the children in need of services or on their families is rooted in a mentality first exhibited during the Progressive Era of the early 20th century. Then, the out-of-home care of children was supported by the emerging *social science paradigm*, which endorsed the idea that children's problems were largely the result of parenting by people who had character and/or genetic flaws and, therefore, caused their children's difficulties and had no moral right to rear them (Collins & Collins, 1990; Petr & Spano, 1990; Turnbull & Summers, 1987). Under this paradigm, the professional's superiority in decision making regarding the care given to these children was assumed, and choice about the nature of this care was removed from the child, the family, and public scrutiny (Petr & Spano, 1990). The *medical model of care* also gained prominence in this era but, in recent years, has been criticized for its focus on the professional or the facility rather than on the consumer, its limitation of consumer choice and responsibility, its concentration on pathology or deficits, and its too-narrow focus on the individual client as the recipient of care and the resource for change (Bazyk, 1989; Donahue-Kilburg, 1992; Dunst, Trivette, Davis, & Cornwell, 1988; Larimore, 1993; Turnbull & Turnbull, 1990). Despite these movements, many professionals in the Progressive Era advocated a return to traditional, more family-oriented views, including "parental authority, home education, rural life, and the independence of the family unit" (Petr & Spano, 1990, p. 230).

With the 1972 *Wyatt v. Stickney* decision that established the concept of least restrictive environment, the development of a range of psychotropic medications, and the fiscal concerns of government bodies, the movement toward deinstitutionalization and community-based care of those requiring human services was strengthened (Foley & Sharfstein, 1983; Schulberg & Killilea, 1982). Then, in 1975, the U.S. Congress passed two bills that specifically reinforced the delivery of community-based services to children.

The Community Mental Health Centers Amendments of 1975, PL 94-63, which required all community mental health centers to establish children's services, and PL 94-142, the Education for All Handicapped Children Act of 1975, led to the creation of better services within schools for children requiring special care (Petr & Spano, 1990). In the mid-1970s, the decriminalization of juvenile status offenses added to the movement to maintain children with special needs in or near their own homes (Frankel, 1988).

Since the 1960s, the elaboration of *systems theory* and its increased application to professional practice has provided a conceptual framework for this increased focus on families. In particular, family systems theory has provided understandings and technologies that are indispensable for family-centered work with consumers (Bryce & Lloyd, 1979; Cunningham & Davis, 1985; Frankel, 1988; Friesen & Koroloff, 1990; Hartman & Laird, 1983; Stehno, 1986). Other applications of systems theory support the creation and maintenance of integrated, comprehensive, community-based service networks, which are characteristic of such work (Langley, 1991).

Langley (1991) suggests that the 1979 White House Conference on Families laid the foundation for political initiatives that focus upon the needs and capacities of families, countering the country's historical focus upon individual rights. By the mid-1980s, the acknowledgment that social problems were emerging that threatened families stimulated a new climate for consensus among conservatives, moderates, and liberals—a climate that encourages the creation of supports for families, including the development of family-centered, community-based, integrated social service delivery systems (Turnbull, Garlow, & Barber, 1991).

Education, Health Care, and Social Work

Since the 1970s, the fields of special education and early childhood education, fueled by several national education initiatives, have done much to explore and explicate the nature of family-centered service delivery. The Head Start program has encouraged parent involvement by providing training to improve parenting skills and by emphasizing parent control of the program. The Education for All Handicapped Children Act of 1975 required parental involvement in educational planning for children with disabilities, while PL 99-457, the Education of the Handicapped Act Amendments of 1986, mandated that states provide early childhood education for children with special education needs from birth to kindergarten. Under the latter law, "early intervention services are designed to meet the strengths and needs of the infant [and young child], as well as the strengths and needs of the family related to enhancing their child's development" (Krehbiel et al., 1991, p. 28).

The Council for Exceptional Children's Division for Early Childhood has established standards for practice that recommend that "parent services and support of parent decision making should be included in all programs that receive federal, state, or local government funds" (Burton et al., 1992,

p. 59). McDonnell and Hardman (1988) have written that exemplary early childhood programs are characterized as being integrated, comprehensive, normalized, adaptable, peer and family referenced, and outcome based.

Outside of special and early childhood education, few efforts have been made to incorporate a family-centered philosophy into the educational process as recommended education practice. However, this approach is making inroads in controversial areas such as parental management of schools (Bailey et al., 1992) and the development of school-linked community services, such as health clinics (Balassone, Bell, & Peterfreund, 1991; Harold & Harold, 1991; Wagner, 1993).

The nursing profession and the medical specialties of family practice, obstetrics, and pediatrics all have been leaders in the area of family-centered health care practice for families with young children since the 1960s. An increasing number of service delivery systems have undergone significant restructuring in order to pursue an approach to caregiving that supports the service recipient's self-determination. In many cases, families are being expected to take more active roles in the health care of their members, consumers are more actively exercising their right of choice, and the needs of multiple family members are being addressed (Pomerantz, 1984; Seltzer, Litchfield, Kapust, & Mayer, 1992).

Such service delivery for families with young children is most evident in the specific areas of maternity care and neonatal intensive care. Based upon needs expressed by child-bearing couples, maternity care units of hospitals have examined their policies and procedures to assess their adherence to consumer wishes. In many situations, those policies and procedures not based upon scientific fact or mandated by state code have been discarded or left to the mother's or couple's decision in order to maximize choices available to new parents (Timberlake, 1975). Neonatal intensive care units (NICUs) also have evolved from child centered to family centered (Brown et al., 1991). These units now consider the relationship between the individual and the environment and among all of the interacting units of the service delivery system, including family members (Thurman, 1991).

Family-centered approaches to care are not limited to newborns. Former Surgeon General of the U.S. Public Health Service, C. Everett Koop, called for the establishment of a national agenda for the care of children with special health care needs, including a focus on the families of these children and the development of a family-centered, community-based, coordinated care system (Brewer, McPherson, Magrab, & Hutchins, 1989). The necessity of involving family members in the care of adults with a chronic illness, of viewing the entire family as the client, has become an accepted principle of care for this population, as well (McIntier, 1979; Nelkin, 1987; Panel on Women, Adolescents, and Children with HIV Infection and AIDS, 1991; Taylor-Brown, 1991; Wetle et al., 1989; Woodruff & Sterzin, 1988).

Family centeredness seems to be a perfect focus for social workers, as its core values (i.e., a belief in client self-determination) are directly relevant to and consistent with principles underlying family-centered practice. Furthermore, this focus on the family dates back to the beginnings of the profession in the late 19th century; as Hartman and Laird (1983) write, "Our profession began in the company of the family and has returned to it once again" (p. vii).

The settlement movement and Charity Organization Societies (COS) both acknowledged the sanctity of the family and supported efforts to maintain family units (Pumphrey & Pumphrey, 1961). Mary Richmond wrote in 1917, "As society is now organized, we can neither doctor people nor educate them, launch them into industry nor rescue them from long dependence, and do these things in a truly social way without taking their families into account" (p. 134). In addition, both COS and settlements utilized, developed, and coordinated the resources of the communities they served.

Social work endured a struggle during the first half of the 20th century between those who affirmed a focus on the family and the growing number, influenced by the mental hygiene movement and psychoanalytic theory, who defined service delivery in terms of individuals. The former position was illustrated by the Home Service, created in 1917 to assist service men and their families with a range of functional problems (Black, 1991). The latter position was supported by the training of social workers to assist psychiatrists in military hospitals. However, interest in the functioning of families and in the provision of more comprehensive services to them has never left social work completely, and the 1950s saw a renewal in the profession's attention to families (Hartman & Laird, 1983).

In the 1950s, the Family-Centered Project of St. Paul, Minnesota, coined the term "family-centered" and established a system of multiple-agency collaboration in the delivery of coordinated, comprehensive social services to multiproblem families (Birt, 1956). Scherz (1953) used the term, before family systems theory was fully developed, to describe a system of individual counseling with multiple family members as a way to address family problems.

In the area of child welfare, PL 96-272, the Adoption Assistance and Child Welfare Act of 1980, has supported the notion of strengthening families so that removing children from their biological homes may be prevented or reduced in duration (Bribitzer & Verdieck, 1988; Bryce, 1979; Frankel, 1988; Nelson, 1984; Nelson et al., 1990; Pecora, Delewski, Booth, Haapala, & Kinney, 1985). Several states have adopted or are exploring the possibility of adopting New Zealand's family group conference process for decision making regarding children at risk, which supports the extended family taking responsibility for developing a plan for the care and protection of the child, usually within the family system itself (Allan, 1991; Firman, 1993). This model extends the concept of family centeredness beyond that currently in use by most American child welfare systems.

Family-centered service delivery also has made advances in the mental health care of children and adolescents. Residential treatment and group care facilities for children have increased the involvement of parents in their children's care and developed interventions to help the child and family learn to live and cope together (Finkelstein, 1980; Martone, Kemp, & Pearson, 1989). The Children and Adolescent Service System Program was initiated in 1984 to further the development of multiagency, coordinated, community-based systems of care for children and adolescents with serious mental health needs, at both state and local levels. It encourages the full participation of parents with children who have emotional disturbances in all areas of service planning and delivery (Allen, 1991; Collins & Collins, 1990). Many communities have begun to experiment with ways to coordinate the multiple service needs of families with children who have emotional disturbances and to increase their capacities to attain goals set by these families, often through the development of *individualized* or *wraparound service delivery systems* (Burchard & Clarke, 1990; Lourie & Katz-Leavy, 1991).

Social work's focus on the family also is evident through its presence in settings dominated by other professions. Within host settings, social work has been the discipline most often assigned responsibility for relating to parents and other family members and for allocating and providing access to community-based resources (Constable, 1992; Pennekamp, 1992; Sefansky, 1990). Social work also has enriched the family-centered service delivery of other disciplines by developing and using service coordination models, such as case management (Bennett, Nelson, Lingerfelt, & Davenport-Ersoff, 1992; Marcenko & Smith, 1992).

FAMILY-CENTERED PRACTICE: CONSENSUS DEFINITION AND CHARACTERISTICS

In order to fully understand the current usage of the term family centered, the authors reviewed more than 120 professional articles from various disciplines, some of which incorporated the views of family members in their exploration of this concept (Collins & Collins, 1990; Cournoyer & Johnson, 1991; Cunningham & Davis, 1985; Dunst et al., 1988; Lee, 1993; Leviton et al., 1992; Mahoney, O'Sullivan, & Dennebaum, 1990; Nelkin, 1987; Ooms & Owen, 1991; Summers, Turnbull, et al., 1989; Turnbull & Turnbull, 1990). A simple content analysis of the 28 definitions of the term found within this literature was performed and used to derive a definition that reflects thinking across disciplines in 1995.

Ten key concepts were identified in this analysis. They are listed here, with a number to indicate how often each appeared in the definitions:

- Regarding the "family" as the unit of attention or concern (28)
- Involving parents or forming a collaboration/partnership between parents and professionals (10)
- Addressing needs of the consumer (9)
- Providing specific types of services (e.g., home-based, comprehensive, integrated, coordinated, community-based continuum of care) (9)

- Relying upon family choice or decision making (8)
- Emphasizing the strengths or capabilities of families (7)
- Maintaining children in their own homes (5)
- Attending to the uniqueness or culture of families (2)
- Empowering families (2)
- Following principles of normalization (2)

Based upon this content analysis, the following consensus definition of the concept was developed, which captures the essence of its meaning for a significant portion of professionals who use the term:

> *Family-centered service delivery*, across disciplines and settings, views the family as the unit of attention. This model organizes assistance in a collaborative fashion and in accordance with each individual family's wishes, strengths, and needs.

Although this may appear to be a simple and straightforward definition, clarification of its key, interrelated components and characteristics is essential to developing an understanding of its implications for service delivery.

Elements of the Consensus Definition

Unit of Attention

Family-centered service delivery, as described above, focuses upon the family as the unit of attention, recognizing that children cannot be served appropriately without consideration of the family or families with whom they have lived. The entire family becomes a focus of assessment, planning, and intervention, even though the presenting concern may relate to only a part of the family.

Family–Professional Collaboration

The definition's next element focuses on organizing assistance collaboratively, pairing family members with professionals in an equal partnership. The concepts of equality, mutuality, and teamwork are used to describe the nature of this partnership (Bailey et al., 1992; Donahue-Kilburg, 1992; Lee, 1993; Marcenko & Smith, 1992; Timberlake, 1975). This conceptualization breaks down the barrier between worker and client, making them both workers with expertise, knowledge, skills, and energy to contribute to the helping process. " 'Equal partners' does not mean that parents and professionals assume each other's roles, but rather that they respect each other's roles and contributions. While professionals bring technical knowledge and expertise to this relationship, parents offer the most intimate knowledge of their children, and often special skills" (Nelkin, 1987, p. 9).

Family Choice

The third component of family centeredness addressed in the definition above is the organization of assistance for families in accordance with their wishes or choices. Although some authors refer to family involvement in decision making (Brown et al., 1991; Woodruff, 1985) or to joint parent–

professional decision making (Collins & Collins, 1990; Roberts & Magrab, 1991; Rushton, 1990), a growing number believe that for service delivery to be considered family centered, the family must, whenever possible, be the primary and ultimate directors of and decision makers in the caregiving process (Bailey et al., 1992; Bazyk, 1989; Donahue-Kilburg, 1992; Kramer, McGonigel, & Kaufman, 1991; Leviton et al., 1992; McGonigel, 1991; Summers, Turnbull, et al., 1989). This latter interpretation expands the meaning of collaboration from working *with* families to working *for* them.

Family Strengths

The definition of family centered next includes a consideration of family strengths—acknowledging them, incorporating them into intervention plans, and building upon them. Although, as Saleebey (1992) notes, "most such nods to building on strengths are little more than lip service," a genuine professional focus on client strengths and their importance to service delivery has been growing during the past decade (Blue-Banning, Lee, Jones, & Turbiville, 1992; Dunst et al., 1988; Saleebey, 1992; Summers, Behr, & Turnbull, 1989). This perspective modifies the view of family members as people who only cause problems and are obstacles to the improvement of clients and it is consistent with the notion of collaboration as a preferred style of family–professional interaction. It may also facilitate the empowerment of families, which often is mentioned as a principle or goal underlying family-centered work (Dunst et al., 1988; Larimore, 1993; McGonigel, 1991; Petr & Pierpont, 1992; Seltzer et al., 1992; Stehno, 1986).

Family Needs

The fifth component of the consensus definition addresses family needs. As noted above, family-centered service is offered and available to all members of a family, not only to the member with the presenting problem, and allows for changes as a family's needs change. This component takes a holistic view of the family's circumstances, concerns, and resources.

Individualized Services

The final element of family-centered service delivery specifically referenced by the consensus definition calls for individualized services to each family. The processes and products of assessment, goal setting, and intervention planning and implementation must be matched to the needs, coping strategies, and formal and informal resources of each particular family, rather than expecting every family to fit into a formulized approach to care (Bazyk, 1989; Dunst et al., 1988; Friesen & Koroloff, 1990; Lourie & Katz-Leavy, 1991; Simeonsson & Bailey, 1991; Turnbull & Summers, 1987). As McGonigel (1991) phrases it, services should be "tailor-made" to each individual family (p. 11).

The concept of individualized services also respects the structural and cultural uniqueness of each individual family. It does not assume that families who have certain structures, lifestyles, socioeconomic statuses, and belief systems are less healthy, functional, or desirable than others (Krehbiel et al., 1991; Thurman, 1991; Woodruff, 1985). It also specifies that racial and ethnic differences among families must be recognized and accepted, and their implications for service delivery must be taken into consideration as care is provided (Allan, 1991; Brown et al., 1991; Ho, 1987; Krehbiel et al., 1991; Mokuau, 1990; Taylor-Brown, 1991).

Additional Characteristics of the Consensus Definition

In addition to service characteristics specifically mentioned in the consensus definition are several others that the literature considers essential to the implementation of this model. Several of these are described below.

Family-Sensitive Information-Sharing Processes

Information exchange reflects the collaborative model, and Collins and Collins (1990) suggest that "full parental involvement" in service delivery includes sharing all relevant information with parents, just as it is shared with other team members (p. 523). This information should be shared in a way that is most useful for a particular family member as well as in a timely fashion, in manageable doses, in the family's primary language without the use of jargon, on a continuous basis, and in a variety of formats (Pecora et al., 1985; Rosenbaum, King, & Cadman, 1992; Rushton, 1990; Summers, Turnbull, et al., 1989). Within this model, the family generally maintains control over what information is shared, with whom, and in what manner, and confidentiality of family information is important.

Normalization

Undergirding the concepts of strengths and empowerment is a normalization perspective—the recognition that much of what service recipients are experiencing is typical, that they can benefit from and have a right to interactions in the community that are typical of others with similar interests, and that services need to be structured and delivered in such a way that the normality of a family's life is disrupted as little as possible (McGonigel, 1991). A normalization perspective dictates that interventions support the functioning of family members in their natural roles (Murphy & Lee, 1991; Panel, 1991).

User-Friendly Service Delivery

The final characteristic of family centeredness relates to the structure in which services are delivered. The dominant features of this structure are 1) maximized accessibility (Collins & Collins, 1990; Frankel, 1988; Pecora et al., 1985; Rushton, 1990); 2) flexibility and customizing of services in as many areas as possible (Bryce, 1979; Leviton et al., 1992; Pierce & Frank, 1992; Turnbull & Summers, 1987; Woodruff & Sterzin, 1988); 3) noncategorical service delivery and funding (Friesen & Koroloff, 1990; Hutchinson & Nelson, 1985; McDonnell & Hardman, 1988); 4) comprehensiveness in scope (Brown et al., 1991; Friesen & Koroloff, 1990; Nelkin, 1987; Panel,

1991); 5) coordination of the service delivery system (Donahue-Kilburg, 1992; Murphy & Lee, 1991; Petr & Pierpont, 1992; Thurman, 1991); and 6) the incorporation and expansion of a wide variety of community-based supports and resources, including both informal networks and formal services (Bribitzer & Verdieck, 1988; Brucker & MacMullen, 1985; Dedmon, 1990; Dunst et al., 1991; Wetle et al., 1989).

Critique of the Consensus Definition of Family-Centered Service Delivery

Although this definition of family-centered service delivery answers many questions, several issues and difficulties still arise as one attempts to operationalize it: how to resolve conflicts among various parts of the definition, how to identify the limits to family choice, how to define family, and how to handle disagreements among family members.

The primary difficulty arises from the family choice element of the definition, which may conflict with other elements in practice. For example, a family may wish to identify only a single member as the unit of concern or recipient of care and ask professionals to leave the rest of the family out of the process. Or, they may choose not to be fully involved in information sharing, in planning for services, or in participation within the policy-making mechanisms of the organization. When these conflicts arise, which element of the definition is to take priority?

The consensus definition presents other family choice-related issues. For example, a consumer's wishes cannot and should not be fulfilled all of the time due to ethical, safety, practical, and legal constraints. Additionally, collaborations seldom are conflict free. When there are disagreements between family members and professionals, some process must enable a decision to be made because mutual consensus is not always possible.

Few authors in the family-centered literature synthesized here address the task of defining the family (Firman, 1993; McGonigel, 1991; "Spreading family-centered care," 1975; Taylor-Brown, 1991). Although professionals may consider the entire family as the unit of attention, in actual practice, involvement and collaboration may be limited to the parents, to a parent–child dyad, or even solely to the primary caregiver, who usually is the mother (Larimore, 1993; Mahoney et al., 1990; Marcenko & Smith, 1992; Panel on Women, Adolescents, and Children with HIV Infection and AIDS, 1991; Sparling, Berger, & Biller, 1992; Turnbull & Summers, 1987). In this light, it may be more accurate to refer to many family-centered programs as "parent centered" or "mother centered" (Drotar, 1991; Simeonsson & Bailey, 1991).

To complicate the matter further, although many references have been made to the family (as decision maker, as recipient of services, and as the unit of attention), it is clear that the family as a whole does not always act in unison. Family members often disagree with each other, and some may be too young or too incapacitated to participate in all aspects of the service delivery process. This makes the family as the unit of attention a concept that is fraught with difficulties.

FAMILY-CENTERED PRACTICE: A NEW CONCEPTUALIZATION

These difficulties, combined with the work of various parents and professionals who are exploring ways to expand the potential of family-centered practice (Firman, 1993; Lee, 1993; Leviton et al., 1992; Turnbull & Summers, 1987), suggest that the concept's current definition requires modification if valid practice standards and measurement tools are to be developed. The family-centered service delivery concept seems to be guided by two indispensable elements: *family choice* and *the adoption of a strengths perspective.* Therefore, a new definition of family centeredness is as follows:

> *Family-centered service delivery,* across disciplines and settings, recognizes the centrality of the family in the lives of individuals. It is guided by fully informed choices made by the family and focuses upon the strengths and capabilities of these families.

The implications of this definition for families with dependent children are described below.

Family Choice: Areas in Which Choice Is Exercised

The first core element of family-centered practice, as defined in this chapter, is family choice. The family is viewed as the director and consumer of the service delivery process, as the party with ultimate decision-making authority (Bailey et al., 1992; Bazyk, 1989; Donahue-Kilburg, 1992; Dunst, 1991; Kramer et al., 1991; McGonigel, 1991; Nelkin, 1987; Summers, Turnbull, et al., 1989). Thus, a family-centered approach would maximize family choice in each of the following areas.

Choice Regarding the Definition of the Family

Webster's New Collegiate Dictionary defines family as "a group of individuals living under one roof and usually under one head" (Mish, 1991, p. 448), which certainly improves upon the dyadic (parent–child or mother–child) view of the family often encountered in practice. In fact, family-centered service delivery requires the family itself to define its boundaries. Therefore, the definition of family proposed by the National Association of Social Workers' Commission on Families better suits family-centered practice: A family is "two or more people who consider themselves family and who assume obligations, functions, and responsibilities generally essential to healthy family life" (Barker, 1991, p. 80).

Many things affect our thinking about family membership and structure, including ethnicity and culture (Ho, 1987). Extended family ties tend to be strong among ethnic minority families and may play a vital part in the functioning of the family. Tribal units may also be considered components of families, as is illustrated by the use of the phrase "family, whanau, hapu, iwi, and family group" to refer to the "family" in New Zealand's Children, Young Persons, and the Families Act[1] (Wilcox et al., 1991). Even nonrelatives, such as pastors and close friends, may be considered and function as members of the family (Taylor-Brown, 1991; Woodruff & Sterzin, 1988). The family-centered practitioner will respect this choice and incorporate it into the design of service delivery.

Choice Regarding Who Makes Decisions

Although ideal, consensus decisions among family members regarding service delivery are not always possible or desirable. Consistent with family systems theory, caregivers of families—usually the parents—are recognized as the heads of the household and, therefore, the primary decision makers for the unit. Family-centered practitioners encourage each family member to be as involved as possible in the service delivery process and acknowledge the normality of conflict that may result (Friesen & Koroloff, 1990); this does not alter the position that the parents or caregivers ultimately must be responsible for making choices regarding care.

Recognizing parents as the primary decision makers in families with children with disabilities does not negate the perspective that family members and professionals need to maximize the self-determination options for those children, especially as they grow into adolescence and adulthood. A family-centered approach needs to guard against *adultcentrism,* the tendency of adults to view children and their problems from a biased, adult perspective (Petr, 1992). Just as professionals should not preempt the roles and choices of parents, parents should not assume responsibilities or make decisions that could be handled by their children. The growth and empowerment of the person with special needs should always be supported.

Group Action Planning provides an example of ways in which families with children with disabilities have exercised their decision-making options.

> Group Action Planning (GAP) occurs when a group of family, friends, and professionals create a "reliable alliance" for the purpose of creatively, energetically, and joyfully translating great expectations into realities and promoting the preferences of the individual and family. (Turnbull & Turnbull, 1993, p. 1)

GAPs create a context for social connectedness and interdependent caring by using this empowering network to share visions of and create action plans for a lifestyle preferred by the individual with disabilities. This approach to care goes beyond various individualized service plans to build a stronger, broader, more intimate base of support for both individuals with disabilities and their families (Turnbull & Turnbull, 1992).

---

[1]According to Williams (1957), "whanau" refers to a family group, although "it is questionable whether the Maori had any real conception of the family as a unit" (p. 487). Barlow (1991) translates the term to mean the extended family (pp. 32–33). The "hapu" is a clan or a section of a tribe (Williams, 1957), while an "iwi" is a tribe (Barlow, 1991).

Choice Regarding the Unit of Attention

The family-centered professional respects the family's right to choose who to involve in the service delivery process. The child–caregiver dyad is a reasonable place to start for the initial engagement between the family and the practitioner. However, over time, the professional must respond to the wishes of the family regarding the expansion or reduction of this unit of attention.

Choice Regarding the Nature of the Family–Professional Relationship

In family-centered service delivery, the family also makes choices regarding the nature of the family–professional relationship (Leviton et al., 1992). The professional serves as a source of information about the options available to the family and a negotiator of roles (Bennett, Nelson, Lingerfelt, et al., 1992), but the limits of these negotiations are still determined by the family and might include any style of interaction ranging from professional directed to parent controlled. In professional-directed approaches to care, the professional is in charge of care and may avoid or minimize involvement with the family, according to the professional's goals (Cunningham & Davis, 1985; Donahue-Kilburg, 1992). The dominant family–professional approach advocated by family-centered practitioners is collaborative, pairing professionals and families as equal partners who work as a team toward mutually defined goals (Collins & Collins, 1990; Friesen & Koroloff, 1990; McGonigel, 1991; Roberts & Magrab, 1991; Thurman, 1991).

A recent emphasis of family-centered models places the family firmly in control of the service delivery process, with the professional serving as an agent for the family (Donahue-Kilburg, 1992; Dunst et al., 1988; Lee, 1993; Tower, 1994). According to professionals at the Kennedy Institute's Department of Family Support Services, parents value professionals' knowledge and clinical expertise in relation to their child but feel that only they have the necessary expertise to determine whether the recommendations of professionals can be successfully incorporated into their own families (Leviton et al., 1992). This model of service delivery conceptualizes the professional role as one of "consultant" (Bazyk, 1989; Donahue-Kilburg, 1992; Roberts & Magrab, 1991), in which the professional works for the family and is at their service.

Choice Regarding the Sharing of Information

In family-centered practice, information flows in both directions, and the family is in control of the information it discloses as well as the information it receives regarding the child's and family's situation, the activities of the professionals involved, and community resources (Brown et al., 1991; Dunst, 1991; Leviton et al., 1992; Nelkin, 1987; Rushton, 1990). Only relevant information is requested by professionals, and the family chooses the form in which the material is provided (i.e., face-to-face interviews, videotaped formats, or filling out a form) (Bazyk, 1989; Dunst, 1991; Leviton et al., 1992; Summers, Turnbull, et al., 1989; Turnbull & Summers, 1987). As members of the intervention team, family members have access to the same information as other team members and control over how information is shared among various sources (Collins & Collins, 1990; Leviton et al., 1992; Roberts & Magrab, 1991). Regardless of format, communication between family members and professionals should be as free of jargon and patronizing, blame-laden language as possible (Collins & Collins, 1990; Leviton et al., 1992; Summers, Turnbull, et al., 1989). It also should match the developmental demands and abilities of the recipient (Kutner, 1994). Professionals must also find the most effective way of establishing and maintaining communication between providers and family members whose primary language differs (Woodruff, 1985).

Choice Regarding the Identification of Needs, Goals, and Intervention

Family-centered practice begins by identifying child and family concerns and goals as the family sees them (Bennett, Nelson, & Lingerfelt, et al., 1992; Dunst et al., 1988; Friesen & Koroloff, 1990; Hutchinson & Nelson, 1985; Krehbiel et al., 1991; Thurman, 1991; Turnbull & Summers, 1987; Turnbull & Turnbull, 1990). The professional may present additional potential areas of concern to the family, acknowledging their right to accept or refuse these ideas. The child's and parents' situations are viewed holistically within the context of the broader family, so that the consideration of needs and goals is as comprehensive as the family wishes it to be. The family also provides suggestions and makes choices regarding the interventions used to reach these goals (Bazyk, 1989; Cunningham & Davis, 1985; Firman, 1993; Hutchinson & Nelson, 1985; Rushton, 1990). Professionals and family members (including the people with special needs, as they are able) together compile an exhaustive list of formal and informal resources needed to meet family goals and of the intervention options (Leviton et al., 1992; Woodruff, 1985). Family members receive a full explanation of each option's potential costs and benefits to help them develop a plan. In the process, the family and professional negotiate their respective responsibilities for implementing the plan (Dunst, 1991; Pierce & Frank, 1992; Roberts & Magrab, 1991).

The family also maintains the right to choose the level and nature of its involvement in the service delivery process (Bazyk, 1989; Dunst, 1991; Firman, 1993; Leviton et al., 1992; McGonigel, 1991; Pierce & Frank, 1992; Woodruff, 1985). As Turnbull and Summers (1987) note, not all families want to be decision makers. Furthermore, only some place a priority on implementing home intervention programs; some like support groups, while some benefit from written self-help materials; some wish to be designated as team leaders or as service coordinators, while others do not want the responsibility. Families may choose to use only a few of the available service options or to totally reject involvement with the formal service delivery system. Family-centered professionals must maintain a flexible perspective on how family members may be involved in the helping process and expect the nature of this involvement to differ from family to family and, within any one family, to change over time (Donahue-Kilburg, 1992; Dunst, 1991; Rushton, 1990).

Family Choice: Limits to Choice

Although family choice is central to the concept of family centeredness, there are limits to any person's self-determination. First, the person must have the capacity to make the choice. Some family members may be too young or have too severe a mental disability to make fully informed choices. However, family-centered practice takes a broad view of capacity, believing in the rights, strengths, and capabilities of families to make reasonable, informed decisions, even if they differ from those of professionals (Finkelstein, 1980; Roberts & Magrab, 1991).

Second, the parent or family must be ready to assume responsibility. In terms of family members of infants who are in NICUs, Krehbiel et al. (1991) suggest that "this concept [parental/family readiness] takes into consideration each family member's ability to take in new information, to become involved in care and decision making, and to receive 'bad news' " (p. 30). Briar (1991) reminds professionals to move at a pace suitable to each family, as their timetable and ability to use services may be different from those of the professional. Research with members of families that include children who have disabilities shows that families want to be introduced gradually to their role of decision maker and to be taught the skills they need to be effective in this role (Summers, Turnbull, et al., 1989). Professionals must be able to determine the readiness of family members to participate in the service delivery process and to offer opportunities for involvement based upon these levels of readiness (Rushton, 1990).

Third, self-determination cannot infringe upon the rights of others. Choices must be made within a legal framework that respects the rights of all parties. For example, professionals do not sanction parents' choices to physically, emotionally, or sexually abuse their children (Cunningham & Davis, 1985; McGonigel, 1991).

Fourth, a person cannot determine how another should behave. Even though the family-centered practitioner is the "employee" of the family, employees cannot and should not always do what the employer asks. Professionals are obligated to inform families when they disagree about means or ends, when they are being asked to do something that they are not capable of doing, when family wishes conflict with limits of the professional's expertise or licensure or with those placed by the organization that employs them, or when they cannot perform or condone certain behaviors because they are illegal or unethical.

Fifth, logistical considerations can limit the choices of families. Often, the resources needed to meet a family's goals may not be available (Kramer et al., 1991). The cost of services can be prohibitive, and difficult decisions sometimes must be made when allocating scarce resources. This fiscal reality also applies to political and nonpolitical entities that could or do fund services.

Strengths and Capabilities

The second core element of family-centered practice is a commitment to family strengths and capabilities. Family-centered practice is virtually impossible without a strong belief in the importance of the family and a strong respect for the inherent strength and capability of family members (Dunst et al., 1988; Simeonsson & Bailey, 1991). Too often, professionals across disciplines have focused upon the deficiencies of children and families, to the extent that families feel under attack rather than supported by the people trained to help them (Briar, 1991; Collins & Collins, 1990; Cournoyer & Johnson, 1991). Family-centered service delivery represents a significant shift in the way professionals and families consider each other and prevents this cycle of family blame.

This approach to service delivery is guided by an awareness of and respect for families' positive attributes, abilities, talents, resources, and aspirations (Saleebey, 1992). Sometimes, the professional needs to encourage family members to adopt this perspective by helping them identify functional, productive aspects of their lives as strengths, aspects of which they lack conscious awareness, take for granted, or have viewed only as problems. Family-centered professionals are committed to using these resources to overcome shortcomings, and to support rather than criticize (Bennett, Nelson, & Lingerfelt, 1992; Collins & Collins, 1990; Dunst et al., 1991; McGonigel, 1991; Nelkin, 1987). Strengths come in a variety of forms, and practitioners must be creative and open-minded in their perspectives of what makes a certain characteristic or behavior a positive contribution to a family's life. This attitude is sometimes challenged when professionals interact with families of a different race, culture, sexual orientation, or socioeconomic status (McGonigel, 1991; Nelkin, 1987). Then the family-centered professional must guard against judging competency through an ethnocentric lens, which could distort or cloud the strengths and competencies of different cultures and lifestyles.

The functional aspects of a particular family's life must be identified, sanctioned, and expanded to those areas which do not work as well. Dunst et al. (1988) point out that professionals may not learn about a family's capabilities because social systems fail to create opportunities for them to be displayed. One of the functions of the professional, then, is to create such opportunities, thereby enabling the family to apply their full repertoire of skills.

Evidence shows that many families feel that their lives have been enhanced and strengthened by the presence of a child with special needs. They report that the experience has strengthened them in the following ways:

- They have a greater appreciation for the simple things in life.
- Their religious faith has been strengthened.
- Their social networks and career opportunities have expanded.
- They feel a greater sense of love and joy in their lives.
- They have a greater appreciation of the value of different kinds of people (Blue-Banning et al., 1992; Kutner, 1994; Pierce & Frank, 1992; Summers, Behr, et al., 1989).

As a family's capabilities are recognized and utilized, the potential for increasing their range of abilities is strengthened (Bennett, Nelson, Lingerfelt, et al., 1992; McGonigel, 1991). Dunst et al. (1988) found that parents receiving services characteristic of the family-centered model, particularly their being allowed to make decisions regarding their families, was associated with their feeling increasingly in control over the care of their children. Thus, the concepts of strength and choice are intertwined and enhance each other—a belief that families possess the strength and capacity to make decisions for themselves leads to the utilization of a service delivery model that maximizes family choice, which itself contributes to an increase in families' sense of competence.

This focus on strengths extends to the identification, use, and building of strengths among families' support networks and broader communities (Roberts & Magrab, 1991). Briar describes one of the benefits of this approach: "The more capacity built through multigenerational families, work groups, and support networks, the less of a capacity crisis the helping systems will experience" (1991, p. 76).

Standards for family-centered practice must be based on the dual, interrelated cornerstones of *choice* and *strengths,* which are both at the core of family-centered practice and establish the context for a variety of other decisions and interactions to take place.

IMPLICATIONS OF FAMILY-CENTERED
SERVICE DELIVERY FOR PRACTICE AND RESEARCH

Implications for the Development of Standards for Practice

According to this model of family-centered service delivery, family members are in the best position to judge whether services are indeed family centered and to determine if they successfully meet their needs. The realization of the vision of service delivery described below requires, for many professionals and parents, a dramatic shift in their views regarding each other's roles, particularly ideas about who is in charge of the service delivery. Professionals must learn to trust families—to trust that they have strengths, that they genuinely and deeply care for their children, that they are interested in and capable of growth, and that they can make effective decisions on their own behalf. They must also actively reinforce the process of sharing information with family members so that their decisions may be as informed as possible.

The potential for conflict within this framework (among family members, among staff, and between family members and professional staff) is acknowledged; therefore, service organizations need to create structures to address grievances and resolve conflicts. Staff must be trained and supported in their efforts to address disagreements with and within families constructively.

In outlining this vision of family-centered service delivery, the authors acknowledge the inspiration provided by the New Life Center of Family Hospital in Milwaukee, the Kennedy Institute's Department of Family Support Services, and New Zealand's family group conferences (Firman, 1993; Leviton et al., 1992; Timberlake, 1975).

Initial Contact

Within a family-centered service delivery system, family members could initially contact a service provider through a variety of means: by telephone, in person with or without an appointment, by e-mail or FAX, or via a third party. Regardless of the means, the family member(s) can easily reach a staff member who will listen to their concerns and wishes and ascertain that the appropriate service provider has been contacted. Families in the service delivery process always are spoken to in easy-to-understand language.

Paperwork at this point is limited to the minimum required to move on to the intake process and/or referral to another provider. Each service delivery system has staff available who are thoroughly familiar with the full range of community resources and who can facilitate easy access to these other resources. Staff always treat family members as competent people with expertise and the best intentions concerning their child. Staff express an attitude of "we are here to work for you" and "let's see how we can get this done."

Intake and Assessment

The intake and assessment process is both efficient and flexible. Family members are able to direct its pace, location, and timing, so that they are as comfortable as possible with the process. Intake and assessment cover as comprehensive a range of life domains as the family members wish, reinforcing the notion that the service provider is there to assist them with whatever concerns or needs they have, regardless of the presenting issue. Because multiple providers and service systems may be involved with a family, an efficient means of coordinating services throughout the service delivery process is established at this point.

During this and all other phases of the service delivery process, family members are provided with all information they want and need, and which legally can be given to them, regarding the service provider, the child's or family's area of special need, community resources, assessment results and care plans, and so forth. It is available to them in a variety of formats (written, visual, oral) and in the everyday language of the consumers. They are given copies of all documents they are required to sign and of all materials available to other members of the service team. They are incorporated as much as possible and as they wish as contributors to the writing of documents pertaining to their care.

Early on, the parents are asked to define who constitutes their family and which family members should be included in the assessment. The specific evaluation instruments, procedures, staffing, scheduling, location, and choice of participants remain flexible, so that family members, with the consultation of staff members, are able to design the assessment around their concerns and wants. The assessment includes a thorough exploration and explication of the family's strengths and resources, as well as their concerns. The observations and understandings of family members are incorporated into the process and given weight that is consistent with their roles as experts about their child and family. Assessment results are shared with family members orally and in writing as soon as possible. Family members are able to edit the reports for accuracy and choose who receives copies.

Care Planning

Care planning focuses upon concerns selected by the family, after they have received their staff members' viewpoints and assessments. The professional staff's primary duties are to provide helpful information to the family as they make decisions about care and to provide the support needed by the family to implement its plans, without pushing its members to make decisions they do not feel ready to make. The family is able to select intervention options from a "menu" of alternatives, while contributing their own ideas to this list of options. The parents attend all care planning meetings and decide which professionals and members of their support network will attend. In addition, they are able to call care planning meetings whenever they feel that plans need to be reviewed and/or revised.

Intervention

Parents and their children with special needs determine the breadth and form of intervention. When negotiations about plans or interventions fail to result in decisions acceptable to all parties, the wishes of the family members prevail over those of staff. Intervention is designed primarily to utilize and build upon existing strengths and capacities of family members, rather than to identify and correct deficiencies. Throughout the intervention process, case records are kept simple, confidential, and available to the parents.

Evaluation and Termination

Ongoing review of the family's situation and experience with the service delivery system is built into the intervention process. Family members take part in the design and implementation of the evaluation plan, including determining the conditions under which intervention will be suspended or ended. If the family and the professional disagree about whether termination should occur, the family makes the final decision. Termination is approached in a planful manner, providing ample time for the family to make adjustments for the approaching end of care, to initiate transitions into other services, and to make decisions regarding such issues as follow-up, evaluation of the service delivery process, and the handling of case records.

Advocacy

Family members are able to participate in the service program's decision-making process as members of committees, task forces, and boards. They are hired to train staff and other parents and are encouraged to organize themselves in order to meet their own goals and needs. Family members are also provided information on service gaps and limitations and are supported in their efforts to advocate for improved services within and outside a particular service system. Staff are willing and able to help them develop the skills and confidence they need for these endeavors.

Implications for Research and Measurement

This model of family-centered service delivery, when operationalized, provides an approach to the evaluation of family support programs. Consumers, policy makers, and program funders are interested in the extent to which these programs are family centered, and whether this concept correlates with or affects the outcomes of services. The Beach Center on Families and Disability has developed a scale that measures the degree of family-centered behavior of service providers who work with families with children who require special resources. The process used to develop the scale illustrates the application of family-centered principles to research.

Consumers were involved in all stages of this family-centered research inquiry. A Constituency-Oriented Research and Dissemination (CORD) Committee (Fenton, Batavia, & Roody, 1993) was created in the initial research design process. The CORD consists of parents of children who require special resources, service providers and policy makers, and the research staff. It meets approximately once per quarter to review and critique the progress of the study and to provide suggestions for the next stages of work.

The study's literature review incorporated references that cited and summarized parental views on service delivery. The conceptualization of family-centered service delivery was discussed thoroughly with three groups of parents and professionals. Next, six focus groups were held to discuss potential items for the Family-Centered Behavior Scale. These groups included 22 parents of children requiring special resources and 20 professionals who work with families. Their comments were used to improve the potential items and select the final scale items; they also made invaluable suggestions for maximizing parental response to the survey. The scale and accompanying materials were field-tested by a group of parents of children who require special assistance. Some focus group participants were paid a small fee for their work, and survey respondents were offered the opportunity to receive the Beach Center's newsletter and a summary of the research findings.

This study made a concerted effort to broaden the range of families receiving the validation study research packets. Strategies were explored to increase the ethnic, gender, and socioeconomic diversity of the respondents, as well as to include parents who receive services from systems with highly confidential consumer lists (i.e., child protection). The research packet was printed in both English and Spanish in an effort to respond to the needs and wishes of the growing population of Spanish-speaking citizens in the United States. Over 450 caregivers of children with physical, developmental, or emotional needs responded to the validation survey.

The scale itself is completed by parents or guardians of children who require special resources (the child could also be asked to complete the questionnaire). Parents are asked to describe the extent to which their service delivery professional performs certain behaviors associated with family-centered practice. The scale items address the *degree of choice* and the *degree of strengths perspective* exercised by the service provider. Two examples of such items are, "The staff member supports my making as many decisions as I choose to about what is done for my child and family," and "The staff member points out what my child and family do well."

The scale is now available to programs for use in assessing their current level of family centeredness and identifying areas in which they are particularly strong or weak.[2] They may be able to compare their performance against that of other programs or against standards of practice which may be established. These results can then be used to inform the program and its consumers of those aspects of service delivery that may need to be changed or initiated. Repeated use of the instruments will allow programs to track their performance over time.

The scale also will be used by the Beach Center as part of a research protocol to test the assumption that family-centered service delivery contributes to improved consumer and service outcomes. As with the scale-development portion of the study, the project's CORD committee will work with the researchers to design this stage of the project. Consumers of the service delivery systems to be evaluated will be consulted regarding the outcomes to be studied and the research methodology to be used.

---

[2]The Family-Centered Behavior Scale is available from the Beach Center on Families and Disability, c/o Institute for Life Span Studies, 3111 Haworth Hall, The University of Kansas, Lawrence, KS 66045.

Chapter Review

CHALLENGES

- Family-centered service delivery has developed simultaneously in several different fields.
- There is no common definition of family-centered practice, which makes it impossible to develop standards of care or measures of evaluation.

CHARACTERISTICS OF HELPFUL PROGRAMS

- New programs should follow this revised definition of family-centered service delivery: Family-centered service delivery, across disciplines and settings, recognizes the centrality of the family in the lives of individuals. It is guided by fully informed choices made by the family and focuses upon the strengths and capabilities of these families.
- New programs should allow for choice to be exercised regarding the following:
  1. Definition of the family
  2. Who makes the decisions
  3. The unit of attention
  4. The nature of the family–professional relationship
  5. The sharing of information
  6. The identification of concerns, goals, and intervention

POLICY IMPLICATIONS

- Intake and assessment methods should be flexible, comprehensive, and provided when, where, and to whom the family chooses.
- Family members should be provided with any information they request during all phases of service provision.
- Care planning should focus on the concerns identified by the family. The family selects interventions from a menu of options and contributes ideas for options.
- Intervention is designed to utilize and build upon the strengths already present in the family.
- Case records are kept simple, confidential, and available to parents.
- Evaluation is ongoing and relies on continuing family input.
- Termination of services is decided by the family.
- Family members should be able to participate in the design and governance of services through membership on boards, committees, and task forces.

References

Adoption Assistance and Child Welfare Act of 1980, PL 96-272. (June 17, 1980). Title 42, U.S.C. 3434 et seq: *U.S. Statutes at Large, 94,* 500.

Allan, G. (1991). Family group conferences: A family lawyer's perspective. In R. Wilcox, D. Smith, J. Moore, A. Hewitt, G. Allan, H. Walker, M. Ropata, L. Monu, & T. Featherstone (Eds.), *Family decision making/family group conferences: Practitioners' views* (Section 6, pp. 1–7). Lower Hutt, New Zealand: Practitioners' Publishing.

Allen, M.L. (1991). Family-centered services in the national policy arena. In A.L. Sallee & J.C. Lloyd (Eds.), *Family preservation: Papers from the Institute for Social Work Educators 1990* (pp. 64–69). Riverdale, IL: National Association for Family-Based Services.

Bailey, D.B., Jr., Buysse, V., Smith, T., & Elam, J. (1992). The effects and perceptions of family involvement in program decisions about family-centered practices. *Evaluation and Program Planning, 15,* 23–32.

Balassone, M.L., Bell, M., & Peterfreund, N. (1991). School-based clinics: An update for social workers. *Social Work in Education, 13,* 162–175.

Barker, R.L. (1991). *The social work dictionary* (2nd ed.). Silver Spring, MD: National Association of Social Workers.

Barlow, C. (1991). *Tikanga whakaaro: Key concepts in Maori culture.* Auckland, New Zealand: Oxford University Press.

Bazyk, S. (1989). Changes in attitudes and beliefs regarding parent participation and home programs: An update. *American Journal of Occupational Therapy, 43,* 723–728.

Bennett, T., Nelson, D.E., & Lingerfelt, B.V. (Eds.). (1992). *Facilitating family-centered training in early intervention.* Tucson, AZ: Communication Skill Builders.

Bennett, T., Nelson, D.E., Lingerfelt, B.V., & Davenport-Ersoff, C. (1992). Family-centered service coordination. In T. Bennett, D.E. Nelson, & B.V. Lingerfelt (Eds.), *Facilitating family-centered training in early intervention* (pp. 143–171). Tucson, AZ: Communication Skill Builders.

Birt, C.J. (1956). Family-Centered Project of St. Paul. *Social Work, 1,* 41–47.

Black, W.G., Jr. (1991). Social work in World War I: A method lost. *Social Service Review, 65,* 379–402.

Blue-Banning, M., Lee, I., Jones, D., & Turbiville, V. (1992). *Family strengths: Annotated bibliography.* Lawrence: The Beach Center on Families and Disability, The University of Kansas.

Brewer, E.J., McPherson, M., Magrab, P.R., & Hutchins, V.L. (1989). Family-centered, community-based, coordinated care for children with special health care needs. *Pediatrics, 83,* 1055–1060.

Briar, K.H. (1991). Promoting new partnerships. In A.L. Sallee & J.C. Lloyd (Eds.), *Family preservation: Papers from the Institute for Social Work Educators 1990* (pp. 70–78). Riverdale, IL: National Association for Family-Based Services.

Bribitzer, M.P., & Verdieck, M.J. (1988). Home-based, family-centered intervention: Evaluation of a foster care prevention program. *Child Welfare, 67,* 255–266.

Brown, W., Pearl, L.F., & Carrasco, N. (1991). Evolving models of family-centered services in neonatal intensive care. *Children's Health Care, 20*(1), 50–55.

Brucker, M.C., & MacMullen, N.J. (1985). Bridging the gap between hospital and home. *Children Today, 14*(4), 19–22.

Bryce, M. (1979). Home-based family centered care: Problems and perspectives. In M. Bryce & J.C. Lloyd (Eds.), *Treating families in the home: An alternative to placement* (pp. 5–11). Springfield, IL: Charles C Thomas.

Bryce, M., & Lloyd, J.C. (Eds.). (1979). *Treating families in the home: An alternative to placement*. Springfield, IL: Charles C Thomas.

Burchard, J.D., & Clarke, R.T. (1990). The role of individualized care in a service delivery system for children and adolescents with severely maladjusted behavior. *Journal of Mental Health Administration, 17*(1), 48–60.

Burton, C.B., Hains, A.H., Hanline, M.F., McLean, M., & McCormick, K. (1992). Early childhood intervention and education: The urgency of professional unification. *Topics in Early Childhood Special Education, 11*(4), 53–69.

Collins, B., & Collins, T. (1990). Parent–professional relationships in the treatment of seriously emotionally disturbed children and adolescents. *Social Work, 35*, 522–527.

Community Mental Health Centers Amendments of 1975, PL 94-63. (1975). Title 42, U.S.C. 2689 et seq.

Constable, R.T. (1992). The new school reform and the school social worker. *Social Work in Education, 14*, 106–113.

Cournoyer, D.E., & Johnson, H.C. (1991). Measuring parents' perceptions of mental health professionals. *Research on Social Work Practice, 1*, 399–415.

Cunningham, C., & Davis, H. (1985). *Working with parents: Frameworks for collaboration*. Milton Keynes, England: Open University Press.

Dedmon, R. (1990). Tourette syndrome in children: Knowledge and services. *Health and Social Work, 15*(2), 107–115.

Donahue-Kilburg, G. (1992). *Family-centered early intervention for communication disorders: Prevention and treatment*. Rockville, MD: Aspen Publishers, Inc.

Drotar, D. (1991). The family context of nonorganic failure to thrive. *American Journal of Orthopsychiatry, 61*, 23–34.

Dunst, C.J. (1991). Implementation of the individualized family service plan. In M.J. McGonigel, R.K. Kaufmann, & B.H. Johnson (Eds.), *Guidelines and recommended practices for the individualized family service plan* (2nd ed., pp. 67–78). Bethesda, MD: Association for the Care of Children's Health.

Dunst, C.J., Johanson, C., Trivette, C.M., & Hamby, D. (1991). Family-oriented early intervention policies and practices: Family-centered or not? *Exceptional Children, 58*, 115–126.

Dunst, C.J., Trivette, C.M., Davis, M., & Cornwell, J. (1988). Enabling and empowering families of children with health impairments. *Children's Health Care, 17*(2), 71–81.

Education for All Handicapped Children Act of 1975, PL 94-142. (August 23, 1977). Title 20, U.S.C. 1401 et seq: *U.S. Statutes at Large, 89*, 773–796.

Education of the Handicapped Act Amendments of 1986. PL 99-457. (October 8, 1986). Title 20, U.S.C. 1400 et seq: *U.S. Statutes at Large, 100*, 1145–1177.

Fagin, C.M. (Ed.). (1970). *Family-centered nursing in community psychiatry*. Philadelphia: F.A. Davis.

Fenton, J., Batavia, A., & Roody, D.S. (1993). *Proposed policy statement for the National Institute on Disability and Rehabilitation Research on constituency-oriented research and dissemination (CORD)*. Washington, DC: National Institute on Disability and Rehabilitation Research.

Finkelstein, N.E. (1980). Family-centered group care. *Child Welfare, 59*, 33–41.

Firman, C. (1993). On families, foster care, and the prawning industry. *Family Resource Coalition Report, 12*(2), 9–11.

Foley, H.A., & Sharfstein, S.S. (1983). *Madness and government: Who cares for the mentally ill?* Washington, DC: American Psychiatric Press.

Frankel, H. (1988). Family-centered, home-based services in child protection: A review of the research. *Social Service Review, 62,* 137–157.

Friesen, B.J., & Koroloff, N.M. (1990). Family-centered services: Implications for mental health administration and research. *Journal of Mental Health Administration, 17*(1), 13–25.

Harold, N.B., & Harold, R.D. (1991). School-based health clinics: A vehicle for social work intervention. *Social Work in Education, 13,* 185–194.

Hartman, A., & Laird, J. (1983). *Family-centered social work practice.* New York: Free Press.

Ho, M.K. (1987). *Family therapy with ethnic minorities.* Beverly Hills: Sage Publications.

Hutchinson, J.R., & Nelson, K.E. (1985). How public agencies can provide family-centered services. *Social Casework, 66,* 367–371.

Kramer, S., McGonigel, M.J., & Kaufmann, R.K. (1991). Developing the IFSP: Outcomes, strategies, activities, and services. In M.J. McGonigel, R.K. Kaufmann, & B.H. Johnson (Eds.), *Guidelines and recommended practices for the individualized family service plan* (2nd ed., pp. 57–66). Bethesda, MD: Association for the Care of Children's Health.

Krehbiel, R., Munsick-Bruno, G., & Lowe, J.R. (1991). NICU infants born at developmental risk and the individualized family service plan/process (IFSP). *Children's Health Care, 20*(1), 26–33.

Kutner, L. (1994, January 12). A sibling's disability can burden children. *Kansas City Star,* pp. 1, 3.

Langley, P.A. (1991). The coming of age of family policy. *Families in Society, 72,* 116–120.

Larimore, W.L. (1993). Family-centered birthing: A niche for family physicians. *American Family Physician, 47,* 1365–1366.

Lee, I.M. (1993). *A validation study of the Family-Centered Program Rating Scale.* Unpublished doctoral dissertation, The University of Kansas, Lawrence.

Leviton, A., Mueller, M., & Kauffman, C. (1992). The family-centered consultation model: Practical applications for professionals. *Infants and Young Children, 4*(3), 1–8.

Lourie, I.S., & Katz-Leavy, J. (1991). New directions for mental health services for families and children. *Families in Society, 72,* 277–285.

Mahoney, G., O'Sullivan, P., & Dennebaum, J. (1990). Maternal perceptions of early intervention services: A scale for assessing family-focused intervention. *Topics in Early Childhood Special Education, 10*(1), 1–15.

Marcenko, M.O., & Smith, L.K. (1992). The impact of a family-centered case management approach. *Social Work in Health Care, 17*(1), 87–100.

Martone, W.P., Kemp, G.F., & Pearson, S.J. (1989). The continuum of parental involvement in residential treatment: Engagement-participation-empowerment-discharge. *Residential Treatment for Children & Youth, 6*(3), 11–37.

McDonnell, A., & Hardman, M. (1988). A synthesis of "best practice" guidelines for early childhood services. *Journal of the Division for Early Childhood, 12,* 328–341.

McGonigel, M.J. (1991). Philosophy and conceptual framework. In M.J. McGonigel, R.K. Kaufmann, & B.H. Johnson (Eds.), *Guidelines and recommended practices for the individualized family service plan* (2nd ed., pp. 7–14). Bethesda, MD: Association for the Care of Children's Health.

McIntier, T.M. (1979). Hillhaven Hospice: A free-standing, family-centered program. *Hospital Progress, 60*(3), 68–72.

Mish, F.C. (Ed.). (1991). *Webster's new collegiate dictionary* (9th ed.). Springfield, MA: Merriam-Webster.

Mokuau, N. (1990). A family-centered approach in native Hawaiian culture. *Families in Society, 71,* 607–613.

Murphy, D.L., & Lee, I.M. (1991). *Family-Centered Program Rating Scale: User's manual.* Lawrence: The Beach Center on Families and Disability, The University of Kansas.

Nelkin, V. (1987). *Family-centered health care for medically fragile children: Principles and practices.* Washington, DC: Georgetown University Child Development Center.

Nelson, J.P. (1984). *An experimental evaluation of a home-based family-centered program model in a public child protection agency.* Unpublished doctoral dissertation, University of Minnesota, Minneapolis.

Nelson, K.E., Landsman, M.J., & Deutelbaum, W. (1990). Three models of family-centered placement prevention services. *Child Welfare, 69,* 3–21.

Ooms, T., & Owen, T. (1991). *Coordination, collaboration, integration: Strategies for serving families more effectively. Part one: The federal role.* Washington, DC: The Family Impact Seminar, The American Association for Marriage and Family Therapy (AAMFT) Research and Education Foundation.

Panel on Women, Adolescents, and Children with HIV Infection and AIDS. (1991). *Family-centered comprehensive care for children with HIV infection.* Washington, DC: U.S. Department of Health and Human Services.

Pecora, P.J., Delewski, C.H., Booth, C., Haapala, D., & Kinney, J. (1985). Home-based, family-centered services: The impact of training on worker attitudes. *Child Welfare, 64,* 529–540.

Pennekamp, M. (1992). Toward school-linked and school-based human services for children and families. *Social Work in Education, 14,* 125–130.

Petr, C.G. (1992). Adultcentrism in practice with children. *Families in Society, 73,* 408–416.

Petr, C.G., & Pierpont, J. (1992). Early implementation of legislative children's mental health reform: The Minnesota/Hennepin County experience. *Journal of Mental Health Administration, 19*(2), 195–206.

Petr, C.G., & Spano, R.N. (1990). Evolution of social services for children with emotional disorders. *Social Work, 35,* 228–234.

Pierce, D., & Frank, G. (1992). A mother's work: Two levels of feminist analysis of family-centered care. *American Journal of Occupational Therapy, 46,* 972–980.

Pomerantz, B.R. (1984). Collaborative interviewing: A family-centered approach to pediatric care. *Health and Social Work, 9,* 66–73.

Pumphrey, R.E., & Pumphrey, M.W. (Eds.). (1961). *The heritage of American social work.* New York: Columbia University.

Richmond, M.E. (1917). *Social diagnosis.* New York: Russell Sage Foundation.

Roberts, R.N., & Magrab, P.R. (1991). Psychologists' role in a family-centered approach to practice, training, and research with young children. *American Psychologist, 46*(2), 144–148.

Rosenbaum, P.L., King, S.M., & Cadman, D.T. (1992). Measuring processes of care-giving to physically disabled children and their families. I: Identifying relevant components of care. *Developmental Medicine and Child Neurology, 34*(2), 103–114.

Roush, J., Harrison, M., & Palsha, S. (1991a). Family-centered early intervention: The perceptions of professionals. *American Annals of the Deaf, 136,* 360–366.

Roush, J., Harrison, M., & Palsha, S. (1991b). Family-centered early intervention: The perceptions of professionals. Appendix. *American Annals of the Deaf, 137,* 6.

Rushton, C.H. (1990). Family-centered care in the critical care setting: Myth or reality? *Children's Health Care, 19*(2), 68–78.

Saleebey, D. (Ed.). (1992). *The strengths perspective in social work practice.* New York: Longman.

Scherz, F.H. (1953). What is family-centered casework? *Social Casework, 34,* 343–349.

Schulberg, H.C., & Killilea, M. (1982). Community mental health in transition. In H.C. Schulberg & M. Killilea (Eds.), *The modern practice of community mental health* (pp. 40–94). San Francisco: Jossey-Bass.

Sefansky, S. (1990). Pediatric critical care social work: Interventions with a special plane crash survivor. *Health and Social Work, 15,* 215–220.

Seltzer, M.M., Litchfield, L.C., Kapust, L.R., & Mayer, J.B. (1992). Professional and family collaboration in case management: A hospital-based replication of a community-based study. *Social Work in Health Care, 17*(1), 1–22.

Simeonsson, R.J., & Bailey, D.B., Jr. (1991). Family-focused intervention: Clinical, training, and research implications. In K. Marfo (Ed.), *Early intervention in transition: Current perspectives on programs for handicapped children* (pp. 91–108). New York: Praeger.

Sparling, J.W., Berger, R.G., & Biller, M.E. (1992). Fathers: Myth, reality, and Public Law 99-457. *Infants and Young Children, 4*(3), 9–19.

Spreading family-centered care. (1975). *American Journal of Nursing, 75,* 1460–1461.

Stehno, S.M. (1986). Family-centered child welfare services: New life for a historic idea. *Child Welfare, 65,* 231–240.

Summers, J.A., Behr, S.K., & Turnbull, A.P. (1989). Positive adaptation and coping strengths of families who have children with disabilities. In G. Singer & L. Irvin (Eds.), *Support for caregiving families: Enabling positive adaptation to disability* (pp. 27–40). Baltimore: Paul H. Brookes Publishing Co.

Summers, J.A., Turnbull, A.P., Campbell, M., Benson, H., Siegel-Causey, E., & Dell'Oliver, C. (1989). *A family-friendly IFSP process: Model outline.* Lawrence: The Beach Center on Families and Disability, The University of Kansas.

Sung, K. (1991). Family-centered informal support networks of Korean elderly: The resistance of cultural traditions. *Journal of Cross-Cultural Gerontology, 6,* 431–447.

Taylor-Brown, S. (1991). The impact of AIDS on foster care: A family-centered approach to services in the United States. *Child Welfare, 70,* 193–209.

Thurman, S.K. (1991). Parameters for establishing family-centered neonatal intensive care services. *Children's Health Care, 20*(1), 34–39.

Timberlake, B. (1975). The New Life Center. *American Journal of Nursing, 75,* 1456–1461.

Tower, K.D. (1994). Consumer-centered social work practice: Restoring client self-determination. *Social Work, 39,* 191–196.

Turnbull, A.P., & Summers, J.A. (1987). From parent involvement to family support: Evolution to revolution. In S.M. Pueschel, C. Tingey, J.E. Rynders, A.C. Crocker, & D.M. Crutcher (Eds.), *New perspectives on Down syndrome* (pp. 289–306). Baltimore: Paul H. Brookes Publishing Co.

Turnbull, A.P., & Turnbull, H.R., III. (1990). *Families, professionals, and exceptionality: A special partnership* (2nd ed.). Columbus, OH: Charles E. Merrill.

Turnbull, A.P., & Turnbull, H.R., III. (1992). Group action planning (GAP). *Families and Disability Newsletter, 4*(2–3), 2–3, 13. (Available from the Beach Center on Families and Disability, The University of Kansas.)

Turnbull, A.P., & Turnbull, H.R., III. (1993). *Group action planning: Families, friends, and professionals.* Unpublished manuscript. The University of Kansas, The Beach Center on Families and Disability, Lawrence.

Turnbull, H.R., III, Garlow, J.E., & Barber, P.A. (1991). *Policy analysis of family support for families with members with disabilities.* Lawrence: The Beach Center on Families and Disability, The University of Kansas.

Wagner, M. (1993). Revisiting the issues: School-linked services. *The Future of Children, 3*(3), 201–204.

Weiner, J.P., & Starfield, B.H. (1983). Measurement of the primary care roles of office-based physicians. *American Journal of Public Health, 73,* 666–671.

Wetle, T., Besdine, R.W., Keckich, W., Morgan, H., Gesino, J.P., Smolski, S.A., & Fulmer, T. (1989). Family-centered detection and management of Alzheimer's disease. *Pride Institute Journal of Long-Term Home Health Care, 8*(4), 3–11.

Wilcox, R., Smith, D., Moore, J., Hewitt, A., Allan, G., Walker, H., Ropata, M., Monu, L., & Featherstone, T. (Eds.). (1991). *Family decision making, family group conferences: Practitioners' views.*. Lower Hutt, New Zealand: Practitioners' Publishing.

Williams, H.W. (1957). *A dictionary of the Maori language* (6th ed.). Wellington, New Zealand: R.E. Owen, Government Printer.

Woodruff, G. (1985). *Planning programs for infants: State series paper* (No. 2). Chapel Hill, NC: Technical Assistance Development System, Frank Porter Graham Child Development Center.

Woodruff, G., & Sterzin, E.D. (1988). The transagency approach: A model for serving children with HIV infection and their families. *Children Today, 17*(3), 9–14.

Wyatt v. Stickney, 344 F. Supp. 373, 387, 396 (M.D. Ala. 1972), *aff'd in part, rev'd in part sub. nom.*, Wyatt v. Aderholt, 503 F. 2d 1305 (5th Cir. 1974).

4

Family Empowerment in a Family Support Program

Theresa M. Jones, Janet A. Garlow,
H. Rutherford Turnbull, III, and Patricia A. Barber

Just as "power to the people" was an activist rallying cry of the 1960s (Alinsky, 1969; Freire, 1973), "empowerment" is the contemporary expression of longstanding, yet not overwhelmingly successful, efforts to cure a variety of social problems (Berger & Neuhaus, 1977; Swift & Levin, 1987), including public housing, education, welfare, mental health programs, and disability services (Garlow, Turnbull, & Schnase, 1991; Knoll et al., 1990; Turnbull, Garlow, & Barber, 1991).

In particular, *empowerment* is a term often used in conjunction with family support policies. Family support services are family-based, family-centered programs that have the avowed goal of supporting families to nurture and care for their children with disabilities at home (Kagan & Shelley, 1987; Knoll et al., 1990; Turnbull et al., 1991). Empowerment is a defining principle of the family support movement. Professionals and families agree that "[family] supports must be administered in ways that enable and empower families and persons with disabilities" (Knoll et al., 1990, p. 5).

Although empowerment is one goal of the family support movement, there is little consensus about what empowerment is and how it operates in a family support system. What does the term mean? Furthermore, how is empowerment operationalized for family support policies, both at the family and service levels (Dunst, Trivette, & LaPointe, 1992; Weiss, 1989)?

Weiss (1989) notes that family support programs are struggling to move professional and family roles, relationships, service practices, and agency coordination beyond the ideal of empowerment to the reality of implementation. Although many programs claim to facilitate and encourage family empowerment with staff experienced in carrying out the empowerment philosophy, little systematic evaluation of these programs has been conducted. In addition, the family research agenda has not yet identified how empowerment is translated into program practices (Dunst et al., 1992).

This chapter describes how the process of empowering families is being carried out in a state-level family support program. It provides a valuable view of empowerment from the professionals' perspective, revealing how professionals can enhance or inhibit families' empowerment. In the chapter, the critical shift from traditional modes of service provision to a family-focused system is the primary mechanism for creating a responsive context for family empowerment.

PROGRAM DESCRIPTION

The particular family support program in this study operates at three levels—the state, the advisory board, and the local service levels. The participants in this study were 17 professionals, five of whom are also parents. However, their responses primarily reflect their professional viewpoints, not their parental roles.

At the state level, participants included the state director of the family support program, the director of the Developmental Disabilities Planning Council, a member of an advocacy coalition, and a parent who helped start the program. Members of advisory boards in three counties and service providers from those same counties comprised the remainder of the participants.

Some providers concentrated solely on family support services, while others performed a variety of professional roles, including service coordination, advocating for families, educating families, and direct service provision. They helped families identify their needs and devise individualized family service plans (IFSPs). Professionals also served as a liaison between the family and other community services.

DATA COLLECTION

Empowerment is a dynamic, subjective transaction between people and their environments, more suited to qualitative and participant action methods of research (Zimmerman, 1992). Within the service system, the following two types of data were examined to describe empowerment:

1. Policy and implementation information from written program documents, including family support legislation and regulations, implementation guidelines, program evaluations, job descriptions, and training manuals

2. Personal interviews with all participants during program site visits and follow-up interviews via telephone

RESULTS

Empowerment Definitions and Conceptual Issues

To understand empowerment's implementation in a family support program, one must examine the framework upon which the concept rests. This section reviews the relevant literature surrounding empowerment, reports how the participants defined empowerment in a family support system, and identifies the definition's conceptual problems.

Literature-Based Definitions of Empowerment

Family empowerment across disciplines generally refers to the goals of policies and programs that aspire to help individuals or families increase control over their lives (Cochran, 1992). For example, sociology interprets empowerment as a process for redistributing power and scarce resources; psychology describes it as a manifestation of psychological health, personal mastery, and self-determination; while community psychology and prevention theory regard it as a process through which individuals or groups gain mastery over their lives by participating in community activities (Jones, 1994). A literature review suggests that empowerment, both at the individual and family levels, consists of the five following ideas:

1. Perceived control and efficacy over the course of life events, including self-efficacy, locus of control, desire and motivation for control, and perceived competence (Cochran, 1992; Dunst & Trivette, 1987; Ozer & Bandura, 1990; Zimmerman, 1990, 1992, in press; Zimmerman & Rappaport, 1988)
2. Effectiveness in influencing life conditions through problem-solving skills, coping strategies, and effective use of resources (Cochran, 1992; Cornell Empowerment Group, 1989; Heller, 1990; Jones, 1994; Turnbull et al., 1993; Zimmerman, 1992), and family involvement in service delivery (Dunst & Trivette, 1987)
3. Family–professional partnerships (Cornell Empowerment Group, 1989) and collaboration (Fine, 1990; Turnbull & Turnbull, 1978, 1990)
4. Community participation, including leadership in organizations (Cornell Empowerment Group, 1989; Florin & Wandersman, 1984; Kieffer, 1984; Zimmerman & Rappaport, 1988)
5. Situational and temporal variability, in that empowerment takes different forms in different contexts, differs across individuals in the same context, and may change over time for the same individual (Zimmerman, in press)

Despite these specifics of empowerment, general consensus labels empowerment as a process. For the family, this process largely depends on their degree of participation in mediating community structures, such as family support systems, schools, churches, and communities. Ideally, families who actively participate in these institutions have a greater sense of mastery, control, and influence over their life events. In addition, they may become more concerned with social influence, political power, and legal rights, and gain greater access to valued resources (Cornell Empowerment Group, 1989; Rappaport, 1987).

Participant-Based Definitions of Empowerment

Before investigating what changes in professionals' roles are needed to empower families, it is crucial to understand how parents and professionals define empowerment. Just as in the literature, no clear, operational definition of empowerment emerged, even among family support program professionals in the study. When asked to define empowerment and illustrate its application to family support programs, each professional had his or her own interpretation (see Table 1).

Professionals describe empowerment in several ways. It can be a process of enabling families to take control of their lives by providing available resources and helping families learn to use them. It may also involve delegating the power that families need to gain control and make decisions. In addition, empowerment implies helping parents develop competence and mastery. Still, an in-depth analysis of all definitions revealed several common components across settings and individuals (see Table 2).

There is a good deal of consistency between the literature's definition of empowerment and the participants' definitions. In both, the common components are control, access to resources, choice, participation, efficacy beliefs, and mastery skills and competency, which shows that families not affected by disabilities view empowerment the same way that families who are affected by disability do. This study, showing how providers and pro-

Table 1.   Definitions of empowerment

Professional	Definition
Beth (family support professional)	*I think that it is giving them [families] the tools they need to make it work for their family. Sometimes, it's helping them to recognize what's available so they can make smart decisions. It also is helping them learn to use what's available.*
Ellen (family support professional)	*Realizing people want to do things themselves, it is necessary to facilitate access to whatever they need in the community, give them information, educate them, and support and encourage them in whatever they need to do things for themselves.*
Karen (advisory board member)	*I believe that it is a process of delegation . . . of delegating power. Delegation has to be based on knowledge, abilities, and strengths.*
Bill (advisory board member)	*Family empowerment means a sense of decision making that comes out of your own capacities. . . . To be empowered means you have the capacities to make those decisions. . . . This may take time to develop.*

Table 2. Components of empowerment definitions

Component	Description of component
Control	Control implies the power to make decisions and have control over the services provided to the family.
Access to resources	Access to resources refers to the resources families need to have control, including services, social support, money, personal psychological resources, and community support.
Choice	Choice allows the family to pick which services to use and how to use them and to refuse them if desired.
Participation	Participation means involvement at all levels, including political activism, social involvement, service systems involvement, and family involvement.
Efficacy beliefs	Efficacy beliefs are people's individual perceptions of their ability to influence their context. These beliefs include self-esteem, perceived competence, and motivation.
Mastery skills and competency	Mastery skills and competencies are needed to successfully master one's environment. These skills include decision-making ability, coping strategies, service systems knowledge, and communication abilities.

vider systems influence the empowerment of families dealing with disability, should also benefit those providers who deal with "generic" or non–disability-affected families.

THE PROGRAM

Empowered and Empowering Organizations

Although theoretical definitions can depict the outcomes of empowerment, only real-life applications can describe how the different aspects of empowerment are manifested in specific programs. Two types of organizations are important in the empowerment process—*empowered* and *empowering* organizations; both have characteristics with relevant implications for studying and implementing empowerment principles (Zimmerman, 1990). Empowered organizations exist because the individuals who make up the organization are experiencing the empowerment process. These organizations, which serve as agents of change and mobilizers of resources for their members, are collective indices of their members' own empowerment. The organization reflects the degree to which individual members are empowered. Examples of empowered organizations include parent coalitions, mutual self-help groups (Rappaport, 1987), parent advocacy groups (e.g., The Arc, the United Cerebral Palsy Association, Inc.), or community-based, grass roots organizations (Florin & Wandersman, 1984).

By contrast, an empowering organization is one that works to remove barriers and provide opportunities for its members (i.e., families). The family support program described in this chapter strives to be an empowering organization. It supports families by meeting their needs collaboratively with the guidance of professional staff. The program also reshapes professionals' attitudes about their roles with families and helps parents become empowered consumers (Barr & Cochran, 1992). In particular, empowering organizations provide an appropriate focus for research about policy and program contexts and their influence on family empowerment. See Table 3 for professional quotes on empowerment program goals.

Making the Shift from Traditional to Family-Focused Philosophies

The family support program has been characterized by a gradual shift from a traditional, deficit-oriented philosophy to a family-centered system in which family members are involved in all aspects of the service provision. Family-centered programs validate each person's feelings and promote family connectedness, thus fostering opportunities for empowerment. Study participants agreed that a family-based philosophy is a prerequisite for promoting empowerment. In a system based on this philosophy, families identify and discuss their needs in order to make choices and decisions. Table 4 describes the essential characteristics of a family-focused philosophy, as professionals report.

What qualities are necessary for a professional to make this shift? In general, the shift is easier for staff members with a range of experience in many service areas who find it easier to be more flexible. In addition, they are usually prepared to deal with the varied needs of families through exposure to many family situations.

More generic program issues also influence this shift toward a family-focused philosophy. Persuading an entire agency to adopt a family-focused philosophy is difficult as bureaucratic structures change slowly and work

Table 3. Explicit and implicit goals of empowerment

Explicit goals	Empowerment has to be a goal for all families, because even though it may not be fully attainable for all parents now, it may have an impact on future generations.
	Empowerment is the basic philosophy of family support.
	[The] family support program is there to help in financial difficulties—that's what's empowering.
	Empowerment should be a program goal.
	It is not the goal to reach some ultimate level of empowerment for all families, but to reach the maximum level possible for that family.
Implicit goals	[The] goal is to help families understand all available resources.
	[A] starting point is to have family dreams and goals so you get a picture of what they look like and where they're going.
	An unconscious goal is to promote empowerment.
	[The goal is to] have families be in control and make sure they have choices.
	One of the goals is to have access to resources and information and to have parent control and decision making.

Table 4. Family support contrasts with traditional support systems

Traditional	Family support
May not be cost-effective because needs are not always met	Cost-effective because only provides what is needed
System provides standard services	System responds to individual family needs
Professional is the expert in the relationship between service provider and family	Collaborative relationship between service provider and family
Standard "rule-driven" service provision	Flexible service provision
Parents given minimal decision power at service and organizational level	Parents active in decision-making process at service and organizational level
Limit access to certain resources	Program is resource broker and provides access to services
Parents are often blamed for their circumstances	No victim blaming by professionals; proactive approach to families
Participation is not always voluntary	Voluntary participation in the program
Child, rather than family, focus	Whole family service
Barriers created by attitudes, inflexibility, and limited resources	Effort made to eliminate barriers

must be done at all levels of the agency. The following are examples of necessary alterations to carry out this change in philosophy:

- Professionals need to incorporate teamwork into their agency that capitalizes on every individual's resources.
- The administration must originate support for changes, while the staff must be convinced to embrace the philosophy.
- Advocates for change must educate other agencies and the community at large, as well as agency professionals.

Parent–Professional Relationships: Example of the Transformed Role

It is not feasible to promote empowerment using traditional roles and strategies. How, then, must professional roles change to facilitate family empowerment? Similarly, what strategies effectively empower families within a service system?

Changes in Professional Roles

Traditionally, three models of help giving (Brickman, 1982; Dunst et al., 1987) have defined service provision roles throughout the 1970s and 1980s. The first—a role-focused model—centers on case manager integration and coordination of services. Role-focused service provision superficially addresses the relationship between families and their goals (i.e., identifying family needs) and service providers. This model can foster dependency and learned helplessness by usurping the family's decision-making power and viewing members as passive and incompetent.

The second model establishes a resource-procurement role that coordinates and provides services for family needs, assuming they cannot accept primary responsibility for resource obtainment. Resource procurement fails to address the positive or negative effects of resource mobilization on families and professionals, as it does not require effective behavior change and learning by families (Dunst et al., 1987).

Empowerment is the final model of helping, which defines and specifies the relationship between family and professional roles, procedural goals, and family outcomes. This model focuses on enhancing family competencies and capacities with the following two goals: 1) to de-emphasize family responsibility for their problems; and 2) to enable families to acquire competencies to solve problems, meet their own needs, and realize personal goals.

As services become family focused, professionals become facilitators and supporters instead of traditional case managers and resource procurers. Families take a more active role in the service system, both at the direct service and the program implementation levels, while professionals serve as resources and collaborators.

Strategies for Empowering Families

Much of the literature concerning strategies for caregiving and the shift in professional roles can be found in the area of effective help giving. For example, Dunst and Trivette (1987) classify effective help-giving behavior in three stages. The preliminary stage, a foundation for effective parent–professional relationships, concerns itself with attitudes and beliefs. This stage involves perceiving families and individuals positively, and believing that they are competent in meeting their needs and solving problems. Once these appropriate attitudes are in place, professionals enter the second stage and begin to practice actual help-giving behaviors such as active, reflective listening skills, and helping the family or individual identify issues and needs and become more competent. The final stage of the effective help-giving process consists of supportive posthelping behaviors, including accepting and supporting decisions, reducing the family's sense of indebtedness, allowing reciprocity, and minimizing the psychological costs associated with accepting help.

According to the participants in the study, changes require a positive attitude by both families and professionals, the development of certain professional skills and competencies, and the acceptance of new roles for professionals. How do these ideas appear in the real world working with families day to day? Are the idealistic values and skills reviewed above really feasible? The next few sections describe the professionals' relationships with families, the skills and attitudes they believe are necessary to fulfill this role, and the roles both play.

Family and Professional Relationships

The assumption that individuals and families are competent and can have mastery and control over important life events provides a foundation for the relationship between the professional and the family in the family-focused philosophy. This relationship then becomes a generative process of identifying, supporting, and building on the family strengths. Families and professionals identified several necessary components of this process:

1. Mutual respect and trust by both professionals and families
2. Specific skills that help the development of empowerment through encouraging and using family strengths
3. Positive, flexible professional attitudes toward service provision and families
4. Changes in roles that put the provider in a supportive role and the parent in a role to make choices and decisions

Mutual Respect and Trust

Two of the Cornell Empowerment Group's (1989) critical elements of an empowering relationship are mutual respect and trust, defined as the "belief that diversity is positively valued, . . . that relations among [stakeholders] should be organized to provide an equal balance of power . . . and play an important role in developing strategies . . . [to] gain control over [their lives]" (p. 2). Translated into the immediate relationship between the service provider and the family, both should feel comfortable sharing ideas and alternate solutions. Professionals can encourage empowerment by cultivating a trusting environment. This trust allows for a freer exchange of ideas without parental fear of manipulation or retribution from the system.

   Professionals and parents described the following two characteristics that foster trust in the parent–professional relationship:

1. The relationship must be open enough so that both sides can speak freely about ideas.
2. Trust is fostered by expressing confidentiality and support.

For example, parents are more likely to identify their true feelings and needs if they do not fear being reported for "bad parenting."

Professional Skills in Developing Parent–Professional Relationships

Participants identified several other essential professional skills that enable parents to work in partnerships with them. These are shown in Table 5.

   Communication skills include listening, verbal communication, the ability to make families feel at ease, and openness to new ideas. Knowledge refers to an understanding of the service system and available resources, parenting skills, and family and child development, as well as specific disabilities. Problem-solving abilities include the ability to identify real needs, generate alternatives, collaborate with parents, and identify solutions to needs. Organizational skills encompass knowledge of how various systems function, the ability to work in the system and collaborate with colleagues, and the skill to coordinate services. Finally, advocacy skills include negotiation ability, public speaking ability, knowledge of the laws and policies surrounding family support, and the ability to work between systems.

Table 5.   Professional attitudes, knowledge, and skills necessary for facilitating successful parent–professional relationships

Skill category	Examples from interviews
Communication skills	*Be able to listen without being judgmental.*
	Support the family by encouraging, planting seeds, being a friend.
	Solicit the ideas of the family. They are truly the experts and know best what their child needs.
Knowledge	*One of our best workers has an incredible knowledge of the service system and what's out there for families. She's a walking resource center.*
	Professionals should have a working knowledge of good parenting skills, child development, families, and different kinds of disabilities.
Problem-solving ability	*You have to be able to communicate different solutions to families and help them choose the best alternative.*
	Professionals have to have good problem-solving skills, be able to identify needs, and then identify what will best meet that need.
Organizational skills	*A critical skill is the ability to work between systems, to effect change at that level.*
	It is necessary to work with other professionals, to try and work together to find a solution.
Advocacy skills	*Negotiation skills are necessary. [Professionals] need to be able to negotiate with and for the family.*

Professional Attitudes

In addition to important skills, participants identified several important attitudes for the professional to have in order to provide an opportunity for families to exhibit strengths. Table 6 lists some categories of responses.

The first category lays the foundation for the parent and professional to develop a productive relationship by showing empathy and genuineness toward the family. Professionals unanimously agreed that they must em-

Table 6.   Professional attitudes necessary for effective parent–professional relationships

Empathy and concern	Flexibility	Role attitudes
Have genuine concern for families.	Maintain flexibility about what works for different families.	Have an attitude of humility.
Understand the family's experiences.	Value and respect the viewpoint of the family.	See self as more than a service worker to individual families.
Be sensitive to the humanity and pain of individual families.	Realize the need for growth.	Have a philosophy of education as part of the process.
Avoid imposing a sense of guilt and shame.	Be sensitive to family needs and cultures.	Be nonjudgmental.
Put oneself in the shoes of the family.	Be patient with families and realize they can get where they need to be with support.	Cannot have a superior "I told you so" attitude.
	Do not push families or impose your own values.	Believe that family has the most knowledge about their needs.
		Be open to learning from families.

pathize with the family's daily experiences. The second category of attitudes involves flexibility, both in practice and in values. Professionals must be able to adapt their style of service provision to address the concerns of a range of families and recognize a variety of values and practices. The key is recognizing that there are many ways to solve the same challenge, depending on the skills and resources of a particular family. The final category describes how professionals should deal with families. The consensus was that professionals should practice nonjudgmental listening, not have a superior attitude, and see the family as knowledgeable and able to make knowledgeable decisions. The major attitudinal barrier to parent–professional relationships is the "professional expert" who does not allow families to participate.

Self-Descriptions of Professional Roles

Finally, to further empower the parent–professional relationship in a shift toward family-focused services, professionals should play a more supportive role, while parents become more directive. A broad range of activities characterize professional duties in a support-oriented role. Table 7 provides a summary of these as seen by professionals in this study.

Many activities and roles reported are not the traditional roles discussed earlier (e.g., Dunst et al., 1987). Instead of seeing themselves as taking an active, powerful role in relationships, providers reported forming more collaborative relationships, the kind typically associated with empowerment (Fine, 1990). Professionals described their roles as facilitative—

Table 7. Reported roles and activities of professional service providers

Roles and activities	Interview examples
Collaborator	*Help parents generate new ideas and alternatives.*
	Help families plan for the future.
	Let families do what they can and help them with the rest.
	Help families redirect their goals.
Advocate	*Advocate for the families within the system and with other systems as well.*
	Be a liaison between the families and the service systems.
Emotional support and encouragement	*Validate families' feelings and choices.*
	Create an atmosphere conducive for families; don't just fill out forms, but be a listener and support.
	Provide emotional support for these families.
Education	*Tell families about what is available to them.*
	Give families information so they can make informed choices.
	Let parents know their rights.
Resources	*Utilize community resources to meet family needs.*
	Serve as a last resort. Help families meet their needs using their strengths and resources; then step in.
	Be accessible and available to families as a resource person.

supporting and enabling families to make choices, generate alternatives, and implement solutions through collaboration, professional and parent advocacy, emotional support and encouragement, and the exchange of information.

When professionals' roles change, families' and parents' roles shift in the process (Barr & Cochran, 1992), meaning when professionals assume a more supportive role, families are able to take on a more active role in addressing their own concerns. A key phrase in family support literature refers to families "taking the lead" (Knoll et al., 1990). The professionals in the study suggested that "taking the lead" meant families should take the initiative in identifying their needs, initiating change, and implementing goals and plans. A local service provider describes her viewpoint: "It means letting them tell you what they need. It also requires that you inform them about long-term impacts and resources that will be available so that they can make informed decisions and choices."

Specifically, the professionals described several areas in which they encourage the family to take an active role.

1. Families must identify their needs, so programs can be designed with the flexibility to address a range of concerns.
2. Families are encouraged to set their service plan goals and develop strategies for achieving these goals.
3. Families should play an active role in the ongoing evaluation and revision of their service plan.
4. Families should be encouraged to become involved in advocacy, first for their own situation and then on a broader level.

Program Elements of Empowerment

What, then, are the elements of empowerment that are facilitated by the program itself? In an earlier section, six elements of empowerment were described—control, access to resources, choice, participation, efficacy beliefs, and mastery skills and competency. Some of these elements are specific to the parents themselves, but others are directly affected by the program itself. For example, mastery skills and competency are directly related to the abilities and behaviors of the parent, while providing access to resources is related to program issues. The next section describes how the family support program supports these components of the empowerment process that directly affect programs.

Control

In the transformation to an empowering organization, professionals face critical issues in their relationships with parents—one of these issues is control. Control implies active participation on the part of the family in influencing the consequences of life events. In a family support system, control translates into decision-making power, both at the direct service provision level and at the programmatic level, and is most clearly delineated in the parent–professional relationship.

Parental control rests on the philosophy that parents are in the best position to identify their families concerns, and assumes they have the ability to do what is necessary to address those concerns. This philosophy also assumes that when parents are unable to control events, it is because of a lack of necessary resources and skills, not inherent inabilities on the part of the parent.

In the family support program, parents are entitled to many types of control:

- They need to have the final say in what they want and do not want for their family.
- They should control what services they receive and from whom they receive them.
- They should govern the needs-identification process and the selection of service providers.
- They should have the ability to alter their service plan when their needs change.
- They should decide the extent of their program involvement.
- They should regulate the legislation and policy concerning families of children with disabilities.

However, several barriers relating to family perceptions and competencies make it difficult for families to have control over their lives. Families may fear taking control because of lack of knowledge or low self-esteem. Problems in the family system such as substance abuse, child protective issues, or lack of parental competence also inhibit control. In addition, program issues limit control. When there are limited resources, families are naturally limited in their ability to control aspects of their lives. For example, a family unable to attain money to put up a fence around their yard (so their child can go outside) will not have control over that part of their lives.

Conversely, the other side of the issue concerns professional control in providing services. Some respondents felt that the professional should always relinquish decision-making control to the parent and believe that they should not involve themselves in other family issues, such as recreational time, school, or medical issues, unless asked. However, others felt that professionals should have a great deal of control concerning resource distribution, program development, and issues involving abuse or neglect of children.

Access to Resources

Resources are key to the empowerment process. For families to have control and make good choices, they must have access to necessary resources to make informed decisions. Access to valued resources provides families with enough options to make choices about what services, supports, and information are needed for them to gain control over their lives. Resources include social support, monetary resources, and services, including information and education about resources. The more families know and understand about their child's disability and available resources, the more they can help themselves. The family support program, besides being a resource itself, links parents with other parents and services. It also provides information and education to parents through various workshops and training programs. These programs provide knowledge and build parents' skills so they become more effective advocates and decision makers for their child.

For families of children with disabilities, one traditional (and perhaps critical) resource is access to formal services. Raising a child with a disability often has tremendous financial, physical, and psychological costs for families. The family support program provides families with access to a variety of service resources, including respite care, mechanical and technological equipment, money for family recreation, medical and insurance costs, and paid opportunities for parents to attend training sessions. If the service is not directly available, the program acts as a "broker" for information and referral services, education, and monetary resources.

In addition to these traditional services, the family support program creatively meets a wide variety of needs, including the following:

- Buying a washer and dryer for a family so the mother would not have to take her child to the laundromat
- Purchasing a used car
- Finding housing for two women with disabilities who were making transitions out of the program
- Providing a deck on a home so a child with autism could be outside safely
- Building a swimming pool for a child with physical disabilities to have therapy at home
- Purchasing a side car for the father's bicycle so the entire family could enjoy biking outings

These informal resources enhance empowerment by allowing families a sense of independence by creating access to needed resources that are often overlooked or not available. In today's transient society, not all families have community and extended family supports, and this isolation can be greater for a family with a child with a disability. These families may lack access to community supports because of the stigma attached to the child's disability, a lack of available community resources and activities, or the limited time and energy of parents to network within the community.

The family support program encourages natural support linkages in a number of ways. Through needs identification, professionals help families see the resources that are already in their natural support system, such as other family members, doctors, school personnel, and child care providers. Parents in similar circumstances help families develop social networks by establishing support groups and creating opportunities for families to socialize together. One county in the program established an extended family program to facilitate friendships between children with and without disabilities in the community. Support groups sponsored by the program are informal support groups that are started to meet specific needs.

Although the program provides access to all of these resources, parents may still experience difficulty obtaining them. Parental language barriers, mental ability, emotional difficulty, and other skill insufficiencies may inhibit parents' acquisition of information. For example, parents may be reluctant to ask for information as a loss of self-respect and dignity often accompanies the help request. Furthermore, the information itself may be irrelevant or presented in an uninteresting way, which renders it useless to parents. Finally, a simple lack of funding is a major program barrier. There is simply not enough money to meet everyone's needs, a fact exemplified by long waiting lists in many counties.

Choice

The next dimension of empowerment that program policies and implementation seek to foster is family choice regarding what services to use and how they are provided. Once the family obtains access to necessary resources, they are able to make choices among several alternatives. Families identify their needs, then choose how services will be provided. Families should have choices in all aspects of the program to maximize opportunity and enhance empowerment as illustrated by the following quote from a parent:

> Choice is really important. Parents need to know there are choices and be able to make decisions. Choice is having the freedom to decide what you need for your family, and to be able to ask for it. Making choices on everyday things are building blocks for empowerment. (Dana, parent)

Sometimes parents' choices benefit the program and other parents by increasing resources. For example; "If families are given choices about how to use their family support money, they are likely to choose to use less of it. Families are empowered to say 'I don't need all of the $3,000, give it to someone else'" (Susan, service provider).

Choice helps empower all families, even those with severe limitations. By providing several acceptable alternatives, professionals give parents choices that will not be harmful to parent or child, allowing families to decide on their own consequences.

Program commitment to family choice occurs in several ways. At the level of the parent–professional relationship, that commitment includes validating decisions, supporting parent choice even when the professional does not agree, allowing families to take responsibility for their choices, and providing encouragement and belief in the parent's decision-making ability. At the service system level, this commitment translates into flexible service provision, whereby families identify their concerns and the program actively seeks to supply what is needed.

Still, these choices have some limitations. For example, parents who themselves have disabilities or emotional problems are sometimes limited in their ability to make the most appropriate choices. In those instances, the professional assumes a more active role in helping parents choose. Another family limitation to choice concerns families who think they should have whatever they want, despite limited resources and underserved populations, as illustrated by the following quote from a professional:

> Families need to realize they can't always have what they want—there is a balance between the general public and your personal wants. Families can't have unreasonable expectations that they will get everything they want. You can't make every choice in life, even without a child with a disability. We all have to learn we can't have everything we want. (Ellen, family support professional)

Barriers to choice exist in the family support system as well. Although the program is quite flexible in its service provision, available resources are limited. The program's spending cap is $3,000 per family, per year, making unlimited choices difficult. For some families, this amount does not even come close to meeting their needs. In addition, not all choices or options are available. For example, options that are detrimental to the child, such as time-out boxes or physical restraints, are not covered by family support funding.

Participation

Participation in the family support program itself promotes empowerment. Participation relates closely to control, access to resources, and choice and traditionally has meant political advocacy, systems change, or support of other families. However, participation may range from being involved in meeting the child's needs to state or national political advocacy.

The distinction between involvement and empowerment is unclear. It is assumed that some involvement is necessary for empowerment, as influence and change are impossible with no active effort. However, this does not mean families have to become involved at all levels of the program to be empowered. Some parents choose not to make their child's disability the focus of their lives and not to become involved in service system advocacy issues. Beth, a family support professional, discusses the fallacy of equating politically involved parents with empowered parents.

> Parents don't necessarily have to have their fingers in everything and be trying to change the whole system. Uninvolved (advocacy-wise and politically) parents can be empowered. They are getting it (advocating for their child) done in their own way. Empowerment doesn't have to be huge and visible.

However, some professionals and families described participation as a necessary component of empowerment. Involvement or participation may be on "a basic level of dealing with services, family issues, or on a broader scope of involvement in political processes. In order to be empowered, people have to participate in some way. Empowerment is a participation process" (Bill, advisory board member).

Many county programs provide opportunities for parents to become active in collective political advocacy. Opportunities may be sponsored by the county, such as a political action committee of parents who lobby for more funding for families, or they may be grass roots organizations, such as a parent empowerment coalition formed by several active parents. There are many opportunities for individual political activity as well. Serving on county boards, writing letters to legislators, speaking at national and state conferences, and lobbying for family support are all activities in which parents can participate.

Participation also happens in social contexts. One goal of empowerment is to create a sense of interdependence as a result of parents developing social networks, participating in mediating supportive systems (e.g., churches, voluntary organizations), and serving as a support for other families. The interdependence encouraged by participation helps families meet the need of reciprocity or giving something in return. Through mutual self-help, families pool their supportive resources for greater influence, and thereby become more empowered.

Different barriers impede family participation. Families may already be involved in many aspects of caring for their child and not want more involvement in their lives, particularly from a service system. The stress level of the family is another barrier to participation. The family may be doing everything possible simply to cope with day-to-day difficulties and may be unable to take on any additional responsibilities.

To summarize, the more systems and professionals create access to needed resources, prompt families to make their own choices, and encourage them to participate in a variety of ways, the more they empower parents. However, provider systems, professionals' behavior, as well as parents' capacities and behaviors, may limit empowerment.

THE FAMILY ROLE

Although program philosophies and strategies set the stage for empowering families, the next section focuses on the actors who actually engage in the empowerment process—the families themselves. Two major aspects of the empowerment process are parent specific. By providing access to resources, choices, and opportunities for participation within the program, parents develop positive beliefs about their personal control and competence. They also learn new skills that increase their ability to deal effectively with the multiple service systems in which their child is involved.

Efficacy Beliefs

Efficacy beliefs refer to the parents' perceptions of the influence they have on their own lives. These beliefs include self-esteem, perceptions of personal control and competence, and the motivation to attempt to change their life conditions. When parents feel in control, they are more likely to act in a way that will change the service system and their life conditions. A family member described these beliefs as a "sense of security in our own ability to make decisions and that our needs are met." Positive personal beliefs give vision and motivation as illustrated by one of the participants: "[Empowerment] gives families a sense of vision. They are able to see what they have—that sense of personal power comes from within." For families in the program, positive personal beliefs consist of a sense of personal power and self-esteem. A parent described the impact empowerment has on her self-worth as, "I feel worthy and competent, not like I am looking for a handout or taking advantage of the government."

Central to these beliefs is a sense of motivation. Although not all positive personal beliefs translate into motivation, one provider observed that, "Some parents are motivated and will see that they get what they need, while other families don't think they are competent enough or don't have the skills to be motivated to act for change." A variety of factors motivate parents to become empowered. For instance, motivation occurs when parents become angry with the system or have trouble acquiring resources needed for their child with a disability. According to one professional, "Motivation is influenced in a variety of ways. Parents are more likely to get involved in things that matter to them and empowerment is being motivated by something significant to get involved and actively do something about it. 'If it matters, then I will do something about it, and I will find the resources to do that.'"

The attitudes of the professionals support parents' positive beliefs about themselves. Families know best what their child needs and have strengths that could be used to meet their needs; families have the ability and the capacity to make competent decisions for themselves. Professionals encourage parents, reinforcing their worthiness and competency, to make good decisions. When asked how professionals support the feelings of competence necessary for empowerment, one provider gave the following example:

> As a professional, you constantly need to reaffirm their value and worth. . .need to have a philosophical view that you [the professional] do not know more than the family about that child. You need to watch for opportunities for them to exhibit competencies, and build on those. (Susan, family support professional)

As in all empowerment components, barriers can either be family oriented or system barriers erected by service providers and program issues. Family barriers may include feelings of guilt and shame. Shame might arise from merely being associated with having a child who has a disability. Parents may feel guilty if they think that they are unable to care for their child without help. They may also think they have limited competencies and skills to deal with the challenges of having a child who has a disability. Changes, decisions, or taking risks are feared, and in extreme cases, a family may exhibit signs of learned helplessness if the system constantly fails to meet their needs.

On the system side, professional attitudes may suppress positive beliefs by blaming families or perceiving families as incompetent. These perceptions risk alienating parents or creating dependency by not allowing parents to develop their skills and positive beliefs. Similarly, inflexible policies and regulations may limit the parents' positive beliefs by making it difficult for them to obtain needed resources and support

Mastery Skills and Competency

Another parent-related component of the empowerment process is the development of skills and competencies necessary to deal effectively with their lives. Several skills are important for parents to cope more effectively with the service system and their child with a disability, including communication skills, problem-solving skills, resource mobilization skills, and advocacy skills.

Empowered parents communicate ideas well and have interpersonal skills that allow them to relate collaboratively with professionals and others. They can negotiate for themselves and are comfortable communicating in an advocacy role, either within the service system or in other settings. Because advocacy is extremely important in finding resources for the parent and family, parents develop knowledge through advocacy training about needed resources.

Parents learn problem-solving skills as they plan and identify their own concerns. As they participate in the service system, they develop critical analysis skills and refine their decision-making abilities. Empowered parents are proactive toward stressful situations and view them as challenges from which to learn. They learn the nature and characteristics of the service system and how to work within it to make changes.

However, personal and family issues, such as alcohol and drug abuse, mental or cognitive disabilities, stress, economic pressure, and poor self-esteem, may become major barriers to the development of decision-making and problem-solving skills. In addition, bureaucratic barriers, such as professional inadequacies in dealing with families, limited funds, and system complexity and inconsistency, may also inhibit skill development by not creating opportunities for parents to learn to deal effectively with the service system.

IMPLICATIONS

Although this particular family support program gives preliminary information from which to draw some implications, further research and in-depth evaluation conducted by the state family support program are still needed.

Policy Comments

Review of the written policies of this program coupled with interviews with professionals at all three levels suggest that the program's policy framework was durable, useful, and understandable to those who used it. The symmetry of the statute, regulations, and program guidelines to professionals' understanding of program goals with the program's family-based philosophy was striking. The state director was a key figure in this symmetry throughout the implementation of the original statute, regulations, and guidelines, bringing continuity and experience to the program—two factors that, together, seem to make family support programs more uniform and more dedicated to empowering families. It appears that putting a responsive policy framework together with family-focused professional interactions facilitates family empowerment.

The three counties studied—despite differences in the professionals' background, experience, and job descriptions—were remarkably unanimous in their grasp of the program's purpose—to place values on families' strengths and capacities. They displayed an unusual level of commitment to the program's vision and goals and were willing to assess current efforts against the original vision of the program. Many of the professionals have been with the program for an extended period of time, and although some frustration with the practical limits of the program, such as funding and waiting lists, was detected, it was not "burnout" frustration. It was clear from the interviews that professionals knew the program limits and their own limits in serving families and were honest with families and themselves about those limits.

Professionals believed in the program's family-based philosophy and trusted their experience with families as valuable, ongoing training. Although some were previously involved in other programs that viewed families quite differently (particularly programs based on child protective services), respondents wholeheartedly supported the family support program's assumption that families were knowledgeable experts of their own concerns and capabilities and quite capable of caring for their own children, given the proper resources and supports. In addition, although respondents were often unclear about the term "empowerment," their comments either explicitly or implicitly showed that they perceived the family support program to be an empowering organization and themselves as transforming agents of change.

Remaining Questions

The "positive belief" component of empowerment identified in the discussion of families also applies to the professionals. Professionals' ability to fulfill their personal and professional roles, involving choice and control, depends upon their access to resources within their own program, as well as their personal training and informal supports and networks. Their perspective of their own power directly related to how powerful they perceived the "system" itself to be and how powerful they perceived other contexts to be, such as the legislature and the community boards. Their sense of mastery and competency was directly related to greater experience and skill in advocating for families and other systems. Similar to families, professionals were also in different stages of empowerment, but were clearer about their need to develop skills and about their roles as advocates—"volunteering" for empowerment in ways that families sometimes did not. A future research agenda should include the parallel or overlapping empowerment processes of professionals and the families they serve.

If the family support program is conceptualized as an empowering organization, then the program must work to remove barriers to professionals, as well as families; these include funding limits, waiting lists, uncooperative county boards, unevenness in programs across the state, and institutionalized services that forestall flexibility and individualization for families. Still, the conceptual literature questions whether a formal system can work to remove its own barriers to empowerment (Rappaport, 1987). Perhaps family advocacy coalitions will be able to use their knowledge to bring pressure on the legislature and county organizations to remove program barriers.

In light of the difficulty involved in shifting from a formal client-based service system to a family-focused empowering organization, it is obvious that skill and philosophy training are required. Some skills and philosophies can be shaped by formal training, but most training is informal and comes from personal and job experience with families. Shifts in professionals' attitudes toward families and in their philosophy on service provision are the most crucial part of achieving the transforming role. Formal training programs need to educate professionals about the family-centered philosophy, teaching that families have strengths, are in the best position to meet the needs of their children, and are competent or capable of meeting those needs on their own with appropriate support. Professionals must learn to provide services flexibly and to relate personally with the families. They must also learn that power should be balanced between families and service providers.

Research Implications

This investigation was the first in a series of necessary research steps to outline the dimensions of empowerment for families of children with disabilities and to delineate factors that empower families within the service context. It focused on only one of the contexts within this system, and its results apply only to the family support professionals and policy makers. To better understand empowerment in family support systems, information needs to be gathered from other stakeholders, such as families, community members, and other service providers. Formal service contexts and informal social contexts for families in these programs should be studied in a balanced way. Only then can well-designed measurement and evaluation studies of empowerment be developed.

Although these results suggest a conceptual framework of empowerment within a family support program, families and other interested people could certainly have a different perspective of empowerment and opinion on whether the family support program is truly an empowering organization. Until other voices are heard, this conceptual framework can only be a sketch.

The next step in the research agenda should conceptualize family support from both a psychological and a social agenda perspective. Psychological components of empowerment and variables associated with them must be identified to provide a theoretical dimension to the empowerment research agenda, as well as provide a more complete understanding of the individual's role in the empowerment process. Longitudinal studies of parents within family support are crucial to understanding how empowerment works in the family context.

A comprehensive research agenda on empowerment would include social agenda research. Rappaport (1987) addresses the sociopolitical importance of studying empowerment, particularly in a group setting. The Cornell Empowerment Group's (1989) definition of empowerment and recent studies include mention of awareness of the political aspects of programs (e.g., Where is the power located in the systems or the communities? What can professionals do to balance the inequities in power?). Research in this area resembles policy research done in political and economic arenas—two areas that also use the rhetoric of empowerment. Researchers should identify important stakeholders, determine the people of concern whose voices need to be heard, familiarize those working in a particular context with people of interest, and study empowerment as a social change mechanism.

CONCLUSION

The Beach Center on Families and Disability[1] conceptualizes family empowerment as having three essential components:

1. Families need to be motivated toward empowerment.
2. Families must have certain skills and resources so they can effectively act on their motivation.
3. Families need responsive contexts that allow them to live in environments where policies, personnel, procedures, and programs are responsive to what families say they need.

---

[1]Since the 1980s the Beach Center program has furnished support that is family centered and consistent with many quality indicators articulated by disability policy advocates.

This study began by focusing on the last of these three elements, the responsive context, in several state-level programs. From conversations with professionals, these programs do seem to be responsive and are dedicated to helping families meet their needs. An understanding of how family empowerment emerges in a responsive context led to an understanding that the context affects families' motivation as well as their skills and resources. The interaction among these three components will become increasingly clear as studies continue.

Not only does the responsive context influence parents, it affects professionals as well. Professionals who seek to empower families must also find ways to empower themselves. Although this responsive context is designed for families, professionals find it inherently responsive to them as well.

Chapter Review

CHALLENGES

- There is little consensus on the meaning of empowerment in family support.
- There has been little systematic evaluation of the extent to which family support programs are empowering.
- Translating an empowerment philosophy into ongoing program practices remains a challenge.

CHARACTERISTICS OF HELPFUL PROGRAMS

- Empowering programs promote perceived control and efficacy, use of skills, coping strategies and resources, family–professional partnerships, and community participation among individuals and families.
- Professional roles are redefined to assist parents to become empowered consumers—professionals use communication, problem-solving, and organizational skills to support family directiveness.
- Agencies adopt a family-centered approach that emphasizes family strengths and competencies, mutual respect and trust, flexible responses, and community-wide systems change.
- Families identify their concerns and goals, develop strategies for achieving goals, and play active roles in advocacy and the evaluation of their service plans.
- Families have access to the formal and informal resources necessary for informed decision making and attainment of needed services and always have choices.
- Resources and support for family skill development and practice are available within programs.

POLICY IMPLICATIONS

- Because families are in the best position to identify their concerns and determine what is needed to meet them, they should determine policy and legislation concerning families of children with disabilities.
- Systems should promote optimal levels of family participation in policy development and implementation.
- Barriers to family participation in policy making must be removed.
- Family choices must be honored regarding participation in policy initiatives.
- Supportive policies and personal commitments are necessary to truly empower families.

References

Alinsky, S.B. (1969). *Revielle for radicals*. New York: Vintage Books.

Barr, D., & Cochran, M. (1992). Understanding and supporting empowerment: Redefining the professional role. *Networking Bulletin, 2*(3), 1–7.

Beach Center on Families and Disability. (1993). *Empowering families: A proposal for a program on families of children with disabilities*. Lawrence, KS: Author.

Berger, P.L., & Neuhaus, R.C. (1977). *To empower the people: The role of mediating structures in public policy*. Washington, DC: American Enterprise Institute for Public Policy Research.

Brickman, P., Rabinowitz, V.C., Kaniza, J., Coates, D., Cohn, E., & Kidder, L. (1982). Models of helping and coping. *American Psychologist, 37*(4), 365–384.

Cochran, M. (1992). Parent empowerment: Developing a conceptual framework. *Family Science Review, 5*(1 & 2), 81–92.

Cornell Empowerment Group. (1989). Empowerment through family support. *Networking bulletin: Empowerment and family support, 1*(1), 1–3.

Dunst, C.J., & Trivette, C.M. (1987). Enabling and empowering families: Conceptual and intervention issues. *Journal of School Psychology, 16*(4), 443–456.

Dunst, C.J., Trivette, C.M., & Lapointe, N. (1992). Toward clarification of the meaning and the key elements of empowerment. *Family Science Review, 5*(1 & 2), 111–130.

Fine, M. (1990). Facilitating home–school relationships: A family-oriented approach to collaborative consultation. *Journal of Educational and Psychological Consultation, 1*(2), 169–187.

Florin, P., & Wandersman, A. (1984). Cognitive social learning and participation in community development. *American Journal of Community Psychology, 12*, 689–708.

Freire, P. (1973). *Education for critical consciousness*. New York: Seabury Press.

Garlow, J.E., Turnbull, H.R., & Schnase, D. (1991). Model disability and family support act of 1991. *Kansas Law Review, 39*(3), 783–816.

Heller, K. (1990). Social and community interventions. *Annual Review of Psychology, 41*, 141–168.

Jones, T.M. (1994). *The development of the Psychological Empowerment Scale: Preliminary investigations*. Unpublished master's thesis, University of Kansas, Lawrence.

Kagan, S.L., & Shelley, A. (1987). The promise and problems of family support. In S.L. Kagan, D.R. Powell, B. Weissbourd, & E.F. Zigler (Eds.), *America's family support programs* (pp. 3–18). New Haven, CT: Yale University Press.

Kieffer, C.H. (1984). Citizen empowerment: A developmental perspective. *Prevention in Human Services, 3*, 9–35.

Knoll, J., Covert, S., Osuch, R., O'Connor, S., Agosta, J., Blaney, B., & Bradley, V. (1990). *Family support services in the United States: An end of decade status report* (summary report). Cambridge, MA: The Human Services Research Institute.

Ozer, E., & Bandura, A. (1990). Mechanisms governing empowerment effects: A self-efficacy analysis. *Journal of Personality and Social Psychology, 58*(3), 472–486.

Rappaport, J. (1987). Terms of empowerment / exemplars of prevention: Toward a theory for community psychology. *American Journal of Community Psychology, 15*(2), 121–148.

Swift, C., & Levin, G. (1987). Empowerment: An emerging mental health technology. *Journal of Primary Prevention, 80*(1 & 2), 71–94.

Turnbull, A.P., Patterson, J.M., Behr, S.K., Murphy, D.L., Marquis, J.G., & Blue-Banning, M.J. (Eds.). (1993). *Cognitive coping, families, and disability*. Baltimore: Paul H. Brookes Publishing Co.

Turnbull, A.P., & Turnbull, H.R. (1990). *Families, professionals, and exceptionality: A special partnership* (2nd ed.). Columbus, OH: Charles E. Merrill.

Turnbull, H.R., III, Garlow, J.E., & Barber, P.A. (1991) A policy analysis of family support for families with members with disabilities. *Kansas Law Review, 39*(3), 739–782.

Turnbull, H.R., III, & Turnbull, A.P. (Eds.). (1978). *Parents speak out: Then and now* (2nd ed.). Columbus, OH: Charles E. Merrill.

Weiss, H. (1989). New state initiatives for family support and education programs: Challenges and opportunities. *Family Resource Coalition Report, 1*, 18–19.

Zimmerman, M.A. (1990). Taking aim on empowerment research: On the distinction between individual and psychological distinctions. *American Journal of Community Psychology, 18*(1), 169–176.

Zimmerman, M.A. (1992). *The measurement of psychological empowerment: Issues and strategies*. Unpublished paper, University of Michigan, Ann Arbor.

Zimmerman, M.A. (in press). Further explorations in empowerment theory: An empirical analysis of psychological empowerment. *American Journal of Community Psychology*.

Zimmerman, M.A., & Rappaport, J. (1988). Citizen participation, perceived control and psychological empowerment. *American Journal of Community Psychology, 16*(5), 725–731.

II

FAMILY SUPPORT
ACROSS POPULATIONS

5

Primary Prevention and the Family Resource Movement

Robert W. Chamberlin

Although most people recognize the need for additional supports to families who have a member with a chronic illness or developmental disability, it is only recently that the notion has come about that many other families can benefit from community-based support systems. Since the 1960s, changing economic and family structures have put increasing stress on families raising children. At the same time, traditional community support systems such as family networks, close-knit neighborhoods, and religious congregations have become increasingly unavailable and underutilized (Weissbourd, 1987). With the erosion of these natural support systems, families experiencing difficulties have had to rely on human services organizations. In the United States, most of these are based on a deficit model, which requires that the family demonstrate it has failed in some way in order to qualify for services (Bronfenbrenner & Weiss, 1983). However, recent reports indicate that increasing numbers of children and youth with health and developmental problems are flooding this system, altering the quality of life in our communities and causing concern in the business community that the United States will not be able to compete in a global marketplace (Carnegie Task Force, 1994; National Commission on Children, 1991; Research and Policy Committee, 1987). Clearly, a different approach is needed.

RATIONALE FOR AN ECOLOGIC APPROACH

Assuming that family risk scores follow a bell-shaped distribution curve, which appears to be the case in many of today's communities, programs targeted only to the families or children at high risk would have little effect on the community as a whole (Chamberlin, 1984; Rose, 1987). Although these programs are helpful to those they reach, they do nothing to alter the underlying conditions that cause families to falter (e.g., changing economy, changing values, changing family support systems, lack of access to community preventive programs). Thus, every family at high risk that receives some form of intensive and expensive intervention is soon replaced by several more families from the much larger, medium-risk pool as their life situation changes—somebody loses a job, undergoes a separation or divorce, becomes pregnant out of wedlock, develops a chronic illness or disability, or moves away from existing support systems (Chamberlin, 1988b).

Furthermore, longitudinal studies on this large, medium-risk group have repeatedly shown that there is no way to accurately predict who will develop problems in the future (Chamberlin, 1987). However, long-term studies have shown that it is usually the accumulation of multiple stresses over time that cause families and/or children to falter (Meisels & Wasik, 1990; Sameroff, Seifer, Barocas, Zax, & Greenspan, 1987). Similarly, categorically funded approaches to specific problems, such as adolescent pregnancy or substance abuse in isolation, have also had only limited effects. This is because early childhood problems so often lead into adolescent problems and then repeat themselves. Targeting resources to only one part of this cycle will have little impact on problem incidence for the community as a whole (Dryfoos, 1990; Schorr, 1988). Figure 1 illustrates this vicious circle.

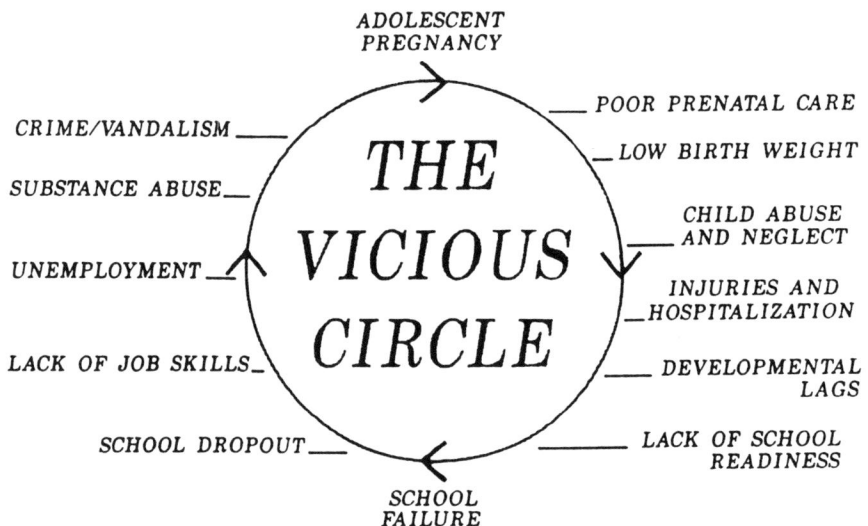

Figure 1.   The vicious cycle that is unaffected by targeting resources to only one problem, as in a categorically funded program. (From Chamberlin, R. [1992]. Preventing low birth weight, child abuse, and school failure: The need for comprehensive, community-wide approaches. *Pediatrics in Review, 13,* p. 65; reproduced by permission of *Pediatrics in Review.*)

A greater understanding of the ecology of human development is currently leading toward an approach that stresses primary prevention and targets services to the community as a whole. This approach recognizes the interdependence of the individual, the family, and the community, and understands that effective change requires modification of all three. In order for a child to develop appropriately, his or her parents must function effectively; in order to function effectively, parents need to have an adequate support system of family, friends, and community organizations; in order for these support systems to function adequately, they must be supported by local government policies and practices; in order for localities to function effectively, they must be supported by the policies and practices of state and national governments. Primary prevention works by keeping families or children at low- and medium-risk from becoming at high risk. Figure 2 illustrates this concept.

To illustrate this point, Western European countries that employ this kind of approach are much more effective than the United States in preventing low-weight births, child abuse and neglect, injuries and violence of all kinds, adolescent pregnancy, and school dropout (Chamberlin, 1988a; Child health in 1990, 1990; Miller, 1987; Williams & Miller, 1991). With this approach, basic primary prevention programs, such as health care, early childhood education, access to higher education, and parent education and support, are made accessible to all children and families as well as those with special needs.

Demonstration projects indicate that this kind of approach will work in the United States, as well. For example, a demonstration program in a school district in Brookline, Massachusetts, found that school functioning could be significantly improved for both low- and medium-income families by developing a community-wide program that includes home visits to new mothers, establishing a neighborhood family resource center, developing an open, center-based early childhood education program, and ensuring that all children have periodic health and developmental screening (Hauser-Cram, Pierson, Walker, & Tivnan, 1991). The home visiting component was found to be essential in reaching families under the most stress.

MOVING TOWARD AN ECOLOGIC FRAMEWORK IN THE UNITED STATES

Once this framework is adopted, communities must begin to develop strategies to move from a deficit model to an ecologic one. Some communities have adopted the African proverb: "It takes a whole village to raise a child," as a symbol of this movement. Nationally, the Family Resource Movement has adopted this framework.

The Family Resource Movement

Following several decades of change in family and economic life and isolated efforts to respond to these changing circumstances around the nation,

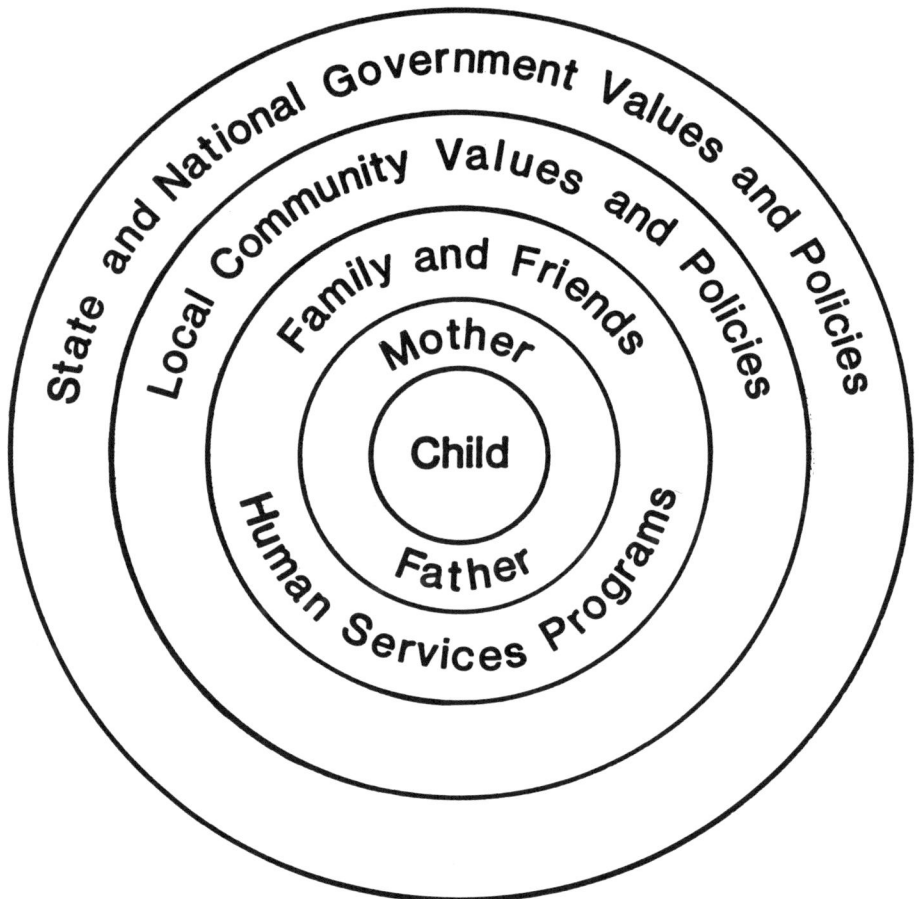

Figure 2.   The ecologic model of caregiving, which recognizes the interdependence of the individual, the family, and the community. (From Chamberlin, R., & Wallace, B. [1995]. Intersectoral approaches to promoting healthy families and children. In B. Lindstrom & N. Spencer [Eds.], *Social Pediatrics* [pp. 469–476]. Oxford, England: Oxford University Press; reprinted by permission.)

Bernice Weissbourd and her colleagues organized several aspects of a growing family support movement to found the Family Resource Coalition in Chicago in 1981 (Weissbourd, 1987). The group's mission is to facilitate the development of family support programs in communities around the nation according to the following six basic principles[1]:

1.   All families need support, regardless of economic status or specific concerns. Most parents want to be good parents no matter what their re-

[1]Weissbourd, B. (1987). A brief history of family support programs. In S. Kagan, D. Powell, B. Weissbourd, & E. Zigler (Eds.), *America's family support programs*. New Haven, CT: Yale University Press, p. 53; reprinted by permission.

sources are. The varying kinds of support provided by family resource programs are determined by the needs of the parents and are responsive to the cultural and social characteristics of the communities in which the families live.

2. The availability of social networks, mutual aid, and peer groups is essential to the family's ability to enhance the child's development.

3. Information on child development, obtained both formally and informally, assists families in their child-rearing role.

4. Support programs increase the family's ability to cope, rather than provide a system on which families become dependent. Support should build on strengths that whole families and individual family members already have. The confidence that family support helps parents build enables families to manage their own lives and participate in shaping the environment in which they live.

5. Providing support during the first few years of a child's life serves a preventive function. Early and continuing support is aimed at strengthening the family unit and preventing family dysfunction.

6. Because families are part of a community, their needs cannot be met in isolation from it. Support is provided in the context of community life and through links with community resources.

Family Resource Centers

Although family support programs come in many shapes and sizes, one of the basic elements is a family resource center. This is a place in the community where parents of young children living in the area can come with their child to socialize with other parents, learn parenting and other basic skills, get temporary relief from child care and help with problems, and develop cooperative arrangements for sharing goods and services. For many families, these centers take the place of an absent family network and provide valuable support. They also give positive recognition to parents, reinforcing their importance in bringing up children. The following are testimonies from parents on the value on family resource centers:

I was just isolated in a small apartment on the third floor. I went out to the park, or I went to the grocery store, or I went shopping; and you see people, but you don't really have a chance to sit down and talk to them if you're really upset about a personal problem. You can't just go to the lady at the check-out counter and say, "My life is falling apart" and expect her to listen. (Parent Interview, Family Resource Coalition Video, Chicago)

It's one of those few places in which you are valued because you are a parent and it says you're right, what you do is important, and we want to help you. (Parent Interview, Family Resource Coalition Video, Chicago)

I used to use spankings more and would scream at the children on a daily basis. I now use consequences and let them make choices. I am also able to compare notes with

*other moms and feel better about my decision to stay home. (Parent Interview, Parent/
Child Centers for Merrimack County, New Hampshire)*

Agencies involved with different aspects of family dysfunction have
discovered that these centers are good places to coordinate services. They
also serve as meeting places for community groups wishing to develop
other types of programs, such as youth centers, and have been used to
upgrade the quality of child care in communities by providing a training
site for family child care workers.

   Levels of Activity   In looking at various programs, one can see three
approximate levels of activity. The lowest level is a program that may meet
once or twice a week for several hours in a borrowed facility, such as a
church basement, community center, or school classroom. Activities are
scheduled for parents and children both together and separately, with a
sponsoring organization often serving as a resource for information and
referral.

   The next level of intensity establishes a permanent facility to serve a
specific area but does little outreach into the surrounding community. This
facility is generally open throughout the week and may have evening and
weekend hours, as well. In addition to level-one activities, it usually provides more opportunities to participate in support groups, learn specific
domestic or prevocational skills, and take part in program planning and
fund-raising.

   A level-three program combines a permanent facility with active outreach into the surrounding community. This could include anything from
providing transportation to and from the center, making home visits, or
establishing toddler play groups in other areas. Program personnel also
participate in community-building activities in surrounding areas and work
closely with area schools and human services agencies.

   Feedback from parents and evaluation studies have shown all levels to
be effective in relieving parental feelings of isolation or loneliness and in
improving parenting skills (Andrews et al., 1982). Level-one centers are
relatively easy to start and maintain but reach only a small number of
families and have little impact on problem base rates for the community as
a whole. Level-two centers reach more families but require considerably
more effort to establish and maintain. Also, because there is no active outreach, they can evolve into programs primarily for middle-class families
who have a regular source of transportation and the energy and confidence
to initiate contact with the center on their own. Adding outreach, as in level
three, considerably increases the ability of programs to engage highly
stressed families and make an overall positive impact on the community.

   Addison County Parent/Child Center   The Addison County Parent/Child
Center serves a rural Vermont county of 32,000 people. It is located in the
largest town, which consists of about 8,000 people. Center-based activities
include a drop-in center where parents can come during the day and have

somebody watch their child while they have a cup of coffee, participate in various support groups or skill-building activities, use the washer or dryer in the basement, or play with their child in an indoor or outdoor play area. Area agencies use the center to coordinate services to families. There is active outreach into the surrounding communities: Vans are available to bring people with transportation problems to and from the center. Home visitors visit new mothers and families with special concerns. Once-a-week toddler play groups have been established in nine other towns; and center personnel work closely with the three high schools in the county to educate teens about child development, parenting, and pregnancy prevention (Chamberlin, 1992).

Dorchester Cares   A similar program, based on an ecologic model, is being used to strengthen families in inner-city neighborhoods in Boston. Dorchester Cares works on a prevention model designed to build strong families: "Our focus is on the whole family living in a whole community, which is diametrically opposed to the idea of individuals going out of their neighborhood to a mental health or child welfare agency for a solution to an isolated problem. We know that families are a critical element in rearing healthy, competent, and caring children. But families cannot fulfill their crucial role unless they have the support of a caring community, one that cherishes its children and their parents." An initial study revealed that the community had overwhelming concerns at the family level, a complex network of providers competing for funding at the community level, and a lack of an infrastructure to provide transportation and child care so that residents could participate in existing programs.

Like the Addison County Program, center-based support and skill-building activities are combined with community outreach, such as knocking on doors to let people know what services are available, home visits to families with newborns and infants under 2, and collaboration with other community agencies such as a local health care center that conducts and supervises the home visitors. The center also works closely with the Family Service of Greater Boston, which provides emergency food and shelter, in addition to running a program for parents with substance abuse problems and a general "Nurturing Program for Parents and Children." The first center was developed in an area of approximately 13,000 families with children; a second center has been opened in another neighborhood with about 10,000 residents (Zabarsky, 1992).

City- and State-Wide Networks   As these centers' value for strengthening families has become recognized, a number of state and city governments have taken steps to facilitate their expansion into other areas. For example, Vermont has established one center in each of its 15 counties (Mable, 1988). Although the services offered by each center vary, all are committed to providing or facilitating services in eight core program areas: child care, drop-in services, parent education, support groups, home visiting, community-based play groups, information and referral, and activities to promote community development. Major emphasis is given to families with young children, but all families are welcome. These programs are now being coordinated with programs for children with special needs funded under Part H of the Families of Children with Disabilities Support Act of 1994. Connecticut, Colorado, and Maryland are currently establishing statewide networks of family resource centers (Weiss, 1989).

School System–Based Programs   Family resource centers have been successfully established in a number of different sites, including trailers, storefronts, flats in housing projects, and neighborhood houses. Using school districts as catchment areas and establishing programs in schools or tied in with school programs has become increasingly popular, helping to promote good parent–school relationships. For example, Missouri has established Parents as Teachers, which is administered through the public school system (Weiss, 1989). This project is a home–school partnership that provides home visits by trained parent educators, on a voluntary basis. The educators assist new parents in developing the skills necessary to promote the social, emotional, and cognitive development of their child from birth to age 3, and is designed to serve all parents.

Minnesota has also established a school system–based program for families with children from birth to age 5, entitled Early Childhood Family Education. Its goal is to strengthen families by enhancing and supporting the parents' ability to promote their childs learning and development (Weiss, 1989). Although the program varies from one community to the next, both in location and content, it always provides opportunities for parents to enrich their relationships with their children through nurturing and playful interaction, learn about child development, develop friendship networks with other parents in the area, and find out where to get help for specific family or personal problems.

Another school system–based model has been developed by Edward Zigler. His program, "Schools of the 21st Century," combines child care and early childhood education programs for preschool children age 3 years and older, after-school programs for those ages 6–12, and parent education and support activities in a facility attached to a neighborhood elementary school (Zigler, 1989).

Kentucky has taken this process one step further by developing a school-based Family Resource Center for families with children 12 and under, and a Youth Service Center for teens (Interagency Task Force, 1994). These programs have now been established in almost 400 school districts around the state, serving communities where at least 20% of the children are eligible for subsidized meals. Once a program is established in a school, however, it is open to all families and children living in the district regardless of income.

The Family Resource Center combines literacy and educational services for parents, with early childhood and after-school programs for children; training is also provided for area child care workers. Rather than initiate new programs, a coordinator is hired by the school system to help families better utilize existing services—an advisory board of prominent local residents, human services providers, and parents also helps choose this coordinator. The centers are usually located in the elementary school itself, in a portable classroom brought in for that purpose or in a nearby neighborhood or housing project. The Youth Service Centers are set up to respond to the needs of students age 12 and older. The coordinator facilitates referrals to health and social services, including family crisis and mental health counseling. In addition, the centers provide employment counseling, training, and placement, as well as summer part-time job development. At least two students serve on the board of the Youth Service Centers.

These programs are based on the premise that 1) all children can learn if barriers are removed; and 2) services must be comprehensive, locally controlled, flexible, innovative, and able to meet the concerns of culturally diverse participants. Although it is too soon to expect any community-wide results, preliminary reports from several school districts have shown more parent involvement, better coordination of services, less student absenteeism, and fewer school dropouts. A more formal long-term evaluation is being conducted.

Neighborhood Networks in Cities   Seattle is developing a neighborhood network of family support centers (Miller, 1993). Under the leadership of the mayor and city council, a levy was passed to fund programs that improve children's education. Strengthening families was incorporated as one of the most critical elements necessary for success. These neighborhood-based family support programs are funded through a request for proposals (RFP). Technical assistance is supplied to help neighborhood groups form broad-based coalitions, apply for funds, and implement programs. Again, programs are based on the principles of being open to all families, building on family strengths, developing self-sufficiency, and cultivating respect for diversity. Other goals are to decrease feelings of isolation in community residents, promote positive parent–child relationships, promote positive school–home relationships, and support positive child development. Centers have been established in four different neighborhood locations—one in a church basement, another in a storefront, a third in a school, and a fourth in a housing project. Four more centers are in the planning stage.

States and cities have been most successful combining a *top-down* and *bottom-up* approach. In top-down, the state or city government provides technical assistance; promotes intersectoral collaboration to coordinate services at the city, county, or state level; and often grants start-up money to initiate new centers. In bottom-up, the local community provides the energy to mobilize local resources and guarantees that local residents will help determine the content of programs, as needed by those living in the area.

Experience from the World Health Organization's Healthy Cities initiative, which now involves more than a thousand cities and communities all over the world, indicates that at least a paid part-time local coordinator is critical for long-term sustainability. Community building and interagency collaboration are very labor-intensive activities and can seldom be maintained by volunteers alone for longer than a year or 2 (Ashton, 1992; Tsouros, 1991).

Steps in Implementing Community-Wide Preventive Programs

In implementing community-wide programs, most communities undergo the following steps, although not necessarily in this order (Chamberlin, 1992):

Defining a Catchment Area   A geographic area of influence must be large enough for efficient program development, yet small enough to maintain a sense of community. In cities, this is often at the neighborhood or elementary school district level. These populations range from 3,000 to 10,000, depending on the density and geographic cohesiveness of the area. For rural areas, this can be a town, several towns, or a county.

Forming a Broad-Based Coalition   Broad-based coalitions need to include human services providers and consumers, community business and local government leaders, members of the religious community, police department personnel, recreation program directors, school personnel, representatives of the media, parents, and teens. In forming coalitions, consideration must be given to who controls the resources necessary to ensure a program's success; this can be in terms of who will provide credibility to the project, who has access to needed data, who has access to the media, and who controls possible funding sources.

Developing a Community Profile and Overall Framework   Either during or after coalition formation, a baseline community profile is generated, which, when put into an ecologic framework, describes the population and economic characteristics of the area, the current status of children and youth, the general level of birthing and parenting skills, feelings of isolation in community residents, and the degree to which current community programs and policies are meeting family needs. This framework is then used to establish short- and long-term priorities for program implementation and coordination.

Implementing Goals   Selling the community on the concept, "It takes a whole village to raise a child," and implementing the previously established priorities become the next focus. Skills in advocacy, social marketing, and fund-raising are essential to this phase of program development (Jackson, 1988; Manoff, 1985).

Establishing Long-Term Sustainability   Once programs are functioning, it is necessary to develop a long-term funding strategy. An advocacy group must also be formed to fend off the inevitable attempts by short-sighted politicians and agency heads to cut back program budgets at the first sign of a budget squeeze.

EVALUATION ISSUES

The difficulty in showing that any one program makes a difference is slowing down the acceptance of a primary prevention approach. Usually, the United States funds an isolated program (e.g., improved obstetrical care, home visiting) in a single community to reduce the incidence of an isolated problem (e.g., low weight births or child abuse). This approach does not even attempt to change the overall community social context in which it is occurring. In addition, these grants are rarely funded for more than 3 years at a time, so although it may be possible to show some modest positive effects on program participants, there is little effect on rates for the community as a whole. One observer from Great Britain describes this approach as taking a full orchestra playing a symphony and trying to determine which instrument is the most important.

With an ecologic model, all the components of each level must be in place before the model gains maximum efficiency—a comprehensive approach that often requires several years to establish and a number more to reap its full benefits. Because the ecologic model requires such a long-term commitment on a community-wide basis, random assignment designs can seldom be used for evaluation. Instead, progress toward long-term goals must be monitored through the achievement of needed changes in community organizations that affect families and children and the identification of evolving knowledge, attitudes, behaviors, and skills in samples of community residents. Contrasting these trends with those in other communities provides a good measure of progress toward eventual reductions in problem incidence.

The need for absolute proof of program effectiveness before implementing large-scale preventive programs is an American attitude. Most Western European countries that have implemented community-wide preventive programs on a national or regional level have not done so because of the results of some study; rather, they have identified a problem and responded to it in terms of what is most likely to be of positive benefit, given the current level of knowledge.

For example, in the 1950s Finland had one of the highest infant mortality rates in Western Europe. On the advice of a prominent pediatrician, the government made a policy decision to develop a nationwide network of maternal and child health centers that would make prenatal and well-child care available to all citizens, despite their location—whether it be in isolated rural areas in the north or in inner cities, such as Helsinki. It took 10 years to complete this network, but during its inception, the infant mortality rate dropped dramatically and remains one of the lowest in the world (Wynn & Wynn, 1979). These changes are, at least in part, related to this network of accessible preventive programs; the fact that the base rates of other preventable problems not made a priority, such as tuberculosis, showed little change over this same period of time supports this assertion. Furthermore, the drop in infant mortality was steeper in Finland than in other Western European countries of similar or better economic status that were not prioritizing maternal and child health.

Another example is a national comprehensive preterm birth prevention program implemented in France. The program was begun on the advice of several physicians, who claimed it would reduce the incidence of birth defects and developmental disorders (Papeirnik, Keith, Bouyer, Dreyfus, & Lazar, 1989). The program included universal access to comprehensive prenatal care through the extensive use of nurse-midwives and risk assessment and specialist care for those at a higher risk for preterm birth. The program also made provisions for educating patients to recognize the signs of early labor contractions and how to avoid them, paying prenatal leave for women working in physically demanding jobs or for those with long commutes, supplying outreach with home visits to women with complicated living situations, and paying for domestic help. Although this approach was put into practice on a community-wide basis, preterm birth rates in well-educated, middle-class women did not decline for 4 years, and in less-educated, lower-income women results did not register for 8 years. Evidence suggested that this comprehensive approach was instrumental in causing the decline in preterm birth rates because 1) changes in birth rates mirrored the willingness of the women to change their lifestyle with the better educated middle-class women leading the way; and 2) preterm birth rates in the United States, Great Britain, and Germany did not decline over this same time period, despite similar levels of technology and living standards.

An attempt in the United States was made to replicate the results of this study by targeting a high-risk pregnancy group with a highly technological approach that emphasized risk assessment, specialist care, and the use of tocalitic drugs to stop early labor. Other parts of the comprehensive approach, such as universal access to care, outreach with home visitors, paid prenatal leave and domestic help, and other various patient education and support features, were not included. Not surprisingly, this study was unable to replicate the French results (E. Papeirnik, personal communication, Spring, 1992).

However, when communities in the United States maintain comprehensive programs over a long period of time, their effects usually parallel those in Europe. For example, an evaluation of the Addison County program, after 7 years of operation, revealed significant progress in the reduction of adolescent pregnancy, low-weight births, child abuse, family violence, and welfare dependency (Chamberlin, 1992). The Brookline, Massachusetts, project, which followed children from birth to second grade, combined home visits, a family resource center, early childhood education programs, and health and periodic developmental screening. Its results showed significant increase in the children's social and academic skills and in the development of enduring, long-term friendships among the adult participants (Hauser-Cram et al., 1991). Other long-term follow-ups of comprehensive programs have documented positive results (Price, Cowen, Lorion, & Ramos-McKay, 1988; Seitz, Rosenbaum, & Apfel, 1985); however, virtually all of these have been small-scale follow-ups of program participants, rather than attempts to demonstrate changes in problem base rates for the community as a whole.

Alternative Evaluation Strategies

For those convinced of the benefits of an ecologic approach, there are other ways to monitor progress toward long-term goals. The three-column model used in the Stanford Heart Disease Prevention study is one such approach (Jackson, 1988). At the start of the intervention, baseline measures are made in three areas: 1) base rates (status indicators) are determined for the problems to be reduced; 2) baseline levels of the individual knowledge, attitudes, behaviors, and skills that affect those base rates are determined from a random sample of parents and adolescents in the community, using survey techniques; and 3) a baseline description of how family-friendly the community is in terms of role models and organizational policies and practices that affect families and youths is established. Figure 3 outlines this overall framework.

A resource inventory of the community would include answers to the following questions: Is there universal access to high-quality, comprehensive health care programs for mothers and children? What percent of major employers have paid pregnancy and child care leave? What is the level of affordability and quality of child care in the community? What percent of

OVERALL FRAMEWORK FOR PROMOTING HEALTHY FAMILIES AND CHILDREN		
ENVIRONMENTAL FACTORS	INDIVIDUAL FACTORS	STATUS INDICATORS
FAMILY AND PEER GROUP ORGANIZATIONAL LEVEL COMMUNITY LEVEL	KNOWLEDGE ATTITUDES BEHAVIORS SKILLS	BASE RATES FOR PREVENTABLE PROBLEMS

Figure 3.   The environmental and individual factors inherent for the promotion of healthy families and children, along with status indicators. (Adapted from Jackson, 1988.)

new mothers have had a home visit; is there the capacity in this support system to sustain these visits over the first 2 years of life if the family has special needs? Is there a parent–child or family resource center in the community that is open to everyone? How accessible and affordable are early childhood education programs for 3- and 4-year-olds? How receptive is local government to supporting programs that strengthen families? What is the level of media coverage in the area for positive approaches to parenting?

Individual factors could be ascertained from a parent survey. Information from the parent survey would reveal the general level of feelings of isolation and loneliness in the community. Other information that can be obtained includes how many mothers entered prenatal care in the first trimester, used cigarettes or alcohol during the pregnancy, and what they are doing now to promote the health and development of their child. For young children, status indicators might be the percentage of low-weight births, immunization levels at age 2, neglect and abuse rates for children under 5, or the school-readiness of children coming into first grade.

A similar procedure is then followed to identify individual, family, and community risk and protective factors related to various status indicators for adolescents, such as school dropout, out-of-wedlock pregnancies, substance abuse, and juvenile crime. Once these baseline measures are established, they can be repeated every few years to follow the progress of the community-wide approach. It is essential for communities to show progress if they are to maintain the long-term funding of these programs that is necessary to produce meaningful changes in problem base rates for the community as a whole.

For families with young children, improvements should first be noted in the development of more family-friendly community services. After these have been in operation several years, one could expect a decrease in feelings of isolation and loneliness in young parents, reductions in risk behaviors that affect pregnancy outcome, and more positive parenting skills. Only after these have been noted for several years could one expect improvements in problem base rates for the community as a whole.

The level of service intensity and duration needed to reduce problem incidence in young children in a given community has not yet been established. However, based on current knowledge, minimum expectations would include universal access to prenatal and well-child care; home visits to families with special needs; a drop-in family resource center that is open to everyone; access to high-quality, affordable child care and early childhood education programs; and family-friendly business benefit packages (Carnegie Task Force, 1994). In some inner-city areas these would need to be combined with access to decent and affordable housing, job training programs and transportation to employment sites, and drug- and crime-free neighborhoods. Both the longer the community has been neglected and the more entrenched the problems increase the length and intensity of community services needed.

IMPLICATIONS FOR PUBLIC POLICY[2]

1. A consensus must be reached on the underlying factors causing the current increase in dysfunctional families and children. Some believe it stems from *both* the changing conditions under which families are trying to function and the failure of most of our communities, businesses, and governments to respond to these changes in constructive ways. As long as a sizable part of the population wants to put all of the blame on single parents, minority groups, or changing family values, without recognizing the contributing role of community and government inaction in meeting these changing needs, the political will necessary to sustain a long-term primary prevention approach will be impossible to attain.

2. A combination of a top-down and bottom-up approach must be more widely used. In this, the political leadership (top) enacts supportive legislation to develop the needed funding and intersectoral collaboration, which is necessary to coordinate existing programs and to facilitate the local community efforts to implement programs that meet local community (bottom) needs. Programs without top support are rarely sustainable over long periods of time, just as programs without bottom support rarely address the most pressing needs of local residents.

3. Comprehensive programs must be kept functioning over the long time periods necessary to produce positive outcomes at the community level. In order to do this, it will also be necessary to monitor progress toward established goals and develop a strong advocacy role to prevent periodic budget cuts by short-sighted politicians and agency heads in times of budget restraints.

4. Every aspect of a comprehensive preventive-promotive package cannot be individually evaluated and justified in relation to health and developmental outcomes. This is unrealistic and unproductive, considering the whole is more than the sum of its parts and outcomes are usually the result of a complex interplay of many different factors.

5. Use family resource centers to coordinate services for children with special needs, such as those with chronic illnesses or developmental disabilities.

---

[2]Good discussions of these and other policy-related issues can be found in Family Resource Coalition (1990) and Kagan and Weissbourd (1994).

Chapter Review

CHALLENGES

- Both family living conditions and traditional community support systems have changed dramatically since the 1960s.
- Families have had to rely on human services organizations that typically function on deficit models.
- Increasing numbers of families and youth with problems are overwhelming communities and the current human services system.
- Focusing on the concerns of populations at high risk fails to address the underlying problems that have placed those people at risk.
- Categorical approaches do not adequately target resources to support the multiple stressors that families face.

CHARACTERISTICS OF HELPFUL PROGRAMS

- Services stress primary prevention and community supports and are more responsive to the cross-categorical, ecologic concerns of most families.
- Programs feature primary prevention, which prevents families at low and medium risk from becoming at high risk.
- Programs are made available to all families and children, regardless of categorical membership.
- Programs are built around the mission of the family resource movement, which is to provide culturally responsive family support regardless of economic status, to promote access to social networks, to promote family coping and self-help, and to facilitate community linkages, with a focus on supporting young children.
- Family resource centers provide places in communities where families can come to learn skills, build social ties, and acquire services, but outreach is also provided.
- Services are comprehensive, flexible, and locally controlled.
- Long-term program sustainability is facilitated by a paid local coordinator who promotes interagency collaboration and community building.

POLICY IMPLICATIONS

- Consensus must be reached on the underlying causes of family dysfunction.
- A combined strategy of top-down and bottom-up supports must be utilized to maintain program viability.

- Programs need to be supported over time to provide sufficient opportunity for components to be established and integrated and long-term impacts to be documented.
- Program effectiveness can be monitored over time by documenting sequential changes in community resources; changes in individual knowledge, attitudes, behaviors, and skills of a sample of parents and adolescents; and, after a number of years, changes in community-problem base rates.
- Family resource centers can be utilized to coordinate services for all children, including those with special needs.

References

Andrews, S., Blumenthal, J., Johnson, D., Kahn, A., Ferguson, C., Lasater, T., Mabne, P., & Wallace, D. (1982). The skills of mothering: A study of the parent-child development centers. *Society for Research in Child Development*, Vol. 47, Monograph No. 6.

Ashton, J. (Ed.). (1992). *Healthy cities*. Philadelphia, PA: Open University Press.

Bronfenbrenner, U., & Weiss, H. (1983). Beyond policies without people: An ecological perspective on child and family policy. In E. Zigler, S. Lynn-Kagan, & E. Klugman (Eds.), *Children, families, and government* (pp. 393–414). New York: Cambridge University Press.

Carnegie Task Force on Meeting the Needs of Young Children. (1994). *Starting points: Meeting the needs of our youngest children*. New York: Carnegie Corporation.

Chamberlin, R. (1984). Strategies for disease prevention and health promotion: The "ecologic" versus the "high risk" approach. *Journal of Public Health Policy, 5*, 185–197.

Chamberlin, R. (1987). Developmental assessment and early intervention programs for young children: Lessons learned from longitudinal research. *Pediatrics in Review, 8*, 237–247.

Chamberlin, R. (1988a). Community-wide approaches to promoting the health and development of families and children: Examples from Scandinavia and Great Britain. In R. Chamberlin (Ed.), *Conference Proceedings, Beyond individual risk assessment: Community-wide approaches to promoting the health and development of families and children* (pp. 176–220). Washington, DC: The National Center for Education in Maternal and Child Health.

Chamberlin, R. (1988b). Rationale for a community-wide approach to promote the health and development of families and children. In R. Chamberlin (Ed.), *Conference proceedings, Beyond individual risk assessment: Community-wide approaches to promoting the health and development of families and children* (pp. 3–13). Washington, DC: The National Center for Education in Maternal and Child Health.

Chamberlin, R. (1992). Preventing low birth weight, child abuse, and school failure: The need for comprehensive, community-wide approaches. *Pediatrics in Review, 13*, 64–71.

Chamberlin, R., & Wallace, B. (1995). Intersectoral approaches to promoting healthy families and children. In B. Lindstrom & N. Spencer (Eds.), *Social pediatrics* (pp. 469–476). Oxford, England: Oxford University Press.

Child health in 1990: The United States compared to Canada, England and Wales, France, the Netherlands, and Norway. (1990). *Proceedings of the American Academy of Pediatrics, Pediatrics, 86* (Supplement), 1025–1127.

Dryfoos, J. (1990). *Adolescents at risk: Prevalence and prevention*. New York: Oxford University Press.

Families of Children with Disabilities Support Act of 1994, PL 103-382. (October 20, 1994). Title 20, U.S.C. 1491 et seq: *U.S. Statutes at Large, 108*, 3937.

Family Resource Coalition. (1990). *Helping families grow strong: New directions in public policy*. Paper presented at the Colloquium on Public Policy and Family Support, Chicago.

Hauser-Cram, P., Pierson, D., Walker, D., & Tivnan, T. (1991). *Early education in the public schools: Lessons from a comprehensive birth-to-kindergarten program*. San Francisco: Jossey-Bass.

Interagency Task Force on Family Resource and Youth Service Centers, Cabinet for Human Resources. (1994). *Annual implementation status report FY93.* Frankfort, KY: Author.

Jackson, C. (1988). A community-based approach to preventing heart disease: The Stanford experience. In R. Chamberlin (Ed.), *Conference proceedings, Beyond individual risk assessment: Community-wide approaches to promoting the health and development of families and children.*

Kagan, S., & Weissbourd, B. (Eds.). (1994). *Putting families first.* San Francisco: Jossey-Bass.

Mable, T. (1988). Vermont invests in parent–child centers. *Family Resource Coalition Report, 3,* 9.

Manoff, R. (1985). *Social marketing: New imperative for public health.* New York: Praeger.

Meisels, S.J., & Wasik, B. (1990). Who should be served? Identifying children in need of early intervention. In J.P. Shonkoff & S.J. Meisels (Eds.), *Handbook of early childhood intervention* (pp. 605–632). New York: Cambridge University Press.

Miller, A. (1987). *Maternal health and infant survival.* Arlington, VA: National Center for Clinical Infant Programs.

Miller, J. (1993). *Seattle's family support centers at one year.* Seattle, WA: Department of Housing and Human Services.

National Commission on Children. (1991). *Beyond rhetoric: A new American agenda for children and families.* Washington, DC: Author.

Papeirnik, E., Keith, L., Bouyer, J., Dreyfus, J., & Lazar, P. (Eds.). (1989). *Effective prevention of preterm birth: The French experience measured at Haguenau.* White Plains, NY: March of Dimes Birth Defects Foundation.

Price, R., Cowen, E., Lorion, R., & Ramos-McKay, J. (1988). *Fourteen ounces of prevention: A casebook for practitioners.* Washington, DC: American Psychological Association.

Research and Policy Committee. (1987). *Children in need: Investment strategies for the educationally disadvantaged.* New York: Committee for Economic Development.

Rose, G. (1987). Environmental factors and disease: The man made environment. *British Medical Journal, 294,* 963–965.

Sameroff, A., Seifer, R., Barocas, R., Zax, M., & Greenspan, S. (1987). Intelligence quotient scores of 4 year old children: Social emotional risk factors. *Pediatrics, 79,* 343–350.

Schorr, L. (with Schorr, D.). (1988). *Within our reach: Breaking the cycle of disadvantage.* New York: Doubleday.

Seitz, V., Rosenbaum, L., & Apfel, N. (1985). Effects of family support intervention: A ten year follow-up. *Child Development, 56,* 376–391.

Tsouros, A. (Ed.). (1991). *World Health Organization Healthy Cities Project: A project becomes a movement: Review of progress 1987 to 1990.* Copenhagen: Fadl Publishers.

Weiss, H. (1989). State family support and education programs: Lessons from the pioneers. *American Journal of Orthopsychiatry, 59,* 32–48.

Weissbourd, B. (1987). A brief history of family support programs. In S. Kagan, D. Powell, B. Weissbourd, & E. Zigler (Eds.), *America's family support programs* (pp. 38–56). New Haven, CT: Yale University Press.

Williams, B., & Miller, A. (1991). *Preventive health care for young children: Findings from a 10-country study and directions for United States policy.* Arlington, VA: National Center for Clinical Infant Programs.

Wynn, M., & Wynn, A. (1979). *Prevention of handicap and the health of women.* London: Routledge & Kegen Paul.

Zabarsky, M. (1992). *Dorchester Cares annual report.* Dorchester, MA: Dorchester Cares.

Zigler, E. (1989). Addressing the nation's child care crisis: The schools of the 21st century. *American Journal of Orthopsychiatry, 59,* 484–491.

6

The Aging Family in a Multigenerational Perspective

M. Powell Lawton

It is very likely that caregiving to frail older adults has been the most researched gerontology issue since the 1980s. This chapter provides descriptive information on caregiving, with particular attention to the implications of caregiving for both public policy and social values. Although the discussion emphasizes the older adult, the underlying themes are interdependence, exchange, and mutual support in multigenerational settings.

It is important to begin by understanding that 1) caregiving is only one aspect of the much larger *mutual support* category; and 2) care may be given either informally (i.e., voluntarily and without charge) or formally (i.e., as a charged-for service).

MUTUAL SUPPORT

Caregiving is one of the many ways in which family members provide for one another's needs, assisting with financial support, housing, help with everyday tasks, and emotional support. These general family assistance operations seem to be distributed among family members generationally, especially regarding the care pattern for frail older adults.

Financial support is perhaps the most crucial aspect of caregiving. Usually, even after a child matures, financial assistance is still almost always from the parent to the child (Cooney & Uhlenberg, 1992). It is only when

A portion of this work was supported by Grant #MH43371 from the National Institute of Mental Health and grants from the Pew Memorial Trust and the Hartford Foundation.

parents reach their 80s that financial assistance *to* the parent begins to exceed that *from* the parent (Hill, Morgan, & Herzog, 1993).

Another extremely important assistance is providing a home—taken for granted during the child-rearing phase, but frequently ignored thereafter. Among all older adults with a living child, approximately 18% live in the same home with the child. Older people who have lower incomes, who are from minority groups, or who have impaired ability to perform activities of daily living (ADL) are more likely to live in the same household with younger family members (Clarke & Neidert, 1992; Soldo, Sharma, & Campbell, 1984). Examining the longitudinal history of the household reveals, though, that this arrangement benefits both generations fairly equally. The adult children benefit primarily from financial aid and social support, especially when they have marital or other problems (Crimmins & Ingegneri, 1990), while older parents usually benefit from the ease and convenience of having their children maintain their care. Of these shared arrangements, about half were not formed at the time assistance was needed by the parent but existed from the adult child's earlier years (Shanas, 1982).

Directly supportive tasks are another form of assistance, usually performed for people who are unable to perform them independently; however, they are also sometimes performed simply as a way of making the everyday life of a family member easier. In fact, of all types of household assistance (e.g., cleaning, yard work, cooking, washing dishes, laundry, shopping, babysitting), 31% of all parents of adult children gave such help and 23% of parents received such help from nonresident children (Eggebeen, 1992). As the parents became older, however, they were more likely to receive help (38%) than give help (23%). In shared households, one estimate showed that an average of 100 household tasks were performed during a month by an older member, compared to 20 by a co-resident adult child (Ward, Logan, & Spitze, 1992).

Psychosocial support is much more difficult to estimate than household support. It should be assumed that some level of support is given within most families, unless some major dysfunction exists. Such support, in the form of sympathetic listening, advice, sympathy, or sharing of experiences, has the great advantage of being deliverable either face to face or at a distance by telephoning or mail.

To summarize, mutual support is highly prevalent in families, provided on demand, and multidirectional across generations. If any imbalance occurs, it is usually on behalf of the parental generation who continue to give until very old age or infirmity interferes; children continue to be nurtured as long as possible. This body of evidence is very important for value-laden questions regarding the equitable division of society's material resources among the generations.

CAREGIVING

When mutual support must address failing abilities and resources, it is referred to as *caregiving*. Caregiving may be defined as assistance given to another person because that person is unable to perform the critical tasks of personal or household care necessary for everyday survival. Caregiving differs from mutual support in that 1) the caregiving activity is in response to a deficit in the care receiver, 2) the care is necessary to the care receiver's survival, and 3) the care may be more costly than mutual support in time or dollars.

More narrowly defined, caregiving is of utmost importance to one segment of older individuals in the United States, the many people who provide care for them, and the citizenry at large because of the high cost of caregiving. Therefore, despite the evidence in favor of the multigenerational and multidirectional quality of support in general, there is good reason to review in depth the type of caregiving directed toward frail older people.

Informal and Formal Care

Informal care is caregiving received at no financial cost through voluntary contributions by family members, friends, or neighbors. *Formal care* is care delivered through profit-making, organizational, or institutional sources, characterized by a formal organizational structure, an explicit cost, and the lack of a prior personal relationship between the caregiver and the care receiver. There may be subsidies to pay for the cost of formal services, but the critical feature is that someone pays.

The best information on the characteristics and prevalence of caregiving comes from the National Long-Term Care Survey (NLTCS) (Macken, 1986), a survey of Medicare recipients who reported any limitation in their ability to perform one or more basic physical ADLs or instrumental activities of daily living (IADLs)—19% of all people 65 and older. A more stringent criterion was used, however, to define caregiving: those who provided help to an elder because of limitations in basic physical ADLs (e.g., bathing, dressing, eating, using the toilet, continence, bed mobility, going outdoors)—13% of people 65 and older. About 10% of older people with impairments reported having no caregiver at all. By this standard, a majority (58%) of older people did not receive care.

An additional survey was conducted on the 13% who displayed limitations in basic physical ADLs—the Informal Caregivers Survey (Stone, Cafferata, & Sangl, 1987). Of this most frail group, 5% had formal help only, 71% had informal caregiving only, and 19% had both paid and unpaid help. Of all the informal caregivers, 80% gave care 7 days per week, with a median of 2.5 hours per day (Stone et al., 1987).

By far, the greatest amount of ADL/IADL assistance is given by household members; 74% of the caregivers in the NLTCS lived in the same household as the care receiver (Stone et al., 1987), and research shows that co-residence is a major predictor of the amount of care given (Tennestedt, Crawford, & McKinlay, 1993). In the NLTCS, 38% of caregivers were adult children, 36% were spouses, and 27% were other relatives, nonrelatives, or paid help. Although spouses are typically the first-line resource for caregiving, recent research suggests that the major factor determining who provides care may be co-residence, rather than spousal commitment (Tennes-tedt et al., 1993). Less than 25% of all those included in the NLTCS received care from paid or formal services, a relatively low percentage considering the long-term care needed by this population.

A more general picture of the formal services used by all older adults is conveyed by two surveys. The first, the Longitudinal Study of Aging (LSOA) (Stone, 1986), sampled all older adults, while the second, the National Medical Expenditure Survey (NMES) (Short & Leon, 1988), studied people over 55 who had one or more ADL/IADL disabilities. The first column in Table 1 shows the proportion of all people 65 and older who used various home- and community-delivered services during the past year, as reported by the LSOA. By contrast, the second column, from the NMES, shows service-use data (i.e., regular use within the past month) for individuals with impairments. The lines drawn by impairment are obvious: The LSOA sample was much more active in utilizing senior centers and group meals, while the NMES group used home health services (e.g., health aides, homemakers, visiting nurses) much more heavily. In both of these surveys, people who lived alone or had substantial ADL impairments used formal services the most frequently.

In fact, the prevalence rate of functional impairment in the older pop-ulation at large far surpasses the number of all people using in-home sup-portive services. Still, the proportions of older people with ADL or IADL impairments using the "heavy" in-home services were 1.6% for home health, 1.4% for homemaker, and 2.9% for visiting nurse (see Table 1, based on the LSOA). These low rates of formal service are compensated for with high levels of informal support, which are more easily delivered and can

Table 1.   Percentages of older community residents in two samples reporting uses of various services

Service	LSOA[a] 1984	NMES[b] 1987
Any service	21.5	31.1
Home health	1.6	17.9
Senior center	15.1	6.8
Group meals	7.8	5.7
Telephone check	unknown[c]	3.8
Home-delivered meals	1.9	5.5
Transportation	4.3	5.9
Homemaker	1.4	N/A[d]
Visiting nurse	2.9	N/A
Adult day care	unknown[c]	N/A

[a]Longitudinal Study of Aging (Stone, 1986), national sample of people 65 and older who used the service in the past year.
[b]National Medical Expenditure Survey (Short & Leon, 1988), national sample of people 55 and older who reported at least one ADL/IADL deficit and used the service regularly and within past month.
[c]Too few cases to estimate.
[d]N/A: Not asked in NMES.

be delivered selectively to people with more severe impairments within the household. Another explanation for the disparity is deprivation—some who clearly need the services are simply not receiving them. Montgomery and Hirshorn (1991) estimated that 7.8% of those 60 and older who are in poor physical health and have an ADL impairment have informal support available. This rate agrees with several other estimates (Grannemann & Grossman, 1986; Stephens & Christianson, 1986).

CONSEQUENCES OF CAREGIVING

Until the fall of 1995 when this book went to press, the heaviest emphasis in caregiving research has been on the burdens associated with caregiving, in the areas of the caregiver's health, lifestyle, and subjective well-being. There is also concern over the progressive permanence of caregiving strain. The *wear-and-tear hypothesis* suggests that caregiving is a chronic stressor that steadily erodes well-being (Townsend, Noelker, Deimling, & Bass, 1989). It has recently become clearer, however, that there are positive outcomes associated with providing care. The *adaptation model* suggests that the caregiver adapts to the stressor, learns better techniques, and therefore either maintains or improves well-being.

This mix of favorable and unfavorable consequences of caregiving is the topic of much contemporary research. Montgomery, Gonyea, and Hooyman (1985) distinguished the effects of caregiving in terms of "objective" features, such as role change, adjustment of daily routines, and other behaviors, as compared to "subjective" features, such as burden. Each of these issues regarding consequences is reviewed very briefly, because there are many factors that affect the quality of life of the person giving care. Most caregiving research has been cross-sectional, a situation that leaves many conclusions necessarily tentative.

Health Outcomes

A number of studies have produced suggestions that caregiving exerts a negative impact on caregivers' health; however, none have definitively established this conclusion with longitudinal research (Wright, Clipp, & George, 1993). A cross-sectional national sample survey found that only one third of caregivers rated their health as being fair or poor (Stone et al., 1987). Still, more focused studies suggest that with better methodologies such effects may be brought to light. Moritz, Kasl, and Berkman (1989) uncovered evidence that giving care to older adults with cognitive impairments raised blood pressure. Kiecolt-Glaser, Dura, Speicher, Trask, and Glaser (1991) found that caregiving was directly associated with poorer immune functioning. This negative psychoimmunological effect continued in caregivers even after the death of the older person (Esterling, Kiecolt-Glaser, Bodnar, & Glaser, 1994).

Lifestyle

Although *lifestyle* is a more general term, it is clear that many changes, such as ceasing to work (Brody & Schoonover, 1986) and limitation of social contacts (Lawton, Kleban, Moss, Rovine, & Glicksman, 1989), have been attributed to caregiving. However, such effects are difficult to assess in longitudinal research because of the lack of data available prior to assuming the caregiver role.

Subjective Well-Being

The subjective outcomes associated with caregiving have been termed *caregiving appraisal* (Lawton, Kleban, et al., 1989), which includes both the positive and negative aspects of caregiving. One study found that 87% of family caregivers of adults with Alzheimer's disease reported some form of subjective distress (Rabins, Mace, & Lucas, 1982). Virtually all caregiving research documents that, with caregiving comes a sense of burden (Deimling, 1994; Schulz, Visintainer, & Williamson, 1990). Similarly, every study documents that depression may frequently accompany the caregiving process, with some estimating *Diagnostic and Statistical Manual of Mental Disorders* (DSM-III-R) (American Psychiatric Association, 1987) depression rates as high as 81% (Wright et al., 1993). However, there is the possibility that these samples have been biased and have selectively recruited the more depressed, because no study to date has successfully sampled groups of caregivers and noncaregivers who represent the universe of these groups. In addition, in studies in which both caregiving-specific feelings of burden and generalized depression have been measured and analyzed, depression has been found to be elevated only in the subgroup who also felt burdened (Lawton, Moss, Kleban, Glicksman, & Rovine, 1991).

It is important to remember that although the majority of caregiving research has concentrated only on uncovering distress, there are benefits derived from the process. Lawton, Kleban, et al. (1989) identified satisfaction as one of the major forms of caregiving appraisal. Furthermore, those who derived greater satisfaction from caregiving also reported a greater frequency of positive feelings about their everyday lives exclusive of caregiving (Lawton et al., 1991). This research showed that a greater feeling of mastery in relation to caregiving enhanced caregiving satisfaction and reduced the feeling of burden (Pagel, Becker, & Coppel, 1985). Although few caregivers frame their experience in completely positive terms, a great many appear to cope with this stressor in a problem-focused fashion (Pruchno & Resch, 1989b). They feel they had no choice other than to assume this role; therefore, they see themselves as making the best of it. Many even believe that their own personality has been strengthened by successfully coping with caregiving and its demands (Rubinstein, 1989).

Many adult–child caregivers frame their roles in a life-span perspective. Caring for the parent is seen as balancing past care from the parent or as providing an example for the next generation to follow (Rubinstein, 1989). In fact, to construe the benefits of caregiving in this way may provide self-affirmation of one's behavior, even when strong social-emotional ties between generations conflict (Lawton, Brody, & Saperstein, 1989).

Predictors of Subjective Well-Being

Although the research on predictors of subjective well-being is too voluminous to review in detail (Wright et al., 1993), consensus shows that caregiving spouses are more burdened than adult children (George & Gwyther, 1986; Lawton et al., 1991; Tennestedt et al., 1993). Also, in a number of measures of caregiving distress, Caucasian Americans have been shown to be more distressed than African Americans (Lawton, Rajagopal, Brody, & Kleban, 1992). The reasons for this difference are not clear, although they have been replicated by other investigators. On a cross-sectional basis, paid employment is associated with less burden (Brody, 1990), as is role diversity outside the family (Stoller & Pugliesi, 1988). In addition, more intense or frequent caregiving behavior is associated with greater burden (Lawton et al., 1991), unless the stressor is measured in terms of the pathology of the care receiver. Behavioral symptoms in the older adult with impairments also seem to lead to caregiver distress (Deimling & Bass, 1986; Pruchno & Resch, 1989b). Yet, the older person's degree of impairment in ADL is rarely related to the caregiver's subjective well-being; degree of cognitive impairment is inconsistently related.

Wear-and-Tear Versus Adaptation

Data on the long-term effects of caregiving are very sparse. Most research has failed to show a relationship between length of time that care has been provided and any of the indicators of subjective burden—a pattern that argues against the wear-and-tear hypothesis. Stability over time in subjective well-being was suggested in several longitudinal studies (Pagel et al., 1985; Townsend et al., 1989; Zarit, Todd, & Zarit, 1986), while a 2-year study by Schulz and Williamson (1991) documented either stable (in women) or increased (in men) depression over time.

However, in reference to adaptation, institutionalizing a relative with impairments (Moss, Lawton, Kleban, & Duhamel, 1993; Townsend, 1990) results in decreased caregiver burden. And, Bodnar and Kiecolt-Glaser (1994) have shown that caregivers continue to be more depressed than noncaregivers for 2 years after the death of their care receivers.

This evidence shows that caregivers do experience wear and tear that may outlast actual caregiving, while others adapt or reconstitute their psychological strength once the caregiving ends.

The evidence is again rather mixed on the effects of social support. The amount of social support received does not regularly decrease psychological distress in all caregivers (Wright et al., 1993), but it does appear to do so among the most burdened (Haley, Levine, Brown, & Bartolucci, 1987). Usually, having more caregivers and more social support is associated with more burden (Bass, Tausig, & Noelker, 1988–1989), as if such help complicates or adds conflict to caregiving.

Interventions for Long-Term Caregivers

Many interventions to assist caregivers have been evaluated. One of the most useful studies was Gallagher-Thompson's (1994) research program based on self-efficacy theory (Bandura, 1982), which suggests that the perception of competence, or self-efficacy, is specific to valued behaviors and is continuously adjusted on the basis of how well one performs that activity in comparison with pre-performance expectations. Positive *performance-based feedback* is central to the enhancement of self-efficacy, as are choosing attainable tasks and goals and providing the necessary skills.

Gallagher-Thompson (1994) designed two programs that sought to enhance the perception of self-efficacy and, ultimately, the subjective state and mental health of the caregiver: The "Life Satisfaction" program taught caregivers how to examine the incidence of positive experiences in their own lives; the "Problem-Solving Class" taught caregivers coping skills to deal with everyday problems. Although not all criteria showed improvement, in a total sample of 111 subjects, both of these programs resulted in a number of indicators of improved efficacy and mental health as compared to waiting-list subjects.

Other approaches have included group-focused activities such as stress management and support (Zarit et al., 1986), group education (Kahan, Kemp, Staples, & Brummel-Smith, 1984), and cognitive-behavioral approaches (Scharlach, 1987).

A quantitative analysis of the results of all individual caregiver interventions and all group interventions led Knight, Lutzky, and Macofsky-Urban (1993) to conclude that individual interventions showed a moderately strong effect. Other types of interventions such as respite care, which allows time off for caregivers, have been shown to be valued highly by caregivers but have little effect on their mental health (Lawton, Brody, & Saperstein, 1989). In light of these results, are services that please caregivers justifiable even if they have no measurable long-term effects? The implications of this knowledge for family policy and social values are the focus of the next section.

FAMILY ECOLOGY AND SERVICE POLICY

In the contemporary life-span view of intergenerational exchange in the United States, autonomy of each generation is not only desired but the norm. Upp's (1982) study of sources of financial support among people 65 and older illustrates the development of this concept since the 1900s. In 1937, two thirds of older people were dependent on relatives or public welfare. By 1978, when Social Security was fully implemented, 97% were self-dependent, 1.7% dependent on children, and 1.3% on public funds. Both generations' growing preference for separate living arrangements has increased the prevalence of nuclear-family households (Lawton, 1992); and the 1.2 million or more publicly subsidized housing units for older Americans have proven to benefit younger families as much as older adults.

Security across the life span represents an equally important goal. Lawton (1985; Parmelee & Lawton, 1990) has interpreted the ecology of later life as a dialectic between autonomy and security, as the balance between them is determined by lifelong individual and social-structural differences, such as the person's level of dependency; habits established on the basis of normative generational hierarchy; learned personal preferences; intraindividual changes across the life span, such as biological health; and cultural, social, and physical-environmental changes. In general, people give up autonomy when faced with intrapersonal or environmental changes that make security more necessary. Although many such changes are imposed on the person, the person also behaves proactively in anticipating or adjusting to such changes (Lawton, 1985).

The *normative life span*—marked by staged, predictable events—and the *happenstance life span*—marked by spontaneous, unpredictable events—rarely follow the classic pattern of development from full support (e.g., childhood) to full autonomy, but the family and social order usually provide the mechanisms to accommodate disturbances in this pattern. In the case of the family, all data show that security, in the form of assistance, is freely provided during times of need. For adult children as receivers, parents provide help for those who are slow to achieve or do not wish full generational autonomy and for those whose autonomy falters through reduced income, disrupted marriages, or illness. For the parental generation, some adult children provide care through much of their own adult lives, while others merely provide support for age-related security needs, such as failing physical or mental health, poverty, social loss as in bereavement, or emotional breakdown.

However, these high needs are extreme. The majority of autonomy and security issues can be enveloped by an elastic exchange zone, where everyday life consists of the normal fluctuations between the enjoyment of helping, being helped, or being free of both roles. Among all parent–adult child households, 56% existed because the child never left home—many by simple preference.

In reference to the exchange of resources across generations, exchanges of time are more equal than those of space and money—need, rather than habit or preference, begins to dominate only when absolutely necessary. Social-emotional exchange is less understood and more difficult to measure, but consensus among investigators documents that this form of assistance most easily bridges geographic separation between generations.

In light of the clearly documented flow of help across generations, it is difficult to understand the rationale behind concerns over generational equity. Two of the largest public subsidies are 1) for education, which primarily benefits children and very young adults; and 2) for the income tax losses that go with home ownership, a benefit to adults in their working years. However, each of these major subsidies could be seen as *life-span subsidies*. People reap the benefits of education for the rest of their lives. Buying a house benefits the worker, the worker's children, sometimes the worker's parents, and virtually always the retired worker. Using the same line of thought, subsidies for Social Security, public housing for older adults, Medicare, and community-based services relieve the working-adult generation of the need to live multigenerationally or to bear the costs of parental livelihood in the pre–Social Security manner.

SERVICE POLICY FOR FRAIL OLDER ADULTS

Considerable political concern has focused on community support, particularly in-home services. Many proposals have been made to add such services to the entitlement package for all people 65 and older. However, because the overwhelming majority of supportive services are already delivered through informal sources, primarily a spouse or adult child, the idea that incentives are needed to entice families to do more—a covert message of the "strengthen the family" initiative of the 1980s—seems quite irrelevant. Ample evidence suggests that adding formal services does not substitute for informally delivered services; additional publicly supported services are used instead to complement existing informal care (Lawton, Brody, Saperstein, & Grimes, 1989).

The distribution of formal services shows that the family is strongly responsive to need. Given this, is it even possible to identify inequities in the form of either underserved groups with unmet needs or overserved groups where reductions of service might be appropriate?

The most obviously underserved group consists of those older people with impairments who live alone without local, informal assistance. This need group is, in a sense, extrafamilial and will not be considered further because, in general, those who live alone and do have an informal support network tend to be relatively healthy, with care needs that fall well within the capability of proximate relatives. Their situation is relatively precarious, however, as a medical crisis can often either reduce them to a deprived life in their own home or precipitate a relocation to an institution. Counteracting this risk status, however, is the fact that the better-educated and perhaps more affluent, caring, network members are also most alert to opportunities for obtaining assistance from the formal service system for their older family member living alone. Thus, there may be some risk that the socially and economically advantaged person who lives alone may receive preferential service.

Among the 69% of older people who share households with others, several disadvantaged groups stand out. Many caregiving spouses are frail themselves. Many spouse and adult–child caregivers experience chronic stress in caregiving. Other caregivers, mainly nonrelatives, have a low level of commitment. Caregivers or household members who are themselves socially deprived in many other ways (e.g., educationally, economically, culturally) are often caregivers by social compulsion. And, although sharing a household with someone requiring care is usually done voluntarily, low household income is an indicator of high potential need for assistance by the care receiver and for support to the caregiver.

Wherever in-home services are provided, it is efficient to offer supportive services to caregivers, such as information and referral, counseling, and respite care. Previous experience attests to the fact that caregivers make relatively small demands on such services (Lawton, Brody, & Saperstein, 1989). For instance, support groups for relatives of people who have Alzheimer's disease exist in many areas, operated at low or no cost by voluntary organizations.

Therefore, it will continue to be necessary to target scarce resources to the most needy and the least economically advantaged. A number of large demonstration programs have been conducted to determine whether services to older adults who are frail could forestall their institutionalization. Among these, two regional long-term care demonstrations (Capitman, 1989), the National Channeling Project (Kemper, 1988), and the Congregate Housing Services Project (Sherwood et al., 1985), have emphasized the need for targeting the most vulnerable but require sharper ADL measurement tools and assessment procedures to better identify which individuals' risk of institutionalization may be cost-effectively reduced. Greene, Lovely, and Ondrich (1993) have demonstrated how this targeting could have been applied to the Channeling client population, turning an otherwise cost-ineffective demonstration (Kemper, 1988) into one that provided services to the most at risk.

More radical approaches than need-group identification and targeting are also needed. For example, a single-agency home care program that allows payments by clients or households for those with the means and subsidies for those meeting a standard criterion, could be combined with the larger long-term care and general health care programs into an *integrated services* system. Along with such a total bureaucratic reorganization would come an ideological reorientation. The intergenerational conception of the family as the philosophical cornerstone of this system would acknowledge and strengthen the mutuality of family needs, while highlighting those groups whose needs fall outside the family. Although the disadvantages of this system should be considered, overall, the system seems politically necessary and ethically defensible, provided its integration of public and private pay systems and its recognition of the underlying equity in family-based service systems.

Chapter Review

CHALLENGES

- Caregiving is an essential form of mutual support for people unable to perform daily tasks without assistance.
- Typically, support is directed from the parent to the child, although this balance may shift as parents reach old age.
- The majority of care for older adults is provided informally by relatives and other care providers.
- Many associate caregiving with increased burden, health risks, and social isolation.
- Home care usage rates are far below the prevalence rates for functional impairment in older adults, which suggests a lack of service availability and a trend toward usage of informal services.

CHARACTERISTICS OF HELPFUL PROGRAMS

- New programs emphasize the fact that caregiving can be a source of satisfaction and mastery.
- New programs assist caregivers in identifying positive life experiences and developing coping skills, thereby bolstering well-being and efficacy.
- New programs benefit from stress management, group education, cognitive behavioral strategies, and respite support.
- Opportunities to demonstrate autonomy, obtain assistance during times of need, and maintain intergenerational exchange of support are important for meeting cross-generational security needs in new programs.

POLICY IMPLICATIONS

- Evaluation methods must be improved to promote capacities to identify caregiver groups at high risk.
- Policy makers need to adopt more radical approaches that promote cross-generational, variable-need, integrated services to encourage mutuality and intergenerational exchange.
- Rather than merely increasing formal supports, programs need to identify and balance the inequities between underserved groups with unmet concerns and overserved groups that could withstand service reductions.
- Private and public payor systems of care should be integrated around the central role of the family—a single community agency should provide assistance to home caregivers, offer in-home paid care, and provide assistance for long-term nursing home care.

References

American Psychiatric Association. (1987). *Diagnostic and statistical manual of mental disorders* (3rd ed., Rev.). Washington, DC: Author.

Bandura, A. (1982). Self-efficacy mechanism in human agency. *American Psychologist, 37,* 122–147.

Bass, D.M., Tausig, M.G., & Noelker, L. (1988–1989). Elder impairment, social support, and caregiver strain. *Journal of Applied Social Science, 13,* 80–115.

Bodnar, J., & Kiecolt-Glaser, J.K. (1994). Caregiver depression after bereavement: Chronic stress isn't over when it's over. *Psychology and Aging, 9,* 372–380.

Brody, E.M. (1990). *Women in the middle.* New York: Springer Publishing Company.

Brody, E.M., & Schoonover, C.B. (1986). Patterns of parent-care when adult daughters work and when they do not. *The Gerontologist, 26,* 372–381.

Capitman, J. (1989). Policy and program options in community-oriented long-term care. In M.P. Lawton (Ed.), *Annual review of gerontology and geriatrics* (Vol. 9, pp. 357–388). New York: Springer Publishing Company.

Clarke, C.J., & Neidert, L.S. (1992). Living arrangements of the elderly: An examination of differences according to ancestry and generation. *The Gerontologist, 32,* 796–804.

Cooney, T.M., & Uhlenberg, P. (1992). Support from parents over the life course: The adult child's perspective. *Social Forces, 71,* 63–84.

Crimmins, E.M., & Ingegneri, D.G. (1990). Interaction and living arrangements of older parents and their children. *Research on Aging, 12,* 3–35.

Deimling, G.T. (1994) Caregiver functioning. In M.P. Lawton & J. Teresi (Eds.), *Annual review of gerontology and geriatrics* (Vol. 14, pp. 257–280). New York: Springer Publishing Company.

Deimling, G.T., & Bass, D.M. (1986). Symptoms of mental impairment among elderly adults of their effects on family caregivers. *Journal of Gerontology, 41,* 778–784.

Eggebeen, D.J. (1992). Family structure and intergenerational exchange. *Research on Aging, 14,* 427–447.

Esterling, B.A., Kiecolt-Glaser, J.K., Bodnar, J.C., & Glaser, R. (1994). Chronic stress, social support, and persistent alterations in the natural killer cell response to cytokines in older adults. *Health Psychology, 13,* 291–298.

Gallagher-Thompson, D. (1994). Clinical intervention strategies for distressed caregivers: Rationale and development of psychoeducational approaches. In E. Light, G. Niederehe, & B. Lebowitz (Eds.), *Stress effects on family caregivers* (pp. 260–277). New York: Springer Publishing Company.

George, L.K., & Gwyther, L.P. (1986). Caregiver well-being: A multidimensional examination of family caregivers of demented elders. *The Gerontologist, 26,* 253–259.

Grannemann, T.W., & Grossman, J.B. (1986). *Differential impacts among subgroups of channeling enrollees.* Princeton, NJ: Mathematica Policy Research.

Greene, V.L., Lovely, M.E., & Ondrich, J.I. (1993). The cost-effectiveness of community services in a frail elderly population. *The Gerontologist, 33,* 177–189.

Haley, W.E., Levine, E.G., Brown, S.L., & Bartolucci, A.A. (1987). Stress, appraisal, coping, and social support as predictors of adaptational outcome among dementia caregivers. *Psychology and Aging, 2,* 323–330.

Hill, M.S., Morgan, J.N., & Herzog, R. (1993, April). *Intergenerational aspects of family help patterns.* Paper presented at the annual meeting of the Population Association of America, Washington, DC.

Kahan, J., Kemp, B., Staples, F.R., & Brummel-Smith, K. (1984). Decreasing the burden in families caring for a relative with dementing illness. *Journal of the American Geriatrics Society, 33,* 664–670.

Kemper, P. (1988). The evaluation of the National Long Term Care Demonstration: Overview of the findings. *Health Services Research, 21,* 167–174.

Kiecolt-Glaser, J.K., Dura, J.R., Speicher, C.E., Trask, J., & Glaser, R. (1991). Spousal caregivers of dementia victims: Longitudinal changes in immunity and health. *Psychosomatic Medicine, 53,* 345–362.

Knight, B.G., Lutzky, S.M., & Macofsky-Urban, F. (1993). A meta-analytic review of interventions for caregiver distress: Recommendations for further research. *The Gerontologist, 33,* 240–248.

Lawton, M.P. (1985). The elderly in context: Perspectives from environmental psychology and gerontology. *Environment and Behavior, 17,* 501–519.

Lawton, M.P. (1992). Generational interdependence: Living arrangements and housing programmes. *South African Journal of Gerontology, 1,* 1–4.

Lawton, M.P., Brody, E.M., & Saperstein, A.R. (1989). A controlled study of respite service for caregivers of Alzheimer's disease patients. *The Gerontologist, 29,* 8–16.

Lawton, M.P., Brody, E.M., Saperstein, A., & Grimes, M. (1989). Respite services for caregivers: Research findings for service planning. *Home Health Care Services Quarterly, 10,* 5–32.

Lawton, M.P., Kleban, M.H., Moss, M.A., Rovine, M., & Glicksman, A. (1989). Measuring caregiving appraisal. *Journal of Gerontology: Psychological Sciences, 44,* P61–P71.

Lawton, M.P., Moss, M., Kleban, M.H., Glicksman, A., & Rovine, M. (1991). A two-factor model of caregiving stress and psychological well-being. *Journal of Gerontology: Psychological Sciences, 46,* P181–P189.

Lawton, M.P., Rajagopal, D., Brody, E., & Kleban, M. (1992). The dynamics of caregiving for a demented elder among black and white families. *Journal of Gerontology: Social Sciences, 47,* S156–S164.

Macken, C.L. (1986). A profile of functionally impaired elderly persons living in the community. *Health Care Financing Review, 7,* 33–49.

Montgomery, R.J.V., Gonyea, J.G., & Hooyman, N.R. (1985). Caregiving and the experience of subjective and objective burden. *Family Relations, 34,* 19–26.

Montgomery, R.J.V., & Hirshorn, B.A. (1991). Current and future family help with long-term needs of the elderly. *Research on Aging, 13,* 171–204.

Moritz, D.J., Kasl, S., & Berkman, L.F. (1989). The health impact of living with a cognitively impaired elderly spouse: Depressive symptoms and social functioning. *Journal of Gerontology: Social Sciences, 44,* S17–S27.

Moss, M., Lawton, M.P., Kleban, M.H., & Duhamel, L. (1993). Time budgets of caregivers of impaired elders before and after institutionalization. *Journal of Gerontology: Social Sciences, 48,* S102–S111.

Pagel, M.P., Becker, J., & Coppel, D.B. (1985). Loss of control, self-blame, and depression: An investigation of spouse caregivers of Alzheimer's disease patients. *Journal of Abnormal Psychology, 94,* 169–182.

Parmelee, P., & Lawton, M.P. (1990). The design of special environments for the aged. In J.E. Birren & K.W. Schaie (Eds.), *Handbook of the psychology of aging* (3rd. ed., pp. 464–487). New York: Academic Press.

Pruchno, R.A., & Resch, N.L. (1989a). Aberrant behaviors and Alzheimer's disease: Mental health effects on spouse caregivers. *Journal of Gerontology: Social Sciences, 44,* S177–S182.

Pruchno, R.A., & Resch, N.L. (1989b). Mental health of caregiving spouses: Coping as mediator, moderator, or main effect? *Psychology and Aging, 4,* 454–463.

Rabins, P.V., Mace, M.L., & Lucas, M.J. (1982). The impact of dementia on the family. *Journal of the American Medical Association, 248,* 333–335.

Rubinstein, R. (1989). Themes in the meaning of caregiving. *Journal of Aging Studies,* *3,* 119–138.

Scharlach, A.E. (1987). Relieving feelings of strain among women with elderly mothers. *Psychology and Aging, 2,* 9–13.

Schulz, R., Visintainer, P., & Williamson, G. (1990). Psychiatric and physical morbidity effects of caregiving. *Journal of Gerontology: Psychological Sciences, 45,* 181–191.

Schulz, R., & Williamson, G.M. (1991). A two-year longitudinal study of depression among Alzheimer's caregivers. *Psychology and Aging, 6,* 569–578.

Shanas, E. (1982). *National survey of the aged* (DHHS Publication No. OHDS 83-20425). Washington, DC: U.S. Government Printing Office.

Sherwood, S., Morris, J.N., Sherwood, C.C., Morris, S., Bernstein, E., & Gornstein, E.S. (1985). *Evaluation of congregate housing* (Final report, Housing and Urban Development Contract AHC-5373). Boston: Hebrew Rehabilitation Center.

Short, P.F., & Leon, J. (1988, November). *National estimates on the use of formal home and community services by the functionally impaired elderly.* Paper presented at the annual meeting of the Gerontological Society of America, San Francisco.

Soldo, B.J., Sharma, M., & Campbell, R.T. (1984). Determinants of the community living arrangements of all unmarried women. *Journal of Gerontology, 39,* 492–498.

Stephens, S.A., & Christianson, J.B. (1986). *Informal care of the elderly.* Lexington, MA: Lexington Books.

Stoller, E., & Pugliesi, K. (1988). Informal networks of community-based elderly: Changes in composition over time. *Research on Aging, 10,* 499–516.

Stone, R. (1986). Aging in the eighties, age 65 years and over—use of community services. *Advance Data* (No. 124). Rockville, MD: National Center for Health Statistics.

Stone, R., Cafferata, G.L., & Sangl, J. (1987). Caregivers of the frail elderly: A national profile. *The Gerontologist, 27,* 616–626.

Tennestedt, S.L., Crawford, S., & McKinlay, J.B. (1993). Determining the pattern of community care: Is coresidence more important than caregiver relationship? *Journal of Gerontology: Social Sciences, 48,* S74–S83.

Townsend, A.L. (1990). Nursing home care and family caregivers' stress. In M.A.P. Stephens, J.H. Crowther, S.E. Hobfoll, & D.L. Tennebaum (Eds.), *Stress and coping in later life families* (pp. 267–285). Washington, DC: Hemisphere Publishers.

Townsend, A.L., Noelker, L.S., Deimling, G.T., & Bass, D.M. (1989). Longitudinal impact of interhousehold caregiving on children's mental health. *Psychology and Aging, 4,* 393–401.

Upp, M. (1982). A look at the economic status of the aged then and now. *Social Security Bulletin, 45,* 16–22.

Ward, R., Logan, J., & Spitze, G. (1992). The influence of parent and child needs on coresidence in middle and later life. *Journal of Marriage and the Family, 54,* 209–221.

Wright, L.K., Clipp, E.C., & George, L.F. (1993). Health consequences of caregiver stress. *Medicine, Exercise, Nutrition, and Health, 2,* 181–195.

Zarit, S.H., Todd, P.A., & Zarit, J. (1986). Subjective burden of husbands and wives as caregivers: A longitudinal study. *The Gerontologist, 26,* 260–266.

7

Early Intervention
and Family Support

Bruce L. Mallory

Can well-designed, carefully conceived, broadly aimed social policies make a difference? This question is of central concern to those who create policies, those who pay for them, and those who are intended to benefit from them; and the answer is not simply derived. As policy analysts typically say, "It depends." What the answer depends on includes the following:

1. Ideological perspectives informed by both values and theory
2. Situational and contextual factors that affect program implementation at the local or "street" level (Lipsky, 1980)
3. The degree of congruence between the design of the policy and the needs of its recipients
4. The nature and use of measures intended to determine the effects of policy

The ambiguities that arise from these multiple variables, however, do not prevent policy makers from taking action. When there is a political consensus that solutions to significant social problems are both needed and wanted, state and federal policy makers respond both out of a sense of altruistic purpose and in their own self-interest as stakeholders in a bureaucratic or elected institutional setting. In fact, some of the most ambitious social policies created in the United States have been based on political conviction, rather than definitive empirical information. Certainly the New Deal represents one such national experiment, as does much of Lyndon Johnson's War on Poverty. Although policy making is usually characterized as incremental, or "muddling through" (Lindbloom, 1959), in hope of stumbling across effective and affordable solutions, it has on occasion been more carefully planned—as in the arena of special education policy, for example, which has been described as a "quiet revolution" (Abeson & Zettel, 1977).

In fact, since the 1970s, disability policy in the United States (and elsewhere) has evolved in dramatic fashion, including the following:

- Both small-scale and large-scale demonstration projects (e.g., the First Chance network that grew from PL 90-538, the Handicapped Children's Early Education Act of 1968)
- Infusion of federal money into capital construction and block funding projects (e.g., PL 88-164, Mental Retardation Facilities and Community Mental Health Centers Construction Act of 1963)
- The development of planning, coordination, and advocacy mechanisms to ensure equitable and easy access to services (e.g., PL 98-527, the Developmental Disabilities Act Amendments of 1984)
- Legislative mandates that guarantee educational services for preschool and school-age children with disabilities, as well as laws that prohibit discrimination in all public accommodations and venues (e.g., PL 101-476, the Individuals with Disabilities Education Act of 1990 [IDEA] and PL 101-336, the Americans with Disabilities Act of 1990 [ADA])

These laws represent radical departures from historical approaches toward people with disabilities, which were characterized by neglect, discrimination, and isolation.

This radical nature of policy development in the field of disabilities must be recognized. Acting often with little or no empirical evidence that a particular policy would achieve its desired ends and without an expressed broad-based consensus that it was the right thing to do, state governments and the U.S. Congress have acted boldly since the early 1970s—these efforts have been expressly intended to reverse the history of both benign and malignant neglect of people with disabilities. This has been particularly true when the focus has been the very youngest members of society. The history of policies and services for infants and preschool children with disabilities demonstrates policy makers' ability to act swiftly and comprehensively. The rapid evolution from small-scale demonstration projects to a national mandate for preschool special education services in a 25-year period "can be seen as a model for the purposeful improvement of services for other populations with disabilities" (Hebbeler, Smith, & Black, 1991, p. 105).

The notion that the history of policy development and implementation for very young children with disabilities can serve as a prototype for similar efforts among other populations is the central thesis of this chapter. Of particular interest is the way in which policies and services for very young children have become family centered to a remarkable degree. Although it has been claimed that there "is no overriding political or social movement [in the United States]" that has led to "a comprehensive rationale and program for supporting caregiving families" (Singer & Irvin, 1989, p. 19), it is the argument here that a particular federal policy, embodied in PL 99-457, the Education of the Handicapped Act Amendments of 1986 and subsequent reauthorizations, is just such a comprehensive development, albeit couched within a service delivery system aimed at children. Part H of PL 99-457 (amended in 1991 under PL 102-119) defines and delineates early intervention services for children from birth to 3 years who have diagnosed disabilities or are at risk for subsequent disabilities. This section of federal special education law may have created a muddle with its comprehensive and ambitious design, but it is not an example of muddling through. Its underlying theoretical framework, its implicit and explicit values, its specific design components, and its implementation history all suggest insights that can be applied to other policies aimed at vulnerable individuals and their families. In short, Part H is an example of federal efforts to support families and its lessons should be heeded.

The following sections, then, examine the relationship between social policy and social change by 1) explicating the theories that are reflected in Part H; 2) identifying the values embedded in its design; and 3) analyzing its specific components with respect to family support, including issues related to the implementation of those components. However, the empirical knowledge of the impact of Part H is still limited; as it undergoes further amendments and as evaluation strategies continue to evolve, claims about the long-term effects, both human and material, must be made with much caution. Still, Part H is far enough along to provide important insights into the concept and practice of family support.

SOCIAL POLICY AND SOCIAL THEORY

The fundamental theoretical framework that is implicit in Part H is that of social ecology (Dokecki & Heflinger, 1989). Social-ecology theory, or ecocultural theory (Bernheimer, Gallimore, & Weisner, 1990), stems from the work of sociologists and anthropologists working in the fields of human development and applied human services (e.g., Bronfenbrenner, 1979; Hobbs et al., 1984; LeVine, 1977; Super & Harkness, 1980; Weisner & Gallimore, 1989; Whiting & Whiting, 1975). For the purposes of understanding the relationship between ecocultural theory and Part H, the central tenets of the theory articulated by Bernheimer et al. (1990) are most useful. Their perspective, that of social constructivism, claims the following:

1. Families derive meaning from and of their circumstances and then construct proactive responses to those circumstances and derived meanings.
2. Daily routines and activity settings are the critical units of analysis used to generate and understand constructed meanings. As these routines

and activities interact with social and cultural forces, they serve as me-
diators between the individual and / or family and the contexts in
which they live and work.

3. These phenomena are observable across cultures; thus, this framework
    can serve to explicate the lives of families from diverse ethnic, cultural,
    and racial groups.

A key concept of this framework is that families are proactive. Families
adapt to their *ecocultural niche* through a process of accommodation, in
which they "exploit, counterbalance, and react to the many competing and
sometimes contradictory forces in their lives" (Bernheimer et al., 1990, p.
223). Clearly this notion is relevant to the lives of families who have a
member with a disability because of its emphasis on active accommodation
and self-constructed meanings. Families are not "hapless victims of im-
placable social and economic forces" (Bernheimer et al., 1990, p. 223), in
this view. Rather, they are capable of defining their own meanings of a
difficult situation and exploiting the available resources to achieve their
own ends. Thus, the individualized family service plan (IFSP) required by
Part H becomes a tool for actively pursuing self-determined goals based on
internally constructed meanings.

Bernheimer et al. (1990) also point out the potential tensions that arise
when the meanings of disability, family competence, need, and support
constructed by professionals differ from those constructed by family members. Essentially, they argue, professionals must accept the family's interpretation of what is meaningful to them. The role of the professional is to
help families use the mediating function of daily routines and activities in
order to enhance their own circumstances and build a better niche. This
may require either modifying those routines or the ecocultural context or
reconstructing existing meanings. Sometimes the modification draws from
all three; for instance, reconstructing existing meanings of disability may
be linked to seeking direct intervention and therapy for a child, so that his
or her competence fits more closely with the family's aspirations, values,
and needs.

This model raises questions about the balance of power between professionals and parents, by casting light on the problems that arise when
one side accuses the other of not valuing their respective expertise, goals,
and methods. As Dokecki and Heflinger (1989) write, there is a "fine line
between intervention and interference" (p. 74). Voluntary participation and
a sense of control over the decision-making process should be at the heart
of family support. "Parents [must] maintain executive control over the decision making. If experts offer advice that parents find unpalatable, they
[the parents] are free to reject it and seek alternative counsel" (Gallagher,
1992, p. 8). In this light, one of the goals of parents is to find professionals
whose constructed meanings are sympathetic with their own. The goodness
of fit between professionals' interpretations of disability and family support

and families' interpretations must be sufficiently congruent to allow for meaningful communication and negotiation to occur.

Illustrating the link between social theory and social policy, Dokecki and Heflinger (1989) provide a succinct description of the relationship between social-ecology theory and the components of Part H.

> 1) In order to reduce educational costs, prevent institutionalization, and maximize citizens' capacity for independent living, 2) financial assistance provided by the federal government to the states 3) enables the development of statewide early intervention systems in order to 4) help marshall early intervention programs throughout the service system from state to local levels and involving both public and private sectors and thereby, to 5) enhance young handicapped children's development and help prevent developmental delay. 6) The strengthening of families helps to bring about these positive developmental outcomes. (pp. 60–61)

Evidence for a conceptual link between theory and policy is unusual and further demonstrates the unique position that Part H has in the social policy arena. In this case, social goals are achieved through economic means intended to enable state and local systems and programs to function so that young children with disabilities and their families may experience enhanced outcomes. The functioning of those systems and programs, in the context of Part H, is guided by an explicit theory that is grounded in the reality of families' lives. The next section explores the values that have informed the design and implementation of Part H, and shows how closely linked these values are to the theoretical framework just described.

SOCIAL VALUES AND SOCIAL POLICY

The role of values in policy making has been addressed cogently by Dokecki (1983) as part of a larger effort aimed at proposing national parent education and child care policies. One result of that effort, based at the Center for the Study of Families and Children at the Vanderbilt Institute for Public Policy Studies, was a comprehensive volume on *Strengthening Families*, which asserts,

> We believe that the strengthening of families within supportive and caring communities is a desirable goal in and of itself. More importantly, however, we believe that competent families and support communities are indispensable elements of any effort to realize the full potential of human development in our society. (Hobbs et al., 1984, p. 2)

Such a statement is clearly normative. It transcends the status quo, creates a vision for social change, and urges a human development perspective not linked to efficiency or investment rationales. The statement strives to balance the multiple and potentially conflicting purposes of individual, family, and social development. By its ambitious and unequivocal stance, it offers a theme that can guide family support policies and programs.

This overriding value is rooted in two other central values that have informed U.S. social policy since the 1960s: equal opportunity for all citizens, regardless of economic, racial, ethnic, or geographic factors; and the concept of *maximum feasible participation* that brings the beneficiaries of social policies into decision-making roles at the local and state level.

> These two core values . . . have served as a foundation for our contemporary commitment to full inclusion in society for people with disabilities. In this perspective, people have a constitutional right to unfettered participation in all social institutions, and their voices are to be paramount in decisions affecting their lives. (Mallory, 1994, p. 46)

The combination of broad political values rooted in constitutional history and more specific developmental values that reflect contemporary societal goals has led to a consensus about the principles that should guide family support policy. Although there are many expressions of this consensus, a representative illustration comes from the Center on Human Policy at Syracuse University:

1. All children, regardless of disability, belong with families and need enduring relationships with adults.
2. Family support services must be based on the principle of "whatever it takes."
3. Family supports should build on existing social networks and natural sources of support.
4. Family supports should maximize the family's control over the services and supports they receive.
5. Family supports should support the entire family.
6. Family support services should encourage the integration of children with disabilities into the community.
7. When children cannot remain with their families for whatever reason, out-of-home placement should be viewed initially as a temporary arrangement and efforts should be directed toward reuniting the family.
8. When families cannot be reunited and when active parental involvement is absent, adoption should be aggressively pursued.
9. While a preferred alternative to any group setting or out-of-home placement, foster care should only be pursued when children cannot live with their families or with adoptive families. (Center on Human Policy, 1987)

These value statements are derived both ideologically and empirically. For example, the assertion that all children belong with families, and support services should reflect a "whatever it takes" principle are ideological statements. The "whatever it takes" approach is radical; it supersedes financial and logistical constraints by advocating flexible, individualized services for diverse families despite narrow bureaucratic or regulatory boundaries. Conversely, concerns related to adoption and foster care stem from experience and empirical research that have revealed the difficulties inherent in nonfamilial care, especially for children with disabilities.

Historical problems in foster care and adoption have led to the prevalent use of *permanency planning* in the disability field, in which long-range plans are developed to ensure the most stable and consistent caregiving

environments possible (Taylor, Knoll, Lehr, & Walker, 1989). This principle is found in Part H, which requires that IFSPs include specific plans for transition to preschool services at age 3, as well as transition plans for older students well before they leave secondary school. Thus, a broad value focused on the stability of caregiving has emerged in general statements of principles as well as specific acts of legislation; it is likely that these values would be especially sustained in a culture that treats nonfamilial care of children with general suspicion and distrust.

Kaiser and Hemmeter (1989) have suggested a framework for evaluating the role of values in Part H, incorporating the earlier work of Hobbs et al. (1984) and Dokecki's (1983) thesis on values in family-oriented social policy. Kaiser and Hemmeter call for a value-based approach to early intervention in order to complement needs-based or categorical approaches, which tend to be deficit oriented and professionally driven. Addressing the inherent tension between general principles and idiosyncratic situations, they believe that a value-based framework would help to resolve parent–professional conflicts, resulting in strengthened family capacities. A value-based approach is "social and relational rather than individual and absolute" (p. 76), thus providing a set of criteria that could transcend particular circumstances when difficult decisions about the nature of intervention must be made.

However, an individualistic perspective is still important. Ecocultural theory recalls the central role of individual circumstances and meanings; but the interpretation of individual needs and the design of appropriate responses to those needs are assisted when there are broader, universal value principles available that can point to more effective policies and programs. This approach thus incorporates the dynamic tension between the individual and the community, rather than ignoring it or deeming it irreconcilable.

Kaiser and Hemmeter's (1989) work effectively translates abstract family support principles into practical guidelines. Table 1 lists the specific questions they believe early interventionists should raise, either as part of the family needs assessment and planning process for evaluating the appropriateness of a particular IFSP and monitoring its implementation, or for assessing overall agency policies and practices. These questions are value based, although they incorporate a social-ecological orientation, and are sufficiently broad in their focus such that they could be generalized to forms of family support other than those found in early intervention.

ESSENTIAL POLICY DESIGN FOR FAMILY SUPPORT

Part H contains a number of components that can serve as models for social policies aimed at families with members who have chronic illnesses or disabilities. These components are linked directly to the theories and values that have guided its design. The nature of these specific requirements and

Table 1.   Value-based criteria for early intervention programs

Part I.   Questions about the intervention:
  1.   Does the intervention enhance the family's participation in the community?
  2.   Does the intervention improve the family's ability to meet its developmental tasks?
  3.   Does the intervention enhance the family's social support?
  4.   Does the intervention provide essential minimum resources?
  5.   Does the intervention promote shared responsibility between parents and service provider?
  6.   Will the intervention provide opportunities for family members to enhance their skills and competence?
  7.   Will the intervention deprive any family member of care or support?
  8.   Does the intervention include only procedures that are nonaversive, safe, and development promoting?

Part II.   Questions about the appropriateness of a particular intervention for a family:
  1.   Is the intervention based on a valid needs assessment?
  2.   Did the family indicate this as a priority need?
  3.   Is the intervention likely to be sufficient to meet the priority need?
  4.   Is the level of intervention appropriate for the problem?
  5.   Does the intervention plan include a comprehensive evaluation of its effects?
  6.   Is the ratio of benefits to costs (resources, time, intrusion) acceptable to the family?
  7.   Are the family members willing and able to meet the costs?
  8.   Is the intervention consistent with the family's values?
  9.   Does the intervention fit with the family's context in the community and the prevailing social norms?
  10.   Is the amount of change, relative to the status quo, required of the family acceptable to them?

From "Value-based approaches to family intervention" by A.P. Kaiser & M.L. Hemmeter, 1989, *Topics in Early Childhood Special Education, 8*(4), p. 84. © 1989 by PRO-ED, Inc. Reprinted by permission.

the process of implementing them must be understood if the history of Part H is to guide policy making in other areas.

Gallagher (1992, pp. 2–3) has identified several underlying assumptions in PL 99-457 that are manifested in the Part H requirements for early intervention programs:

1. *The earlier the treatment, the better.* This assumption is the basis for the Child Find provisions that require the earliest possible screening and assessment of newborns, infants, and young children suspected of having a developmental delay or disability. Once assessment has occurred and eligibility for services determined, then services must begin in order to ameliorate the problem as quickly as possible. It should be noted that although families may, in general, support this concept of early identification and treatment, it can be problematic with respect to parents of infants and very young children because of the emotional dimensions and constructed meanings associated with the early diagnosis of a significant developmental problem.

2. *The more professional disciplines that participate, the better.* This assumption supports not only traditional multidisciplinary approaches to early intervention, but has also been the rationale for the transdisciplinary

models that have grown increasingly common; some have argued that the transdisciplinary model is consistent with recommended practice in early intervention (Odom & McEvoy, 1990). Part H requires a team-based service delivery approach that can respond to the multiple and complex needs of young children with developmental difficulties. Consequently, families must work with many professionals, which can have positive results because of the additional expertise made available, as well as negative results because of the coordination and communication tasks that inevitably arise.

3. *Families are important.* This assumption clearly is at the heart of many of the Part H requirements, including those focused on family assessment, family participation in decision making, and service coordination aimed at assisting families to gain access to available resources. This simple belief statement, derived from theoretical, empirical, and ideological sources, now permeates the early intervention service delivery system and the literature that describes it.

4. *Qualified personnel are needed.* There are many assumptions supported by empirical evidence and a consensus about recommended practice related to this belief. For example, it takes well-prepared professionals to deliver early intervention services. Currently, there are insufficient numbers of such personnel. If there were more personnel and programs to prepare them, there would be more accessible and higher quality programs for the children and families who need them. As more family-based services are implemented, then the definition of qualified will need to change, so that professionals are not only competent clinicians or teachers, but also are capable of working within complex family systems.

5. *Children who are defined as at risk should be helped.* This statement assumes that some children who do not currently demonstrate developmental problems are likely to do so in the future. It also assumes that those children are identifiable and can be assisted in order to prevent more serious problems later. With respect to family support, this is one of the more sensitive assumptions, as it requires that parents agree with professionals' assessment of risk, and it often implies that the nature of the risk is environmental or familial, rather than intrinsic to the child. Too often, risk is categorically correlated with ethnic or racial minority status or economic disadvantage (Swadener, 1990). Damaging assumptions about family or parental pathology may be made in the absence of careful, nonbiased assessment of particular children and their caregivers (Sheehan & Sites, 1989).

Other fundamental assumptions or elements found in Part H include 1) the importance of natural environments for service delivery, 2) the central role of states in policy implementation, and 3) the need for an infrastructure that can support the implementation process. These design elements, although found most often in early intervention policies, can serve as prototypes for programs and policies in other arenas, such as mental health and aging.

Natural Environments

When PL 99-457 was amended in 1991, the term *natural environments* was added to the description of services for infants and toddlers. Essentially, this language emphasizes the need to provide services in home and community settings where children without disabilities participate (Office of Special Education Programs, 1993). The language can be seen as part of a larger "natural supports" movement (Nisbet, 1992, p. 5) that explicitly rejects the concept of a continuum of services, interventionist approaches, and professional domination of decision making and service design. The locus of services is always assumed to be in the child's and family's proximal and natural social context. This is particularly important for families with very young children with significant developmental disabilities who face tremendous obstacles to participation in their local, community support systems (both formal and informal). If parents begin their child-rearing careers isolated from friends, neighbors, and community services because of their child's disability, it will be very difficult for them to establish a more natural ecocultural niche among those resources as the child gets older. Thus, the principle of natural supports must be considered for any social policy affecting families.

The Role of the States

The way in which the balance of power between federal and state governments is apportioned is a critical element in the design of Part H. Although Part H, and PL 99-457 in general, may be viewed as highly prescriptive policies, great care was taken in their conception to respect the role of states in decision making and service delivery. This can be seen in three interrelated areas—planning, implementation, and discretionary decision making.

First, Part H gave states an extended initial planning period, allowing them up to 5 years to provide all of the entitlements and services described in the law. Even when using federal dollars for initial planning purposes, state participation is discretionary. Prior to the fourth year of planning, states may choose whether they will participate in and comply with the provisions of Part H. This phased-in implementation process has worked well, with all states and most territories fully participating in Part H by 1995 and federal appropriations exceeding $300 million.

The flexibility of "second Year 3" provides a reasonable planning phase without undue pressure from the federal government. In regions with a historic resistance to federal mandates, such as New Hampshire and other rural states, the strategy of gentle nudging has been effective. This flexibility has made a difference in New Hampshire, where the "second Year 3" convinced the governor to move into Years 4 and 5 and subsequently embark on full implementation.

A second aspect of state-level decision making is the designation of a *lead agency* (state agencies charged with receiving, distributing, and monitoring Part H funds). States may choose whatever lead agency they believe will most appropriately manage the planning and implementation of Part H. Although state departments of education, health, human services, and developmental disabilities are most often chosen, some states have selected the governor's office itself (e.g., Maryland) or interagency groups (e.g., Texas) as the lead agency (Office of Special Education Programs, 1993). Although this opportunity to make state-level decisions about governance can lead to initial disputes over boundary lines and fiscal matters, it may increase the likelihood of state participation. The process of designating the lead agency may become, in fact, an exercise in interagency cooperation and compromise, preparing states for more substantive decision making.

The third aspect of state-level decision making concerns definitional and eligibility issues. Within broad guidelines, states are expected to develop their own definitions of developmental delay and then decide to whom early intervention services should be extended—a significant departure from Part B of the amended Education for All Handicapped Children Act of 1975 (PL 94-142), which relies on a categorical classification system of rather precise, although controversial, definitions of who may be served in school-age special education programs. By granting this power and responsibility to states, policy makers hope that early intervention systems will more closely reflect the nature of regional and local populations and thus be more responsive to their concerns. This is an empirical question that should be addressed in the future.

Finally, states may select whatever mix of funding for early intervention they deem necessary and appropriate. Currently, states use an average of 21 different funding sources to support their service delivery systems. State appropriations are blended with federal dollars in a number of ways, through existing mechanisms such as Medicaid, Chapter 1 of the Elementary and Secondary Education Act (ESEA, PL 89-313), Maternal and Child Health block grants, mental retardation and mental health programs, and federal and state Social Security allocations (Clifford, Bernier, & Harbin, 1992). Local early intervention programs also rely on fees for services, philanthropic sources such as United Way, and payments from third-party insurers.

The Need for an Infrastructure

Since the 1970s, the designers of early childhood special education law have recognized that full achievement of the various statutory mandates would occur only if there were an infrastructure in place to support the programs developed from legislation. The major components of the early intervention and preschool infrastructure that have been established include 1) preservice and in-service personnel preparation programs to increase the availability of competent professionals, 2) model demonstration programs to test a variety of service delivery strategies, 3) evaluation studies to determine the effects of both pilot and broadly aimed programs, 4) the use of incentive grants to states for planning and implementation, and 5) mechanisms for interagency coordination. In many cases, these infrastructure components exist at both the federal and state level.

Personnel Preparation

The major focus of personnel preparation has been on new or experienced professionals who work in educational, therapeutic, or administrative roles with young children and their families. Since the implementation of PL 99-457, increased emphasis has been placed on improving professionals' family support skills. Bailey (1989) notes the particular importance of family support skills in early intervention with respect to three responsibilities—helping parents cope with and learn about their child's diagnosis, helping parents obtain needed services, and preparing parents to take on decision making and caregiving tasks relative to their child's formal program. Essential skills for professionals identified by Bailey include those related to family assessment, effectively communicating with parents, providing child-related services within the family context, and acting as service coordinators when appropriate.

Personnel preparation funds have also been dedicated to supporting parents directly, through the creation of Parent Training and Information Centers. The centers operate as a network of parent-to-parent assistance projects that emphasize parents' roles as advocates for their own children. For example, the centers give specialized training and information to parents serving on interagency coordinating councils (Ziegler, 1989). Under PL 99-457, these centers now must serve parents of children not yet in school as well.

Model Programs

One of the most significant accomplishments of early childhood special education policy has been the creation of a national network of model demonstration programs. Beginning in 1968 and funded by PL 90-538, the First Chance Network has led to the establishment of hundreds of local, regional, and state-level programs for children from infancy to primary-school age that focus on the inclusion of family members in the design and delivery of services. Hebbeler et al. (1991) note that the programs have become "an important force for shaping future early childhood policy at the state and federal levels" (p. 109).

Efficacy Studies

The First Chance Network has promoted the proliferation of a number of important small- and large-scale efficacy studies of services for very young children and their families. The evidence concerning whether parent participation in early intervention services makes a difference is mixed. Castro and Mastropieri (1986) found that parental involvement had minimal effects on children's cognitive outcomes, based on pooled analyses of more than 400 different studies. However, Shonkoff and Hauser-Cram (1987), in a separate analysis, found significant positive effects on children's development when family involvement is combined with early program entry.

Evaluation research methodologies have been problematic, giving narrow emphasis to cognitive gains. When studies have focused on other contextual variables, more consistent results emerge. A classic example, relative to the maximum feasible participation principle discussed earlier, is the Kirschner Associates report (1970) on the impact of parent involvement in Head Start on community institutions. This national survey found that communities with Head Start centers were more likely to have educational, health, and welfare organizations that included low-income parents in positions of power as either staff or board members. Head Start seemed to serve as a model and catalyst for enfranchisement and participation. This finding, within the context of family support concerns, can be viewed as significant as the measurement of developmental gains in young children.

Planning and Implementation Grants

By the early 1980s, more qualified professionals were becoming available, model programs were becoming stabilized and receiving ongoing state and local funding, and evaluation studies were beginning to provide some guidance as to the most effective means of designing services. Starting in 1983, the federal government began to shift its focus from small-scale experiments to large-scale mandates. An important precursor to the mandates established in PL 99-457 was the funding of state planning grants to help states expand their services to infants and preschoolers with disabilities. These planning grants were funded on a formula basis, so that virtually every state and territory received assistance. Activities that occurred at the state level included provision of direct services and diagnostic centers; development of interagency agreements; establishment of technical assistance centers; and parent and professional training (Hebbeler et al., 1991). Thus, the planning grants were an important component of the growing infrastructure, and the model of multi-year planning was later replicated in the phased-in implementation of Part H.

Interagency Coordination

One final assumption of Part H not mentioned previously is, "interagency coordinating committees (ICCs) should help in the coordination of services" (Gallagher, 1992, pp. 2–3). The designers of Part H were careful to ensure service coordination at the state level. The requirement for interagency coordination is intended 1) to facilitate the implementation of the law, and 2) to increase its efficacy through planned use of appropriate services. This aspect of Part H can advance the goal of family support by mandating that parents of young children with special needs serve on the ICCs in a decision-making capacity and by creating a more coordinated, effective, and accessible service delivery system. Thus, the two fundamental value tenets described previously—maximum feasible participation and equal opportunity to benefit from public resources—are sustained and reified in the law.

The need for interagency coordination has also been recognized at the federal level. In 1992, a landmark federal interagency agreement was signed by the Secretaries of Education and Health and Human Services in order to foster cooperation among seven federal agencies responsible for managing or delivering services to very young children with disabilities and their families (Office of Special Education Programs, 1993). The agreement involved the following agencies:

- Office of Special Education Programs
- Maternal and Child Health Block Grant
- Administration on Children, Youth, and Families
- Health Care Financing Administration
- Administration on Developmental Disabilities
- Social Security Administration
- National Institutes of Mental Health

The ability of this disparate group of high-level agencies to come together committed to coordinating their resources through collaboration and cooperation bodes well for similar efforts in such areas as mental health and aging.

Two central principles contained in the federal interagency agreement are as follows: 1) services should be family centered, and 2) identification of special needs should be individualized and culturally competent (Office of Special Education Programs, 1993). The principle of cultural competence in the delivery of early intervention and special education services, which implies professional abilities related to linguistic and ethnic variation among families receiving services, has also been addressed by Harry (1992) as well as Lynch and Hanson (1992). This concept has received increased attention as children and families from diverse ethnic and racial groups participate in early childhood and special education programs (e.g., Mallory & New, 1994). Any efforts to create family support policies or programs must be designed so as to be *culturally appropriate* (Phillips, 1994), which ensures maximum congruence between the formal world of the school and other social institutions and the lived world of the child and family. The principles of a culturally competent staff and culturally appropriate or culturally responsive (Harry, 1992) services are essential to the design and implementation of family support, whether in the early intervention arena or other areas of disability policy.

These five ingredients of the Part H infrastructure—personnel preparation, model programs, efficacy studies, planning and implementation grants, and interagency coordination—have played key roles in the successful implementation of the law; while the other design elements discussed previously—beginning as early as possible, including multiple disciplines in treatment, helping children at risk, and striking a balance between state and federal authority—are also generalizable to other categories of social policy. This overview portrays a comprehensive, well-conceived, thoughtfully planned, broadly aimed policy that neither muddles nor meddles.

Part H has been implemented largely because 1) it addresses a population that elicits some public sympathy; and 2) its policy contains complementary, integrated components that build on earlier experimental efforts. There is, in fact, an integrity that binds what is believed, what is known, and what is viewed as effective within the structure of Part H. In other fields, such as mental health and aging, this kind of integrity has not yet developed. The diversity of the populations, the unresolved ethical dilemmas, the magnitude of the costs, and the power of traditional belief systems, with respect to these groups, may be inhibiting the kind of progress seen in early intervention. However, the design elements outlined here can be applied more broadly.

CONCLUSION

Lessons about family support can be gleaned from Part H of PL 99-457 that are applicable to other areas of social policy, in general, and disability policy, specifically. Two responses emerge when the following question is posed: Can well-designed, carefully conceived, broadly aimed social policies make a difference? On the one hand, there is not yet conclusive evidence that Part H has significantly improved the lives of very young children with disabilities and their families. There is evidence, on the other hand, that there has been considerable program development, professional preparation, installment of new infrastructures, and systemic change aimed at creating more family-centered services. This process has evolved from a coalescence of ecocultural theory building, aggressive policy making, innovative interagency collaboration, and effective advocacy by and for parents of young children.

So perhaps the answer to the question is that the policy-making process can make a difference, not only for those intended to benefit from the policy, but for those implementing the policy as well. Therefore, policy making in one arena (e.g., early intervention) can serve as a prototype for policy making in other fields. If this is true, then it may be that the concerns of diverse interest groups in our society may be more similar than originally believed. Such an understanding could motivate efforts to establish national family support policies—a goal the United States has been unable to achieve although other nations, developed as well as developing, have long ago done so.

It should also be recognized that the conception and implementation of Part H has occurred within a larger societal context. Since the 1970s, the United States has seen significant achievements in the sciences of human development and organizational behavior, new forms of medical technology and treatment, increased concern for the rights of individuals with disabilities and their families, and the recognition that people who once were viewed as passive recipients of social interventions (i.e., victims of their own circumstances) must be seen as active participants capable of constructing their own destinies. The postmodern search for new forms of helping that do not demean, oppress, or patronize, but rather liberate and empower, is clearly seen in the early intervention field and its struggle to collaborate with families. This struggle is driven by ideological, theoretical, political, economic, and cultural forces, which are applicable across generations.

Chapter Review

CHALLENGES

- The design and goals of social policies are a function of ideological perspectives, contextual factors, theoretical and empirical paradigms, and evaluation frameworks. As such, the effects of such policies on families and children are difficult to determine and subject to varying interpretations.
- Social policy related to young children with disabilities and their families has evolved dramatically rather than incrementally, unlike efforts in other social policy arenas. Thus, the lessons learned from early intervention policy must be understood in this context.

CHARACTERISTICS OF HELPFUL PROGRAMS

- Equal opportunities for having access to and maximum control over decision making are fundamental to family support programs.
- Effective programs support proactive family involvement based upon the meanings constructed by families about their own needs and concerns.
- Professionals' and families' interpretations of disability and family support are congruent.
- Theories that guide program design are rooted in family experience, emphasizing family competence and supportive communities.
- Programs emphasize early detection and intervention, family support and participation in governance, participation in integrated community-based programs, high-quality professional preparation, state-level decision making, the establishment of a strong early intervention and preschool infrastructure, and interagency coordination.

POLICY IMPLICATIONS

- The design of high-quality programs requires ecocultural theory building, comprehensive and aggressive social policy, innovative interagency collaboration, and effective advocacy for and by families.
- Early intervention policy making may serve as a prototype for policy making in other fields.
- New forms of helping that emphasize liberation and empowerment are applicable to support programs targeted across generations and populations of vulnerable citizens.

References

Abeson, A., & Zettel, J. (1977). The end of the quiet revolution: The Education for All Handicapped Children Act of 1975. *Exceptional Children, 44,* 114–128.

Americans with Disabilities Act of 1990 (ADA), PL 101-336. (July 26, 1990). Title 42, U.S.C. 12101 et seq: *U.S. Statutes at Large, 104,* 327–378.

Bailey, D.B. (1989). Issues and directions in preparing professionals to work with young handicapped children and their families. In J.J. Gallagher, P.L. Trohanis, & R.M. Clifford (Eds.), *Policy implementation and PL 99-457: Planning for young children with special needs* (pp. 97–132). Baltimore: Paul H. Brookes Publishing Co.

Bernheimer, L.P., Gallimore, R., & Weisner, T.S. (1990). Ecocultural theory as a context for the individual family service plan. *Journal of Early Intervention, 14*(3), 219–233.

Bronfenbrenner, U. (1979). *The ecology of human development: Experiments by nature and human design.* Cambridge, MA: Harvard University Press.

Castro, G., & Mastropieri, M. (1986). The efficacy of early intervention programs: A meta-analysis. *Exceptional Children, 52,* 417–424.

Center on Human Policy. (1987). *A statement in support of families and their children.* Syracuse, NY: Author.

Clifford, R.M., Bernier, K.Y., & Harbin, G.L. (1992). *Financing Part H services: A state-level view.* Chapel Hill, NC: Carolina Institute for Child and Family Policy.

Developmental Disabilities Act Amendments of 1984, PL 98-527. (October 19, 1984). Title 42, U.S.C. 6000 et seq: *U.S. Statutes at Large, 98,* 2662–2685.

Dokecki, P.R. (1983). The place of values in the world of psychology and public policy. *Peabody Journal of Education, 60*(3), 108–125.

Dokecki, P.R., & Heflinger, C.A. (1989). Strengthening families of young children with handicapping conditions: Mapping backward from the "street level." In J.J. Gallagher, P.L. Trohanis, & R.M. Clifford (Eds.), *Policy implementation and PL 99-457: Planning for young children with special needs* (pp. 59–84). Baltimore: Paul H. Brookes Publishing Co.

Education for All Handicapped Children Act of 1975, PL 94-142. (August 23, 1977). Title 20, U.S.C. 1401 et seq: *U.S. Statutes at Large, 89,* 773–796.

Education of the Handicapped Act Amendments of 1986, PL 99-457. (October 8, 1986). Title 20, U.S.C. 1400 et seq: *U.S. Statutes at Large, 100,* 1145–1177.

Elementary and Secondary Education Act (ESEA), PL 89-313. (September 23, 1950). Title 20, U.S.C. 631 et seq: *U.S. Statutes at Large, 79,* 1158.

Gallagher, J.J. (1992). The role of values and facts in policy development for infants and toddlers with disabilities and their families. *Journal of Early Intervention, 16*(1), 1–10.

Handicapped Children's Early Education Act, PL 90-538. (September 30, 1968). Title 20, U.S.C. 621 et seq: *U.S. Statutes at Large, 82,* 901–902.

Harry, B. (1992). *Cultural diversity, families, and the special education system: Communication and empowerment.* New York: Teachers College Press.

Hebbeler, K.M., Smith, B.J., & Black, T.L. (1991). Federal early childhood special education policy: A model for the improvement of services for children with disabilities. *Exceptional Children, 58*(2), 104–112.

Hobbs, N., Dokecki, P.R., Hoover-Dempsey, K.V., Moroney, R.M., Shayne, M.W., & Weeks, K.H. (1984). *Strengthening families.* San Francisco: Jossey-Bass.

Individuals with Disabilities Education Act of 1990 (IDEA), PL 101-476. (October 30, 1990). Title 20, U.S.C. 1400 et seq: *U.S. Statutes at Large, 104,* 1103–1151.

Individuals with Disabilities Education Act Amendments of 1991, PL 102-119. (October 7, 1991). Title 20, U.S.C. 1400 et seq: *U.S. Statutes at Large, 105,* 587–608.

Kaiser, A.P., & Hemmeter, M.L. (1989). Value-based approaches to family intervention. *Topics in Early Childhood Special Education, 8*(4), 72–86.

Kirschner Associates, Inc. (1970). *A national survey of the impacts of Head Start on community institutions.* Washington, DC: Office of Child Development, Department of Health, Education, and Welfare.

LeVine, R. (1977). Child rearing as cultural adaptation. In P. Liederman, S. Tulkin, & A. Rosenfeld (Eds.), *Culture and infancy* (pp. 15–27). New York: Academic Press.

Lindbloom, C. (1959). The science of "muddling through." *Public Administration Review, 19,* 79–88.

Lipsky, M. (1980). *Street-level bureaucracy.* New York: Russell-Sage.

Lynch, E.W., & Hanson, M.J. (Eds.). (1992). *Developing cross-cultural competence: A guide for working with young children and their families.* Baltimore: Paul H. Brookes Publishing Co.

Mallory, B.L. (1994). Inclusive policy, practice, and theory for young children with developmental differences. In B.L. Mallory & R.S. New (Eds.), *Diversity and developmentally appropriate practices: Challenges for early childhood education* (pp. 44–61). New York: Teachers College Press.

Mallory, B.L., & New, R.S. (Eds.). (1994). *Diversity and developmentally appropriate practices: Challenges for early childhood education.* New York: Teachers College Press.

Mental Retardation Facilities and Community Mental Health Centers Construction Act of 1963, PL 88-164. (October 31, 1963). Title 42, U.S.C. 2670 et seq: *U.S. Statutes at Large, 77,* 282–298.

Nisbet, J. (Ed.). (1992). *Natural supports in school, at work, and in the community for people with severe disabilities.* Baltimore: Paul H. Brookes Publishing Co.

Odom, S.L., & McEvoy, M. (1990). Mainstreaming at the preschool level: Potential barriers and tasks for the field. *Topics in Early Childhood Special Education, 10*(2), 48–61.

Office of Special Education Programs. (1993). *Fifteenth annual report to Congress on the implementation of the Individuals with Disabilities Education Act.* Washington, DC: U.S. Department of Education.

Phillips, C.B. (1994). The movement of African-American children through sociocultural contexts. In B.L. Mallory & R.S. New (Eds.), *Diversity and developmentally appropriate practices: Challenges for early childhood education* (pp. 137–154). New York: Teachers College Press.

Sheehan, R., & Sites, J. (1989). Implications of PL 99-457 for assessment. *Topics in Early Childhood Special Education, 8*(4), 103–115.

Shonkoff, J.P., & Hauser-Cram, P. (1987). Early intervention for disabled infants and their families: A quantitative analysis. *Pediatrics, 80,* 650–658.

Singer, G.H.S., & Irvin, L.K. (1989). Family caregiving, stress, and support. In G.H.S. Singer & L.K. Irvin (Eds.), *Support for caregiving families: Enabling positive adaptation to disability* (pp. 3–26). Baltimore: Paul H. Brookes Publishing Co.

Super, C.M., & Harkness, S. (Eds.). (1980). *Anthropological perspectives on child development: New directions for child development* (Vol. 8). San Francisco: Jossey-Bass.

Super, C.M., & Harkness, S. (1986). The developmental niche: A conceptualization at the interface of child and culture. *International Journal of Behavioral Development, 9,* 454–569.

Swadener, B.B. (1990). Children "at risk": Etiology, critique, and alternative paradigms. *Educational Foundations, 4*(4), 17–39.

Taylor, S.J., Knoll, J.A., Lehr, S., & Walker, P.M. (1989). Families for all children: Value-based services for children with disabilities and their families. In G.H.S.

Singer & L.K. Irvin (Eds.), *Support for caregiving families: Enabling positive adaptation to disability* (pp. 41–54). Baltimore: Paul H. Brookes Publishing Co.

Weisner, T.S., & Gallimore, R. (1989). *Ecocultural influences on development and developmental delay.* Paper presented at the Biennial Meeting of the Society for Research in Child Development, Kansas City, MO.

Whiting, J., & Whiting, B. (1975). *Children of six cultures: A psychocultural analysis.* Cambridge, MA: Harvard University Press.

Ziegler, M. (1989). A parent's perspective: Implementing PL 99-457. In J.J. Gallagher, P.L. Trohanis, & R.M. Clifford (Eds.), *Policy implementation and PL 99-457: Planning for young children with special needs* (pp. 85–96). Baltimore: Paul H. Brookes Publishing Co.

8

Family Support in Cases of Child Abuse and Neglect

Steve Kairys

This chapter discusses the rapid emergence of family support systems that assist children who are physically abused and neglected. These systems have blossomed under strong state and community governmental support, which provides alternatives both economically and in response to the foster care focus of the 1970s and 1980s.

In order to understand the debate around this paradigm shift from foster care to family unification, this chapter first describes the current set of assumptions relating to the epidemiology of abuse and presents a synthesizing etiological model for child abuse. It then briefly reviews the short- and long-term impact of abuse in order to illustrate the absolute necessity for developing models of intervention that will be of long-term benefit. The chapter then presents the history of family support services in the United States, describes in detail some of the models of family support services, and discusses the controversy surrounding their benefits and potential risks.

Family support services have become integral components of the social service systems' armamentarium of intervention. With quantitative evaluation, perhaps these services will set a standard for the future and not simply become another intervention fad as the United States continues to struggle with the epidemic of violence toward children.

THE EPIDEMIOLOGY OF CHILD PHYSICAL ABUSE

Each year, more than 2 million reports of child physical abuse in the United States are filed, a number that represents only a small fraction of the actual

yearly incidence (Straus & Gelles, 1986). In two separate surveys, one in 1975 and a second in 1985, 10%–15% of families interviewed reported at least one episode of severe violence (e.g., hitting with a fist or object, beating up, kicking, biting, threatening with a gun or knife, using a gun or knife) toward a child in the 3 months prior to the interview. This translates into approximately 16 million episodes per year. Even though 98% of the families reported to child protection agencies have low incomes, Straus and Gelles found a 10% incidence rate in the middle-class families surveyed. Physical abuse knows no economic restrictions, but middle-class families tend to have enough defenses to prevent them from easy detection.

Minor physical violence (e.g., slapping, spanking) is almost universal at all socioeconomic levels in the United States. The violence is particularly prevalent in the first 3 years of a child's life, but even teenagers experience a minor violence occurrence rate of 40%. Most of this violence is intimate violence, occurring within the family unit. Even though females have far more contact with children than males, perpetrators are just as likely to be male.

Some data suggest that the rate of severe violence is less now than in the 1970s, but no other studies have verified this. The staff in child protection systems believe that the abuse being reported is severe and that new patterns of abuse are emerging that were overlooked in the past. For example, in New York City, as many as 10% of sudden infant death syndrome (SIDS) cases are the result of infant homicide from suffocation, poisoning, or drowning (Meadow, 1990). More and more cases of *munchausen by proxy* (i.e., parental fabrication or active inducement of illness in a child) are being seen (Sullivan, Francis, Bain, & Hartz, 1991). Of these cases, 25% involve deliberate poisoning by a parent in order to produce mysterious symptoms that enable the parent to use the child as a medical entrance ticket to the health care system.

The rate of physical violence toward children is 5 times as high as asthma and 200 times as high as childhood cancer, with effects that may be more damaging and lifelong in their impact. These rates may still be increasing.

THE ETIOLOGY OF PHYSICAL ABUSE AND NEGLECT

A clear definition of the problem and a consensus on the cause or causes, supported by experimental investigation, comprise the foundation for designing specific interventions. For example, cancer interventions have made major strides only after better delineation of the disease etiology and cycles. The etiology and life cycles of child physical abuse and neglect, however, are still poorly defined and often hotly contested. The current preventive and therapeutic paradigms are not based on scientifically proven risk factors and causes; thus, the debate for best policy is often based on opinion

and incomplete data. An understanding of family support systems must be seen in the context of this causal uncertainty.

Violence in Society

The social theory of child abuse attributes violence to societal attitudes that condone the use of physical force to solve problems. The United States is a violent society, depicting violence in fiction, in the movies, and on the nightly news. All levels of society condone physical violence as a problem-solving technique, with the belief that sparing the rod does spoil the child. Gelles (1978) compared U.S. data on violence with more pacifistic countries such as Sweden where spanking children is outlawed. Sweden's already low rates of child abuse have dropped even lower since passage of the law. In the United States, over 95% of families accept spanking, compared to 35% in Sweden.

Poverty and Violence

Theorists often cite poverty and its effect on family life as a cause of child abuse. Poverty produces multiple impediments to effective child development. It limits access to health care; it uncovers and magnifies the vulnerabilities in parents; and it places stress on parents and children that only adds many new stresses, such as inadequate or impermanent housing, unsafe neighborhoods, persistent economic instability, and the intrusion of social service and police systems. Also, as some people are impoverished because of inadequate interpersonal skills, poverty skews the numbers of parents with inadequate self-esteem and unstable relationships. Yet, a study in Pittsburgh, Pennsylvania (Elmer, 1977), discovered that characteristics found in families reported for child abuse (e.g., witnessing violence in the home, being threatened with a gun or knife) were no different from samples of nonabusing families from the same neighborhoods. Moreover, the results of cross-sectional surveys by Straus and Gelles (1986) demonstrate a high rate of violence toward children in middle-class families also. Although poverty certainly catalyzes the reactions that lead to violence, it does not appear to be causal.

Family Stress

Family stress is another theorized cause of child abuse; it postulates that every family has a breaking point and that the amount of stress is more important than whether the stress is eustress or distress (Justice, Calvert, & Justice, 1985). *Eustress* is stress from positive changes, such as a new house, a new child, or a new and better job. The theory predicts that *distress*, which includes such stressors as loss of employment, social isolation, physical isolation, an unwanted child, a child with physical impairment, a highly temperamental child, and multiple moves, is additive in effect and its cumulative damage can lead to abuse. As with poverty, stress in family life is not predictive of abuse, although it certainly increases the risk of abuse. Poverty is a family stressor, but, according to the poverty theory, the family dysfunction and parental inadequacies often caused by poverty are more causal than the actual stress of living in poverty. This stress appears to be associated with, but not causal of, abuse.

Learned Behavior

Learning theories attribute many cases of child abuse to learned behaviors (Newberger & Newberger, 1982). Thus, parents who were abused as children are more likely to abuse because they learned that physical actions toward children are the way to discipline them. This theory asserts that the learning of new parenting skills will produce the changes necessary to prevent and reduce the incidence of child abuse.

Psychological Factors

All of the theories mentioned above have little sensitivity or specificity in predicting child abuse as child abuse most likely occurs on a continuum or bell-shaped curve. There are certainly fairly stable families who will abuse if the stressors are high enough, just as there are parents who experience a moment of dysfunction and harm their children. Much of child abuse, however, is long-term and multimodal, involving physical, verbal, and psychological abuse. As many as 60% of the parents seen by mental health or medical professionals appear to have long-term intrapsychic problems that may be closer to the cause of abuse than the theories just described.

In the late 1970s and 1980s, medical and psychological research suggested that long-term personality structure dysfunction is key to identifying abusive individuals from others of the same socioeconomic status (SES) or environmental stress level. Frodi and Lamb (1980) found that child abusers were more physiologically aroused by videotapes of crying children than the control group. Anderson and Lauderdale (1982), among others, found that abusive parents had poorly integrated personalities and struggled with issues concerning basic sense of self. These parents were socially isolated, mostly because of poor social skills, and got little enjoyment from their parenting role. At an extreme, these parents with characteristics of personality disorder were both antisocial and exhibited self-injurious behaviors.

Much of the current literature discusses these long-term personality and psychological characteristics found in clinical samples of abusive parents. This view of etiology has led to the intrapsychic model of abuse (Salter & Kairys, in press), which states that in order for abuse to occur, the following four interactive components must be present:

- Accelerator—negative affect toward the child
- Mediator—worldview that rationalizes the abuse
- Brakes—inability to control impulses
- Reinforcer—payoff of abusive behavior

Thus, abusive parents must have some negative construct toward the child(ren) in order to abuse. For example, they may be uncomfortable in the presence of children, may project unrealistic expectations onto the child, or may see their child's actions as malicious or premeditated. They must also hold a worldview that gives them the right to use physical force, because they then act on their impulses without the necessary social brakes that would prevent such behavior. This lack of impulse control is closely connected to the poor social skills, lack of self-esteem, and internal rage that are so prevalent in the clinical samples. This aggression often reinforces a feeling of power for these parents who, otherwise, feel powerless in all aspects of their lives. It also can turn family or spousal attention away from other issues and maintain a precarious, but useful, homeostasis in a troubled family. Of families connected with spousal abuse, 25% also abuse their children (McKibben, DeVos, & Newberger, 1989). Those working to reduce the incidence of abuse need to understand and envelop each component part of this intrapsychic model.

Present clinical protocols aimed at screening for child abuse are both insensitive and nonspecific, usually based only on SES determinants. A prior history of being abused is the highest risk factor available, yet only 30%–40% of physical abuse occurs in families with a history of abuse in the parent's childhood.

Because there is this spectrum of etiological risks, many call for ecological models of prevention (Chamberlin, 1988)—programs geared toward an entire community, instead of a selected high-risk category (Belsky, 1980).

THE EFFECTS OF PHYSICAL ABUSE ON THE CHILD

Although violence toward children has some physical effects, the most dramatic and long-lasting damage is psychological in nature. Briere (1992) and Herman (1992), among others, have recently begun labeling many of these effects as the *trauma syndrome*, which involves a range of secondary repercussions, including the following:

1. Isolated symptoms of somatic complaints
2. Anxieties
3. Alcohol and drug abuse

This blends, then, with aspects of the posttraumatic stress syndrome:

1. Hyperarousal—anxieties, sleep disorders
2. Intrusion
3. The imprinting and constriction of the trauma—nightmares, flashbacks, and reenactment
4. Defenses to protect—numbness, amnesia for the events, and pathological methods of continuing the attachments to those who abuse

One method of constriction is double-self or double-think, in which victims dissociate their love for their parents from their terror by vertical splitting (Herman, 1992). They continue to love the ones who hurt them by keeping the bad–good issues psychically separate. Some victims enlarge double-self and double-think and develop multiple personality disorders.

Studies of abused children also uncover an array of physical and cognitive disturbances. For example, children may have growth retardation; there is a syndrome of growth hormone deficiency secondary to chronic abuse, wherein developmental milestones are delayed and specific speech-language problems arise, such as scanning speech in which a child's language appears adequate on first impression but lacks specificity and detail and is more a protective defense (Martin, 1976). When children grow up in an environment where the people who love them are also the people who abuse them, they can never be sure what will trigger the next abuse. They spend much of their learning time being hypervigilant and wary and have little enjoyment for living. They also experience many secondary somatic problems, such as pain syndromes, sleep disturbances, attention-deficit/hyperactivity disorder (ADHD), and resultant school failure, that are often lifelong and lead to difficulties with relationships, self-esteem, and success in the workplace and in the home. In fact, as many as 80% of adults using mental health services will describe an abusive background as children (Mullen & Roman-Clarkson, 1988).

The effects of abuse can be ameliorated by a strong constitution, a high IQ, or other positive attributes, as well as by a long-term caring adult figure and a home environment that is not continually dangerous. Although not every child victim is damaged, the majority do experience long-term problems that even the best treatment services cannot help—especially if the abuse has been long term and began at an early age (Cline, 1988).

FAMILY SUPPORTS IN CHILD ABUSE

Models of family support have arisen for many aspects of abuse and neglect. Some of the systems are ecological and aimed at primary prevention, working to prevent abuse from ever occurring; some are geared toward secondary prevention, working to detect abuse as early as possible; and some offer tertiary prevention, working to prevent further psychological or physical damage from the abuse. Although some are local, private systems, more and more are state supported and associated with child protection agency activities. At times, these services are voluntary; often they are court ordered. In some areas these services are interdisciplinary, unconditional, and individualized and are termed *wrap-around services* (see Chapter 13).

The current enthusiasm for family support models stems from the common belief that the child protection model used since the 1960s has not worked. The U.S. Advisory Board on Child Abuse and Neglect released a report in 1990 that stated the following:

The most serious shortcoming of the nation's system of intervention on behalf of children is that it depends upon a reporting and response process that has punitive connotations, and requires massive resources dedicated to the investigation of allegations. State and county child welfare programs have not been designed to get immediate help to families based on voluntary requests for assistance. As a result, it has become far easier to pick up the phone to report one's neighbor for abuse than it is for that neighbor to request and receive help before the abuse occurs. If the nation ultimately is to reduce the dollars and personnel needed for investigating reports, more resources must be allocated to establishing voluntary, non-punitive access to help. (p. 8)

Family support services focused on child abuse and neglect are actually a century old. In the 1880s, private charity organizations dispatched friendly visitors to the homes of the urban poor in an attempt to transform their behaviors. As many as 4,000 such workers regularly worked with families in the major cities of the northeastern United States. The architect of the movement, S. Humphrey Gurteen, described the work of the visitors in language not unlike that used for today's model:

The chief need of the poor today [is] not almsgiving, but the moral support of true friendship—the possession of a real friend, whose education, experience, whose general knowledge of life are placed at the service of those who have neither the intelligence, tact, nor the opportunity to exact the maximum of good from their slender resources. (Weiss, 1993, p. 116)

Home visiting was considered the panacea for poverty, until it did not produce the expected changes. It was gradually abandoned by the turn of the century, giving way to the settlement houses of the early 20th century.

A vast array of programs and philosophies are lumped together as family support, making it difficult to evaluate the effectiveness of family support services for child abuse. Some programs focus primarily on child outcomes and offer child services only; others target adult outcomes and provide adult and child services. Some assume that all families need help; others target groups at high risk. Some target parenting as the vehicle for change; others look to improve the environment in which the family lives. Some programs emphasize interpersonal relationships between worker and family as the strategy for change; others see education and information exchange as the dominant strategy. Some programs have single goals, such as parent–child interactions; others focus on multiple goals and look at the broad ecology of family functioning. Some services are infrequent and end after a few months; others are of higher intensity and may last, in some form, for several years (Powell, 1993).

Family support services are tailored to different cycles of the abuse spectrum. There are a wide array of programs around the United States aimed at the prevention of abuse. There are programs, called *family preservation programs,* that are tertiary prevention services aimed at working with families after abuse has occurred. And there are some newer programs developing aimed at using family support techniques for reuniting families separated by abuse. This review focuses on each of these different aspects of family support, describes the salient general principles, presents some specific program examples, and then critiques the available data about the outcomes provided by the programs.

Primary Prevention

Family support services are deeply rooted and universally supported in primary prevention for abuse and neglect. By nature, these are voluntary services that are often originated at the community level and supported by local funding and volunteerism. Most often these services have an ecological philosophy and offer services to any family in the community, including traditional parenting education programs as well as more integrated home visitor models. The following characteristics are integral to such preventive programs:

1. Services should be voluntary to all families. Those programs that target only a labeled population (e.g., risk lists for poverty or abuse) are considered special programs for selected groups. This model appreciates the fact that all parents, particularly first-time parents, can benefit from community services. Eighty percent of countries in Europe routinely provide family support services for all newborns, a concept that is just now gaining ground in this country. The more a voluntary service is offered to all, the more likely it is to be used by those in need of the help. Also, existing risk factors for abuse are still too insensitive and nonspecific to devise a valid screening tool, providing further support for the concept of universal availability of services.
2. Family support services should have multiple goals. Those programs that target only parenting education or offer information and referral services, for example, are far less likely to have the impact of a delivery system that works with the family system and offers education, psychological support, child care, and medical services.
3. Services should be flexible in intensity and duration.
4. Programs should be sensitive to the unique characteristics and circumstances of their clients. Cultural diversity, poverty, and racial differences, to name a few, must be understood so that a message of inadequacy is not inadvertently sent to the family.
5. Programs require a well-trained and dedicated staff.
6. Expectations of the family should be realistic. Even intensive programs spend very few hours with families and must compete with the ongoing stresses and premorbidity of the family.
7. Cost-effectiveness needs to be a feature of the evaluation process. It is often very difficult to promote prevention programs at a time of budgetary restraint. Careful delineation of costs and benefits is crucial to successful governmental and private support (Behrman, 1993).

Many of these characteristics are evident in successful state programs, including Hawaii's Healthy Start Program; the Elmira, New York, program; the Addison County, Vermont, Parent/Child Center (PCC); and Healthy Families America (Elliott, 1993).

Hawaii's Healthy Start Program

Hawaii is widely known for its home visiting system entitled "Healthy Start" (Powell, 1993), which, over the past 8 years, has demonstrated the ability to reduce rates of reported physical abuse. The program began in 1976 as a small, $200,000 demonstration project in Leeward, Oahu. It is now statewide and supported by state funds. The goals of the program are 1) to ensure that all families have a primary health care provider, 2) to ensure proper use of community resources, 3) to promote positive parenting, 4) to enhance parent–child interaction, 5) to enhance child health and development, and 6) to prevent child abuse and neglect.

Healthy Start uses a risk-assessment tool to define the amount of services required, but services are voluntary and available to all. Core services are home based and are supplemented with other supportive services. Services can be long term and address a variety of factors including child development, discipline skills, use of health care, economic and emotional support, and respite care. Home visits are conducted by trained aides who emphasize developing a trusting relationship with the parent(s) and working together to improve parenting skills. Families are interviewed in the hospital shortly after birth. Services are offered to all families with the frequency and intensity of services varying based on needs. Services continue with some frequency until the child is 5 years old.

The initial evaluation of the first demonstration project showed no incidence of physical abuse during the first 2 years of services. Studies are now underway to explore long-term effects of the program.

The Elmira Study

Elmira is a small city in New York with a population of 40,000; in 1980, it was rated as the worst area in the United States in terms of economic conditions. The Elmira Study (Olds, 1992) is a nurse visitation program aimed at pregnant women and newborns. The study set up four treatment groups. The group in need of most intensive supports received health and developmental screening for children at ages 1 and 2, free transportation for health visits, home visits by a nurse during pregnancy, and home visits by a nurse during the child's first 2 years of life, while the other groups received one, two, or three of these services. The home visits were weekly for the first few months and then of diminishing frequency. The nurses worked with the women on infant care, personal development, problem-solving skills, and health habits. After 2 years, the group receiving all services had an abuse incidence of 4%, compared to 19% in the groups with one or two services. The cost of the service was $3,200 per family, on average; costs for the families in the control groups were double this.

Addison County Parent/Child Center

The Addison County Parent/Child Center (PCC) uniquely offers preventive family support and family preservation services (Russell, 1994). The Center was funded in 1979 through a grant from the Federal Office of Pregnancy Programs but is now primarily state funded. The PCC believes that parents know best what supports they need; that all parents are doing the best job they are capable of; and that families in distress are struggling with stress, lack of support, and lack of education about child care skills.

Services include a therapeutic child care program, meals for parents and children, counseling and support groups, a drop-in crisis center, transportation, and parenting classes, such as Learning Together and Dads programs. These classes are a 20-hour per week training program and parents are paid a small stipend for the time that they are at the Center.

There are also home-based services for pregnant and parenting teens, and for parents of children with disabilities. The Center also promotes community activities, including drug and alcohol prevention, family-life education in the schools, and weekly play groups. Families with varying levels of need are integrated in the programs, in part to have families teach each other.

Other Primary Prevention Programs

The National Committee for the Prevention of Child Abuse in partnership with the Ronald McDonald Children's Charities has launched "Healthy Families America," in an effort to replicate Hawaii's model. An advantage of a state-based system is that a centrally based resource center can help develop training programs for staff, advocate for state support, organize data systems to evaluate process and outcome, and initiate new approaches to the community systems.

One further example of a state-based primary prevention program is the "Ounce of Prevention Fund" in Illinois, which supports 40 community programs that are ecological and family centered. These projects offer an array of services, including parent group services, home visitors, and family support services. The programs also include churches, schools, and businesses in the goals and activities of the program.

Primary Prevention and the Self-Help Movement

A few primary prevention programs are part of the self-help movement. The model program is "Parents Anonymous," a nationwide program that has worked to empower parents since 1972. Jolly K., a parent with abuse problems, began Parents Anonymous to offer parents help before abuse occurred. Groups have two leaders: 1) a volunteer facilitator who is a parent from the group, and 2) a professional in the human services. Any parent can join in the group, although many are referred by social and medical service professionals. The groups work best when the members become the healers and supporters. Every state has chapters in Parents Anonymous that are funded by local and state agencies. The program has never had a true measure of effectiveness, but its tenets of support and empowerment make it a program with strong governmental support.

Secondary Prevention

Whereas primary prevention services are available to all families, secondary prevention programs are targeted to specific groups at risk. Family support services for families identified as being high risk for abuse and neglect have slowly been developing across the United States. Many areas are recognizing that attention to families in need can greatly reduce subsequent abuse and neglect. Family support programs for targeted families at risk of abusing include parent aide programs and wrap-around services—the broader relative of home-based programs.

Parent aide programs are the oldest secondary prevention programs, offering concrete supports and role models. There are currently 800 parent aide programs in the country serving 48,000 families per year (Hornick & Clarke, 1986). A recent 9-year study in North Carolina of 200 such families showed no evidence of abuse in 93% of the families (Bryan, 1993).

Vermont Parent/Child Centers
Vermont has developed statewide Parent/Child Centers in 14 communities. These centers offer an array of family support services—child care, parent education, parent support, drop-in services, home-based services, playgroups, and community development. The program is a model of state–grassroots cooperation that enhances the commitment of local communities to the well-being of families, and has been recently praised by the Harvard Family Research Project in its report, "Innovative States: Emerging Family Support and Education Programs" (Kajan, 1994).

Wrap-Around Services
The latest evolution in secondary prevention has been the development of wrap-around services. By current definition, *wrap-around service* involves an interdisciplinary services team including the parent, service coordinator, advocate for the child and/or parent, and other professionals important to the family. The services are community based, flexible, and unconditional, meaning that the team agrees never to deny services and to change services as the concerns of the family change. The services are individualized, not categorical, and include traditional services (e.g., therapy) and nontraditional services (e.g., hiring a special friend, special recreational services). The services must include at least three of the following life domain needs:

residential, family, social, educational, medical, emotional, legal, and/or safety. Vermont, for example, is using this concept to work with families at risk and in need of mental health services. A huge barrier to such a system is the categorical funding and expense tracking used by state bureaucracies. Some states, such as Alaska, have set aside a percentage of state agency dollars to be used as a pool of resources for wrap-around services.

Tertiary Services

The major controversy surrounding family support services for families connected with abuse and neglect involves family preservation services for families with substantiated abuse and neglect: Do such services safeguard the child who has been abused? Family preservation services are used for families newly identified as abusive, or for families involved with child protection who attempt to reunite with their children after a period of time in foster care.

The major trend in the child protection services that arose in the 1970s was "child rescue" services. The primary goal of these services is to secure the safety of the child, often through foster care; working with the family in an attempt toward reunification often seemed to be a secondary goal, at best. Services were often poorly coordinated and children frequently stayed in foster care indefinitely, which is highly destructive to an already damaged self. This model was also very expensive: Foster care alone can cost the state $10,000 per year per child (Barnett, 1993).

The roots of family preservation begin in the 1950s in St. Paul, Minnesota, with the "Family-Centered Project." The movement gathered momentum after the Adoption Assistance and Child Welfare Act of 1980, PL 96-272, which states that every child has a right to a permanent home with the biological parents, if possible, or with adoptive parents, if not. This led to the least restrictive environment doctrine of today's child welfare systems that attempts to use foster care as a last resort. The 1980s also saw Reagan-generated cutbacks in the social welfare system. As a result, initial reductions in foster care placement due to family preservation were lost. The rosters of foster children grew from 276,000 in 1985 to 429,000 in 1991. Since then, the numbers have been declining, primarily because most states have seen increased development of family preservation programs, most modeled after the "HomeBuilders Program" of Tacoma, Washington. The movement achieved a major triumph in 1993 with the passage of the Family Preservation and Family Support Act, the first new federal child welfare legislation since 1980. The act provides $1 billion (over 5 years) for states to use as a new capped entitlement, which allows them to provide a variety of child welfare services that protect children and strengthen, support, and preserve troubled familes—reunifying them when placement is necessary.

Family preservation, thus, is the paradigm shift of the 1990s, generating new practice methods and values and a commitment to promoting competence rather than "curing" the dysfunctional family. Family preservation is modeled around intensive home-based services. Its services are an extension of parent aide programs; they incorporate social workers and psychologists who spend 4–10 hours per week in the home of an abusive family using a non–deficit-based approach to help families develop new competencies to care for their children. Drawing on crisis intervention, lifespace intervention, ecological theories, and cognitive-behavioral theories, family preservation is family centered—it is delivered in the home and is available 24 hours a day for a limited period of 6–9 weeks. Workers have an average caseload of two to four families. Guided by a belief in family resources and priorities, workers provide or connect families to services and other resources, instruct in parenting skills, model behavior, help resolve family crises, and provide on-site monitoring of family members at risk.

Initial results from the early programs documented reduced out-of-home placements, with no increase in child abuse reports (Berry, 1992). Costs of care also were reduced, with an average family preservation costing about $2,500 per year compared with a cost of over $10,000 for a child in foster care. Connecticut has followed 591 families for 2 years. During this time, 82% of the children remained with their families and were never placed outside the home. Child well-being scales were used to assess family functioning. The scores improved in most areas, with the greatest improvement in parenting (McDonald, 1993). Family preservation also seems to protect children during the period of service delivery. Michigan's "Family First Program" detailed only one case of abuse in the 2,500 families it served in its first year, as compared to 30 children abused per 1,000 in out-of-home foster care placements.

These initial reports have not been matched by subsequent studies, which have found that the short-terms gains do not always last and that the rates of children in placement begin to climb after services are removed (Wells & Biegel, 1992). In some cases, the emphasis on saving money has led to poorly organized programs. These outcome evaluations, however, are just now being conducted, long after the family preservation approach has been institutionalized in most states. Unfortunately, true measurements will be difficult as the standards and characteristics of programs vary widely.

Although home-based services may be more constructive and less damaging than the old child protection, child rescue system, the movement cannot solve all of the problems associated with the treatment of child abuse. The etiology of abuse suggests that family psychopathology is often very high, which requires years of support—much more than the typical 6 weeks of home-based services. If substance abuse is present, little progress will be made in any area until the addictive behavior is arrested. Additionally, studies looking only at recidivism in terms of physical abuse overlook the psychological damage that may continue to increase if the environment remains threatening and malevolent.

Family preservation, if done successfully, will probably be as expensive or more expensive than the old model. Each child and family unit must have a formal assessment of resources and limitations in order to place them on the continuum of psychopathology and child damage. Services, then, must be tailored to those individual needs. The best interest of the child demands a careful and comprehensive initial evaluation and then regular reevaluations to chart progress or problems, all of which take money.

Still, family preservation systems do include components that have been missing from the child protection system of the past, such as high worker morale and commitment. These programs also create an opportunity for professionals to walk in the shoes of families being served so they can more meaningfully understand their resources, their crises, and their life stories. Evaluation of Michigan's Family First Program showed a 89% worker satisfaction rating and worker belief that the program was effective. Client families' reactions were also positive, with 98% of those surveyed stating they would recommend the services to other families (Weiss & Jacobs, 1988).

Family-based services have extended their reach to the reunification of families separated by child abuse. One program in Utah compared the results of 57 families receiving in-home family-based services to a group of 53 families receiving routine reunification services (Walton, Fraser, Lewis, Pecora, & Walton, 1993). Families were picked by random assignment. The family-based services were based on the following principles:

1. The client–service coordinator relationship should be mutually supportive.
2. Primary needs should be met with concrete services.
3. The whole family should be the focus of treatment.
4. Priority should be on parenting, household management, and relationships, rather than on psychopathology.

The services were limited to 90 days with 3 visits per week, for an average of 6 hours per week. At the end of 90 days, 93% of the treatment families were reunited, compared with 28% of the control families. The program is too new to evaluate effectiveness at or beyond 1 year.

SUMMARY

Family support services are a critical component of care for families who abuse their children. These services should be multidimensional and incorporate primary, secondary, and tertiary prevention strategies. Primary prevention services need to be ecologically based and available to all. The services that work best appear to use professionals rather than lay workers, provide multidimensional supports for all members of the family, and be flexible enough to provide services for periods as long as 5 years. Services should respect the families that they serve and work with their priorities, but be objective enough to call for help when problems arise. The best of these models are centrally supported and funded as state or national systems. Secondary prevention is perhaps best illustrated by Vermont's Parent/Child Centers, which use state funds and local direction to develop a menu of support services for families in need. Tertiary services are employed by state child protection agencies. For most states, now, the services are family centered and philosophically based on family abilities and family preservation. Using intensive home-based services as the principal service delivery tool, these services are appealing for their family orientation and for their fiscal economy. However, they have not been studied in enough detail to be universally applicable to the scenarios found in families who abuse. If the effects of abuse, parental psychopathology, and addictions were fully documented at the beginning of service delivery, family support programs would be further strengthened, as the data could be used to define the types of services to be delivered, the length of service delivery, and the measures of success to be evaluated.

There are many professions, bureaucracies, advocates, and opinions involved in shaping public policy about the prevention and treatment of child abuse. Unfortunately, the many factions have not been able to reach a consensus about the services needed for effective interventions. Federally funded consensus panels consisting of representatives from those professions and agencies dealing with child safety and children should be organized to dispassionately review the data currently available and make policy and research recommendations that can be developed, adequately tested, and evaluated. Until more formal inquiry takes place, programs will continue to be based on prevailing theory and economic incentives.

Chapter Review

CHALLENGES

- Ten percent to 15% of all families will experience extreme violence between family members within a 3-month period, totaling as many as 16 million violent family episodes a year.
- Family violence toward children is 5 times more prevalent than asthma and 200 times more prevalent than diabetes.
- Child abuse has severe and long-lasting psychological effects on children.
- Advocates and professionals generally agree that the current system of child protective services is ineffective, emphasizing reporting and investigation of allegations over treatment and prevention.
- The current system is a hybrid of many different elements and approaches, and services are crisis driven and usually result in an out-of-home placement for the child.

CHARACTERISTICS OF HELPFUL PROGRAMS

- Helpful programs provide treatment and support services to families that emphasize protection of children as well as treatment for the family.
- Helpful programs have multiple goals, address many family concerns, and are sensitive to the unique characteristics of their clients.
- Helpful programs have staffs who are well-trained and dedicated, and have realistic expectations of families.
- Helpful programs evaluate cost-effectiveness and treatment outcomes.
- Helpful programs offer primary prevention services to all families in a community, and secondary prevention and treatment services to families at high risk.
- Helpful programs provide intensive family- and child-centered treatment for verified cases of abuse, including in-home services.

POLICY IMPLICATIONS

- Cost-effectiveness studies should evaluate different service models, and family support services should be intensively studied to determine their efficacy.
- The federal government should convene consensus panels to encourage uniform recommendations about the design of services and treatments.
- The long-term effects of child abuse should be more thoroughly studied.
- Studies should determine the contribution of parental psychopathology and substance abuse in child abuse and neglect.

References

Adoption Assistance and Child Welfare Act of 1980, PL 96-272. (June 17, 1980). Title 42, U.S.C. 3434 et seq: *U.S. Statutes at Large, 94,* 500.

Anderson, S., & Lauderdale, M. (1982). Characteristics of abusive parents. *Child Abuse and Neglect, 6,* 285–293.

Barnett, W. (1993). Economic evaluation of home visiting programs. *The Future of Children, 3*(3), 93–113.

Behrman, R. (1993). Home visiting: Analysis and recommendations. *The Future of Children, 3*(3), 6–22.

Belsky, J. (1980). Child maltreatment: An ecological integration. *American Psychology, 35,* 320–335.

Berry, M. (1992). An evaluation of family preservation services: Fitting agency services to family needs. *Social Work, 37,* 314–321.

Briere, J. (1992). *Child abuse trauma.* Beverly Hills: Sage Publications.

Bryan, G. (1993). Parent aide programs in the United States. *Common Ground, 10,* 10.

Chamberlin, R.W. (1988). Rationale for a community-wide approach to promote the health and development of families and children. In R.W. Chamberlin (Ed.), *Beyond individual assessment.* Washington, DC: National Center for Education in Maternal and Child Health.

Cline, F. (1988). *Understanding and treating the severely disturbed child.* Denver: Foster Cline.

Elliott, B. (1993). Community responses to violence. *Primary Care, 20*(2), 495–502.

Elmer, E. (1977). A follow-up study of traumatized children. *Pediatrics, 59*(2), 273–279.

Family Preservation and Family Support Act of 1993, PL 103-66. (August 10, 1993). *U.S. Statutes at Large, 107,* 312.

Frodi, A.M., & Lamb, N.E. (1980). Child abusers responses to infant smiles and cries. *Child Development, 51,* 238–241.

Gelles, R. (1978). Violence toward children in the United States. *American Journal of Orthopsychiatry, 48*(4), 580–592.

Herman, J. (1992). *Trauma and recovery.* New York: Basic Books.

Hornick, J.P., & Clarke, M.E. (1986). A cost-effective evaluation of lay therapy treatment for child abusing and high-risk parents. *Child Abuse and Neglect, 10,* 309–318.

Justice, B., Calvert, A., & Justice, R. (1985). Factors mediating child abuse as a response to stress. *Child Abuse and Neglect, 9,* 359–363.

Kajan, J. (1994). *Innovative states: Emerging family support and educational programs. Harvard Family Research Project.* Cambridge, MA: Harvard University Press.

Martin, H. (1976). *The abused child.* Cambridge, MA: Ballinger Publishing.

McDonald, W. (1993). Connecticut evaluates intensive family preservation services. *Common Ground, 11,* 10.

McKibben, L., DeVos, E., & Newberger, E. (1989). Victimization of mothers of abused children: A controlled study. *Pediatrics, 71,* 531–535.

Meadow, R. (1990). Suffocation, apnea, and sudden infant death. *Journal of Pediatrics, 117,* 351–357.

Mullen, P.E., & Roman-Clarkson, S.E. (1988). Impact of sexual and physical abuse on women's mental health. *Lancet, 8590,* 841–845.

Newberger, C.M., & Newberger, E.H. (1982). Prevention of child abuse: Theory, myth, and practice. *Journal of Preventive Psychiatry, 1*(4), 443–451.

Olds, D. (1992). Home visitation for pregnant women and parents of young children. *American Journal of Disabled Children, 146,* 704–708.

Powell, D. (1993). Inside home visiting programs. *The Future of Children, 3*(3), 23–38.

Russell, H. (1994). Vermont center integrates family support and family preservation services. *Common Ground, 11,* 1–4.

Salter, A., & Kairys, S. (in press). *Treatment of child physical abuse.* Beverly Hills: Sage Publications.

Straus, M.A., & Gelles, R.J. (1986). Societal changes and change in family violence from 1975 to 1985 as revealed by two national surveys. *Journal of Marriage and the Family, 48,* 465–479.

Sullivan, C.A., Francis, G.L., Bain, M.V., & Hartz, J. (1991). Munchausen syndrome by proxy: 1990. *Clinical Pediatrics, 30,* 112–116.

U.S. Advisory Board on Child Abuse and Neglect. (1990). *Child abuse and neglect: Critical first steps in response to a national emergency.* Washington, DC: U.S. Government Printing Office.

Walton, E., Fraser, M.V., Lewis, R.E., Pecora, P.J., & Walton, W.K. (1993). In-home family-focused reunification: An experimental study. *Child Welfare, 72,* 473–487.

Weiss, H.B. (1993). Home visits: Necessary but not sufficient. *The Future of Children, Winter,* 113–129.

Weiss, H.B., & Jacobs, F.H. (Eds.). (1988). *Evaluating family programs.* New York: Aldine de Gruyter.

Wells, K., & Biegel, D. (1992). Intensive family preservation services research: Current status and future agenda. *Social Work Research and Abstracts, 25,* 220–228.

9

Charting Unknown Territory with Families of Children with Complex Medical Needs

James A. Knoll

This chapter documents a fundamental social change now being evidenced in the lives of real families. In their lives, concepts such as comprehensive, coordinated, family-centered, community-based care (Koop, 1987; Maternal & Child Health, 1988; Nelkin, 1987) are central, as their day-to-day existences are shaped by public policy decisions that most people know only as abstractions with names like "Home- and Community-Based Waiver," "Katie Beckett Waiver," and "Home Care." These families represent a new frontier where social policy meets individual lives, being the

Preparation of this chapter was supported in part by Project No. MCJ-365004 from the Maternal and Child Health program (Title V, Social Security Act), Health Resources and Services Administration, U.S. Department of Health and Human Services. All opinions expressed herein are solely those of the author and should not be taken as expressions of policy of the U.S. Department of Health and Human Services.

The research reported in this chapter was conducted under a subcontract from Sick Kids (need) Involved People (SKIP) of New York, Inc., while the author was employed by Human Services Research Institute of Cambridge, Massachusetts. Numerous individuals participated in the activities that made this document possible. They include Margaret Mikol, Kathy Schwaninger, Carmen Soto, and Natalie Giuffi at SKIP of New York; the members of the project advisory board: Karen Buckholtz, Nina Daratsos, Aaron Favors, Gary Fitzgerald, Luann Kennedy, Kathryn Kirkhart, Barbara Kenefick, Suzanne Leach, Katie McKaig, Barbara Donaghy, Linda Reese, and Ed Walsh; and Valerie Bradley, John Agosta, Kathleen Moore, Lasell Whipple, and Paul Nurczynski at Human Services Research Institute. Although these individuals contributed to this project, the author alone should be held responsible for any opinions expressed in this chapter.

first generation of families to confront the implications of a community-based system of services within their homes and daily lives. Through their ongoing interaction with individual professionals, service providers, and state agencies, the meaning of *family support* is being defined. Their experiences merit careful scrutiny from anyone concerned with building community systems that maintain and support the integrity of families.

METHOD

In this chapter, the interview data collected during a study of caregiving families has been used to present an overview of the day-to-day realities of raising a child with complex medical needs and to highlight the challenges involved in providing truly family-centered, community-based care. The study documented in this chapter had two principal aims:

1. It was intended to evaluate the pilot service coordination and advocacy service provided to these families by Sick Kids (need) Involved People (SKIP) of New York, Inc.
2. Family-centered home- and community-based services for children with complex medical conditions create completely new relationships between families and service providers. This study sought to understand these new realities and communicate them to policy makers and service providers.

In order to achieve these dual objectives, a detailed 56-page data collection protocol, originally designed to conduct a national study on the experiences of families raising children with disabilities and chronic medical conditions, was adopted (Knoll, 1992). This form was slightly modified, in consultation with the project advisory panel, to include a subset of questions that focused on evaluation of the pilot project activities. The protocol integrated standard forced-choice questionnaire items that are amenable to statistical analysis with open-ended items that allowed the families to respond in detail.

This protocol was administered by a project worker who was familiar with each family. In this way, the usual problems related to establishing rapport are eliminated, although this approach is somewhat limiting as it involves the agency under evaluation in the process. However, the benefits derived from the already-established relationship seemed to far outweigh this limitation. During the interview the data collectors kept detailed notes of the families' responses and their own observations. The interviews lasted from 3 to 7 hours and yielded an incredible amount of rich, descriptive information.

The unprocessed data forms and field notes were then submitted to the author, who coordinated the data analysis and prepared the final report. All interview notes were transcribed into a standard form for management and analysis, after the data were read at least three times by the evaluation coordinator. During these readings, recurring topics and common experiences were identified in an effort to organize the common themes that capture the experiences of these families. A final report that integrated statistical data and interview information into a summative evaluation of the project and an overview of the challenges confronting the families served by the project was prepared (Knoll, 1989).

RESULTS

This chapter tells the stories of 48 families who represent the range of cultural, ethnic, religious, and economic diversity found in New York State. They live in run-down, public housing in New York City where they lock themselves in for their own protection; they live on acres of land in rural upstate New York. They range from anonymous single-parent families barely subsisting on welfare to a nationally known celebrity with a six-figure income. Still, their stories are surprisingly similar—the experience of raising a child with complex medical needs has transcended their differences.

In a very real sense, these families are the authors of this chapter. They were willing to open their homes and their hearts to the interviewers, indirectly giving readers a glimpse into some of the most private areas of life. This effort, along with so much else that these families have endured, has unquestionably exacted a cost from them—an invaluable expenditure of self. By pooling that most personal of resources, their own stories, these families have provided a scenario that demonstrates a pattern of policy and professional behavior that seriously threatens families. The testimony of these families calls on policy makers across the public and private spectrum to examine whether the ever-present rhetoric about the centrality of home and family life is supported by the day-to-day practices of their organizations.

Wherever possible, the presentation of findings relies on direct quotations from the field notes in the form of parents' comments or observations by the data collector. These quotes have been modified to ensure the families' anonymity and clarify any comprehension problems that could result if quotes were taken out of context.[1] Also, an effort has been made to ensure that despite the specifics of each situation, the central point stands as an

---

[1]Each quotation is followed by a two-digit number in parentheses. This is a randomly assigned identifier to assist in the management of data and to allow the reader to identify quotations from the same source.

exemplar for the experiences of the entire group by consciously avoiding quotations that describe a set of circumstances entirely idiosyncratic to one family or a very small group of families.

The Families and Their Children

The 48 families included in this study represent 25% of all families served by the SKIP service coordination pilot project. Of this group, nine lived in the Bronx, eight in upstate urban or rural areas, seven in Queens, six on Long Island, six in Westchester and other northern suburban communities, four in Brooklyn, and two on Staten Island. The average household in the study group had four residents. In 21% of the cases there was a single parent, while the remaining 79% had two or more adults in the home. In 43 of the 48 cases, one of the birth parents of the child with special needs was interviewed for this report. Responses indicate that in 71% ($n = 34$) of the cases, the mother was the primary caregiver. The father fulfilled this role in two cases, and grandparents in one case. The remaining respondents (23%, $n = 11$) indicated "other" (usually a nurse or home health care worker) as the primary caregiver. The households in the study group had incomes that averaged in the $20,000–$29,999 per year range.

Children with Special Needs

The children with special needs in the study group were relatively evenly distributed across a range of 1–14 years of age. All of the children had their disabilities identified before age 10—17% were diagnosed by age 5 and 75% were diagnosed at birth or shortly thereafter. The study group contained slightly more females (54%, $n = 26$) than males (44%, $n = 22$). Most of the children in the study group had complex medical histories, with 81% considered to have multiple diagnoses. The specialized nature of this group of children is captured by the figures presented in Table 1. The largest single diagnostic category is "other," reflecting the fact that the children in this group represented people with low-incidence, rare disorders; these include such conditions as sleep apnea (Oendine Curse), osteogenesis imperfecta, Rett syndrome, Dandy-Walker syndrome, CHARGE association, and nemaline mypopathy, among others.

The reality of raising a child with a low-incidence condition emerges from the descriptions provided by the parents and / or the interviewers. The six examples that follow give some sense of the diverse nature of the children in this report:

Ryan *She is 2 and very age-appropriate, starting to get interested in the potty. She is now standing on a stool at the kitchen sink, playing with water. Ryan needs to be watched as any 2-year-old, but unlike all 2-year-olds, Ryan has Oendine Curse and cardiac anomalies. She has a tracheotomy that must be watched and*

Table 1.   Number of study group members with various disabling conditions

Condition	Primary diagnosis	Secondary diagnosis
Other	14	13
Cerebral palsy	6	3
Birth defects	6	
Mental retardation	5	8
Heart disease	3	1
Acquired brain injury	3	
Muscular dystrophy	3	
Bronchopulmonary dysplasia	2	6
Spina bifida	2	
Asthma	1	3
Autism	1	1
Neuromuscular disease	1	
Cystic fibrosis	1	
Visual impairment		14
Epilepsy		8
Hearing impairment		6
Orthopedic impairment		4
Learning disability		2
Emotional disturbance		1
Tuberous sclerosis		1

Thirty-seven informants identified one or more secondary diagnoses, 13 identified at least two conditions, and six indicated three or more conditions.

cared for, and she must be on the ventilator while sleeping or else she will go into respiratory arrest. (03)

Michelle   *For 9 months Michelle appeared healthy. Then she developed uncontrollable seizures. At 3 years she was diagnosed as autistic with an uncontrollable seizure disorder. Michelle now lives in her own world and is fascinated by letters on cans and road signs. She can sit for hours obsessed with letters. Her father says she requires at least 4–6 weeks of constant contact with someone before communication can occur. She uses physical directions (i.e., pointing) and has some receptive language skills. If she is told to pull up her pants she will sometimes do so but will not dress on her own. (11)*

George   *George is 17 years old and has muscular dystrophy. He cannot move at will and requires total support—someone has to dress him in bed and even lift him to the commode. He communicates well with others and loves to play chess. George's family has adapted, by themselves, a stick with a toilet paper roll that he puts over the chess piece and then moves by moving his chair. George also loves to watch TV late and requires constant moving every hour, on a good night. He knows that his disorder is progressive and wants to be in control of the outcome. He sat in during most of the interview and interjected that these questions make him too much of a doctor's client. His mom says he has "too big a mouth" but never complains. (23)*

Pam   Pam is 2 years old and has Dandy-Walker syndrome, a genetic disorder. Because of this, she is classified as profoundly retarded. She also has bronchopulmonary dysplasia and hydrocephalus but no shunt—as yet, she has not had to have any fluid extracted. Physicians have told her parents that Pam has very little brain mass—most of her brain consists of a tumor. Still, she is a very active and alert child. Physicians are not sure how she is able to survive so alertly with such a small amount of brain tissue. (34)

Eva   Eva, age 7, has brain injury and is in a semicomatose state because of a loss of oxygen during a drowning incident. She is unable to speak or move any part of her body but will make faces and blink her eyes in order to communicate or in response to loud sounds. At times, Eva becomes very frustrated and will cry when feeling uncomfortable. (44)

Stanley   Stanley is 4 years old. Just before his third birthday he was struck by an automobile, which left him with severe learning and motor disabilities. Although he will need assistance for the rest of his life, he does not require 24-hour hands-on care. He does need to be watched and requires a lot of physical intervention. In addition, he is stubborn and impulsive—he gets on a topic and cannot get off it and refuses to do anything you ask. Stanley has no sense of where things end. For example, if he were climbing stairs, when the steps ended, he would continue climbing in mid-air. He is unaware of danger. (47)

Daily Routine

The level of day-to-day care that these families must provide for their children emerges when they describe their daily routines in the home. Here the emphasis is solely on the amount of support the child needs in the regular activities of daily life, not on any specialized care that may be required because of his or her condition. Concerning the degree of care or supervision the child needed during various periods of the day, 70%–80% of the respondents consistently reported giving "complete supervision."

Complete supervision is a very dry measure on a Likert scale. The reality in the lives of the families in the study group shows that complete supervision means they are engaged in the hard work of personal care for most of their waking day, as the summaries presented here indicate.

Gini   One-year-old Gini has osteogenesis imperfecta and will require diapers for the rest of her life. She is a fussy eater, only eating foods she likes and will not eat for new people, so achieving a proper nutritional balance is difficult. She is subject to bone fractures but loves bathing, so her mom has to be careful and always use two hands because Gini's bone structure also does not allow self-grooming. She has specially made clothes with Velcro so that none of her bones are damaged while she is being dressed. She is not very mobile and she cannot turn herself, so she *must be manually repositioned in her infant seat. She is starting to babble and will say "Hi" to her grandma on the telephone but is wary of new faces and will not speak to new people. Still, she likes company and will not play alone. She wakes every 2 hours and gets nasal gastric feeding at night. (02)*

***Morris**   Morris bounces out of bed quite early each morning, but knows he must be quiet and plays alone for about 2 minutes before he bursts out of his room. Because of his tracheotomy he can aspirate and must be closely watched. His mother, Lisset, gets up and monitors him at night and organizes his meals. Two months ago Morris was yelling and choked on rice, which knocked him unconscious. Lisset had to bag him and change his tracheotomy to remove a rice plug— a new law of quiet and calm was then set for mealtimes. Morris must also be watched in water. He loves bubbles and bubble baths but cannot blow bubbles because of his tracheotomy. (04)*

***Amy**   Amy is a 12-year-old with Rett syndrome. Amy's mom bathes her twice a day, in the morning and evening. Mom weighs 107 pounds and daughter weighs 60 pounds, making it difficult for Mom to lift her in and out of the tub. (12)*

***Jake**   Jake, age 4 with a variety of pulmonary problems, never sleeps through the night—he disconnects; he needs suctioning; his tubing has to be monitored; his lungs require half-hour checks. In all, he is checked 8 times each night! His parents report that no one period of the day is the most stressful because his care is constant. (20)*

Specialized Care

The parents' responses about the exact nature of their child's specialized care fell into the following three categories: 1) medication administration, 2) medical monitoring procedures, and 3) specialized treatments or procedures that are performed on a regular basis. These specialized activities are in addition to the regular supports the families provide to the children.

***Gini**   The experience of Gini, age 1, and her mom is very typical of the other families in this study: Gini is essentially immobile—she requires stimulation and many interventions. She can move her hands to her face but cannot roll from side to side. She has to be carried, along with her heart monitor, Delee traps, feeding tube, stethoscope, special seat, and adapted stroller. If she is not strapped she will slide down, so positioning is crucial. Positioning her is also very tricky because her bones fracture easily and must always be supported. In addition, Gini's respiratory status is compromised as a result of her chest deformities. A licensed practical nurse (LPN) is needed for 8 hours each day to monitor Gini's respiratory status and feedings, as well as to monitor her bones for fractures and problems. Gini gets nasal gastric feedings at night when she has not taken in enough food during the day. She is also on antibiotics, to prevent infection, and a cardiac monitor.*

When she first came home, her monitor was not set correctly and went off constantly. Now, everyone in the family can operate it and things are running more smoothly. Her mother takes Gini everywhere she goes. (02)

Loss of Privacy

Another factor that complicates the lives of these families is the loss of privacy they experience as a constant parade of outsiders traipses through their homes.

Pat   Pat is a baby with hydrocephalus. It has not yet been determined how much supervision he will require as he grows, but currently a registered nurse (RN) comes in three times per week to check Pat's vital signs. Pat's mother gives him oxygen twice a day and medicine three times a day. Pat has oxygen and suctioning machines (portable and plug-in). His mother carries along the portable oxygen machine when Pat goes out, although he doesn't always need it. (14)

Sissy   They used to have 24-hour nursing for 2-year-old Sissy, but the family got tired of the lack of privacy and are taking more primary caregiving responsibilities. (18)

Additional Primary Care Responsibilities

Taking more "primary care responsibilities" entails a major responsibility for these children.

Margie   At age 3, Margie is being weaned from the respirator but still needs constant monitoring for infection. Her care is rather straightforward, unless she is sick. Then, the need for monitoring her is much more stringent—requiring 12–24 hours of detailed and involved registered nursing treatment per day. Margie's condition can "turn sour" in a second and require full intervention for immediate treatment. For example, she is subject to bronchospasm and has underlying allergic reactions. She also requires constant medication—including Lasix-Digoxin, Alupent Inhalant, and Cromalyn, four times per day. All medications are as needed to gastrostomy, except inhalants, which only slightly elevate her heart rate. Her specialized medical equipment includes oxygen, tracheotomies, mist at night, suctioning equipment, portable oxygen, a compressor, a heart and oxygen monitor, an ambubag, an accumulator, suction catheters, a portable nebulizer, tracheotomy strings, a stethoscope, saline, sterile water, a 60-cc syringe, other syringes for epinephrine, and tracheotomy filters. Her mom is so used to it, these procedures do not phase her but the deliveries are not well coordinated and Mom has to scream a lot. (17)

Specialized Equipment and Medication

The extensive care needs of the children in this study group can be found in a mere inventory of the specialized equipment or medication in each home. The vast majority of families (87.5%) reported having such equipment and often cited extensive lists of equipment or medications. For families with children on oxygen, this "specialized equipment" included such things as running tubing throughout their home so the child would not be restricted in the house. Of families with equipment, such as Margie's, 32% reported problems with monitoring it and 42% reported problems in getting service.

One family's inventory of equipment and supplies gives some sense of what all of these families deal with:

- Suction machines—one battery operated, one stationary
- Two compressors
- Oxygen tank and backup
- Big battery and two battery packs
- Ventilators
- Syringes
- Tubing and saline
- Sterile water
- Delee—traps and filters
- Humidifier
- Saline ampules
- Peep valve, saturation machine wires, and tapes
- Vapor phase
- Cardiac monitor
- Gloves (03)

Another family's list of medication gives some meaning to the care needs of these children:

- Phenobarbital (30 mg)—one every morning, two tablets every evening
- Ditropan (5 mg)—twice a day (enhances muscle control in bladder)
- Vitamin C (500 mg)—one tablet twice a day
- Carafate (1 gm)—twice a day (ulcers)
- Prednisone (2.5 mg)—once a day (for swelling in head)
- Multivitamin—once a day
- Collace (100 mg)—twice a day
- Urinary tract prophylactic, Septra DS—one tablet every night for 10 days
- Ultraceph (500 mg)—one tablet at night for 10 days, then back to Septra
- Senecot laxative—prescribed as needed (PRN) for constipation
- Tylenol (325 mg)—two tablets PRN for headache
- Codeine—one tablet every 4 hours
- Motrin (40 mg)—PRN for arthritic pain

- Mylanta/Antigel (30 cc)—PRN every 2 hours (when she has blood in stool) (48)

Crises Requiring Extraordinary Intervention

A further measure of the specialized care needs of these children and a sense of the subtle tension these families live with is illustrated by the 31% of families who reported that, within the last month, their child had experienced some sort of crisis that required an extraordinary intervention. However, remember events that most people regard as life threatening are often routine to these parents; for example, some of their children need assistance with their breathing several times each day. When these families describe an "extraordinary event," it usually entails a major accident, illness, equipment breakdown, or other truly life-threatening event. The following event, which took place during the interview, is *not* considered by the parent to be extraordinary, but just one of the little day-to-day crises of life.

Sukari Four-year-old Sukari was choking on a thick piece of mucous that could not be suctioned. The nurse was not able to clear her properly, so Sukari's mom jumped in and turned the child carefully, giving several pats in the right spots. She then grabbed the suctioning tube, put it in the tracheotomy, and got the piece out within seconds. Sukari stopped coughing immediately and began breathing normally. Throughout the entire process, Sukari's mom remained calm and unphased. (32)

However, these families encounter situations that quite often do precipitate crises that are seen as very serious. As in the cases that follow:

Sally Sally is 6 years old and has brain damage. The respiratory therapists were trying to get Sally on a home ventilator. They tried switching from one system to another, which took 2 weeks to straighten out, as Sally was not responding well to the switch. (15)

Pam Pam, a 2-year-old with Dandy-Walker syndrome, was with her parents in their apartment one night at 11 P.M. when she began having a seizure. The seizure lasted for 3 minutes, and Pam turned blue and lost consciousness. Mom administered oxygen, which returned Pam to semiconsciousness and restored some of her color. Her parents then immediately rushed her to the hospital, where a doctor Pam's dad had called during the seizure was waiting in the emergency room. After an examination, the doctor reported that whenever the weather warms up and the temperature rises, Pam is going to have seizures. (34)

Jim Some high-tension crisis scenarios become a way of life for these families, as with Jim, a 4-year-old who is respiratory dependent with cardiac problems. Jim's condition can change so rapidly it is dangerous, as he can arrest in no time at all.

When this happens, Jim needs extraordinary interventions very quickly and without warning. He needs someone to monitor him and his equipment constantly—someone who knows his baseline status well enough to clinically evaluate him. This person also needs to be able to troubleshoot his pacer, ventilator, and various other equipment. (20)

Pete *Pete requires constant skilled care and continuous 24-hour monitoring. His clinical condition is highly unstable and influenced by weather, fatigue, activity, and so on. He has sudden episodes of severe wheezing and active distress and has required emergency resuscitative care on several occasions during the past year. He and his mother have dealt with the following:*

1. *A choking episode on solid food where Pete lost consciousness—the Heimlich maneuver resuscitated him within 1 minute, but on the advice of their doctor, his mother kept a bedside vigil all night, watching for a sudden onset of respiratory distress.*
2. *A severe midnight asthma attack with minimal BS cyanosis—although Pete responded to a 40% oxygen, Alupent mist IV aminophylline drip, the episode lasted throughout the night.*
3. *A milder asthmatic attack requiring additional medication or Alupent mist—one of which lasted 4 hours.*
4. *Viral gastroenteritis, along with a fever of 102 degrees, became an all-night affair, as it put Pete in danger of aspirating from vomiting while asleep.*

Impact on the Family

As for how the demands of home care affect the families' daily lives, the unique stories of each family best illustrate this.

As an example of the "opportunity cost" these families face, 73% of respondents said their child's disability had influenced where the family lived. Some families consciously chose to live in an area that they thought had good services. Some families chose to live in a neighborhood close to a hospital or clinic that would treat their child. Many families found the expenses associated with the care of their child either made it impossible for them to move into the kind of housing they wanted or forced them to move out of a home and live in an apartment or less expensive house.

Jim *As a result of 3-year-old Jim's complex needs, his mom had to quit work in order to be home at all times. Because of Jim's extra expenses, they live in a house with four generations of the family, which cuts down on costs. It also allows Jim's mom to care for her aging parents and grandmother, although she cannot spend nearly enough time with them as a result of Jim's health care needs. The family is at the mercy of 15 different service systems but cannot relocate as they are unable to fix or sell their house. (08)*

In addition to some of the obvious costs of care that have modified their lifestyles, a number of families speak of more subtle factors at work within their homes.

Margie *Margie's family's cultural difference made them acutely aware of the need to be looking over their shoulders at the various professionals, who have a different value system and were always "evaluating" them. Three-year-old Margie requires a lot of nursing as a result of her dependence on technology. However, this is putting undue stress on her family, as the home service is so invasive. With nurses and therapists around all the time, they can never seem to find enough family time. They feel like the nurses talk about them, like they talk about other cases, and would like more discreet nurses who could better understand what a "big Spanish family" is like. "We laugh, we shout, we hug—we are just a typical family," they say. (17)*

The families experience a global transformation, which usually begins at birth or shortly thereafter when the child's condition becomes evident. Many families tell similar stories of being overwhelmed by the whole experience—a feeling often intensified by the hospital environment and the demeanor of the professionals at birth. They also tell of professionals who dealt with them in a cold, detached manner, which only contributed to the confusion they were already feeling. Some professionals even blame parents for their child's condition, through subtle innuendos or direct accusations. The attitude of the immediate and extended family is often formed by this initial negative experience, although in many cases the family changes its attitude toward the child.

Gini *Gini's mom had a long and difficult labor and the baby's deformities were visible at birth. The obstetrician and pediatrician told Gini's mother that it was her fault because she had smoked while pregnant, although the condition is, in fact, a genetic defect that is inherited or simply a chance occurrence. Doctors kept Gini in the neonatal intensive care unit without showing her to her mom. After 2 days, the nurses came in to tell her that babies are taken care of very well at institutions, which is also easier on the parents. They then brought Gini in. At this point in the interview, Gini's mom could not even begin to describe her emotions or confusion. She thought about putting Gini up for adoption, at the hospital's suggestion. Then, Gini's father said that Gini's mom had to choose between him and Gini, so Gini's grandma went to visit a long-term care home. Her reaction to this place greatly affected Gini's mom's decision and she broke up with Gini's father as he still refused to get involved with the care of the child. Gini's mom then began to find out about the services available to home caregivers. (02)*

Many other families recount a similar story that strengthened or actually formed their resolve to take their child home.

Steve When Steve, a 5-year-old with neurofibromitosis, was in the hospital, he required ventilator assistance 24 hours each day—a condition his parents did not want to bring into the home. They were overwhelmed by the tracheotomy, tube feeding, and ventilator dependency they had witnessed this past year while their son was in the hospital. A social worker and a nurse both suggested they institutionalize the child at Miller Memorial Hospital, a local long-term care facility. His parents were thinking about placing him in Miller Memorial until he could breathe on his own. On SKIP's advice, they visited the hospital before making their final decision. Immediately following their visit, they called the hospital saying under no circumstances would they place their son in such an environment. They were shocked by the lack of stimulation and care children there received and felt it would be irreparably harmful to their son. Instead, they chose to take him home, despite the ventilator. Very shortly after, the hospital was able to wean him off the ventilator, so he only required it during the night or while sleeping. His parents still cannot believe that professionals would recommend a place like Miller Memorial Hospital for their son. Regardless of the ventilator, he remains an active, alert child who needs a healthy, caring, and stimulating environment. (07)

After families recover from their initial shock and decide to care for the child at home, most of them report that they were still totally unprepared for the radical changes that follow. Jim's family provided a detailed inventory of physical, social, and psychological changes that are associated with the care of their child.

Jim We have borne all expenses and have provided most of the specialized supplies and equipment needed ourselves. We have had to purchase the following: a van, small eating trays, stands, paper towels, peroxide, food, telephone bills, travel expenses to Chicago, electricity, extra telephones, and intercoms. In addition, our lifestyle has had to be drastically altered. We have run tubes in the walls for oxygen, cleared closet space for supplies, and measured oxygen daily. We have no flexibility as far as coming and going, and we seldom entertain—there is no privacy to be had with home care nursing services. (20)

His father emphasized how caregiving had affected the other children in the family, which was a special area of concern in every family in which the child with special care needs had siblings.

Jim Jim's dad says he can write a book on all the changes Jim's dependence on a ventilator has brought to their lives. They have lost all flexibility and a sense of family because they can no longer simply get in the van and go—there is no *spontaneity in their lives. Jim's older brother did not have typical third and fourth years of childhood, as he spent most of that time in the hospital with his baby brother. As a result, he is very sensitive and withdrawn, often wanting to stay home and help take care of Jim. The family is trying to compensate, but the brother is still too young to fully comprehend Jim's disability. He is, however, starting to learn the names of certain equipment and can help in a pinch.*

Jim's mom has had to drop out of school and cannot work now, as she is needed at home; yet, she cannot even consider having another baby. As for home, the entire family is moving back to the city to be closer to the hospital, family, friends, and support.

Now that Jim is at home, though, he is happier and well adjusted, striving toward being a typical kid. Jim's brother loves him and is glad he is home, while Jim's mother feels like the entire experience has made her a stronger person and also strengthened her marriage. It has prioritized things, and their lives are now better defined. Despite the sacrifices, they report, "Jim is a joy." (20)

This extensive list of disabilities, complex care needs, daily crises, effects on the family lifestyle, and other factors related to providing home care are powerful data. No family exposed to these forces can avoid profound stress and major changes. Yet, caring for a child at home does reap positive results, as well. This positive impact often comes through in the parents' stories.

The majority of families speak of the enormous improvement in their child's physical and psychological condition once he or she comes home as the most tangible affirmation of their decision to provide care at home. This is accompanied by an emerging awareness of their own capacity and competence as parents. Some less concrete outcomes of home care include getting to know the child as a person, seeing him or her as a contributing member of the family, experiencing a sense of togetherness and a growing sense of personal strength, the reordering of life's priorities, and siblings learning to be caring people, among other factors.

One family reported that their decision to care for their daughter at home finally allowed them to accept her as their daughter.

Sissy *Sissy's mom and dad felt enormous stress as a result of her tracheal mylaseasin. As they look back, they realize they once considered Sissy only as an extension of her equipment. Last winter their 24-hour nursing assistance was cut back, obliging them to provide the care. At first, Sissy's mom thought she would have a nervous breakdown, but even though she was exhausted and nervous, she soon realized that she could meet the care demands and started bonding with Sissy for the first time. Although a smoother transition to fewer hours of nursing would have been better, she survived and feels good about the situation. Sissy's mom feels that this is a very bad way to learn a good lesson. Now, even though the financing* *problems have been resolved, her mom schedules less nursing so she can spend more one-to-one time with Sissy. (18)*

As the following excerpts from the interview with Pete's adoptive mother testify, this need to see the child as a child—a unique, growing human being—may be one positive outcome that all of these parents experience, as it seems that it is this awareness that gives the families the strength to endure all they must confront.

Pete's Mom   *"Most stress and dissatisfaction come from outside sources. Pete has been a joy, despite his problems, and I have never regretted my decision to adopt him. I have learned and am still learning from him everyday, both as a professional and as a mother. Pete's excitement about life and learning, despite his severe problems and his past, is remarkable. His achievements—emotionally, academically, and artistically—over the past 3 years are amazing, considering that he was hospitalized in the intensive care unit (ICU) for 4½ years. Best of all, Pete is a funny, bright, loving child who gets into lots of mischief to keep me busy, but who constantly makes me laugh, often at myself. Pete has enriched our family in a way that no one else could, and each of us has learned something about ourselves through him. Not one of us would trade a single hour with Pete for a winning lottery ticket. We're all very proud of him. Pete is the most loved member of his immediate and his extended family." (38)*

Many of the parents, particularly the mothers, speak of the whole experience of fighting for their child as totally reordering their value system and giving them a very different perspective on their own competence as well as both self-awareness and social awareness.

Charlene   *Charlene's mom has saved her life. Her mom also feels that Charlene, age 12, has saved her life and put things in order. Charlene has made her mom realize just what life means. Charlene has taught her mom about the practical application of health care. Charlene's mom has learned patience, how to be frugal, how to keep a budget, self-reliance, independence, and survival. (21)*

John   *Five-year-old John has taught his mother the beauty of the power of each human life. He has made her a more socially conscious person, spurring her to help others and sharpening her compassion for all people with disabilities and advocacy efforts, as none of us is without a disability. John's mom now has the best sense of self-worth of her entire life, as John has introduced her to God and helped her understand unconditional love. He enunciates the condition of U.S. society. (25)*

Although the families clearly understand the extensive costs associated with their decision to care for their children at home, they are, as a group, also very clear on the dividends they are accruing.

Informal Supports

Family support literature increasingly emphasizes the need for support services to be community based and built on the already-existing resources of the family and the community. With this in mind, it is important to get some measure of how this informal system supported the families in the study group.

Unfortunately, in many cases, the primary caregiver told of instances in which other family members were unable to accept the child with special needs or were resistant to the idea of home care. In several cases, this led to divorce; however, the informants indicated that they felt the relationship was already headed in that direction and the added pressures associated with the child's needs only hastened the inevitable. In most cases the responses were very short and without much elaboration.

Mary's Family "*Husband and father pulled away. The rest of the family was shocked but relatively supportive. Mom's cousin is helping with direct care. Still, Mom is tired of explaining everything and now avoids the subject. She stays in contact, but without details.*" (36)

While almost every family has at least one tale of callousness, neglect, obfuscation, or arrogance on the part of professionals, many also tell of long-term relationships where the professional went far beyond the limits of his or her job description. Families identify these professionals as some of the people they can depend on as "informal" supports.

Ishtara's Physician "*Our physician is excellent and goes beyond the call of duty. I had an emergency on her wedding day. Although she was dressed and ready to go down the aisle, she got on the phone and made sure that everything was taken care of for Ishtara.*" (40)

Concerning the rather intangible psychological sense of community, the members of the study group did not feel particularly well connected to their communities and neighborhoods. In general, the interviewees indicated that this sense of isolation can be at least partially attributed to their intense involvement in the daily care of their child. However, a number of families cited specific instances in which they felt the active resistance of their neighbors to accepting their child.

Jose's Community   When a woman on the street chastised her for keeping her son in a carriage, Jose's mom was reminded that people have to be educated about the needs of people with disabilities. She believes that such children should not be institutionalized, and that no one has a right to say that a child born with a disability should be automatically put away. She also feels that children have the right to be with their families. *(13)*

Margie's Community   Margie's parents once took her to the public pool and the community "went crazy," so they are "nervous" to try that again. They say, "We can be happy at home, so why try that again?" *(17)*

For the most part, the families' interaction with the community is dominated by a sense of being "the outsider." Linked to the extensive demands that are associated with the care of their children, it is little wonder that the parents are not more aggressive in trying to connect with their communities.

Pam   Pam's mom is Hispanic and has a child with a disability—she doesn't really feel accepted. She has a couple of neighbors who will come over at times, even with gifts, but still feels uncomfortable and out of place. She lived there for 3 years before people acknowledged her existence. It would be hard for her to even take Pam across the street to the park because of the way people would stare at her and Pam, sometimes making ignorant remarks. Pam's mom would rather not go to the park, than have to listen to those comments. *(34)*

Star   "I can't get involved in the community because I must be home with Star, unless I get someone to help me watch over her. But the community doesn't understand Star, they just look at her." *(42)*

Several families have tried to assist their child to develop some relationships beyond the family. Unfortunately, most of these efforts have not been particularly successful.

John's Friends   John and his family live in a sparsely populated area, where access is difficult. Occasionally his sister brings friends home from school and sometimes his mom will invite school friends for a party. However, the community they live in is not too accepting. Last year, the superintendent cancelled a party in John's home at the last moment. The Arc organizes recreation only for children with mild mental retardation and has not done anything for children with more involved conditions. *(22)*

Paying the Bills

The majority of the families (69%) are covered by Medicaid because most of the significant expenses associated with the needs of their child are not covered by many traditional insurance carriers. Families consistently report major concerns about retaining eligibility for the program, which also contributes to the degree to which the family's lifestyle is determined by the care needs of their child. They are not just affected by the demands and the out-of-pocket costs of care, but must also keep the family income at a certain level so they do not become ineligible for Medicaid coverage.

Yet, even with extensive insurance coverage, many families experience additional major household expenditures that increase the financial pressure they feel.

Hank   Hank's family has had to cover many costs associated with his quadriplegia. As he is too heavy to carry but unable to walk on his own, the family has installed a chair lift on the stairs. They must supply him with diapers, formula, kangaroo pumps, tubes, gauges, and a van, which was an added cost of $21,500. (01)

Ryan   Ryan's sleep apnea requires her room to be on a separate box. In order for her family to accommodate her, they had to install a new driveway (a $5,000 expenditure) and electrical wiring (a $500 expenditure). In addition, they must pay her electric bill, gas bill, and telephone bill—even when nurses make long-distance calls. (03)

John   John is 7 years old and has paraplegia and is "dead weight" for his mom who is only 5 feet tall. He can only be made mobile with the assistance of one to two adults using a crane system, as he cannot turn from stomach to back. John is getting too big for his current system, but the family has to build on to their house to accommodate a larger system. (22)

For some families, expenses of the type listed above appear to be a luxury because of their lack of medical insurance coverage. For these families, meeting basic medical costs pushes them to the fiscal limits.

Star   Star has no Medicaid or SSI coverage, so her mom must buy her the following supplies:

Pampers—$90 per case
Nutrmegin milk—$16 per can, two cans per week
Bibs, towels, baby powder, and constant changes of clothing—$300 per season
Camp—$400 (Star's mother was unable to get a stipend for this)

In addition, all medical appointments must be paid for, which entails even more costs:

Appointments—$21 per visit
Transportation to the doctor's office—$16 per visit
Neurologist—$21 per visit
Dental—$30 per visit

Star has outgrown her braces and desperately needs new ones, as her heels are bleeding. But, they would cost $2,000, and there is no money for them. (42)

A major problem for many families is the lack of complete information on insurance coverage.

Insurance   One child's parents were sent out to a research center that specializes in their child's rare disorder without ever being told that they would have to cover certain costs or that insurance would not cover certain research needs. They then began receiving bills that totaled $7,000. No one would offer them any assistance. By putting bills through insurance agencies again and again, half of the bills have been covered. The parents are awaiting word from the insurance company as to who will be covering the rest. (43)

A universal issue is the drawn-out payment process for home care providers. Almost every family in the study group told of problems in obtaining or retaining services simply because the providers must wait so long to be paid.

Payments for Home Service   All insurers have delayed payments, and usually the enrollment process is a mess and poorly defined. Outstanding bills mean interrupted nursing services, because many nurses leave if they must wait too long for their payments. In addition, nurses notes must be sent first to Medicaid and then to the health care plan. Parents must photocopy (at their expense) two sets of notes to submit to the health care plan, even though the allowed financial amounts are known. (31)

When this slow payment and lack of information is further complicated by the bureaucratic maze that seems to confront these families, parents can find themselves without services, even those who have followed the system.

Bureaucratic Stipulations   The major medical is slow to reimburse, but the nurses won't work for Medicaid either because it takes them too long to get paid. "In our community, St. Joseph's is the service coordinator. When Billy was hos-

pitalized for 2 weeks in the winter, St. Joseph's told us that home care services can only be reimbursed through BC/BS (a New York State–licensed home care provider) if they are contacted upon discharge." The day of his discharge, Billy's mom called St. Joseph's to let them know that Billy was home; they acknowledged this and took a message. Billy's mom then received a $15,000 home care services bill. When Mom called St. Joseph's to inquire about the billing, she was told again that BC/BS could not be billed for services (equipment and supplies) unless St. Joseph's was informed about Billy being home. She told St. Joseph's that she had called, but they didn't believe her, so she called BC/BS for help. BC/BS said that they had to be notified within 24 hours of discharge to approve payment but would assist if St. Joseph's wrote them a letter describing the "mitigating circumstances." Billy's mom called St. Joseph's and asked them to write a letter to this effect but they refused—she really feels that they do not care. (05)

For some families stretched way beyond their financial means, mere survival demands that they develop expertise in "gaming" the system.

"Gaming" the System   *"All of our savings were gone. We were forced to hide money; I worked as a waitress off the books to make ends meet, even though I am an RN—you just don't make it on SSI and food stamps. We also had a lot of difficulty with doctors. They have refused services because my child has Medicaid. We have been reduced to tricking doctors to get the services, then later telling them they will be paid through Medicaid; otherwise they would not help us." (48)*

It is surprising that these parents are not more cynical, particularly in their dealings with the Medicaid system. They are exposed daily to arbitrary, apparently capricious decisions, accompanied by seemingly irrational regulation.

Eva   *Medicaid would only approve one box of Pampers per month, so Eva's mom had to buy the rest at $55 per box. (44)*

Stanley   *Stanley's dad says that the way reimbursements are handled is weird. For example, Pampers are less expensive than Depend adult diapers, but Medicaid will approve the Depend diapers instead of the Pampers. (47)*

One of the most frustrating experiences for these families is acquiring the needed support. Professionals and insurers routinely ignore parents' assessments of the supports that are needed to adequately care for their children.

Morris   Four-year-old Morris needs to be watched constantly, because if he goes to sleep he will arrest. His mom, Lisset, has been asking for an adaptive stroller for him for almost a year now so that she can transport his ventilator. She wants the family to be more mobile, as they now have to take a crash bag along whenever they go out. So far, nothing has happened. (04)

Jose   Medicaid will only cover certain things, not necessarily what the doctor recommends or what Jose's mom feels is necessary. For example, a walker is desired, but the physician will not prescribe it; suction is used to remove seizure-causing mucous from his lungs, but the physician will not prescribe a machine for their home either. (13)

These families soon find that services and benefits coordinators are also misinformed about necessary coverage and basic procedures. This experience is so universal and recurs so frequently among these parents that often they begin to see an organized threat to the welfare of their child and family.

Jim   Jim's family is about to experience insurance burnout because of the high rates they pay. They were never informed of lower-cost services and were misinformed about the services they were eligible for. They have also had to do most of the paperwork themselves. After the county service coordinator tried to force the family to pay for additional expenses, the service coordination project intervened and helped negotiate a solution by which the insurers take care of the costs. On several other occasions the state has misinformed them and tried to take away or scale back their services. This has made the family suspicious of the state. (08)

Insurers seem to affirm these suspicions, as families sometimes see themselves as targeted for loss of benefits after their costs have exceeded some apparently predetermined ceiling of acceptable risk.

Brian   Brian's insurance company is giving his family problems, and their coverage is pending review. Brian's father was laid off from work for 2 months and the insurance company is using this and the baby's preexisting conditions as possible reasons for denying their claims. (10)

Sissy   Sissy's dad was covered with unlimited insurance through the workplace; even major medical was covered with no cap. He felt, from an insurance perspective, that all of the bases were covered. Recently, he was told that the employer would become self-insured and there would be new restrictions placed on services; nursing would be capped at $50,000 per year per client and co-payments would be tripled. Under state law this is not legal. The primary carrier must remain *intact for a minimum of 365 days on preexisting conditions until the new insurer can assume the case.*

The family was devastated. They took their story to the newspaper. They had to devote 200 hours of advocacy work to ensure that the insurer would comply with the state regulations. Because the care supports were withdrawn due to lack of funds, Sissy also had to spend 30 days in the hospital to meet the model waiver requirements so that the nursing hours could be paid for while the insurance battles were being decided. The family also had to have an outside attorney because Sissy's dad was getting a lot of pressure from the union that he felt was based on Sissy's medical cost to the Welfare Fund. He felt like his job would be in danger if he did not get legal advice, as his employers have tried to change his work schedule on several occasions. (18)

Even when the family is able to negotiate some form of coverage that seems to adequately meet their needs, they often find that it is a real battle to ensure that cost control does not take priority over quality care.

__Jim__   Getting nursing for 4-year-old Jim has always been very difficult because the insurance company obligated the family to use their home care team, through an exception to policy. This team is a subsidiary of BC/BS and run out of the hospital. The family feels that these burgeoning agencies represent a conflict of interest because the payer is the manager, the monitor, and the provider. This was felt most acutely when they were trying to negotiate direct insurance payment for the nurses. The family wanted to hire the nurses directly to avoid the agency overhead, but the insurer refused. After an unskilled nurse who was caring for Jim almost caused him irreparable damage, the family threatened to start legal action. As a result, the rates were slightly increased and only RNs are on the case, but the shifts are rarely filled. The family has to put a great deal into training new nurses, and the turnover is high. (20)

Services to the Child

Many of the families reported extremely positive interactions with individual therapists and physicians who have known them and their children for a long time. These providers have acted as major sources of support and advocates within the system, developing a real responsiveness to the unique characteristics of these families and attempting to provide truly individualized family-centered services.

__Pete__   Pete's condition is often too unstable to transport him safely by car, but he responds well to treatment and has not required hospitalization since discharge. Pete's pediatrician is very sensitive to his fear of hospitals and often makes house calls for hospital, doctor's office, or outpatient clinic appointments. Pete's pediatri-

cian sees him at home for everything but regular well-child care, which may be because the pediatrician has been emotionally involved with Pete since Pete was 6 months old, also providing services free of charge. After spending 4½ years in a pediatric ICU, Pete's biggest fear is having to return to the hospital; clinic and dental visits cause sleep and behavioral changes in him for weeks afterward. (38)

Unfortunately these good stories are far outweighed by instances of "detached" professional behavior or, worse, professional providers who, in the parents' perception, are callous.

Ryan *Ryan's doctor is still not up front with the family. Her mom feels that he does not respond to her, whereas if Ryan's dad gets involved, they get the answers they need. (03)*

Fatima *Fatima's family has had problems with equipment failure; the ventilator stopped working, and no nurses were there to take care of the problem until Fatima's dad noticed the situation. Often the nurses also fail to change the baby, leaving her wet and unattended. (09)*

Sally *Sally's care has been inconsistent. There is a lack of communication between her mom and the staff. There has been improper supervision and nonobservation; Sally is constantly dirty and her mom cleans her all the time. Sally's mom feels frustrated by dealing with these issues on a daily basis. (15)*

Furthermore, many parents recount incidents in which the "treatment plan" seemed misinformed and their understanding of the child ignored.

Barbara *Barbara has cystic fibrosis and an eating disorder, but she is decanulated and now weaned from the ventilator. During her prolonged hospitalization, Barbara was force-fed. Her parents objected and tried to fight this method, but were told that she could not go home unless they got a certain amount of calories into her per day. Barbara vomited at every meal; mealtime was a horror. Now, Barbara is doing better with food intake, but it will take a while to get over the "punishment of what the doctors prescribed." (19)*

Supporting the Family

The types of supports usually identified as components of a comprehensive system of family supports (Bradley, Knoll, & Agosta, 1992; Knoll et al., 1990; Taylor, Knoll, Lehr, & Walker, 1989) were rarely fully used by the families in this study. The majority (62%) of families indicated the pilot service coordination project as their sole source of support. The next most commonly used support service was membership in traditional parent advocacy organizations, such as The Arc, the Autism Society of America, and so forth (e.g., parent network, newsletter, parent instruction, parent advocacy/ training).

The experience and concerns articulated by many of these families indicate that although the system has, to a certain extent, been able to respond to some of the children's highly specialized needs, it has not addressed some basic supports that are currently available to families of less seriously involved children.

Hank's Mom   *"We need respite—time when Mom and Dad can be together to rest, relax, and go out. Grandparents used to babysit, but my son's care needs are becoming more intense and he has grown too large for them to move him." (01)*

The SKIP Pilot Project

As far as many of the families are concerned, the only "service" they have received that can appropriately be called "family support" has been their involvement with the SKIP pilot project. Many of the other organizations and professionals involved in their lives have approached families either as the all-knowing professional or as the fraud investigator, out to ensure that the families do not defraud the state, the insurance company, or the provider. Only in their interactions with SKIP did the families consistently feel like they were treated as equal partners, collaborating with professionals to serve the best interests of their children. SKIP helped them to work through the maze of information about support services and payment mechanisms, in an effort to get the child and the family the supports they needed. This relationship between the SKIP project and the families outlines the characteristics that make a truly family-centered approach to providing support.

From the interviews, it is clear that some of the families would not have been able to maintain their children at home without SKIP. In other instances, SKIP has made the difference in obtaining services, receiving insurance coverage, ensuring services met minimal standards of quality, and preventing vendors from overcharging. In addition, all of this was achieved in a supportive atmosphere, which is so different from the families' experience with the majority of "service coordinators" and "discharge planners."

Lucy   *Lucy's family has a service coordinator and a discharge planner, yet the only organization that responds to their needs is SKIP. Without SKIP, they would never have known how to get her home—SKIP is the only group that seems to care if Lucy lives at home. Her mom and dad do not understand why SKIP is doing all of the tracking of the discharge plan when they are supposed to have service coordination through the care-at-home (model waiver) program, but these people have lost two sets of eligibility papers. The hospital is putting a lot of pressure on the family to place Lucy because they want the bed. Lucy's mom and dad feel like they have four providers: the hospital, their service coordinator, equipment suppliers, and SKIP; only SKIP converses with all of the others. (27)*

Perhaps one of pilot project's greatest strengths is its independence. It is able to look to the best interest of the child and family, is knowledgeable about the system, and is willing to do the legwork needed to build a case for private insurers or state funders. In this regard, it captures the essence of the ideal of independent service brokerage.

Jim *Jim's family first contacted SKIP many years ago because they wanted to bring their son home and reunite their family. He had been in the hospital for 6 months. Although the hospital was in favor of discharging Jim, they had no success in actually doing so. SKIP finally stepped in and negotiated an exception to the family's insurance policy that allowed for the hospital-based dollars to be applied to home care. It was underwritten by Blue Cross and Blue Shield, but SKIP collected all of the data. Jim's mom feels that if the pressure to bring Jim home had not come from the outside, Jim would still be in the hospital. (20)*

SKIP's independence has enabled it to monitor many of the other caregiving professionals involved in the lives of these families and ensure they do not violate any basic rights.

Landon *Landon's mom feels that SKIP monitored Landon's discharge planning process and aborted unnecessary screw-ups, omissions, and misinformation. SKIP also got the family's insurance reinstated because the insurer did not present the family with the option to self-carry per COBRA and violated the law. His mom feels that only SKIP would have assisted them with an issue like this. (31)*

Often, SKIP affirms parents' instincts, particularly when they encounter nonresponsive professionals. This level of support, when everyone else seems to oppose them, may be the single most valuable contribution SKIP makes to these families.

Ryan *Ryan's family has had many fights with her doctor. When the family wanted to transfer Ryan home, the doctor could not assure them that he would maintain the same level of coverage. Ryan's mom was hysterical and called nurses who assured her that Ryan would be safe. Still, she was afraid to make waves because she felt as if her daughter were being held hostage. In addition, the family was never told about any entitlement programs. The hospital made many service provider decisions without consulting the family. They linked the family to the most expensive providers and their insurance was about to reach the annual cap. The family decided to direct the hiring and the agency sued them. Usually, when Ryan's mom presses doctors for answers, they tell her to seek counseling. SKIP gets her questions answered and gives her peace of mind, knowing she is asking the right questions. (03)*

SKIP's central credo establishes a system of working with parents by providing information, support, and critical feedback, rather than trying to manage them.

Morris   Morris's mom likes to be independent and appreciates that her case advocate helps her to "run" things and does not try to "social work" her. She likes to do her own thing and is glad that SKIP supports those efforts. She feels more in control that way. She says that SKIP is very reasonable when she has no place to turn and calls on weekends. And although SKIP does not always agree with her expectations of providers, it always has a nice way of letting her know. She says that the most important thing is that SKIP is on her side, and even though she was skeptical and unsure because it is a new organization, it has always given her very accurate information. (04)

The Families' View of the Future

Hank's Family   Don't look at the long-term picture—live day by day. (01)

The future is a difficult issue for many of these families. The major traumas they have endured thus far—the child's disability, the constant battle to obtain support services, the financial strains, the re-ordering of their social world, and especially the day-after-day care needs of their children—have led them to adopt a perspective that takes life one day at a time.

This "live-for-today" attitude, which is consistently reported throughout the interviews, is further reinforced by the uncertain future all of these families face. First, the parents of children with degenerative or terminal conditions, while not denying this reality, consciously choose not to dwell on it and devote their physical and psychological energy to making the most of the present moment.

Pat's Mom   Pat's mom wants to make the rest of Pat's life as happy as possible. She recently saw a 12-year-old boy with the same disease as Pat (hydrocephalus), which gave her hope that Pat will live for a long time, especially considering the fact that she was told in the beginning that Pat would be "a vegetable" all his life. (14)

Second, families of children who will need lifelong supports also share this attitude. In these cases, not thinking about the future is one way the parents can conserve their energies for the battles yet to be fought.

George's Mom   *George's mom says, "Stop punishing parents for keeping their children at home." She feels like she has been told at least 80 times that all of this would be less stressful if she would just place George in an institution. His mom is drained, but parents have to fight because others do not. "Since my husband was in the hospital 3 years ago, not a day goes by that I don't wonder what would happen to George if anything happened to my husband. This must make us the smallest minority in the world: Parents who think, 'Please God, let him go before us.' " (23)*

Charlene's Mom   *"I am terrified. She deserves comfort and security. She deserves to learn and live in a supportive environment, but all of this depends on income. Utopia does not exist, but even the simple practical things I want for her do not exist. There is a constant battle to get the smallest things. How to face puberty? How can we find skilled people who really care? Where is a medical system that can truly be responsive? Are there alternatives to the lousy group homes or the hellholes of institutions? There is a natural phenomenon of a child leaving the nest—but what I've seen are dumping grounds. This is the most neglected minority group known to man. The entire issue raises complex moral questions. The lack of support makes a parent weigh the value of their child's life and that is so fundamentally wrong." (21)*

Pete's Mother   *Pete's mother laments the fact that what she regards as an acceptable future for Pete demands some fundamental changes in society's basic attitudes toward people with significant disabilities, specifically the artificial limits our culture places on the ability of these people to achieve their full potential. She says, "I can't bear to think about the future. If Pete did not have a disability, his prospects would be wonderful. Pete is a great kid; he works hard and is talented as an artist, and academically. Pete scored second in a class of 30 normal kids on a standardized achievement test; his scores were in the 97th–99th percentile in all areas at the end of his first grade. His aspirations are tremendous. He will undoubtedly have much to contribute to society, if he ever gets the chance. Realistically, I doubt that Pete will get the chance in our present society. If he does, what will it cost him in lost Medicaid coverage? Will he be able to pursue a career?*

One of my chief sources of stress is what will happen to Pete when I am gone. If money or property is left to Pete he will probably lose Medicaid coverage. Then what? Who will advocate for him and protect him? Who will ensure that he is cared for? Is this bright, funny, loving little boy doomed to live on welfare? Or will he choose not to continue living at all when he finally realizes that his hard work and achievements are all for naught? I hope that by the time Pete reaches adulthood, our society will provide him with other choices—like being a contributing, functioning member of the community who can use his skills to remain self-sufficient without losing medical services and care he needs.

It is traditional in our country for parents to work hard in an effort to help their children attain a better position in life. Most parents promote the best opportunities for growth and learning in an effort to help their children develop. When parents die their children are usually left with the benefits of their parents' hard work. Why is a child with a disability not entitled to this? Why must he choose between the health care he needs to survive and a decent home to live in or the self-esteem that comes from self-sufficiency and earning a living at a challenging job that allows him to use his exceptional talents?" (38)

Battles on the Frontier of Social Change

Consistently, parents report that the care of the child with a disability is worthwhile. Most parents don't see the demands of care as a "burden," but simply part of being a parent and loving a child. What they consistently identify as their burden is the continual struggles they must go through to get the supports they need to appropriately care for their child.

George's Parents   George's parents told the interviewer, "The system can really wear you down, even if you are used to being the pioneer." This sense of frustration can become intensified, if the battles continue even after years of effort, particularly as the family is confronted with a progressive degenerative disorder, like George's muscular dystrophy. George's mom told the interviewer, "You know, I am so tired of being a pioneer. I fought for accessible school buses; we got George into the accelerated classrooms; we were in court for the first 5 years [after diagnosis] more than we were at home. I just want to follow for now because my son is failing and I want this time to be special and uncomplicated." His mom feels that George will need nursing eventually, so, for now, she wants quiet and calm time. (23)

Jim's Mom   "I do not understand why they fight us tooth and nail for every little thing but would not ask us a single question if we left and abandoned him to an institution. Our newest battle is the school system. We are now in court, at great expense to our family, so that Jim can get the nursing he needs at school. I am a little tired of being a pioneer. We are fighting like this to get him into Board of Cooperative Education Services—can you imagine what it is going to be like to get him into elementary school? His dad sits on a lot of statewide coalitions and even with his visibility things are a struggle." Both parents are tired and would love to go back to just being a family. (20)

Parents also routinely experience frustration and, in many cases, anger over the incredible lengths they have had to go to in order to get even minimal support and assistance in their efforts to care for their child at home. Also disturbing is the arbitrary manner in which the state, health care providers, local education authorities, insurance companies, and home care providers deal with these families. Again and again, the families report being treated as if they were trying to steal something from these individuals and agencies that are supposedly there to offer assistance to them.

The inadequacy of professional and staff preparation is underscored by the frequency with which families encounter providers who are completely out of touch with the idea of community-based, family-centered care.

Gini's Mom   *Gini's mom was not completely trained in the hospital. She went home with a service provider (the hospital-based home health provider) who made many initial promises as their service coordinator. This person did not understand community-based care but was full of opinions, and seemingly more interested in making Gini's mom compliant than providing support. She did not know how to obtain many of the necessary nursing services for Gini and so took a great deal of additional time to arrange the services. When the family decided to bring Gini home, they were discouraged at every turn. One social worker even went so far as trying to have the child taken by the Bureau of Child Welfare and placed. (02)*

This lack of support is often accompanied by a clearly stated judgment that the family's decision to take the child home is not valued. Indeed, some families find themselves abused in the name of service planning.

Eva's Mom   *"Discharge planning for Eva was a mad house—all the equipment, everything was arriving at the same time as Eva did and we didn't know what to do. Everything was chaos. Two nurses came home with the child. Although later I would have to wait for nurses, and many times they wouldn't arrive at all. The social worker who was supposed to have planned everything had not. She would make me cry by saying things like 'Benefits would be denied' or 'You have no right to welfare.' The discharge planner in the hospital social service department told me that I would never be able to take my child home, that I wouldn't be able to care for her at home. She did a terrible job—any confidential information I gave, she would write down in her book and then later expose it. I trusted her because she was the social worker and she treated me badly and disrespected me by writing the personal things I would tell her." (44)*

George's Parents   *George's mom told the staff, "It isn't the child or young person that makes you crazy; it is the system." She says that all she needs is an extra set of hands so that George's dad could go to work and she could get a break and does not understand why just a little support is so hard to come by. She feels that simply caring for a child with a progressive illness is enough stress and wants to understand why it is further complicated. She also doesn't understand why the social workers at the hospital for the past 17 years have not connected her with some kind of supports.*

Once, when the paperwork for billing had to be completed and sent back to the insurer by the social worker at the university clinic to start payment for the home health care agency, this process was so delayed that the family almost lost their services.

George's dad does not understand why the service coordination project had to intervene to get these issues resolved: "Why are our services always dependent on the good will of a particular social worker when the family assumes they are doing their job?" He wants to understand why you have to monitor people who are supposed to be helping you. (23)

This lack of consistency and the apparently arbitrary actions of multiple public and private professionals intensifies the families' feelings of living on the fringe. They must deal with the ever-present fear that someone will do something to topple their carefully constructed support system, which they all realize is little more than a house of cards. This tension effectively subverts one of the basic principles of family supports: to enable a family to be a family, where parents can devote their principal energies to parenting.

Landon's Parents *Landon's parents would like to have time as a family, as well as quiet time alone just as husband and wife. They would like to be able to take the kids to grandma's and sleep late once in a while, or to get away on weekends and leave the children home. Landon's mom is pregnant and would like some time to herself, but she won't do it. She is convinced that if she leaves it up to the "system," something dreadful will happen. She says she also doesn't understand the role of all the state players who come to her home, but every time they make a visit, some of her services are in danger of being cut. (31)*

The families also tell of the professional attitude that consistently assumes incompetence on the part of the parents and family. Usually this attitude changes only because the parents' awareness showed the professionals some area in which they had made a mistake. The experience of Billy's mother captures this quite well.

Billy's Mom *Initially, the hospital fought Billy's mom over taking him home, mistaking her easygoing and relaxed manner for an attitude of noncaring. They thought she was not up to the challenge, an opinion that took a long time to change. The turnabout came when the staff made a serious judgment mistake. His mom knew that Billy was getting septic, but the staff dismissed her and told her she was overreacting—she should let them "make those calls" and stick to being a mom. As a result, they almost lost Billy to an infection. After this, things changed dramatically for the better. The staff have all told his mom they now have new respect* *for parents and their capacity to take care of their kids. And Billy is at home and thriving. (05)*

One of the basic forces driving this "nonsystem" of home care is the principle of the squeaky wheel. In other words, if parents are vocal, well informed, and politically well connected, then eventually they will get some response from the programs that are supposedly there to assist them, while other families will not get what should be available to them because they do not have the knowledge, strength, or connection to endure. Furthermore, the fact that these services are driven by an essentially adversarial process means that even the "empowered" family cannot take the pressure off the system. This, of course, puts them under tremendous psychological pressure, which is itself a very effective strategy for controlling the demand for services. John's mother confirms the experience of many families:

John's Mom   *John's mom has been asking for help since his birth. She is really her own best advocate, finding out about programs and going for them. And, although she is tired, she will be inexhaustible where John is concerned. "You are a parent who should have no problems because you know so much and are so strong," a social worker once told her. His mom says, "I would rather see a little action than hear that nonsense." During one interminable wait for supports, she had her husband call the county government agency to say she was "cracking up and needed help." Their response was, "We can put him on the waiting list, which extends over 2 years for out-of-home placement." She is furious and says, "I can't even go crazy because they simply do not care." His mom also says the people who did the waiver forms have known John since birth (they live in a small rural upstate county) but are now asking for his entire medical care history since birth. "The question I have is, what have they been doing in my home all these years?" (22)*

SUMMARY AND CONCLUSIONS

This chapter represents an effort to examine the experience of families of children with highly specialized needs who, as the pioneers in home care, are defining the future of services. Of necessity, it also looks at the services that are supposed to support the families in their efforts. On the one hand, this chapter has exposed the tension between a very traditional approach to services for children with complex medical needs and parents on the forefront of a ground-breaking effort. On the other hand, the information here testifies to the development of a new definition of the parent–professional relationship as individual professionals and the SKIP service coordination project strive to work out what it means to support families.

The testimony of these families leaves the impression of a disjointed system of public and private supports for home care for children with severe disabilities and specialized health care needs. The rhetoric of those heading these systems continually affirms the primacy of the family, yet the experience of these families is otherwise. Again and again, the families tell of benefits managers, service coordinators, discharge planners, and social workers whose actions indicate that they regard the families as welfare junkies out to milk the system for everything it's worth. An attitude is conveyed, even in dealing with entitlements and plans to which the parents have long contributed, that the families are the beneficiaries of some benevolent charity and should be happy with what they are given. Families struggling to come to terms with their child's disability and the care demands associated with it find themselves stigmatized, impoverished, and degraded. In a society of rugged individualists they are forced to ask for help, which, in itself, is more than some parents can deal with. And yet, the system in its machinations throws these requests back in their face.

It should be clear that these parents are not asking for charity—no one here is out to "milk the system." In its simplest form, these families affirm human community and simply seek community support in meeting some of the extraordinary demands associated with raising their children. As parents, they are not looking for the state to assume their responsibilities. Rather, they seek supports that will enable them to devote their energies to being parents instead of exhausting themselves by battling for a few services. They are calling on the state to recognize support for the family as an entitlement that affirms the family as the cornerstone of our society, based on the fact that support for families is the most cost-effective service the state can provide. By supporting families and aiding the integration of children with disabilities and special health care needs in their home communities and neighborhood schools, the state will shape the future demand for adult services in a manner that places much greater reliance on the already existing resources of our communities and less requirement for expensive specialized service settings.

Chapter Review

CHALLENGES

- Caregiving often involves heavy lifting, sleep disruption, and continual vigilance.
- The boundaries of the family are disrupted by many outsiders coming into the home; as a result, families lose privacy.
- Children require specialized equipment that is hard to obtain, service, and monitor and have frequent medical emergencies.
- Families must choose where they live based on proximity to medical care; they often must deal with extreme financial hardship.
- Parents' employment opportunities are curtailed, as are opportunities for community involvement.
- Families often feel blamed by professionals or feel they are treated in cold and unhelpful ways.
- Insurance companies and Medicaid often give incomplete information, are too slow to pay providers, and do not cover many essentials. Service coordinators are often uninformed and insurers drop many families from coverage.
- Service providers are often resistant to giving help, arbitrary, and unhelpful.

CHARACTERISTICS OF HELPFUL PROGRAMS

- Support workers recognize that children who are medically fragile give their families opportunities for positive growth and adaptation.
- Helpful professionals show dedication to the families, and their support often increases through the years.
- Effective professionals and services believe and trust the parents as experts about their child and his or her condition, are responsive to the unique concerns of this group, and listen to parents and affirm their instincts about their children's needs.
- Effective programs assist families in dealing with the maze of information about support services, financial assistance, and other resources.
- Effective programs monitor the quality of services that families receive, insist that service providers live up to quality standards, and prevent providers from overcharging.

POLICY IMPLICATIONS

- The state must actively assist families to carry out their role as caregivers with the creation of a unified, accessible, and caring system.

- Professionals must be educated about the daily concerns of families of children with complex medical needs.
- Professionals must recognize that families are their own experts.
- Support funding must cover the extraordinary financial costs of home care.
- Supports must be given in ways that respect family boundaries, offer rest and free time to all family members, and deal with the tension created by frequent crises through effective crisis and emergency services.

References

Bradley, V.J., Knoll, J., & Agosta, J.M. (Eds.). (1992). *Emerging issues in family supports* (Monograph Series No. 18). Washington, DC: American Association on Mental Retardation.

Knoll, J. (1989). *Come together: The experience of families of children with severe disabilities or chronic illness.* Cambridge, MA: Human Services Research Institute.

Knoll, J. (1992). Being a family: The experience of raising a child with a disability or chronic illness. In V.J. Bradley, J. Knoll, & J.M. Agosta (Eds), *Emerging issues in family supports* (Monograph Series No. 18) (pp. 9–56). Washington, DC: American Association on Mental Retardation.

Knoll, J. Covert, S., Osuch, R., O'Connor, S., Agosta, J., & Blaney, B. (1990). *Family supports in the United States: An end of decade status report.* Cambridge, MA: Human Services Research Institute.

Koop, C.E. (1987). *Surgeon General's report: Children with special health care needs.* Rockville, MD: Public Health Service, U.S. Department of Health and Human Services.

Maternal & Child Health. (1988). *Family-centered care.* Rockville, MD: Public Health Service, U.S. Department of Health and Human Services.

Nelkin, V. (1987). *Family-centered health care for medically fragile children: Principles and practices.* Washington, DC: Georgetown University, Child Development Center.

Taylor, S.J., Knoll, J.A., Lehr, S., & Walker, P.M. (1989). Families for all children: Value-based services for children with disabilities and their families. In G.H.S. Singer & L.K. Irvin (Eds.), *Support for caregiving families: Enabling positive adaptation to disability* (pp. 41–53). Baltimore: Paul H. Brookes Publishing Co.

10

The Relative
Nature of Brain Injury

Janet M. Williams

There is increased recognition that all families require community support to carry out their roles, whether the support is from community centers, churches, schools, or other community resources. When an individual experiences a brain injury, that person and his or her family are likely to require additional support in the form of professional services, training, and skill building. The nature and location of available services is often dependent upon funding availability. In the field of brain injury, some funds have been available for institutional care and inpatient rehabilitation, but few options have developed to address individual concerns in a person's own community.

This chapter addresses the issues, challenges, and opportunities for people with brain injuries and their families to receive in-home supports as soon as possible after an injury. Social policies that support and hinder this process are explored. Examples from the Home- and Community-Based Services Medicaid Waiver in Kansas are used to look at how community-based services are developing.

THE INCIDENCE OF BRAIN INJURY

There are no accurate statistics regarding the number of people with brain injuries in the United States at any given time (DeJong, Batavia, & Williams, 1989). Increasing survival rates, prevention efforts, and the lack of a consistent definition or counting mechanism have compounded the dilemma. Nonetheless, the National Head Injury Foundation (NHIF) estimates that

500,000 people are hospitalized each year with brain injuries and some 300,000 have symptoms that interfere with daily living (National Head Injury Foundation, 1993). At least 70,000 of these individuals will require some form of ongoing support that will address the myriad of challenges they may face.

Brain injury is a significant insult to the brain by physical force or trauma (Levin, Benton, & Grossman, 1982). *Open brain injuries* are those in which the skull is actually penetrated (e.g., from gunshot wounds, other objects). *Closed brain injuries* are those in which there is a blow to the brain (e.g., from auto wrecks, falls, violence), often resulting in a period of unconsciousness. It is important to note that brain injury can occur in either instance without loss of consciousness. Recently, the term *minor brain injury* has been given to brain injury without coma (Kay, 1988). Although the terms *head injury, brain injury, acquired brain injury, traumatic head injury,* and *brain damage* have all been used in this newly developing field, this chapter uses only the term *brain injury.*

The consequences of brain injury also vary, making it difficult to develop a standard regimen of support. Among people diagnosed with brain injury, challenges and strengths can differ dramatically from one person to the next, as well as fluctuate within the same person from one day to the next. For example, someone with a memory challenge may remember something quite well one day only to have great difficulty the next; a list of challenges may include memory, problem solving, judgment, and impulse control. Developing one program that meets the needs of all people with brain injuries is not possible. Individual services must be flexible enough to adapt to each person's concerns and allow for variance from day to day over time.

EVOLUTION OF SERVICES

Most people with brain injuries and their families enter the service delivery system in the emergency room of a hospital (Williams & Kay, 1991). This will be the first in a long series of encounters with the medical system, within which the medical model is considered reality, rather than a representation (Mishler, 1981). Families are taught to expect that the medical system will diagnose the problem, fix their family member, and send him or her back to life as before the injury. But as the family will come to realize, there is a paradox in coping with the sometimes dramatic changes brain injury can cause, while being grateful that the person is alive (Corbin & Strauss, 1988). Roles and relationships change, often many times, and the entire family must adapt; they must deal with losing some of that person's previous personality, while negotiating a new place for him or her within the family.

Once a person is medically stable, physicians continue to direct treatment, prescribing therapy for a myriad of physical, cognitive, and behavioral challenges, which are usually defined within a medical context and environment.

The Medical Model

Like other conceptual models, the medical model defines, classifies, and specifies roles and relationships among events in particular ways (Mishler, 1981). As a result, families and friends perceive and interpret the person's behavior in light of the illness, even after the acute symptoms subside (Riessman, 1983). Attention is centered on defects, deformities, and disease within the individual, instead of focusing on how the system may contribute to a person's challenges. For example, a person who has a short attention span or is easily distracted may be expected to perform in a room with several other people who add to the individual's confusion. The person may become frustrated, labeled a behavior problem, and prescribed medication or put on a *behavior management plan,* all of which change the person, rather than decrease commotion in the room.

Sick Role

These common medical model images led Parsons (1951) to develop the theory of the sick role. In short, when people get sick, they are excused from social responsibility—their only job is to get better. They are also excused from fault or blame for anything associated with the illness. Additionally, as the role of patient is considered undesirable, they must want to shed this role. In this undesirable state, a person is supposed to get technical and competent help for the illness.

The sick role is temporary, undesirable, and socially disruptive. This understanding is based upon achieved technical expertise, which labels the patient as passive and dependent and the physician as expert (Bloom & Wilson, 1979)—one needing protection and the other needing control. In the medical model, the professional is the expert who legitimizes the claim to illness and is responsible for returning people to their customary roles in society.

The Medical Model and Brain Injury   All four themes in Parson's (1951) theory of the sick role are applicable to people with brain injuries.

1. People with brain injuries are immediately excused from social responsibility, especially if they have been hospitalized and can prove by neurodiagnostic testing that significant brain injury has resulted.
2. Because of their dire circumstances, individuals are immediately excused from fault or blame for the brain injury. The immediate priority is to attend to the medical needs of the person, regardless of the circumstances.
3. The role of patient is clearly undesirable and families hope that the role will be a temporary one.

4. People with brain injuries have many opportunities to attain technically
    competent help.

However, brain injury is seen as a medical problem long after a person
is medically stable. This medicalization of brain injury often becomes a
lifelong quest for a cure by knowledgeable experts, which leaves patients
and families dependent upon them.

For many people who experience brain injury, the realization that they
are not sick comes early. They strive to get out of the sick role but find
themselves indefinitely categorized as such by the funding and service delivery system, which also forces their family and social network to define
them as sick. The sick status they are forced into often reflects funding
dilemmas rather than any real need.

Being a brain injury patient sometimes becomes a career, forcing an
individual to be compliant to avoid punishment and learn how to go along
with professionals (Goffman, 1963). People with brain injuries who question
the medical model may find that noncompliance stereotypes them as inappropriate and lacking judgment as a result of their brain injury, not as a
result of inappropriate institutionalization. The longer people with brain
injuries are forced to stay in the institution, the more the community per-
ceives them as too sick to live in the community, creating a stigma of in-
definite duration.

There are various reasons the medical model has so much influence in
the provision of services to people with brain injuries. Funding for people
with brain injuries comes from health and liability insurance, as well as
settlements; for some people, state and federal funding has become available. However, all too often, funding only pays for health-related challenges
and the medical model becomes predominant in a person's life—forcing an
individual to continue the sick role in order to receive money for services.
Furthermore, because the hospital is the point of entry into the system,
transitions to other models of service provision can be difficult. There is
also some safety in an institutional environment that discourages risk taking. However, these dilemmas have driven the development of services for
people with brain injuries.

The Medical Model, Families, and Brain Injury

The medical model also puts families in a difficult predicament. Initially,
families are forced to make life-and-death decisions for which they are not
prepared. Naturally, they want to protect their family member from further
harm. Because traditional thought dictates that being surrounded by technology and professionals equals protection, families logically want people
to stay in this protective environment.

This natural protective instinct is repeatedly reinforced as the person
progresses and wants to take more risks. The family begins to realize that
funding will end if the person leaves the institution, again inhibiting the

ability to make any moves toward independence. Furthermore, the structure of the system leads to the assumption that a person cannot function outside the institution, even though the person may be working hard and wish to leave. Families are caught in the middle—wanting independence for their relative while wanting financial support for themselves.

Families, at this time, have been described as overprotective (Lezak, 1978), unrealistic (Rosenthal & Muir, 1983), and in denial (Romano, 1974). This deficit and problem approach to labeling families often leaves questions unanswered: What are the chances of another occurrence of brain injury? Why has this happened to us? Why can't the person be as he or she was before? Why can't we grasp the enormity of the current life changes?

Research with families after brain injury similarly follows the deficit and problem approach common within the medical model. For example, several studies have been conducted on the high divorce rate after brain injury (Bond, 1983; Lezak, 1988). None of these studies looks at whether brain injury was the cause of a divorce or whether the couple would have divorced anyway. Furthermore, not one study looks at the couples who stay together and why.

Services to people with brain injuries have become an anomaly for both the medical and disabilities communities, making service provision an ongoing challenge. For so long, brain injury has been defined as a medical problem within the realm of the medical model with terminology and situations so very different from those for people with physical disabilities.

The Development of Community Services

The shift in practice and policy from defining community life in terms of institutions, caregiving, and residential facilities toward more flexible, consumer-responsive approaches presents several challenges to the individual, the family, professionals, and society. People with brain injuries often look to three existing community support systems for help. Each may offer a patchwork of services the individual may need, but no one system can adequately address all of their concerns. The three systems include home-care agencies, community-based programs for people with developmental disabilities, and independent living centers (ILCs). The next section addresses each of these systems and explains how people with brain injuries can acquire these services.

Home-Care Agencies and Brain Injury

Home-care agencies are considered the mainstay of caregiving. Yet, home-care for people with brain injuries presents several distinct challenges for traditional providers and agencies. First, the majority of people who experience brain injuries are between the ages of 18 and 44 years old (National Head Injury Foundation, 1993), a significantly younger group of people than most home-care agencies are accustomed to or even prepared to serve. Second, people with brain injury may continually improve over time. Rather than requiring more care and preparing for additional services, agencies must prepare for fewer services and greater independence. Third, home-care agencies usually permit a limited number of home visits and do not usually provide the long-term rehabilitation therapy some people with brain injuries require. Additionally, many of the services for people with brain injury are needed in the community, not in the home. Fourth, financing home care can be a great challenge for someone who is under 65 and not yet eligible for Medicare. Private insurance has limited home-care benefits and only people with very limited financial means can qualify for state assistance or Medicaid.

Community-Based Programs for People with Developmental Disabilities and Brain Injury

The developmental disabilities movement began the first move away from the medical model for people with disabilities. Parents of individuals born with cognitive, behavioral, and physical challenges began to realize that their children did not have medical problems that needed to be fixed, but disabilities requiring supports and services. Institutions were established in an effort to create comprehensive supports and services, but it soon became clear that institutions could not replace the role of the family, which led to a move to deinstitutionalize people with developmental disabilities. Since then, many milestones have been accomplished in the area of community-based services and supports, and today, the movement recognizes that all people have gifts and strengths to share in the community.

Some individuals with brain injury look to the developmental disabilities model for support, while others have encountered certain obstacles. First, the definition of *developmental disabilities* currently includes people who experience disability before the age of 21 (Berkowitz, 1987). If a person experiences a brain injury after that age, he or she is not eligible for services in the community. Second, people with brain injuries who do not have families or do not want their families involved may encounter problems under the developmental disabilities model. Some innovative adoption and foster family situations have been set up for people with developmental disabilities, but this approach is more challenging for older people who do not have access to the same funding streams. Third, if a spouse or sibling becomes the significant decision maker in a person's life because of a brain injury, they face different issues than if a child experiences a disability. For example, management of assets, guardianship, and competency may require different regulations and tests.

Independent Living Centers and Brain Injury

In the late 1960s, people with physical disabilities began to reject the medical model—the first wave of the independent living movement (DeJong,

1979). A philosophy of consumerism, self-direction, self-help, peer support, civil rights, and improved quality of life for people with disabilities marks the movement. People with physical disabilities want to control their own lives separate from the medical domain.

Those with brain injuries who ascribe to an independent living philosophy are considered to be exploring a new paradigm; because some people with cognitive disabilities experience challenges in judgment, reasoning, and problem solving, most assume that these people cannot control their own lives—an assumption used to justify the control characterized by the medical model. There are four primary areas of focus for people with brain injuries who are exploring the independent living movement. First is the concept of self-directing services, which traditionally has meant hiring, managing, and firing staff who work for the person with a disability; the control, decision making, and problem-solving requirements a person has in self-directing services can be quite new for people with brain injuries who have never hired and fired their own staff. Second is learning compensation techniques. Developing ways to compensate for challenges in scheduling, remembering, and other daily tasks is an area yet unexplored by most ILCs. ILCs have cited limited time and financial resources as obstacles to learning what compensation techniques are and how they can be used to help someone become more self-sufficient (Jones, White, Ulicny, & Mathews, 1988); however, they are important skills for people with brain injuries and provide much promise for future development. Third is family support. People with physical disabilities in the independent living movement are accustomed to advocating for themselves and have not relied on their families to help. Many people with brain injuries choose to have their families involved, but the independent living movement does not address the issue of guardianship and surrogate decision making. Fourth is involvement in the operation of ILCs. In a 1991 survey of 63 ILCs, 37% of the centers employed at least one staff member with brain injury and 44% had at least one board or committee member with a brain injury (Hermalyn, Breen, Harris, & Aguda, 1993). The ILCs that had a paid staff member or board member with brain injury were more likely to advocate for services for people with brain injury. Overall, the attitude of doing for oneself and making cognitive (instead of physical) substitutions will be an ongoing challenge to the independent living movement and people with brain injuries involved in it.

RECOMMENDED PRACTICES

At least five prominent issues affect the future development of home- and community-based services for people with brain injuries. They are best exemplified by explaining how they apply to the lives of two individuals with brain injuries living in the community.

Larry Phillips Larry Phillips is a 26-year-old man who was shot in the head 1 year ago in an argument with another man. As a result, one eye was removed and he lost vision in his other eye. He has paralysis on the left side of his body and uses a wheelchair. Planning and organizing a day's events and remembering details are more difficult than before the shooting and are attributed to his brain injury. He participated in intensive rehabilitation for 3 months and then was moved to a nursing home where he stayed for 6 months. He described the nursing home, which was often short staffed, as a hellhole. Larry slept most of the day and was awake all night. He has nine brothers and sisters who seldom visited the nursing home. He learned about the Home- and Community-Based Services Medicaid Waiver from a speech-language pathologist doing contract work for the nursing home.

Maggie Mills Maggie Mills is a 38-year-old woman who has had a seizure disorder since the age of 9. She is a recovering alcoholic. During her third marriage, she fell, hit her head, and had a seizure that lasted between 4 and 6 hours. She was alone at the time and when she regained consciousness in the hospital 3 days later, she thought she was still married to her first husband. She has significant short- and long-term memory loss, but no physical challenges. She continues to have prolonged seizures despite many trials on various medications.

Larry and Maggie want similar things: They both want to live in their own home, they both want to work, and they both want significant relationships that support their lifestyle. However, the way they want those things to happen and the concerns they have differ dramatically. The following five issues are an integral part of their day-to-day lives and the future development of home- and community-based services for persons with brain injuries:

1. *The use of compensation techniques, rather than a focus on fixing people:* Compensation techniques are strategies people use to build on their strengths to overcome existing challenges. For example, a person with a physical disability may use a wheelchair in place of walking. For people with brain injuries, compensation techniques must address both cognitive and physical disabilities and be adaptable—therapy to change the challenges that exist may lose their effectiveness over time.

Larry Larry uses many compensation techniques. For his visual challenge, he uses magnifying glasses and has a reader attend school with him while he studies for his general equivalency diploma. He also uses devices at home, like a reacher to get things from the cabinet and a bowl with a suction cup on the bottom to mix food. Additionally, he makes many notes in large print to organize things he previously kept in his head, such as frequently called telephone numbers and lists of things to do. Without these compensation *techniques, he would be dependent on others for many details in his life he has learned to manage himself.*

Maggie   Maggie has as many compensation techniques, but they address issues very different from Larry's. First, Maggie uses a day timer to record every event in the past, present, and future of her day-to-day life to compensate for her significant memory challenge; she continually refers to it and is literally lost without it. Second, Maggie has a watch with the month, day, and year, and an alarm. She frequently refers to the date and sets the alarm to remind her to take her seizure medication. It took several weeks for her to remember that the alarm goes off to remind her of her medication, but with repetition, structure, and consistency she no longer forgets her medication.

2. *A balance between inclusion in community life and specialization:* One of the greatest dilemmas in supporting individuals and families after brain injury concerns specialization. How much technical knowledge do community support agencies and services need to have about brain injury? In what areas do people need to know specifics about brain injury and in what areas is this not necessary? Can these areas be specified? If not, how can the area of family support be addressed? How can physical, cognitive, emotional, and financial issues be supported?

Larry   The staff that Larry has hired have had to learn specific things about brain injury to help support him in the community. Because of his dual challenge (i.e., memory challenge and the need to write things down), Larry often has conversations with people that he forgets, and he forgets he needs to write them down. He is now comfortable telling people he has a memory challenge and has asked the staff to remind him to write down things he says he wants to remember. He said he really had to swallow his pride to tell neighbors and relatives that he needs help.

Maggie   The two main areas of specialization for Maggie are her memory challenge and her seizures. It took Maggie 4 months to remember her address after she moved to her new apartment. It was important for staff to learn that quizzing her repeatedly and playing games did not help her remember; she needed to develop and learn her own strategies. Staff also learned that rewards and reprimands had no effect on her memory but significant negative effects on her mood. She remembers the aura of the encounter, but not the details. Maggie also continues to have seizures that can last from 1 minute to several hours. If a seizure lasts for more than 3 minutes, staff must call 911 and explain her history to the emergency medical technicians. The staff must also know seizure procedures.

Still, there are many things in Larry's and Maggie's lives that do not need specialized training: Knowing how to treat someone as an equal, asking people what they want, and privacy are a few.

3. *Supporting self-sufficiency and interdependence:* Self-sufficiency means learning what one can do for oneself and who one can depend upon for support. Interdependence implies interconnectedness, the linkage of people to people (Condeluci, 1991). In practical terms, self-sufficiency and interdependence mean learning to do things with people, not for people. It does not mean doing everything on one's own, nor does it mean having someone else do everything. Therein lies the challenge for consumers, staff, and families.

Larry   At 26 years old, Larry is living in his own apartment for the first time. He had paid staff with him most hours of the day when he first started to live in his own place but now requires assistance only in the early morning and late at night. Early on, he realized that the more he learned to do for himself, the less staff time he would require. But he decided that he did not want to lose staff hours because he was afraid of being lonely and started refusing to do things for himself. After some negotiation, he decided that staff would help him make connections in the community before they started to decrease their hours. As he made friends and felt more comfortable getting around on his own, he started to change staff hours.

Maggie   Maggie needs to have someone with her all the time because her seizures give no forewarning and can last for hours if no one intervenes. However, it is extremely frustrating for her to have someone with her all of the time and she often she feels like "June Cleaver" entertaining her staff. After tracking her seizure frequency and times, a plan was put in place for Maggie to have 3 hours alone each day. She now calls the staff answering service every hour during those 3 hours. If she does not call by 15 minutes after the hour, staff call her. If she answers, things proceed as usual; if she does not answer, an emergency plan is in place. Maggie now protects her time alone and says it is the best part of her life.

---

4. *Self-direction of services:* Self-directing services means learning to hire and fire staff and learning how to teach someone about personal needs. It is a constant negotiating process. There are many potential pitfalls, but the benefits far outweigh the difficulties. The entire process of dealing with staff often provides as many skills as any therapy or job training. It also provides individuals with staff they like and know to help them to reach their goals.

Larry   Larry has had eight staff people in 7 months. Recently, he reviewed his own record and decided that he was very demanding in the beginning and did not take staff feelings into account. His current staff have been with *him for 8 months—he says he approaches things more professionally now.*

> ***Maggie*** *Maggie has had some staff leave for other jobs but has only had two staff members in the past year that she did not want working for her. In both situations, it was only after a great deal of thought and consideration.*

5. *Funding:* Rehabilitation for people with brain injuries has been documented as the most expensive in the United States (Congressional Report, 1992), as a result of a lack of consistent therapeutic intervention, many sources of health insurance, and a for-profit health care system. For those with insurance or funds, rehabilitation is available, but community services are limited. In some states, Medicaid waivers have been developed for community-based services. In any instance, a person's previous and current income can greatly affect benefits.

> ***Larry*** *Larry had a limited work history before his brain injury and does not qualify for Social Security Disability Insurance (SSDI). He receives a Supplemental Security Income (SSI) check for approximately $446 per month. The Medicaid Waiver pays for services, and his monthly check must cover all other expenses, including food, rent, utilities, telephone, fun, and transportation. If he falls short 1 month, it takes several months for him to catch up. He is job hunting but knows that any income above $200 per month will affect his SSI.*

> ***Maggie*** *Maggie had an extensive work history before her brain injury and receives an SSDI check for $892 each month. She can only keep $500 per month to qualify for Medicaid and the waiver services she needs. Recently, she set work goals that enabled her to participate in a Plan for Achieving Self Support (PASS) through Social Security to use the SSDI for work-related goals.*

SUMMARY AND CONCLUSIONS

Overall, there is increasing recognition that people with brain injuries have been relegated to the medical model. But, as medical funds become increasingly scarce, people with brain injuries have had to search elsewhere for services. As health policy changes and public policy explores who is responsible for supporting people with brain injuries in the community, the need to look at community supports and services is at a critical stage.

Because people with brain injuries live in every community, the type, flexibility, and access to resources can make the difference between dependence, self-sufficiency, and quality of life. Social policies and services that support increased opportunities for people with brain injuries to receive support in the community are proving cost-effective and practical and increasing community participation.

Chapter Review

CHALLENGES

- Every year approximately 70,000 people experience brain injuries so severe that they will require some form of ongoing support.
- Services for people with brain injuries have been dominated by the medical model, which is often not appropriate for people who need long-term accommodations to live as typical a life as possible.
- People with brain injuries are stigmatized.
- Often families' needs for information, emotional support, and assistance in caring for their member with brain injury go unmet.
- Home-care services are not used to working with younger people and often fail to prepare people for more independence.
- Independent living programs usually serve people with physical, rather than cognitive, disabilities.

CHARACTERISTICS OF HELPFUL PROGRAMS

- Programs support self-sufficiency in everyday activities.
- Programs focus on compensation techniques for, and accommodations to, the person's cognitive disabilities.
- Programs encourage family involvement and assist families to better support their relative with brain injury.
- Programs have board members, staff members, and employees with brain injuries.
- Programs aim to include people in community life, while disseminating specialized information about brain injury to the community.
- Funding from public sources is used to foster independence.

POLICY IMPLICATIONS

- Brain injury should be redefined as a long-term, biological, psychological, and social challenge that requires assistance from several sectors of society, not just the medical sector.
- The central role of families in supporting people with brain injuries should be recognized and supported.
- Agencies that traditionally serve people with disabilities must reexamine their basic assumptions.
- Policies, such as income restrictions on Medicaid eligibility, should be reexamined if they inhibit employment or independence.
- People with brain injuries and their families should be involved in the governance of programs that assist them.

References

Berkowitz, E.D. (1987). *Disabled policy: America's programs for the handicapped.* New York: Cambridge University Press.

Bloom, S.W., & Wilson, R.N. (1979). Patient–practitioner relationships. In H.E. Freeman, S. Levine, & L.G. Keeden (Eds.), *Handbook of medical sociology* (3rd ed., pp. 275–296). Englewood Cliffs, NJ: Prentice Hall.

Bond, M. (1983). Effects on the family system. In M. Rosenthal, E. Griffith, M. Bond, & J.D. Miller (Eds.), *Rehabilitation of the head injured adult* (pp. 209–217). Philadelphia: F.A. Davis.

Condeluci, A. (1991). *Interdependence: The route to community.* Orlando, FL: Paul M. Deutsch Press.

Condeluci, A., & Gretz-Lasky, S. (1987). Social role valorization: A model for community reentry. *Journal of Head Trauma Rehabilitation, 2*(1), 49–56.

Congressional Report. (1992, February 19). *Hearing on rehabilitation facilities for people with head injuries.* Washington, DC: U.S. Government Printing Office.

Corbin, J., & Strauss, A. (1988). *Unending work and care: Managing chronic illness at home.* San Francisco: Jossey-Bass.

DeJong, G. (1979). Independent living: From social movement to analytic paradigm. *Archives of Physical Medicine and Rehabilitation, 60,* 435–446.

DeJong, G., Batavia, A.I., & Williams, J.M. (1989). Who is responsible for the lifelong well-being of a person with a head injury? *The Journal of Head Trauma Rehabilitation, 5*(1), 9–22.

Goffman, E. (1963). *Stigma: Notes on the management of spoiled identity.* Englewood Cliffs, NJ: Prentice Hall.

Hermalyn, D.P., Breen, M.U., Harris, E., & Aguda, C. (1993). Mail and telephone surveys of services for people with TBI. *American Rehabilitation, 19*(2), 48–57.

Jones, M.L., White, G.W., Ulicny, G.R., & Mathews, R.M. (1988). A survey of service by independent living centers to people with cognitive disabilities. *Rehabilitation Counseling Bulletin, 31,* 244–248.

Kay, T. (1988). *Administration manual: New York University head injury family interview.* New York: NYU Medical Center Research and Training Center on Head Trauma and Stroke.

Levin, H., Benton, A., & Grossman, R. (1982). *Neurobehavioral consequences of closed head injury.* New York: Oxford University Press.

Lezak, M.D. (1978). Living with the characteriologically altered brain injury patient. *Journal of Clinical Psychiatry, 39,* 592–598.

Lezak, M.D. (1986). Psychological implications of traumatic brain damage for the patient's family. *Rehabilitation Psychology, 31,* 241–250.

Lezak, M.D. (1988). Brain damage is a family affair. *Journal of Clinical and Experimental Neuropsychology, 10,* 111–123.

Mishler, E. (1981). Viewpoint: Critical perspectives in the biomedical model. In E. Mishler (Ed.), *Social contexts of health, illness and patient care* (pp. 141–168). New York: Cambridge University Press.

National Head Injury Foundation. (1993). *The silent epidemic.* Washington, DC: Author.

Parsons, T. (1951). *The social system.* New York: Free Press.

Riessman, C.K. (1983). Women and medicalization: A new perspective. *Social Policy, 14*(1), 3–18.

Romano, M. (1974). Family response to traumatic brain injury. *Scandinavian Journal of Rehabilitation Medicine, 6,* 1–4.

Rosenthal, M., & Muir, C.A. (1983). Methods of family intervention. In M. Rosenthal, E. Griffith, M. Bond, & J.D. Miller (Eds.), *Rehabilitation of the head injured adult* (pp. 407–419). Philadelphia: F.A. Davis.

Williams, J.M., & Kay, T. (1991). *Head injury: A family matter.* Baltimore: Paul H. Brookes Publishing Co.

11

Developing Family-Centered Care for Families of Children with Special Health Care Needs

W. Carl Cooley and Ardis L. Olson

WESLEY A.

Wesley A. is a 3-year-old boy with Down syndrome and spastic quadriplegic cerebral palsy due to a fluid-filled cyst that occupies most of the left side of his brain. He also has myoclonic seizures, moderate sensorineural hearing loss, myopia that requires corrective lenses, and a neurogenic bladder requiring intermittent clean catheterization four to six times per day.

Wesley's birth followed an unplanned pregnancy; he was conceived while his mother was taking birth control pills. During the seventh month of the pregnancy, his mother experienced abdominal pain, went to the hospital for evaluation, and was diagnosed as having a bladder infection. She delivered Wesley precipitously at home later that evening. He was stabilized by emergency medical technicians and transported to a nearby tertiary care medical center where he was hospitalized in the intensive care nursery. Although he sustained few serious complications of prematurity, Down syndrome was suspected and chromosome analysis confirmed trisomy 21. Overwhelmed by multiple stresses, his birth parents considered relinquishing him for adoption. However, his paternal aunt and her family agreed to provide guardianship of Wesley. His aunt obtained physical custody, but Wesley's birth parents maintained some financial responsibility and legal custody. Wesley now lives with his aunt, uncle, and two cousins, ages 11 and 13.

Wesley began having generalized seizures at 7 months of age resulting in hospitalization at a tertiary care medical center. During that hospitalization, a magnetic resonance imaging (MRI) scan of his brain revealed that a large fluid-filled area was replacing normal brain tissue. At that time, neurological findings included spastic quadriplegia, which led to the diagnosis of cerebral palsy. Hearing and vision evaluations documented moderate hearing loss and visual impairment. A referral to a functional vision program was made to supplement his regular early intervention services. In addition, a pediatric cardiologic consultation revealed an abnormal aortic valve, which has trivial clinical significance, but requires periodic cardiologic follow-up.

In December 1990, Wesley was seen for the first time in a Down syndrome clinic. During that visit, an abdominal mass was noted that proved to be an enlarged bladder with a thickened muscular wall. A pediatric urologic follow-up revealed no evidence of bladder outlet obstruction on an anatomical basis, but intermittent clean catheterization was advised. His caregivers were trained to perform this procedure at least twice a day. An MRI scan of the entire spine ruled out the presence of a spinal cord abnormality to explain the bladder problem. The clinic provided Wesley's guardian with reading and supportive information about both Down syndrome and cerebral palsy, put her in contact with other parents through the Parent-to-Parent Program and through the regional Down syndrome parents organization, and connected her with the family support services coordinator for the region. Information about possible Supplemental Security Income (SSI) and Medicaid benefits was also provided.

Since his third birthday, Wesley has undergone the transition from early intervention to preschool special education services. He currently attends a Head Start program 3 half-days per week with additional, separate visits for physical therapy, occupational therapy, and speech-language therapy.

Wesley A. has a complex cluster of challenges that have no definable boundaries in his physical body or with regard to his psychological well-being, his family's functioning, or his community's capacity to provide both natural and formal supports. His challenges are not simply defined by the events of his birth, the diagnoses of professionals, or the criteria that entitle him to special supports and services. Wesley may be rare, perhaps unique, with respect to the specific details that challenge him, but he exemplifies the patchwork of policy solutions that have evolved in the United States. Wesley, and others like him, have generated a categorical approach to support for families affected by special or complex health care needs.

Lacking an overriding policy of generic supports that strengthen and empower all families for their essential task of mutual caregiving, the United States has historically used a residualist approach to family support policy and family support in health care. This approach assumes that most families are healthy, self-sufficient, and self-supporting, but makes exceptions for the residual number of families who will always require societal supports (Singer & Irvin, 1989). Support systems developed from the residualist perspective were inherently oriented toward social control rather than family empowerment and embodied a crisis management rather than preventive approach. Families in need of support were not regarded as competent assessors of their own needs, resulting in a rigid and limited menu of supports that were determined by service providers rather than consumers.

Beyond a history of paternalism and control, family support policy in the United States has been fragmented and without coordination. In fact, this poorly integrated system has fostered the necessity of a whole new social services profession, that of service coordinator. Many families now have multiple service coordinators, under titles varying from care coordinator to benefits facilitator, prompting the suggestion of a manager of the managers role. Policy makers have developed programs based on chronic condition categories (e.g., Title V programs), socioeconomic status (e.g., Early and Periodic Screening, Diagnosis and Treatment; Head Start), or demographic region (e.g., rural health initiatives). Some programs provide health insurance (e.g., Medicaid, Title V), some provide services such as care coordination, some provide financial benefits (e.g., SSI), and some provide combinations of supports (e.g., SSI plus Medicaid) in some states but not others. In fact, families who must move from one state to another may experience dramatic changes in their eligibility for services and in the nature and extent of available services. In many other developed countries, paid maternity and child care leave and universal health care are the foundations for all families upon which other supports are built. In the United States, families must fend for themselves until circumstances demand that they seek help. They then must demonstrate their exceptionality through what is often a demoralizing and degrading eligibility determination process. Furthermore, many families must endure similar (but never identical) eligibility procedures for multiple programs in order to patch together a viable system of supports. Often families begin this process long after the threshold for cost-effective, successful, prevention-oriented interventions has been passed.

This chapter outlines the development of family supports in the health care of children with chronic conditions and disabilities in the United States. The diversity and complexity of social policies that have affected the health of children and the relative absence of a long-term, integrated agenda valuing family strengths make the task difficult in both organization and scope. As unifying threads, the discussion focuses on both public and private trends that have promoted family-centered, community-based care, a medical home for every child, and the importance of family empowerment to healthy outcomes for children.

Through networking, advocacy, political action, and litigation, families of children with disabilities and chronic illnesses have led the movements that have closed institutions, opened classrooms, and challenged discrimination against their children in multiple arenas. Meanwhile, family research has documented the improved outcomes that come from family-driven therapeutic agendas, rather than agency or professional-driven ones (Cooley, 1992; Singer, 1991; Stein & Jessop, 1984). At the same time, some health care providers have begun to recognize the value of seeing health care from the patient's perspective and have accumulated data documenting improved outcomes through patient-centered care (Gerteis, Edgman-Levitan, Daley, & Delbanco, 1993). These interwoven developments have centered attention on family issues as a crucial focus for service providers and as integral to the planning of policy makers. As a consequence, new terminology, such as family-centered care, family support, individualized family service plan (IFSP), parent–professional partnership, and family empowerment, have become regular elements of the vocabulary of change for children with challenges. Such developments warrant some attention to definitions for the purposes of this chapter.

Family

Family is defined in many ways and clearly has taken many forms in contemporary life. The definition of family determines what family-centered care encompasses and incorporates the values by which we develop policies and services. The New Mexico Advocates for Children, Youth, and Families (1994) developed the following definition of family:

> We all come from families. Families are big, small, extended, nuclear, multigenerational, with 1 parent, 2 parents, and grandparents. We live under 1 roof or many. A family can be as temporary as a few weeks, or as permanent as forever. We become part of a family by birth, adoption, marriage, or from a desire for mutual support. As family members, we nurture, protect, and influence each other. Families are dynamic and are cultures unto themselves, with different values and unique ways of realizing dreams. Together, our families become the source of our rich cultural heritage and spiritual diversity. Each family has strengths that flow from the individual members and from the family as a unit. Our families create neighborhoods, communities, states, and nations.

Family-Centered Care

Family-centered care refers to services for children and families as envisioned in the Surgeon General's report of 1986, which includes the nine elements defined by the Association for the Care of Children's Health and illustrated in Table 1.

Parent–Professional Partnership

Parent–professional partnership is one of the elements of family-centered care in which families and professionals collaborate as equals in the evaluation and decision making about a child and share responsibility for outcomes.

Table 1.   The key elements of family-centered care

1.   Recognizing that the family is the constant in a child's life, while the service systems and personnel within those systems fluctuate

2.   Facilitating family–professional collaboration at all levels of health care

3.   Honoring the racial, ethnic, cultural, and socioeconomic diversity of families

4.   Recognizing family strengths and individuality and respecting different methods of coping

5.   Sharing with parents, on a continuing basis and in a supportive manner, complete and unbiased information

6.   Encouraging and facilitating family-to-family support and networking

7.   Understanding and incorporating the developmental needs of infants, children, and adolescents and their families into health care systems

8.   Implementing comprehensive policies and programs that provide emotional and financial support to meet the needs of families

9.   Designing accessible health care systems that are flexible, culturally competent, and responsive to family-identified needs

From Johnson, B.H., Jeppson, E.S., & Redburn, L. (1992). *Caring for children and families: Guidelines for hospitals* (1st ed.). Bethesda, MD: Association for the Care of Children's Health, p. 3; reprinted by permission.

Family Support

Family support encompasses all of the natural and formal sources of strength that allow families under stress to cope and find resiliance (Cooley, 1994b). Natural supports include spouses, extended family, friends, neighbors, and community resources that families have used in the past or have identified as helpful. Formal supports are those services that a family may be entitled to as a consequence of a child's chronic condition (Karp & Bradley, 1991). Formal family support services include respite and child care, help with making home and vehicle adaptations, parent-to-parent and family support groups, in-home assistance, training for parents, recreation, information and service coordination, and direct financial assistance. Formal support services are often defined under a state's family support policy but may be categorically limited. For example, a service may be available to families of children with disabilities, but not chronic illnesses.

From the standpoint of health care services, the adoption of a family-centered approach not only entails attention to a family's need for natural and formal supports, but becomes a family support in itself through the empowerment implicit in family-centered and patient-centered health care. Health care programs, health care financing, and, as it unfolds, health care reform must acknowledge family support as part of any individual health care plan for a child with a chronic condition or complex health challenges.

THE DEVELOPMENT OF FAMILY-CENTERED CARE

The origins of the family-centered approach to providing health care or, for that matter, any professional services affecting families, are diverse, with multiple influences.

Advocacy and Consumer Organizations

Beginning in the 1950s, advocacy groups were formed, giving families a sense of empowerment. The foundation of many parent and family organizations began with informal encounters that often occurred when parents were thrust together in hospital pediatric wards or in the waiting rooms of specialty clinics. These chance meetings provided parents with validation of their common needs and concerns, a valuable empowerment tool that was often missing from their relationship with professionals. Such informal contact has remained an important source of family support and provided the model for developing more structured and reliable parent-to-parent networks. However, episodic encounters among parents may also have originated the development of more formal, enduring, and influential advocacy groups with a local and national focus.

Organizations such as The Arc, the Autism Society of America, United Cerebral Palsy (UCP), The Association for Persons with Severe Handicaps (TASH), the Federation for Children with Special Needs, the National Alliance for the Mentally Ill (NAMI), as well as networks of family leadership and advocacy groups such as Technical Assistance for Parent Programs (TAPPs) have developed an evolving consensus for the meaning of family-centered care. These organizations and many others have sought to include the voice of families in policy making, program planning and development, quality assurance, research, training, and direct care at the federal, regional, state, and community levels. In fact, Family Voices is the name chosen by a loosely organized, but influential, national network of families whose aim is to ensure that the current national debate about health care reform includes the input of families of children with special health care needs.

Family and parent advocacy organizations have influenced changes in federal policy to include family-centered approaches in areas such as the federally funded, state administered Title V programs for children with special health care needs, and Part H of the Individuals with Disabilities Education Act of 1990 (IDEA), PL 101-476. Advocacy organizations have also been positioned to respond to state and regional agencies that, in implementing new family-centered policies, are required to seek participation of parents on boards, advisory groups, and planning councils. One successful and landmark product of such collaborations was *Enhancing Quality: Standards and Indicators of Quality Care for Children with Special Health Care Needs* produced by New England SERVE, a collaborative of representatives from the Title V programs of the six New England states working with parents from the region, professionals from many disciplines, hospitals, and community organizations (Epstein, 1989).

Health Care Services

A number of developments in direct health care have influenced the evolution of family-centered principles since the 1970s. Alternative approaches to childbirth, the involvement of parents in care, attention to the developmental needs of children during pediatric hospitalizations, the use of home and adaptive practices for children with chronic conditions, and the growth of training programs for physicians in family medicine are examples of specific health care practices that have paved the way for the wider acceptance of family-centered care.

In the early 20th century, 95% of births in the United States occurred at home and were attended predominantly by female midwives or nurses. By 1945, nearly 80% of births were in hospitals, and by 1969 this figure rose to 99% (Mathews & Zadak, 1991). Although hospital births have given physicians better control over complications of labor, prevention of infection, and initial care of a sick newborn, they have also disengaged childbirth from the family and redefined the process in medical terms, as if birthing involved the treatment of an illness. In the 1950s and 1960s, the notion of prepared childbirth helped prospective parents regain some control over the labor process, as concern for the welfare of the fetus reduced the utilization of general anesthesia during labor and delivery. By the late 1970s emphasis on maternal–paternal–infant bonding prompted hospitals to room babies with their mothers, which led to a more family-oriented approach in labor, delivery, and postpartum care (Gjerdingen & Fontaine, 1991). Finally, scientific evidence began to emerge that documented fewer obstetrical complications and better outcomes for newborns when family-centered approaches to labor and delivery were practiced (Klaus, Robertson, Kennell, & Sosa, 1986), which helped to convince and move medical professionals toward family-centered care. These developments not only acknowledge that the birth of a child is a family event, but set the stage for family involvement should a newborn require more than routine care.

Meanwhile, hospitals caring for children as inpatients began redefining their rules and procedures. Visiting hours were expanded and then abandoned altogether in favor of the constant presence of family members. Pediatric hospital units hired recreational therapists, child life experts, and educators to make the hospital environment and experience less threatening to children. Input from parents about their child's preferences and needs, food, and the timing of tests and blood drawing has become commonplace, and parents are often included during treatment room procedures. Parents are invited to participate in their child's daily care, and older children are encouraged to provide some of their own care. The duration of hospitalization has decreased partly as a result of economic pressures, but has been accepted by most parents who willingly assume more responsibility for home care. Finally, economic pressures toward same-day surgery for common childhood procedures (e.g., removal of tonsils, placement of ventilation tubes in ears, eye surgery) have also shifted the focus of postsurgical care from the hospital to the home and from professional caregivers to parents. As more hospitals have explicitly subscribed to the elements of family-centered care illustrated in Table 1, parent advisory councils and the use of trained parent consultants have emerged (Stewart & Covington, 1992).

Children with chronic conditions such as asthma, diabetes, cystic fibrosis, and hemophilia must contend with a loss of control over part of their lives, as their chronic illnesses dictate certain daily care requirements and precipitate crises from time to time. Families of such children also lose some mastery over their lives. Parents experience stress and siblings are upset when the family member with a chronic illness must be hospitalized or requires time-consuming care at home. Such issues are compounded in the home care of children with complex, technology-assisted needs, such as tracheostomy care, supplemental oxygen requirements, or tube feedings.

Since the 1980s, the care of children with chronic conditions has been subjected to the combined scrutiny of parents, medical professionals, and funding sources, in order to determine what elements could safely be provided at home (Biggert, Watkins, & Cook, 1992; Richardson, Student, O'Boyle, Smyth, & Wheeler, 1992). Furthermore, with data suggesting that adaptive skills enhance self-esteem and healthier outcomes for children with chronic conditions, efforts have been directed at making children with asthma, diabetes, spina bifida, or hemophilia responsible for more of their own care, sometimes involving them more in the home management of their illness. A good example is diabetes for which the work of nurses and diabetes educators has resulted in appropriate learning materials for children of all ages and their parents, as well as guidelines for the knowledge needed and for the management activities the child performs, based on a child's developmental level.

For some conditions, new procedures requiring frequent application promoted parent and child involvement. For example, the efficacy of earlier and more frequent use of intravenous medication to treat traumatic bleeding in hemophilia promoted parental involvement in the home administration of hemophilia treatments. Similarly, the demonstration that daily catheterization in children with spina bifida prevented deterioration of renal functioning led to parents performing catheterization procedures at home.

Once the involvement of parents in such procedures was established, the next step became gradually shifting the responsibility to the child as he or she grew. However, much less work has been done to provide standardized and widely accepted guidelines about when it is appropriate for the child to assume responsibility. Rather, guidelines vary considerably from one program or location to another. Only recently have efforts been made in common conditions (e.g., asthma) to involve the child in daily assessment and decision making about treatment. For children with a seizure disorder, involvement in self-management is just beginning. The training and support for families to assume more responsibility for illness management usually involves nursing personnel who specialize in chronic illness care, as well as physicians in pediatric specialties. Efforts to shift some of the parent and child training activity to the primary care setting have barely begun. Thus, the extent and availability of home management programs for chronic conditions depend on the belief of local health professionals in the benefits of home care by families and adaptive behaviors by people with disabilities, as well as the resources invested in these programs by state Title V programs and by tertiary care medical and training centers.

Family-oriented primary health care has always existed sporadically, where the values, personality, and experience of the individual physician allows for collaboration with patients and families to overcome the paternalistic tendencies engendered by traditional medical training. In 1966, the American Medical Association (AMA) convened two committees whose reports supported the idea of specialized training in family practice. With these reports from the Willard Committee and the Millis Commission, AMA's Council on Medical Education endorsed the development of family practice residency training programs (Ventres & Frey, 1992). Subsequently, family medicine has developed training standards, a board certification process through the American Board of Medical Specialties, as well as national and local professional organizations and publications for the dissemination of knowledge and establishment of practice standards. During debates about the need for a specialty in family medicine, other primary care professionals (e.g., pediatricians, internists, obstetrician-gynecologists) have been challenged to examine their attention to the family as a whole. Although there is much to be done to enhance the family centeredness and consumer orientation of all medical training, the growth of a new specialty in family medicine has helped to focus attention on the issue.

Trends in Health Policy and Research

Changes toward family-centered care for health policy and research have involved a diversity of federal agencies and their counterparts in the individual states. Programs as diverse as Head Start, special education, maternal and child health, SSI, and Medicaid are involved. There is no single point of departure or convenient way to organize a history of these developments, although they have been clearly influenced by the aforementioned consumer advocacy movement and developments in direct health care services. The continuing process of deinstitutionalization and decentralization of services has moved children with chronic conditions back to their families and moved many of the services they require back to their home communities. Research about families and individuals with chronic conditions has also influenced policy development.

Title V of the Social Security Act (PL 74-271) was enacted in 1935 to ensure that children with chronic conditions could have access to the best specialized care possible for their condition. Title V greatly improved the lives of children with chronic illnesses and has proved remarkably durable as it has evolved over the years. However, for the first 50 years, it focused services on the child and the illness, with little regard to broader family issues or needs; its orientation was largely curative and rehabilitative in a medical sense.

Then in July 1980, the Institute for Public Policy Studies at Vanderbilt University began a study jointly funded by the U.S. Office of Maternal and Child Health in the Department of Health and Human Services and the Office of Special Education and Rehabilitative Services in the Department of Education. Known as the Vanderbilt Study, this 5-year project focused on the existing systems of care for children with special health care needs. The publications arising from the Vanderbilt Study provided professionals, researchers, teachers, and policy makers with comprehensive data about the status of children with special health care needs. It also emphasized the issues facing these families that were affecting access to services, adherence to care plans, and overall outcomes, for the first time (Hobbs, Perrin, & Ireys, 1985).

Meanwhile, Congress passed PL 94-142, the Education for All Handicapped Children Act of 1975, that guaranteed a free and appropriate public education in the least restrictive environment to all children. This legislation did not address family issues directly, but it did ensure that many children with chronic conditions affecting school performance could attend school in their home community even if certain medical procedures (e.g., administration of medication, intermittent clean catheterization of the bladder) needed to be carried out at school. Furthermore, the reauthorization of PL 94-142 during the late 1980s and early 1990s, as the Individuals with Disabilities Education Act of 1990 (IDEA), PL 101-476, has strongly endorsed the notion of family-centered services at least for infants, toddlers, and preschool children.

In 1977, the SSI program of the Social Security Administration, which provided benefits for adults with disabilities too severe for them to work, was expanded to include children with disabilities. This program now provides financial benefits to poorer families of qualifying children. Following a 1990 Supreme Court decision in a class action suit (*Sullivan v. Zebley*) claiming an unfair and unequal eligibility determination process for children, access to SSI benefits for children with special health care needs has been significantly expanded. Also, in the early 1980s through the exhaustive efforts of the parents of Katie Beckett, a child with complex health care needs, a change in federal Medicaid policy allowed families with children like Katie Beckett to benefit from Medicaid's considerable range of benefits. This Katie Beckett option has allowed many families to provide needed care for their children at home instead of in hospital settings, without consuming all of a family's financial resources (Hostler, 1991).

With the Vanderbilt Study documenting the need for a new agenda and foregoing developments pointing the way, the U.S. Maternal and Child Health Bureau—under the leadership of Vince Hutchins and Merle McPherson—began forging a new agenda for services to children with special health care needs. This culminated in a series of conferences between

1982 and 1988 for children with special health care needs convened by former Surgeon General C. Everett Koop. These conferences focused on the promotion of self-sufficiency and autonomy for children with special health care needs and their families, and the development of a new set of national guidelines against which policies and programs would be measured. In 1987, the *Surgeon General's Report on Children with Special Health Care Needs* articulated the concept of family-centered, community-based, coordinated, culturally competent care for children with special health care needs (U.S. Department of Health and Human Services, 1987). In 1989, family-centered care first appeared in the *Federal Register* as one of the criteria to be met by applicants for Special Projects of Regional and National Significance grants from the U.S. Maternal and Child Health Bureau.

The Importance of a Primary Care Medical Home

Chronic health impairments affect the lives of nearly 10 million children in the United States. Nearly 4 million children experience chronic conditions severe enough to disrupt daily activities of childhood at home, school, or play (Perrin, Shayne, & Bloom, 1993). Although high-quality, specialized services have become widely available (though not always easily accessible) in the United States, the health care of children with chronic conditions has become more fragmented and uncoordinated.

Community-based primary health care providers (e.g., pediatricians, family physicians, nurse practitioners, physician's assistants) have often been excluded from the management of chronic illnesses. At best, their involvement has been either peripheral or poorly integrated with the care provided in specialty clinics. The notion of co-management of chronic conditions shared between primary care and specialist professionals has only recently received attention.

For example, a child with diabetes may require quarterly chronic illness management visits. By present standards, these monitoring visits are often provided in a diabetes clinic or a pediatric endocrinologist's office. All aspects of chronic illness management including health monitoring and parent and child education are provided in the specialty setting, while the primary physician provides all other aspects of well-child and acute illness management. The primary physician might also be called upon to respond when an acute complication of diabetes occurs or when the child's parents are unable to reach their endocrinologist. In such circumstances, the primary physician is poorly prepared to intervene, having been excluded from the diabetes management in the past. Under co-management, the primary physician would assume a larger role in the monitoring of diabetes by alternating monitoring visits with the specialist. Certain patient education tasks would be assigned to the primary care setting, while the specialty visits would focus on fine-tuning the illness management and educating the child, family, and primary physician on the latest developments in diabetes research or care. Community-level communication about the child's illness, such as with school nurses, would be the responsibility of the primary physician, not the specialist who may be located in another community.

Pediatricians have complained that their training has not emphasized the long-term management of chronic illnesses, the health consequences of developmental disabilities, behavioral pediatrics issues, or the skills required of service coordinators (Cooley, 1994a). At the same time, pediatricians providing primary care agree that service coordination needs to be provided in the primary care setting. Primary care physicians have requested more continuing education about chronic illness, more information about community resources, better reimbursement for service coordination activities, and better communication between physicians and parents (Liptak & Revell, 1989).

These policy initiatives that emphasize family-centered care practices have also endorsed community-based, coordinated care for children with special health care needs. State agencies administering Maternal and Child Health Block Grants have been required to submit plans and implement system changes that would emphasize community-based services for children with chronic conditions. As a result, Title V-funded tertiary clinic systems are pressured to relinquish some care responsibility back to the community and the primary care level, and help develop the capacity of communities to provide first-rate services for children with complex health needs.

At the same time, the emergence of managed care and health maintenance organizations in the funding of health services has designated the primary physician as the gatekeeper to specialty services. Many proposed plans for universal health care reform in the United States are based on concepts of managed care, with primary care as the point of origin and coordination of services. Primary care providers must be prepared for these new responsibilities, and their practices must be supported in the provision of care and service coordination. Primary care providers must be assisted in acquiring new knowledge about the long-term care needs of children with chronic conditions, the educational and support needs of the families of such children, the implications of these conditions for learning and schools, and the other community resources available for families of children with special health care needs.

However, despite wide public acceptance of the concept of primary care as the point of entry and coordination for one's health care needs, the U.S. health care delivery system has been slow to provide the supports for all families to receive such care, in part because of the inadequate physician supply and insufficient financing of care for lower-income families. Still, in the 1970s, many communities developed neighborhood health centers that provided a variety of services in one community setting for families.

More recently, the American Academy of Pediatrics has strongly supported the concept that all children should have a primary care medical home. The Academy's CATCH program offers small grants for local community efforts to improve children's access to care. Recently, many states have implemented managed care systems for recipients of Medicaid benefits. Some of these efforts even provide additional family support and care coordination services. In addition, private foundations like the Robert Wood Johnson Foundation and the Kaiser Family Foundation have funded service models that provide better access to primary care, better care for chronic illnesses, and care aimed at meeting families' needs.

During the early 1990s a number of projects supported by the U.S. Maternal and Child Health Bureau provided both definition and implementation to the concept of a primary care medical home for every child (Sia, 1992), which would ensure access to good primary care by health care professionals willing to collaborate with families in making health care plans. Such professionals need to be knowledgeable enough about chronic conditions to make effective use of specialists, but not have to abandon responsibility for all management. Ideally, a medical home provides help to parents for coordination of health services and has established communication links to schools, family support services, and other community-based resources involved with children and families.

Efforts to promote primary care systems that function effectively as medical homes need to be incorporated into pre- and postgraduate medical education, office management supports, health care financing systems, and specialty clinic organization and behavior. State Title V programs need continued encouragement to develop community-based capacities and expertise, and to identify obstacles and disincentives to the involvement of primary care professionals in the care of children with special health care needs. Most important, barriers to acquiring a primary care medical home for all children and families need to be identified and removed.

Family Empowerment and the Parent–Professional Partnership

One of the reasons that families fare better with services driven by the family agenda instead of the professional agenda is empowerment. Just as children feel a loss of control over their lives when they experience a chronic health condition, families similarly lose self-esteem and confidence when a member is affected by illness or disability. The restoration of self-confidence is an intrinsic part of any long-term therapeutic process that, if disregarded, seriously impairs the chances of an optimal outcome (Dunst, Trivette, & Deal, 1988; Stein & Jessop, 1991).

It is now possible to envision a continuum of empowerment for children or families made vulnerable by a disability or chronic condition. This process begins with a parent–professional partnership based on the care required. This partnership implies a shared stake in all aspects of care including the gathering of information, the pursuit of an explanation or diagnosis, the decision making about treatment, and the responsibility for outcomes. Beyond this individual consumer–professional interaction, parents have become partners with researchers, teachers, and policy makers.

A recent review of family participation in state Title V programs for children with special health care needs provides ample evidence of this trend (Wells, Anderson, & Popper, 1993). In 50 out of 50 states and the District of Columbia responding, family members were involved on advisory committees and task forces; 35 respondents involved families in in-service training; and 46 states included families in the Maternal and Child Health Block Grant planning process. While 47 state programs supported parent activities (e.g., parent-to-parent services, categorical parent support groups), only 21 states actually hired parents as paid staff consultants. There is also further progress to be made in the area of including adults who have chronic illnesses or disabilities in state program and policy activities.

The fruits of the parent and consumer advocacy movement, grass roots networking, class action litigation, and other examples of citizen-driven political action are clearly embodied in the statutes and policies of the last 20 years, including the Americans with Disabilities Act of 1990 (PL 101-336), the Individuals with Disabilities Education Act of 1990 (PL 101-476), the Omnibus Budget Reconciliation Act of 1990 (OBRA) (PL 101-508), and new public health policies emphasizing family-centered, community-based care. The current debate over health care reform and the widely accepted need for universally guaranteed access to affordable health care for all Americans provides the latest and, in many respects, most important opportunity for the confluence of recent developments into important systems change.

Health care reform provides a crucial opportunity for linking advocacy and political reform to disability and chronic illness in a process that affects every American family. Universal access to care under health care reform applies to all citizens and would therefore be one of the first examples of family support legislation that is generic for all families. The provision of a minimum package of universally available health benefits would move everyone's health care firmly in the direction of health promotion instead of crisis intervention.

Advocates for children with special health care needs support universal access to health care, but do not want to lose their accomplishments of the past 20 years (e.g., Katie Beckett option, Title V, SSI, state-level insurance reforms). They would like a health care reform package that would provide comprehensive, long-term care benefits in keeping with the natural history of chronic conditions and their impact on children's health. Families would also, for once, like to have the same insurance plan for all of their family members without having to go to extraordinary ends to find piecemeal coverage through private insurance, Title V programs, Medicaid, individual education plans, SSI, family support systems, and major out-of-pocket payments for their child with special needs. Families would like to avoid a demeaning, demoralizing, and often hopelessly complicated application and eligibility determination process in order to obtain each of the pieces of their child's patchwork of coverage (Vohs & Propper, 1994).

CONCLUSION

The story of Wesley A. epitomizes the fragmentation of health care and health-related support services currently available for families in the United States who have children with special health care needs. However, Wesley's family has gradually become informed negotiators on his behalf, has become skilled mobilizers of needed supports, and has even become a stakeholder in the support system itself—Wesley's aunt and legal guardian is chairperson of the family support council for his region. Communication between specialists and Wesley's primary care physician has developed into a system of co-management with more clearly defined roles, expectations, and information sharing among those involved. In some respects, the evolution of care and services supporting Wesley and his family provides a single case model of the development of family-centered care and family support policies relating to health care services in the United States. Because services and supports have always been fragmented from the standpoint of funding, purpose, or focus, it is unlikely that even the process of health care reform will provide unification of family support resources into a generic whole. However, as the systems become increasingly responsive to consumers and reflect a more family–patient driven agenda, families and communities will steadily expand their capacities to provide local support and services close to home, where flexibility, responsiveness to individual needs, and emphasis upon natural support systems can thrive.

Chapter Review

CHALLENGES

- The service system for children with special health care needs is fragmented and difficult for parents to navigate.
- Traditional services have been based on a residualist model that does not empower families and tends to view them as sources of problems rather than as essential sources of support for children with special health care needs.
- Families often feel voiceless in medical decision making and policy development.
- Primary care physicians have not been trained in the long-term management of chronic and rare conditions—often, their communication with specialists is problematic.
- Reimbursement for the extra time and services that children with special health care needs require is often not provided by insurers.

CHARACTERISTICS OF HELPFUL PROGRAMS

- Helpful programs provide a medical home for children in the community, which is a primary care physician who provides long-term care to the child and family.
- Physicians and health care providers develop partnerships with family members that are reciprocal—communication and planning care is a two-way street.
- Parents are active participants in making policy, designing services, and evaluating programs.
- Primary care physicians receive necessary consultation and support from medical subspecialists.
- Children learn medical self-management skills appropriate to their developmental level.
- Programs provide coordination that mobilizes formal and informal sources of assistance for families.
- Health care providers address the social and emotional impact of illness, as well as physical symptoms.

POLICY IMPLICATIONS

- Medical school training for primary care physicians should teach young physicians to manage the long-term needs of people with special health care needs.

- State Title V programs should continue to develop and expand the capacity of community health care providers to serve children with special health care needs and their families.
- Universal access to health care must be established in order to ensure that all children with special health care needs will receive comprehensive care.
- Programs should make family empowerment a primary part of their mission.
- A uniform system of care should replace the present patchwork of services.
- Quality control standards should include measurement of family satisfaction and family participation in decision making.
- Categorical family support programs should be extended to serve all families of children with special health care needs.

References

Americans with Disabilities Act of 1990 (ADA), PL 101-336. (July 26, 1990). Title 42, U.S.C. 12101 et seq: *U.S. Statutes at Large, 104,* 327–378.

Biggert, R.A., Watkins, J.L., & Cook, S.E. (1992). Home infusion service delivery system model: A conceptual framework for family-centered care in pediatric home care delivery. *Journal of Intravenous Nursing, 15*(4), 210–218.

Cooley, W.C. (1992). Natural beginnings–unnatural encounters: Events at the outset for families of children with disabilities. In J. Nisbet (Ed.), *Natural supports in school, at work, and in the community for people with severe disabilities* (pp. 87–120). Baltimore: Paul H. Brookes Publishing Co.

Cooley, W.C. (1994a). Pediatric training and family-centered care. In R. Darling & M. Peter (Eds.), *Families, physicians, and children with special health care needs: Collaborative medical education models* (pp. 109–122). Southport, CT: Greenwood Press.

Cooley, W.C. (1994b). The ecology of support for caregiving families. *Journal of Behavioral and Developmental Pediatrics, 15,* 117–119.

Dunst, C., Trivette, C., & Deal, A. (1988). *Enabling and empowering families: Principles and guidelines for practice.* Cambridge, MA: Brookline Books.

Education for All Handicapped Children Act of 1975, PL 94-142. (August 23, 1977). Title 20, U.S.C. 1401 et seq: *U.S. Statutes at Large, 89,* 773–796.

Epstein, S. (1989). *Enhancing quality: Standards and indicators of quality care for children with special health care needs.* Boston: New England SERVE.

Gerteis, M., Edgman-Levitan, S., Daley, J., & Delbanco, T.L. (Eds.). (1993). *Through the patient's eyes: Understanding and promoting patient-centered care.* San Francisco: Jossey-Bass.

Gjerdingen, D.K., & Fontaine, P. (1991). Family-centered postpartum care. *Family Medicine, 23*(3), 189–193.

Hobbs, N., Perrin, J., & Ireys, H. (1985). *Chronically ill children and their families.* San Francisco: Jossey-Bass.

Hostler, S.L. (1991). Family-centered care. *Pediatric Clinics of North America, 38*(6), 1545–1560.

Individuals with Disabilities Education Act of 1990 (IDEA), PL 101-476. (October 30, 1990). Title 20, U.S.C. 1400 et seq: *U.S. Statutes at Large, 104,* 1103–1151.

Johnson, B.H., Jeppson, E.S., & Redburn, L. (1992). *Caring for children and families: Guidelines for hospitals.* Bethesda, MD: Association for the Care of Children's Health.

Karp, N., & Bradley, V. (1991). Family support. *Children Today, 20*(2), 28–31.

Klaus, M.H., Robertson, S.S., Kennell, J.H., & Sosa, R. (1986). Effects of social support during paturition on maternal and infant morbidity. *British Medical Journal, 293,* 585–587.

Liptak, G.S., & Revell, G.M. (1989). Community physician's role in the case management of children with chronic illness. *Pediatrics, 84*(3), 465–471.

Mathews, J.J., & Zadak, K. (1991). The alternative birth movement in the United States: History and current status. *Women and Health, 17*(1), 39–56.

New Mexico Advocates for Children, Youth, and Families and New Mexico Young Children's Continuum. (1994). *Kids Count/New Mexico.* Algodones, New Mexico: Author.

Omnibus Budget Reconciliation Act of 1990 (OBRA), PL 101-508. (November 5, 1990). Title 5, U.S.C. 4712. *U.S. Code Congressional and Administrative News, 2,* 104 Stat. 1388-187–1388-190.

Perrin, J.M., Shayne, M.W., & Bloom, S.R. (1993). *Home and community care for chronically ill children.* New York: Oxford University Press.

Richardson, M., Student, E., O'Boyle, D., Smyth, M., & Wheeler, T.W. (1992). Establishment of a state-supported, specialized home care program for children with complex health care needs. *Issues in Comprehensive Pediatric Nursing, 15,* 93–122.

Sia, C.C.J. (1992). Medical home and child advocacy in the 1990s. *Pediatrics, 90*(3), 419–423.

Singer, G.H.S. (1991). *The evolution of models of family adaptation to disability.* Unpublished manuscript, Hood Center for Family Support, Dartmouth Medical School, Lebanon, New Hampshire.

Singer, G.H.S., & Irvin, L.K. (1989). Family caregiving, stress, and support. In G.H.S. Singer & L.K. Irvin (Eds.), *Support for caregiving families* (pp. 3–25). Baltimore: Paul H. Brookes Publishing Co.

Social Security Act of 1935, PL 74-271. (August 14, 1935). Title 42, U.S.C. 301 et seq: *U.S. Statutes at Large, 15,* 687–1774.

Stein, R.E., & Jessop, D.J. (1984). Relationship between health status and psychological adjustment among children with chronic conditions. *Pediatrics, 73,* 169–174.

Stein, R., & Jessop, D.J. (1991). Long-term mental health effects of a pediatric home care program. *Pediatrics, 88*(3), 490–496.

Stewart, E.S., & Covington, C. (1992). Parent consultants in the health-care system: A new approach in the care of children with special needs. *Issues in Comprehensive Pediatric Nursing, 15,* 123–139.

Sullivan v. Zebley, 88 U.S. 1377 (1990, February 20).

U.S. Department of Health and Human Services. (1987). *Surgeon General's report on children with special health care needs.* Rockville, MD: Author.

Ventres, W.B., & Frey, J.J. (1992). Voices from family medicine: Lynn Carmichael. *Family Medicine, 24*(1), 53–57.

Vohs, J., & Propper, B. (1994). Health care reform: A primer for families and advocates. *Coalition Quarterly, 11*(2), 1–4.

Wells, N., Anderson, B., & Popper, B. (1993). *Families in program and policy: Report of a 1992 survey of family participation in state Title V programs for children with special health care needs.* Boston: CAPP National Parent Resource Center.

12

Family Support in Child and Adult Mental Health

Barbara J. Friesen

The philosophy and concept of family support, as well as actual resources and services for families, have been slow to develop in the mental health field, as compared to other disabilities. Reviewing the state of family support for families whose children have developmental disabilities, Karp and Bradley (1991) note that families whose children have serious emotional or behavior disorders are traditionally underserved, and recommend that family support services be extended to them. A review of state-of-the-art family support in children's mental health conducted in 1989 (Freud, 1990) provided a good conceptual beginning but uncovered very few actual program examples. This relative lag in the development of family support services in mental health is related to a number of factors, among them the theoretical approaches that hold families responsible for their children's psychiatric problems, the consequent stigma and lack of public and professional understanding and support for family concerns, and until relatively recently, the lack of organized and effective advocacy.

A BRIEF HISTORY OF PROGRAM DEVELOPMENTS

Since the 1980s, a number of developments have helped to establish a climate conducive to the development of family support services in the mental health field. Although this work is still in its beginning stages, there is reason for guarded optimism. The development of family organizations at the national, state, and local levels—federal initiatives and corresponding state-level activities and a few notable programs of private foundations are among the contributing forces.

Family and federal initiatives have been closely linked in both adult and child mental health arenas. The Community Support Program (CSP) of the National Institute of Mental Health (NIMH), initiated in 1974, provided a model of support for people with chronic mental illness who were moving out of mental hospitals and into communities. The CSP model gave assistance in securing basic needs (e.g., housing, food, health care, vocational services), as well as access to mental health services, including the management of psychotropic medications. At that time, the CSP framework marked a significant departure from the services generally provided within the mental health system, which largely focused on psychotherapeutic interventions.

Partially stimulated by state and local CSPs, and often supported by state and county mental health associations, local support groups for families of people with schizophrenia and other major mental illnesses grew in number and focus during the 1970s. In 1979, representatives of these local groups convened at the Wingspread Conference Center in Racine, Wisconsin, and formed a new organization, the National Alliance for the Mentally Ill (NAMI). This organization was designed as a family-driven group focused on information, support, and advocacy for families of people with severe mental illness (Hatfield, 1981). Since it was founded, NAMI has grown tremendously in both size and its ability to influence the national agenda on behalf of people with mental illness and their families. NAMI and the National Mental Health Association, which has a broader focus, often participate in joint advocacy efforts.

The Child and Adolescent Service System Program (CASSP) was begun at NIMH in 1984 to improve services for children and adolescents with serious emotional disorders and their families (Lourie & Katz-Leavy, 1985). Through a program of grants to states, CASSP focused on state-level, system-building activities, and on the support of state and local service innovations. CASSP also funded a Technical Assistance Center at Georgetown University, and with the U.S. Department of Education, two Research and Training Centers focused on improving services to children and families. Since 1985, all grantees have been mandated to develop and implement goals related to family participation. Since that time, families have increasingly become organized at the local, state, and national levels (Friesen, 1993). Through a variety of activities, the number of state and local family support and advocacy organizations exclusively focused on children's mental health issues have grown from 9 in 1986 to more than 200 in 1993 (Friesen, 1991). These include national conferences designed to improve parent–professional collaboration, promote planning and implementation of a family support agenda, promote respite services, and provide information about case management[1] (McManus & Friesen, 1986; Schultze & Friesen,

---

[1]Although the developmental disabilities field favors the term *service coordination*, in the arena of child and adult mental health, *case management* remains the accepted terminology.

1992; Thomas & Friesen, 1989); state-level activities designed to promote the development of family support organizations (Rowe, 1991); and CASSP-funded development and evaluation of statewide family support organizations (Koroloff & Friesen, 1990). The number of organizations that provide support to families of children with emotional disorders, along with other disability groups, has increased from 200 to more than 600 during this time period.

At the national level, two new organizations for children with mental or emotional disorders and their families were formed in 1988. The Child and Adolescent Network of the National Alliance for the Mentally Ill (NAMI-CAN) and the Federation of Families for Children's Mental Health both work to improve services for children and families at the national, state, and local levels. Although formal, comprehensive, family support programs for these families are still rare, the availability of state and local family organizations that can provide information, support, and advocacy is beginning to have an impact on the lives of individual children and families. Through advocacy for policy change, family organizations are also positively influencing the climate for children's mental health services and family support.

Two national initiatives sponsored by private foundations have also added to the impetus for innovation in children's mental health and the development of family support services. Through partnerships with state and local public mental health authorities, the Mental Health Services Program for Youth of the Robert Wood Johnson Foundation (Beachler, 1990) collaborated with state and local organizations in eight communities to develop individualized, flexible, community-based services for children with serious emotional disorders and their families. Many of these programs are able to provide family support components, such as respite services, that are generally not available within the public mental health system. The Annie E. Casey Foundation also supports a children's mental health initiative in five urban communities and funds the Federation of Families for Children's Mental Health to develop training and technical assistance on family support issues for these demonstration sites.

Private foundations such as the Ittleson Foundation and the McArthur Foundation have contributed to the advancement of information and services for families whose adult members have psychiatric disabilities.

FAMILY SUPPORT IN THE MENTAL HEALTH FIELD

One consequence of the lack of family support services is that there is very little literature that either describes existing family support programs or reports the findings of family support research in the mental health field. The immense need for family support, however, is clearly reflected in both the conceptual literature and the small body of research that examines the concerns, experiences, and preferences of families with members who have serious mental or emotional disorders. This literature addresses the following three broad categories:

1. Theoretical perspectives about mental illness and emotional disorders
2. The experiences and concerns of families whose adult or child members have a mental or emotional disorder
3. Specific program examples of family support efforts in the mental health field

This literature provides a foundation for further policy and program development and suggests further research directions.

Theoretical Perspectives in Mental Health

The major theoretical frameworks that have been used as a basis for understanding and treating mental and emotional disorders during the 20th century have had a profound influence on the way that services and interventions have developed, including those directed at the family. Although a wide variety of theories have been used over the years, an examination of four contrasting approaches contained in Table 1 will help to understand the attitudes, interventions, and family support issues that are related to each of them.

Psychoanalytic Theory

Beginning in the 1920s, *psychoanalytic theory* has profoundly influenced the mental health field in the United States. This theory is strongly associated with ideas that hold families responsible for the psychiatric problems of their children. Central to psychoanalytic theory is the idea that emotional disorders and mental illnesses result primarily from early childhood experiences, which may include disturbances or inadequacies in primary relationships, especially with the mother, as well as traumatic events at crucial developmental stages. Although the parents are not necessarily seen as deliberate pathogenic agents, their inadequacies have chilling consequences for their children within this framework. For example, it was from within this perspective that Frieda Fromm-Reichmann developed her concept of the *schizophrenogenic mother*—where the mother's emotions and behaviors were thought to cause schizophrenia (Fromm-Reichmann, 1948). Similarly, Bruno Bettleheim recommended *parentectomies*—complete separation from parents—for children with autism (Whittaker, 1976). These and other parent-blaming constructs persist; the concept of schizophrenogenic parents is still included in textbooks for mental health professions (Wahl, 1989), despite a number of studies that reveal the limitations of these theories (Arieti, 1974; Erickson, 1968; Garfinkel et al., 1983; Hingtgen & Bryson, 1972; Miller & Keirn, 1978; Waxler & Mishler, 1972).

Although Sigmund Freud warned against any attempts to gain the confidence or support of parents or relatives by educating them about psychiatric treatment (Freud, 1952), child guidance clinics often employed out-

Table 1. Theories of etiology and family support issues in mental health

Theory/framework	Role assigned to parents	Professional role	Likely choices of intervention	Role of family support
Psychoanalytic theory: Emotional and mental disorders result from deficits in early childhood experiences in primary relationships, especially with mother.	Patient/client: Parents are (often unwitting) agents of mental or emotional disorder. They are responsible for the child's developing problems because of their own ignorance, emotional immaturity, or confusing communication.	Expert, educator, therapist	Move the child from the pathogenic family environment to a benign and/or therapeutic setting: residential, group care, or foster home.	Minimal
Systems theory: Emotional or mental disturbance reflects problems in the structure, communication patterns, and functioning of the family. Behavior of the identified patient has a function related to preserving or restoring the family as a unit.	Patient/client: Parents (usually unknowingly) participate in family patterns and processes that are skewed, disturbed, or unbalanced. Parents, along with the rest of the family, need treatment to help align family structure, clarify roles, and improve communication.	Expert, educator, therapist	Increase availability of treatment services for families. Work to shift services from residential and inpatient settings to community programs that feature treating the whole family.	Therapeutic tool, incidental
Neurobiological factors: Mental illness results from chemical disturbances, imbalances in the brain. Some conditions may be genetic. Behavior resulting from the brain disorder is extremely stressful for the family, sometimes resulting in nonadaptive coping mechanisms.	Client, advocate, partner: Parents are not to blame for the illness of their children. They need services for themselves and for their children. Subjected to the stress of living with difficult behavior, they need respite and support. They may join with professionals in advocating for improved services.	Medical expert, service provider, advocate, partner	Treatment for the disorder consists of attempting to correct or neutralize the chemical imbalance with psychotropic medications. Special educational and vocational services are needed to maximize the person's ability to learn and function in the community. Also need social, medical, and other supports.	Central, high priority
The ecological paradigm: Mental or emotional disorders are varied and result from biological, psychological, and social factors. The family's environment affects the health and quality of family life. Stressors such as poverty and discrimination, as well as interpersonal issues, need intervention.	Client, student, partner: Parents are both the agents and the recipients of interpersonal interactions with children, other family members. Influences are transactive, and perhaps cumulative. Parents need support, skills, and information in order to perform effectively in tough role.	Teacher, facilitator, partner, service provider	Interventions tend to be multifaceted, with attention given to comprehensive needs of families. Emphasis on provision of basic resources, as well as on skills training, social and emotional support. Compatible with whatever it takes philosophy of family support and individualized approach to service.	Central, logical, essential

263

patient treatment for both the mother and the child, each seen by separate clinicians (Bremner, 1972). The psychoanalytic perspective has historically supported out-of-home settings which remove the child from the unhealthy influence of the family and provide an opportunity for corrective, therapeutic experiences (Whittaker, 1980). In conjunction with out-of-home services, parents are sometimes offered treatment and / or educational services designed to better prepare them to fulfill their parental responsibilities. But, Burford and Casson (1989) believe that psychoanalytic models mitigate against the full inclusion of families in residential treatment programs. Aside from emotional support provided by therapists in the context of treatment, family support is not considered an important issue within this framework. In the literature, attention is almost entirely focused on the effect of the family environment on the child / patient and on remedial interventions.

Systems Theory

Although still based on psychoanalytic thought, new approaches to understanding mental illness through *systems theory* gained momentum and acceptance during the 1950s and 1960s. Through the work of Gregory Bateson (1972) and others, mental and emotional problems of the *identified patient* are seen as symptomatic of family conflict and disorganization. Concepts such as *double-binding* and *scapegoating* were developed to describe *dysfunctional* family communication patterns and processes that, according to this perspective, are expressed through the symptoms of one or more family members.

The application of family systems theory has a number of implications for professional attitudes and beliefs about desirable interventions. Proponents often emphasize the importance of family therapy for all families in which a member has an emotional or mental disorder and favor interventions such as day treatment that allow children to remain in their own homes while the entire family receives treatment. Family support services such as respite care are sometimes recommended, but usually emphasize the therapeutic ramifications of such services; examples of this include diluting intense family relationships or allowing appropriate individuation. Atwood (1992) provides an overview of family therapy approaches associated with this perspective.

The positive contribution of family systems theory lies in its inclusion of the entire family in the treatment process, rather than focusing exclusively on the person with a mental disorder. Critics of applications of this theory, however, point out that it may simply shift the blame from the parents to the family system, engendering guilt and alienation from professionals (Woesner, 1983), or neglecting other important explanations for the mental disorder (Johnson, 1986).

Neurobiological Factors

Since the 1970s, scientific evidence has increasingly supported theories linking *neurobiological factors* to mental disorders such as schizophrenia and manic-depressive illness, which has led to a radical shift in assumptions and practices regarding appropriate treatment for people with those conditions as well as in the ways their families are viewed (Johnson, 1989). Although these disorders constitute a relatively small proportion of all mental and emotional problems, they are the most severe, devastating, and persistent and are more likely to affect adults, although manifestations may occur in late adolescence. There is also evidence that some childhood mental disorders may have a neurobiological component (Institute of Medicine, 1989; Peschel, Peschel, Howe, & Howe, 1992), but research in this area lags behind that focused on adult disorders.

With the advent of the CSP model, many publicly funded interventions for adults with major mental illnesses shifted from an emphasis on psychotherapeutic approaches designed to cure or remediate, to supportive services such as medication management, case management, supported education and living, vocational training, and self-help groups. For family members, family support and advocacy groups, accurate information, respite care, and psychoeducational interventions are considered central (Hatfield & Lefley, 1987). The impact of the disorder and its ramifications on the family, often characterized in the adult literature as *family burden* (Goldman, 1982; Lefley, 1989), are emphasized within this perspective; there is also a growing body of research in this area that documents family problems and needs (Doll, 1976; Holden & Lewine, 1982; Lefley, 1987).

In addition to efforts to secure and maintain appropriate community support services, related advocacy efforts focus on funding basic brain research in the hope of finding a cause and, ultimately, a cure for mental illness.

This theoretical framework, which explicitly excludes interpersonal processes and family relations as major causal agents in the development of specific mental disorders, is the focus of a great deal of research funded by the NIMH. People with neurobiological disorders and their families are also the focus of education and advocacy efforts of the NAMI.

The Ecological Paradigm

The *ecological paradigm* (Bronfenbrenner, 1979; Weiss, 1986), while acknowledging the importance of interpersonal processes within the family, emphasizes the impact of environmental factors on the health and well-being of families. This perspective includes a wide variety of elements—emphasizing the harmful consequences of poverty, discrimination, and social isolation, as well as such issues as parenting skills and mother–infant bonding (Weissbourd & Kagan, 1989; Whittaker & Garbarino, 1983). Whereas traditional services have focused only on changing children and families, the ecological paradigm adds environmental intervention.

The ecological perspective is not a theory of mental illness specifically, but a framework for understanding human development. It is also applied to prevention programs for child abuse and neglect (Whittaker & Garbarino,

1983), and to general family support programs designed to enhance the well-being of all families (Weissbourd & Kagan, 1989). The ecological paradigm is the basis for understanding human behavior in many professional education programs, although the degree to which various aspects of the framework are emphasized (e.g., biological, psychological, social) varies greatly (Johnson et al., 1990).

Interventions for children with emotional disorders developed within this perspective include assessment and modification, if necessary, of all relevant environments (e.g., family, school, peer group), so that they more closely match the needs and capacities of the child (Whittaker & Garbarino, 1983; Young, 1990) in addition to helping children and families achieve goals for change. Family support is a logical program consequence of the ecological perspective, and these concepts are central to the general family support movement, represented by the Family Resource Coalition (Weiss, 1986; Weissbourd & Kagan, 1989).

COMPARISON OF CHILD AND ADULT MENTAL HEALTH ISSUES

Public service systems for children with severe emotional disorders and adults with severe and persistent mental illness have developed along different tracks and within different time frames, both at the national and state levels.[2] These differences are summarized in Table 2.

Population Definition

The first contrast between adult and child mental health services, especially public services, is the definition used to determine access to services. Although specific definitions vary from state to state, the definition of severe emotional disturbance developed by the CASSP and the NIMH in 1985 (Lourie & Katz-Leavy, 1985) includes age (birth–17); difficulty in functioning in home, school, or peer settings; a *Diagnostic and Statistical Manual of Mental Disorders* (DSM-IV) diagnosis (American Psychiatric Association, 1994); and involvement with two or more service systems. The definitions contained in PL 94-142, the Education for All Handicapped Children Act of 1975, and its reauthorization, the Individuals with Disabilities Education Act of 1990, PL 101-476, refer to behavioral, emotional, and psychological factors that interfere with educational functioning and do not include any reference to diagnostic categories, except to note that children with schizophrenia are included (Forness & Knitzer, 1991). These two definitions include children with a range of emotional, behavior, and mental disorders that emanate from a variety of possible causes, constitute a heterogeneous group, and are estimated to represent between 12% and 15% of all children (Institute of Medicine, 1989).

---

[2]An analysis of the reasons for these differences is beyond the scope of this chapter, but some very good accounts are available: The development of children's mental health policy and services is summarized by Petr and Spano (1990). For a review of the history of mental health services for adults and the development of the CSP, see Carling (1984).

Table 2.   Similarities and differences: Child and adult mental health issues

Population definition		Primary service systems	Major treatment/rehabilitation goals
Child	Functionally derived Inclusive Heterogeneous	Public education Mental health Child welfare Juvenile justice Health	Developmentally appropriate experiences, activities, skills; preparation for adulthood Inclusion Family living Major roles: family, peers, school
Adult	Diagnostically derived Exclusive Homogeneous	Mental health Public welfare Corrections Health	Maximize quality of community life—social, vocational, and recreational skills; support maximum development Community integration Issues: medication management, appropriate housing, vocational and educational opportunities Major roles: social, vocational, family

The CSP's definition is much more circumscribed, including those with major mental illnesses such as schizophrenia, manic-depressive illness, and major depression (Carling, 1984). This more homogeneous population is estimated to be between .5% and 3% of the adult population.

Primary Service Systems

Children and adults with serious mental or emotional disorders are also served by different service systems. In addition to the public education system, children and families may receive services from public and private mental health agencies, state or local child welfare and juvenile justice systems, and the health system; but, in many communities, services tend to be fragmented and sparse. Although the child welfare system is associated in the public mind primarily with aid to poor families and the protection of children from abuse and neglect, many families whose children have serious emotional disorders become involved with it as a way of gaining access to publicly funded residential treatment, group homes, or therapeutic foster care programs. Parents are often required to relinquish custody of their children as a condition of service (Cohen, Harris, Gottlieb, & Best, 1991; Ervin, 1992; McManus & Friesen, 1989).

State and local mental health systems tend to be a major source of services for adults with serious and persistent mental disorders; and the community support programs that have been instituted almost always provide some form of case management, although resource limitations often mean that all people who need services do not get them. In addition, some innovative programs provide comprehensive, coordinated systems of service, usually within specific geographic boundaries (Brekke & Test, 1987; Reinke & Greenley, 1986). Eligible adults with psychiatric disabilities may also receive financial support and services through the adult welfare system. Those who come into contact with the law are often inappropriately placed in the adult corrections system or may be served by the mental health system, depending on their circumstances.

Major Treatment/Rehabilitation Goals

Differences in treatment and rehabilitation goals for adults and children are related to the developmental needs of children, as well as the major roles that are considered developmentally appropriate for each group. Goals for children tend to focus on healthy physical, social, psychological, and cognitive development; the remediation or reduction of emotional and behavior problems; and preparation for adulthood. The family and the educational system assume major responsibility for helping children accomplish these tasks, ideally through inclusion in regular educational, social, and recreational activities in the community. It is generally expected that children will live at home with their families, and current child mental health and child welfare policies emphasize keeping children with their families whenever possible, although practice does not always parallel policy.

Two age-related differences in goals for adults with psychiatric disabilities are an emphasis on living independently of their parents (Grosser & Vine, 1991; Lefley, 1987) and a focus on work, adult education, or other structured activity. Therefore, the location of appropriate, affordable housing and access to vocational training or supported education programs are major issues. In a survey of families of adults with psychiatric disabilities (Grosser & Vine, 1991), appropriate housing was identified as the greatest need. Medical supervision of psychotropic medications, as well as access to general health and dental care, are also common needs.

FAMILY EXPERIENCES AND SUPPORT NEEDS

Until recently, there was little research that directly asked families about their concerns and experiences. But since the 1990s, a small number of studies have been designed to elicit family members' points of view, including what services they currently receive (Friesen, 1989; Grosser & Vine, 1991; Tarico, Low, Trupin, & Forsyth-Stephens, 1989), and family satisfaction with services (Greenley & Robitschek, 1991; Grella & Grusky, 1989; Kotsopoulos, Elwood, & Oke, 1989; Loff, Trigg, & Cassels, 1987; Petr & Barney, 1993). This research provides some foundation for the assessment of the common experiences and family support needs of families whose minor or adult children have serious emotional or mental disorders. Table 3 summarizes these issues.

Table 3.   Family experiences and support needs

| Common family experiences | Family support needs | |
	At home	Out-of-home
Child: Stigma and blame Adult: Prolonged uncertainty Re: diagnosis, prognosis, appropriate services Need to deal with difficult behaviors, interpersonal interactions Severe financial problems	Specific: transition planning; educationally oriented services and information Common: respite care; crisis service; behavior management; emotional support; accurate information; transportation; homemaker service; life-planning assistance; financial assistance Specific: vocational services	Specific: maintain family connection; prepare for return home; transition services Common: emotional support; accurate information; life-planning assistance Specific: housing assistance; maintain family connection

Common Family Experiences

Despite the differences in goals and services for adults and children with serious emotional or mental disorders, the families of each group share a number of common experiences including stigma and blame, and uncertainty about diagnosis, prognosis, and appropriate services. The manifestations of the disorders themselves also pose particular challenges when they involve difficult-to-manage behaviors and emotionally draining interactions. And when the emotional or mental disorder is severe and long standing, many families face serious financial problems.

Stigma and Blame

Most family members have experienced stigma and blame as a result of their loved ones' problems. Because of the impact of Freudian theory, beliefs that family, and especially parents, are key to the development of emotional and mental disorders permeate the popular and professional literature. In the absence of better information, family members are likely to blame themselves; may be criticized by relatives, friends, and neighbors; and often feel directly or indirectly blamed by the professionals with whom they come in contact.

Wasow and Wikler (1983) provide a striking example of how families with a member who has a mental or emotional disorder are stigmatized, compared to those with a member who has mental retardation. Included is a discussion of a professional literature analysis conducted by Moroney (1980): The research category, "families as a part of the problem," received the heaviest emphasis in literature on mental illness and the least in literature dealing with mental retardation. The scores were reversed for the category, "family members as a part of the team."

In reaction to feeling stigmatized, family members have become interested in changing the attitudes of both professionals and the general public.

They have also begun to focus on the emotional and interpersonal aspects of encounters between family members and representatives of the service system. Thus, there is considerable conceptual literature about family–professional relationships in both adult (Backer & Richardson, 1989; Hatfield, 1986) and children's mental health (Collins & Collins, 1990; Friesen & Koroloff, 1990; Vosler-Hunter, 1989).

A small body of research also exists on parent–professional relationships in the mental health field (Bernheim & Switalski, 1988a; Cournoyer & Johnson, 1991; Friesen, Koren, & Koroloff, 1992; Spaniol, Jung, Zipple, & Fitzgerald, 1987; Tessler, Gamache, & Fisher, 1991). This research generally reveals that family members are often frustrated with the lack of information about the cause, treatment, and probable outcome of their family member's disorder; want to be involved in decisions about care and treatment; and value honesty and want support from professionals for their children, themselves, and other family members. DeChillo (1993) found that higher levels of collaboration between mental health professionals and families of adult psychiatric patients were associated with increased family involvement in discharge planning and higher levels of family satisfaction. Lefley (1989) summarizes research addressing family concerns and identifies possible sources of iatrogenic damage to families through their relationships with professionals. These include professionals' rebuffs of families' requests for information and support, double-binding messages, interventions that may worsen relationships between patients and family members, and negative self-fulfilling prophecies about family–provider interactions. Petr and Barney (1993) also report that families of children with emotional disorders identified such system-induced crises as professionals' recommending placement when parents believed that more or better in-home supports were indicated.

Prolonged Uncertainty
Many families involved with the mental health field also experience *prolonged uncertainty* about diagnosis, prognosis, and appropriate services. Many parents whose children's emotional, behavior, or mental problems began at an early age report extreme frustration because they feel that their concerns are often not heeded by pediatricians or other primary care providers (Friesen, 1989). Even when their child's emotional or behavior problems are apparent to teachers and health care providers, parents report that obtaining an accurate assessment and clear information about appropriate next steps in very difficult (Friesen, 1989; Tarico et al., 1989). The uncertainty about diagnosis may complicate the process of coming to terms with a family member's serious mental or emotional disorder, but there is little research in this area (Miller, Dworkin, Ward, & Basrone, 1990). Although these problems are widespread and related to the state of knowledge in children's mental health, they still may result in frustration and lack of satisfaction with specific professional services on the part of parents (Friesen et al., 1992).

Although major mental illnesses in adolescents and adults may be somewhat easier to diagnose, Grella and Grusky (1989) summarize a number of studies in which family members report widespread dissatisfaction with mental health services, especially linked to lack of information about mental illness and lack of involvement in the treatment process of their family members. Hatfield and Lefley (1987) also review much of this research.

Dealing with Difficult Behaviors and Interpersonal Interactions

Dealing with difficult behaviors and interpersonal interactions constitutes a major source of concern for many families of children and adults with emotional disorders. Dealing with difficult behaviors, including sleep disturbances, was reported to be more stressful than the routine—but demanding—physical care of people with developmental disabilities (Quine & Paul, 1985). In the mental health arena, Lefley (1989) points out that "behavior management issues are ongoing tensions between patients and families" (p. 557) and describes problems with abusive or assaultive behavior, unpredictability, socially offensive or dangerous behavior, and sleep disturbances, among other problems that create enormous stress for families.

In a study involving nearly 1,000 parents of children with severe emotional disorders, 44% of the families said that they had, at some time, felt physically threatened by their children (Friesen, 1989). More than half said that information about practical child-rearing techniques was a "very important" need, while more than 90% said they needed information about raising a child with an emotional disorder. In research involving professionals who are also relatives of adults with mental illness, help with behavior management and appropriate housing were given high priority (Lefley, 1987).

Financial Problems

Financial problems—related to the high cost of medical care—also plague families whose members have a serious emotional or mental disorder. Insurance coverage, for the most part, inadequately covers hospitalization and residential care, and it often does not cover noninstitutional alternatives. Additionally, many family members must quit or limit employment to provide care for their minor or adult children (Asarnow & Horton, 1990; Lefley, 1987). Although financial problems are mentioned in almost every article that addresses the concerns and experiences of families in the mental health field, there is very little research about the extent of these problems, the conditions under which they occur, and what steps families take to address them. Informal reports from families suggest that the problem is widespread and severe; that mothers are the most likely to give up their employment; and that a variety of problem-solving steps including multiple jobs, second mortgages, other loans, and bankruptcies are not uncommon.

Family Support Needs

Both research and family advocacy organizations in mental health have identified family support services as a major need. In children's mental health, the national support and advocacy organization, the Federation of Families for Children's Mental Health (1992), has given a high priority to the development of family support services. Its statement on family support defines it as the following:

> A constellation of formal and informal services and tangible goods that are defined and determined by families. It is "whatever it takes" for a family to care for and live with a child or adolescent who has an emotional, behavioral, or mental disorder. It also includes supports needed to assist families to maintain close involvement with their children who are in out-of-home placements and to help families when their children are ready to return home. (p. 1)

The statement emphasizes family-defined, comprehensive, and flexible services designed and delivered according to the concerns and preferences of the family. Family strengths and resources, including existing social networks and informal supports, should be the foundation upon which new supports are provided (Federation of Families, 1992).

Although no specific statement of family support principles was identified in the adult mental health literature, a number of authors identify challenges faced by families and their need for support. For example, Howe (1988) emphasizes the need for family support and describes NAMI's efforts to stimulate the development of such programs. Bernheim and Lehman (1985) provide an analysis of the needs and preferences of families of adults with mental illness.

This examination suggests that specific needs for intervention and support depend upon where the person with a mental or emotional disorder is living as much as his or her age, development, or behavior.

Common Family Support Needs

Families of children with emotional, behavior, or mental disorders and those whose adult members have mental illnesses share a number of common family support needs. These include emotional support for all family members, accurate information about a number of vital topics, and a range of other tangible and intangible services and resources.

Emotional Support   Emotional support, a seemingly universal family need, can be provided through informal means, as well as through organized family support groups or parent-to-parent programs. In a study of parents of children with serious emotional disorders (Friesen, 1989), respondents identified partners (spouse—51%, significant other—6%) as the people who had been most helpful in raising their child with an emotional disorder, followed by the child's grandparents (13%), and friends (10%). When asked to identify the most helpful type of support provided by these persons, an overwhelming 72% identified emotional support; babysitting (9%) and financial help (7%) lagged far behind. Using the same data set to compare the experiences of family members in support groups for parents of children with emotional disorders with those who were not, Koroloff and Friesen (1991) found that both support group members (80%) and non-members (34%) identified involvement with other parents as helpful in coping. Rowe (1991) reported that most family members who participated in support groups for parents of children and adolescents with emotional disorders in Virginia found them supportive and rewarding.

Accurate Information   The need for accurate information about the nature of mental disorders, prognosis, appropriate treatment, and service availability is also mentioned almost universally in reports of family-identified needs (Friesen, 1989; Petr & Barney, 1993; Tarico et al., 1989). The need for accurate and complete information is not easy to meet, given the imperfect state of knowledge and general lack of services in the mental health field. However, even an accurate assessment of the limited state of knowledge is useful to families, as are recent research findings, information about innovative programs, and so forth.

Other Common Support Needs   Other common family support needs for families whose minor or adult children live at home may include respite care, crisis service, and assistance with behavior management through a variety of means, including training in behavior management techniques and in-home assistance. Locating and obtaining reliable respite care is difficult because of the need for special training and skills in respite providers. Because of this problem, the development of specialized respite curricula and provider training programs is a high priority in the children's mental health field (Butler & Friesen, 1988a, b; Friesen, Griesbach, Jacobs, Katz-Leavy, & Olson, 1988). The need for crisis services is related to the cyclical nature of many emotional and mental disorders (Lefley, 1989; Olson, 1988) and may include support for family members struggling with the difficult decision and process of involuntary commitment. Other family-defined needs include transportation, homemaker service or other in-home service, financial assistance, and life-planning assistance.

Specific Family Support Needs—Children

One unique concern of families with minor children is obtaining appropriate general and special educational services (Forness & Knitzer, 1991; Knitzer, 1982; Nelson, Rutherford, Center, & Walker, 1991; Petr & Barney, 1993). Parents report that it is often difficult to get accurate assessments, access to general and special education services, and inclusion in decision making and planning about their child's educational program. These difficulties exist despite legislative mandates for parent participation in educational planning (Knitzer, 1982; Petr & Barney, 1993).

For families whose children are living away from home, major issues include preserving social and affectional ties with their children, participating in planning and decision-making about their children's lives, and preparing for their return home. Jenson and Whittaker (1987) assert that residential treatment programs should be considered a support system for and an extension of the family, rather than a substitute. Although they suggest a number of specific ways that families can involve themselves in their children's residential treatment, along with Burford and Casson (1989), they also identify a number of barriers to full participation. Furthermore, they suggest a number of parental involvement issues that need systematic study, including the impact of family-based interventions and the effects of the frequency and duration of family involvement on the child's adaptation upon leaving residential treatment.

Specific Family Support Needs—Adults

Families of adults who are living away from home also require assistance in maintaining a balanced relationship with their relatives (Howe, 1988), while retaining various degrees of responsibility for their well-being. Family members may also need ongoing information and assistance in obtaining appropriate housing and support.

FAMILY SUPPORT INITIATIVES AND PROGRAM EXAMPLES

Although family support programs are increasingly being developed in both children and adult mental health areas, only a small number of program descriptions, and even fewer research reports, exist in the literature.

The aforementioned definition of family support (Federation of Families, 1992) sets a standard of designing services to fit the needs of each family, rather than matching family needs to existing programs—the component approach. In reality, this ideal is far from being a standard of practice; most communities do not even have basic components of family support, such as respite services, family information and support systems, or case management. Therefore, the following review of developments in and examination of the few family support programs that exist should be weighed against the ideal of a flexible, family-centered system with resources to meet the needs identified by families.

Currently, family support groups and organizations provide the bulk of personal support and information to families. Family support groups are available in many communities through groups affiliated with organizations such as the Federation of Families for Children's Mental Health, NAMI and NAMI-CAN, the National Mental Health Association, groups organized for families whose children have specific disabilities (e.g., attention deficit hyperactivity disorder, learning disabilities, attachment disorders), and a host of unaffiliated parent groups and organizations. In addition to family support groups, many parents participate in other parent-to-parent activities such as warm lines or buddy systems, only some of which are formally organized.

Currently, 28 statewide organizations for parents of children with emotional disorders are funded by the Center for Mental Health Services (CMHS), Substance Abuse and Mental Health Services Administration (SAMHSA) to provide information, support, advocacy, training, and technical assistance to local groups and individual families. These programs have collected family-specific information about the usefulness and acceptability of their services and are now compiling it. This information will be among the first outcome data available about the impact of these services (Briggs & Richards, 1993). A review of these programs suggests that the ability of family organizations to be supportive to families is dependent upon, and interacts with, the availability of appropriate services in the community. In addition to the 28 programs funded by the CMHS, statewide organizations have been formed recently with funds from a variety of sources, although many have no stable source of funding.

State-level family organizations are also involved in advocacy activities, both at the case and systems level. For example, family-focused, comprehensive mental health legislation for children has been passed in Kansas, Montana, Virginia, and Wisconsin, supported by the energy and initiative of family members. Minnesota, Georgia, and Oregon have passed legislation addressing the problem of parents having to relinquish custody of their children, and family advocacy efforts focused on this issue are underway in Ohio, Pennsylvania, and Tennessee, among others.

The activities of these family organizations are supported primarily by small, temporary grants and contracts, and by a substantial amount of volunteer labor on the part of paid and unpaid staff. The demands for service at both state and local levels often surpasses the abilities of these organizations. Requests from families for assistance with family crises or school-related problems, and needs for concrete services such as transportation and financial assistance far outweigh organizational resources. Nonetheless, many families receive support, information, and material assistance through the growing network of family organizations.

Wrap-Around Services

Within the formal service system, the concept of *wrap-around services* (Burchard & Clarke, 1990; VanDenBerg, 1993) most closely approaches the ideal of family-centered support services. This approach also begins with an individualized assessment, tailoring services in response to the needs of the child and family, although it tends to be more child centered than family centered in operation. Central to this service approach is the need for flexible funding so that services that are not available can be developed and purchased. However, in reality wrap-around services are often subjected to resource limitations and the vested interest of the current service system, which tends to exert forces away from individualization and toward component services, and shift attention away from the needs of all family members to focus more exclusively on the child or adolescent with an emotional disorder. This tendency, however, is related to the fact that many wrap-around services have been applied in circumstances where children were already in out-of-home placements and, in many cases, estranged or disconnected from their families.

Respite Care

Respite care is among the key components of family support services; however, it is not available to most families whose adult or minor children have emotional or mental disorders. Although the need for respite service is frequently mentioned in the adult literature, only one outcome study of respite care for adults with psychiatric disabilities was located. Noteworthy is Geiser, Hoche, and King's (1988) report that a program allowing regularly scheduled admission to an inpatient unit for respite care was associated with significant decreases in hospitalization.

A U.S. Government Accounting Office (GAO) (1990) study of respite care for children at risk of abuse and neglect, defined as including children with disabilities, revealed that respite services were specifically identified as available to children with serious emotional disorders in 11 states, 6 of which indicated that they did not have statewide services available. It should be noted that statewide availability is a reference to geography, and not to universal access. Most of the states that specifically identified children with emotional disorders as eligible did not have data on the numbers of families served. A number of states maintained that eligibility for respite services was broad, indicating that children with emotional disorders might be eligible.

From the data available, there is one example that illustrates the state of service development for families whose children have emotional disorders. According to the GAO report, New York state provided respite care through the state mental health authority to 177 families with children who have behavior or emotional disturbances or mental retardation. By comparison, 13,000 families of children with developmental disabilities received respite services through the state developmental disabilities / mental retardation authority.

Although respite services are not widely available to families whose children have serious emotional disorders, considerable attention has been given to developing concepts and specialized training related to respite care (Friesen et al., 1988), and to sharing information with providers and family members through conferences and workshops (Schultze & Friesen, 1992). Respite care is also included as a part of core services available through specialized demonstrations, such as the programs within the Mental Health Program for Youth funded by the Robert Wood Johnson foundation (Beachler, 1990). This inclusion is possible because of the emphasis on flexible funding within these projects; respite care is not traditionally seen as a mental health service, so obtaining it usually involves program development or new funds for purchase of service.

Psychoeducational Approach

In the field of adult mental health, considerable research has been conducted on a controversial psychoeducational approach that can be interpreted as a family support service but is not usually labeled as such. Research related to the concept of *expressed emotion* (EE) (Leff & Vaughn, 1985) focuses on the relationship between the emotional climate surrounding the person with a psychiatric disability and the rate of relapse. Briefly, the theory holds that people with psychiatric disabilities who live in families with a high degree of expressed emotion, particularly critical or negative emotion, are more likely to relapse than those who live in calm, supportive, less expressive environments (Lefley, 1992). The issue of blaming families makes this theory controversial (Hatfield, 1987).

As with all services, the psychoeducational approach's appropriateness and supportiveness must be determined by the families who choose to use it. It can show family members how to deal with difficult behaviors and reduce the number of negative family interactions, which may help to address some of the behavior management needs identified by families. Parallel psychoeducational approaches for families whose children have mental or emotional disorders have not been widely implemented or reported in the literature, but many families suggest that such approaches are sorely needed.

Case Management

In order for states to retain eligibility for mental health block grant funds, case management for children defined as having serious emotional disturbances must be provided (State Mental Health Services Comprehensive Plan, 1986, PL 99-660). Because of scarce resources for human services programs, however, development of these services is spotty across the United States. In a recent study, Franks-Jacobs (1992; 1995) reported that only 9 (26%) of 35 states surveyed were judged to have considerable development in case management services. Furthermore, although the policy requiring case management services exists, there are powerful incentives to limit the amount of resources that must be devoted to this service (and other children's mental health services) by defining serious emotional disturbance very narrowly, and case management very broadly.

Case management is a well-established and widely available service for adults with psychiatric disabilities that has been considerably researched (Anthony & Blanch, 1989; Chamberlain & Rapp, 1991; Rubin, 1992). However, it is generally not considered to be a part of family support services in the field of adult mental health, especially if the person with a psychiatric disability does not live with his or her parents, despite the fact that case managers often assume tasks and roles that would otherwise be assumed by family members and often provide other support to families. This point is underlined by the finding that family members' satisfaction with mental health services was directly related to the amount of contact that they had with a case manager (i.e., those with more contact were more satisfied) (Grella & Grusky, 1989).

Home-Based Services

Home-based services are another service component that can be a part of a comprehensive family support system. Programs, such as Homebuilders

(Fraser & Haapala, 1988; Nelson, Landsman, & Deutelbaum, 1990), combine in-home family therapy with a variety of other possible interventions, including skill building and concrete services. Home-based services were originally developed to intervene in family crises where the placement of a child in out-of-home care was imminent, and many states have adopted this eligibility criterion (Nelson et al., 1990). As Small and Whittaker (1979) write, however, enthusiasm for this service has tended to focus on the in-home location, which is difficult to separate from the content, purpose, and process of service. In-home services may be enormously supportive to families, or they may be intrusive, disruptive, and unwelcome. Because home-based services are increasingly being implemented in the field of children's mental health, vigilance is needed to guarantee that they, and other services labeled "family-based," are not oppressive (Reed & Jacobson, 1992). Research is needed to sort out such issues as the interaction of location, content, process, and family characteristics and preferences with outcomes.

Family Support Programs

A few programs labeled family support were located in the adult mental health literature. Craig et al. (1987) describe a program in a regional mental health system that is designed to be family centered and individualized. Program goals include promoting communication between families and professionals, developing mutual support systems among families, and enhancing family coping skills and problem-solving abilities. Family support groups are the primary vehicle used in these programs. As many other mental health programs have most likely implemented similar programs, a systematic evaluation of their acceptability and effectiveness, then dissemination of evaluation results, is needed.

Bernheim and Switalski (1988b) report on an innovative program that sought to build family support into all aspects of families' contact with a psychiatric inpatient institution through engaging families and staff in a program of organizational change. A joint committee of family members and staff, along with two consultants, worked together to conduct an assessment of family and staff attitudes toward family involvement, develop staff training and policies designed to increase the institution's supportiveness of families, implement family-oriented services, and engage in ongoing evaluation. The authors describe this program as very successful; it was so well accepted by families and staff that the joint meetings were made an ongoing part of the hospital program, which demonstrates the possibility of a partnership between staff and families, the ability to operate family support programs without a substantial infusion of funds, and the feasibility of institutional change.

In the children's mental health field, VanDenBerg and Minton (1987) describe an approach to developing an entire Alaskan village as a support system for children with mental or emotional disorders and their families. The process builds on the resources and culture of the people who live in the villages and supports them in designing a needs assessment and providing their own solutions.

Three Oregon counties, as part of a federal demonstration project, assisted low-income families in gaining access to mental health services for their children through the creation of a paraprofessional role called a *family associate*. This program was designed to test the effectiveness of support in improving the accessibility of services and preventing service discontinuance in the Early and Periodic Screening, Diagnosis, and Treatment (EPSDT) program (Koroloff, Elliott, Koren, & Friesen, 1994). The family associate provided information, emotional support, assistance with arranging appointments, and a flexible fund to help with the cost of child care, transportation, or other resource needs identified by families as barriers to using services. The intervention, which focused on the period from the initial referral for mental health services through the first three appointments, was successful in increasing the rate of enrollment in services.

Family support is a central feature of a research demonstration project in New York state, the Family-Centered Intensive Case Management program (FCICM) described by Armstrong and Evans (1992). This project is designed to compare therapeutic foster care with intensive family support in families whose children have serious emotional disorders. Families who participate in FCICM receive an array of services, including intensive case management, access to respite care, family support groups, and other family support services, including recreation and the services of a paid family advocate.

Perhaps, though, the most fully developed family support program in children's mental health is the Finger Lakes Family Support Program in New York state. Designed as a collaborative effort of parents and professionals in nine rural counties, this project includes parent support groups with on-site child care, respite care provided by workers who are selected and trained by a team of parents and professionals, a newsletter, an annual conference, and parent retreats. Overall planning is done by a joint committee of parents and professionals. Decisions, such as how to spend the discretionary funds for the project, selection of training topics and speakers, and respite program issues, are made by the 150 participating parents in their support groups. The parent coordinator for this project recently wrote the following:

> Family support is here to stay. . . . Professionals who work with our families report that family support actually makes their job easier. Many have become supportive and active in our efforts. It's so exciting to see professionals treating parents with respect and recognizing their expertise. . . . Every time I hear a parent say that this project has changed their lives, I want everyone to be fortunate enough to be a part of it! My dream is for no parent to be or feel alone, and to have parents empowered to help themselves. (Friesen & Wahlers, 1993, p. 12)

Recommended Practices

It is evident that, aside from the important work of family organizations, family support services for families whose adult or minor children have serious mental or emotional disorders are severely underdeveloped. Almost any service that is supportive to families would be an improvement in many situations. For this reason, recommended practices extracted from the program examples presented in the previous section should be accepted as the best (and nearly all) that there is at the present time, and future assessment standards should employ the following principles of family support:

- Build on family strengths.
- Acknowledge families as the primary source of information about their child's and their own needs.
- Tailor services to fit the family's needs and preferences.
- Focus on the whole family.
- Be appropriate for the family's culture and traditions.
- Utilize formal and informal supports.
- Respect the family's choices about the nature, timing, and location of services.

Recommended practices should also address the following common challenges of families:

- Stigma and blame—address families with respect and involve them as partners
- Prolonged uncertainty—provide up-to-date and complete information
- Difficult behaviors and interpersonal interactions—provide emotional and tangible support, information, and skills
- Financial problems—provide assistance so that family members can keep their jobs if they choose to be employed, work to change policies and funding approaches that mitigate against families and children staying together (Federation of Families, 1992)

IMPLICATIONS FOR POLICY DEVELOPMENT AND POLICY REFORM

The most basic recommendation is to acknowledge and act on the urgent need for services; people with serious mental or emotional disorders are not included in most federal and state family support programs. A first step is to expand eligibility criteria for existing key components such as respite care, in-home support, and other programs. Being added to existing component programs, however, will not accomplish the goal of family-centered services. Current policies and any new policies should be examined in relation to the principles of family support to anticipate the impact that they will have on families. Specific steps are given below:

- **Review current policies against the principles of family support and family-centered service:**

1. **Identify blatantly harmful policies and institute programs for reform.** For example, the requirement in many states that parents whose children need out-of-home placement must relinquish custody in order to gain access to publicly funded services must be abolished (Cohen et al., 1991; Ervin, 1992; McManus & Friesen, 1989). Addressing this issue will require coordinated policy change at federal, regional, and state levels.

2. **Identify policies and funding approaches that mitigate against state-of-the-art practice.** Examples of such policies include Medicaid and Title IV-E funding regulations that encourage out-of-home placement.

3. **Identify opportunities where policy can be used to increase family input and choice.** The requirement in PL 99-660 for family participation in the development of state plans is a positive example of this principle. The implementation of this requirement needs better monitoring, however, because often family involvement is solicited in the initial planning meetings and review of early drafts, but the final product is not returned to the planning body for review and may be substantially different from the expressed preferences of families. Some states (e.g., Louisiana, New York, Virginia) are also instituting mandatory participation of family members in mental health and interagency service planning.

4. **Identify areas where family strengths and informal supports can be promoted, rather than eroded, by policy.** Paying relatives to provide foster care is a good example of this issue. Although federal policy allows states to pay relatives to provide foster care, which at least in principle should utilize a family's informal support system and preserve family ties, many states have instituted administrative rules that do not take advantage of this option.

- **Develop policy initiatives that directly address the principles of family support and family-centered service:**

1. Build principles of family support into all children's mental health legislation.
2. Model collaboration by promoting federal interagency initiatives for family support and family-centered service.
3. Build requirements for collaboration and family participation into new initiatives (e.g., planning for services and research).
4. Provide training and support for change—people can only do what they know how to do.

IMPLICATIONS FOR RESEARCH

Current research demonstration programs in the area of family support are promising. Knowledge building in family support should be able to proceed rapidly, given the foundation that has been laid in other fields, and the excellent communication that exists among researchers working in the area of mental health family research. Current research cycles, however, do not provide sufficient time to conduct solid research in areas such as family support, where new services must be developed, implemented, and stabilized, in addition to the central research tasks of data collection and analysis. Furthermore, there is a need for instrument development to keep pace with new concepts and issues of interest. Although the development of measures is expensive and time consuming, resources should be devoted to this activity, as well.

In November 1992, a group of family members and researchers met to develop recommendations about research priorities in the area of family research in children's mental health (Friesen, Koroloff, & Koren, 1993). Recommendations regarding priorities and methodological issues were generated in four areas: 1) parent–professional collaboration and training, 2) family support and family advocacy, 3) multicultural competence in working with families, and 4) financing of family support and family-centered service.

Several general themes emerged from this meeting that are of particular relevance. First, family members should be involved as full and active participants in all phases of research. Family members have much to offer in the generation and refinement of research topics, development and review of questionnaires, review and interpretation of research findings, and planning for dissemination of results, as well as in more traditional roles as respondents and consumers of research.

Second, outcomes should be mutually valued by the various constituencies interested in mental health research. These include policy makers who are interested in issues such as cost-effectiveness, public acceptance of need and of the means of delivering services, and reasonable cost, among others. Service providers and researchers, who often share the same professional training, have tended to emphasize the clinical aspects of family research, focusing on issues such as improved child and family functioning, placement in least restrictive options, and similar objectives. Family members are often concerned about issues such as affordability and accessibility of services, improved child functioning, improved family relationships, a balanced life for all family members, and acquiring needed supports to keep their children at home. Although these outcomes are not necessarily in conflict, they do reflect different perspectives and preferences about what dependent variables are chosen for specific studies. Hunter and Friesen (in press) suggest convening groups of policy makers, providers, researchers, and family members to discuss and negotiate the issue of acceptable outcomes. This process is one way of involving those who have an ultimate interest in mental health research, and moving the issue of family support to a central position in the minds of policy makers and providers who are in positions to influence the course of mental health services.

Chapter Review

CHALLENGES

- Families of children with emotional or behavior disorders are traditionally underserved.
- Family support, as a policy and service initiative, has been slow to emerge in mental health.
- Stigma associated with mental health disorders and the lack of societal understanding of the challenges facing families with members who are mentally ill have slowed the development of family advocacy.
- There is little literature available that describes family support research or programs in mental health.
- Traditionally, theoretical approaches to children's mental health have either emphasized the family as pathology or disregarded the roles of families in treatment or health promotion.
- Despite many differences in goals and services for adults and children with serious mental health challenges, families of children and adults share many common experiences, including stigma, uncertainty regarding diagnosis, difficult behaviors and interactions, and financial problems.

CHARACTERISTICS OF HELPFUL PROGRAMS

- Effective interventions focus on systems change at the state level and the design of flexible, individualized, ecologically based services for children and their families.
- Programs emphasize family-defined, comprehensive services that promote family coping and informal supports.
- Services include emotional support, service coordination, financial help, respite care, crisis support, in-home assistance, and help with behavior management.
- Programs facilitate family support groups and parent-to-parent support and advocacy.
- Ideally, wrap-around services with flexible funding are tailored to address individual needs.

POLICY IMPLICATIONS

- People with serious mental disorders must be included in federal and state family support programs.

- Current policies and practices should be evaluated for their impact on families and modified to promote family strengths, family decision making, informal supports, and home-based services.
- Major research needs exist in family support and family advocacy, parent–professional collaboration, financing of family-centered services, and multicultural competence.
- Research should be designed and undertaken through partnerships among researchers, families, service providers, and policy makers.

References

American Psychiatric Association. (1994). *Diagnostic and statistical manual of mental disorders* (4th ed.). Washington, DC: Author.

Anthony, W.A., & Blanch, A. (1989). Research on community support systems: What have we learned? *Psychosocial Rehabilitation Journal, 12*(3), 55–81.

Arieti, S. (1974). *Interpretation of schizophrenia* (2nd ed.). New York: Basic Books.

Armstrong, M.I., & Evans, M.E. (1992). Three intensive community-based programs for children and youth with serious emotional disturbances and their families. *Journal of Child and Family Studies, 1*(1), 61–74.

Asarnow, J.R., & Horton, A.A. (1990). Coping and stress in families of child psychiatric inpatients: Parents of children with depressive and schizophrenia spectrum disorders. *Child Psychiatry and Human Development, 21*(2), 145–157.

Atwood, J.D. (Ed.). (1992). *Family therapy.* Chicago: Nelson Hall.

Backer, T.E., & Richardson, D. (1989). Building bridges: Psychologists and families of the mentally ill. *American Psychologist, 44*(3), 546–550.

Bateson, G. (1972). *Steps to an ecology of the mind.* New York: Ballantine.

Beachler, M. (1990). The mental health services program for youth. *Journal of Mental Health Administration, 17*(1), 115–121.

Bernheim, K.F., & Lehman, A.F. (1985). *Working with families of the mentally ill.* New York: Norton.

Bernheim, K.F., & Switalski, T. (1988a). Mental health staff and patients' relatives: How they view each other. *Hospital & Community Psychiatry, 39*(6), 663–665.

Bernheim, K.F., & Switalski, T. (1988b). The Buffalo family support project: Promoting institutional change to meet families' needs. *Hospital & Community Psychiatry, 39*(6), 663–665.

Brekke, J.S., & Test, M.A. (1987). An empirical analysis of services delivered in a model community support program. *Psychosocial Rehabilitation Journal, 10*(4), 51–61.

Bremner, R.H. (Ed.). (1972). *Children and youth in America: A documentary history.* Cambridge, MA: Harvard University Press.

Briggs, H., & Richards, K. (1993). *Statewide family organization demonstration projects: Interim report.* Portland, OR: Research & Training Center on Family Support and Children's Mental Health, Portland State University.

Bronfenbrenner, U. (1979). *The ecology of human development.* Cambridge, MA: Harvard University Press.

Burchard, J.D., & Clarke, R.T. (1990). The role of individualized care in a service delivery system for children and adolescents with severely maladjusted behavior. *Journal of Mental Health Administration, 7*(1), 48–60.

Burford, G., & Casson, S.F. (1989). Including families in residential work: Educational and agency tasks. *British Journal of Social Work, 19*(1), 19–37.

Butler, T.E., & Friesen, B.J. (1988a). *Respite care.* Portland, OR: Research & Training Center on Family Support and Children's Mental Health, Portland State University.

Butler, T.E., & Friesen, B.J. (1988b). *Respite care: An annotated bibliography.* Portland, OR: Research & Training Center on Family Support and Children's Mental Health, Portland State University.

Carling, P.J. (1984). *The National Institute of Mental Health Community Support Program: History and evaluation.* Washington, DC: National Institute of Mental Health.

Chamberlin, R., & Rapp, C. (1991). A decade of case management: A methodological review of outcome research. *Community Mental Health Journal, 27*(3), 171–188.

Cohen, R., Harris, R., Gottlieb, S., & Best, A.M. (1991). States' use of transfer of custody as a requirement for providing services to emotionally disturbed children. *Hospital & Community Psychiatry, 42*(5), 526–530.

Collins, B., & Collins, T. (1990). Parent–professional relationships in the treatment of seriously emotionally disturbed children and adolescents. *Social Work, 35*(6), 522–527.

Cournoyer, D.E., & Johnson, H.C. (1991). Measuring parents' perceptions of mental health professionals. *Research on Social Work Practice, 1*, 399–415.

Craig, T., Hussey, P., Kaye, D., Mackey, K., McCreath, J., Tremblay, J., & Vedus, M. (1987). Family support program in a regional mental health system. *Hospital & Community Psychiatry, 38*(5), 459–460.

DeChillo, N. (1993). Collaboration between social workers and families of patients with mental illness. *Families in Society, 74*(2), 104–115.

Doll, W. (1976). Family coping with the mentally ill: An unanticipated problem of deinstitutionalization. *Hospital & Community Psychiatry, 27*, 183–185.

Education for All Handicapped Children Act of 1975, PL 94-142. (August 23, 1977). Title 20, U.S.C. 1401 et seq: *U.S. Statutes at Large, 89*, 773–796.

Erickson, M.T. (1968). MMPI comparisons between parents of young emotionally disturbed and organically retarded children. *Journal of Consulting and Clinical Psychology, 32*, 701–706.

Ervin, C.L. (1992). Parents forced to surrender custody of children with neurobiological disorders. In E. Peschel, R. Peschel, C.W. Howe, & J.W. Howe (Eds.), *New directions for mental health services: Neurobiological disorders in children* (No. 54, pp. 111–116). San Francisco: Jossey-Bass.

Federation of Families for Children's Mental Health. (1992). *Principles on family support*. Alexandria, VA: Author.

Forness, S.R., & Knitzer, J. (1991). *A new proposed definition and terminology to replace "serious emotional disturbance" in Individuals with Disabilities Education Act*. Alexandria, VA: National Mental Health Association, National Mental Health and Special Education Coalition.

Franks-Jacobs, D. (1992). Children's case management state-level survey. In K. Kutash, C.J. Liberton, A. Algarin, & R.M. Friedman (Eds.), *A system of care for children's mental health—expanding the research base: 5th annual conference proceedings* (pp. 315–322). Tampa: Research & Training Center for Children's Mental Health, Florida Mental Health Institute, University of South Florida.

Franks-Jacobs, D. (1995). States' policy response to the need for case management. In B.J. Friesen & J. Poertner (Eds.), *From case management to service coordination for children with emotional, behavioral, or mental disorders* (pp. 373–385). Baltimore: Paul H. Brookes Publishing Co.

Fraser, M., & Haapala, D. (1988). Home-based family treatment: A quantitative-qualitative assessment. *Journal of Applied Social Science, 12*(1), 1–23.

Freud, E. (1990). *Family support programs for families who have children with severe emotional, behavior, or mental disabilities: The state of the art*. Cambridge, MA: Human Services Research Institute.

Freud, S. (1952). Recommendations to physicians. In *The complete works of Freud* (Vol. 12). London: Hogarth Press.

Friesen, B.J. (1989). *Survey of parents whose children have serious emotional disorders: Report of a national study*. Portland, OR: Research & Training Center on Family Support and Children's Mental Health, Portland State University.

Friesen, B.J. (1991). *Organizations for parents whose children have serious emotional disorders: Report of a national study*. Portland, OR: Research & Training Center on Family Support and Children's Mental Health, Portland State University.

Friesen, B.J. (1993). Creating change for children with serious emotional disorders: A national strategy. In T. Mizrahi & J. Morrison (Eds.), *Advances in community organization and social administration* (pp. 137–146). New York: Haworth Press.

Friesen, B.J., Griesbach, J., Jacobs, J.H., Katz-Leavy, J., & Olson, D. (1988). Improving services for families. *Children Today, 17*(4), 18–22.

Friesen, B.J., Koren, P.E., & Koroloff, N.M. (1992). How parents view professional behaviors: A cross-professional analysis. *Journal of Child and Family Studies, 1*(2), 209–231.

Friesen, B.J., & Koroloff, N.M. (1990). Family-centered services: Implications for mental health administration and research. *Journal of Mental Health Administration, 17*(1), 13–25.

Friesen, B.J., Koroloff, N.M., & Koren, P.E. (1993). *Family symposium: Developing a research and demonstration agenda for services in children's mental health: Conference report.* Portland, OR: Research & Training Center on Family Support and Children's Mental Health, Portland State University.

Friesen, B.J., & Wahlers, D. (1993). Respect and real help: Family support and children's mental health. *Journal of Emotional and Behavioral Problems, 2*(4), 12–15.

Fromm-Reichmann, F. (1948). Notes on the development of treatment of schizophrenics by psychoanalytic psychotherapy. *Psychiatry, 11*, 263–273.

Garfinkel, P.E., Garner, D.M., Rose, J., Darby, P.L., Brandes, J.S., O'Hanlon, J., & Walsh, N. (1983). A comparison of characteristics in the families of patients with anorexia nervosa and normal controls. *Psychological Medicine, 13*, 821–828.

Geiser, R., Hoche, L., & King, J. (1988). Respite care for mentally ill patients and their families. *Hospital & Community Psychiatry, 39*(3), 291–294.

Goldman, H.H. (1982). Mental illness and family burden: A mental health perspective. *Hospital & Community Psychiatry, 33*, 557–560.

Greenley, J.R., & Robitschek, C.G. (1991). Evaluation of a comprehensive program for youth with severe emotional disorders: An analysis of family experiences and satisfaction. *American Journal of Orthopsychiatry, 6*(2), 291–297.

Grella, C.E., & Grusky, O. (1989). Families of the seriously mentally ill and their satisfaction with services. *Hospital & Community Psychiatry, 40*(8), 831–835.

Grosser, R., & Vine, P. (1991). Families as advocates for the mentally ill: A survey of characteristics and service needs. *American Journal of Orthopsychiatry, 61*(2), 282–290.

Hatfield, A.B. (1981). Families as advocates for the mentally ill: A growing movement. *Hospital & Community Psychiatry, 32*, 641–642.

Hatfield, A.B. (1986). Semantic barriers to family and professional collaboration. *Schizophrenia Bulletin, 12*(6), 325–333.

Hatfield, A.B. (1987). The expressed emotion theory: Why families object. *Hospital & Community Psychiatry, 38*, 341.

Hatfield, A.B., & Lefley, H.P. (1987). *Families of the mentally ill: Coping and adaptation.* New York: Guilford Press.

Hingtgen, J., & Bryson, C. (1972). Recent developments in the study of early childhood psychoses: Infantile autism, childhood schizophrenia, and related disorders. In S. Chess & A. Thomas (Eds.), *Annual progress in child psychiatry and child development* (pp. 503–576). New York: Brunner / Mazel.

Holden, D.F., & Lewine, R.J. (1982). How families evaluate mental health professionals, resources, and effects of illness. *Schizophrenia Bulletin, 8*(4), 626–633.

Howe, J.W. (1988). Commentary. In M. Harris & L.L. Bachrach (Eds.), *New directions for mental health services: Clinical case management* (No. 40, pp. 51–52). San Francisco: Jossey-Bass.

Individuals with Disabilities Education Act of 1990 (IDEA), PL 101-476. (October 30, 1990). Title 20, U.S.C. 1400 et seq: *U.S. Statutes at Large, 104* (part 2), 1103–1151.

Institute of Medicine. (1989). *Research on children and adolescents with mental, behavioral, and developmental disorders: Mobilizing a national initiative.* Washington, DC: Institute of Medicine, Division of Mental and Behavioral Medicine, National Academy Press.

Jenson, J.M., & Whittaker, J.K. (1987). Parental involvement in children's residential treatment. *Children and Youth Services Review, 9,* 81–100.

Johnson, D.L. (1989). Schizophrenia as a brain disease: Implications for psychologists and families. *American Psychologist, 44*(3), 553–555.

Johnson, H.C. (1986). Emerging concerns in family therapy. *Social Work, 31*(4), 299–306.

Johnson, H.C., Atkins, S.P., Battle, S.F., Hernandez-Arata, L., Hellelbrock, M., Libassi, M.F., & Parish, M.S. (1990). Strengthening the "bio" in the biopsychosocial paradigm. *Journal of Social Work Education, 2,* 109–123.

Karp, N., & Bradley, V. (1991). Family support. *Children Today, 20*(2), 28–31.

Knitzer, J. (1982). *Unclaimed children.* Washington, DC: Children's Defense Fund.

Koroloff, N.M., Elliott, D.J., Koren, P.E., & Friesen, B.J. (1994). Connecting low-income families to mental health services: The role of the family associate. *Journal of Emotional and Behavioral Disorders, 2*(4), 240–246.

Koroloff, N.M., & Friesen, B.J. (1990). *Statewide family organization demonstration project, 1988–89: Final report.* Portland, OR: Research & Training Center on Family Support and Children's Mental Health, Portland State University.

Koroloff, N.M., & Friesen, B.J. (1991). Support groups for parents of children with emotional disorders: A comparison of members and nonmembers. *Community Mental Health Journal, 27*(4), 265–279.

Kotsopoulos, S., Elwood, S., & Oke, L. (1989). Parent satisfaction in a child psychiatric service. *Canadian Journal of Psychiatry, 34*(6), 530–533.

Leff, J.P., & Vaughn, C. (1985) *Expressed emotion in families: Its significance for mental illness.* New York: Guilford Press.

Lefley, H.P. (1987). Impact of mental illness in families of mental health professionals. *Journal of Nervous & Mental Disease, 175,* 613–619.

Lefley, H.P. (1989). Family burden and family stigma in major mental illness. *American Psychologist, 44*(3), 556–560.

Lefley, H.P. (1992). Expressed emotion: Conceptual, clinical and social policy issues. *Hospital & Community Psychiatry, 43*(6), 591–598.

Loff, C.D., Trigg, L.J., & Cassels, C. (1987). An evaluation of consumer satisfaction in a child psychiatric service: Viewpoints of patients and parents. *American Journal of Orthopsychiatry, 57*(1), 132–134.

Lourie, I., & Katz-Leavy, J. (1985). *Severely emotionally disturbed children and adolescents.* Rockville, MD: Child and Adolescent Service System Program, National Institute of Mental Health, U.S. Department of Health and Human Services.

McManus, M.C., & Friesen, B.J. (1986). *Families as allies. Conference proceedings.* Portland, OR: Research & Training Center on Family Support and Children's Mental Health, Portland State University.

McManus, M.C., & Friesen, B.J. (1989, June 1). *Relinquishing legal custody as a means of obtaining services for children who have serious mental or emotional disorders.* Testimony before Subcommittee on Human Resources, Committee on Ways and Means, U.S. House of Representatives.

Miller, F., Dworkin, J., Ward, M., & Basrone, D. (1990). A preliminary study of unresolved grief in families of seriously mentally ill patients. *Hospital & Community Psychiatry, 41*(12), 1321–1353.

Miller, W.H., & Keirn, W.C. (1978). Personality measurement in parents of retarded and emotionally disturbed children: A replication. *Journal of Clinical Psychology, 24,* 686–690.

Moroney, R.M. (1980). *Families, social services, and social policy.* Rockville, MD: National Institute of Mental Health, U.S. Department of Health and Human Services.

Nelson, C.M., Rutherford, R.B., Center, D.B., & Walker, H.M. (1991). Do public schools have an obligation to serve troubled children and youth? *Exceptional Children, 57*(5), 406–415.

Nelson, K.E., Landsman, M.J., & Deutelbaum, W. (1990). Three models of family-centered placement prevention services. *Child Welfare, LXIX*(1), 3–21.

Olson, D. (1988). A developmental approach to family support: A conceptual framework. *Focal Point, 2*(3), 2.

Peschel, E., Peschel, R., Howe, C.W., & Howe, J.W. (Eds.). (1992). *New directions for mental health services: Neurobiological disorders in children* (No. 54). San Francisco: Jossey-Bass.

Petr, C.G., & Barney, D.D. (1993). Reasonable efforts for children with disabilities: The parents' perspective. *Social Work, 38*(1), 247–253.

Petr, C.G., & Spano, R.N. (1990). Evolution of social services for children with emotional disorders. *Social Work, 35*(3), 228–234.

Quine, I., & Paul, J. (1985). Examining the cause of stress in families with severely mentally handicapped children. *British Journal of Social Work, 15,* 501–517.

Reed, C., & Jacobson, Y. (1992, July 19). *Families' perspectives on wrap-around services.* Workshop presentation: Developing local systems of care, sponsored by Georgetown CASSP Technical Assistance Center, Breckenridge, CO.

Reinke, B., & Greenley, J. (1986). Organizational analysis of three community support models. *Hospital & Community Psychiatry, 37*(6), 624–629.

Rowe, K. (1991). *Study of groups for parents of children with serious emotional disorders in Virginia.* Richmond, VA: Department of Mental Health, Mental Retardation, and Substance Abuse Services.

Rubin, A. (1992). Is case management effective for people with a serious mental illness? A research review. *Health and Social Work, 17*(2), 138–158.

Schultze, K.H., & Friesen, B.J. (1992). *Respite care: A key ingredient of family support: Conference proceedings.* Portland, OR: Research & Training Center on Family Support and Children's Mental Health, Portland State University.

Small, R., & Whittaker, J. (1979). *Residential group care and home-based care: Toward a continuity of family services.* Springfield, IL: Charles C Thomas.

Spaniol, L., Jung, H., Zipple, A., & Fitzgerald, S. (1987). Families as a resource in the rehabilitation of the severely psychiatrically disabled. In A.B. Hatfield & H.P. Lefley (Eds.), *Families of the mentally ill: Coping and adaptation* (pp. 167–190). New York: Guilford Press.

State Mental Health Services Comprehensive Plan, PL 99-660. (November 14, 1986). Title 42, U.S.C. 300 et seq: *U.S. Statutes at Large, 100,* 3794–3797.

Tarico, V.S., Low, B.P., Trupin, E., & Forsyth-Stephens, A. (1989). Children's mental health services: A parent perspective. *Community Mental Health Journal, 25,* 313–326.

Tessler, R.C., Gamache, G.M., & Fisher, G.A. (1991). Patterns of contact of patients' families with mental health professionals and attitudes toward professionals. *Hospital & Community Psychiatry, 42*(9), 929–934.

Thomas, N., & Friesen, B.J. (1989). *Next steps: Toward a national agenda for families whose children have serious emotional, behavioral, or mental disorders: Conference proceedings.* Portland, OR: Research & Training Center on Family Support and Children's Mental Health, Portland State University.

U.S. Government Accounting Office. (1990). *Respite care: An overview of federal, selected state, and private programs.* Washington, DC: Superintendent of Documents.

VanDenBerg, J.E. (1993). Integration of individualized mental health services into the system of care for children and adolescents. *Administration and Policy in Mental Health, 20*(4), 247–257.

VanDenBerg, J.E., & Minton, B. (1987). Alaska native youth: A new approach to serving emotionally disturbed children and youth. *Children Today, 16*(5), 15–18.

Vosler-Hunter, R.W. (1989). *Changing roles, changing relationships: Parent–professional collaboration on behalf of children with emotional disabilities.* Portland, OR: Research & Training Center on Family Support and Children's Mental Health, Regional Research Institute, Portland State University.

Wahl, O.F. (1989). Schizophrenogenic parenting in abnormal psychology textbooks. *Teaching of Psychology, 16*, 31–33.

Wasow, M., & Wikler, L. (1983). Reflections on professionals' attitudes toward the severely mentally retarded and the chronically mentally ill: Implications for parents. *Family Therapy, 10*(3), 299–308.

Waxler, N.E., & Mishler, E.G. (1972). Parental interaction with schizophrenic children and well siblings: An experimental test of some etiological theories. In S. Chess & A. Thomas (Eds.), *Annual progress in child psychiatry and child development* (pp. 568–589). New York: Brunner/Mazel.

Weiss, H. (1986). Family support and education programs: Working through ecological theories of human development. In H. Weiss & F. Jacobs (Eds.), *Evaluating family programs* (pp. 3–36). New York: Aldine de Gruyter.

Weissbourd, B., & Kagan, S. (1989). Family support programs: Catalysts for change. *American Journal of Orthopsychiatry, 59*(1), 20–31.

Whittaker, J.K. (1976). Causes of childhood disorders: New findings. *Social Work, 21*(2), 21–26.

Whittaker, J.K. (1980). Family involvement in residential treatment: A support system for parents. In A.N. Maluccio & P.A. Sinanoglu (Eds.), *The challenge of partnership: Working with parents of children in foster care.* New York: Child Welfare League of America.

Whittaker, J.K., & Garbarino, J. (1983). *Social support networks: Informal helping in the human services.* New York: Aldine De Gruyter.

Woesner, M.E. (1983). A professional's guide to books for families of the mentally ill. *Hospital & Community Psychiatry, 34*(10), 925–938.

Young, T.M. (1990). Therapeutic case advocacy: A model for interagency collaboration in serving emotionally disturbed children and their families. *American Journal of Orthopsychiatry, 60*(1), 118–124.

13

Individualized
Wrap-Around Services
for Children with Emotional,
Behavior, and Mental Disorders

Naomi Karp

Since the 1970s, the field of developmental disabilities has undergone major changes. For example, the family advocacy movement has surged ahead. And, as a result of families' hard work, the quality of opportunities available to people with developmental disabilities and their families has improved dramatically. Families whose children had developmental disabilities were quick to organize and develop services for their youngsters when none were available. They also were leaders in litigation and legislative initiatives to improve services and opportunities for their daughters and sons. With the 1975 passage of the Education for All Handicapped Children Act, PL 94-142, families received a Congressionally mandated right and responsibility to have a voice in their children's educational services. A second related change has radically shifted service provision from professionals in restrictive, human warehouses (Blatt & Kaplan, 1974) to families, friends, neighbors, professionals, and/or nonprofessionals in the family home and other community places. Customizing supports to meet each family's needs is state-of-the-art practice in a growing number of states.

This article was written by the author in her private capacity. No official support or endorsement by the U.S. Department of Education is intended or should be inferred.

Still, the field of children's mental health has been reluctant to change the way it provides services to youngsters with emotional, behavior, and mental disorders and their families. Many professionals still recommend expensive hospitalizations and restrictive residential schools as the treatments of choice. Additionally, some professionals still blame and shame, rather than support and encourage families. Until recently, there has been a family advocacy vacuum, with few advances in the field. In the mid-1980s, however, changes slowly began, resulting in new ways of thinking about services. Families and professionals started adapting successful ideas from the developmental disabilities field. One new way of supporting this population of children and their families is with individualized wrap-around services. This chapter describes the evolution and components of wrap-around services, discusses research and social policy implications related to wrap-around services, and makes recommendations for future research.

THE EVOLUTION OF WRAP-AROUND SERVICES

History

Although families whose children had emotional and behavior disorders were slow to respond to the call for advocacy and involvement (Karp, 1992), beginning in 1982, the following five separate, but interrelated, events brought about a chain of dramatic changes in children's mental health.

Unclaimed Children Report

In 1982, Jane Knitzer prepared the report, *Unclaimed Children,* for the Children's Defense Fund. This seminal report called attention to the dismal and archaic state of policies and programs for children with serious emotional disorders. It revealed a total lack of family advocacy for, professional support of, and public commitment to model services that needed to be addressed immediately. At that time, state mental health systems had no contact with child welfare, juvenile justice, and/or education, all of which had mandates to serve children (Knitzer, 1982). Furthermore, and perhaps most important, the study found the following:

- The traditional, existing services simply did not meet the needs of the children and their families. A 50-minute office visit was insufficient, but hospitalization was excessive. Between 40% and 60% of hospitalized children did not need to be there.
- Between one third and one half of the children hospitalized in many states were actually in custody of child welfare agencies, a fact that remains true today. Families actually relinquish custody to the state in order to get services that are usually inappropriate, ineffective, and out-of-home for their children.

- Those youth not hospitalized usually received a series of evaluations as their only services; few, if any, community-based services were available to meet their needs.

Unclaimed Children quickly became the rallying point for children's mental health advocates (Karp, 1992). There was an urgent need to design a system that would support and respond to the children and families who would use it. This meant, according to Knitzer (1993), providing services that were not the ineffective, traditional inpatient and outpatient treatments. Rather, a new system was needed to provide help with housing, education, and other survival tasks, including support for families (Knitzer, 1993).

Children's and Adolescent Service System Program

In 1984, the Children's and Adolescent Service System Program (CASSP) was established by Congress. As a response to *Unclaimed Children* and the pleas of mental health advocates, the National Institute of Mental Health (NIMH) received $1.5 million from Congress to begin a federal program that would enable states to develop multilevel systems to meet the needs of children with emotional, behavior, and mental disorders (Boyd, 1992; Stroul & Friedman, 1986). According to Lourie and Katz-Leavy (1992), Congress established this innovative, but small, program because 1) the services at that time were fragmented; 2) children in need of services were being served by mental health, child welfare, juvenile justice, and special education; and 3) the children who had the most severe problems were served by one agency even though their actual needs crossed several service systems. Furthermore, the goal of CASSP was to improve multiagency state-level services for children with, or in danger of developing, emotional and mental disorders.

In order for children to be eligible to receive services under this system of care, CASSP developed the following criteria:

- Be under 18 years of age
- Have an emotional disability based upon social functioning criteria, not just diagnosis
- Have multiagency service needs
- Have a mental health problem diagnosable under DSM-IV (American Psychiatric Association, 1994) or another system used by the state
- Have a mental disability that lasts or is at risk of lasting at least 1 year (Stroul & Friedman, 1986)

Similarly, CASSP funds would be awarded to states on a competitive basis if the following certain criteria (Knitzer, 1993) were met:

- The states had to develop leadership for children and adolescent programs and policies within their departments of mental health.

- The state mental health departments had to demonstrate a collaborative relationship with other state child-serving agencies.
- The states had to include new principles of service delivery in the development of a range of community-based services.
- The states had to encourage and strengthen family advocacy in order to build networks of change agents.
- The states had to make mental health service systems responsive to the varied cultural, racial, and ethnic populations of children and families needing to use the systems.

In 1985, the first competition for CASSP grants was conducted, with 44 states applying for funds. Ten states received funding, but by 1989, all 50 states had received CASSP support to develop and/or improve children's mental health services (Knitzer, 1993).

Research and Training Center

In 1984, the National Institute on Disability and Rehabilitation Research (NIDRR), in the U.S. Department of Education, announced that it intended to fund a Research and Training Center dedicated to children's mental health issues. As a result of the CASSP competition, the CASSP program staff initially approached NIDRR and offered to jointly fund the winning proposal, but then NIDRR and CASSP actually funded two Research and Training Centers focusing on children's mental health. One center, at the University of South Florida at Tampa, focused on systems change; the other, at Portland State University in Oregon, focused on family support and mental health. Both centers became major change agents in the field. In addition, CASSP funded a Technical Assistance Center, located within the Georgetown University Child Development Center.

The center at the University of South Florida began investigating ways to integrate the public service systems that primarily dealt with children with emotional disorders. These systems may include juvenile justice, child welfare, maternal and child health, education/special education, mental health, and/or vocational rehabilitation. Frequently, a youngster may be enrolled in a special education class, receive group therapy from a community mental health center, and be on probation for a juvenile offense. Rarely, however, do the adults working for the various public systems know that the child is a customer of all of their services. Thus, there is virtually no coordinated effort to provide integrated, comprehensive services and supports to the child and his or her family (Boyd, 1992). The Florida center began researching ways to bring together a coordinated system of care in order to yield better outcomes for children with emotional, behavior, and mental disorders.

At the same time, the Portland center began developing strategies to improve relationships and collaboration between families and mental health professionals—a difficult feat as there were no easily identifiable and viable advocacy organizations solely for families whose children had emotional disorders. After scouring the country for families, the Portland State staff convened the first Families as Allies conference in 1986. The purposes of the conference were threefold: 1) to develop a knowledge base about professional and family advocacy efforts on behalf of children with serious emotional disturbances, 2) to stimulate activity in each state in order to increase the degree of professional–family collaboration, and 3) to develop and disseminate conference products about family–professional collaboration (McManus & Friesen, 1986). Mental health professionals and families from 13 western states attended this landmark conference that revolutionized the idea of families and mental health professionals working together toward common goals, and Families as Allies gradually began to spread to the midwest, south, east, and northeast regions of the country.

Parent–professional collaboration became a new password in state-of-the-art thinking. Suddenly families were demanding to be included in decisions about their children's treatments, and they wanted to be respected by mental health professionals. Families were tired of being told that they were the source of their children's problems and wanted to be included as part of the solution. No longer did they accept shame and blame therapy; instead, they wanted support for themselves and their children. Families were starting to view themselves differently, to stand up, to speak out, and to be counted. Family advocacy was taking hold (Karp, 1992) and professionals began listening and responding in positive ways.

Next Steps Conference

In December 1988, the family advocacy movement became formalized at the Next Steps Conference. Throughout the 1980s, there was a growing recognition that family involvement is necessary if children and youth are to have improved outcomes (Karp, 1993b). In tandem with, and as a result of, the series of Families as Allies conferences and the Next Steps Conference, a national advocacy organization composed of families whose children had emotional, behavior, and mental disorders evolved (Karp, 1992).

The purpose of the Next Steps Conference was to set a national children's mental health agenda, based on Portland State's 4 years of research for families. One of Next Steps' purposes was to lay the groundwork for an ongoing national coalition of families, professionals, and citizens concerned with improving services for children with emotional, behavior, and mental disorders and their families (Friesen, 1990). At the end of the meeting, 17 family members from across the country decided to meet again in February 1989 in order to form a national organization (Karp, 1992), which was the genesis of the Federation of Families for Children's Mental Health, the first national advocacy organization dedicated solely to children's mental health and family support issues.

Since 1989, the Federation of Families has played a key role in improving services, policies, and laws affecting children with mental health disorders and their families (Karp, 1992). The Federation has served as an impetus for organizing and supporting families, particularly families of different ethnicities who traditionally have been overrepresented in the service systems but have received little real support. The Federation also has worked intensely to erase the term *dysfunctional families* from the repertoire of mental health professionals. According to the Federation of Families' philosophy statement, families view service systems as dysfunctional when their needs are not met, which adds extra and unnecessary stress on them. The Federation asks professionals to build on families' strengths and respect each family's values and choices. Additionally, the Federation has helped establish a strong, active national network of families who are becoming forceful change agents in their communities. Slowly, but surely, families are coming forward to assist in the planning, delivery, and evaluation of their daughters' and sons' mental health services (Karp, 1992).

Family-Centered Services

In the mid-to-late 1980s, the concept of family-centered services appeared in the field of health care for children with chronic illnesses and disabilities (Shelton, Jeppson, & Johnson, 1987). Family-centered attitudes are based on the idea that the family and child with special needs are at the center of the delivery system; services revolve around and support the family unit (Turnbull & Summers, 1987). The Association for the Care of Children's Health convened working groups of families and developed principles upon which family-centered health care service delivery systems should be built. The specific elements of family-centered care state the following:

- The family is a constant in the child's life, but the professionals within the service system are transient.
- There should be parent–professional collaboration at all levels of care.
- Professionals should share unbiased and complete information with parents about their child's care on an ongoing basis and in a supportive and appropriate way.
- Policies and programs should be comprehensive and provide emotional and financial support to meet families' needs.
- Each family's strengths, individuality, and different coping styles should be recognized and respected.
- The developmental needs of all children and their families should be incorporated into the delivery system.
- Parent-to-parent support should be encouraged and facilitated.
- Delivery systems should provide services that are flexible, accessible, and responsive to family needs.
- Services should be respectful of each family's ethnic, racial, and cultural background.

Family centeredness began to revolutionize how health care professionals perceived and communicated with families. This model also has been permeating the field of developmental disabilities, and now family-centered approaches are being incorporated into mental health services, policies, and practices (Karp, 1992).

These five events of the 1980s documented and highlighted the fact that traditional children's mental health services are grossly inadequate and ineffective in supporting children and their families. This, in turn, prompted the development of the CASSP system of care philosophy and the move to individualized, wrap-around services.

Systems of Care

As mentioned previously, the Research and Training Center at the University of South Florida began to investigate multiple systems serving children with a range of emotional and behavior disorders. The CASSP Technical Assistance Center's Advisory Board also began to develop a conceptual framework upon which CASSP services could be built. In 1986, based upon the work of the Advisory Board and the Research and Training Center, Stroul and Friedman published *A System of Care for Severely Emotionally Disturbed Children and Youth*. The CASSP system of care is built on two concepts: 1) it is child/family centered, and 2) it is community based. Its guiding principles are as follows:

1. Emotionally disturbed children should have access to a comprehensive array of services that address the child's physical, emotional, social, and educational needs.
2. Emotionally disturbed children should receive individualized services in accordance with the unique needs and potentials of each child and guided by an individualized service plan.
3. Emotionally disturbed children should receive services within the least restrictive, most normative environment that is clinically appropriate.
4. The families and surrogate families of emotionally disturbed children should be full participants in all aspects of the planning and delivery of services.
5. Emotionally disturbed children should receive services that are integrated, with linkages between child-caring agencies and programs and mechanisms for planning, developing, and coordinating services.
6. Emotionally disturbed children should be provided with case management or similar mechanisms to ensure that multiple services are delivered in a coordinated and therapeutic manner and that they can move through the system of services in accordance with their changing needs.
7. Early identification and intervention for children with emotional problems should be promoted by the system of care in order to enhance the likelihood of positive outcomes.
8. Emotionally disturbed children should be ensured smooth transitions to the adult service system as they reach maturity.
9. The rights of emotionally disturbed children should be protected, and effective advocacy efforts for emotionally disturbed children and youth should be promoted.
10. Emotionally disturbed children should receive culturally competent services that are sensitive and responsive to cultural differences and special needs and are provided without regard to race, religion, national origin,

> sex, physical disability, or other characteristics. (Stroul & Friedman, 1986, p. vii)

In addition to the principles, the system of care framework contained seven components and a range of specific services, as shown in Table 1.

THE MOVE TO INDIVIDUALIZED SERVICES

This inclusion of the family was radical for mental health. The system concept of care principles and service components was a dramatic departure from traditional, mental health treatment programs based on the medical model. The focus on designing and customizing services to meet the specific needs of individual children was an important advancement. Yet, in all too many instances, children and families still were being forced into traditional programs and offered the same ineffective treatments. Families, advocates, and many mental health professionals began adopting the CASSP principles

Table 1.   Components of the system of care

1. **Mental health services**	4. **Health services**
Nonresidential services	Health education and prevention
Prevention	Screening and assessment
Early identification/intervention	Primary care
Assessment	Acute care
Outpatient treatment	Long-term care
Home-based services	
Day treatment	5. **Vocational services**
Emergency services	Career education
Residential services	Vocational assessment
Therapeutic camp services	Job survival skills training
Independent living services	Vocational skills training
Residential treatment services	Work experiences
Crisis residential services	Job finding, placement, and retention
Inpatient hospitalization	services
	Supported employment
2. **Social services**	
Protective services	6. **Recreational services**
Financial assistance	Relationships with significant others
Home aide services	After-school programs
Respite care	Summer camps
Shelter services	Special recreational programs
Foster care	
	7. **Operational services**
3. **Educational services**	Case management
Assessment and planning	Self-help and support groups
Resource rooms	Advocacy
Self-contained special education	Transportation
Special schools	Legal services
Home-bound instruction	Volunteer programs
Residential schools	
Alternative programs	

From Stroul, B.A., & Friedman, R.M. (1986). *A system of care for severely emotionally disturbed children and youth.* Washington, DC: CASSP Technical Assistance Center, Center for Child Health and Mental Health Policy, Georgetown University Child Development Center; reprinted by permission.

as guidelines for measuring the appropriateness of newly developing state systems.

However, as with all concepts and philosophies, time and practice led to revisions and adaptations to the original system of care principles and components. Time and experience are showing that the original principles and components are sound but require modifications if they are to continue to be the basis for planning and delivering state-of-the-art services.

In addition, recent advances and philosophical changes in the field of developmental disabilities again have had an effect on the practices in children's mental health, slowly infiltrating and altering current theories. For example, families whose children have developmental disabilities speak of inclusion in neighborhood schools; thus, segregated classes and special schools are being increasingly rejected (Martin, 1992). Additionally, in a quickly expanding number of states, families whose children have developmental disabilities have access to family support programs, which provide *whatever it takes* for families with special needs to live as typically as possible (Bradley, Knoll, & Agosta, 1992; Karp & Bradley, 1991).

Families and many mental health professionals are now realizing that there are options other than expensive out-of-home placements, restrictive segregated schools, and devaluing self-contained classes. They are asking for in-school and/or in-home supports to enable children with emotional, behavior, and mental disorders to remain at home in nurturing environments. Finally, the idea of whatever it takes has reached the mental health profession. Many professionals and families are literally interpreting the individualization principle and demanding that flexible, custom-designed supports and services be wrapped around the children and their families. These services are always flexibly funded and unconditional, are usually coordinated, and can be intensive—a support strategy that should foster, and often result in, typical, productive lives (Boyd, 1992). Thus, the individualization of services is expanding, both as a philosophy and a process, as more and more communities implement systems of care (Katz-Leavy, Lourie, Stroul, & Ziegler-Dendy, 1992). The process of individualizing services has four main components: 1) flexible funding and services, 2) service coordination, 3) interagency collaboration, and 4) wrap-around services. In order for wrap-around to be successful, the other three components must be functioning well.

What Is Wrap-Around?

The term wrap-around originated in North Carolina, where the use of flexible funds allowed service coordinators to wrap the services around children and their families, rather than forcing children into existing service programs. In this approach, the service coordinator, treatment team, or service program administrator can, with the family, add or delete any services and supports to tailor a program to meet the child's and/or family's specific needs at that time in order to meet specific goals that have been mutually agreed upon in a service plan (Katz-Leavy et al., 1992).

In addition, wrap-around services use all the regular community resources available—informal and formal, nontraditional and traditional. The International Initiative on the Development, Training, and Evaluation of Wrap-Around Services (Boyd, 1992; Katz-Leavy et al., 1992) defines wrap-around as having the following attributes:

- *Community-based and unconditional*—Restrictive or institutional care is used only for short-term stabilization procedures. The team agrees never to deny services because of the severity of the disability, never to dismiss or reject a child or family from appropriate services, and to change services only as the needs of the child or family change.
- *Developed by a team of interdisciplinary service providers*—This includes the family/surrogate family, an advocate, systems' representatives, and other people who are important in the child's and family's life.
- *Focused on the strengths of the child and family*—The team meets with the family to determine their strengths and ascertain what supports will provide the family with normalizing experiences.
- *A package of coordinated, custom-made services in three or more life domains of a child and family*—Life domain areas include family life, residential, social, educational, medical, recreational, psychological, community life, and safety.

These concepts were pioneered, developed, and are continually being refined by three leaders in the wrap-around movement. Karl Dennis of the Kaleidoscope program in Chicago successfully works with inner-city youngsters and firmly believes in the no eject–no reject policy. John Vandenberg, one of the creators of the Alaska Youth Initiative, understands how to pool resources, build teams, and improve outcomes for children who usually have rotten outcomes (Boyd, 1992). And John Burchard, of the University of Vermont, was one of the first to document and validate the benefits of wrap-around services.

Katz-Leavy and her colleagues (1992) identified criteria used by several communities to include children as eligible for individualized and wrap-around services: Many states require that the children fulfill the following conditions:

- Have serious emotional or behavior disorders
- Have functional impairments
- Need multiagency services
- Be placed, or at risk for placement, in restrictive residential treatment settings
- Have difficult and complex needs that are not being met within the framework of the existing service system

Successful individualized wrap-around services are dependent on flexible funding. There are numerous examples of creative ways in which flexible interagency funding streams have been wrapped around children and their families. For example, funds have been used to provide the following (Katz-Leavy et al., 1992):

- Buy a washing machine for a family whose child has a severe bed-wetting problem
- Provide a classroom aide to enable a girl with a bipolar disorder to attend her neighborhood school rather than have to go to an out-of-city school
- Buy a membership at the YMCA after-school recreation program for a boy with a conduct disorder
- Pay to fix the family car so that a boy could then get to the YMCA
- Pay a neighbor to be a big sister to a girl who is extremely withdrawn
- Hire a job coach so that a high school student with a panic disorder can work at a small factory
- Pay the monthly tuition at a community preschool for a 4-year-old who has depression and needs to have playmates without disabilities
- Hire a high school student to come in every morning to help a child with a severe attention deficit disorder and a tendency for truancy to get ready for school

The list of options is infinite, limited only by each team's flexibility and creativity. Perhaps one of the best uses of wrap-around services is to design individualized packages of supports that will bring children back from restrictive out-of-home or even out-of-state placements.

The Alaska Youth Initiative illustrates this benefit perfectly. Alaska was paying up to $500 per day for children with severe and persistent emotional disorders to go to expensive, private, out-of-state psychiatric facilities. In 1985, in an effort to find ways to cut costs and still effectively treat the children with the most difficult problems, the senior staff from the state's departments of education, mental health, and developmental disabilities and the division of family and youth services formed the Interdepartmental Team (IDT) (Boyd, 1992). IDT began implementing wrap-around service principles, and the costs per child per year were reduced from $72,000 to $40,000 in the first year of their return to Alaska; the second year also showed a cost savings, with better services (Burchard & Clarke, 1990). Of 117 children, only two had to be placed out-of-state during the first 2 years of the project; subsequently, both children have returned to Alaska (Boyd, 1992).

Vermont, North Carolina, Alaska, and other states are confirming that intensive service coordination is also an essential ingredient to the success of individualized, wrap-around services (Boyd, 1992; Katz-Leavy et al., 1992). The coordinator's role is multifaceted: marshalling resources, bringing the team together, helping the family identify its resources, developing a mutually agreed-upon interagency plan, ensuring coordination across agencies, and being ready when and if crises or problems arise.

Perhaps the most crucial element in successful wrap-around services is strong interagency collaboration. In a recent survey of 15 programs that provide individualized services, the greatest percentage of respondents (42%) said that interagency collaboration was the most important factor in the program's success (Katz-Leavy et al., 1992). Burchard and Clarke (1990) found that an interdisciplinary team that tracks services across agencies makes individualized care easier to implement, promotes shared ownership, and decreases the likelihood that one agency will do something without agreement from the other agencies. The interagency team concept illustrates how a group of people working together to achieve the same goals can dramatically improve results.

Since the early 1980s, the publication of *Unclaimed Children*, the birth of the CASSP program at the federal level, the growth of the family advocacy movement, the swift implementation of systems of care, and the growing demand for individualized wrap-around services have greatly altered the world of children's mental health, resembling changes in the developmental disabilities field. The major differences between children's mental health and developmental disabilities are that 1) families in developmental disabilities have been organized and vocal for a much longer period of time, and 2) families have been a major force in bringing about changes in supports and services.

SOCIAL POLICY IMPLICATIONS RELATED TO WRAP-AROUND SERVICES

As systems try to meet families' and professionals' demands for more flexible fiscal and physical resources and state-of-the-art training to increase the availability of individualized wrap-around services, many questions and issues are arising that have implications for policies in education as it is the only mandated, zero-reject system with professionally trained personnel.

When considering social policy implications, it is important to remember that every current piece of disability-related federal legislation focuses on two themes (Karp, 1993a):

1. People with disabilities have a right to take part in classes, programs, and other activities that people without disabilities have access to.
2. People with disabilities may need to have supports, aides, services, and other types of accommodations so that they are able to benefit from classes, programs, and other activities in the community.

This means that under the Individuals with Disabilities Education Act of 1990 (IDEA), PL 101-476, the Americans with Disabilities Act of 1990 (ADA), PL 101-336, and the Rehabilitation Act Amendments of 1992, PL 102-569, children and youth with emotional, behavior, and mental disorders and their families must have opportunities to be fully included and supported in school, employment, and community activities. The language in these laws sets the tone for social policies for years to come.

Education—Social Policy Issues

Schools are not addressing the needs of children with emotional, behavior, and mental disorders. They are grossly underserved and inappropriately served, even under IDEA. According to the *Fourteenth Annual Report to Congress on the Implementation of the Americans with Disabilities Act of 1990* (Division of Innovation and Development, 1992) by the U.S. Department of Education, 392,559 children termed as having serious emotional disturbances (SED) were served in the 1990–1991 school year. This is only 9.3% of the more than 4 million total children served. In 1982, Knitzer estimated that over 3 million children were in need of mental health services. Other facts in the *Fourteenth Annual Report to Congress* (1992) are shocking:

- The percentage of students with SED served in regular schools went down 4.2% from 1980 to 1992. There has been a longitudinal decrease in the numbers served in regular buildings.
- In the 1989–1990 school year, 43.2% of the students with SED dropped out of school, almost twice the rate of any other category.
- Only 37% of students with SED graduated, compared to 57% for all students with disabilities.

Additionally, Koyanagi and Gaines (1993) found that this population of children are placed on home-based instruction more often than any other category. They also have lower grades, fail more frequently, and have a lower rate of promotion than children in any other category of disability. Also, these youngsters are underidentified, are sent to restrictive placements more frequently than any other students, and are low priorities for community and state mental health programs.

This population of youth also has a low employment rate, even 5 years after leaving school. They are enrolled in postsecondary programs at rates that are significantly lower than the general population and lower than any other disability category, except students with mental retardation. Involvements with juvenile justice are frequent, as are problems of substance abuse. They also use the public welfare, public health, and public mental health systems at a high rate (Koyanagi & Gaines, 1993).

From these alarming data, it can be concluded that schools are failing to meet the needs of students with emotional, behavior, and mental disorders (Koyanagi & Gaines, 1993). Educational, mental health, health, welfare, and justice systems must work together to correctly identify, evaluate, and then serve these students. The term *seriously emotionally disturbed* needs to be changed to *serious emotional/behavioral disorder*, as recommended by the Mental Health Special Education Coalition (Koyanagi & Gaines, 1993), to bring order to the chaos that exists because states vary so greatly in identifying and serving this population.

Individual wrap-around services are desperately needed to accommodate and support children with emotional disorders in inclusive classrooms, not in restrictive settings. Although no data indicate that restrictive placements yield better outcomes, professionals still overuse this placement. This change requires flexible funding streams so that creative teams can develop and carry out individualized, multiagency services that will support the child in the classroom, at work, and in social settings. Without the flexibility in funding, one system receives the brunt of the cost for the needs of a child that span several systems. The result is that the child usually does without needed supports and services. There has to be a shift from loading financial resources at the restrictive end of the service scale (e.g., residential treatment centers) and moving them to the community to pay for respite care, educational aides, service coordination, and a range of child and family supports (Katz-Leavy et al., 1992). One solution is to expand Medicaid reimbursement options to make more nonmedical services reimbursable (Koyanagi & Gaines, 1993).

Full implementation and enforcement of IDEA and the ADA also are imperative, meaning that families have to receive ongoing and effective education and information about their rights under the laws. Additionally, families need to know that they do not have to relinquish custody in order to get services for their children and support for the family, nor that they have to accept restrictive and/or traditional services. Families also need to learn strategies that will enable them to negotiate the public policy arenas so that they can become informed policy makers. They will then be able to develop legislation improving supports and services.

Professional Training—Social Policy Issues

The rate of attrition for teachers trained to work with children who have SED is the highest for any group of special education teachers. Koyanagi and Gaines (1993) found that while the vacancy rate for all special education teachers is 8.25%, there is a 12.4% vacancy rate for teachers of children with mental health disorders. This 12.4% may be even higher because all too frequently shortages are filled with untrained teachers.

Related services personnel issues are just as discouraging. The National Association of School Psychologists suggests that there be 1 school psychologist per 1,000 school children; the number of school psychologists is currently 1 school psychologist for every 2,221 school children (Koyanagi & Gaines, 1993). The National Association of Social Workers, Inc. suggests that there be at least 1 school social worker for every 2,000 students, or 1 social worker for every 500 students in schools with special education enrollments; the actual ratio is 1 social worker for every 4,763 students (Koyanagi & Gaines, 1993). With these types of work loads, how can professionals be expected to be active, creative members of wrap-around service planning teams?

The need for culturally competent, well-qualified staff to work with the children of different ethnicities who are overrepresented in the public systems is a pressing issue (Isaacs & Benjamin, 1991). This need extends across systems, across positions, and across disciplines. Burchard and Clarke (1990) and McFarquhar and Dowrick (in Katz-Leavy et al., 1992) report that negative professional attitudes are the greatest barrier to implementing wrap-around services. University training programs still offer traditional medical model mental health courses, with virtually no exposure to community alternatives. Burchard and Clarke found that once professionals saw wrap-around actually implemented, they began to change a little, but still could not erase the idea that funding has to be attached to categories and specific services. Thus, professional training is a major social policy issue, in need of immediate attention. Without adequate personnel, wrap-around will not be implemented.

IMPLICATIONS FOR FUTURE RESEARCH

These social policy issues create multiple research implications for individualized wrap-around services. An overarching concern is that the vast majority of children's mental health research is conducted by the National Institute of Mental Health (NIMH), which tends to focus on biomedical, experimental, clinical trial research. Under the recent NIMH reorganization, a new entity was created by Congress—the Substance Abuse Mental Health Services Administration (SAMHSA). Within SAMHSA is the Center for Mental Health Services (CMHS) that conducts only evaluation research. However, there is an enormous gap between traditional, clinical trial studies and evaluation research.

There is, unfortunately, very little solid data to validate the effectiveness of both long-term outcomes and cost savings related to wrap-around services. To gather these types of data, researchers need to use research methodologies that are not traditionally funded by NIMH and CMHS. It is difficult to collect information when services for each child will differ as will behaviors (Burchard & Clarke, 1990). This means that the mental health funding agencies should consider accepting proposals with single subject designs, qualitative research, and longitudinal case studies, in addition to traditional experimental group designs. Specific research questions to be addressed cut across systems and disciplines, but education and mental health need to take the lead.

Recommendations for Education

Under this new system, the education field should do the following:

- Develop and evaluate collaborative models in which multiagency wrap-around support services are coordinated by the schools and emphasize funding and service coordination.
- Develop and evaluate interventions and alternative curriculum models that will reduce the dropout rate of students with emotional disorders and increase employability.

- Conduct a state-by-state analysis of how many children with emotional disorders are in restrictive public settings with no educational programs in place.
- Develop and evaluate materials and strategies for educating social workers, juvenile justice personnnel, psychologists, and other professionals about the rights of students under IDEA, the ADA, and the Rehabilitation Act.
- Develop and evaluate curricula for interdisciplinary training, retention, and promotion of culturally competent professionals.
- Investigate the long-term outcomes for children and cost savings when children with emotional disorders are supported in regular education.

Recommendations for Mental Health

Under this new system, the mental health field should do the following:

- Investigate how changes in the public mental health system affect the private system.
- Investigate what financing and organizational change strategies promote integrated service delivery.
- Investigate the policy, attitudinal, and legislative disincentives to individualized services and develop solutions to overcome the barriers.
- Develop, with education departments, strategies for preventing burnout in both professionals and families.
- Develop functional assessment instruments for evaluating children with emotional disorders.

These suggestions merely touch upon what is needed to document and validate the outcomes of individualized wrap-around services. As Burchard and Clarke (1990) have stated, "There has been little systematic research demonstrating the cost-effectiveness of individualized care" (p. 59). Researchers across the United States are now challenged to develop and conduct a relevant, multidisciplinary, rigorous research program, the results of which will improve policies and strategies for child- and family-centered services in the community. The task is large, but the rewards, in terms of restoring dignity and value to children with emotional, behavior, and mental disorders and their families, will be even larger.

Chapter Review

CHALLENGES

- Prior to the 1980s, the field of children's mental health was operating on an outmoded paradigm that emphasized hospitalization and professional control.
- Parents are often blamed for their children's mental illnesses and emotional and behavior problems.
- Community-based services are only beginning to be created in many parts of the country.
- Services have been fragmented so that children are served by mental health, child welfare, juvenile justice, maternal and child health, vocational rehabilitation, and special education systems; often, there has been little communication or coordination among services.
- Unlike other disability fields, families have only recently organized advocacy groups and emerged as an influential group in children's mental health.
- Less than 20% of all children with serious emotional disturbances receive public school services; over 40% of all high school students with SED drop out before graduating.

CHARACTERISTICS OF HELPFUL PROGRAMS

- Helpful programs base their teams and services in the community.
- Restrictive or institutional care is used only for short-term stabilization.
- The team includes interdisciplinary service providers as well as the family or surrogate family, a child advocate, representatives from key service systems, and other people who are important to the child's and family's life.
- The team never denies services because of the severity of the disability—choosing instead to focus on the child's and family's resources.
- The team meets directly with the family to decide what experiences will create valued social roles for the child and family.
- The team establishes a package of coordinated and custom-made services in three or more life domains using flexible funding and will change these services only as the concerns of the family change.
- Strong interagency collaboration is the foundation of effective wraparound services.

POLICY IMPLICATIONS

- The same principles that guide policy for people with disabilities should be applied to children with serious emotional/behavior disorders.
- Full implementation of the ADA for children with emotional disabilities is essential, as is full implementation of IDEA.
- Families of children with emotional/behavior disorders must assume roles in policy making.
- Flexible funding mechanisms must be created, and funding allotted to research teams evaluating wrap-around and community-based services.
- Schools must increase personnel qualified to meet the concerns of children with emotional/behavior disorders, including school psychologists and social workers.
- Policy should be directed at recruiting and retaining more culturally competent professionals in all service systems.
- University programs must train human services workers to staff community service programs, including wrap-around services.

References

American Psychiatric Association. (1994). *Diagnostic and statistical manual of mental disorders* (4th ed.). Washington, DC: Author.

Americans with Disabilities Act of 1990 (ADA), PL 101-336. (July 26, 1990). Title 42, U.S.C. 12101 et seq: *U.S. Statutes at Large, 104,* 327–378.

Blatt, B., & Kaplan, F. (1974). *Christmas in purgatory: A photographic essay on mental retardation.* Syracuse, NY: Human Policy Press.

Boyd, L.A. (1992, July). *Integrating systems of care for children and families.* Tampa: Department of Child and Family Studies, Florida Mental Health Institute, University of South Florida.

Bradley, V.J., Knoll, J., & Agosta, J.M. (1992). Emerging issues in family support. *Monographs of the American Association on Mental Retardation, 18.*

Burchard, J.D., & Clarke, R.T. (1990). The role of individualized care in a service delivery system for children and adolescents with severely maladjusted behavior. *The Journal of Mental Health Administration, 17,* 48–60.

Division of Innovation and Development. (1992). *Fourteenth annual report to Congress on the implementation of the Individuals with Disabilities Education Act of 1990.* Washington, DC: U.S. Department of Education.

Education for All Handicapped Children Act of 1975, PL 94-142. (August 23, 1977). Title 20, U.S.C. 1401 et seq: *U.S. Statutes at Large, 89,* 773–796.

Friesen, B.J. (1990, June). *Introduction: Next Steps conference proceedings.* Portland, OR: Portland State University Research and Training Center on Family Support and Children's Mental Health.

Individuals with Disabilities Education Act of 1990 (IDEA), PL 101-476. (October 30, 1990). Title 20, U.S.C. 1400 et seq: *U.S. Statutes at Large, 104,* 1103–1151.

Isaacs, M.R., & Benjamin, M.P. (1991). *Towards a culturally competent system of care* (Vol. 2). Washington, DC: CASSP Technical Assistance Center, Center for Child Health and Mental Health Policy, Georgetown University Child Development Center.

Karp, N. (1992) *Building collaborative partnerships with families.* Unpublished paper.

Karp, N. (1993a, March). *Collaborating with families: Program leadership for serving students with disabilities.* Blacksburg: Virginia Polytech Institute and State University.

Karp, N. (1993b). *Inclusion: A right, not a privilege.* Farmington: University of Connecticut Health Center.

Karp, N., & Bradley, V.J. (1991). Family support. *Children Today, 20*(2), 28–31.

Katz-Leavy, J.W., Lourie, I.S., Stroul, B.A., & Ziegler-Dendy, C. (1992, July). *Individualized services in a system of care.* Washington, DC: CASSP Technical Assistance Center, Center for Child Health and Mental Health Policy, Georgetown University Child Development Center.

Knitzer, J. (1982). *Unclaimed children.* Washington, DC: Children's Defense Fund.

Knitzer, J. (1993). Children's mental health policy: Challenging the future. *Journal of Emotional and Behavioral Disorders, 1*(1), 8–16.

Koyanagi, C., & Gaines, S. (1993). *All systems failure.* Alexandria, VA: National Mental Health Association.

Lourie, I.S., & Katz-Leavy, J.W. (1992). New directions for mental health services for families and children. *Families in Society: The Journal of Contemporary Human Services, 72,* 277–285.

Martin, R. (1992). *Special education law—1992–1993: A year of changes.* Urbana, IL: Baxley Media Group/Reed Martin Conferences.

McManus, M.C., & Friesen, B.J. (1986, July). *Families as Allies conference proceedings.* Portland, OR: Portland State University, Research and Training Center to Improve Services for Seriously Handicapped Children and Their Families.

Rehabilitation Act Amendments of 1992, PL 102-569. (October 29, 1992). Title 29, U.S.C. 701 et seq: *U.S. Statutes at Large, 100,* 4344–4488.

Shelton, T.L., Jeppson, E.S., & Johnson, B.H. (1987). *Family-centered care for children with special health care needs.* Washington, DC: The Association for the Care of Children's Health.

Stroul, B.A., & Friedman, R.M. (1986). *A system of care for severely emotionally disturbed children and youth.* Washington, DC: CASSP Technical Assistance Center, Center for Child Health and Mental Health Policy, Georgetown University Child Development Center.

Turnbull, A.P., & Summers, J.A. (1987). From parent involvement to family support: Evolution to revolution. In S.M. Pueschel, C. Tingey, J.E. Rynders, A.C. Crocker, & D.M. Crutcher (Eds.), *New perspectives on Down syndrome* (pp. 289–306). Baltimore: Paul H. Brookes Publishing Co.

III

ISSUES AND INNOVATIONS
IN PUBLIC POLICY

14

Family Participation in New Community Schools

Wayne Sailor,
Jeannie Kleinhammer-Tramill,
Thomas Skrtic, and Brenda K. Oas

Family support is emerging as an important policy initiative across many arenas. This chapter addresses its importance within educational policy developments, because as conditions change for families, educational systems are affected. Often, communities are slow to respond to these changed family conditions in constructive ways. But if families are to provide supports to their members, then communities need to look at new ways to support families. Just as the social-ecological perspective places families within the larger community, schools are nested within that community as well and operate as significant service systems to families with children.

The school is one element of the community that is making some initial steps to respond more appropriately. Because schools are perceived to be relatively neutral entities in neighborhoods and are often viewed positively by families with children, they are looked to as institutions capable of organizing supports for families. Schools are typically closer and more accessible to families than are other agencies. Although educational services have typically been very child focused, schools offer an infrastructure that is adaptable to serving families also, as demonstrated by the many family resource center movements across the country that are using schools as host sites. The field of education demonstrates a growing awareness that childhood is changing and that schools' roles must change to keep pace.

FAMILIES IN SCHOOL POLICY REFORM

The school restructuring movement heralds changes in the relationships among families, communities, and schools. Traditionally, families have delegated the responsibility of educating their children to professional educators, while educators have expected families to assume responsibility for the health, nutrition, shelter, safety, and socialization of children. With few exceptions, both educators and families have accepted their respective contributions to the lives of children as *separate spheres of influence* (Epstein, 1992).

Conley (1993) describes the manner in which families and communities have delegated responsibility for schooling to professional educators:

> The structure of public education has evolved over the past 150 years based on much the same rationale used to develop common fire, police, sanitation, and public welfare systems. Once government creates a system, citizens have only to pay taxes and hold elected officials accountable for the efficient and effective delivery of the services. Well-trained professionals are to make the day-to-day technical decisions that drive the system and ensure provision of high-quality services to all. (p. 89)

Since the 1980s, however, the challenges of educating an increasingly diverse population of students, together with a changing economy and the need to prepare students with the skills to enter the postindustrial job market, have forced public attention on education, spawning intense dialogue about what schools can and should be responsible for doing and how they should be managed. This dialogue has produced consensus that professional educators cannot solve the myriad of social and economic problems that influence how children achieve in school, but, at the same time, they cannot perform their roles effectively without solutions to these problems. Thus, there is increasing recognition that education can effectively address these challenges only through meaningful interfaces—based on flexibility and permeability—with families and communities.

Recent Legislation

Recent legislation, Goals 2000: Educate America Act of 1994, PL 103-227, speaks directly to the need for greater involvement of families in the governance and process of education. Section 2(8) of the act states that one purpose of Goals 2000 is to provide assistance to "every elementary and secondary school that receives funds under this Act to actively involve parents and families in supporting the academic work of their children at home and in providing parents with skills to advocate for their children at school." Clearly, the intent of Goals 2000 is to increase opportunities for families to have a voice and collaborate in the education of their children. Goals 2000 also paves the way for schools to provide direct support to families through adult literacy classes, parenting or Parents-as-Teachers classes, school completion programs, and school-linked services, as described later in this chapter.

Another policy opportunity is offered by the Families of Children with Disabilities Support Act of 1994, PL 103-382, passed by Congress in October 1994, as part of the reauthorization of the Elementary and Secondary Education Act of 1965, PL 89-313. The new law provides a springboard for initiating a range of family-centered strategies for families who have children with disabilities. Under the law, the family support strategies selected by planners within each state are to be determined by the needs of families and are to be coordinated across agencies, including schools. Possible categories include training and technical assistance, policy studies, public awareness and education, or pilot demonstration projects. The Family Support Law offers families opportunities to become involved in identifying their own needs and collaborating with agencies to design appropriate supports. In some cases, these supports might be provided or coordinated by schools.

Family Participation Strategies

Conley (1993), Johnson (1993), and Wagstaff and Gallagher (1990) describe the range of strategies typically employed to engage families in education. Those strategies, ranging from passive participation of families to active participation and advocacy, include reports on achievement and educational programs, volunteer activities, home visits, family participation in site-based management, and challenges to family participation.

Reports on Achievement and Educational Programs

Wagstaff and Gallagher (1990) identify the most passive level of family involvement as that in which parents are merely recipients of information about their child's educational program and level of achievement within that program. Conley (1993) similarly identifies knowledge of learner outcomes as a way of monitoring and supporting student performance, also a passive strategy for family involvement. In either case, the communication process is often one way, and families have few opportunities to reveal the extent of their cognitive engagement with the information or their response to that information in terms of home activities. Furthermore, they have little or no voice in validating or disputing the information about their child's knowledge or in building a more complete picture of the child's interests and abilities based on interactions at home.

School and family interactions become somewhat more collaborative when families participate in setting learning goals for their child through the development of individualized education programs (IEPs) as mandated by the Education for All Handicapped Children Act of 1975, PL 94-142, for children with disabilities. Similar processes may be adopted by individual teachers or schools (Conley, 1993). Ideally, the process of developing the IEP involves collaboration between families and professionals to identify the child's resources, concerns, and current level of educational performance. Based on that information, families and professionals develop goals for the

individual child. Turnbull, Turnbull, Bronicki, Summers, and Roeder-Gordon (1989) have found, however, that IEP meetings often provide little real opportunity for parental voice in determining either their child's needs or the goals and / or content of instruction.

Volunteer Activities to Relieve Teachers of Noninstructional Tasks

Wagstaff and Gallagher (1990) classify noninstructional volunteer activities as another strategy that involves families in passive relationships with the school. Traditional parent–teacher organization activities may require parents to invest time and / or financial resources in the school; however, they do not offer families the opportunity to participate in decisions that affect school governance or instruction. Furthermore, traditional relationships between families and educators were built on the assumption that caregivers—usually mothers—were available during the day to engage in volunteer activities to support the school and, at the end of the school day, to monitor homework. The increase in the number of single-parent families and families in which both parents work severely limits this type of involvement (Johnson, 1993; Wagstaff & Gallagher 1990). Still, the family member who can volunteer during the school day has the advantage of experiencing and / or shaping the school culture, as well as observing his or her child in the social and learning context of the school.

Home Visits

During the 1940s and 1950s, schools often reached out to families by teacher visits to students' homes. This practice gradually faded as teachers' unions grew stronger; schools were consolidated into larger, more efficient units; social conditions for many students grew worse; and students were more frequently transported to distant school sites to achieve racial desegregation or to acquire specialized services. Current recognition that family support is integrally related to student achievement has revitalized this strategy (Conley, 1993). In addition, current emphasis on school readiness has spawned programs such as Parents-as-Teachers where educators provide information related to child development, emergent literacy, and behavior management to families. For young children with disabilities or those who are at risk for disabilities as defined by the Education of the Handicapped Act Amendments of 1986, PL 99-457, educational or therapeutic interventions are provided to both families and children in *natural environments*, which include the home, preschools or child development centers, and child care settings.

Family Participation in Site-Based Management

A core feature of current efforts to restructure schools involves participatory, site-based management that is designed to make schools more responsive to the concerns of the community and to empower parents to join administrators and teachers in a variety of planning, governance, and instruc-

tional tasks. Guthrie (1986) describes the rationale for site-based management of schools when he states, "A school faculty and its Principal constitute—or should constitute—a natural team. Moreover, parents and students usually give their allegiance to a school, rather than to a district or to a statewide educational system. Thus, it seems only logical that the school should be the primary decision-making unit in an educational system" (p. 306).

Governance of schools through site-based management typically involves development of site resource management teams (Sailor, Anderson, Halvorsen, Doering, Filler, & Goetz, 1989), site advisory councils, or similar team configurations consisting of families, community representatives, and educators. These site teams provide opportunities for collaboration and, thus, development of a shared vision of education. Team members ideally serve dual roles by representing the concerns of their constituent groups in managing schools and by disseminating information about the school to those whom they represent. Team members should also represent the community's needs and resources in terms of cultural, ethnic, and economic diversity.

The scope of issues addressed by site teams varies widely. At one end of the continuum, site councils may serve as merely an extension of the parent–teacher organization to address such issues as raising funds for specific school functions or building improvements. The other end of the continuum is represented by site resource management councils that are empowered to make key decisions about instruction, personnel, and allocation of resources to accomplish school improvement. The team's scope of authority and composition (including the inclusion of families on the site council) is often determined by the willingness of educators, particularly the building principal, to share authority (Conley, 1993).

Challenges to Family Participation

Regardless of the strategy for family involvement in schools, the school restructuring movement and related legislative programs, including those embodied in Goals 2000, acknowledge that schools can be successful only to the extent that partnerships with families and communities are forged. Although building new relationships with families is a core task in school restructuring, it poses challenges for both educators and families.

Family participation necessitates a willingness to abandon the delegation model of education and acknowledge that professionals cannot accomplish the task of education in isolation. It also means that families must learn advocacy and negotiation skills, as well as educational skills, for supporting their child's learning. The feasibility of family participation in education may depend upon the development of broader community supports, such as employers providing released time from work, schools providing extended hours of operation, and compensation for professionals and staff who meet the scheduling needs of working parents.

Professionals will, likewise, need to learn new roles and accommodate the extended work scope involved in family participation. Professional educators have become accustomed to the hierarchical roles that have been traditionally assigned by the education bureaucracy; educators have typically been socialized to see themselves as providers of information but must now learn to collaborate with students and their families in planning and delivering instruction. Educators will also need to learn to appreciate the diversity of values and cultures that families will bring to the collaborative process.

Conley (1993) cautions that opportunities for families to engage in school governance activities may be limited to safe family members who are not likely to challenge professionals. There is also concern that family participation in school governance might enable particular groups to forward agendas that conflict with larger societal goals. Still, the very energy and investment of people who wish to influence schools could serve as an impetus for the development of highly participatory site advisory teams; and representative site teams might, in turn, help to allay fears and misconceptions based on lack of information.

SCHOOL-LINKED SERVICES INTEGRATION

In spite of the tremendous efforts to improve schools through restructuring, there is growing recognition that change in education, alone, cannot withstand the tide of poverty and social problems that place a growing population of students at educational risk. Children who arrive at school in marginal or poor health will not respond positively to even the most innovative curriculum and teaching. Therefore, social welfare systems need to become more responsive to the day-to-day, real-life problems of individual children and families. It has been proposed that social and health services should be provided in the school setting or, at least, be coordinated with the school (Kirst, 1992). This movement toward site-based management is a critical first step toward implementing community-based, school-linked services. Site-based management allows for more flexible use of resources and for more localized decision making that is approached holistically, rather than on isolated areas of need. School-linked services integration offers a means for addressing root causes of educational risk (e.g., hunger, poverty, poor physical and/or mental health, abuse, neglect) by creating a single point of contact for all school and community services, and by locating services, when possible, in schools to promote access for families with multiple needs (Crowson & Boyd, 1993; Kirst, 1992).

The Need for School-Linked Services Integration

Many children and their families are in dire need of assistance in order to end the cycles of poverty, violence, abuse, malnutrition, and chronic health problems that can have lasting impact on future generations. The crises

affecting so many of our nation's children and families are compounded by the fact that poverty, illness, lack of education, and powerlessness make it difficult for many families to gain access to or use existing social services. Child abuse, health, income support, and housing statistics suggest that families' access to support services for children is actually declining (Kirst, 1989; 1992). During the economic stress of the 1980s, budgets for social services declined, making the caseloads of individual service providers unmanageable. As caseloads have grown, the quality and availability of service to individuals has declined. Furthermore, existing human services systems, funding patterns, and service delivery are typically organized around categorical needs so that children and families may or may not qualify under various programs for the full array of services they need.

Many families who would initiate access to health care or social welfare assistance fail to do so because of patterns of *learned helplessness* (Seligman, 1975). That is, when poverty prevents a family from gaining access to necessary transportation to reach service providers or, worse, when service providers and their respective agencies respond to these families by imposing rigid and incomprehensible eligibility guidelines, long waiting periods, attitudes of blame, or helpfulness only when the right family pathology is exhibited, the family is apt to feel as if they have lost control—completely helpless and at the mercy of an irrational system.

For families of children with disabilities, this attribution of helplessness may be compounded by chronic challenges posed by the disability. The family who is reluctant to go to church or other public places because of a child's behavior, who receives blame by extended family members and neighbors, who is unable to obtain respite care, or who is unable to envision a future of autonomy for their child may experience increased helplessness (Turnbull, Ruef, & Reeves, 1993). These families may, in addition, experience poverty, engage in violence against their children, or face separation or divorce as a result of the disability. Families of children with disabilities often confront an overwhelming and fragmented array of services, ranging from neonatal intensive care and various therapies after the child is born to the need for legal and financial counseling when faced with issues related to the child's transition to adulthood (Turnbull et al., 1989).

The Promise of School-Linked Services

School-linked services integration is a promising strategy for bringing families into contact with the services they need. Within a school-linked services integration model, education (and all of its specialized support categories), health and its subsystems, employment (business and industry as active participants), social and recreational systems, judicial systems, housing support systems, and religious supports, among others, are made accessible to the family and child through a single point of contact linked with or even located in the school. This means that agencies that have typically functioned quite independently agree to work in a coordinated fashion to meet

families' concerns. In ideal situations, funding and services that are typically earmarked by category of need are used flexibly to ensure that no child or family falls through the cracks of categorical services. School-linked services integration is prevention, rather than crisis, oriented; and it addresses problems from neonatology to the school years, including the period of transition from school to adult status. The model provides for a single point of contact, service coordination, and long-term progress evaluation, and provides a seamless web of support services that cuts across all of the service systems that characterize the community served.

This service transformation must be driven by the makeup of particular neighborhoods in the community and, in turn, be a source of resources and assistance to those communities (Gerry & Certo, 1992). Where services to children and their families have previously been agency focused in scope and application, the services must become family focused and community managed. Under such a configuration, emphasis is placed on actual service delivery events and specifiable outcomes, rather than on narrowly defined agency services. A problem-solving approach becomes possible, particularly when the integrated services structure permits flexible funding to meet particular unanticipated needs at the community level (Sailor, 1991).

Growing Commitments to School-Linked Services Integration

Efforts to improve the delivery of health, education, social, and welfare services to children and their families through interagency coordination and collaboration are currently being hailed as novel approaches to serving clients in both an efficient and cost-effective manner. Although currently gaining a great deal of attention, these efforts are not new. Kagan and Neville (1993) have traced the history of integrating human services in America back to the colonial period. Historians and policy analysts cite numerous, but isolated, examples of federal and state attempts at services integration prior to the 1960s. However, there is general consensus that the current focus on services integration started in the 1960s.

Crowson and Boyd (1993) state, "Few ideas have caught on in public education as rapidly or as widely as the notion that public schools and other social and health agencies should collaborate to provide more effective services for children" (p. 143). Indeed, interagency agreements and efforts to stimulate the development of school-linked services integration range from federal efforts, such as those of the U.S. Department of Education (USDOE) and U.S. Department of Health and Human Services (HHS) (Melaville, Blank, & Asayesh, 1993), to state and local efforts.

However, the spread of school-linked services integration has not always been accompanied by reasonable efforts to evaluate success. Crowson and Boyd caution,

> in the case of coordinated services for children, all manner of arks are being launched into poorly understood weather and waters. Not surprisingly, this sense of "damn the torpedoes, full speed ahead" has exacted a price. A number

of coordinated ventures have foundered on the shoals of interagency relationships. (p. 141)

As school-linked services integration provides a means for addressing the critical problems facing many families and overshadowing the future of many children, it is essential to begin to develop a set of properly evaluated practices for effective implementation. This includes an understanding of the policies that facilitate or impede delivery of school-linked services integration and an understanding of its impact on children with disabilities.

In some communities, family resource centers have been established as the conduit for integrating services. Such centers may be located in or near a school or at another convenient neighborhood site. In this model, personnel are hired to serve as a single point of contact and service coordinator for families. An individual family would visit with the contact person to explain their situation and to discuss appropriate options. This contact person would make the necessary inquiries to clarify options with agencies or other services thus streamlining what is often a frustrating or confusing process for families. The family would then make a decision based on the options available.

In some cases, it may be possible to get needed services at the family resource center. For example, a public health nurse or employment counselor might be at the center 2 days each week and be available for family consultations. In other cases, the family's contact person might arrange transportation so the family can obtain services available elsewhere in the community. The family's contact person would typically communicate with the family as a follow-up to determine if the services received were satisfactory. In the family resource center model, it is advantageous for the same contact person to work with the family over time to better understand the family's needs and to develop a trusting relationship.

School-linked services integration appears to offer tremendous promise for bringing families into contact with the services they require. Yet, the challenge of achieving collaborative systems where fragmentation and specialization abound are great (Skrtic, 1991). Furthermore, relatively little is known about the impact of these emerging efforts on the lives of children with disabilities and their families.

Key Components of Effective Services Integration

Models (New Beginnings, 1990; Sailor, 1991) that demonstrate relationships among school restructuring, inclusive education, and school-linked services integration are particularly useful in considering the impact of school-linked services integration on children with disabilities and their families.

To review briefly, *school restructuring* allows schools to function with relative autonomy through site-based management and, thus, involves teachers and parents in the use of resources to stimulate student outcomes. As a result, management of restructured schools is participatory so that teachers, support staff, and family members come together in collaborative

team arrangements at the school. There, they plan how to use all of the resources at the school in a way that would benefit all children. Categorical services, including special education, Chapter 1, and bilingual education are reconfigured and coordinated to the benefit of all of the students at the school. Furthermore, the school and community are brought closer together through collaborative planning activities.

Inclusive education for students with disabilities means that these students receive the services they need in age-appropriate general education classrooms and other fully integrated school and community settings, rather than in segregated special education classrooms; students with disabilities are served in their neighborhood schools or the attendance centers that they would participate in if they did not have disabilities; and students with disabilities are represented in natural proportion, rather than clustered in one or a few schools. Furthermore, eligibility requirements and services for students with disabilities are organized around student need rather than categories of exceptionality, and special education exists as a support service to the general education classroom so that the context of education is made appropriate and accessible to the student rather than the student to the context. Thus, general education classrooms better accommodate students with disabilities and also acknowledge that all students have special needs of varying intensity and duration.

The *school-linked services integration* component of this interactive model acknowledges that many students, including those with disabilities, have needs that directly affect their ability to participate effectively in education. Under this arrangement, children and families become the focus of the service system, not the agencies that provide the services. Under this reform effort, it is recognized that investing early in the lives of children may prevent significant social, educational, and health problems later in life. Agency supports are provided in a decentralized fashion through a community, family-assistance planning council. This council is made up of service agency representatives from all human assistance systems in the community, representatives of families who use these services (e.g., families with low income, parents of children with disabilities), and service coordinators who link the family service planning efforts in the community to the special assistance programs that operate in the schools. Under this arrangement, all support systems in the school and the community operate in accordance with each other; there is no duplication of services, nor do children fall through the gaps in the various systems of support. A single family services plan is generated at the local community level that wraps around the child in school, and the child and family in the community.

INCLUSIVE EDUCATION

As evidenced by the current controversies surrounding reauthorization of the Elementary and Secondary Education Act—Improving America's

Schools Act, PL 103-382—a revolution in service delivery systems and related educational practices for children with special needs is occurring. This revolution takes several forms. First, based on the recognition that children who are at educational risk are more alike than different, many have proposed merging the resources of special education with those of remedial and compensatory education, bilingual education, and migrant education to provide more comprehensive services for all (Reynolds & Lakin, 1987; Reynolds & Wang, 1981; Will, 1986). Second, based on both ethical and philosophical arguments and effectiveness research, many have proposed ending pullout services for children with remedial or compensatory educational needs (Eyler, 1982; Johnston, Allington, & Afflerbach, 1985; National Institute of Education, 1978; Walberg, 1984).

The trend toward inclusive education for students with special needs and infusion of resources from programs such as Chapter 1, special education, limited English proficiency, migrant education, and so on represents a critical step in involving families for several reasons.

Decategorizing Resources and Services

Traditionally, the challenge of educating diverse populations of students has meant an attempt to carve out homogeneous subgroups of the student population. Thus, programs for children in poverty, for children who speak languages other than English, for children whose families are migrant workers, for children with disabilities, and for other subgroups of children have developed through legislation that entitles them to educational services that might remediate or compensate for problems caused by these circumstances.

However, there is widespread acknowledgment that, in spite of these programs, many students fall through the cracks of service delivery because they or their families do not meet categorical eligibility requirements. Students who do receive services under such programs often experience curricular fragmentation. For example, remedial reading services under Chapter 1 are not coordinated with the reading curriculum in the general education class. Likewise, classification of students is erratic and varied; a student with a disability may not be recognized as such, and, therefore, not eligible for special education. Furthermore, remedial and compensatory categorical services tend to be focused on learning pathology, which is based on environmental, cultural, or physical etiology, rather than on the assumption that diversity is natural and valuable to the human condition. Under such conditions, parent–teacher communications are apt to focus on determining the cause and extent of a learning difficulty, and the parent's contacts with the schools may focus around the special program, its eligibility requirements, and compliance with its statutory and regulatory requirements, rather than around the student's citizenship in the overall school culture. The particular focus on a child's learning difficulties may produce guilt in the parent of a child with disabilities or the parent of a

child with limited English proficiency. These parents may be alienated by interactions with teachers whose role is to counteract the effects of non-English cultural and linguistic experiences.

Families are less likely to participate in school governance under such circumstances. Wagstaff and Gallagher (1990) note that families began to assume activist roles in education only when federally mandated compensatory or remedial services legislated in the 1960s and 1970s began to include them. Many of these programs include requirements for some form of family participation in planning services for their child. Requirements for the type and degree of family participation vary; they include parent advisory boards, periodic conferencing requirements, the full range of IEP notification, and consent procedures (required as part of due process protections by the Education for All Handicapped Children Act of 1975, PL 94-142).

Wagstaff and Gallagher (1990) note, however, that efforts to involve families in such roles have typically failed because, "Unfortunately, many non–English-speaking families, single parents, and working parents cannot or do not participate in parent advisory committees" (p. 110). Furthermore, where family participation does occur, all too often families become disaffected with schools when they receive only bad news from these programs about their child's behavior and performance. When family members become discontented with the school, the attitude is subtly passed on to the child who may then begin to disconnect from the program.

Yet, decategorization and infusion of resources in restructured and inclusive schools means that teams of teachers, parents, and staff have primary responsibility for educating all students, including those with special needs. The specialty teacher model used previously gives way to broader general education responsibility for all students. In many restructured school models, every student is assigned to general education, and all of the specialized services personnel participate in teams that are responsible for every student's needs. According to Sage and Burrello (1994), in a restructured and inclusive school, the principal, in agreement with the school site team, exercises control over all of the resources available to the school, including special education, in a manner that benefits all of the students at the school (Sailor & Skrtic, 1995).

Parent participation can be dramatically different in the restructured and inclusive school where services are decategorized and infused into general education. For parents of children with special needs, the focus of schooling is the classroom and the school, not the specialty service designed to improve the child or his condition. Individualized planning in collaboration with families occurs for every student, not just for those children with special needs; thus, the process potentially becomes more normalized and less bound by legalistic procedures for both families and teachers. Particular care must be taken to recruit and include families representing a diversity of cultures, disabilities, and economic statuses for membership on

school site councils. Families are likely to be more willing to participate in such activities when the focus and scope of these outcomes center on meeting the learning needs of all children rather than on remediating the specific problem area that affects their child.

Inclusion in Community Schools

When PL 94-142, the Education for All Handicapped Children Act, was passed in 1975, it held great promise for ensuring that every child with a disability would receive a free and appropriate public education and, when possible, be integrated into the mainstream of general education. Since its enactment, the spirit of PL 94-142 has often been overshadowed by the separate system established to carry out special education.

As in general education, many current issues in special education are being framed around implementation of Goals 2000. Senate Report 103-85 directly addresses the educational needs of students with disabilities in the context of the eight national goals contained in the Act (S.1150). The report ties the Act directly to previous legislation and states the following:

> In far too many districts around the country, two separate educational systems have developed with little or no coordination—one system for regular or general education and a separate and distinct system for special education. This isolation and lack of coordination creates artificial barriers to achieving the promises of Part B of IDEA, the ADA, and Section 504 of the Rehabilitation Act of 1973. (U.S. Congress, 1993, p. 20)

Remedial and compensatory programs, such as Chapter 1 and programs for students with limited English proficiency, have also developed separate educational systems for serving eligible students. Like special education, these services frequently separate the students they serve from mainstream education, their age peers, and full participation in natural community environments. Eyler (1982) argues that certain students are, in effect, racially and economically segregated for significant portions of the school day because of pullout services for remedial or compensatory education. While limited pullout services are still widely used, a 1992 Chapter 1 implementation study showed that 62% of school districts are providing some integrated, or in-class, instruction.

The inclusion of students with special needs in neighborhood schools provides a direct incentive for parent involvement. For example, traditional categorical special education services have, for economic reasons, often transported groups of students from a single disability category to a central location where they can be served in a segregated, self-contained classroom. Such an arrangement makes family participation in planning for the individual child difficult, and families have little incentive to participate actively in broader advocacy and governance for a school that might be across town or in a different town. But, if a student who is deaf-blind attends her neighborhood school and is included in a broader range of school activities than just special education, her parents are far more likely to become in-

volved in the school as advocates, volunteers, and / or participants in school governance, supports, and assistance.

Early Childhood Education

When inclusive education is tied to fundamental shifts in the organization and governance of schools through school restructuring and integrated services, family participation may be qualitatively different. Two federal programs that provide services to young children with special needs, Head Start and PL 99-457, the Education of the Handicapped Act Amendments of 1986, may partially form the basis for a comprehensive redefinition of the family's role in education. Both Head Start and Part H of PL 99-457 acknowledge that families may need to hold dual roles, both providing and receiving the interventions that promote the development of young children.

Head Start, initiated under the Elementary and Secondary Education Act of 1965, was designed to promote the development and school-readiness of young children who live in poverty. Head Start services target preschool children, acknowledging that the development of cognitive, social, and linguistic skills is also facilitated or limited by the child's overall environment. Thus, when a child is served by Head Start, his or her family members receive interventions, such as training in nutrition and child care, as well as work-related skills. Families of children served by Head Start participate in both planning for their child and providing governance to the program.

Part H of PL 99-457, the 1986 amendments to PL 94-142, both consider the family integral to the successful development of young children. PL 99-457 mandates that services for children with disabilities be extended to encompass the preschool years, Part H of the Act provides incentives to states for serving infants and toddlers who have disabilities or are at risk for disabilities and their families.

Like Head Start, PL 99-457 views families as recipients of interventions as well as interventionists. Services for infants, toddlers, and young children with disabilities are somewhat unique as they empower families through transdisciplinary approaches to service planning and delivery. Effective services for young children with disabilities frequently necessitate collaboration among professionals from a variety of disciplines, and the challenges of intervening with an infant or toddler demand that professionals work closely with families and one another to minimize the psychological and physical demands on both the young child and the family. The family, of necessity, must be trained to participate in interventions with the young child. Thus, support to families may range from training a father or grandmother to stimulate language during feeding times to coordinating the services for an infant who needs intensive medical and cognitive interventions.

Formal communications between families and professionals under PL 99-457 are designed to empower families. Unlike PL 94-142, which provides

families with the opportunity to participate in development of the IEP, Part H of PL 99-457 allows for development of individualized family service plans (IFSPs). Ideally, the IEP planning process for elementary and secondary school children with disabilities involves collaboration with families to identify the child's learning needs and goals of the education program. However, the bureaucratic structure of schools is often replicated in IEP team meetings: School psychologists or building principals lead the meeting, educators provide well-prepared documentation of the child's learning difficulties and needs, and the parents only provide consent rather than information or alternatives. In the context of the IFSP, the parent's role as interventionist potentially legitimizes the family's participation as equal partners in the assessment and planning process. Furthermore, the IFSP allows families to participate in assessing their resources and needs for support and mandates coordination of the health, social welfare, and educational services, which may be necessary to support effective interventions for a young child with disabilities or at risk for disabilities.

While systems for implementation of PL 99-457 are still emerging, evolving models for family participation in the education of their children may be supported by family-focused and family-driven systems for serving young children. Parents who have participated in these systems may become vocal advocates for change in school–family relationships in the elementary and secondary school years.

NEW COMMUNITY SCHOOLS

These three significant processes of policy reform affect public education and families with children who have disabilities. But can these processes operate in relative isolation? Can there be effective inclusive education at a school site, for example, without school restructuring and/or without school-linked, services integration? Increasingly, the evidence contradicts this: The three processes belong together and are *interdependent* to a large extent. When all three processes are present at a particular school site, the *culture* of the school changes dramatically. This process is called the *New Community School,* which suggests that such schools offer a path to *empowerment* for family members of students with disabilities who attend the school (Sailor, 1996; Sailor & Skrtic, 1995).

The Emergence of New Community Schools

New Community Schools are not part of a franchise process, nor are they identified with any particular educational consultant, university, or other agency. The term is simply a name to describe school–community partnership arrangements that exhibit certain key processes. These processes include the following:

1. *School restructuring*—to emphasize team governance procedures with full resource infusion and management

2. *Inclusive education*—wherein children at the school are not treated categorically, nor grouped separately, on the basis of needing special assistance

3. *School-linked services integration*—conducted in accordance with a special school–community partnerships arrangement that has service coordination within the school for the child, and between the school and community for the child and family

The New Community School thus reflects each of these interdependent processes. First and foremost, it is a unified school. Special education support services at the school are fully integrated (as are their students) and coordinated so that each program benefits all of the students at the school, while still addressing the needs of children with disabilities.

Second, New Community Schools are governed in accordance with collaborative team processes that both empower and draw from family members of the children at the school. Services within the school are coordinated for children through single point-of-contact service coordinators functioning at the school site and participating on resource management teams; services are wrapped around children and families in the community through service coordination linkages between school and community.

Finally, through direct participation in community service integration councils, New Community Schools are integrally linked to emerging processes for the coordination and integration of all special assistance programs at the community level for children and families. The principal hallmark of the New Community School is its posture as one component in the web of community support systems available to children and families. As such, it performs its educational functions collaborating and in accordance with community health and social support systems (Melaville et al., 1993), empowering families to better cope with the stresses of a changing society, and equipping children to overcome the many factors that increasingly place them at risk for social problems and even disability.

Such schools really do exist in a number of states and communities (Kagan & Neville, 1993), and more are emerging all the time. The challenge for the immediate future is to move from the level of isolated, single school–university partnerships, to whole districts and even states. Two states, Indiana and West Virginia, have created state policy agendas to facilitate these kinds of efforts (Sugarman, 1994). Other states, such as California, Kentucky, and Vermont, have large-scale, statewide initiatives underway that are leading to New Community School types of arrangements. For families of children with disabilities, the potential for positive change and meaningful involvement is promising as the year 2000 approaches.

Chapter Review

CHALLENGES

- Schools are traditionally organized as standard services to deliver a standard product.
- Children with special concerns are peripheral to the basic mission of the school.
- Schools are not able to adapt quickly to changes in the student population, which are increasingly occurring.
- Educators and families operate in what they consider separate spheres of influence.
- Schools have not been preparing a work force for a postindustrial economy.
- Separate special education services divert parental focus from their neighborhood schools.

CHARACTERISTICS OF HELPFUL PROGRAMS

- Families participate as members of site-based governing councils for building-level policy making, serving as advocates, policy makers, and supporters of children's learning.
- Professionals learn new roles as collaborators with families.
- Effective programs provide school-based linkage services that are prevention oriented to an array of social services that include specialized services.
- Children and families are the central concern of school-linked services, not the agencies that provide the services.
- Every student is assigned to a general education classroom, and services and resources are decategorized.
- Care is taken to recruit and include parents representing a diversity of cultures, disabilities, and economic statuses.

POLICY IMPLICATIONS

- New Community Schools should be created, incorporating the following three major reforms:

  1. School restructuring to transfer power to site-based management teams that empower building-level administrators, teachers, and parents

2. Inclusive education to serve all children in age-appropriate, general classrooms with necessary accommodations and supports to meet the educational needs of all children

3. School-linked services integration to bring diverse social services together in the school and provide coordinated team planning to meet family and child concerns

- New Community Schools should coordinate services for all children through single point-of-contact service coordinators at the school site.

References

Conley, D.T. (1993). *Roadmap to restructuring: Policies, practices, and the emerging visions of schooling.* Eugene, OR: Eric Clearinghouse on Educational Management.

Crowson, R.L., & Boyd, W.L. (1993). Coordinated services for children: Designing arks for storms and seas unknown. *American Journal of Education, 101,* 140–170.

Education for All Handicapped Children Act of 1975, PL 94-142. (August 23, 1977). Title 20, U.S.C. 1401 et seq: *U.S. Statutes at Large, 89,* 773–796.

Education of the Handicapped Act Amendments of 1986, PL 99-457. (October 8, 1986). Title 20, U.S.C. 1400 et seq: *U.S. Statutes at Large, 100,* 1145–1177.

Elementary and Secondary Education Act (ESEA), PL 89-313. (September 23, 1950). Title 20, U.S.C. 631 et seq: *U.S. Statutes at Large, 79,* 1158.

Epstein, J.L. (1992). School and family partnerships. In M.C. Alkin, M. Linden, J. Noel, & K. Ray (Eds.), *Encyclopedia of educational research* (6th ed., pp. 1139–1151). New York: Macmillan.

Eyler, J. (1982). *Resegregation: Segregation within desegregated schools.* (ERIC Document No. ED 216 075). Nashille, TN: Vanderbilt University.

Families of Children with Disabilities Support Act of 1994, PL 103-382. (October 20, 1994). Title 20, U.S.C. 1491 et seq: *U.S. Statutes at Large, 108,* 3937.

Gerry, M.H., & Certo, N.J. (1992). Current activity at the federal level and the need for service integration. *The Future of Children, 2*(1), 118–126.

Goals 2000: Educate America Act of 1994, PL 103-227. (March, 1994). Title 20, U.S.C. 5801: *U.S. Statutes at Large, 108,* 125–280.

Guthrie, J.W. (1986). School-based management: The next needed educational reform. *Phi Delta Kappan, 68*(4), 305–309.

Improving America's Schools Act, PL 103-382. (October 20, 1994). Title 20, U.S.C. 6301 et seq: *U.S. Statutes at Large, 108,* 3518.

Johnson, V.R. (1993). *Parent/family centers: Dimensions of functioning in 28 schools in 14 states* (Report No. 20). Baltimore: Center on Families, Communities, Schools, and Children's Learning.

Johnston, P., Allington, R., & Afflerbach, P. (1985). *Guidelines and recommended practices for the individualized family service plan.* Washington, DC: Association for the Care of Children's Health.

Kagan, S.L., & Neville, P.R. (1993). *Integrating human services: Understanding the past to shape the future.* New Haven, CT: Yale University Press.

Kirst, M.W. (1989). *The progress of reform: An appraisal of state education initiatives.* New Brunswick, NJ: Center for Policy Research in Education.

Kirst, M.W. (1992). *Financing school-linked services* (Policy Brief #7). Los Angeles: Center for Research in Education Finance, University of Southern California.

Melaville, A.I., Blank, M.J., & Asayesh, G. (1993). *Together we can: A guide for crafting a profamily system of education and human services.* Washington, DC: U.S. Government Printing Office.

National Institute of Education. (1978). *Perspectives on the instructional dimensions study, U.S. Department of Health, Education, and Welfare.* Washington, DC: Author.

New beginnings: A feasibility study of integrated services for children and families. (1990). City of San Diego Public Schools, California.

Reynolds, M.C., & Lakin, K.C. (1987). Noncategorical special education: Models for research and practice. In M.C. Wang, M.C. Reynolds, & H.J. Walberg (Eds.), *Hand-*

book of special education: Research and practice: Vol. 1. Learner characteristics and adaptive education (pp. 331–356). Elmsford, NY: Pergamon.

Reynolds, M.C., & Wang, M.C. (1981). *Restructuring "special" school programs: A position paper.* Paper presented at the national invitational conference on Public Policy and the Special Education Task of 1980s, Racine, WI.

Sage, D.D., & Burrello, L.C. (1994). *Leadership in educational reform: An administrator's guide to changes in special education.* Baltimore: Paul H. Brookes Publishing Co.

Sailor, W. (1991). Special education in the restructured school. *Remedial and Special Education, 12*(6), 8–22.

Sailor, W. (1996). New structures and systems change for comprehensive positive behavioral support. In L.K. Koegel, R.L. Koegel, & G. Dunlap (Eds.), *Positive behavioral support.* Baltimore: Paul H. Brookes Publishing Co.

Sailor, W., Anderson, J.L., Halvorsen, A.T., Doering, K., Filler, J., & Goetz, L. (1989). *The comprehensive local school: Regular education for all students with disabilities.* Baltimore: Paul H. Brookes Publishing Co.

Sailor, W., & Skrtic, T. (1995). American education in the postmodern era. In J.L. Paul, H. Rosselli, & D. Evans (Eds.), *Integrating school restructuring and special education reform* (pp. 418–432). San Diego: Harcourt Brace Jovanovich.

Seligman, M. (1975). *Helplessness: On depression, development, and death.* San Francisco: W.H. Freeman.

Skrtic, T.M. (1991). *Behind special education: A critical analysis of professional culture and school organization.* Denver: Love Publishing.

Sugarman, J.M. (1994). *Mobilizing communities for children, youth, and families.* Unpublished manuscript, Center on Effective Services for Children, Washington, DC.

Turnbull, A.P., Ruef, M., & Reeves, C. (1993). *Family perspectives on lifestyle issues for individuals, a problem behavior.* Unpublished manuscript, Beach Center on Families and Disability, University of Kansas, Lawrence.

Turnbull, H.R., Turnbull, A.P., Bronicki, G.J., Summers, J.A., & Roeder-Gordon, C. (1989). *Disability and the family: A guide to decisions for adulthood.* Baltimore: Paul H. Brookes Publishing Co.

U.S. Congress. (1993, July). *Goals 2000: Educate America Act, Senate report 103-85 to accompany S. 1150,* 103d Congress, 1st Session, Senate Committee on Labor and Human Resources.

Wagstaff, L.H., & Gallagher, K.S. (1990). Schools, families, and communities: Idealized images and new realities. In B. Mitchell & L.L. Cunningham (Eds.), *Educational leadership and changing contexts of families, communities, and schools: 89th yearbook of the National Society for the Study of Education.* Chicago, IL: University of Chicago Press.

Walberg, H.J. (1984). Improving the productivity of America's schools. *Educational Leadership, 41,* 19–30.

Will, M.C. (1986). Educating students with learning problems: A shared responsibility. *Exceptional Children, 42,* 411–415.

15

Decentralizing Services in Three Scandinavian Countries

Valerie J. Bradley and Bruce Blaney

A profound revolution in the delivery of welfare and other governmental services is taking place in the industrialized democracies of Western Europe. Country after country has shifted the locus of responsibility for previously centralized functions to subgovernmental units (Bennett, 1990). This diminution of central authority and control is mirrored in the United States, where the respective roles of government—federal, state, and local—and the private sector are being reappraised (Osborne, 1988).

The changes implied by decentralization have broad ramifications for the future of welfare and human services, in general, and for services and supports to people with disabilities and their families, in particular. Human services planners, policy makers, and advocates in the United States must understand this phenomenon in its various permutations in the European community and assess its relevance to the debate surrounding the roles of government and the private sector. Although the political traditions differ, the forces that have spurred change in Western Europe are also present in the United States, including escalating budgets, frustration with bureaucracy, and dissatisfaction with a monopolistic public sector.

This chapter outlines a study designed to assess the phenomenon of decentralization in three Scandinavian countries—Denmark, Norway, and Sweden—and to determine the preliminary impact of these changes on the structure of the service system. These three countries were chosen because

The study discussed in this chapter was supported by Grant #90PD001740 from the Administration on Developmental Disabilities, U.S. Department of Health and Human Services.

1) they illustrate the radical changes taking place in Europe, and 2) they have provided significant leadership in the field of disabilities. The study was conducted from 1991 to 1993 and included site visits to each country, an analysis of policy materials and research literature, a three-country symposium, and the preparation of a final report.

THE SCANDINAVIAN INFLUENCE

The principles that govern the delivery of services to people with disabilities in the United States are largely due to the influence of the Scandinavian experience and the popularization of the theoretical construct of normalization (Wolfensberger, 1972). The acceptance of this concept among leaders in the disability community has profoundly changed attitudes about the capabilities of people with disabilities, as well as assumptions about the content and location of services. As first defined by Bengt Nirje (1969) of Sweden in the early 1950s, *normalization* means supporting people in community settings that are as typical as possible. Its aim is to reduce stigma through natural, accepted service arrangements and to eliminate infantilization by serving people with disabilities in an age-appropriate fashion.

Initially, the normalization principle provided a powerful critique of large, remote, and custodial institutions. More recently, it has spurred a reassessment of community programs, stressing more individualized supports and the exercise of consumer choice (Taylor, 1988). The ultimate aim of the normalization principle is true community integration, along with the development of natural, as well as specialized, supports for people with disabilities. However, developing individualized services and building on natural supports, such as families, friends, and neighbors, are difficult to accomplish in highly bureaucratized systems. In the 1990s, therefore, the disabilities field will be challenged to find ways to direct resources closer to the person in need while ensuring that his or her special needs are met.

Karl Grunewald, one of the designers of the Swedish mental retardation system, described the following four phases in the evolution of the principle of normalization in a speech before the World Federation for Mental Health in 1971:

1. *Diagnostic stage*—the focus on the diagnosis and formulation of needs
2. *Specialization*—as services became specialized, the tendency toward centralization
3. *Differentiation*—the increasing difficulty of standardization and stress on individualization
4. *Decentralization and integration*—the involvement of people in their own communities helping services to be specialized

Using Grunewald's model, the development of services in the United States is poised at level three, differentiation. As in the Scandinavian countries, services in the United States have centered around large, remote in-

stitutions until quite recently when, as a result of pressure from advocates, the courts, and disability professionals, institutions have come under attack and service development has moved to the community level (Bradley, 1978). As Knoll (1990) has noted, reforms in the United States began with institutional improvements, shifted to a concern with diagnosis and specialized services, and are now beginning to focus on individualization.

Recommended Practices from Scandinavia

Just as the Scandinavian experience provided an impetus for the development of community services in the 1960s, recent events in these countries are once again a source of innovation and direction. The national laws of Denmark, Norway, and Sweden have been changed to move the control of resources and programs closer to communities and away from highly centralized national agencies. This study was designed to assess whether these larger shifts in authority and responsibility have removed some of the policy and structural constraints from Grunewald's fourth stage of normalization, allowing for a more individualized and integrated system of supports. The analysis proceeded from the following set of assumptions about the nature of recommended practices and the trends that are emerging in the United States:

- Choices about the nature of services and supports should be vested in the person with a disability.
- Families of children with disabilities should be supported, and they should be treated by professionals as collaborators and partners.
- The aim of the service system should be to provide functional supports to individuals in their own homes and in their chosen workplaces instead of moving people through a continuum of residential and vocational programs.
- Planning for people with disabilities should begin with the individual's aspirations, preferences, and dreams, rather than with the imperatives of the service system.
- The outcomes of publicly supported interventions should be measured in terms of their ability to increase the individual's quality of life, to enhance participation in the community, and to assist in establishing and maintaining human relationships.

In order to structure the inquiry into the experiences of the three countries, several areas of exploration were developed. These areas were selected because of their relevance to issues that the researchers hypothesized would be important to policy makers and planners in the United States.

Decentralization and Quality Assurance Mechanisms

After decentralization, how will localities ensure the quality of the services provided, and what role will the central government continue to play? What methods will be used to ensure that people with disabilities and their families can petition to an authority beyond the locality if they are dissatisfied with the services and supports they receive?

Decentralization and More Individualized Funding Mechanisms

Will decentralization of service delivery make it possible to develop more flexible and individual means of funding services? Will local control of funding mean that a broader menu of services will be available? Current funding for disability services in the United States is geared to the support of programs and providers, rather than individuals; only a few small models of individualized funding exist in this country (Ashbaugh & Nerney, 1990).

Decentralization and Interagency Coordination

Under decentralization, will the integration of previously specialized staff in generic social services agencies result in increased coordination among agencies at the local level? People with disabilities, in order to live in communities, require a range of supports. In some places in the United States, these supports are provided under a variety of auspices (e.g., health care, job training, residential services, income support, recreation), and coordination and collaboration are difficult to implement. Consumers and their families are faced with a confusing array of public and private agencies and eligibility requirements. Assuming that the authority and decision making for the multiple agencies involved have been uniformly transferred to the same sublevel of government, service access and coordination may be easier in the decentralized systems.

Decentralization and Family Support Services

Will decentralization increase supports to families at home? In the United States, supporting families is still a low priority in a service system dominated by expensive residential arrangements. In a recent survey of family support programs in the 50 states, the Human Services Research Institute determined that only 6 states have comprehensive family support programs. Furthermore, the total amount of money spent on family support at the state level represents only 1.5% of all funds spent on services to people with developmental disabilities (Knoll et al., 1990).

Decentralization and the Availability of Training and Technical Assistance

Will decentralization dilute the availability of expertise? How will staff training be organized and information on recommended practices be communicated across agencies and jurisdictions?

Decentralization and Inequities in the Distribution of Resources

Will the devolution of decision making to the local level result in uneven distribution of resources for people with disabilities across localities?

Service Systems in the Three Study Countries

As shown in the summary of findings, these issues, although important in the United States, were not always directly relevant to the Scandinavian experience. For example, the concept of *quality assurance* was a somewhat alien notion in countries where the service system is almost 100% publicly operated (either at the county or local level). Furthermore, some of the issues had not yet fully emerged as the reforms in the three countries—especially Norway and Sweden—were still quite new and still evolving.

According to Juul (1984), the histories of services for people with disabilities in the Scandinavian countries have many common features:

> During the 19th and first half of the 20th century the mentally retarded were mostly cared for in private and charitable residential institutions. Treatment was of a custodial nature, and the large majority of the handicapped received no help at all... After the Second World War dramatic changes began to take place. The public conscience was aroused. Laws were passed in all the countries requiring the formation of programs and services. The national plans were originally for . . . a limited number of central institutions. (p. 2)

Denmark

Pressure for service reform in Denmark (population 5,100,000) began with the formation of a national parents organization in 1952. By 1954, the government had created a committee to draft new legislation based on the principle of normalization. The committee was chaired by N.E. Bank-Mikkelsen. As a result, a law was passed in 1959 that created a new State Mental Retardation Service, and Bank-Mikkelsen was appointed director. The new agency created modern institutions with small units in 12 regions that became a model for visitors from around the world. In the 1970s, this model subsequently gave way to more typical forms of community living, including hostels, smaller group homes, and apartments (Dybwad, 1989).

Bank-Mikkelsen took the next, more radical step in the 1970s when he determined that true normalization and integration of people into more generic services would require that his central state agency be dissolved (Juul, 1984). As a result of his efforts, the Social Assistance Act was passed in 1974, to be implemented by 1980. The new law significantly altered the Danish service system—all services were decentralized, and authority was turned over to the 16 counties and 275 municipalities. This policy change has dramatically altered the delivery of services to people with disabilities in Denmark and provides a key focus for the comparative analysis.

Norway

The modern system of services for people with disabilities in Norway (population 4,200,000) began with a 1950 law that mandated the creation of 10 regions, each with a central residential institution for comprehensive care. At the time, they were considered models of humane treatment and were designed to serve several hundred residents each (Juul, 1984). In 1970, the

Hospital Act gave the counties full responsibility to plan, establish, and run all health care institutions, including those for people with mental retardation.

By 1976, the Norwegian Parliament had approved a government report on the future direction of services to people with developmental disabilities. The major objectives outlined in the report included decent education and treatment, suitable occupations, housing, meaningful leisure-time activities, and rights similar to those of other citizens. The report also recommended that services be provided by local government and coordinated across agencies. After the report was adopted, the use of residential institutions declined, family-scale homes were developed in the community, and supports were provided to families with children with disabilities (Dybwad, 1989).

In 1982, a law was passed (effective in 1984) that gave local communities responsibility for providing ordinary health and social services for all residents; special services remained a county obligation. Finally, with the passage of the decentralization and deinstitutionalization reforms of 1987–1988, decentralization became the primary theme within disabilities services. This centralized, county-based, institution-centered system of services to people with mental retardation was mandated to devolve to the municipal and precinct level within 2 years. Under the same legislation, all institutions for people with mental retardation were slated to be closed by 1994.

Sweden

A landmark change in the Swedish (population 8,300,000) system came when the Act on Provisions for Certain Retarded Persons was passed in 1967. This statute gives people with mental retardation the same rights as other citizens and other people with disabilities. In addition, the act contains provisions for the following special rights: free medical and dental care; support services for parents who have a family member with mental retardation living at home; preschool and child nursery services; compulsory education for children and adolescents with mental retardation; residential services in institutions or group homes; and day activity centers for adults who are not living in institutions and are not competitively employed (Sterner, 1976).

In Sweden, as in Denmark, the use of institutions has declined dramatically since the 1970s. Increasingly, integrated apartments are used, and small, family-style student homes are provided for young people from rural areas of the country to stay during the week while attending school (Juul, 1984). In 1986, the Swedes passed a new welfare law for people with disabilities that transfers responsibility for specialized services to county councils. Although the central government retains monitoring and oversight responsibilities, all special services are now provided by the 23 counties and 2 municipalities. Most recently, other local municipalities have begun to take some of the county responsibilities, and services have become even more decentralized as a result.

Defining Decentralization Issues

Before analyzing the Scandinavian experience, it is important to define what is meant by *decentralization* in this context, as the term is highly general and encompasses a variety of structural arrangements. At its most basic, "to decentralize is to disperse or distribute power from the center" (Wolman, 1990, p. 29). Wolman also notes that this definition covers the following three potential forms of decentralization:

1. *Political decentralization* entails the devolution of decision making regarding "policy issues, including the policy to be pursued, the amount of revenues to be raised, and the allocation of available revenues" (p. 29).
2. *Administrative decentralization* refers to the delegation of authority to decentralized entities to make decisions regarding the interpretation and execution of general policy directives and guidelines, leaving the central authority to monitor and oversee implementation.
3. *Economic decentralization* refers to dispersal of economic decision making from government to consumers through market mechanisms.

The decentralization pursued by these three Scandinavian countries is primarily political and administrative; economic decentralization is in an embryonic stage, insofar as services to people with disabilities.

According to Bennett (1990), decentralization occurs on two axes: 1) localized power—centralized power, and 2) governmental resource allocation—market resource allocation. The first dichotomy is based on the extent of intergovernmental power and ranges from highly centralized public sector models to highly localized public sector models. The second dichotomy ranges from models of resource allocation determined by governmental policy to models of allocation driven by market forces. Bennett places Scandinavia firmly on the localized, governmental resource allocation end of the continuum.

Rationales for Decentralization

The decentralization movement has appeared during a pervasive and converging critique of the welfare state that pre-dates World War II, both in the United States and Western Europe. The inexorable growth of welfare state expenditures and the bureaucracy created to manage welfare state programs has led to a new wave of post–welfare state reforms. Bennett (1990) summarizes the major elements of the indictment as follows:

1. Public perceptions of governmental programs as pork barrel
2. Increasing doubt about the ability of administrators and politicians to manage and deliver services
3. Increasing conviction that welfare state programs have perpetuated dependency, rather than fostering self-sufficiency

4. Growing conviction that centralized governmental authority has stifled local initiative and innovation
5. Inability to gain meaningful control over welfare expenditures
6. Suspicion that growing public expenditures will freeze out other activities (pp. 12–13)

The critique of centralization is clearly not limited to the traditional welfare state bureaucracies in countries like Sweden and Great Britain but has also begun in the United States. One of the most recent observers of post–welfare state America has been David Osborne. Like his European counterparts, Osborne describes an emerging new paradigm in the public sector that stresses partnership with the private sector, customer responsiveness, innovation and investment, and, most importantly, decentralization (Osborne, 1988; Osborne & Gaebler, 1992).

In support of decentralization, Wolman (1990) identifies several values that proponents have advanced, including increased responsiveness and accountability, enhancement of diversity and innovation, reduction in the gap between individual preferences and the allocation of public goods and services, growth in political participation and leadership development, and the creation of countervailing political power; Bennett also adds the potential for increased governmental responsiveness to customers and broadened external accountability.

Ideological and Political Rationales

Decentralization has attracted supporters from the political left and right because, as Bennett (1990) notes, "as a new paradigm, it is attracting both socialist and conservative governments as a means of better responding to consumer demands" (p. 25). The conservative right views decentralization as a means to diminish central bureaucracy and control; it reasons that such a course will result in "less government—more market" (Olsson, 1990, p. 247). This rationale is based on the assumption that the increased taxes necessary for a burgeoning public sector divert investment from the private sector and thwart private initiative. Conversely, the progressive left views highly centralized government and regulation as a threat to a more interdependent, community-based society. From this vantage point, decentralization means "less state—more civil society" (Olsson, 1990, p. 247). This rationale is based on a suspicion of a highly regulated state that diminishes the autonomy of its citizens and their ability to participate in ordinary life spheres.

Decentralization Versus Privatization

Because the argument for decentralization often stresses that the private sector should provide increased public services, it is important to address the concomitant trend of privatization. Osborne and Gaebler (1992) address the need to move away from monopolistic governmental enterprises by advancing the notion of competition among levels of government, and between government and the private sector. In sum, their proposals state, "Competition that is structured carefully, however, can produce more equitable results than service delivery by a public monopoly" (p. 105).

In 1987, the U.S. Office of Economic and Community Development listed the following forms of privatization that can serve as alternatives to the public provision of services:

1. Regulation of private-sector contractors by a) "contracting out," b) developing contracts, c) controlling standards, d) using competitive bids, and e) using vouchers
2. Cooperatives, associations, trusts, not-for-profit organizations
3. Voluntary and charitable bodies
4. Public–private partnerships
5. Para-state sectors (Bennett, 1990, p. 16)

It is important to keep in mind that decentralization and privatization are not necessarily synonymous, nor must they occur in tandem. Decentralization has many supporters who do not subscribe to wholesale privatization of welfare services. Such groups include emerging social movements, such as environmentalists and feminists, who see the central state as too remote and out of touch with the concerns of the local citizenry. The rallying cries of these groups include "democratization, de-bureaucratization, participation, voluntarism, self-management, mutual aid, and local decision-making" (Olsson, 1990, p. 252). Conversely, staunch supporters of privatization argue that the solution to the "welfare crisis" is "deregulation and commercialization of previously publicly provided goods, services, and transfers, all of which should be switched from bureaucratic agencies to competitive private enterprises" (Olsson, 1990, p. 249).

Although decentralization and privatization can certainly work together in a synthesis of public–private partnership, privatization is still a somewhat negligible feature of the decentralization initiatives in Denmark, Norway, and Sweden.

SUMMARY AND IMPLICATIONS

Similarities Among Scandinavian Countries

There are several similarities and differences in the ways in which decentralization has evolved in Scandinavia, generally, and in the character of services to people with developmental disabilities, in particular. Some of the major similarities are noted below.

Part of Larger Movement

In each of the three countries, decentralization of services to people with disabilities is the logical extension of a broader social and political reform movement. The diminution of bureaucracy and a return to community and local participation were among several motivating factors that drove decentralization. Some suggest that there were also more hidden and potentially corrupting reasons for the shift to localities, including cost cutting and a desire to shift tough resource decisions to the local level (Vetvik, 1992).

Although driven by larger social service reforms, the decentralization of services to people with disabilities in these three countries is consistent with long-standing commitments to serve people according to the principle of normalization—that is, people with disabilities should receive services under the same auspices and in the same ways as people without disabilities, which seems to be the logical extension of this broadly accepted value. The unresolved issue, then, is whether services and supports available to the citizenry without disabilities will be sufficient to meet the needs of people with disabilities.

Public Sector Services

Services and supports to people with disabilities in all three countries are predominantly provided by public sector employees. Although charitable and voluntary organizations played a role in the early 1900s, the emergence of the welfare state created almost total reliance on publicly provided services. The fact that program and administrative staff are primarily public employees facilitated decentralization because employees could move easily from one public entity to another (e.g., county to municipality) without loss of benefits or salary levels.

In each of these countries, privatization was emerging in such areas as child care and health, but was not a consideration in the area of mental retardation and related disabilities. What remains to be seen is whether and to what extent privatization will become a factor in the future. If so, issues surrounding monitoring, training, and quality assurance will almost certainly arise.

Welfare of the Group Versus the Individual

The welfare state in all three of the countries is based on an underlying commitment to the welfare of the group, rather than the maximization of individual opportunity. The move to decentralize has raised concerns that the atomization of services to people with disabilities and the blurring of distinctions between specialized and generic services may put people whose needs are highly complex at a disadvantage. Another concern is that cost-conscious municipalities will be reluctant to fully fund the supports needed by a relatively small number of their constituents. These concerns have led to a new thrust of reform aimed at the development of special legislation in Denmark and Norway, and to the enhancement of special legislation in Sweden. Also, increased attention is being paid to the administrative procedures by which families and people with disabilities appeal decisions made at the local level. This increasing focus on individual rights is a departure from the collective norms that informed the development of the welfare state.

Focus on Training

Each of the countries places a premium on staff training and professionalism. In Denmark, for instance, group home and vocational rehabilitation staff are trained as social pedagogues in a 3-year curriculum. Although the focus of training varies from country to country, all three devote substantial resources to personnel preparation and see it as the major cornerstone in any quality assurance mechanism.

Role of Parent Organizations

In all three countries, parent organizations play a predominant and collaborative role. They participate on national policy-making bodies and on local users councils. Their role is legitimized through law, as well as administrative practice, even though self-advocacy has only recently been explored. In Denmark, for instance, *kultur conferences* have been held by self-advocates to explore their own agenda. In Norway and Sweden, the parent organizations have changed their composition to include people with disabilities, as well as parents. With respect to decentralization, parent organizations, such as the FUB national organization in Sweden, have provided a counterbalance to the reforms by raising concerns about the impact of the reforms on people with disabilities and their families.

Diminution of Central Leadership

Until the initiation of decentralization, leadership in the three countries was primarily located in the central government. Figures, such as Niels Bank-Mikkelsen of Denmark, or Karl Grunewald and Bengt Nirje of Sweden, developed international reputations. But as services have moved to municipalities both the reliance on and the need for strong central leadership has diminished. As one participant in the forum held in Oslo noted, "There are no more heroes."

Tension Between Cost and Programmatic Concerns

As in any major political reform, the influences that brought about change in these three countries reflect a mixture of efficiency and cost concerns on the one hand, and programmatic and philosophical concerns on the other hand. It can clearly be argued that in all three countries the decentralization movement began before any fiscal problems surfaced during the late 1980s—especially in Denmark where the reform is now 10 years old. It is also clear that acceptance of decentralization, especially among more conservative political forces, was premised on assumptions that spiraling costs could be more easily controlled at the local level and that difficult political decisions regarding priorities could be avoided if control were placed at the municipal level.

Being alert to these competing influences is important in the long-term evaluation of the reforms. However, such evaluation may be somewhat hampered, as in Norway, where no systematic data on expenditures by type of program or type of client are currently being collected.

Differences Among Scandinavian Countries

In addition to the general similarities discussed above, some important differences among the three countries should be noted also.

Impetus for Reform

The impetus and approach to decentralization varied among the three countries. In Norway, the reform was very much a top-down phenomenon driven by the central government and facilitated through funding from the central authority. In Denmark, the shape of the reform, though mandatory, was left almost entirely to localities to determine. In Sweden, the reform was approached much more cautiously and was initially left to the discretion of localities to pursue.

Approach to Evaluation

Each of the three countries has developed varying approaches to evaluating the decentralization effort. Denmark has invested very few resources in a systematic assessment of the phenomenon. Norway, at the other extreme, has invested a significant amount of money in projects run by researchers in various parts of the country. Sweden's efforts, although somewhat more modest than Norway's, reflect a deeper interest in feedback on the status of the reform.

Approach to Innovation

Denmark has relied heavily on the use of pilot programs to demonstrate innovative approaches, while Norway has tended to advance a national policy direction with modest reliance on pilots or experimentation. Sweden has allowed counties to proceed with decentralization, based on approved plans.

Approach to Integration

Denmark again stands out somewhat from the other two countries in its approach to integration. As characterized by those interviewed, Denmark uses an approach that supports people with disabilities in developing a cultural affinity and identification, theorizing that such an identity will give them the strength and capacity to, over time, reach out to others who do not have disabilities and to participate in the life of the community. The approaches to integration in Norway and Sweden are more similar to notions of inclusion as expressed in the United States, which primarily relies on a rejection of segregated activities.

Approach to Personnel Preparation

Although all three countries have training programs, the social pedagogues in Denmark seemed better prepared to work in a decentralized system.

They are trained in ways that build the capacities of local communities. Compared to Norway where professional roles remain more relevant to a centralized, categorical system, Denmark's social pedagogues are really on the leading edge of the reform.

Findings

In each of the three countries, central government officials were grappling extensively with their ongoing role in a decentralized system. Typical roles, such as providing technical assistance and quality assurance oversight, had not yet taken shape, and it was not clear that these options would be pursued. The policy makers strongly felt that technical assistance would be seen as an intrusion by those at the municipal level. And quality assurance did not seem necessary as much of the system was still publicly managed and staffed, and those staff were well trained.

By the end of the project, however, some trends were beginning to emerge. Specifically, each of the countries was interested in developing centers of specialized expertise, as well as developing or enhancing special legislation. In Denmark, the role of the National Council on the Handicapped was being expanded with a watchdog, or national oversight, function. In Sweden, legislation had been passed to develop centers of expertise and to strengthen entitlements for people with disabilities. Similar considerations were taking place in Norway.

All three countries also had a deepening interest in a more rights-oriented approach to ensuring that people with disabilities receive appropriate and needed services. This trend is especially profound in Denmark and Norway, which until recently had eschewed special legislation in favor of broad-based social services program mandates. A more individualistic or rights orientation is also being discussed in Denmark and Sweden regarding the responsibilities of the ombudsman's office in a decentralized system, particularly with respect to protecting the prerogatives of people with disabilities. All three countries also intensely discussed grievance or complaint mechanisms at the municipal level, and the extent to which they can become viable safeguards against inequitable or capricious decisions by local policy makers.

The move to decentralize also poses challenges to parent organizations in the three countries. Specifically, the family representatives interviewed noted that more local organizing will be necessary, as well as a concerted effort to educate municipal politicians who typically have not dealt with disability issues. At the national level, parent organizations increasingly have been raising concerns regarding the impact of decentralization on people with disabilities and have been calling for more legal protections.

The countries are also concerned about diluting their expertise, as habitation teams are split up to work in decentralized municipalities and parts of municipalities. Dilution also results from the loss of collegiality and information sharing that happens in more centralized work environments. As service areas become smaller, the likelihood that all the relevant expertise will be present in a locality is small. Some of the family members interviewed in Stockholm noted that these jurisdictional lines had constrained their ability to obtain certain specialized services that they felt their family members required. A local politician in Denmark noted that some families had actually moved across jurisdictional lines in order to get services. Administrators interviewed in Halmstad, however, did not foresee any problems in sharing resources across municipal lines. It remains to be seen whether expertise can be secured in smaller jurisdictions, when necessary, and whether some specialized functions can be absorbed by more generic, community-based human services workers.

It is important to remember that the decentralization reform, particularly in Sweden, was not tied explicitly to deinstitutionalization or to disability issues. However, most observers agree that the decentralization would facilitate deinstitutionalization, especially in light of recent explicit national policies to downsize public institutions. Furthermore, the political context of deinstitutionalization in the three countries appeared to be somewhat different from the typical set of political issues surrounding institutional phase-downs in the United States. First, the Scandinavian unions are not automatically cast as opponents, as most community services are publicly staffed. Second, the parents of people in institutions do not seem to be as confrontational and resistant. However, as in the United States, a renewed push seemed necessary in order to move the last of the residual population into the community.

Some areas of inquiry emerged as central issues and others remained more relevant to an American context.

Decentralization and Quality Assurance Mechanisms

Quality assurance mechanisms were not directly relevant to concerns in the three countries because of the public character of services and the high levels of training in personnel. However, interest is growing in quality of life issues, as well as in issues of equality and appropriateness; these issues are being addressed through legislation and training. If privatization becomes more prominent in the disability field, quality assurance and monitoring may become more significant concerns.

Decentralization and More Individualized Funding Mechanisms

Scandinavian funding mechanisms have changed, not by nature but by jurisdiction. Because most of the services that had previously been run by the county were being moved to the municipal level, not enough services had been developed at the local level to determine whether approaches had become more individualized. It should be noted that funding for people with disabilities has traditionally been more individualized in Scandinavia, where there is a broader range of income and housing supports.

Decentralization and Interagency Coordination

Where decentralization has taken place, previously specialized personnel are usually now based in generic social services agencies at the municipal level. It should be noted, however, that many social services available to people with disabilities (e.g., attendant care) have been delivered by generic agencies at the municipal level for many years. It remains to be seen whether there will be intergovernmental coordination and collaboration both among municipalities and among various levels of government.

Decentralization and Family Support Services

It is clear that families of people with disabilities in Scandinavia receive a broader array of income, health, and housing supports than those in the United States. Thus, Scandinavian families have more of their basic needs met through public programs. However, whether decentralization will create a more collaborative and supportive approach to the provision of services and supports remains to be seen. Anecdotal information from families suggested that the need to develop more family-driven and family-controlled services concerns Scandinavians as much as Americans. It also showed interactions between families and the formal service system are still characterized by more paternalistic approaches.

Decentralization and the Availability of Training and Technical Assistance

Scandinavians make the training of front-level staff a more prominent priority than Americans, and there is no reason to think that such training will be diminished as a result of decentralization. The more valid question is whether training will equip staff for skills such as developing community capacity and mobilizing generic supports.

Decentralization and Inequities in the Distribution of Resources

An important difference that bears on the issue of equity is the fact that Scandinavian counties and localities have ceilings on their taxation authorities. Any inequities arising out of maldistribution of income across localities are compensated for by the central government. Thus, the most obvious source of unequal distribution, differential tax bases, is not a consideration as it would be in the United States. However, there will certainly be differences in the ways in which municipalities allocate resources. The question is whether these differences will reflect varying local priorities and broad-based community input or, rather, disregard of the needs of people with disabilities. The emergence of special legislation that will provide a threshold of mandatory requirements should diminish the possibility of significant inequalities.

In the final analysis, the most significant tension that emerges in these three countries is between the ideal of normalization in ordinary communities and the reality that questions the ability of ordinary communities to provide the extraordinary supports that many people with disabilities need to fully participate. The end of the 20th century should show whether a balance can be reached between these two aspirations—a balance that may require somewhat uncharacteristic attention to individual rights and prerogatives.

IMPLICATIONS FOR THE UNITED STATES

From Disability to Society: Patterns of Welfare Reform in the United States

In Scandinavia, sweeping social reforms preceded disability reform; the United States has not yet established the social welfare platform needed to build supports for people with disabilities. In the United States, the generic system of health care, housing, income supports, and employment policies simply cannot provide the standards of quality sought by advocates in the disability community.

However, significant social reform is underway in the United States. Reformers within the American disability community have, of necessity, undertaken both disability and social reform simultaneously. This pattern is apparent in the family support movement, given the absence of a larger, social movement. The discussion and growing literature on the new paradigm of personalized supports, circles of support, personal futures planning, and community membership all reflect the effort to mobilize and improvise quality of life supports in housing, health care, employment, income, and recreation. These supports constitute welfare reform in its real sense—one person at a time. Innovations in housing, such as housing cooperatives, other homeownership innovations associated with supported living, and the Community-Supported Living Arrangements of partial Medicaid reform are social reforms within the domain of disability policy and practice.

However, the primary learning domain for sweeping social reform is developing within the comparatively circumscribed realm of innovative and often small-scale pilot projects and centers of excellence within the U.S. disability community. One of the more vivid examples of the movement from disability reform to social reform is the recent work of Martha Minnow on comprehensive legal reform. Based on the analysis of the evolution of disability law since the 1970s, Minnow proposes a sweeping reform of the paradigm that defines the entire legal system, shifting the U.S. justice system from a difference- and deficit-focused approach to a community-based and social relations approach (Minnow, 1990).

Since the 1980s, the disability community has also shifted from a service system, featuring an agency-centered approach, toward a community-first strategy, in which human services professionals aim for building the capacities of and improving the quality of life in communities. This mission clearly builds on the core theme of Norway's social reform—universal commitments to quality of life—by viewing inclusion not as an act of charity, but as a qualitative enrichment of community life, a society for all. This commitment can also be seen in the quality of life movement in Denmark and in the training of social pedagogues.

Social reformers in the Unites States, both in the generic welfare system and disability services, should be aware of this uniquely American pattern of social reform, which goes far beyond the superficial influence of the American penchant for individualism, as opposed to comprehensive and coordinated reform efforts. That these efforts have often been on a small scale and person focused should not detract from the richness and depth of the knowledge, values, and experience base they bring to disability and societal reform movements. Scandinavia can learn much from the United States regarding personalized approaches to supported living, employment, and community membership. Indeed, merging the Scandinavian and U.S. platforms for change would be ideal—the former grounded in the visions and practice of creating a universalist and revivified democracy, the latter in learning individually (Schorr & Schorr, 1988) how to support inclusion within the relationships and opportunities that signal quality of personal and community life.

Creating effective supports to improve the quality of life for people with disabilities goes against the prevailing notions of subsistence for the undeserving poor. In fact, such supports are seldom seen in the generic welfare environment. The disability arena has successfully created supports by mobilizing the untapped capacities of communities and the range of resources that already exist to support all citizens. All of these various experiments constitute a rich base of knowledge upon which a new conception of the role of government regarding people with disabilities, families, and communities can be built.

The Family Support Movement in the United States: Toward a Universalist and Nonbureaucratic Welfare State

Family Focus: From Special Interest to Universalism

The family support movement gained national momentum in the late 1980s, and differed from the parents movement of the 1950s in its core demand: Disability policies and services should be family focused, not disability focused. This demand is for nothing less than the quality of family life enjoyed by the typical family.

Explicit in this demand is the deeply felt and compelling conviction that "our families are valuable." When a family with a member with a disability is unable to contribute fully and effectively, the entire community suffers (Bradley & Blaney, 1990). The quality of family life, therefore, is defined as one of the implicit goals of social policy. Conversely, previous social policies regarding families with members with a disability have been repudiated as derogating the family, particularly the mother, to the role of a social instrument, providing unpaid services at the cost of enormous social and personal opportunity.

In adopting a family focus, this socially broad-based and cross-disability movement has articulated perhaps the clearest universalist social policy in the United States. The family support movement is committed to the quality of American family and community life, a sharp contrast to the welfare conceptions of constricted eligibility and the provision of bare subsistence to those regarded as different.

An Activist State, an Engaged Citizenry

Pierson (1991), in his assessment of the key challenges to renewing the welfare state as an effective institution, calls for "simultaneous democratization and strengthening of the state" (p. 219). One of the major criticisms of the decentralization of both the generic welfare system and the mental retardation system in Scandinavia is that the democratization of decision making was not accompanied by a strong state presence that could guarantee the political and economic framework of the reform. Within the mental retardation reform, the absence of state presence was felt acutely in the areas of quality assurance, the lack of policy and economic commitments to the communal planning process for deinstitutionalization, and the failure to provide strong leadership through training and technical assistance on the local level. Many of the current reforms also feature this paradox between inclusion and empowerment and the democratization of politics, which requires a strong, although selective, state presence.

The family support movement in the United States is using both a bottom-up strategy by creating family-run policy and planning bodies, and a top-down strategy guaranteeing the implementation of a family-controlled and family-focused system of supports through legislation that develops a strong role for the state. Federal legislation, especially in early intervention and proposed federal family support legislation, relies on central government at the state or federal level to support families as the key decision makers within education and family support.

The family support councils, mandated by family support legislation in New Hampshire and replicated by many states, comprise voluntary boards of parents who advise regional funding agencies, assist in developing the annual family support plan, and hire the family agents who assist families in negotiating the system and in developing a future plan for their family. Within the context of welfare reform, the councils engage a significant number of citizens in planning supports and allocating resources—those citizens who are most knowledgeable regarding families and local communities. And while the councils call for a reasonable level of involvement, they do not require the total mobilization that may undermine representative and sustained participation by typical citizens.

The councils rely upon the state's capacity and will to guarantee legislatively mandated policies. They are supported by the authority of state bureaus and have done much to shape these bureaus' mandates and political frameworks. Yet, they resemble voluntary associations more than bureaucracies and are responsive to personal and community needs. The future configuration of the welfare state in the United States may well lie with the intersection of centralized authority and local democratic councils.

Despite its recent emergence, the family support movement in the United States constitutes one of the richest learning domains for the implementation of an effective welfare state. That such a movement initially evolved around disability issues underlines a key finding: The field of developmental disabilities has generated numerous disability and social reform movements based on a vision of community membership and quality of life. These projects can also serve as models for reforming and renewing the welfare state.

REDEFINING THE ROLE OF PROFESSIONALS AND PROFESSIONAL EDUCATION: BUILDING THE CAPACITIES OF COMMUNITIES

In 1992, Norway established a national task force on the mission and content of professional education within the decentralization and deinstitutionalization reforms. The task force is drawing on and elaborating the role of the social pedagogue within a decentralized system committed to universalist approaches. The role of the social pedagogue is similar to that of the support or service coordinator in the United States, a generalist role anchored in knowledge of advocacy, the local community, and systemic negotiation and change. However, the roles significantly differ in the categorical nature of service coordination and the universalist role of the social pedagogue: The service coordinator is located within and functions out of a mental retardation or developmental disabilities agency. The proposed role for the social pedagogue is to enhance the capacities of the general and local welfare system to include and effectively respond to people with mental retardation. This is quantitatively and temporally probably the most ambitious deinstitutionalization effort ever undertaken by any nation. The social pedagogues will be located within housing, health care, social service, employment, and income support agencies, bringing specialized knowledge to these organizations without creating categorical structures.

Education must now focus on issues of community organization and the ideologies and activities of community-based, generic agencies, in addition to the current focus on clinical and specialized knowledge and skills. The education of social pedagogues may be one of the first opportunities to operationalize a community-first strategy by training to build family and community capacities rather than focusing on individual deficit and rehabilitation. As educational reform proceeds and a body of practice develops,

professional educators in the United States, as well as those committed to
the revival and relevance of the service coordination role, will have much
to learn from the Norwegian reformers.

CONCLUSION

In assessing the reforms of the welfare state and supports to people with
disabilities, both Scandinavia and the United States are recovering from
encounters with crisis-driven pessimism and are embarking on the incremental tasks of building effective and inclusive democracies. Both societies
have impressive accomplishments that they can teach each other. The
intersection of the two sets of experiences may provide the most fruitful
pathway to achieving quality of community life and effective welfare
democracy.

U.S. policy makers must decide how to harness the forces that are
already at work. A cursory review of developmental disabilities systems in
states around the country suggests that decentralization is moving swiftly,
stimulated by budget deficits, the elimination of significant staff at the control level, and a philosophical commitment to build capacity at the community level and enhance inclusion of people with developmental disabilities. A systematic understanding of this change and its ramifications in
public systems is needed, and the lessons provided by the experiences in
Scandinavia will be invaluable.

Chapter Review

CHALLENGES

- The locus of responsibility for welfare and other services in Western Europe is moving from central governmental authority and control to subgovernmental units.
- Decentralization and the principles of normalization have led to significant changes in the structure of the service delivery systems in Denmark, Norway, and Sweden.
- Decentralization presents challenges for quality assurance and family recourse.
- More individualized and varied funding may not be possible with the decentralization of services to those with disabilities.
- Decentralization has the potential to enhance interagency coordination and family support, but can dilute expertise and unevenly distribute resources.
- Decentralization can cause changes in power, policies, and administrative authority, as well as change the allocation of resources to local consumers.
- Decentralization may occur with or without privatization.

CHARACTERISTICS OF HELPFUL PROGRAMS

- Decentralization in Denmark, Norway, and Sweden was motivated by a broadly held value of normalization, desire for local participation, and the diminution of bureaucracy.
- Concerns about the quality of local service delivery have led to legislation allowing appeal of local decisions and continued substantial support for staff training.
- Parent organizations play an important national policy role.
- With decentralization in place, Denmark, Norway, and Sweden are developing centers of specialized expertise and legislation ensuring the rights of people with disabilities.
- Equity in the distribution of resources in Scandinavian countries is assisted by distribution of income across municipalities and legislation for mandatory local requirements.

POLICY IMPLICATIONS

- Social welfare reform should precede disability reform.
- Countries should employ community-first strategies that focus on the

well-being of the community, while including the concerns of those with disabilities.

- Communities should build their capacity for improving the quality of life for all citizens.
- The quality of family life and community membership should be used as broad social values to influence services for those with disabilities, especially with volunteer–state collaboration on a local level.
- The United States needs to upgrade its efforts for inclusion and support to comprehensive reform efforts.

References

Ashbaugh, J.W., & Nerney, T. (1990). Findings and implications of a study of the costs of providing residential and support services to individuals with mental retardation in two substate regions of the United States. *Mental Retardation, 28*(5), 269–273.

Bennett, R.J. (Ed.). (1990). *Decentralization of local governments and markets: Towards a post-welfare agenda.* Oxford, England: Clarendon Press.

Bradley, V.J. (1978). *Deinstitutionalization of developmentally disabled persons.* Baltimore: University Park Press.

Bradley, V.J., & Blaney, B.C. (Eds.). (1990). *The family support legislative projects: Proceedings of a national meeting on lessons learned from nine states.* Washington. DC: Administration on Developmental Disabilities.

Dybwad, R. (Ed.). (1989). *International directory of mental retardation resources.* Washington, DC: President's Committee on Mental Retardation.

Grunewald, K. (1971, March / April). *The guiding environment: The dynamic of residential living.* Paper presented at the first regional conference of the United Kingdom Committee of the World Federation for Mental Health, in association with the National Society for Mentally Handicapped Children, Dublin, Ireland.

Juul, K. (1984). *Programs, progress, and problems in services for mentally retarded persons in Scandinavia.* Unpublished manuscript, Southern Illinois University, Carbondale.

Knoll, J. (1990). Defining quality in residential services. In V.J. Bradley & H. Bersani (Eds.), *Quality assurance for individuals with developmental disabilities: It's everybody's business* (pp. 235–262). Baltimore: Paul H. Brookes Publishing Co.

Knoll, J., Covert, S., Osuch, R., O'Connor, S., Agosta, J., & Blaney, B. (1990). *Family support services in the United States: An end of decade status report.* Cambridge, MA: Human Services Research Institute.

Minnow, M. (1990). *Making all the difference: Inclusion, exclusion, and American law.* Ithaca, NY: Cornell University Press.

Nirje, B. (1969). The normalization principle and its human management implications. In R. Kugel & W. Wolfensberger (Eds.), *Changing patterns in residential services for the mentally retarded.* Washington, DC: President's Committee on Mental Retardation.

Olsson, S.E. (1990). *Social policy and welfare state in Sweden.* Lund: Arkiv.

Osborne, D. (1988). *Laboratories of democracy.* Boston: Harvard Business School Press.

Osborne, D., & Gaebler, T. (1992). *Reinventing government: How the entrepreneurial spirit is transforming the public sector.* Reading, MA: Addison-Wesley.

Pierson, Christopher. (1991). *Beyond the welfare state?* University Park: Pennsylvania State University Press.

Schorr, L.B., & Schorr, D. (1988). *Within our reach: Breaking the cycle of disadvantage.* New York: Doubleday.

Sterner, R. (1976). *Social and economic conditions of the mentally retarded in selected countries.* Brussels, Belgium: International League of Societies for the Mentally Handicapped.

Taylor, S.J. (1988). Caught in the continuum: A critical analysis of the least restrictive environment. *The Journal of The Association for Persons with Severe Handicaps, 13,* 41–53.

Vetvik, E. (1992, August). *The case of Norway: Transition from institution to open care, planning under financial stress in a welfare state.* Paper presented at the 9th World

Congress, International Association for the Scientific Study of Mental Deficiency, Broadbeach, Queensland, Australia.

Wolfensberger, W. (1972). *Normalization: The principle of normalization in human services*. Toronto, Ontario, Canada: National Institute on Mental Retardation.

Wolman, H. (1990). Decentralization: What it is and why we should care. In R.J. Bennett (Ed.), *Decentralization, local governments, and markets: Towards a postwelfare agenda*. Oxford, England: Clarendon Press.

16

Coalitions for Family Support and the Creation of Two Flexible Funding Programs

Susan Yuan, Tanya Baker-McCue, and Karen Witkin

Since the early 1990s, there has been growing support for a family-based approach to the development and delivery of health and human services. This support has developed from an increasing awareness that families are the primary source of support and sustenance for their members. In addition to this pragmatic perspective, the family support movement has been fueled by a value-based philosophy of service provision, which challenges many long-held assumptions about health and human services by viewing families and their members as interdependent partners in the development and implementation of care, and an invaluable resource for meeting their identified goals. These guiding beliefs are buttressed by strongly held values and assumptions about families themselves, which view families as the following:

- Benevolent—attempting to act in the best interest of their members
- Trustworthy
- Experts on their own children
- Unique—each with their own set of resources and abilities
- Entitled to support in ways that allow them to maintain their integrity

Commitment to a family support philosophy means viewing families positively and recognizing parents' commitment to their children and desire to raise them at home. Most parents do not view the demands of care as burdens, but they do consistently identify the continual struggles they face in order to get the supports they require to appropriately care for their children as burdens (Knoll, 1993). A family support philosophy acknowledges the fundamental principle of mutual obligation—a family assumes a great deal of responsibility in taking care of their member with special needs, thereby relieving the taxpayer of the substantial monetary burden of institutionalization. In turn, the government must keep faith with families by supporting them in ways that enable them to survive intact. A family support philosophy affirms that, "Families of children with disabilities enrich the lives of all citizens through their contributions to the economic health and social fabric of their community, state, and nation" (Families of Children with Disabilities Support Act of 1994, PL 103-382). Finally, a family support philosophy means that every person has a right to a family, and that every child has the right to be raised within and be an integral part of a family unit. Government and the community have the complementary obligation to support that right.

The acceptance and implementation of this philosophy by service providers, agency administrators, and policy makers would be revolutionary; currently, in 1995, the revolution is stirring. Caution is predictable, however, for a minimum of four reasons. First, family support obligates professionals to relinquish their roles as experts who give pronouncements and prescriptions for families to follow. Family support challenges the balance of power (e.g., expertise) in family–professional relationships by requiring partnership, collaboration, and symmetry in decision making. Second, family support puts context back into the family–professional relationship. Individuals can no longer be extracted from their families, communities, and cultures, fixed, and placed back into their natural environment. All of these contexts are part of, and must be incorporated into, the professional relationship. Third, program responsiveness should not depend on families being vocal, well informed, politically connected, or persistent, but on the agencies and professionals they employ. These agencies must assume the responsibility of informing families about the resources available to them—moving from the practice of the squeaky wheel to entitlement. Fourth, family support requires replacing largely system-based and deficit-oriented services with those that are family and community based and strengths oriented.

Although this vision of family support has yet to reach fruition, an increasing number of programs are demonstrating its viability. This chapter describes two such programs that grant flexible funding to families. Although neither program alone addresses all of the above issues, each expresses some of the core values necessary for a truly family-centered approach. In doing so, each supports the possibility and desirability of family-centered services.

A NATIONAL OVERVIEW OF FLEXIBLE FUNDING

Policy and Principles

Flexible funding in family support is an outgrowth of policies and practices that respect families' identification of their own needs, recognize that those needs are unique and change over time, and acknowledge that power is in the hand that holds the purse strings. As early as 1986, a conference of family support policy leaders held at Syracuse University's Center on Human Policy included in its list of principles, "Family supports should maximize the family's control over the services and supports they receive."

In 1990, a national conference of parents and staff of developmental disabilities councils included the principle, "Family supports should be flexible" (Bradley, 1993, p. 5). The National Conference on State Legislatures declared in 1991, "Families should be allowed to control resources, making the system less 'provider driven' and more 'consumer driven'" (Bradley, 1993, p. 6).

Joint research on quality indicators for family support by Family and Integration Resources and Human Services Research Institute found that "very important" ratings were given by 82% of national family respondents to "program is flexible," 83% to "change as needed," and 86% to "family makes decisions" (Karp, Faison, Agosta, & Melda, 1992, p. 6). In the final version of the quality indicators, three overarching principles emerged:

1. Family driven—Each family leads the decision-making process concerning the type and amount of support they receive.
2. Easy-to-use—Families are not overwhelmed by paperwork and red tape.
3. Flexible—Families can choose supports and services based on their individual needs and preferences. (*Expecting Excellence in Family Support*, 1993, p. 1)

The Families of Children with Disabilities Support Act states, "It is the policy of the United States that all programs, projects, and activities receiving assistance under this Part shall be family centered and family directed." Among the principles governing policy are the following: "Family needs change over time and family support must offer options that are flexible and responsive to the unique needs and strengths and cultural values of individual families"; and "Families are the primary decision-makers regarding services and supports they receive and play decision making roles in policies and programs that affect their lives" (p. 3).

The bill defines the term *family support* to include "financial assistance, which may include discretionary cash subsidies, allowances, voucher or reimbursement systems, low interest loans, and/or lines of credit" (p. 6). This bill gives states the right to specify a lead agency to coordinate the application of systems change grants offered. Under this bill, the lead agency has the ability "to promote and facilitate the implementation of family support services that are family-centered and family-directed, and flexible, and that provides families with the greatest possible decision-making authority and control regarding the nature and use of services and supports" (p. 13).

Prevalence of Financial Assistance and Cash Subsidy Programs

Financial assistance is not a new concept in family support. Michigan has implemented a cash subsidy program for families since July 1, 1984. By September 1991, 16 states had cash subsidy legislation in place (Dunst, Trivette, Starnes, Hamby, & Gordon, 1993). And, adding states with pilot programs and family support initiatives without legislation, the number of states with financial assistance programs had grown to 25, according to one study (Knoll et al., 1993), and 33 according to another (Dunst et al., 1993). Changes in state programs are taking place so rapidly that the discrepancies between studies may reflect the most recent checks of state practices rather than disagreement over criteria.

Issues in the Implementation of Flexible Funding

Beyond the philosophical issues of family control and flexibility are the practical issues of program costs, effectiveness, and sources of funding. Among the most difficult questions states struggle with as they redesign their delivery of services to families to include flexible funding are those related to eligibility. When funds are limited, does a state divide funds equally among the broadest number of families, ensuring, as one father quipped, "a chicken wing in every pot," or does it triage families, serving only those with the most intense needs—a practice reflecting crisis-oriented services; one honest program director said dryly, when asked by a friend what she had to do to qualify her son for a Medicaid waiver, "It would help if you died." Families working on the proposed draft of the national family support bill recommended the addition of a statement under policy declaring family support to be precrisis, proactive, and preventive, "not a response to crisis only" (National Family Support Legislation, 1994, p. 3).

Although cash subsidy programs began with eligibility limited to one disability group, current discussions favor broadening eligibility. Michigan's annual report to the governor and legislature for 1989–1990 recommended that they "expand the subsidy program to families with children who have severe physical, health, or emotional impairments" (Arneaud & Herman, 1991, p. 25). This broader, cross-disability approach may be easier to achieve when no program is yet in place and no one has anything to lose rather than later when an existing program with narrow eligibility is in place. According to Knoll et al. (1993), "In at least 10 states, the issue of who should be a beneficiary of a family support program was and is a problem" (p. 90). The influence of Part H of the Individuals with Disabilities Education Act of 1990 (IDEA), PL 101-476, with its emphasis on family-centered, family-identified services and interagency coordination, lays the groundwork for thinking about supports in broader, less categorical ways. When needs of families show commonalities across disabilities, dividing families into haves and have-nots on the basis of categorical labels seems senseless.

Some states have limited program costs by establishing income ceilings for eligible families. Michigan's program was established in the early 1980s with a ceiling of $60,000 on total family income. According to the report on fiscal years 1989–1990, "During the seven years since enactment of the Subsidy, spending power has eroded. We recommend that the Legislature consider removing the cap or raising it"(Allard, Gottlieb, & Hart, 1993, p. 25). In the 3-year Family Cash Assistance Project in Massachusetts, evaluated by the Shriver Center, the 30 families selected were required to have incomes below $70,000 (Allard et al., 1993). Ohio's ceiling is $78,000. Connecticut's pilot cash subsidy program ceiling is set at $58,800, Illinois's at $50,000, Iowa's at $40,000, and Georgia's at $30,000. Rhode Island's figure for financial assistance is set at 400% of the federal poverty level; Texas requires families to make a co-payment above the state median for its voucher/debit program (Knoll et al., 1993, pp. 63–71).

Another question in the financing of flexible funding is the extent to which a state can or should convert existing service dollars into flexible use, rather than budget new money for cash subsidies and continue to provide existing services. According to Knoll et al. (1993), 17 states provide both financial assistance and services. Knoll et al. also suggest three principal components of family supports: services, service coordination, and financial assistance; taking funding from the first two components to strengthen the third requires careful consideration of the possible impact within a state. When the state of Maryland passed a family support bill extending subsidies to families caring for adults with disabilities at home, the governor took the opportunity to withdraw other services from those individuals with disabilities because their families were being supported, which left them increasingly dependent on their families (Bergman, 1992).

Although studies have determined states' level of fiscal effort for family support programs using a formula that computes the amount of family support program funds per $1,000 of personal income in the state (Dunst et al., 1993; Knoll et al., 1993), determining where that funding comes from has proven to be a daunting challenge. Most programs creatively use their Medicaid funding to maximize the impact of state funds, which has complicated efforts to determine how much goes to administrative costs instead of going directly to families. Direct cash subsidy programs, however, cut checks at the state level and are reputed to have very low administrative costs. Michigan's program serves more than 4,000 families with two full-time employees; there, eligibility is determined by educational placement, and program administrators handle only billing, record keeping, and satisfaction surveys (Bergman, 1994).

SYSTEMS CHANGE IN VERMONT

Coalition: Working Together

Realizing early that competition for resources would sap limited energy, parent organizations across disabilities in Vermont began to network, share ideas, conduct joint trainings, and ultimately, form a unified group—the Family Support Committee of the Vermont Coalition for Disability Rights. Once formed, the committee undertook the tasks of defining family support for Vermont and articulating an ideal system of supports for families toward which all work.

Inspired by the passage of the New Hampshire Family Support Bill, members of the Family Support Committee began to explore questions inherent in defining a version of cross-disability family support legislation for Vermont. The Vermont Arc and the Division of Mental Retardation conducted focus forums in every mental health center in the state, asking families directly what they wanted for supports.

Overlapping boards is one way to strengthen consensus among organizations. In Vermont, where there are only so many parents available to serve on various councils, members of the Family Support Committee also served on the Vermont Developmental Disabilities Planning Council and its Research Committee. They encouraged the Research Committee to take on a thorough study of existing services offered to families caring for members with disabilities by the Agency of Human Services and the Division of Instructional Support Services (Special Education). Using definitions and a survey matrix designed by the Family Support Committee, teams consisting of one member of the Family Support Committee and one member of the Research Committee interviewed administrators of state programs and compiled a comprehensive Developmental Disabilities Planning Council report with recommendations, *Family Support for People with Disabilities: Why We Need Legislation* (Vermont Developmental Disabilities Planning Council, 1993).

With consultation from the Human Services Research Institute, the Family Support Committee struggled through the issues and decisions involved in designing Vermont's Family Support Bill, which was introduced in both houses of the 1993 Legislature with 26 sponsors. By the time of the hearing in the House Health and Welfare Committee, all legislators had copies of the Developmental Disabilities Planning Council report as background, many hand-delivered by constituent families.

History of Flexible Funding in Vermont

On an informal, individual family level, flexible funding in Vermont has been practiced for many years. Long before policies for flexibility were in place, respite coordinators at both the regional and state levels responded to emergency or crisis situations as needed with tacit approval, providing assistance that addressed actual needs, rather than presuming that only hours of respite were needed. These needs included such basics as food, utilities, and transportation (D. Bombard, personal communication, December 31, 1993).

As respite was completely state funded, greater flexibility was possible than with federal funds such as Medicaid. The importance of this was underlined when the Family Support Committee of the state Mental Retardation Advisory Board recommended that Vermont not apply for the competitive Community and Supported Living Arrangements Medicaid Waiver (CSLA) in 1990, as it would have taken all the state respite money to use as match funds. Although it would have brought federal dollars into the state, this waiver was viewed as creating excessive bureaucratic restraints on existing flexibility. The grant application, already written and ready to go, was not submitted.

Different from the individual, flexible supports that occurred in emergencies, the flexible funding emerging in Vermont is now policy, not an exception to the rule. Before, in order to use respite funds flexibly, a family had to live in a region of the state with a respite coordinator who recognized the logic of flexibility and was supported by the agency administration; a certain level of crisis had to be reached and acknowledged; the family had to ask for help; and everything had to be done quietly, under the table. Decisions even to consider granting flexible use of funds were made by individual coordinators and could be interpreted as arbitrary.

With a strong tradition of independence in Vermont, many families find acknowledging the need for help to be difficult; some care for children and adults in their homes for decades—one family interviewed, for 45 years—before accepting even respite. For flexible family support to be successful in Vermont, it must be simple, easy to gain access to, fair, and respectful of the dignity, capability, and privacy of families (*Family Support in Vermont,* 1990).

SPECIFIC PROGRAM EXAMPLES

Two programs that attempt to meet these characteristics have been instituted in Vermont: a parent-run endowed fund, and a pilot of the state-funded respite program involving two regional community mental health agencies that serve people with mental retardation and their families. Although these programs are distinct from one another, it is important in Vermont's history of flexible funding to be aware of the human interconnections between them—both arose out of the caring and energy of families combined with the commitment of professionals.

The move toward coalition of the family support groups in Vermont began in earnest at the same time that flexible funding was started by Parent to Parent of Vermont. The death of many children that year drew families closer together in support of one another and helped them to overcome some of their previous differences. No one advocated for a privately funded program versus a publicly funded one; the programs developed side by side and involved many of the same families, both as recipients and designers of policy.

Brookes Baker Family Support Fund

Parent to Parent of Vermont, a nonprofit organization offering support and information to families with children who have chronic illnesses or disabilities, established a family support fund in 1989 with an initial $5,000 seed grant from the University of Vermont's Department of Social Work. This was the first formal financial assistance grant program in Vermont.

The program had a few eligibility requirements and stipulated that parents identify their own priorities. It was important to the mission of the fund that families not lose their dignity or privacy. They were required only to write or call the request personally to the Parent to Parent office to apply for up to $200 each year. The amount of funding per family was limited in order to meet as many requests as possible. Each request received an individual response, guided by the belief that everyone knew what they needed for support.

In 1990, $50,000 from the Brookes Baker Trust was awarded to Parent to Parent by Tim and Tanya Baker, parents of Brookes, who died in 1988 at 8 years old. Fund-raising efforts in Vermont had previously collected over $75,000, enabling Brookes to be one of the youngest people with cystic fibrosis to receive a heart/lung transplant. The fund was aptly renamed the Brookes Baker Family Support Fund (BBFSF) to commemorate this child whose courage and strength helped to provide this unique opportunity for families in Vermont. As an endowment fund, 80% of the income or interest generated from the principal is distributed to families each year. The fund also benefits from ongoing donations of Parent to Parent staff honoraria and memorial gifts.

Parents comprise the BBFSF Review Committee and determine the individual family awards each year. Priority is given to families who have not been funded previously. In addition, families are helped to identify and obtain other resources.

State-Funded Community Mental Health Center Pilots for Flexible Family Support

With the experience of the Brookes Baker Fund and the efforts of the Family Support Committee of the Vermont Coalition for Disability Rights and the Vermont Mental Retardation Advisory Board, leadership of the state Division of Mental Retardation began a pilot program in July 1992 in two areas of the state—the Northeast Kingdom and southeastern Vermont. These areas cover five counties and include both prosperous small cities and some of the poorest rural areas in Vermont. The two community mental health agencies chosen had similar respite budgets and numbers of families using respite care. Each agency involved had a coordinator with primary responsibility for the respite program; these coordinators invited family members in the region to form a Family Support Board. The guiding principles of the pilot specifically stated "Keep it simple, easy to access," and "Trust families" (Wood, 1993, p. 1).

Families were notified by letter of the changes in the program, and coordinators discussed the program with families when they had occasion to contact them. Families using the respite portion of the program filled out the usual respite forms that were already familiar to them. To apply for flexible funds, families simply turned the respite form over and wrote the item or service requested and the cost, up to the yearly allotment of $1,200 per family. The coordinators were instructed not to second-guess the families, but to offer help in finding the best possible deal available. They would also help gain access to other sources, if families wanted that. Requests were to be processed and checks sent as quickly as possible, without requiring receipts or other proofs-of-purchase.

Coordinators submitted records of specific requests to the state quarterly in order to regularly monitor the budget, as no one knew ahead of time what the impact of the flexible funding option would be on program usage. Lists of specific uses were kept at both the regional and state respite/family support program levels, with summarized reports to the state Agency of Human Services organized in general categories.

A qualitative evaluation of the project was conducted by interviewing nine families at the beginning and end of the pilot year. Table 1 gives demographic profiles for those families interviewed. Families were chosen by targeted sampling and represented both pilot regions of the state, urban and rural settings, single and two-parent families, varying degrees of disability severity, varying ages of parents and children, and varying employment status. These characteristics were identified to ensure that the breadth of family circumstances was represented, but do not reflect the philosophy or practices of the two Vermont programs, which oppose characterizing families on the basis of needs. These interviews, each averaging 1½ hours, were carried out as part of a dissertation by a Vermont mother whose young adult son has significant disabilities—a fact that families were aware of. The interviewer was acutely aware of the possibility that her own ideas might influence the interview process and worked to maintain a neutral position throughout the information gathering and analysis. In this ongoing research, the scope of the interview questions extends beyond the evaluation to seek the opinions of the families on policy directions for support in Vermont (see Appendices A and B at the end of this chapter). For the purpose of the pilot evaluation, however, only those responses relating to use, impact, satisfaction with the process, and suggestions for improvement of the flexible family support programs will be represented and discussed here.

Table 1. Community mental health center flexible family support pilot project: Family demographic profiles

Family 1

    Single-parent family, two children
    Two people currently living at home
    Mother, age 62, has diabetes
    Son, age 16, has Down syndrome
    Home located in small city
    Mother retired, on Social Security

Family 2

    Single-parent family, three children
    Two people currently living at home
    Mother, age 54, has diabetes
    Son, age 15, has Down syndrome and orthopedic problems
    Home located in small town
    Mother working part time

Family 3

    Two-parent family, one child
    Three people currently living at home
    Mother and father in early 50s
    Son, age 20, has multiple disabilities
    Home located in rural area
    Father and mother do piece-work in the home

Family 4

    Two-parent family, two children
    Four people currently living at home
    Mother and father in late 40s
    Son, age 13, has autistic characteristics
    Home located in rural area
    Mother has professional position; father is between jobs

Family 5

    Two-parent family, three children
    Five people currently living at home
    Mother and father in late 30s
    Son, age 7, has degenerative terminal disorder
    Home located in small town
    Father works full time; mother works part time

Family 6

    Two-parent family, two children
    Four people currently living at home
    Mother and father in early 40s
    Son, age 17, has seizure disorder, severe allergies, orthopedic problems, and mild learning impairment
    Home located in small town
    Father works full time; mother works part time

Table 1. (*continued*)

Family 7

Two-parent family, two children
Four people currently living at home
Mother and father in early 40s
Son, age 8, has autism
Home located in rural area
Father works full time; mother works part time

Family 8

Two-parent family, two children
Four people currently living at home
Mother and father in 30s
Son, age 5, has Down syndrome and orthopedic problems
Son, age 4, has congenital heart defect requiring multiple surgeries
Home located in rural area
Father works full time; mother is a homemaker

Family 9

Two-parent family, one child
Three people currently living at home
Mother and father in early 70s; mother has diabetes
Daughter, age 46, has diagnosis of both mental retardation and manic-depressive disorder
Home located in rural area
Parents retired, on Social Security

Summary and Discussion of Data on Flexible Funding in Vermont

The BBFSF and the state-funded pilots have several differences:

- Length of operation: BBFSF—5 years, pilots—1 year
- Yearly accessible amount per family: BBFSF—$200, pilots—$1,200
- Method of application: BBFSF—letter or telephone call, pilots—respite form
- Nature of program: BBFSF—private and parent-run, pilots—statewide and state-funded

Nevertheless in both the quantitative data on the categories of type of use and the qualitative data from the BBFSF letters and the pilot project interviews, there were apparent similarities. The aggregate data presented in Table 2 represent the most comprehensive picture available of the use of flexible funding by families in Vermont, their impressions of its impact, and the processes involved.

In January 1994, the BBFSF had provided a total of $20,695 of assistance to 83 families over 5 years, approximately 10% of the families involved with Parent to Parent across Vermont. In the experience of the fund, parents have consistently researched items for the best offer and made requests for the exact purchase price, even though a receipt or proof-of-purchase is never required. Table 3 shows exact figures. Many of the requests from families come with offers of reciprocal support, either to the fund, organization, or fellow parents.

Table 2. Flexible funding in Vermont

Category	Total frequency	Brookes Baker Family Support Fund—5 years	Community Mental Health Center Pilot—1 year
Care	119	14	105
Recreation and education	105	49	56
Camps, community activities, aides for camps	40	8	32
Toys, Christmas presents	26	16	10
Vacations, conference	23	16	7
Lessons	12	8	4
TVs, VCRs, tape recorders	4	1	3
Assistive technology or services	72	44	28
Medical care, therapy, special equipment	42	20	22
Medical travel	21	17	4
Computers and software	9	7	2
Household necessities	42	23	19
Utilities	28	14	14
Fuel, heating, a/c	15	6	9
Telephone	13	8	5
Household expenses	5	3	2
Food	4	4	0
Home adaptations	3	1	2
Toilet	1	0	1
Cleaning expenses	1	1	0
Individual necessities	37	16	21
Clothes and shoes	22	11	11
Beds, mattresses, bedding	12	4	8
Car seats	2	1	1
Place setting	1	0	1
Other	6	4	2
Counseling	3	1	2
Legal fees	1	1	0
Driver's license	1	1	0
Funeral expenses	1	1	0

At the beginning of the flexible funding pilots, there was concern that families might spend all their resources early in the year, leaving insufficient funds available for later needs. Would families who had underused respite in the past "come out of the woodwork" once they could use funds as they wished and create excessive demands on the resources? Fortunately, this did not happen in the programs. The actual spending, including adminis-

Table 3. Brookes Baker Family Support Fund: Statistics

Number of families eligible	850
Number of families using fund	83
Instances of use (over 5 years)	150
Amount available yearly per family	$200
Total expenditure (over 5 years)	$20,695
Average spent per eligible family (over 5 years)	$24.35
Average for families using fund (over 5 years)	$249.34
Average per instance of use	$138

trative costs, of the two pilot programs was slightly less with flexible funding than the previous year with only traditional respite (in the southeast region, $74,000 in 1993 versus $76,000 in 1992; in the northeast, $72,500 in 1993 versus $74,000 in 1992). Families tended to be conservative with program use, saving their allotment until the latter part of the year. In the Northeast Kingdom, by the end of the third quarter, less than half the funds available had been used; the spending in the fourth quarter was greater than the first three quarters combined. The average use per family of flexible funding for the 109 families involved in the pilot program was $245. This, however, represented use by 38 families, only 34% of those eligible, with the others using only traditional respite. The average flexible funding use for those 38 families was $702, still less than half the amount available. Those parents who used flexible funding researched the best prices on items purchased and, in several cases, opted to buy used equipment to save money. In at least one new region opting to convert its respite program to flexible funding after the pilot year, the same phenomenon of frugal use is reported (D. Bombard, personal communication, December 31, 1993).

For Vermont families to become comfortable allowing themselves to use the flexible funding option, more time and experience with the program may be necessary. It also may help to give families the opportunity to discuss the program among themselves or with coordinators. Of the nine families who took part in the interviews, 100% used the flexible funding option, although they received no particular encouragement to do so. Table 4 shows how flexible funding was used within the pilot program.

Categories of Use and Descriptions of Impact

Instances of use in both programs are calculated by 1) use of traditional respite or child care as indicated by each family and counted only once, whether it was used for 1 hour or more than 100 hours; 2) use of flexible funding, counted by individual use, under the category of the item or service purchased. This difference in recording data sometimes disguises the importance of respite, which emerged as the highest category of use. Ag-

Table 4. CMHC pilot use of flexible funding:
Program statistics

Number of families eligible	unavailable
Number of families served	109
Number of families using respite	105
Number of families using flexible funding	38
Instances of total use	231
Instances of use of flexible funding	126
Amount available per family yearly	$1,200
Total amount spent in fiscal year 1993—minus administrative costs	$122,200
Average spent per family	$1,121
Average spent on respite per user	$910
Average flexible funding per eligible family	$245
Average flexible funding by families	$702
Average flexible funding per instance of use	$212

gregate figures for both programs combined are given in Figure 1. Usage fell into six categories.

Care

Care, including traditional respite, child care for other children in the family, and specialized nursing care, was the largest category of use with 119 instances. This frequency has two possible explanations. Respite dates back to 1976 and is the most familiar service available to families; therefore, most families are comfortable with using it; or, help with care may truly be the greatest need experienced by families, regardless of their familiarity with it.

In Vermont, respite workers are enlisted from the natural community and extended family members. No particular training is provided other than that given by the family. The amount paid, $4.25 an hour, is more than the going rate for most child care, but many families have to supplement this rate in order to find people willing to accept the greater responsibility of caring for someone with a disability. The greatest problem for families in rural areas is finding workers, to say nothing of trained respite providers.

Respite is not always used by parents for rest and recreation. One family, retired parents caring for their 46-year-old daughter with both mental retardation and manic-depressive disorder, used it when the mother, who has diabetes, was hospitalized for an operation on her foot. "Someone stayed at night because J. [father] doesn't hear well. We've used the program more because of R.'s [mother's] health rather than going out and

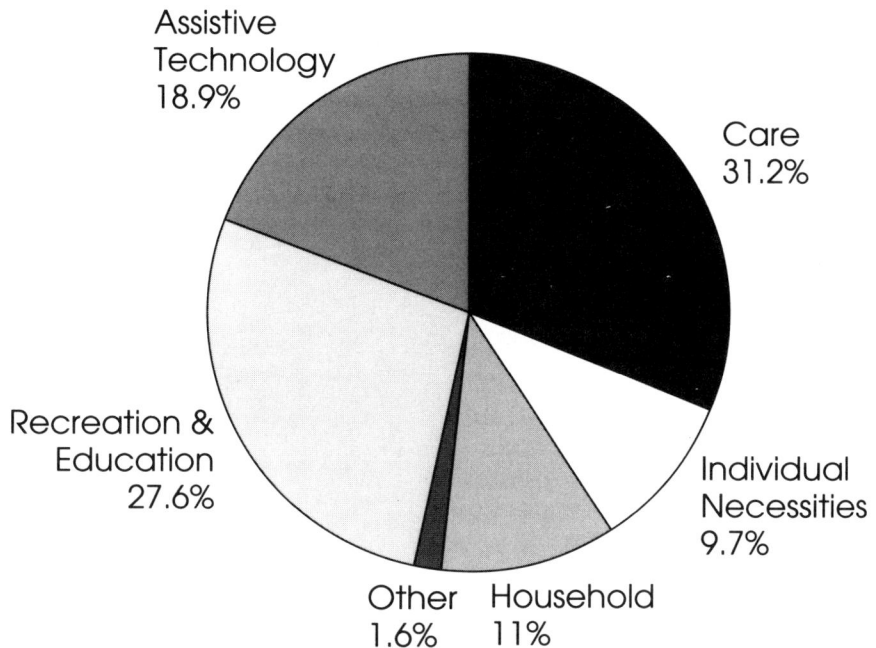

Figure 1.   Aggregate uses of flexible funding for both the Brookes Baker Family Support Fund and the Community Mental Health Center pilot program.

enjoying ourselves. It's been a good help in this situation. People say they'll come and do things, but it's nice not to have [to ask]."[1] These parents have not spent a night away together alone since 1968 because of their daughter's problems with sleep.

Recreation and Education

Recreation and education, the second most frequent use with 105 instances, included a number of subcategories, the largest being camp fees, personal assistants for camp, and community activities with 40 instances of use. This may reflect the importance of summer camps for respite when school is out, but it also provides enriching opportunities for the individual with a disability. In some cases, the brother or sister of the child with a disability went to camp, reflecting the family-centered nature of the program.

Toys, Christmas presents, bikes, and educational materials were the next most frequently purchased with 26 instances. A single parent of a teenage son with Down syndrome bought a used three-wheeler bike so that

---

[1] Any quotes not cited can be attributed to comments generated in interviews with participants of the BBFSF or the Vermont pilot program.

he could ride with his friends in the neighborhood. Sometimes the line between recreational equipment and assistive technology blurred. A climbing gym "for our son . . . would greatly benefit his gross motor development and coordination." A 6-month-old child "has been using a swing in the hospital and really enjoys it. He now weighs 7 pounds and is developmentally behind, so I am sure that he would use it for a long time." The parents of a young man with multiple disabilities bought "a portable hammock-type of thing that has a roof and screened-in sides . . . which we plan on using outside because he can't stand the sun, because his eyes bother him, plus the bugs; he doesn't have the defense to swat off the bugs. This will give us a chance to maybe go down to the garden. . . . It's going to free us up a lot. It is just so nice to be able to buy something instead of having to think that we've got to go out or something. To me, it has just been a Godsend." A family with two preschoolers, one with a serious heart condition and the other with hip dysplasia, used flexible funding to buy a double stroller. "It's been a big help. There were several months that D. spent a lot of time not walking. We had to carry him all over the place."

Travel unrelated to medical care, such as vacations and conferences, was the next largest subcategory under recreation, with 23 instances. One parent said, "We used it to go home [to England] when my mum died, to have enough for S.'s ticket so he could come with me. . . . It also helped me with my ticket, too. . . . I think there's a big impact. I would have had to get a sitter for him and as it was, he went with me." Another woman shared this: "My husband and I would like a night away, just the two of us. . . . I was lucky enough to win a weekend to Quebec. Our problem is . . . our car is not reliable for that distance. We were hoping to rent one so that we could go."

Lessons also fell under the category and included gymnastics, horseback riding, and swimming for the child with a disability, and in one case, piano lessons for the mother. "I feel relaxed and at peace when I play. To nurture this within myself and our home would be very healing for all of us." According to the mother of a 7-year-old boy with autism, "I'd like M. to do swimming lessons this summer . . . with the rest of his peers. . . . We need a one-to-one respite worker to do lessons at [the lake]. . . . It's going to make things a lot easier for us, because we can't do it."

Two televisions, a tape recorder, and the repair of a VCR completed the requests in this category.

Assistive Technology or Services

Assistive technology or services was the next largest category, with 72 instances of use, including all medically related equipment, special technology, medical care, or related travel. One family used it this way: "When L. was in the hospital for 70 days, we drove down and back (150 miles) every day. We were able to use the money to buy gas to go down." Another said, "We have a son . . . who needs to go to Toronto for surgery. This will be our fourth trip flying to Toronto. . . . We are in hopes to obtain a grant to help offset our expenses . . . for airfare . . . as well as helping with the cost of lodging for approximately 1 week, food, and other miscellaneous expenses such as taxis or buses. . . . In the future, we would gladly speak to any other parents to help answer any questions regarding the Hospital for Sick Children in Toronto, the most inexpensive place to stay, etc., including emotional support."

Special equipment ranged from computers to electric wheelchairs, to Medic-Alert bracelets and nursery monitors. "I am asking please for some money to buy a nursery monitor so I won't need to check on [my 20-month-old daughter] every hour as she no longer has any night nurses. . . . At least this way I could sleep at night."

Parents sought out the best cost on equipment whenever possible. "The prone stander that he could use is a locally made device. The cost of the materials is $75. The labor cost is donated." Or, "We know of a used and discounted portable pulmonary aid for $360 and the vendor would allow us to have it for monthly installment payments."

Household Necessities

Household necessities formed the next category, with 42 instances. In some cases, ensuring the safety of the family member with disabilities required household changes, such as adaptations and fences. The family of a young boy with a degenerative terminal illness recently "had to purchase new safety gates. . . . The house we moved to had stairs, a lot more doors and entry ways. . . . It's been really good. . . . I think mostly knowing that in the middle of the night we don't have to worry about S. trooping out into the living room or outside even, right out the door."

This category was frequently used, 28 instances, for help with utility costs—fuel, heating or air conditioning equipment, and telephones. Nine of the families in the pilot program used the program for heating (e.g., cords of wood, tanks of propane), which has raised the question of the extent to which a family support program should pick up the slack for inadequate generic social programs, such as fuel assistance. Do families use a family support program because it is more family friendly and they are uncomfortable using programs perceived as welfare, or are such programs simply inadequate to meet the need? Should program administrators require families to exhaust all other social resources first? One family reported withdrawing their application for SSI for their daughter until they retired and received Social Security themselves, because an office worker had told the mother that SSI "is something like welfare." Until these issues are resolved by family support boards committed to a family-centered approach, coordinators will continue to respond by sending the funds requested.

In some cases, utility costs are related to the special needs of the family member. "I have high electric bills as my son has machines that are plugged in at all times. My phone bill has been high as I need to call doctors far away." Another mother illustrates this point: "If [my son] is hot or warm, his skin massively blisters—200 blisters per day. A specialist in New York indicated that his condition will be much more severe without an air conditioner. Medicaid has denied this support. . . . They are currently on sale at Sears for $299.99 until Saturday."

Four families found it necessary to use family support funds for food. A widow on Social Security caring for a teenage son who had trouble with his weight said, "I like to get him special stuff, a lot of fruit, because I want him to eat healthy. Well, fruit costs. Once, I said maybe I'll take some of the respite and save it aside. See, you can't buy lettuce and tomatoes and expect that's going to last you a month; you've gotta go day by day. My money is gone."

Perhaps the most basic need of all is illustrated in a story from the pilot program. One morning a son tried to flush his mother's false teeth down the toilet. The lowers went down, but the uppers jammed. "He [the plumber] said we were going to have to have another toilet. I'm thinking of my money. I said, 'I guess the kid won't eat this month if I have to buy a toilet.' . . . My money is basically out. Every cent that I have. I can't afford to have bills." Flexible funding bought the toilet, creating what is known, tongue-in-cheek, as the t-test for family support programs (Agosta, 1993b).

Individual Necessities

Individual necessities accounted for 37 instances of use (10%), which contrasts with Michigan's patterns of use in 1990, where 85.2% of subsidy families purchased clothing (Allard et al., 1993). The most common need was clothes and shoes, with 22 instances of purchase. One mother said "We've got S.'s sneakers with a support hook on them and we thought what if halfway through the year we go completely broke and we don't have the money to get him new sneakers and they're $20, but we just don't have it. What are we going to do?" Another family reported, "My son . . . wears a helmet to reshape his head, but the helmet is too big to put regular shirts on. I have to buy button-down shirts . . . This has become extremely difficult since I do not work and we have a limited income." Two of the interview families in the pilot reported that their sons shred their shirts almost daily, creating a steady financial drain. "Would it be too much to ask you for help for a new winter jacket, hat, and gloves? My son just had a back operation this summer and his old jacket is too short."

Beds, mattresses, and bedding were requested 12 times. For one pilot family the flexible funding came a year too late. Their son, who spends most of his time in bed, had outgrown the crib that served him for many years. The parents priced lumber to build a new bed but found it beyond their means. For the next 6 weeks, the father searched the nearby woods for trees and branches the right size. He cut them down, peeled, and dried them. Then, working continuously for 3 weeks on the front porch, he shaped and fitted the rails and spindles together until he had built a bed worthy of his son. In answer to a comment that he could earn a great deal making furniture like this, the mother said, "He wouldn't sell them to parents with kids like ours. He would give them away."

Other

The final category, other, contained three requests for counseling and one for legal fees. A family that was originally homeless finally got a small apartment "so that our baby could be released home from the hospital. . . . My biggest dream is to get my driver's license . . . so that I can transport my family to appointments, church, etc., without relying on people. I have obtained a grant to take driving classes, but still need the fee to obtain the license itself." Also, just before Christmas came a request for funeral expenses for a child.

Differences in Program Usage

Because of the inherent differences in the two flexible funding programs, patterns of usage did not reflect the same values. Figures 2 and 3 illustrate the specific patterns of use in each program.

Incidental Benefits

An unexpected benefit from the pilot program with the families interviewed was the sense of security the availability of flexible funding provided. One parent said that it is "nice to know that if he needs something and we're broke and we don't have the money, we can fall back on this for it." Using the program as a "rainy-day fund" may account for the initial underuse of the flexible funding option and the subsequent rush for funds later in the year. As one parent illustrates, "I also understand that like if the car broke down, the respite program would help with that, which is great. I don't know what we would have done this summer if the car had broke down."

Satisfaction with the Process

Families in the pilot program generally reported satisfaction with the process of obtaining funds. One parent said, "There was really no process. It was very easy; just on the back of the respite form I wrote in the need, the amount of the item to purchase and the reason . . . That was it." Another reported, "She said to just go ahead and buy it and I had the check back within a week. It was wonderful. . . . We've had to deal with other state agencies and they take so long, but this was great." Overall, satisfaction was overwhelming. One family said, "I think we've found it perfect so far."

Some commented on the ability to choose. "It seems like what the [family support] committee has done in shaking [the funding] loose has probably unbureaucratized it and given people some flexibility and that's great!" One family captured the consensus of the group by saying, "I just think it makes life a lot more pleasant to be able to spend the money on something that we want rather than to have to do what somebody tells us is going to be better for us."

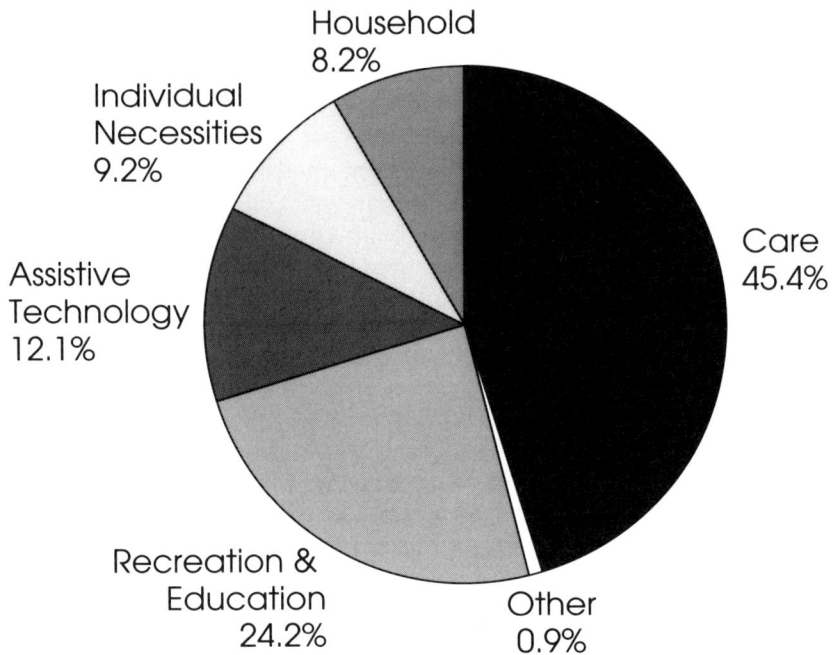

Figure 2.   Specific patterns of flexible funding usage for the Brookes Baker Family Support Fund.

Suggestions for Improvement

Families interviewed were asked for specific suggestions for improving the existing program and speculation about better ways the program might operate in the future. As expected, one family identified the need for "appropriately trained respite services." Also highlighted was the perennial need for "more money, of course. I understand not everybody can get on. There's a waiting list now." The last point was made by a member of the regional family support advisory board, in discussing a decision-making dilemma—should she extend double benefits to a family with two children with disabilities or open up the program to another family on the waiting list? The benefits were finally extended to an additional family, hoping the family with two children could double-up on benefits. Here, the program sought to serve two families, rather than two children.

Although no one used the term *cash subsidy,* several families identified the concept in their suggestions for other ways support could be delivered. One parent said, "I've heard of one state where they took all the money and evenly divided it and sent a check to every family once a month. That's the fairest way. It's got to be the same way for every person." Another parent made the following suggestion: "I think the only other way would

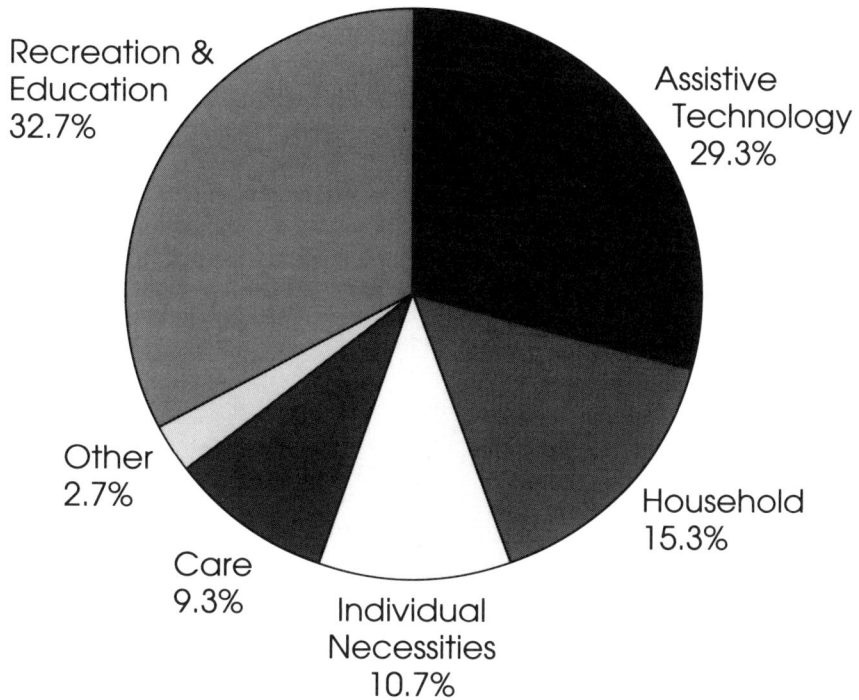

Figure 3. Specific patterns of flexible funding usage for the Community Mental Health Center pilot program.

be either a monthly or bimonthly or yearly amount. I think the monthly thing is good. . . . Unless, if a person were to say, 'I have a big thing I need now and it will use up my respite money for the year, but I need it now.' I think that option is nice."

One mother expressed her general frustration with the various rules that accompany direct payments to parents. "I wanted to go to work a long time ago, and they were willing to give you (an) aide for your child at school, but they won't pay you to be the child's aide in school. Why not pay the mother? She can't work; you're sending her out away from her kid and giving somebody else the job and paying them. It seems silly to me."

Opinions About Reporting

Neither of the two programs required receipts or proofs-of-purchase. Even the application and preapproval in the pilot program was regarded as a formality, as coordinators were instructed not to question the requests. Nevertheless, as plans proceed to extend flexible funding to the larger state respite system, there is considerable debate regarding methods of ensuring accountability. Some families interviewed focused on the concept of trust.

"I would guess that the families that keep their children and take care of them are trustworthy."

Another regarded reporting as limiting the choice of the family. "But who decides how it's spent anyway? That's one of the things that's always been upsetting to me, that you have to use the money for what somebody tells you that you need, even if you don't want to do that. It should be an individual family's decision as to what they are doing with it, but then again, you don't want them spending it on the horses."

Others regarded reporting as a safeguard against misuse, "In any type of flexibility there is always the possibility of misuse. I think that so that one doesn't get in a pickle and so the agency doesn't try to limit it in the future, there probably should be some minimal standards or criteria somehow set up because otherwise, as soon as somebody blows it, or as soon as there is [a] question, then it might blow everybody's [chance]." Other families simply accept it, acknowledging the value of reporting. "I think that as long as it's being used then no one would object to it, to reporting. I see no reason why a family should not report what they are using it for."

Irreplaceable Services

When asked what services they would not like to have replaced by money if the program ever moved toward a cash subsidy, several families expressed the need for a service coordinator or family support facilitator. "We still need a person to talk to. . . . human contact means too much to me. The money, the check would supply a lot, but I wouldn't necessarily know where to get services . . . not without the human side too." "The human contact, the being able to talk to someone or know that I can call so and so and if she doesn't know, she knows someone who does, or just to say, 'gee, it sounds like you had a bad day.' "

One family found a related program irreplaceable, commenting, "The home health services . . . I'd just as soon have them than the money. They try to keep the continuity. The service is better than the money. It would be a pain in the neck to arrange it." And, finally, the basic health care safety net was identified, Medicaid.

IMPLICATIONS FOR FUTURE POLICY DEVELOPMENT AND RESEARCH

Although funding for respite programs remains inadequate, the Vermont pilot program reports that converting existing respite programs to flexible funding does not create any additional demand. In fact, if the same patterns of use persist, allowing respite funds to be used for other purposes may alleviate some of the pressure that is expected to limit funding if the minimum wage is raised in Vermont. If the funds were available only for respite hours at minimum wage, the number of such hours available to each family would be reduced with a higher wage. However, if funds were used for other family support purposes identified by the family, the amount of money for each family would remain unaffected by changes in the minimum wage and would be affected only as inflation affects the prices of items or services purchased.

Another problem in the experience of the Vermont pilots was that families did not make full use of available flexible funding. If full use of the program provides the greatest preventive effects, then several questions need to be addressed. What are the individual and social restraints preventing families from making full use of this option? What is the role of the program coordinator or family support facilitator in helping families achieve a level of comfort in using flexible funding? How effective is modeling in encouraging program use? What would be the impact of having families speak in family support forums about their use of flexible funding? Would the effects be greater than just having families write their experiences in a newsletter?

The pattern in which families save their allotment until close to the end of the program fiscal year merits further study. Is this pattern characteristic of families in a certain income bracket or does it extend across economic lines? Is this pattern rural or urban? If no emergencies arise, do families consistently use up the money at the year's end? If they were given the option of allowing the money to go back into the general coffers for the other families with more intense needs to use, would they choose this option? Is social comparison even a factor in families' patterns of use of flexible funding?

What is the impact of flexible funding on families' self-efficacy perception? Does the experience of making choices that are respected by the system build greater efficacy and empowerment over time, as the Massachusetts Family Cash Assistance Program found in its evaluation of 3 years of subsidy (Allard et al., 1993)?

A nationally established principle of the family support movement is that family support should supplement—not supplant—other, more generic social programs (Families of Children with Disabilities Support Act of 1994). In the attempt to keep family support pure, some programs place restrictions on using family support funds for basic needs, such as food and utilities (Allard et al., 1993). In suggestions for program improvement, however, several Massachusetts families indicated they would like to be able to use funds for basic needs. Research is necessary to answer the following questions: Is there a correlation between funding cuts in generic social programs and use of flexible funding for basic needs? Does data indicating that nine pilot families used the flexible funding for heat suggest a correlation with cuts in the state fuel assistance program during the year of the pilot? Are families who use flexible funding for basic needs eligible for more generic programs? If they are eligible for both flexible funding and generic programs, do they favor the use of flexible funding over the more generic program to meet basic needs? If this is the case, why do they prefer the use of flexible funding? Are there characteristics of flexible funding programs that make families more comfortable using them for basic needs than other programs?

The Families of Children with Disabilities Support Act of 1994 allows for family support funding to be acquired first "to prevent a delay in the receipt of family support," but requires "the entity or agency responsible" to reimburse the family support program. If a family is not eligible for generic programs, yet still uses flexible funding for basic needs, what additional costs is the family incurring that require them to need assistance in meeting basic needs? What restrictions on employment and earning are they experiencing? Recent evaluations of programs in other states have looked at program effects on opportunity costs, such as giving up education and employment opportunities, experienced by families (Agosta, 1993a; Allard et al., 1993; Knoll, 1993). Should generic social programs take additional expenses and opportunity costs into consideration in eligibility determination for families caring for children with disabilities? Should principles of affirmative action apply to these families?

Current Efforts of the Family Support Movement in Vermont

Members of the coalition and involved professionals continue to move forward toward a family-centered system on a number of fronts. With the closing of Brandon Training School, no more institutional placements for people with mental retardation or autism exist in Vermont. This frees the state from the burden of supporting two systems—institutional and community based. Efforts are underway to completely rewrite the statute authorizing services for people with mental retardation, with the new law taking into consideration the role played by families in the care of their family members.

Flexible funding is now an option extended to all regions of the state respite program, with individual community mental health centers creating family support advisory boards.

The state Agency of Human Services and the Department of Education are collaborating to create a joint vision of services for children and families in Vermont. State principles of family support are in the drafting and approval stages, with participation of both state personnel and members of the family support coalition, using the proposed guiding principles of the Vermont family support bill as a reference point.

Vermont is moving forward in full implementation of Part H services to infants, toddlers, and their families, with interagency collaboration in implementing the family-centered policies of this program. Parent to Parent is playing a vital role in the training of community resource parents who bring the experience of being a family member to the service coordinator role.

The Family Support Project of the University Affiliated Program (UAP) of Vermont received a 3-year training grant from the federal Administration on Developmental Disabilities to develop and conduct training in all areas of the state on new approaches to family support. This program is offered each year in six regions of the state and is targeted primarily at service coordinators across agencies; the curriculum, however, could be used as leadership training for family support councils in Vermont and other states. As implemented in Vermont, a train-the-trainers component is built in, with each regional course team-taught by a UAP-based coordinator of the family support project and a family member from the local area. The objective is to build a core of parents available as local trainers, both to continue training when the grant is over, and to be available as informed representatives on state and local family support policy boards.

As Vermont moves family support policy forward on all fronts, the coalition recognizes the need to continue to work from a base of consensus, renewing its shared vision and direction.

Chapter Review

CHALLENGES

- Family support services have a need for predictability in funding use, which works against flexibility and family determination.
- Family supports are not always initially designed by coalitions of families across disability categories; where existing supports favor one group over another, achieving balance may require one group to give up an advantage.
- Family support services are divided in philosophy between those serving families identified as functional and dysfunctional.

CHARACTERISTICS OF HELPFUL PROGRAMS

- Helpful programs are proactive and preventive, rather than crisis driven.
- Helpful programs give parents and family members the power to decide how to use resources.
- Helpful programs provide services, service coordination, and financial assistance, marked by flexibility and low administrative costs.
- Helpful programs encourage coalitions across groups of families concerned with different disabilities.

POLICY IMPLICATIONS

- Professionals will have to relinquish their roles as sole experts, and services must be changed to allow family members to make key decisions.
- Individuals with disabilities and their families are typically viewed in a decontextualized fashion; family support requires policy makers and professionals to view them in the context of their culture and community.
- Family workers must move away from serving only the most vocal parents or the most troubled families to providing an entitlement to all families of people with special needs.
- Family support services must move from a deficit orientation to a strengths-based orientation.
- Family services must be community based rather than centralized in certain locales, and states must overcome narrow eligibility categories.
- As of the mid-1990s, programs are categorical and have rigid rules; family support services must become flexible with the attitude of "Do what it takes to get the job done."

- Families and family organizations must train and mentor one another to achieve the highest levels of effectiveness in individual and systems advocacy.
- Service providers and agencies must overcome territoriality and protectiveness around funding to allow pooled resources across categories.
- Service providers and agencies must reconfigure their structures and boundaries to fit natural communities.
- Service coordinators must reexamine their own motivation and personal satisfaction in serving families by understanding and embracing a philosophy of family empowerment.
- Service coordinators must rethink their roles, becoming service brokers or sources of information for families, with responsibility to families rather than agencies. This may require that service coordination become independent of agencies to avoid conflict of interest.

References

Agosta, J. (1993a). Evaluating family support services: Two quantitative case studies. In V.J. Bradley, J. Knoll, & J. Agosta (Eds.), *Emerging issues in family support* (pp. 99–150). Washington, DC: American Association on Mental Retardation.

Agosta, J. (1993b, Spring). Teleconference on family support. Salem, OR: Human Services Research Institute.

Allard, M.A., Gottlieb, A., & Hart, D. (1993). *Impact study of the Family Cash Assistance Project: Year three results.* Waltham, MA: The Shriver Center.

Arneaud, S., & Herman, S.E. (1991). *Family support subsidy program: Annual report to the governor and legislature, fiscal years 1989 and 1990.* Michigan Department of Mental Health.

Bergman, A.I. (1992, December 2). Parent-to-parent conference, Burlington, Vermont.

Bergman, A.I. (1994, January 16). Meeting on national family support legislation, Washington, DC.

Bradley, V.J. (1993). Overview of the family support movement. In V.J. Bradley, J. Knoll, & J. Agosta (Eds.), *Emerging issues in family support* (pp. 1–8). Washington, DC: American Association on Mental Retardation.

Brookes Baker Family Support Fund. (1993). *Records.* Winooski: Parent to Parent of Vermont.

Center on Human Policy. (1986). *A statement in support of families and their children.* Syracuse, NY: Author.

Dunst, C.J., Trivette, C.M., Starnes, A.L., Hamby, D.W., & Gordon, N.J. (1993). *Building and evaluating family support initiatives: A national study of programs for persons with developmental disabilities.* Baltimore: Paul H. Brookes Publishing Co.

Expecting excellence in family support (Vols.1 & 2). (1993). Salem, OR: Human Services Research Institute.

Families of Children with Disabilities Support Act of 1994, PL 103-382. (October 20, 1994). Title 20, U.S.C. 1491 et seq: *U.S. Statutes at Large, 108*, 3937.

Family support in Vermont. (1990). Position paper presented at the meeting of the Family Support Committee, Vermont Coalition for Disability Rights, Montpelier, VT.

Family support pilot project. (1993). *Records.* Waterbury: Vermont Department of Mental Health and Mental Retardation.

Individuals with Disabilities Education Act of 1990 (IDEA), PL 101-476. (October 30, 1990). Title 20, U.S.C. 1400 et seq: *U.S. Statutes at Large, 104*, 1103–1151.

Karp, N., Faison, K., Agosta, J., & Melda, K. (1992). *Toward positive family policy: Assessing "quality" in family support programs.* Arlington, VA: Family and Integration Resources and Cambridge, MA: Human Services Research Institute.

Knoll, J. (1993). Being a family: The experience of raising a child with a disability or chronic illness. In V.J. Bradley, J. Knoll, & J. Agosta (Eds.), *Emerging issues in family support.* Washington, DC: American Association on Mental Retardation.

Knoll, J., Covert, S., Osuch, R., O'Connor, S., Agosta, J., & Blaney, B. (1993). Supporting families: State family support efforts. In V.J. Bradley, J. Knoll, & J. Agosta (Eds.), *Emerging issues in family support* (pp. 57–98). Washington, DC: American Association on Mental Retardation.

National Family Support Legislation. (1994, January 16). *Minutes of the special meeting to draft legislation*. Washington, DC: Author.

Vermont Developmental Disabilities Planning Council. (1993). *Family support for people with disabilities: Why we need legislation*. Waterbury, VT: Author.

Wood, T. (1993). *Family support pilot project*. Waterbury: Vermont Department of Mental Health and Mental Retardation.

Appendix A

Family Interview 1

The following interview is designed to capture the visions, perceptions, and responses of families caring for members with developmental disabilities. The responses gathered are applicable to evolving models of support. These forms, although slightly edited, are taken directly from actual interviews.

INSTRUCTIONS

These questions are guidelines to help you gather as complete a perspective from the family as possible in an initial interview, which attempts to get to know the family and find out about their experience with family support. They should not be used rigidly, but modified to fit each situation. Follow-up questions should be asked when appropriate. Families should be encouraged to contribute additional information they consider relevant to family support. If a question provokes discomfort, skip it until the end, then ask if they would like to try to answer it. Their choices must be respected. Interviews should be audiotaped if possible. If participants are unwilling, notes may be taken. If more than one family member is participating in the interview, each speaker should be clearly identified at the beginning of the tape and in the text of transcriptions.

INTERVIEW INFORMATION

Date:
Place of interview:
Interviewer:
Names and ages of participants:
Relationship to family member with a disability:

QUESTIONS

1. Please tell me a little about your family. Who are the people living at home?

2. Please tell me about _____ (the family member with a disability—e.g., what kind of disability, how old, in or out of school, etc.).

3. What is it like for you with _____ living at home?

4. What are your thoughts about _____ continuing to live at home (e.g., how long, what would make it possible, what reasons for changing, etc.)?

5. Who supports you in your efforts to care for _____ living at home?

6. How do they support you?

7. How long have you been in the respite program?

8. How have you used your respite in the past (e.g., going out for dinner, taking an occasional overnight trip, using it to hire an aide for different programs, using it for camp, etc.)?

9. How has that felt for you? (e.g., comfortable, rushed, relieved, etc.)

10. What has been your experience in getting respite workers (e.g., difficulty finding, willingness to work for minimum wage, quality, availability, time flexibility, etc.)?

11. How has the program coordinator from the agency helped you?

12. How much contact do you like to have with your family support / respite coordinator?

13. What do you think about this new flexible funding plan in your agency (e.g., what sounds good, what questions or concerns do you have, etc.)?

14. What do you think you would like to use the funding for?

15. What is the most important issue you are dealing with right now?

16. What specific kinds of support could help you deal with this?

17. How do you think decisions about family support should be made (e.g., in your own family, in your mental health agency, at the state level, etc.)?

18. If you could choose one or two characteristics you would like your support provider (e.g., agency, respite coordinator, etc.) to have, what would they be?

19. If the amount of money available for each family for family support / respite stays the same, are there other ways to organize it that would be more effective than the way things are done now?

20. Is there anything else you would like us to know right now?

Appendix B

Family Interview 2

Follow-up on Flexible Funding and Family Support Systems Design:

1. Now that flexible funding has been in place for more than half a year, how have you used it?
2. What impact have these uses made on your family?
3. What was the process of getting the money like for you?
4. Do you have any suggestions on how the process might be improved?
5. If all the family support services you need were provided only through a monthly check, would this check suffice? What size would it be?
6. If you were to keep all the existing family support services your family has and add a monthly check so that all your needs would be met, what would the size of the check be?
7. Which, if any, services would you not like to have replaced by money?
8. If a monthly subsidy would become part of the system of services, what groups of families should be eligible?
9. If too many families were eligible, how would you choose who receives it?
10. Should there be income guidelines? If so, what should they be?
11. Should everyone get the same amount?
12. Should there be some measure of severity of disability?
13. What type or types of disability should make a family eligible for the subsidy?
14. Should there be some measure of family stress?
15. Do you think families should have to report on how they use the money?
16. If there were a Family Support Board for the state, what would you see as its duties?
17. Who should serve on such a board? What groups should be represented?

17

The Role of Education and Community Services in Supporting Families of Children with Complex Health Care Needs

Chris C. Clatterbuck and H. Rutherford Turnbull, III

Assume for a moment that you are a teacher and have just been advised that you will have a new student—one whose life depends on a ventilator that he transports with him from place to place. Also assume that, except for the ventilator and the fact that the student has missed 2 years of schooling because he has been hospitalized to stabilize his medical conditions, the student has no other disabilities and presents no cognitive, emotional, or other challenges. What can and should you do to provide this student with a free appropriate public education, as required by PL 101-476, the Individuals with Disabilities Education Act (IDEA) of 1990.

Assume a different role: You are the student. For the first time in 2 years you are leaving the hospital and returning to school. You are intellectually competent, but at least two grades behind your peers. You are leaving an environment where your health was far more important than your education, where you had a reliable staff and technological backups so that you did not have to worry about your ventilator malfunctioning.

Now, assume a third role: You are this student's mother. You have received a thorough, and often frightening, in-service education about health care systems, your son's medical needs, and his life prospects. Still, no one has discussed with you what your son's education might be like or what rights he might have to even receive an education.

Now, assume a final role: You are the superintendent of the school district required to educate this young man. You knew him as a younger, much healthier person, before he was injured in an automobile accident and required ventilator support. Never before has a student come to your school district using any form of technology to enhance his education, much less to sustain his life.

None of the roles in this scenario are farfetched. Today, children with ventilator support are surviving their medical challenges. Technologies that keep them alive and enable them to live outside hospitals and attend schools in their communities are sophisticated, effective, expensive, and increasingly available. Schools clearly have the obligation to educate these children, including the provision of related services, which may involve some medical care.

However, these children who depend on technology to survive, especially those who depend on ventilators, represent a paradigm case of new challenges posed to families, schools, and other social institutions by medical, technological, and social policy advances. As such, this class of students, and the ways that their families and schools respond to them, warrants careful scrutiny. What is known about these children—their medical needs, the technologies they use, their education, and the processes and criteria by which decisions about their education are made—will inform, but certainly not dictate, what is done in the future as more of these students—and others with equally complex medical and technological attributes—present themselves for an education.

There is more to these students and their education than the convenient presentation of a paradigm case; there is a very important issue about the roles of schools in responding to them. Clearly, IDEA and its related services provisions have transformed the schools into multifunctional systems, requiring them not only to educate, but also to provide a range of services that make a student's education beneficial. The dividing line between an *educational service* and a *health care service* has yet to be clearly defined.

The role of the school is equally ill-defined. Schools are essential to students; they hold much of the students' futures in their hands. However, for these children, the school's role has changed. Now, it is a place for academic and social development, as well as health maintenance. In a sense, the school is a social services system, one with the capacity to develop and expand beyond its present state.

Just as the school provides an interlocking system of services to students, it also provides a resource for families. The school becomes the place to which they turn so that their children may receive an education and opportunities for associating with other students. The school's ability to provide for physical, social, and academic inclusion for the student with a disability is the key to the student's future. No one understands this more clearly than the family of a child with a disability. Indeed, the family's stress

seems to accelerate in proportion to the child's aging-out of school eligibility; an indicator of the extent to which a family relies on schools as a source
of stability is the concern the family expresses when their child becomes
eligible for *transition services*.

That is not to say that the school is always a comforting place. All too
often the school is at odds with the student and family. But, lacking any
other service system except the health care system for students who are
supported by technologies, schools provide students and families with
some continuity and certainty of service. Whether that certainty and those
services enable or disable students and their families to meet the challenges
of living and learning while being supported by technologies is a different
and highly individualized matter. Still, the fact remains that for many students and families, schools are places that enable them to cope.

Seeing schools as places is seeing them as environments with which
families interact. They are not, of course, the only environments. Families,
especially families of children with ventilator assistance, interact with other
environments, namely health care provider and health payor systems and
the communities where they live, which are the equivalents of other
environments.

One issue is how the family fits, or accommodates, in these environments. A related and equally important issue is how these environments
accommodate the family and the person with a disability. This issue has
civil rights nuances (addressed through such laws as IDEA and the Americans with Disabilities Act [ADA] of 1990, PL 101-336), attitudinal or prej-
udicial nuances (addressed through efforts to erase the stigma of disability),
and architectural nuances (addressed through concepts of universal and
ergonometric design). When children with disabilities move from hospitals
to their families' homes, local schools, and communities, they must face
dual accommodation issues: the need that they and their families may feel
to fit into these new environments and the need that these environments
have to accommodate them.

In this situation, the schools are the primary point of accommodation.
Whether they make accommodations and whether the students and their
families accommodate to the schools, how these accommodations occur,
what facilitates them and what impedes them, and what must be done by
the families and by these new and relatively unfamiliar environments are
poignant issues that have been somewhat unaddressed previously. However, the schools are good laboratories for understanding more about dual
accommodations. And they may be good models for understanding how
to advance the accommodations.

Despite the universal-education/zero-reject principle of IDEA, the
nondiscrimination provisions of the ADA, and the technological advances
and support systems that health care systems have developed, creating a
suitable fit between students and families and the schools remains a for-
midable challenge. This is due, in part, to the failure of schools to develop
policies, practices, and capabilities to accommodate these students.

Meeting the educational needs of children who are ventilator assisted poses an enormous challenge as public policy makers strongly favor placement in the *least restrictive environment (LRE),* presumably in the local educational agency where the student would have been educated if he or she did not have a disability (IDEA, 1990). The LRE doctrine also assumes that the student will live at home and receive home- and community-based services (Developmental Disabilities Assistance and Bill of Rights Act of 1990, PL 101-496; Social Security Administration Reform Act of 1994, PL 103-296). The issue is not so much whether this assumption is inappropriate, but whether families, educators, health care providers, and social services providers have the will or ability to execute it, as they face major challenges in doing so.

This chapter reviews the issues that families, local educational agencies, and health care providers face when attempting to comply with IDEA's requirements for a free appropriate public education in the least restrictive environment, and with other public policies favoring home- and community-based services. This chapter is based on data that define a child who is ventilator assisted as an individual between the ages of 5 and 20 who has a chronic disability that necessitates the use of mechanical ventilation for the purpose of breathing. All of the children included in the study were enrolled in a public or private educational agency during the 1990–1991 school year.

This chapter provides an introduction to the nature of the disability faced by children requiring ventilator assistance, and the nature and effect of the technology they use. It then reports on the methodology used, describing in detail the interview procedures employed; the characteristics of the children; and the problems and solutions found by their families, educators, and health care providers in complying with IDEA and other public policies. It concludes with a general discussion of policy implications.

These issues are not simple in nature, nor are they simple to resolve. But, this research—the first that has emerged from interviews of the families themselves—has resulted in an optimistic assessment. It suggests that a dedicated family and professional team can devise its own solutions and secure an appropriate education in the least restrictive environment, even in the absence of specific federal policy.

It may well be argued that the absence of federal policy, presumably an undesirable status, actually facilitates locally devised solutions. Still, scant federal policies seem to result in a great cost in terms of time, uncertainty, negotiation, and anxiety for families. As the United States faces the prospect of health care reform, it also confronts the opportunity to clarify the policy issues that arise from other laws (e.g., IDEA, Social Security Act), issues that clearly need resolution.

Two other issues arise from this research: One concerns the very nature of the school as a provider system, the other the relationships that professionals in that system have with the consumers of the system—the families and the students needing ventilator assistance.

As Sailor and colleagues argue in Chapter 14, some school systems are taking on new and considerably expanded roles. Whether under the rubric of new community schools with school-linked, integrated services or under other names, these developing systems attempt to serve students and their families far more comprehensively than ever before. Kagan and Neville (1993) note that the school-linked services model can be confused with family support programs: "[The] many strategic similarities [between school-linked services and family support] often lead people to use these terms interchangeably, but equating them obscures subtle but critical differences in the origins and priorities of the school-linked service and family support movements" (p. 4).

Schools and families have difficulty providing an appropriate education in the least restrictive environment for students with ventilator needs. Will this change under the new community schools model and under developing state and federal family support laws? At this point, the answer remains unclear.

The second issue emerging from this research relates to the relationship between the families and the educators. As Allen and Petr make clear in Chapter 3, family centered is an attractive, but still elusive, concept and goal. Policy and professional perspectives about family empowerment assume a new role for organizations and professionals alike (see Chapter 4); and the concepts of family centered and empowering may become standard by the late 20th and early 21st centuries. However, achievement of these goals will depend to a large degree on how policy makers, system designers, and program implementers learn the lessons that this research reveals.

THE POLICY CHALLENGE

Much of the challenge in implementing family-centered goals and projects stems from a lack of policies regarding provision of services to children supported by medical technology. Although IDEA ensured educational and related services for students with disabilities, its policies were never intended to address all of the education (and certainly few of the health-related) requirements of children with chronic illnesses or reliance upon technology assistance (Turnbull, 1993; Walker & Jacobs, 1984). Consequently, schools and families must make difficult decisions regarding education and service provision without sufficient guidance and support. Given the general absence of other policy mandates and more explicit regulations or guidelines from the federal government, it is not surprising that many state and local educational agencies have refused to admit or have inappropriately placed or served children with complex health care needs (U.S. Department of Health and Human Services, 1988).

THE NATURE OF THE DISABILITY

Children who are ventilator assisted comprise one of several subgroups of students classified as technology dependent (U.S. Department of Health and Human Services, 1988). They require mechanical ventilation to sustain them in the face of life-threatening respiratory disorders. Conditions that sometimes necessitate ventilator support include bronchopulmonary dysplasia (BPD), neuromuscular disease (e.g., muscular dystrophy), and injuries (e.g., spinal cord injuries, brain stem contusions). As with other children who rely on technology assistance, children who are ventilator assisted require daily ongoing care and/or monitoring by trained personnel (U.S. Department of Health and Human Services, 1988).

The Nature and Purpose of Ventilator Assistance

Neuromuscular and respiratory paralysis result from damage to some part of the nervous system. The paralysis can be either central or peripheral. In children, central paralysis is most frequently the result of improper intrauterine development or injuries to the brain. Peripheral paralysis is caused by such conditions as poliomyelitis. Other common causes of paralysis in children are damage to the spinal cord as the result of injury, infectious disease, or tumors (Miller & Keane, 1983). Conditions that cause restrictive lung disease, such as tuberculosis and kyphoscoliosis (i.e., curvature of the spine), are also common conditions that necessitate ventilator use (Fischer & Prentice, 1982).

Mechanical ventilation is necessary for people with neuromuscular diseases or conditions that prevent the lungs from receiving or exchanging adequate levels of oxygen. Examples of such conditions include respiratory paralysis, alveolar hypoventilation syndrome, or distributive hypoxia. In alveolar hypoventilation, gas exchange within the blood is not adequate to fully remove carbon dioxide and, as a result, an insufficient supply of oxygen is delivered into the pulmonary system. In distributive hypoxia, there is interference with the intrapulmonary distribution of the inspired air and large amounts of carbon dioxide are removed from the blood, causing inadequate oxygenation of the blood (Miller & Keane, 1983).

Ventilator Technology

The advent of ventilator technology is not recent. The first prototype iron lung (i.e., tank respirator) for newborn infants was designed and built by Alexander Graham Bell in 1889 (O'Leary et al., 1979). The ventilators most commonly used today are negative pressure and positive pressure ventilators. Bearing little resemblance to the original iron lung, today's negative pressure ventilators work on a similar principle, exerting negative (subatmospheric) pressure on the exterior chest wall. This external pressure creates a suction in the lungs. Examples of this type include the full body ventilator or iron lung and the cuirass, which is a molded plastic shell that covers only the chest (Miller & Keane, 1983).

The negative pressure ventilators typically require relatively normal lung tissue and are the ventilator of choice when an individual's main problem is muscle weakness. The advantage is that this type of ventilator does not require a tracheostomy, an operation that frequently restricts the child's ability to generate speech. However, the iron lung inhibits virtually all mobility, as the tank structure restricts all movement except that of the individual's head. The cuirass, by contrast, is portable and allows mobility of the arms (O'Leary et al., 1979). In general, these negative pressure devices are relatively inexpensive and easy to use (Frates, Splaingard, Smith, & Harrison, 1985).

The positive pressure ventilator forces air directly into the lungs under positive (supraatmospheric) pressure. This type of device is most regularly used for conditions of respiratory insufficiency. The advantage of this type of equipment is its portability. However, because it is a more powerful method of moving air, the positive pressure ventilator can harm the circulation and antidiuretic hormone balance; as a result, frequent measures of vital signs and accurate record keeping are required. Although positive pressure ventilators can be attached with a mouthpiece for short-term use, long-term use usually necessitates a tracheostomy (Frates et al., 1985). When a tracheostomy is used, special care is required to maintain a proper airway and prevent infections (Miller & Keane, 1983).

Life Expectancy of Children Who Are Ventilator Assisted

Predicting the life expectancy of children who are ventilator assisted is difficult at best. The prognosis for these children varies greatly and is linked to both etiology and severity of the child's condition. Severity reflects an interaction between physiological severity and the environment, including medical treatment (Stein et al., 1987).

Aday and Wegener (1988) report that among the group of children 5 years and older in one study, half with congenital anomalies and one third with diseases of the nervous system, one fourth were expected to improve, one fourth were expected to worsen, and the remaining half were expected to remain relatively stable over time.

In the Frates et al. (1985) study of 54 older children who used either positive or negative pressure ventilators at home between 1962 and 1983, 17 children (31%) died prior to the end of the study. There was an 84% 1-year survival rate, and a 65% 5-year survival rate. Four of the deaths reported were caused by a disconnection of the ventilator and failure of the alarm to trigger, or an unnoticed nighttime power failure. At least half of the deaths were attributable to the progression of the primary illness.

Shifting Locus of Care

Until 1980, most children supported by mechanical ventilation lived in hospitals or long-term care facilities. Major improvements in the portability of ventilator equipment and the increased availability of home nursing support, however, have now made home placements a viable option for many families (Lynch, Lewis, & Murphy, 1992). Concerns about costs have also spurred the transition from hospital to home and community care.

Consequently, more and more school systems are being challenged to provide services to students who are ventilator assisted. The most accurate, recent count estimates that between 700 and 2,000 school-age children in the United States require ventilator assistance on either a full- or part-time basis (Office of Technology Assessment, 1987). Although these children represent a small proportion of the total student population, it is likely that the continued refinement and broader application of medical technology will steadily increase the number of school-age children who are ventilator assisted.

Providing appropriate educational services in the least restrictive environment for these children is highly dependent on available resources. These resources may be affected by the child's geographical location, the degree to which services are coordinated (Office of Technology Assessment, 1987), the availability of competent staff, the attitudes of educational service providers, funding limitations, legal liability, and state and federal educational policy (Walker, 1987; Walker, 1991).

Families' Challenges

Although a variety of factors related to public policy and the educational system may affect the provision of educational services for children requiring ventilator assistance, the family's role in this process has been poorly defined. In a study of children who are ventilator assisted, parents reported feeling confident in their skills as medical caregivers, but less secure in their knowledge of the developmental and educational needs of their children (Burr, Guyer, Todres, Abrahams, & Chiodo, 1983). This finding suggests that families need to have up-to-date information about school and community services. In fact, parents' access to appropriate information affects the educational resources available to children (Office of Technology Assessment, 1987). Unfortunately, parents face a fragmented system of community services and often receive limited information regarding available resources and the educational rights of their children (Jones, Clatterbuck, Barber, Marquis, & Turnbull, 1993).

In a study of school and family perspectives on the needs of children who are ventilator assisted, Jones et al. (1993) found that parents were generally satisfied with educational programs established for their children. Parents reported, however, that they were less satisfied with the schools' ability to meet student therapy needs. Furthermore, parents strongly emphasized the need for educators to better understand the pervasive effects of chronic illness on families and students.

THE TECHNOLOGY SUPPORT PROJECT

Considering all of the factors that can affect educational services for children who are technology assisted, little is known about specific influences on educational outcomes. Without such information, it is difficult to develop policies and practices that respond to the needs of these students

(Palfrey, DiPrete, Walker, Shannon, & Maroney, 1987). Therefore, researchers at the Beach Center on Families and Disability designed the Technology Support Project (Tech Project) to gather information on the provision of educational services for children who are ventilator assisted. The Tech Project's work began in early 1989 with a national search for students who used ventilators and their families, and concluded with final data analysis during the summer of 1993. The issues presented in this chapter and the policy implications that follow derive solely from that project.[1]

The Tech Project's research revealed a number of areas that both parents and educators agree are problematic in the process of establishing educational services for children supported by ventilator technology. Because of the broad scope of parent concerns, it is unrealistic to discuss each individual issue and its policy implications. Instead, various issues have been combined and summarized into four clusters, based on naturally occurring themes that emerged from the individual interviews:

1. Problems that result from the inexperience of schools and school personnel in planning and implementing services for students using ventilators and other technologies
2. Personnel problems—particularly shortages of qualified personnel to work with these students, and the attitudes that professionals have toward the students
3. Problems resulting from the lack of an organized transition system, which facilitates hospital-to-home and home-to-school transitions for students who are ventilator assisted and other technology users
4. Problems that arise in securing funding for nursing and other ongoing routine health care during school hours

This chapter is based solely on 18 interviews conducted with parents of children who are ventilator assisted. The following paragraphs provide a brief description of the interview process and detail some of the basic characteristics of the students who are ventilator assisted on which these data are based.

Interview Procedures

Interviewees were selected from among Tech Project survey respondents. To ensure representativeness, they were placed in groups based on their responses to selected survey questions dealing with service satisfaction and whether parents had to fight to obtain services. From the selected questions, a simple index was established to classify respondents into four groups: 1) those who were satisfied with educational services and did not have to fight for such services; 2) those who were satisfied with services, but did have to fight to obtain them; 3) those who were dissatisfied with services and had to fight to obtain the services presently received; and 4) those respon-

---

[1]For a full explanation of project funding, sample characteristics, methodology, and specific research questions, see Jones et al. (1993).

dents with students in home-based education. Within each group, the respondents were stratified by the age of their child. A randomization procedure was then used to select respondents from each group, and invitations were issued for participation in the interview phase of the study. Of 30 invitations, 18 families agreed to participate in a telephone interview.

The interviews lasted approximately 1 hour and consisted of both closed- and opened-ended questions designed to clarify issues emerging from the Tech Project surveys and further define the policy issues involved in obtaining educational services.

Characteristics of Children Who Are Ventilator Assisted

The sample of children who were the source of data for this chapter had the following characteristics: The majority of children were male (67%), and Caucasian (72%); however, 17% were African American, and 11% were Hispanic. Most of the sample (78%) reported IQ levels in the normal range. Because of the many variables involved with this population, it is not possible to identify a typical student who was ventilator assisted, but a summary of student demographic information is provided in Table 1.

PROBLEMS WITH INEXPERIENCED SCHOOLS

The issues outlined in the following pages were identified as typical barriers faced by families and educators in implementing home- and community-based educational programs consistent with the doctrine of the least restrictive environment. In some cases, the issues are presented in aggregate form with comments from many interviews combined. In other cases, direct quotations that provide examples of major issues are presented directly. Where possible, details of how families were able to successfully overcome these barriers are described. In those cases where families failed to provide generalizable solutions to these issues, recommendations have been provided, based on recommended practices collected from research with various educators and families of individuals with disabilities.

Planning Problems

The Incidence Problem

Some argue that every issue facing educators and families of children who are ventilator assisted stems from one common factor—the relatively low incidence of these students in the general population and particularly in the school population. Because portable ventilator technology and home health care services that allow children who are ventilator assisted to live in home- and community-based settings and attend local schools have only recently become available, the students in the Tech Project sample were often the first students requiring technology assistance ever to be served by their respective school districts. As a result, educators and families of children who are ventilator assisted are constantly forced to break new ground

Table 1. Characteristics of students who are ventilator assisted in the Tech Project study

Student age	Range	Mean
Age in years	5.5–16	8.6
Gender		
Male	12	67%
Female	6	33%
Race		
Caucasian	13	72%
African American	3	17%
Hispanic	2	11%
IQ level		
Within normal range of cognitive abilities	14	78%
Some degree of cognitive disability	3	17%
Unknown	1	5%
Ventilator use		
Continuous (24 hours per day)	12	67%
Fewer than 24 hours per day Ventilator not used during school hours	3	17%
Fewer than 24 hours per day Ventilator used during school hours	3	17%
Impact of ventilator on learning		
Very little interference with day-to-day learning	5	28%
Some interference with learning due to unusual episodes or some routine care	8	44%
Moderate interference with learning due to frequent crises or time-consuming routine care	4	22%
Severe interference with learning due to the need for special medical care on a nearly continuous basis	1	5%
Diagnosis		
Congenital anomalies (e.g., spina bifida)	7	39%
Diseases of the nervous system (e.g., muscular dystrophy)	5	28%
Injuries (e.g., spinal cord injury, near-drowning)	3	17%
Bronchopulmonary dysplasia	2	11%
Other (phrenic nerve damage during emergency heart surgery)	1	5%

Note: Of the 18 students in the survey, 75% began using a ventilator prior to age 5.

in their attempt to establish and provide educational services for these students.

The Missing-Policy Problem
The Tech Project data revealed that few local policies or recognized procedures are in place for parents and school officials to follow when beginning

to establish educational plans for students who are ventilator assisted. This lack of basic local policy or protocols frequently made initial planning meetings chaotic and unproductive. And because this population is so new in the schools, educators, too, have considerable difficulty establishing a basic starting point for the educational plan. Parents looking to schools for guidance lack any useful compass for traversing this new territory. Parents and educators consistently voiced their feelings that each step in the planning process was another movement into uncharted territory. One parent characterized the problem in this way:

> In the school setting, ventilator-assisted students are often the most involved students ever served in the district—not the sickest, but the most involved—and with so many things to do, the planning team has a hard time knowing where to start.

Overall, the typical first response of the school planning team is bewilderment or mystification at the vast scope of the task at hand. An initial period of polarization within the planning team frequently develops: At one end of the spectrum are those team members who argue that students who are ventilator assisted do not belong in the school setting; at the other end are those who acknowledge that the students belong in the school. Interestingly, although both camps hold strong opinions regarding the best placement for these youngsters, their arguments are frequently emotionally based and lack the needed facts for responding to and implementing the public policy of least restrictive, home- and community-based education. Rather than breaking the problem of rights implementation into practical steps, there is a tendency for educators and parents to be initially overwhelmed by an emotional reaction that shapes and dominates their thinking. Yet, the planning process seldom remains at this highly charged, polarized status for extended periods of time. In fact, after the initial emotional period has passed, the planning process generally becomes less confrontational and hectic and more productive.

Paradoxically, the process of emotional exchange and the voicing of fears and concerns are actually key steps in the planning process. Through this sharing of concerns, team members begin to form working relationships and then operationally define the problems they must address in order to achieve successful educational outcomes. Once educators acknowledge that their planning goal is to find solutions and establish procedures that minimize the health risk to the child and provide an appropriate education in the least restrictive environment, they shift their thinking away from fixating on barriers or limitations to conceiving possibilities. With this shift, the planning process takes on a new focus and productivity. Parents can take comfort in the fact that although the planning process is time consuming and labor intensive, the educational outcomes that result are generally positive (Clatterbuck, Jones, & Turnbull, 1993).

The Practical Solutions

Clatterbuck et al. (1993), having studied the planning process in detail, suggest that the likelihood of positive outcomes can be increased through some very simple steps, such as introducing the planning team to the student directly. This face-to-face introduction helps remind those involved that the focus of their work is a child who needs an education. Another factor that facilitates the planning process is the flexible exchange of information and ideas across disciplines. Although cross-disciplinary communication can be difficult as a result of differing communication styles and approaches, the benefits of finding a common language within the planning team are very valuable to the overall process. Clatterbuck et al. (1993) propose that planning will be most effective if the planning team adopts an approach similar to the transdisciplinary model described by Campbell (1987). In this approach, parents and professionals function as a team to assess students and then design, implement, and evaluate programs for these students. As one physician stated, "In our team approach, everyone had to be willing to move together—the parents, doctors, and educators—it [educational planning] was a team effort the whole way through."

Personnel Problems

Shortages of Qualified Teachers and Therapists

Once placement and appropriate instruction have been agreed upon, new problems arise with respect to personnel. A large majority of school personnel have little or no experience serving children who depend on technology, particularly students using ventilators. In the school-based setting, parents complain that the lack of experienced teachers and therapists places severe limits on the child's educational options.

Parents report that finding teaching personnel with experience working with youngsters who have complex health care needs was often impossible and that they were regularly forced to settle for the person who was willing to learn to teach their children. Although it is refreshing to see that educators are willing to rise to a new challenge, the fact exists that most general and special education teachers simply have never been prepared to work with students with the complex medical needs and multiple involvements characteristic of students who are ventilator assisted.

Staffing shortages are also problematic in the area of related services personnel, such as occupational and physical therapists. Because of the extreme levels of physical involvement characteristic of many students who are ventilator assisted, parents were concerned that their child receive a specific amount of physical and/or occupational therapy as part of their educational program. This issue of school-furnished therapy services becomes a source of tension between school officials and parents because few schools have the needed personnel to provide students with the levels of therapeutic service parents desire. In many of these cases, parents reported that the school district did not have the funds to purchase the services of full-time occupational and physical therapists at each individual school building.

Budget limitations generally resulted in hiring one therapist to provide treatments on a rotating basis in multiple buildings within the district. Parents reported that the time limitations inherent in this type of scheduling resulted in therapy being performed on a less frequent basis than they desired.

Shortages of personnel for home-based instruction are even more critical, as one parent explained:

_____

We are very happy to have our child in home-based education, but it is often difficult to find good teachers for the home-based instruction—there seems to be a shortage of special education teachers who can adjust to home-based instruction effectively. In the last district (the family has recently moved to a new school district in another city), it was so bad that they would send you whoever was left on their list, one of the last teachers they sent us wasn't even credentialed—she was a media resource person. It's a constant struggle, even when you do get a credentialed teacher you still have to roll the dice. In the previous district there were a lot of "flaky teachers" who would take the assignment and then quit after a week. Meanwhile, our son would lose six sessions of instruction.

_____

A second parent who discussed the problem of finding skilled home instruction complained of a related issue:

_____

When you find a good teacher, there's no guarantee that they will be around the next year, because when they're good they [the special education teachers] get placed back in the classroom, or they are offered better pay or perks to teach in specialized institutions.

_____

The Fear Factor and Staff Attitudes

The second most frequently voiced parental concern regarding personnel problems is related to a phenomenon called the *fear factor*. The fear factor is an exaggerated and unwarranted fear that the student who is ventilator assisted will experience a medical crisis while at school and die. For the administrators, the fear appears to revolve around the legal repercussions, while the teachers simply do not want to take the risk of losing a student who is under their direct supervision. This fear is often exaggerated. This research has not revealed any children who were ventilator assisted who died while at school, and the Frates et al. (1985) study suggests that the incidence of school-site death is low.

Often these concerns are discussed openly in team and parent meetings; in other cases, the issue is alluded to but is never fully expressed. It is clearly a good practice for every team member and the team as a whole to discuss all of their fears openly and as often as necessary. Data show that when teachers' concerns are addressed directly and incorporated into the emergency plan for the students, their fears of having a child who is ventilator assisted in school are alleviated (Clatterbuck et al., 1993).

Another concern raised by teachers is that the addition of a student who is ventilator assisted to their classroom will divert time from teaching. In many cases, this concern was voiced in the following form: "If they place a ventilator-assisted student in my classroom, I will have to perform special procedures that will distract me from my other teaching activities." Although this argument appears to make logical sense at a surface level, the facts simply do not support the teachers' fears. Most students who are ventilator assisted attend school with a full-time health care aide or nurse who is responsible for completing all medical procedures needed by the student. Jones et al. (1993) report that only 4% of teachers were required to perform any type of routine health care for their students who are ventilator assisted. Despite this fact, teacher concerns still persist.

The Stereotype and Discrimination

Many parents related stories of general discrimination and stereotypical thinking on the part of school personnel. Educators' discriminatory acts ranged from general insensitivity by teachers and other school personnel to attempts to deny students any access to the school environment. Clearly, ignorance regarding the needs and abilities of individuals with technology supports still abounds in the school systems.

Lack of an Organized Service System

Limited Transition Services

Data from the Tech Project clearly show that formal transition systems are lacking. Typically, there is no one individual or group available to assist parents in establishing educational services for their children following hospital discharge. As one parent reported, "One of the problems we had at the beginning [is that] we were kind of thrown into the system without much background and we just had to fend for ourselves." Another parent reported that "I just sat down with the phone book and started calling anyone and everyone that I thought might help get my child in school." These and other similar comments demonstrate that parents are far too often left to their own devices, without emotional support, needed resources, or information.

The Tech Project's data suggest that to be successful, parents need emotional support and information concerning the educational rights of their children. Some of this is provided through early intervention programs and parent groups, but these sources do not adequately fill the void. The current system simply misses too many individuals. One parent put it quite simply, "The current system is simply not supportive enough. If it weren't for some good people who helped us out, we would have been overwhelmed. It is easy to feel like a victim of the system."

Although peer support appears to be a very important component in a successful transition, many parents reported that their contact with other families was seldom systematic and tailored to their concerns, but more likely the result of a chance meeting with a sympathetic stranger in the education system.

Lack of Flexibility Among Service Systems

Parents also complained that the existing support networks and government agencies working with families of children with disabilities have trouble adapting to children who are ventilator assisted. As one parent put it:

_____

The "system" has to be more generic—they need to see each child as an individual. The current "system" is made up of a number of poorly connected agencies that were set up to address the needs of children from specific disability groups. The programs assume that participants will share common needs. Our children [children assisted by ventilator technology] do not typically share one common set of involvements. As a result, many of our children's needs go unmet by the service systems that are available at this time.

_____

The current service system is set up to place individuals into programs intended to address specific needs. Unfortunately, the programs available frequently do not fully address the diverse needs of the children who are ventilator assisted.

Funding Problems

Parents also commonly complained about the difficulty of finding adequate funding for school and health care services. Complaints usually take two forms.

The Hot-Potato Issue

A number of parents have to fight with various funding agencies to secure nursing care during school hours. Typically, the education system argues that nursing care does not qualify as a related service under IDEA and, therefore, refuses to provide funds for nursing care. Yet, private funding agencies (e.g., insurance companies) argue that the care is necessary for the child to learn and should qualify as an IDEA-related service paid for by the school system funds.

While the funding agencies debate over responsibility, parents and children are left to their own devices. In some cases, parents will attend school with their child and act as the child's nurse. In other cases, parents will spend sleepless nights working as the child's night nurse in order to use their alloted nursing hours for school coverage.

Exclusionary Eligibility Criteria

Concerning eligibility requirements for supplemental services or funds from state or federal agencies, parents complain that strict eligibility criteria for many of the current assistance programs frequently exclude or limit access for children who are ventilator assisted and their families.

Parents agree that it is important for government assistance programs to have a means of controlling fraud and ensuring that access to these programs is limited to individuals and families with legitimate needs. They report, however, that the current selection/inclusion criteria for many programs actually result in exclusion of children who are ventilator assisted and their families, despite their obvious need.

Theoretically, one would expect to find that children with multiple involvements, like those found in the population of individuals who are ventilator assisted, would be eligible for a wide range of assistance programs and generally receive more services than other students with less complicated disabilities. Data, however, suggest that this is simply not the case. Parents reported that they were frequently deemed ineligible for funding or other assistance because their children did not have the right involvements. One common reason was that children who have cognitive abilities in the normal range are considered ineligible for certain early intervention programs and other assistance programs. This is particularly problematic for students in the ventilator-assisted population because a large majority of them have cognitive abilities in the normal range. Jones et al. (1993) report that less than 21% of the population of students supported by ventilator technology have any cognitive impairment.

According to parents, the current practice of basing program access on one specific criteria, such as IQ level, needs to be modified because it excludes a large number of individuals with very legitimate needs from programs that could have significant impact on their lives. One parent of a 15-year-old boy who has quadriplegia and requires 24-hour ventilation and around-the-clock nursing stated the following:

It is ridiculous to exclude my son from supplemental funds because he has intact cognitive functions. I don't mean to be disrespectful or make light of children with cognitive impairments, but if a low IQ was our only concern I think it would be a relief. My son's needs should qualify him for supplemental funds but, unfortunately, the legislation here says that if the individual does not have a cognitive deficit, then they don't qualify. It's not a lot of money but it would go a long way toward the purchase of a computer which could give my son the ability to have increased independence.

Parents of children who are ventilator assisted argue that program eligibility should not be determined by any one involvement, but rather on an individual, case-by-case basis in which the extent of the child's needs, not the nature of the disability, would be the basis for supplementary assistance. An individualized approach would still allow for controlled access to these programs, while simultaneously decreasing the likelihood that a child with legitimate needs would be excluded from those beneficial programs.

POLICY IMPLICATIONS

Implications for Planning

Although planning is a labor-intensive and time-consuming process, the educational outcomes that result are generally positive (Clatterbuck et al., 1993). The practical solutions and planning model proposed by Clatterbuck et al. (1993) are a first step in making the process less difficult. Planning for educational services must not be looked upon as a single, one-time event, but for students who are ventilator assisted and other students with chronic illnesses, planning truly needs to be approached as an ongoing process. Thinking must be flexible and team members must be willing to adjust and adapt to feedback from one another, as well as changes in a student's condition. To facilitate this type of planning, the current model and frequency of individualized education program (IEP) meetings may need to be altered for children who are technology supported, particularly during initial implementation when medical personnel are such essential members of the process. Although increasing the frequency and nature of IEP meetings may place a greater strain on personnel time resources, in the long run the planning process will be more responsive to the changing needs of students.

Implications for Personnel Shortages

Shortage of experienced personnel is a very real problem that limits the options available to students who are supported by technology. Although this problem does not lend itself to a quick resolution, there are some initial steps that could currently be instituted.

First, state and educational agencies must acknowledge that the population of students who are technology supported is growing and is likely to continue to grow as advances in medicine continue. Once they accept this fact, then it follows that institutions of higher education and school systems will need to train increased numbers of teachers and therapists to work with these students. Training programs at colleges and universities need to increase both the number and quality of their graduates. Students graduating in these fields need to be familiar with individuals who are technology supported. The addition of classroom and field experiences with a greater emphasis on working with students supported by technology is critical. Also, training programs are well advised to sponsor seminars or guest lecture series presented by individuals who have experience working with these students so that the experiential knowledge can be shared with future educators and clinicians. Naturally, federal personnel preparation money will be desirable and justifiable.

In the professional setting itself, there is a clear need for more in-service training for all school personnel. In-service training should focus on sensitivity training with respect to students with multiple involvements, severe disabilities, and technology support. Other topics of interest for these in-service seminars is the technology itself; providing educators with hands-on exposure to the technology that causes them apprehension and fear will help them to see beyond the equipment to the child it sustains.

Implications for Resolving Fear and Ignorance

Although people with disabilities have made great gains in the area of acceptance, there is still a great deal of public fear and ignorance that does not stop at the doorways of our school buildings. Teachers and other professionals still hold stereotypical views of individuals with disabilities. Nowhere is this fact more clear than within the population of educators who are currently serving students who are technology supported.

There is no better tool to combat these discriminatory attitudes than information and experience with individuals with disabilities. To that end, adaptations to teacher-training curricula to provide both increased exposure to and experience with individuals with disabilities are recommended.

Implications for Lack of Transition System

Clearly, there is a need for better communication and transition planning by educators and health care providers. Although some interaction and communication occur in a limited scope as part of hospital-based education programs, meeting the needs of the students who are technology supported requires a more regularized, systematic means of communication. Although this may seem like a new role for hospitals and schools, medical and school social workers are already in place who could take on these new joint communication and planning responsibilities. The existence of a clearly defined pathway from hospital to school will help ensure that the needs of students and their parents are met during the transition process.

Other recommendations for ways to provide increased support to parents during periods of transition come in the form of other parents. Parent support groups, such as Parent to Parent, are quickly spreading across the country (Santelli, Turnbull, Marquis, & Lerner, 1993). These groups may be suitable vehicles for forming specialized sections to deal exclusively with students who are technology supported and their families. These parent support groups are not only excellent sources of emotional support, but also can provide parents with success stories and concrete detailed advice for working in the educational system (Santelli et al., 1993).

Implications for Resolving Funding Problems

There needs to be a formal resolution to the debate between medically necessary and related services under IDEA. At present, there is little distinction between these two types of services, which allows schools and private insurance agencies to defer responsibility at the expense of parents. Legislation and litigation have failed to provide a clear resolution to this issue of funding responsibility for specific services, whether as IDEA-related services or Social Security Act entitlements under Title XIX (Medicaid) or Title V (Maternal and Child Health) (Turnbull, 1993).

Until a clear resolution is adopted, creativity seems to be one of the most effective tools parents have at their disposal. Data show that bringing together private and public sources in joint funding ventures has been successful in many cases. It is very seldom that one funding body will step forward and volunteer to provide full funding, but compromises and joint funding arrangements have allowed funding sources to avoid long, costly litigation.

Getting the child's physician involved in the jurisdictional funding disputes is another powerful strategy. Clatterbuck et al. (1993) suggest that physicians can play an important and even decisive role in cases when disputes regarding the funding or necessity for specific related services occur (e.g., occupational therapy, nursing services during school hours). A carefully worded physician's recommendation and / or prescription for such services often helps to resolve disputes in favor of increased services and identify a logical funding source for the physician-prescribed service.

CONCLUSION

This chapter has outlined some of the issues facing children who are ventilator assisted and their families as they attempt the transition to home- and community-based care. Problems arise from inadequate or nonexistent policies, personnel shortages, stereotypes and discrimination, and conflicts concerning funding of services. These problems call for systemic responses and coordination of policy between education and health care systems, which are not easy to obtain. In addition, the current health care policy focus offers little hope, as the issue of schools' responsibilities is not even included in that agenda.

Even lacking these responses and coordination, families and professionals can create workable solutions with due diligence. A policy that favors home- and community-based care, and assumes that an education in the least restrictive environment will accompany that type of care, is in place in two critical respects: It is policy on the books, and it is policy in practice. The gap between what is on the books and how it is in practice, however, is intolerably wide. Families, educators, and health care providers can devise responses, but a child's education and health care should not depend solely on good will. There must be policy movement beyond good will and toward more rights. Advocates for school-linked services, family-centered services, and empowering systems and professionals must acknowledge this and further the movement in order to give children who are ventilator assisted the rights they deserve.

Chapter Review

CHALLENGES

- New community school models and family support laws are going to affect schools' and families' abilities to provide children who are ventilator assisted an education in the least restrictive environment.
- In 1995, the delivery of appropriate educational services in the least restrictive environment for children who are ventilator assisted varies greatly by geography, service coordination resources, attitudes and skills of school staff, funding, and legal liability.
- Family empowerment changes the roles of both professionals and families.
- Families believe that school inexperience in planning and implementing services; a shortage of qualified personnel; unorganized transitions among hospital, home, and school; and a shortage of funding for health care services in the school are all key issues in providing services to them and their children.
- School planning teams are usually bewildered by the nature of the disability, and discussions with families often become emotion-laden and polarized.
- Parents desire school-furnished therapy, while schools lack experienced teachers and therapy services.
- School staff irrationally fear a medical crisis, or even death, while a child who is ventilator assisted is under their supervision—policies and federal regulations to guide educators need to be developed.

CHARACTERISTICS OF HELPFUL PROGRAMS

- Programs first introduce the school planning team to the student to keep the members focused on the child's needs.
- Teachers' fears about medical crises are discussed openly, and an emergency plan developed.
- Programs view the planning process as ongoing and flexible.
- Programs assess children individually for supplemental funding to ensure those with legitimate concerns are included, regardless of eligibility requirements.
- Programs provide emotional support to parents through early intervention programs and parent groups.
- Parents promote creative joint efforts between public and private funding efforts, while physician support helps obtain increased related services and identifies logical funding sources.

POLICY IMPLICATIONS

- IDEA must formally resolve the controversy between medically necessary services and related services in order to clarify funding issues.
- In-service training for staff caring for children who are technology supported needs to be augmented.
- A teacher-training curriculum that increases exposure to and experience with disability should be adopted to dispel the current fear and ignorance surrounding disabilities.
- Planning mechanisms for children with complex medical needs should establish forms of support.

References

Aday, L.A., & Wegener, D.H. (1988). Home care for ventilator-assisted children: Implications for the children, their families, and health policy. *Children's Health Care, 17*(2), 112–120.

Americans with Disabilities Act of 1990 (ADA), PL 101-336. (July 26, 1990). Title 42, U.S.C. 12101 et seq: *U.S. Statutes at Large, 104,* 327–378.

Burr, B.H., Guyer, B., Todres, I.D., Abrahams, B., & Chiodo, T. (1983). Home care for children on respirators. *The New England Journal of Medicine, 24,* 1319–1323.

Campbell, P.H. (1987). The integrated programming team: An approach for coordinating professionals of various disciplines in programs for students with multiple handicaps. *Journal of The Association for Persons with Severe Handicaps, 12*(2), 107–116.

Clatterbuck, C.C., Jones, D.E., & Turnbull, H.R. (1993). *Planning educational service for children who are ventilator assisted.* Unpublished manuscript, University of Kansas at Lawrence, Beach Center on Families and Disability.

Developmental Disabilities Assistance and Bill of Rights Act of 1990, PL 101-496. (October 30, 1990). Title 42, U.S.C. 6000 et seq: *U.S. Statutes at Large, 104,* 1191.

Fischer, D.A., & Prentice, W.S. (1982). Feasibility of home care for certain respiratory-dependent restrictive or obstructive lung disease patients, *Chest, 82*(6), 739–743.

Frates, R.C., Jr., Splaingard, M.L., Smith, E.O., & Harrison, G.M. (1985). Outcome of home mechanical ventilation in children. *Journal of Pediatrics, 106,* 850–856.

Individuals with Disabilities Education Act of 1990 (IDEA), PL 101-476. (October 30, 1990). Title 20, U.S.C. 1400 et seq: *U.S. Statutes at Large, 104,* 1103–1151.

Jones, D.E., Clatterbuck, C.C., Barber, P.A., Marquis, J., & Turnbull, H.R. (1993). *Educational placements of children who are ventilator assisted.* Unpublished manuscript, University of Kansas at Lawrence, Beach Center on Families and Disability.

Kagan, S.L., & Neville, P.R. (1993). Family support and school-linked services: Variations on a theme. *Family Resource Coalition Report, 1993–1994, 12*(3 & 4), 4–6.

Lynch, E.W., Lewis, R.B., & Murphy, D.S. (1992). Educational services for children with chronic illnesses: Perspectives of educators and families. *Exceptional Children, 59*(3), 210–220.

Miller, B.F., & Keane, C.B. (1983). *Encyclopedia and dictionary of medicine, nursing, and allied health* (3rd ed.). Philadelphia: W.B. Saunders.

Office of Technology Assessment. (1987). *Technology dependent children: Hospital v. home care—A technical memorandum.* Washington, DC: U.S. Government Printing Office.

O'Leary, J., King, R., Leblanc, M., Moss, R., Liebhaber, M., & Lewiston, N. (1979). Cuirass ventilation in childhood neuromuscular disease. *Journal of Pediatrics, 94*(3), 419–421.

Palfrey, S.J., DiPrete, L., Walker, D., Shannon, K., & Maroney, E., (1987). School children dependent on medical technology. *Rehabilitation Research Review.* Washington, DC: The Catholic University of America, D: *ATA Institute* Monograph.

Santelli, B., Turnbull, A.P., Marquis, J., & Lerner, R. (1993). Parent-to-parent programs: Ongoing support for parents of young adults with special needs. *Journal of Vocational Rehabilitation, 3*(2), 25–37.

Social Security Administration Reform Act of 1994, PL 103-296. (October 1994). Title 42, U.S.C. 8301 et seq. (1994 Sup.).

Stein, R.E.K., Perrin, E.C., Pless, I.B., Gortmaker, S.K., Perrin, J.M., Walker, D.K., & Weitzman, M. (1987, December 26). Severity of illness: Concepts and measurements. *The Lancet, 2,* 1506–1509.

Turnbull, H.R., III. (1993). *Free and appropriate education: The law and children with disabilities* (4th ed.). Denver: Love Publishing.

U.S. Department of Health and Human Services (HHS), Health Care Financing Administration. (1988). *Report of the task force on technology-dependent children: Fostering home- and community-based care for technology-dependent children* (HCFA Publication No. 88-02171). Washington, DC: U.S. Government Printing Office.

Walker, D.K. (1987). Chronically ill children in schools: Programmatic and policy directions for the future. *Rheumatic Diseases of Childhood, 13*(1), 113–121.

Walker, D.K., & Jacobs, F.H. (1984). Chronically ill children in school. *Peabody Journal of Education, 61*(2), 28–74.

Walker, P. (1991). Where there is a way, there is not always a will: Technology, public policy, and the school integration of children who are technology-assisted. *Children's Health Care, 20*(2), 68–74.

18

Family and Consumer Activism in Disability Policy

Laurie E. Powers

The 20th century has been a period of remarkable advancement in technology and medicine in the United States. For people with disabilities and their families, advancements in technology have resulted in the design of lightweight wheelchairs, communication and environmental control devices, scanners, and numerous other aids that have significantly promoted independent living and inclusion in society. Likewise, advancements in medicine have resulted in the prolongation of life for many people with formerly acute life-threatening injuries, people with chronic conditions, older adults, and premature infants (Estes & Swan, 1993; Newacheck & Taylor, 1992). As a result, the proportion of citizens who have chronic health challenges or disabilities has risen to an unprecedented level.

This period has also been marked by the emergence of increasingly progressive social policy regarding people with disabilities and their families. Until the mid-1950s, the progressive movement was primarily focused on preventing harm and assisting those perceived to be less fortunate and incapable of helping themselves (Boggs, 1994). Assistance was typically provided by voluntary organizations until 1933 when New Deal policies initiated a rapid shift toward government responsibility for the support of disadvantaged citizens. The Social Security Act of 1935, PL 74-271, provided the first national program of ongoing government assistance to adults with disabilities, which was, perhaps, the most notable indicator of government's growing role. Federal funding of rehabilitation centers following World War II further promoted the design of comprehensive programs emphasizing the complete rehabilitation of individuals with physical disabilities to typical community living. However, institutions continued to be regarded as effective caretaking facilities for people with developmental disabilities and mental health problems.

During this time of rapid change, the medicalization of disability catalyzed a societal shift toward an emphasis on treatment, rehabilitation, and more humane caregiving practices. However, it also promoted a societal interpretation of disability as pathology, which emphasized the necessity for individuals to acquiesce to treatment plans designed by medical professionals, and the importance of individual responsibility for overcoming functional limitations and achieving optimal normalization (Zola, 1991).

During the second half of the 20th century, social benevolence toward people with disabilities and their families has given way to increasing emphasis on highlighting and enhancing autonomy and personal rights (Boggs, 1994; Singer & Powers, 1993). As a result, there has been growing public support for community-based living and employment, the enactment of legislation to provide flexible mechanisms for family support, and the emergence of the disability rights movement. Historically, stereotypes of dependence, incompetence, and biological inferiority have been considered inherent attributes of people with disabilities and their families. Yet, contemporary perspectives increasingly define disability as a social construct that is shaped by both individual and societal responses to the differences imposed by the disability (Zola, 1991). This redefinition has resulted in the acceptance of minority group status among people with disabilities and fostered growing support for the importance of public accommodation; it has also called attention to the discrimination that prevents people with disabilities from functioning as full members of society (Hahn, 1985). The focus on civil rights advocacy has embraced tenets of personal choice, inclusion, and access to and control of supports.

Two major factors have contributed to this shift in societal perception and public policy. First, the increasing number and visibility of people with disabilities in our society has stimulated recognition that "the disabled" are indeed people who can assume typical roles within society. Although responses of fear and pity toward people with disabilities and their family members continue to pose serious obstacles to inclusion, much progress has been made through increased exposure. Many people without disabilities have become sensitized to the physical, attitudinal, and social barriers that impede the success of those with disabilities.

The second, and perhaps more critical, factor fueling the shift in social policy from benevolent care to societal accommodation has been the emergence of powerful parent and consumer movements. Historically, advancements in individual treatment and adoption of progressive social policy have both been largely catalyzed by the intensive efforts of people with disabilities and their family members. Parents have successfully advocated for appropriate educational services; consumers with disabilities have won hard-fought personal battles to gain access to typical employment, transportation, and colleges. At the systems level, individuals with disabilities, their families, and organizations of parents and consumers have spearheaded efforts to pass virtually every piece of contemporary disability legislation, including the Individuals with Disabilities Education Act of 1990 (IDEA), PL 101-476, the Americans with Disabilities Act (ADA) of 1990, PL 101-336, family support legislation, and reauthorizations of the Rehabilitation Act of 1973, PL 93-112.

The rapid emergence of parent- and consumer-driven movements has been critical to the success of sociopolitical change in the portrayal and treatment of people with disabilities and their families. This chapter reviews the history of these movements, explicates the principles that provide their foundations, discusses some of the current challenges to the integration of consumer- and family-centered perspectives, and reviews the recent emergence of collaborative agendas for social change between people with disabilities and family members.

THE RISE OF PARENT AND CONSUMER ADVOCACY

Although organized parent and consumer advocacy have achieved unprecedented levels of influence during the second half of the 20th century, it is important to acknowledge the earlier influence of advocates in the establishment of services and enactment of legislation. For example, the emergence of deaf and blind advocacy groups in the 1880s, and their subsequent influence upon the passage of blind relief laws in the 1920s, were an early signal of growing consumerism among parents and people with disabilities. The establishment of the League for the Physically Handicapped to protest exclusion of people with disabilities from the Works Progress Administration during the Depression provides another example of early consumer organizing.

With regard to contemporary parent and consumer influence, two interrelated waves of advocacy can be delineated. The first wave, initiated in the 1950s, was spearheaded by parents of children with physical, sensory, and developmental disabilities; parents of children with mental health disabilities subsequently assumed activist roles. The second wave emerged in the 1960s and was led by people with physical and sensory disabilities; again, consumers with developmental and mental health disabilities became increasingly active during the 1980s.

The First Wave of Parent Activism

The rise of the parent movement is most often traced to the formation of key disability organizations, such as the United Cerebral Palsy Associations, the National Association of Parents and Friends of Mentally Retarded Children (later renamed the Association for Retarded Citizens and, most recently, The Arc), and the Muscular Dystrophy Association. Initially, the primary operational goals of these groups were to solicit charitable contributions to support research in prevention and treatment, to promote improved medical care, to create more humane conditions in public institutions, and to expand educational services for children with disabilities. By 1960, parent-led organizations had promoted the establishment of special education services in most states, additional outpatient and community-based services, summer camp programs, and the expansion and enhancement of institutions. Parents were also successful in advocating for a shift in terminology: Mental deficiency became mental retardation, and crippled became handicapped. Through these organizations, parents were able to solicit public support, gain additional control over their lives, and create a platform for responding against societal stereotypes. At the time, society often perceived parenting a child with disabilities as maladjusted or shameful, while it considered the children subhuman and incapable of sensitivities or typical living (Boggs, 1994; Shapiro, 1993).

During the 1960s, parent organizations were increasingly influential in establishing disability research and training initiatives, promoting the design and establishment of comprehensive habilitation and rehabilitation programs, and leveraging federal funding to support the provision of expanded services. The Division of Handicapped Children and Youth was also given prominence within the federal government, an event significant for the later passage of educational legislation on behalf of children with disabilities.

During the 1970s, many parent organizations were active in advocating for passage of legislation, such as the Education for All Handicapped Children Act of 1975, PL 94-142, the Developmental Disabilities Assistance and Bill of Rights Act of 1975, PL 94-103, and Title XVI (SSI) of the Social Security Act of 1935, PL 74-271. This was a period of growing legal advocacy for adults with disabilities, as well. Legislation passed during this era was landmark in asserting the rights of children and adults with disabilities.

These efforts continued through the 1980s, with parent groups instrumental in the establishment of early intervention efforts, family support initiatives, and mandates for community-based services to provide expanded alternatives to institutional care (Covert, MacIntosh, & Shumway, 1994; Farber & Marcel, 1994). A stronger parent voice in mental health also emerged at this time through the establishment of groups such as the National Alliance for the Mentally Ill (NAMI), the Federation of Families for Children's Mental Health, and support and advocacy programs such as the Parent Involved Network Project in Pennsylvania (Fine & Borden, 1991).

Numerous other parent organizations have been established to advocate for and provide support to families of children and adults with a variety of disabilities and chronic health conditions. Family Voices, the National Parent Network on Disabilities, the Alliance for Technology Access, and the Federation for Children with Special Health Care Needs are just a few such organizations. The Parent to Parent self-help movement has also flourished with more than 300 local parent-to-parent programs currently functioning across the country (Santelli, Turnbull, Lerner, & Marquis, 1993).

In addition to shaping national and state policy, parents have increasingly assumed leadership roles in organizations established through such policies. Parent-directed centers for educational advocacy and parent-governed family support programs have been established in most states. Parent groups have also gained increasing respect among professional organizations, resulting in the establishment of partnerships between parents and professionals in advocacy and service delivery efforts (Dunst, Trivette, Starnes, Hamby, & Gordon, 1993).

One of the most notable examples of growing parent power is the family-centered care movement in pediatrics. Key elements of family-centered care include recognizing family strengths and individuality, facilitating parent–professional collaboration at all levels, designing health care systems that are responsive to family-identified needs, and encouraging family-to-family support and networking (Shelton, Jeppson, & Johnson, 1987). These principles represent a major divergence from traditional medical models of support that emphasize professional control and the assessment and treatment of dysfunction. The Family Advocacy Case Management Model is an example of a similar shift in mental health; influenced by family constituencies, the model seeks to promote partnerships between parents and professionals in service provision (Poertner & Ronnau, 1989).

A great deal of diversity exists among parent organizations over focus and approach. Some parent organizations have made legislative reform focused on expanding rights and removing barriers to societal inclusion as their top priorities; other groups maintain their focus on soliciting charitable support to improve treatment and rehabilitation efforts; and still other groups have directed their efforts toward establishing programs for family-directed services. The variation in focus among parent organizations has, in part, been driven by different organizational structures, perceptions of need, and attitudes within different disability constituencies. In general, parent groups have become increasingly focused on promoting the quality of life and personal rights for children and families with disabilities in their communities.

However, some parent organizations, such as the Muscular Dystrophy Association, have remained closely affiliated with traditional medical professionals and focus on promoting cure and treatment of disease by raising funds for research and medical support services. Fund-raising efforts for this group have been particularly controversial because they have perpetuated the public attitude that children and people with disabilities lead tragic lives and amelioration of disease is the only way to help them. Likewise, some parent activism in adult mental health has maintained a focus on treatment, care, and decision making for consumers, instead of focusing on addressing discrimination and maximizing consumer autonomy.

Inconsistencies in public attitudes and policy toward different disability constituencies have affected the focus of parent organizations. One example involves parent activism and deinstitutionalization. In developmental disabilities, the deinstitutionalization movement was accompanied by public support for the establishment of community-based service alternatives; whereas in mental health, deinstitutionalization typically resulted in the dumping of people into their communities with few services available. As a result, parents of people with developmental disabilities have been able to focus many of their efforts on promoting inclusion and quality of life for consumers in their communities, while mental health parent organizations have been more preoccupied with advocating for the establishment of safety net services to provide hospitalization alternatives and basic shelter and care needs for consumers.

These inconsistencies have fostered categorical perspectives of disability and provided disencentives for parent group collaboration. For example, activists representing people with developmental disabilities and blindness have achieved notable enhancements in services and supports for these groups that are not available to people with other disabilities. As a result, these groups have been somewhat reluctant to support efforts to expand benefits to other groups, fearing that their services would be threatened. Similar tensions exist between organizations for older adults and disability groups in the current debate over distributing health care resources. Differential public regard and treatment have fostered resentment among organizations and reinforced separate group identities and perceptions of need. These differences, along with inconsistent public policies, have also created barriers between parent and consumer groups that have impeded their collaboration, particularly with respect to defining and promoting policies and services for adults with disabilities. Full understanding of this issue requires consideration of the history of the second wave of activism— the consumer advocacy movement.

The Second Wave of Consumer Activism

As with the parent movement, the emergence of consumer activism can be traced to specific events. (A detailed presentation of the history of the disability civil rights movement is found in Shapiro, 1993.) However, beyond the influence of specific events, history and research findings clearly point to an association between parent advocacy and consumer advocacy (Powers et al., 1996; Shapiro, 1993, 1994). The skills, commitment, and perseverance of many contemporary consumer advocates can be traced to their early experiences in families who fought to create opportunities for people with disabilities to attend typical schools and become active members in their communities.

In addition, government programs and rehabilitation centers' increasing emphasis on independence and community integration for adults with physical disabilities helped to further the consumer activism movement. For example, in 1950, the University of Illinois was one of four universities that created a program to assist veterans with disabilities who wished to attend college (Crewe & Zola, 1983). By 1961, there were 163 students in the program; these students started a newspaper, got buildings ramped, and established an accessible transportation system. The program was not designed to promote consumer activism or self-help. However, by providing opportunities for people with disabilities to move toward increasing levels of independence, such programs sensitized them to societal barriers impeding their typical living, some of which were intrinsic to the design and operation of the programs themselves.

Much consumer activism has continued into the 1990s as a reaction against medical models of rehabilitation and independent living that emphasize professional control, amelioration of illness, personal responsibility for overcoming disability, and the importance of "adjustment" to "normal" life. For this reason, the consumer advocacy movement has historically been more distrustful of collaboration with professionals and more focused on advocating specifically for consumer control over policies and services than the parent movement.

A third factor that shaped the direction of early consumer activism was the activism evident in the civil rights movement, the antiwar protests of the 1960s, the gay rights movement, and the women's movement. The philosophies and strategies of these movements provided a framework for consumers to both interpret and respond to the barriers they faced in assuming typical societal roles. It is a meaningful coincidence that in 1962 James Meredith was the first African American student to enter the University of Mississippi, while Ed Roberts was the first person with quadriplegia to enter the University of California at Berkeley—an event generally regarded as the start of consumer activism for independent living. When Ed Roberts indicated he wanted to attend Berkeley, the California Department of Rehabilitation refused to provide funding because it deemed his disability too severe for him ever to work. Roberts' case was reported in the local newspapers, and the agency eventually relented and agreed to support his schooling. The University then resisted his admission because the buildings were inaccessible and the dormitories floors were not strong enough to support the weight of his iron lung. Roberts assured University officials that he could arrange for attendents to carry him into inaccessible buildings and the director of the student infirmary agreed to provide Roberts living space on the third floor. Roberts met his personal care needs by hiring attendants, funded through the first attendant program in the nation.

News of Roberts' admission to the University spread; by 1967, there were 12 students with quadriplegia attending Berkeley and living in the infirmary. These students became increasingly discontent with their segregated living situation and formed a support group called the Rolling Quads to help each other find and manage independent living. In 1970, they were able to get funding to create a program for peer mentoring from a Department of Health, Education, and Welfare anti-dropout program for minorities. People with disabilities were thought to experience obstacles, such as presumptions of biological inferiority, stereotyping, segregation, and discrimination, that impeded other minority groups. In reality, adults with disabilities had the highest unemployment rates, lived primarily in poverty, and usually were forced to lead segregated lives—facts that made acceptance of minority group status a logical outcome (Hahn, 1985).

The Physically Disabled Students Program (PDSP) was established as the first university-based peer support service in the nation directed by people with disabilities. Program services were gradually expanded to include advocacy and wheelchair and van repair. Independence was defined as control over life; the program's basic tenets included self-help, self-sufficiency, promoting access to typical living, and opposing discrimination. Disability was defined in sociopolitical terms, which emphasized the role of attitudinal and physical barriers in restricting the lives of people with disabilities, rather than focusing strictly on functional limitations.

In 1972, the efforts of the PDSP were expanded through the formation of the Center for Independent Living (CIL), the first consumer-directed, community-based independent living program in the nation. CIL was governed by people with disabilities and the majority of its employees had disabilities. Currently in 1995, there are more than 300 independent living centers in the United States. Centers remain committed to consumer control and advocacy. Many also provide extensive services, such as personal assistance, transportation, peer support, and interpreters. Core federal funding for independent living is now provided to many centers.

Since its inception, consumer activism has been inextricably tied to civil rights and the independent living movement through its focus on advocacy and support of social protest. Concurrent with his CIL activities, Ed Roberts was active in teaching community organization strategies to ethnic minority groups in the San Francisco Bay area. Judy Heumann, the Deputy Director of CIL from 1975 to 1982, was drawn into disability activism after being denied a license to teach in the New York City Public Schools in 1970. She formed the first consumer group focused exclusively on advocacy, Disabled in Action (DIA). DIA actively protested the lack of federal support for disability programs in partnership with veterans with disabilities.

Heumann was also a leader of the most powerful consumer social protest activity in the history of the disability rights movement. In response to federal unwillingness to release regulations for Section 504 of the Rehabilitation Act of 1973, a group of cross-disability activists occupied the San Francisco Health, Education, and Welfare offices for 25 days. Officials attempted to force them out by denying food, telephones, and access to attendants. However, widespread support from state officials—including Ed Roberts who was then State Director of Rehabilitation—other civil rights groups, and local businesses and organizations bolstered the group's resistance. In response to this protest, the federal government relented and the regulations were signed for both the Rehabilitation Act and the Education for All Handicapped Children Act of 1975—another major piece of legislation for which regulations were held up. This marked a critical step forward in ensuring that children would have access to public schooling and adults could not be discriminated against in federally funded education and employment programs.

Consumer activists have been instrumental in catalyzing the shift in social attitudes and policy toward people with disabilities in the 1980s and 1990s. On the policy level, activists spearheaded the development of federal requirements for state rehabilitation agencies to establish consumer advisory boards, federal funding of independent living programs, granting of federal Medicaid waivers to states to enable funding for personal assistance services and other community-based supports, and passage of the ADA. Organizations such as American Disabled for Attendant Programs Today (ADAPT) have demonstrated consumers' capabilities to organize for and successfully achieve policy change through civil disobedience. Although sometimes considered on the fringe due to their endorsement of protest and mass arrest, ADAPT has created additional leverage for political negotiation by drawing attention to discrimination in transportation access and nursing home treatment for people with disabilities.

With regard to promoting attitude change, consumer advocates have led efforts to change the language of disability: "Handicapped" has been changed to "disability," "wheelchair bound" has been changed to "wheelchair user," and "patient" has been changed to "consumer." Many activists have also reacted against language such as "differently abled" and "physically challenged" because it distances society from the reality of disability and the reality of discrimination (Zola, 1993). Consumer activists within government have also promoted funding for initiatives to promote consumer direction. For example, initiatives developed by the Department of Education, Office of Special Education Programs to promote the self-determination of youth in education have been the outgrowth of efforts by officials with disabilities (Ward, 1988). People with disabilities have assumed increasing visibility and influence in society (e.g., riding public buses, assuming key roles in government agencies and professional organizations). In conjunction, attitude change efforts have begun to stimulate public acceptance of disability as diversity and heighten sensitivity to the impact of discriminatory practices.

The deaf community has been very successful in focusing attention on the sociopolitical nature of disability. Rejecting the notion that being deaf is a disability, activists have shifted the debate to society's unwillingness to accommodate difference. Although sometimes considered radical, the proliferation of this perspective has helped many consumers to question the lengths to which they should go to adapt to and overcome barriers. A qualitative study of 35 adults with various physical disabilities found that, as a result of their exposure to the disability rights movement, informants emphasized their personal transformation from striving for social role valorization to emphasizing renegotiation and accommodation (Phillips, 1992). Their realization that personal worth is not defined by perseverance or constantly proving one's ability by achieving societally defined outcomes is echoed by Zola's (1991) recount of his personal evolution in response to the disability rights, women's, and independent living movements of the 1970s and 1980s.

Although much consumer activism has been by people with physical and sensory disabilities, self-advocacy is emerging as an important force among consumers with developmental and mental health disabilities. Initially established in 1974, People First continues to develop and gain power as a national self-advocacy organization for people with developmental disabilities. Through chapter development and national conferences, People First provides opportunities for self-advocates to frame the issues with which they are confronted, provide one another with peer support, and identify strategies for social action. Self-advocates have engaged in a variety of activities including conducting strikes at sheltered workshops, demonstrating for deinstitutionalization, and advocating for inclusion in policy making within developmental disability organizations. In response to self-advocate activism, the Association for Retarded Citizens changed its name to The Arc in 1991; and advisors, people who do not experience cognitive disabilities who support People First chapters, are becoming increasingly aware of the capabilities and power of self-advocates (Bowen, 1994). Partnerships are also gradually being developed between advocacy organizations in developmental disabilities and independent living (Jones & Ulicny, 1986). Fractionalization continues to exist, however, among disability consumer groups for the same attitudinal and policy problems associated with parent organizations.

Although professional models continue to dominate policies and supports for older adults with disabilities, programs such as Peer Counseling for Older Adults and Concepts in Community Living provide opportunities for older Americans to support one another and to make choices regarding the nature of services they receive (Estes & Swan, 1993). Interventions focused on promoting personal control have been shown to promote self-esteem and functional well-being among older adults (Rodin, 1989). There is a growing recognition among professionals that the promotion of self-help and advocacy groups that serve their self-defined concerns is essential (Bernard & Phillipson, 1991), through organizations such as the Gray Panthers and the American Association of Retired Persons.

THEMES OF CONSUMER AND PARENT MOVEMENTS

Diversity within consumer and parent advocacy movements makes the identification and comparison of philosophies and practices difficult and somewhat controversial. Yet, there are thematic trends underlying these movements that are essential to understanding their perspectives, potential tensions that exist between them, and opportunities for enhancing partnerships. This section discusses three major issues that are sources of both tension and opportunity for consumer and parent activists.

Influence of Perspective

At the most basic level, it is important to acknowledge the inherent difference in locus of perspective between people with disabilities and their family members: a difference between other and self. Parents are typically perceived as like others, and stigmatized only by the association of having to cope with the tragedy of parenting a child or adult with a disability. In contrast, people with disabilities are stigmatized by societal reaction to the reality of what they look like, how easily they blend into the social milieu, which services they use, and so on.

Despite current trends toward defining disability as one aspect of personhood, there is still an important distinction between being judged as different because of an association with someone who is different and being that someone yourself. This distinction may help to explain why successful parent activism emerged ahead of consumer activism. It may also have facilitated parent linkages with professionals and policy makers—a process that has been more difficult for consumer activists. In a sense, families can be viewed as committed arbiters between society and people with disabilities. They have the most intimate understanding of disability possible for people without disabilities. Because they do not experience disability, they also have the capacity to advocate as members of the society they are trying to influence.

As most parents of people with disabilities have little intimate exposure to disability until parenthood, they are also likely to have been socialized to accept attitudes of stigma and tragedy. As such, they are at risk to adopt societal biases that impede their support of the acceptance of positive notions of disability by their family members with disability. Although the parent movement has done much to challenge prevalent negative perceptions of disability at the sociopolitical level, some parent-dominated organizations continue to perpetuate negative stereotypes through both active and passive support of activities such as telethons. Additionally, at the individual level, some families continue to perceive disability as tragedy—a perspective that is reinforced through interaction with friends, relatives, and professionals who hold such views. They continue to question whether their children with disabilities are capable of being happy, living independently, holding real jobs, marrying, or having children, even if resources are available that enable them to achieve these outcomes.

Independent living staff and activists who interact with such families often encounter negativity and resistance. As a result, families are sometimes viewed as negative influences on their members with disabilities, and as enemies to those trying to help. In turn, consumer advocates are perceived as insensitive to family concerns and provocateurs of consumer–family conflict. Unfortunately, such tension between consumer advocates and families at the individual level has perpetuated perceptions of antagonism and distrust at the organizational level, a factor that has discouraged collaboration between parent and consumer organizations. This tension is more reflective of the incremental nature of societal change than irreconcilable differences in perspectives between parent and consumer organizations; however, it must be acknowledged if shared visions and partnerships are to be fostered between parent and consumer groups.

Differences in perspective between parents and consumers underlie conflicts regarding several specific issues. One issue that centers on the self–other distinction is medical intervention to save the lives of newborns with disabilities. This issue has been the focus of major division between the women's movement and the disability movement (Blackwell-Stratton, Breslin, Mayerson, & Bailey, 1988). Parent advocates argue that privacy rights of parents in making personal family decisions should take precedence in policy, whereas consumer advocates argue that protection of children's rights should guide decision making.

A second issue that has historically promoted divisiveness is deinstitutionalization (Asch & Fine, 1988). Some family advocates argue that the best interests of people with disabilities and their families are served by supporting the availability of institutional options, whereas consumer advocates argue that it is better to serve them by developing community-based resources. Most consumer and family organizations now agree that community-based support is the best alternative.

A third issue that is emerging as a source of potential tension between consumers and families relates to control over resources. For example, subsidies provided to families for supporting members with disabilities can create disincentives for families to promote consumer independence. This problem is complicated further when guardianship is at issue and consumers do not have the legal authority to make their own decisions.

For each of these issues, policy makers must decide whose interests to emphasize. In most cases, policies strive to promote the joint satisfaction of consumer and family interests; however, further dialogue is needed to develop methods for resolving issues that stimulate conflicting interests. Solutions to these conflicts may be found in both the development of uniform policies and the identification of problem-solving approaches that consumers, parents, and professionals can use to discuss and resolve conflicts.

A related issue of concern is the current emphasis on supporting caregiving families. Although focusing on the care demands associated with having a member with a disability appears to be a successful strategy for mobilizing public attention to the concerns of families, it also reinforces perceptions that people with disabilities are dependent, incapable, and must be looked after—in other words, the notion that people with disabilities must receive care and their families must provide care. This perspective underestimates the capabilities of families and people with disabilities by suggesting that families do not have the right to expect typical lifestyles for all their members and people with disabilities do not have the right to assume typical adult lifestyles and interdependent roles within their families.

Parents of teenagers with disabilities have a right to expect that their teenagers will establish independent lives and they will be able to resume their educations, careers, or any other activities they have deferred while fulfilling their parenting roles. Likewise, adults and older adults with disabilities have a right to maintain desired levels of personal independence and assume desired levels of interdependence within their families. Finally, society has a right to expect that people with disabilities will function as contributing members and optimize their capabilities. Although promoting the welfare of families is important in fulfilling these expectations, maximizing mutual support within families and promoting public support for all family members to live typical lives is even more essential.

Welfare Versus Autonomy

Historically, parent activism has centered on promoting the welfare of children with disabilities and their families. In contrast, consumer activism emphasizes advocating for the rights of people with disabilities to control their lives and have access to the same life opportunities as people without disabilities. These agendas are not mutually exclusive. In fact, they have been integrated in some recent advocacy efforts. However, their approaches diverge enough to have a direct bearing on the formulation of disability policy and the collaboration between parent and consumer activists.

At a conceptual level, this divergence is, to some extent, a conflict between autonomy and paternalism (Cicirelli, 1992). Paternalism typically derives from a desire to promote the welfare and happiness of another and a belief that one knows what is best for the other person, even if the person does not. Paternalism is generally based on genuine caring about another's well-being; however, it fails to respect the autonomy and decision making of the individual to whom care is directed. Personal welfare is considered to be more important than individual choice.

Parent activism's historic focus was somewhat reflective of paternalistic concerns for people deemed unable to care for themselves. Although the paternalistic flavor of this movement has dissipated, paternalism is still prevalent, particularly in advocacy efforts on behalf of people with developmental and mental health disabilities and older people with disabilities (Hofland, 1988). Because the consumer movement was defined, in part, as a reaction to professional and family paternalism, most consumer activists are highly sensitive to the negative effects of paternalism on their attempts to advance societal regard for the capabilities and autonomy of people with disabilities. This sensitivity has successfully catalyzed consumer activism to counteract policies of paternalism. However, activist sensitivity has also prompted some reluctance either to engage with professionals and parents who might have shifted their views or to take on complicated issues that intertwine paternalism with disability-related limitations.

This conflict has led to debate over such issues as whether people with developmental disabilities can or should have access to control over their personal assistance services. Traditionally, professionals and family members of people with developmental disabilities have advocated for the design of services that would not be dependent on consumer control: A consumers' concerns would be met by caregivers who were supervised by someone thought to understand the consumer's concerns and preferences. Generally, services have been designed in this way to ensure that consumers' needs were met and prevent harm from befalling a person who could not direct his or her personal care. Although well-meaning, this emphasis has resulted in the establishment of expensive, vendor-driven systems of personal care services that provide only basic care, reinforce paternalistic attitudes, and provide little incentive for shifting to consumer-directed models.

In contrast to this service-focused approach, consumer advocates have argued for and successfully established policies and funding mechanisms that enable consumers to hire, train, and supervise their personal assistance services, in a consumer-directed approach (Litvak, Zukas, & Heumann, 1987). However, such programs typically require consumers to demonstrate the capacity to independently direct their assistance, which excludes many people with developmental disabilities who may need training or support to manage their personal assistants. Ironically, both consumer advocates, by responding against paternalism, and family and professional advocates, by adopting paternalistic service models, have avoided finding solutions that serve the needs of people who require support but desire autonomy.

It is essential that consumer, family, and professional advocates work together to identify creative solutions that maximize welfare and personal autonomy in all issues, especially guardianship. Traditionally, policy makers debate whether to ensure welfare or personal autonomy, instead of identifying the strategies and supports necessary to promote consumer autonomy while ensuring personal welfare, as defined by the consumer. For example, Cicirelli (1989) suggests that autonomy be considered as having a number of levels, such as directive autonomy, consultative autonomy, joint autonomy, delegated autonomy, and surrogate autonomy. In reality, every person, regardless of disability, exercises his or her autonomy at most of these levels. We choose to direct some parts of our life, whereas we rely on assistance to manage other parts. It is most important to decide which level of autonomy is most appropriate.

People with disabilities also have the right to exercise autonomy at various levels and decide which level of autonomy is most appropriate for addressing their specific concerns. This perspective suggests that efforts should be directed toward providing them with the information, skills, and experiences necessary to promote informed decision making. In addition, those in supportive roles need to permit consumers to take risks and assist them to productively learn from experience the consequences of making bad decisions. This would demonstrate increasing respect for consumers' abilities to manage problems and learn from failure. Although some truly life-threatening experiences can result from poor decisions, most consequences are not permanently damaging.

Control in Policy Making

Understanding and resolving issues of control is critical for the development of interdependent partnerships between consumers and families, at both personal and systems levels. Historically, parent organizations have focused their efforts on child issues, whereas consumer organizations have focused on adult advocacy. Activists in both movements have argued strongly for respective parent and consumer governance in policy making and service delivery (Crewe & Zola, 1983; Knoll, 1990).

Basing support on consumer age has enabled both movements to assert greater control over policies and services that most directly affect them. However, policies and services to address the needs of some consumers, most notably adults with mental health and developmental disabilities and older adults with disabilities, have been significantly controlled by caregiver organizations with little consumer participation. Furthermore, the division of control has also promoted the establishment of different, sometimes conflicting, policies and service systems for children and adults, and put parent leaders and consumer leaders in adversarial positions when resolving issues that pertain to both constituencies. For example, the proliferation of family support programs across the nation has promoted parent governance of policies and services that affect families, children, and adults. Parents often make decisions regarding expenditures for adult services and recreation programs, as well as respite care and service coordination. Although principles of family-centered care were originally advanced by professionals and families of young children, its basic tenets (including parent control and parent–professional collaboration) are now being generalized to older children and adults. Finally, although services provided by independent living centers affect both consumers and their families, there are typically not mechanisms for family participation in their governance.

A climate has been fostered that suggests adults with disabilities are not useful participants in policy design and service delivery for families and children, and parents are not important participants in the formulation of policies and services for adults. Yet, families are often the primary source of support for family members, regardless of age. Children grow into independent adults, and interaction among children with disabilities, their families, and adults with disabilities can have a remarkable impact on the well-being of all participants.

It appears essential that the constituencies for which policies and services are designed assume major responsibility for directing those policies and services. This suggests that issue and context be defining factors in determining who should assume control, rather than age or nature of disability.

Adult consumers are probably the appropriate constituency to make decisions regarding policies and services to support adults, regardless of the nature of their disabilities. When policies are considered that directly affect the families who support those consumers, parents and siblings should be invited to participate in decision making. Likewise, policies and services to support children are appropriately informed by parents and older children. However, to the extent that policies have ramifications for transitions to adult living or conflict with analogous policy initiatives supported by adult consumers, adult consumers should be invited to participate in decision making. Such governance decisions are complex to sort out and implement. This discussion is not intended to propose specific solutions, but rather to suggest that it is essential for consumer and parent activists to acknowledge current governance challenges, and together formulate guidelines for their constituencies that provide creative solutions and promote partnership where it is mutually advantageous.

THE EMERGENCE OF THE THIRD WAVE: COLLABORATIVE AGENDAS FOR SOCIAL CHANGE

A third wave of advocacy has gained momentum since the 1980s, defined by increasing collaboration among parent and consumer constituencies and cross-disability advocacy efforts. Leveraging support for policy and service responsiveness to the unmet needs of people and families with disabilities remains a major agenda for third-wave activists. However, there is increasing consensus among parent and consumer constituencies on the importance of advocating to promote inclusion and access to typical life options, bolster the supportive capabilities within families and communities, and ensure civil rights. Professional allies are supporting this by highlighting the capabilities of families and consumers, and advocating for more extensive collaboration with them in research and programmatic activities (Turnbull et al., 1993).

The most notable achievement in the third wave of activism is the passage of the ADA, which was marshalled through unprecedented collaboration between family and consumer activists representing a range of disability constituencies. The ADA was endorsed by 180 national parent, consumer, and professional organizations. Major support was provided by legislators with personal disability connections and traditional rehabilitation organizations, such as the National Rehabilitation Association (Shapiro, 1993). At the organizational level, the Consortium for Citizens with Disabilities (CCD) has become a major national force for cross-categorical advocacy. The CCD has been involved in advancing a number of policy initiatives, including the ADA and efforts to leverage increasing federal support for families and personal assistance services. Similarly, the Partners in Policymaking initiative based in Minnesota has increasingly emphasized parent and consumer collaboration and cross-categorical community organization. Among consumer and professional advocates, there is also growing recognition that the future success of advocacy efforts will hinge on the ability of different constituencies to join forces. Particular attention is being focused on highlighting common concerns among families of children with developmental and mental health disabilities, adults with disabilities, and older adults with disabilities (see Chapter 12; Racino & Heumann, 1992; Zola, 1988).

The success of the third wave of activism will depend upon a number of factors beyond the external economic and political realities that shape all contemporary movements for social change. The development of shared visions and agendas for change between consumers and families will necessitate collaborative discussion and problem solving to resolve potential tensions regarding differences in perspectives, the philosophy and goals of advocacy, and constituency control over policy and service design. It is also likely that competing interests among families, consumers, and specific disability constituencies will continue to arise. Acknowledgment of competing agendas among constituency groups and the formulation of strategies to enable groups to advocate individually, call on partnerships for additional support, and mobilize cross-categorical efforts is essential if long-term collaboration is to be fostered.

A final major challenge that will have to be addressed is the development and support of new leaders. Many of the original advocates for disability rights, independent living, and family empowerment now work within the system or function in professional roles. There is a growing need to identify and develop new leaders who understand the struggles, lessons, and accomplishments of those leaders they will succeed and are prepared and willing to carry the torch into the 21st century. Experiences from the 20th century suggest that our new leaders will most likely be committed consumers with disabilities and their families. These future leaders may be currently employed in parent information centers or independent living centers. They may be volunteers who are providing parent-to-parent support or mentoring youth with disabilities. In many cases, they will be young people with disabilities who were the first generation to have participated in inclusive education and been transitioned into college, independent living, and naturally supported employment. The future direction of disability advocacy will depend upon these second- and third-generation leaders who will lead the United States into the fourth wave.

Chapter Review

CHALLENGES

- Inconsistencies in public attitudes and policies toward different disability groups have influenced the focus of parent and consumer activism, promoted categorical approaches, and acted as disincentives to collaboration.
- Parent activism has historically emphasized caregiving and well-being, whereas consumer activism has focused on civil rights and promoting autonomy.
- There are differences in perspectives among some parent and consumer activists related to disability stigma, welfare and autonomy, and control over decision making.

CHARACTERISTICS OF HELPFUL PROGRAMS

- Helpful programs feature consumer and parent collaboration in policy development and program governance.
- The deaf community has focused attention on the sociopolitical nature of disability.
- The family-centered care movement in medical care emphasizes family needs and strengths; the independent living movement emphasizes consumer control and self-direction.
- Partnerships are gradually being developed between advocacy organizations in developmental disabilities, independent living, services for older adults, and mental health.
- Interventions that promote self-esteem and functioning for older people have led professionals to increasingly recognize the importance of self-help and advocacy groups.

POLICY IMPLICATIONS

- Policies need to be developed that satisfy both family and consumer interests and promote joint governance.
- Policy makers need to provide supports and incentives for consumers to control their lives.
- Consumer, family, and professional advocates need to work together to identify creative solutions that maximize both well-being and personal autonomy.
- Efforts should be directed toward providing consumers with the information, skills, and experiences necessary to make informed decisions.

References

Americans with Disabilities Act of 1990 (ADA), PL 101-336. (July 26, 1990). Title 42, U.S.C. 12101 et seq: *U.S. Statutes at Large, 104,* 327–378.

Asch, A., & Fine, M. (1988). Shared dreams: A left perspective on disability rights and reproductive rights. In M. Fine & A. Asch (Eds.), *Women with disabilities: Essays in psychology, culture, and politics* (pp. 297–305). Philadelphia, PA: Temple University Press.

Bernard, M., & Phillipson, C. (1991). Self-care and health in old age. In S. Redfern (Ed.), *Nursing elderly people* (2nd ed., pp. 405–415). New York: Churchill Livingstone.

Blackwell-Stratton, M., Breslin, M.L., Mayerson, A.B., & Bailey, S. (1988). Smashing icons: Disabled women and the disability and women's movements. In M. Fine & A. Asch (Eds.), *Women with disabilities: Essays in psychology, culture, and politics* (pp. 306–332). Philadelphia, PA: Temple University Press.

Boggs, E.M. (1994). Benchmarks of change in the field of developmental disabilities. In V.J. Bradley, J.W. Ashbaugh, & B.C. Blaney (Eds.), *Creating individual supports for people with developmental disabilities: A mandate for change at many levels* (pp. 33–58). Baltimore: Paul H. Brookes Publishing Co.

Bowen, J.N. (1994). The power of self-advocacy: Making thunder. In V.J. Bradley, J.W. Ashbaugh, & B.C. Blaney (Eds.), *Creating individual supports for people with developmental disabilities: A mandate for change at many levels* (pp. 335–346). Baltimore: Paul H. Brookes Publishing Co.

Cicirelli, V.G. (1989, December). *A measure of family members' belief in autonomy and paternalism in relation to caregiving practices toward elderly parents.* Final report to the Retirement Research Foundation. West Lafayette, IN: Purdue University, Department of Psychological Sciences.

Cicirelli, V.G. (1992). *Family caregiving.* Beverly Hills: Sage Publications.

Covert, S.B., MacIntosh, J.D., & Shumway, D.L. (1994). Closing the Laconia State School and Training Center: A case study in systems change. In V.J. Bradley, J.W. Ashbaugh, & B.C. Blaney (Eds.), *Creating individual supports for people with developmental disabilities: A mandate for change at many levels* (pp. 197–212). Baltimore: Paul H. Brookes Publishing Co.

Crewe, N.M., & Zola, I. (1983). *Independent living for physically disabled people.* San Francisco: Jossey-Bass.

Developmental Disabilities Assistance and Bill of Rights Act Amendments of 1975, PL 94-103. (October 4, 1975). Title 42, U.S.C. 6000 et seq: *U.S. Statutes at Large, 89,* 486–507.

Dunst, C.J., Trivette, C.M., Starnes, A.L., Hamby, D.W., & Gordon, N.J. (Eds.). (1993). *Building and evaluating family support initiatives: A national study of programs for persons with developmental disabilities.* Baltimore: Paul H. Brookes Publishing Co.

Education for All Handicapped Children Act of 1975, PL 94-142. (August 23, 1977). Title 20, U.S.C. 1401 et seq: *U.S. Statutes at Large, 89,* 773–796.

Estes, C.L., & Swan, J.H. (1993). *The long-term care crisis: Elders trapped in the no-care zone.* Beverly Hills: Sage Publications.

Farber, A., & Marcel, K. (1994). Parent power: Change through grassroots networking. In V.J. Bradley, J.W. Ashbaugh, & B.C. Blaney (Eds.), *Creating individual supports for people with developmental disabilities: A mandate for change at many levels* (pp. 373–386). Baltimore: Paul H. Brookes Publishing Co.

Fine, G., & Borden, J.R. (1991, February 18–20). Parents involved network project (PIN): Outcomes of parent involvement in support group and advocacy training activities. In A. Algarin & R.M. Friedman (Eds.), *A system of care for children's mental health: Expanding the research base* (pp. 25–30). Fourth Annual Research Conference Proceedings. Research and Training Center for Children's Mental Health, Florida Mental Health Institute, University of South Florida, Tampa.

Hahn, H. (1985, January–February). Disability policy and the problem of discrimination. *American Behavioral Scientist, 28*(3), 293–318.

Hofland, B.F. (1988). Autonomy in long-term care: Background issues and programmatic response. *The Gerontologist, 28*(Suppl.), 3–9.

Individuals with Disabilities Education Act of 1990 (IDEA), PL 101-476. (October 30, 1990). Title 20, U.S.C. 1400 et seq: *U.S. Statutes at Large, 104*, 1103–1151.

Jones, M.L., & Ulicny, G.R. (1986). The independent living perspective: Applications to services for adults with developmental disabilities. In J.A. Summers (Ed.), *The right to grow up: An introduction to adults with developmental disabilities* (pp. 227–244). Baltimore: Paul H. Brookes Publishing Co.

Knoll, J. (1990, Fall). Legislative advocacy: Fourteen essential components of a comprehensive system of family support—The new era. *Family Support Bulletin*, 4–5.

Litvak, S., Zukas, H., & Heumann, J. (1987). *Attending to America: Personal assistance for independent living*. Oakland, CA: World Institute on Disability.

Newacheck, P., & Taylor, W. (1992). Childhood chronic illness: Prevalence, severity, and impact. *American Journal of Public Health, 82*(3), 364–371.

Percy, S.L. (1989). *Disability, civil rights, and public policy: The politics of implementation*. Tuscaloosa: University of Alabama Press.

Phillips, M.J. (1992). Try harder: The experience of disability and the dilemma of normalization. In P.M. Ferguson, D.L. Ferguson, & S.J. Taylor (Eds.), *Interpreting disability: A qualitative reader* (pp. 213–227). New York: Teachers College Press.

Poertner, J., & Ronnau, J. (1989, February 27–March 1). The family advocacy case management model: An innovative approach to meeting the needs of families caring for youth with emotional disturbances. In A. Algarin, R.M. Friedman, A.J. Duchnowski, K. Kutash, S.E. Silver, & M.K. Johnson (Eds.), *Children's mental health services and policy: Building a research base* (pp. 133–142). Second Annual Conference Proceedings. Research and Training Center for Children's Mental Health, Florida Mental Health Institute, University of South Florida, Tampa.

Powers, L.E., Singer, G.H.S., & Todis, B. (1996). A retrospective study of the emergence of self-esteem. In L. Powers (Ed.), *Making our way: Building self-competence among children with disabilities*. Baltimore: Paul H. Brookes Publishing Co.

Racino, J., & Heumann, J. (1992, Winter). Independent living and community life: Building coalitions among elders, people with disabilities, and our allies. *Aging and Disabilities, 16*(1), 43–47.

Rehabilitation Act of 1973, PL 93-112. (September 26, 1973). Title 29, U.S.C. 701 et seq: *U.S. Statutes at Large, 87*, 355–394.

Rodin, J. (1989). Sense of control: Potentials for intervention. *Annals of the American Academy of Political and Social Science, 503*, 29–42.

Santelli, B., Turnbull, A.P., Lerner, E., & Marquis, J. (1993). Parent to parent programs: A unique form of mutual support for families of persons with disabilities. In G.H.S. Singer & L.E. Powers (Eds.), *Families, disability, and empowerment: Active coping skills and strategies for family interventions* (pp. 27–58). Baltimore: Paul H. Brookes Publishing Co.

Shapiro, J.P. (1993). *No pity: People with disabilities forging a new civil rights movement*. New York: Times Books.

Shapiro, J.P. (1994, January 10). The mothers of invention: How a mighty grassroots movement of parents with disabled kids is changing the nation. *U.S. News & World Report*, 4–8.

Shelton, T.L., Jeppson, E.S., & Johnson, B.H. (1987). *Family-centered care for children with special health care needs* (2nd ed.). Washington, DC: Association for the Care of Children's Health.

Singer, G.H.S., & Powers, L.E. (1993). Contributing to resilience in families: An overview. In G.H.S. Singer & L.E. Powers (Eds.), *Families, disability, and empowerment: Active coping skills and strategies for family interventions* (pp. 1–26). Baltimore: Paul H. Brookes Publishing Co.

Social Security Act of 1935, PL 74-271. (August 14, 1935). Title 42, U.S.C. 301 et seq: *U.S. Statutes at Large, 15,* 687–1774.

Turnbull, A.P., Patterson, J.M., Behr, S.K., Murphy, D.L., Marquis, J.G., & Blue-Banning, M.J. (Eds.). (1993). *Cognitive coping, families, and disability.* Baltimore: Paul H. Brookes Publishing Co.

Ward, M.J. (1988). The many facets of self-determination. *National Information Center for Children and Youth with Handicaps: Transition Summary, 5,* 2–3.

Zola, I.K. (1988, September–October). Aging and disability: Toward a unifying agenda. Special issue: Aging and disabilities. *Educational Gerontology, 14*(5), 365–387.

Zola, I.K. (1991). Bringing our bodies and ourselves back in: Reflections on a past, present, and future "medical sociology." *Journal of Health and Social Behavior, 32*(3), 1–16.

Zola, I.K. (1993). Self, identity, and the naming question: Reflections on the language of disability. *Social Science and Medicine, 36*(2), 167–173.

19

The Thinking
Behind New Public Policy

Allan I. Bergman and George H.S. Singer

All great establishments in the nature of boarding schools, where the sexes must be separated; where there must be boarding in common, and sleeping in congregate dormitories; where there must be routine, and formality, and restraint, and repression of individuality; where the charms and refining influences of the true family cannot be had—all such institutions are unnatural, undesirable, and very liable to abuse. We should have as few of them as possible, and those few should be kept as small as possible. (Samuel G. Howe, 1866)

The 1994 passage of the Families of Children with Disabilities Support Act, PL 103-382, marked a milestone for public policy efforts aiming to establish support services for families of people with disabilities. The culmination of 8 years of effort, this law represents a landmark in broader efforts to reform disability policy that could be termed the evolution of common sense in public policy. Because it is important to understand the context in which new family support policies have been created, this chapter briefly reviews disability policy in the United States.

DISABILITY POLICY IN THE UNITED STATES

Family support efforts represent a paradigm shift in public policy toward people with disabilities and their families. Public policy refers to laws, regulations and rules, budgets, and court decisions, all of which reflect widely held societal values. An examination of public policy is one way to understand how society has valued people with disabilities and their families.

Institutionalization

During most of this nation's history, policy for people with disabilities reflected the notion that disability meant a negative difference from the norm
that required exclusion from the typical community, both to protect the
community and to protect people who were viewed as weak and vulnerable. For a period of 120 years, beginning in 1850, the dominant paradigm
emphasized removing and separating people with disabilities regardless of
the type or cause. The standard approach to people with mental retardation,
seizure disorders, deafness, blindness, cerebral palsy, and mental illness was
to send them away with their own kind. They usually were sent to remote
places away from family and home communities. Large encompassing care
facilities, called schools, hospitals, or institutions, received virtually all of
the public funds for people with disabilities. An important element of this
early paradigm, medical professionals dominated the labeling, caregiving,
and decision making for people with disabilities; most states had statutes
requiring that the director of state institutions be a physician. At their peak
in 1967, institutions for people with mental retardation and other disabilities housed over 194,650 children and adults (*Family Support Bulletin,*
1992–1993).

For a long time, policy makers believed that institutions saved money
through economies of scale. However, experience eventually showed that
money could only be saved by sacrificing the most basic standards of decency. Reformers during this 120-year period usually focused on trying to
make institutions safe and clean, and provide treatment, as well as custodial
care. However, when institutions try to meet these basic standards, economies of scale are dwarfed by the costs of creating an entire surrogate community of services, professionals, activities, and worksites. By 1995, costs
often ran over $100,000 per year per resident; with over 70,000 people still
in public institutions, these places consumed over half of the public budget
for people with developmental disabilities (*Family Support Bulletin,*
1992–1993). Yet, paradigms are hard to dissolve; they develop vested interests that make dissolution of old models and programs politically difficult.
Still by 1994, there were three states in the United States that had completely
closed their public institutions—New Hampshire, Rhode Island, and Vermont—and the District of Columbia.

Deinstitutionalization and the Parent Movement

After World War II, parents began to challenge the dominant exclusion
model. As early as 1948 and in the 1950s, they began organizing local chapters of the Association for Retarded Citizens (The Arc) and United Cerebral
Palsy Associations (UCP). These early parent activists strongly opposed the
state, as well as dominant social attitudes. Medical textbooks written prior
to the mid-1960s advise physicians to recommend institutional placement
at all times for people with mental retardation. For people with moderate
and severe disabilities, the books told physicians to urge parents to put the

children in institutions at birth. Recent historical research has shown that the practice of putting infants away dates back to the Romans and continues through the Middle Ages to early modernity (Boswell, 1988).

By the 1950s, however, parents were no longer content to follow expert opinion about removing their children from the family and community and formed an early grass roots movement. The first UCP meeting in New York City and the first meeting of The Arc in San Francisco were publicized in the newspapers with small advertisements reading "Are you a parent of a child with mental retardation or cerebral palsy? If you are, come and meet other parents and let's talk." In both of these instances, 250–300 people showed up, which proved that parents had a tremendous need to talk to someone who understood what they were experiencing. Originally, The Arc and UCP were informal parent groups with no paid staff, no buildings, and no legislative agenda. Despite such obstacles, these parents organized the first early intervention programs and the first preschools.

This was a new generation of parents who resented the messages that bombarded them, advising them to put their children away—out of sight and out of mind. Their early programs were funded on shoestring budgets, often in basements of churches with borrowed equipment. At the time, the small number of professionals trained in rehabilitation were working almost exclusively with the many injured veterans of war. Therefore, these programs lacked professional expertise and other current indicators of quality. Still, parents' underlying values and instincts influenced the way programs were established and run, which generated quality education and care. The most important of these basic values was that children should be able to live at home with their families, instead of hidden away because of shame.

Parents and the Push for Public Education Programs

Parent organizations began lobbying for public education programs in the late 1960s and 1970s. By the mid-1970s, many states provided public educational services to children with disabilities as discretionary programs, which did not recognize a common right to education or community services. A milestone in this early community movement came through the courts in a class action lawsuit, *PARC v. the Commonwealth of Pennsylvania*. Attorney Thomas K. Gilhool developed the PARC parents' legal argument in that case, under the agreement that he would argue it on federal constitutional grounds; this meant it would be tried in federal court, propelling parent organizations onto a national stage. Gilhool argued that children with disabilities were protected under the liberty and due process clauses of the Constitution and the right to equal protection under the law. At the time the idea that people with disabilities were protected under the same rules as other citizens of the United States was revolutionary. The three-judge court in the PARC case approved a far-reaching consent decree, saying that children with disabilities should have the same right as other children to attend a neighborhood school with their peers and should be provided with compensatory services to allow them to benefit from participation in the mainstream. However, this ruling was not widely adhered to. If it had been, many of the disputes that have arisen over the policy of inclusion in public schools would have been prevented.

Gilhool's legal strategy was used in lawsuits in over half the states by the mid-1970s. Repeatedly, the courts ruled in favor of the parents, recognizing that school exclusion constitutionally questioned the country's most basic values of equal protection and liberty. Thus, by 1975, there was pressure on Congress to pass a national special education law based upon the civil and constitutional rights of these children. The passage of PL 94-142, the Education for all Handicapped Children Act of 1975, now PL 101-476, the Individuals with Disabilities Education Act of 1990 (IDEA), was a true watershed as it established a right to a free, appropriate public education of special education and related services for *all* children in the least restrictive environment. The PARC standard is found in Congressional intent: "It is in the national interest that the federal government assist state and local efforts to provide programs to meet all the education needs of handicapped children in order to assure equal protection of the law." Once it became possible for parents to send their children with disabilities to the same schools as their brothers and sisters, the idea of sending them away from the community began to fall out of favor. The school day also provided mothers with 5–6 hours of respite 5 days per week.

Parents and Institutions

These same parent organizations launched a new round of lawsuits in the 1970s, targeting the institutional system. They pursued a two-tract policy: The plaintiffs in some suits argued for a right to treatment in institutions; whereas, in other suits, they demanded closure of the institutions altogether. As a result of suits in Alabama, Massachusetts, Michigan, New Hampshire, and New York, among others, two policies emerged: 1) closure or downsizing of many institutions, and 2) upgrading of their quality of care. As the upgrading was enormously expensive, states continue to use over half of their budgets for people with developmental disabilities for the care of the small percentage of people who still live in these places. Much of the institutions' expensive maintenance is encouraged by federal policy that allows states to charge more than half of their costs to the federal Medicaid program. Some believe that this money is being wasted and that these same funds could be providing an excellent quality of life in the community for those 70,000 people still living in state facilities. Daily costs for institutional care in some states are $400 per day. At this price, a person could live in the finest hotel, eat in a restaurant or order food from room service, and have a personal attendant with a doctoral degree around-the-clock. In retrospect, some policies that have come from the combination of federal funding streams, federal regulations for "active treatment," and court-imposed standards of care make little sense.

Specialized Programs

Efforts to downsize or even close institutions have also led to a new phase of program development in communities. The former Pennsylvania Commissioner of Mental Retardation, Steven Eidelman, has described this new policy phase: "We relocated the institution, made it smaller, and changed the ZIP code." This phase of public policy was marked by the creation of many new, separate programs within the community: separate schools and preschools, sheltered workshops, activity centers, and large group homes and living centers. As a result, there was an enormous expenditure on real estate and buildings. An infrastructure was created for a system that most advocates now believe is outmoded. These new services were still segregated and viewed as special. They were dedicated to a group of people who were labeled and publicly acknowledged as different from ordinary citizens.

But again, as in the case of the institutional movement, this old model created an enormous inertia. It is difficult to give up the special school or the sheltered workshop once it has become the standard method of service delivery. However, the services were in the community, rather than in remote rural sites, which was a major improvement that fueled the development of new skills among professionals and a new emphasis on community living. Two elements of this second phase of public policy have been particularly influential and difficult to change: the idea of a continuum of services and the emphasis on rehabilitation, or habilitation through behavioral programming, as preparation for life in typical environments.

The concept of a continuum of services and facilities incorporates the notion that people with disabilities should have available a range of environments, including ones that are segregated and inclusive in education, residential, and adult day services. For example, most state residential systems created intermediate-care nursing homes, group homes, small group homes with simulated apartments, clusters of apartments in one building, and separated apartments. Graduates of such a program would, in theory, move from the most segregated to the most typical residence as they mastered new skills, according to readiness criteria. This system was created according to an educational model in which access to the next stage has to be earned by attaining a given skill level.

The training model for this continuum was a behavioral–developmental model that teaches skills hierarchically (i.e., earlier learning makes more complex and advanced skills possible). Although this approach has some merit, in many cases it led to an unfortunate emphasis on teaching skills that were not very functional or interesting for the learners. In turn, the skills sequences and tests of attainment evoked the sense of earning access to the next step on the continuum. The continuum also defined the least restrictive/most independent settings as the least staff supported and the least costly.

This model of skill hierarchies combined with a continuum of settings has been particularly problematic for people with severe intellectual or physical impairments and multiple disabilities—the people still disproportionately represented in the institutional population. One of the primary characteristics of severe mental retardation, as defined by the American Association on Mental Retardation in 1983,[1] is difficulty in generalizing from one setting to another or from one task to another. For example, a person might have been taught to operate a washing machine in a group home but be unable to use a somewhat different machine at the neighborhood laundromat. Based upon extensive experience, many educators now realize that it is best to teach the task that is the ultimate goal in the natural setting from the beginning. Or, a second successful option has been to structure the instruction from the beginning to include experience with a range of, in this case, washing machines. In either solution, the ideals of readiness skills and learning hierarchies are now considered a significant mistake in the history of designing community options for citizens with disabilities, as are the notions that only people with low-cost support needs can earn their way into the community.

However, the second phase of disability policy, the facility-based continuum phase, has made a valuable contribution by creating conditions that allowed people with disabilities and their advocates to see that there are more desirable approaches to creating a valued quality of life in the community for people with disabilities. But, once again, it created considerable inertia that had to be overcome.

Individual and Family Support Programs

The new, third public policy phase is marked by the emergence of family support programs; supported work and living arrangements; and an emphasis on community membership, self-determination, and self-advocacy by people with disabilities. Table 1 gives a taxonomy of family support. This shift is marked by some important trends, beginning with the decoupling of supports.

Prior to 1987, services provided assistance to people with disabilities in segregated places—a special school, a separate classroom, a sheltered workshop, or a separate house in a neighborhood. But, with the help of parents, self-advocates, visionary professionals, and advocates, it began to make more sense to use places that already existed for everyone else. That is, if everyone else in a town goes to the public swimming pool, the race

---

[1]New terminology adopted in 1992 by the American Association on Mental Retardation (AAMR) (Luckasson et al., 1992) does not utilize the classification scheme of mild, moderate, severe, and profound retardation.

Table 1. Taxonomy of family support

Core services	Traditional developmental services
Respite and child care	Behavior management
Child care	Case management/service coordination
Respite	Evaluation/assessment
Sitter service	Financial assistance
Environmental adaptations	Allowances
Adaptive equipment	Discretionary cash subsidy
Home modification	Line-of-credit
Supportive	Reimbursement
Family counseling	Vouchers
Family support groups	Individual counseling
In-home assistance	Medical/dental
Attendant care	Nursing
Chores	Occupational therapy
Home health care	Physical therapy
Homemaker services	Skills training
Extraordinary/ordinary needs	Speech therapy
Health insurance	
Home repairs	
Rent assistance	
Special clothing	
Special diet	
Transportation	
Utilities	
Vehicle modification	

Source: Human Services Research Institute (1990).

track, the skating rink, the place of worship, and the movie theater, so should people with disabilities. And if they need supports or accommodations to enjoy these places, they should be provided there at the typical site.

This shift has profound implications. Instead of creating new human services, the shift emphasizes opening up the community and expanding the capacity of typical community institutions to accommodate all citizens. Presently, this shift is in the early learning phase. Still, many places now provide supports to families to raise their children at home, and it is possible to see people with disabilities being provided with the necessary supports to participate in typical preschools and child care centers, neighborhood schools, community jobs, homes of their own, and public recreational activities.

However, there is still a great deal to learn about accomplishing these accommodations. It is very important to keep in mind that this approach has not yet affected the lives of most people with disabilities. The great majority are still being served under the first- and second-phase models. An essential part of this effort is providing the right kinds of accommodations and supports so that all children with disabilities can grow up in a typical home with a family. Thus, the family support movement is intimately linked to phase three of public policy, in which services are decoupled from a fixed setting and supports are provided in natural environments.

True Individualization

Another hallmark of phase three is *true individualization*. Phase two, which created new segregated community services, gave plenty of lip service to individualization with programs such as individualized family service plans (IFSPs), individualized education programs (IEPs), individualized habilitation plans (IHPs), and others. Each part of the system developed its own individualized plan. However, these programs are rarely truly individualized; in reality, they simply function as program designs. That is, these plans end up being a description of the standard service that is offered to most, if not all, the people who are served by a particular organization. If the organization has people trained in Piagetian approaches, it will have goals and objectives that reflect a belief in phased development. If the organization is steeped in behavioral methodology, it will have a lot of language about observable, measurable, task-analyzed learning. If the service is a sheltered workshop that offers six different kinds of work activities, it will have objectives that explain how the individual will do one or more of those six activities. In other words, the individualized plan has become a way of saying how each person's activities will be shaped by the existing structure and content of the service.

This is individualization in a very strange and limited sense. There is rarely room in these plans for people to express their preferences; explore different opportunities and develop new interests; or change what they do, with whom, and when. This kind of program planning does not involve a dialogue or conversation. The direct observation studies that have been done, for example, of the IEP process show that parents rarely make active suggestions or talk as much as any other member of the team. How people with disabilities and their families participate in the design of their daily experiences and life plans is one of the main problems with the phase two model.

In 1995, there is symbolic individualization. The language that people use and the ways that they talk during meetings to develop these plans do not reflect two-way communication. Instead, meetings are a kind of technocratic ritual in which people talk the specialized languages of their professions—a language and communicative system so far removed from how parents and citizens talk and think that these professionals often are not even able to think clearly about how to make a plan relevant to their customers' typical activities, wishes, hopes, and dreams.

The emerging model will not have planning team meetings, but multiple dialogues and conversations in a variety of settings. Perhaps then, people with disabilities and their families will do more talking than the professionals. However, when the person with the disability does not have the skills to take part in the dialogue, parents and family members assume a greater responsibility. This necessitates that professionals truly listen to and trust parents' understanding of their family member's wishes. At times, when programs dominate the design of accommodations, parents' wishes are marginalized, and in many cases, the person with the disability could be providing far more input than is presently recognized. Unfortunately, professionals operate under narrow definitions that do not always acknowledge the ways that people with severe disabilities carry out dialogue. Perhaps some people can only express their desires and preferences through their actions. Perhaps dialogues with people with severe cognitive disabilities should take into account the day-to-day reality of their lives. In the same way, parents may need to contribute to the dialogue by telling family stories and sharing their dreams about their child's future, although they might not want to do these things at a formal meeting, and it might take more than one occasion for their story to take shape and become clear.

Fostering Dreams and Hopes

Dreams and hopes for all people with differences, including those with disabilities and their families, are essential. One of the most damaging aspects of the social system for families of people with disabilities in the United States is that, all too often, it has destroyed parents' capacities to dream about their children—often from the beginning of the child's life. Research shows that most parents imagine an ideal child during pregnancy (Seligman & Darling, 1989). As soon as a child is born with a disability, a message is conveyed that something disastrous has happened; frequently, the first information that medical professionals give to parents is about their child's future limitations.

Also, there are centuries of culturally transmitted messages about disabilities that are evoked when a child is labeled. Professionals often seem to feel that they have to reinforce the child's inabilities, which is never done for a newborn without a disability. Never do doctors say, "Look, statistically, chances are he is going to have an average IQ; he's not going to be a genius. And as far as being in the major leagues or the NBA, forget it; the chances are less than getting struck by lightning. We just want you to be realistic." Since Freud, psychological thought has considered it very unhealthy to have unrealistic dreams or perceptions. Denial is viewed as the primary roadblock to be cleared.

Fortunately, new parents are increasingly being put in touch with veteran parents who have the ability to comfort; saying, for instance, "Your hopes for this child might have to be changed, but here are some other dreams that you can have." Professionals are also beginning to understand that their role is not to shatter dreams, but rather to give information with the humility that limited powers of prediction require and a vision of how to acquire a valued lifestyle for all children. This shift should allow service programs to become much more flexible and responsive.

Flexibility

Once professionals begin thinking in these terms (e.g., going to the person's home for a meeting, carrying on a conversation that might unfold over a long period of time, letting a family's understanding of their needs really drive the design of accommodations), program administrators start to get very nervous; these kinds of processes are not as convenient and predictable as the old model, which was dominated by routine planning. It becomes necessary to design ways of providing accommodations and supports that are maximally *flexible*. Flexibility requires the ability to respond quickly with novel responses to a changing environment. It also requires a sustained dialogue between the person who is served and the person providing the service.

In the phase-three model, the people most affected by the services and accommodations are put in charge of their design and implementation. Families are allowed to express their concerns. For some families, it is help repairing a car so they can drive their child to therapy sessions; for others, it is a chance to talk with other parents or an opportunity to go on a vacation. In this approach, professionals must consider it their duty to facilitate the capacities of families or people with disabilities to determine their own needs and realize their own wishes.

Self-Determination

Professionals are still learning how to behave and think under this approach. For example, they are beginning to understand that people may need supports and accommodations in order to gradually become aware of their own desires and plans, as with the person who has lived his life in an institution or gone to school solely with other people with disabilities and has been so protected and taken care of that his behavior exemplifies what has been defined as *learned helplessness*; he may not know that he is interested in swimming in a lake or in working in an office instead of a factory. In order for some people to determine their own choices, service systems may need to provide special ways for them to explore their options, communicate, and form special relationships with people who can be maximally responsive to them. Thus, *self-determination* is a key element of the third phase, and creating the proper circumstances for promoting self-determination is an essential goal.

Dignity of Risk

Bob Perske defined another key element of this new phase in the 1970s by coining the term *dignity of risk*. Taking the community imperative seriously requires acknowledging the costs of emphasizing protection and safety, as opposed to choice, dignity, and inclusion, which involves taking some risks in supporting the quality of life for people with disabilities. Opening up the community for people with disabilities entails the risks inherent in any open society and requires that people work to make the community safer for everyone.

In summary, thinking about people with disabilities, their place in society, and the kinds of societal accommodations that are necessary has evolved dramatically. Historically, the single approach was one of removal, exclusion, and protection, dominated by remote, congregate care institutions. After World War II, emphasis shifted to creating new, but still segregated, organizations and places for people with disabilities. Recognizing their rights under the Constitution, schooling and employment opportunities began to open up. However, this phase of disability policy was dominated by the demands of programs and services. More recently in the third phase of thinking, it is being recognized that the goal should be to build an inclusive community where society is responsible for creating accommodations that allow any citizen access to a typical life of shared rights and responsibilities. Family support is an essential component of this new approach.

THE DEVELOPMENT OF FAMILY SUPPORT PROGRAMS

The values behind new family support programs were first articulated at a meeting sponsored by the Center on Human Policy at Syracuse University in 1986. Based upon family support initiatives underway in several states (see Table 2), a group of forward-thinking advocates and parents generated a statement of commitments, shown in Table 3. This commitment to a home life for every child with a disability was the driving motive behind new family support services. Recognizing the primacy of the family for children with disabilities also logically led to the belief that families should control the kinds of supports that they receive, rather than the service system. One way to ensure that the family is the locus of control is to give resources directly to them in the form of money or vouchers.

Cash Subsidy Programs

In reviewing state policy and practice regarding families with children with developmental disabilities, the first recognition of respite care—one type of

Table 2. States with family support legislation between 1988 and 1995

Alabama	Missouri
Arizona	Nebraska
California	New Hampshire
Colorado	New Jersey
Connecticut	New York
Illinois	Ohio
Indiana	Oregon
Iowa	Tennessee
Louisiana	Texas
Maine	West Virginia
Maryland	

Note: Massachusetts, Vermont, and Virginia have family support legislation pending, as of 1995.

Table 3.   A statement in support of families and their children

These principles should guide public policy toward families of children with developmental disabilities. . .and
the actions of states and agencies when they become involved with families:

All children, regardless of disability, belong with families and need enduring relationships with adults.
   When states or agencies become involved with families, permanency planning should be a guiding
philosophy. As a philosophy, permanency planning endorses children's rights to a nurturing home and
consistent relationships with adults. As a guide to state and agency practice, permanency planning requires
family support, encouragement of a family's relationship with the child, family reunification for children
placed out of home, and the pursuit of adoption for children when family reunification is not possible.

Families should receive the supports necessary to maintain their children at home.
   Family support services must be based on the principle "whatever it takes." In short, family support services
should be flexible, individualized, and designed to meet the diverse needs of families.

Family supports should build on existing social networks and natural sources of support.
   As a guiding principle, natural sources of support, including neighbors, extended families, friends, and
community associations, should be preferred over agency programs and professional services. When states or
agencies become involved with families, they should support existing social networks, strengthen natural
sources of support, and help build connections to existing community resources. When natural sources of
support cannot meet the needs of families, professional or agency-operated support services should be
available.

Family supports should maximize the family's control over the services and supports they receive.
   Family support services must be based on the assumption that families, rather than states and agencies, are in
the best position to determine their needs.

Family supports should support the entire family.
   Family support services should be defined broadly in terms of the needs of the entire family, including
children with disabilities, parents, and siblings.

Family support services should encourage the integration of children with disabilities into the community.
   Family support services should be designed to maximize integration and participation in community life for
children with disabilities.

*When children cannot remain with their families for whatever reason, out-of-home placement should be viewed
initially as a temporary arrangement and efforts should be directed toward reuniting the family.*
   Consistent with the philosophy of permanency planning, children should live with their families whenever
possible. When, due to family crisis or other circumstances, children must leave their families, efforts should
be directed toward encouraging and enabling families to be reunited.

*When families cannot be reunited and when active parental involvement is absent, adoption should be
aggressively pursued.*
   In fulfillment of each child's right to a stable family and an enduring relationship with one or more adults,
adoption should be pursued for children whose ties with their families have been broken. Whenever possible,
families should be involved in adoption planning and, in all cases, should be treated with sensitivity and
respect. When adoption is pursued, the possibility of "open adoption," whereby families maintain involvement
with a child, should be seriously considered.

*Although a preferred alternative to any group setting or out-of-home placement, foster care should only be
pursued when children cannot live with their families or with adoptive families.*
   After families and adoptive families, children should have the opportunity to live with foster families. Foster
family care can provide children with a home atmosphere and warm relationships and is preferable to group
settings and other placements. As a state- or agency-sponsored program, however, foster care seldom provides
children the continuity and stability they need in their lives. Although foster families may be called upon to
assist, support, and occasionally fill in for families, foster care is not likely to be an acceptable alternative to
fulfilling each child's right to a stable home and enduring relationships.

Source: Center on Human Policy, Syracuse University (1987).

family support—appears in the budget of the Commonwealth of Pennsylvania in 1973. Other states may have allowed such expenditures prior to this but it was not declared public policy. Beginning in 1976, Minnesota began to experiment with cash subsidy programs for 50 families of children with disabilities. In 1983, in response to strong parent advocacy, the Michigan legislature passed a cash subsidy entitlement, modeled after the 1972 federal law creating an entitlement to cash assistance (up to $458 per month in 1995) called Supplemental Security Income (SSI). Both programs have narrow eligibility requirements but have given maximum autonomy to families regarding the use of the funds. In Michigan, families of children from birth to age 18 with the most severe disabilities receive $243 a month. At the end of each year, they are asked to fill out a simple form saying how they spent the money. In addition, they are given a consumer satisfaction survey that asks how they liked the program. They are treated like customers whose satisfaction matters to the state.

By giving resources directly to the consumer, the locus of control shifts from the service provider to the consumer. If all services were operated this way, the service system could be dramatically renovated and reinvented. Imagine if the $100,000 spent to keep a person in an institution went directly to that person and his or her family. The meeting to decide on the spending of the funds might look very different than current individualized program plan (IPP) meetings. The state of Michigan has kept data on family satisfaction with its stipend program and has consistently found that families consider the program to be helpful in assisting them to raise their children.

Whatever It Takes Motto

However, family support is not simply a matter of giving families money or vouchers. It entails a range of assistances that are flexibly designed to meet individual family needs. Early in the family support movement, the term *whatever it takes* became an important motto because it expresses the commitment to provide whatever is needed to make home life possible for children with disabilities and their families. Part of this flexibility means relying on the family's definition of membership, as the family can take many forms in present-day society. Programs must be able to equally help a single- or two-parent family, a large multigenerational family, or same-sex parents. They have to respond to families as they exist now, not upon an idealized image. This flexibility is particularly important in recognizing the needs of divorced and unmarried mothers who now make up a large and growing percentage of all families.

Additionally, family support aims to target the needs of all family members. Thus, family support workers need to ask after the well-being of grandparents and brothers and sisters, as well as the mother and father in two-parent families. In stepfamilies, they ask after the well-being of the stepparent and even the ex-spouse because these people, over the long term,

can represent some of the most important resources for a family member
with disabilities.

Investing in Human Capital

The economists have a term they use for investing resources in people—
human capital. Human capital means that investing in the education, training, and health of people provides long-term payoffs, as a result of having
more skilled and capable workers. Family support services represent an
investment in human capital. The community provides resources to family
members so that, over the long term, they are better able to provide support
to people with disabilities. One of the key characteristics of human capital
is that it requires early investments in order to yield later gains. In this case,
an investment in the family unit, early in a person's life, enables the family
to better provide a lifelong social network to the member with a disability.

In fact, this kind of family-based social network is typical for a majority
of people in the United States. Recent studies, for example, of intergenerational transfers of wealth and social support indicate that the majority of
elderly people give both financial and social assistance to adult children
and grandchildren until their very last years of life. It is clearly in the interests of society, as well as people with disabilities who have historically
been vulnerable because of stigma and discrimination, to try to bolster these
kinds of support in collaboration with government. Otherwise, the duties
of family and friends devolve upon the state, which often does not do a
very good job of meeting human needs.

This flexible commitment of resources and services to the family does
not imply that the family should always be the locus of control. In this
respect, support should follow the norms established by the family's culture
regarding when and how the older child starts to become the director and
focus of services. By adulthood, people with disabilities should assume the
maximum control possible for the design of accommodations and supports
they need in order to exercise their choices and preferences and participate
in desirable community life. This transition of the locus of control also needs
to be fine-tuned and will require more attention from professionals, parents,
family members, researchers, and advocates.

What happens in the case of a child who has no home? There are some
parents and families who cannot or will not live with a child with severe
disabilities. According to the principles outlined in Table 3, the best option
is adoption. Some of the larger service regions in Michigan even have a
policy that no child will be placed in a nursing home, group home, or long-
term foster home. Every effort is made to provide whatever supports are
needed to keep children in their own homes. Sometimes this involves extremely costly services because the alternatives are understood to be either
highly expensive in dollars or extremely costly in terms of the child's well-
being. This policy agrees with the prominent notion in child protective services based on permanency planning for the child that foster homes should

be only used as temporary expedients while getting the family ready for reunification with the child. It says that it is best to put every possible resource into the home before removing the child; if removal is needed and reunification cannot be accomplished, the child should be put up for adoption as soon as possible so that he or she will have a permanent home.

In the new approach to family support, families have maximum flexibility and control in deciding how resources will be used to benefit them. However, some fear that people will be dishonest and misuse public resources after hearing countless stories of welfare fraud and misuse of public funds. Experience with family support for families of children with disabilities in states like Michigan and Minnesota provides evidence to the contrary. Table 4 shows an evaluation of support services in Michigan. It lists the ways that families have made use of public money. A number of parents used the funds to buy clothing, educational aids, and toys. Comparing the costs of child's blue jeans at a discount store with the costs in mail order catalogs for jeans made for children who must wear diapers past age 2 shows that the price tag is almost triple for the special pants. In the same way, the cost of even the simplest adapted toy is at least $30 more than regular toys. Tables 5 and 6 show families' reactions to the Michigan subsidy.

Table 4. Categories of use for the Michigan subsidy

Category	Percent
Clothing (1)	83.8
Educational aids and toys (2)	63.4
General household expenses (3)	60.6
Sitters for child with handicaps (4)	56.1
Medical expenses and health related needs (5)	54.6
Diapers (6)	50.3
Transportation expenses (7)	43.1
Special foods (8)	37.9
Adaptive equipment for child with disability (9)	28.4
Respite care for child with disability (10)	23.1
Home renovation projects (11)	10.7
Care for children without disabilities (12)	10.3
Camp (13)	9.7
Physical or speech therapy (14)	6.8
Counseling services (15)	5.1
Nursing respite care (16)	3.6
Home nursing care (17)	2.2

$N = 1,283$.

Parenthetical notations indicate rank.

In the actual survey, *handicap* was used in place of *disability*.

Table 5. Impact of subsidy on families: Distribution of responses

| | Participant responses | | | | |
Areas of impact	Very greatly	Greatly	Some	A little	Not at all
Improved overall lifestyle of family	20.9	33.7	33.0	9.2	3.1
Improved ability of family to care for child with disability	28.5	35.2	25.8	6.5	3.9
Helped family do more things together	27.3	28.0	27.7	9.8	7.2
Eased family's financial worries	33.0	26.5	26.0	9.9	4.6
Reduced family's level of stress	25.3	23.8	31.4	12.0	7.5

Note: Figures represent percentages of the distribution of answers of the 1,283 families participating in the subsidy.

Respite Care

Michigan parents also use these discretionary funds to pay for "sitter services." This kind of respite care provides an important example of how giving resources directly to the family can make a service more accessible and typical for families. If families are given the funds directly, they can arrange their own sitter service and have the stability and continuity of a regular sitter; they have the flexibility to pay a grandparent, neighbor, high school student who lives across the street, or family friend to take care of their child. By contrast, if those funds are given to an agency that disperses respite services to families, the agency has to set up training programs and, in many cases, certification requirements, limiting the pool of people available to the family to a select list of approved providers. Once the supply

Table 6. Satisfaction with subsidy: Distribution of responses

| | Participant responses | | | | |
Areas of satisfaction	Very dissatisfied	Dissatisfied	Neutral	Satisfied	Very satisfied
Amount of subsidy	2.1	6.3	22.7	52.2	16.8
Initial application procedure	1.8	2.0	10.3	55.1	30.7
Yearly reapplication procedure	2.4	3.7	11.7	52.0	30.2
CMH's handling of application	2.4	1.4	6.0	47.7	42.7
Information received about the program	3.3	3.6	8.4	49.0	35.8

Note: Figures represent percentages of the distribution of answers of the 1,283 families participating in the subsidy.

of respite workers is limited in this way, the family's choice is reduced dramatically. The family is likely to have to schedule 3–4 weeks ahead of time, thereby distorting the typical process of obtaining child care so that a family must learn to operate under a completely different set of rules and standards simply because they have a child with a disability.

Giving funds directly to parents also enables families to draw upon natural sources of social support in the community. In most neighborhoods, there is a pool of people who help with child care—high school students, college kids, men or women who provide care in their homes for children, and relatives. These people make up a network of informal supports to families who may be excluded if respite providers are professionalized and certified. Instead, these existing social support networks should be open to all children, regardless of their special caregiving needs. Sometimes people in these networks will need some special training, which can usually be provided by family members. Or, if the family really needs someone with special training, they can use their extra funds to purchase the time of a trainer to work with neighborhood or family members who could be respite providers if they had the skills.

Leveraging Existing Resources

Allocating resources to families and generic community institutions in family support programs has another kind of economic benefit. Building upon and leveraging existing resources, programs can be multiplied. For example, opening up an after-school YMCA latchkey program to kids with disabilities by adding staff and providing extra training, instead of building a separate center for kids with disabilities and hiring a whole new staff, leverages the existing community resources—the YMCA's building and staff, in this case. Economists view this change as cost shifting—the costs of care are shifted from a narrow stream of funding to a broader pool of economic resources. In the long run, there may not be cost savings in cost shifting, but the benefits may extend to more people and the community may become a very different, more open and inclusive place than it would have been otherwise. Providing respite, stipends, and whatever it takes, instead of replacing the family with a whole new social system (a 24-hour-a-day staff, a new house, monitoring personnel) leverages the natural or expected care that a family provides by enlisting them as partners in care—one of the strongest arguments for shifting public policy to enhance the capabilities of families and communities to meet the needs of people with disabilities.

Customer Satisfaction

Another important practice that the people in Michigan have adopted is conducting customer satisfaction surveys, treating families as the consumers of a service that the state provides. Again, this approach to evaluation of customer satisfaction represents a considerable change in orientation from the attitude of many human services. The practice of evaluating customer satisfaction is used widely in the private service sector. Most restaurants and hotels have an evaluation form that asks about how customers were treated and whether the service lived up to their expectations. The people in these corporations have learned to pay attention to the results of these surveys as their income is dependent upon pleasing their customers.

The Role of Family Support Professionals

Is there a place for family support professionals in this system? Some states have chosen a somewhat different model of family support that provides a family support worker/broker, in addition to having flexible funds available to families. These states have been careful to avoid calling these workers case managers because they do not want the workers to carry out the roles of traditional, service-oriented social workers who often focus upon eligibility, protection against fraud, and social control. Families also tell us they do not want to be referred to as "cases" and they do not want their lives "managed." Family support for families of young people with disabilities has to be designed for people in all social classes; it is not a poverty program. Middle- and upper-income families have children with disabilities and also encounter many unusual expenses and demands that require some assistance from the larger society. However, these families are not used to being treated as cases. They expect services that are responsive to the customer because, if they do not get the kind of service they desire, they can take their dollars elsewhere.

Disability family support services are provided across social classes, and the models and methods that have been applied in many poverty programs are not palatable to this larger group of consumers. Families do not want to be asked a lot of personal questions that ensure they have the right motives. They do not want the power to be in the hands of professionals. Services designed to apply across social classes are different from services designed as part of a safety net for the poorest of families and children. As a result, the states that have personnel to provide family support services have chosen to call these front-line workers *family support coordinators/brokers* or *family support workers*, whose work is dramatically different than traditional case managers.

EXAMPLES OF STATE-RUN FAMILY SUPPORT PROGRAMS

In states like Wisconsin and New Hampshire, the new family support coordinators see their job as assisting families to identify their goals and unmet needs through conversation, not formal assessment. The family support coordinator is someone who is extremely knowledgeable about the resources, both formal and informal, that are available in the community. This information and referral role is one of the most important parts of the job.

In addition to providing information and linking families to other sources of support, family support coordinators aim to enable or empower a family—leaving them better equipped to handle their own problems. Empowerment incorporates many different interactions with the family, including linking them to other families who can model coping skills, coaching a family member on how to handle the situation so that he or she acquires new skills, informing a family member of his or her legal rights, or going with the family to a difficult meeting and modeling how to interact in an assertive way. The family support worker also strives to integrate the family into the community by helping them build social ties. Community integration activities may include convening a group of potential supporters who could work together to assist the families, arranging child care so that parents can participate in religious services regularly, or connecting siblings to other brothers and sisters of children with disabilities.

The design of family support services differs from state to state. Some states, such as Iowa and Michigan, have emphasized transferring funds directly to the families via a state-run program.

Table 7 summarizes data from Iowa about how families have chosen to use funds in their family support program. Comparing Iowa with Michigan shows that families used the funds differently. Iowa is a more rural state, while Michigan has more large urban areas. Thus, the families in Iowa used more of their support funds for transportation. These summative figures, however, tend to average out the individuality that marks these family support programs.

For example, one family, served by one of the new family support services, has a son with serious behavioral challenges—labeled as autism or emotional disorders. This family receives a variety of services through

Table 7.   Usage for the Iowa cash subsidy

Service/item purchased	Frequency of purchase
Sitter for child	83
Educational aids or toys for child	79
Transportation	77
Medical expenses and health-related items	75
Recreation	65
Respite care for child	54
Diapers	48
Adaptive equipment	47
Special foods	42
Home renovation	29
Insurance	22
Camp	18
Parent training	15
Individual or family counseling	14
Clothing	14
Therapy (physical, occupational, or speech)	11
Household expenses (to pay bills)	8
Homemaker services	6
Household items (miscellaneous household expenses)	3
Home nursing care	1

Note: The survey question was as follows: "Listed below are some services and items that may help families care for the special needs of their child with disabilities. Please indicate which of them your family has purchased with your family support subsidy."

school and the mental health system. With their family support funds, they chose to repair the walls and doors in their home. When their son is upset, he kicks the house and often makes holes in the walls or knocks the doors off their hinges.

These expenses would never be approved at a traditional IEP or IPP meeting—the professionals would say, "Sorry, that's a problem for the housing authority. We can't use our funds for home repairs." Because human services funds are always constrained and targeted to narrow categories, the formal service system has little flexibility to meet the unique needs that arise for families. One of the benefits of having funds that are earmarked to be used according to the wishes of the family is that of lived reality—the 24-hour-a-day experience that families have with disability. The needs and concerns that are embedded in this lived reality can be the target for support because the family is given charge. As a result, a family who wants to have a repair person come and put plaster over holes in the wall so that they feel comfortable having friends over for dinner can have their needs met.

Other states have created regional or local family support workers who have the authority to issue vouchers or purchase services for family members. In Wisconsin, the services are administered at the county level and center around a family worker who can issue vouchers to families. In New Hampshire, the services are regionalized and located in nonprofit agencies set up to serve people with developmental disabilities. Each regional program has a council of family members who are authorized to decide how a family support budget will be used by their agency. These councils are intended to provide families with a direct voice in policy making and the allocation of funds to families. These states are serving as a kind of national laboratory for the development of new kinds of assistance to families. Figure 1 outlines Colorado's Family Support Council.

However, as new states begin to establish family support services, there will undoubtedly be some new designs. The innovative states are already beginning to furnish some important public policy data. Figure 2 presents evidence from Minnesota, comparing the numbers of people served and dollars expended before and after the court order and policy decision to downsize its state institutions to create family support services. In 1980, prior to the court order to reallocate funds to the community, 830 children under 18 years of age were being served in public and private institutions at a cost of $20 million a year. After a court decision and major policy change in the state, by 1990 there were 291 children remaining in institutions and specialized foster care and 1,827 at home receiving family supports (Minnesota Disability Law Center, 1992). Adjusted for inflation, the state was actually spending less money ($24 million) for more children. In addition, the state provides 3,800 middle-income families with supplemental health insurance under Medicaid; they experienced an eligibility option available to all states (TEFRA 142–Katie Beckett) that allows them to waive

---

Colorado's family support council

Family support council is the group of people within the designated Community-Centered Board (CCB) local service area who have the responsibility for providing guidance and direction to the CCB for the implementation of the Family Support Services Program.

Membership:
- Each Council must have at least three members.
- The majority of the Council must be family members.
- The chairperson of the Council must be a member of an eligible family.
- Membership includes:
  - People with developmental disabilities
  - Members of families with a member with a developmental disability living at home

Responsibilities:
- Make recommendations to the CCB for the overall direction of the Family Support Services Program in the local service area.
- Be aware of the local community resources available to families.
- Provide guidance and assistance to the CCB in the development of a Family Support Plan and monitor the implementation plan.
- Prepare an annual written report to the Department of Institutions describing their involvement, including any recommendations or concerns.
- In cooperation with the CCB, set budget parameters for the program, including the maximum amount any one family may receive through the program in any given fiscal year and the distribution of funds across the four service categories.
- Make recommendations to the CCB for gathering information from the families who are enrolled or in need of the four service categories.
- Make recommendations on how to assist families transitioning out of the program.
- Make recommendations regarding proposed family supports or services not specifically listed in statute (Title 27-10.5-401, C.R.S.).
- Identify with the CCB the training needed by the members of the Council.
- Make recommendations for policies and procedures that are not provided for by the state.

Note: The local Family Support Council is *not* responsible, nor encouraged, to become involved in decisions regarding individual families. The Council's actions should be broader and address issues that impact families in general. The CCB is responsible for actual implementation of the Family Support Services Program.

Recruitment: The CCB is responsible for advertising, recruiting, and training the initial members of the Family Support Council. This initial selection process should include family participation. After the initial set-up, the Family Support Council will be responsible for establishing a process for maintaining an ongoing membership. There are no specific agencies or positions that must be represented on the Council other than members of eligible families. The nominations for the Council are subject to approval by the Board of Directors of the CCB to ensure that the minimum composition of the Council is maintained and that there is fair representation from a cross-section of families, including people of different cultures.

Monitoring:
- The effectiveness of public awareness and the services and supports provided in meeting the intent of the legislation
- The diversity of the families using the program in comparison to area demographics
- Family satisfaction with regard to the program over time
- The administrative practices of the CCB regarding the Family Support Services Program, including the implementation of the eligibility criteria

---

Figure 1.   An outline of Colorado's Family Support Council.

1980 FY actual spending	1990 FY actual spending

Over decade
20% Increase in spending
240% Increase in children served

$24.3 Million

$10,844,880
RTC 3 @ $233/day
ICF/MR 161 @ $110/day
MA Waiver Out-of-Home
127 @ $89/day
291 children in ICF/MR
(Public & Private) 1990

$13,433,314
MA CHO TEFRA (1523)
@ $14.15/day
Waiver in-Home 304
@ $40/day
Family Subsidy 418
@ $ 7.40/day

1827 children
served at home

$20.4 Million

RTC 245 @ $97/day = $8.7 Million
Private ICF/MR
585 @ $60/day = $11.7 Million
$20.4 Million
for 830 children

880 Children

Family Subsidy   50
Out of Home   830
Children Served   880

2118 Children

Family Supports 1827
Out of Home   291
Children Served 2118

1990 Cost if MN had not instituted Family Support and Community Services	1990 Cost with Family Support and Community Services

Projected Total
WITHOUT
Family Supports

$44.3 Million

Family Subsidy   50
Out of Home   830
Children Served   880

Actual FY 1990 Total
WITH
Family Supports

$24.3 Million

Family Supports 1827
Out of Home   291
Children Served 2118

$13,433,314

$13,433,314
MA CHCO TEFRA (1523)
@ $14.15/day
Waiver In-Home 304
@ $40/day
Family Subsidy 418
@ $7.40/day

1827 children
served at home

$44,343,775

RTC 245 @ $233/day
Children
Private 585 @ $110/day
830 children in ICF/MR
(Public & Private) 1980

$150,000 = 50 families
Family Subsidy
1980

$10,844,880

RTC 3 @ $233/day
ICF/MR 161 @ $110/day
MA Waiver Out-of-Home
127 @ $89/day
291 children in ICF/MR
(Public & Private) 1990

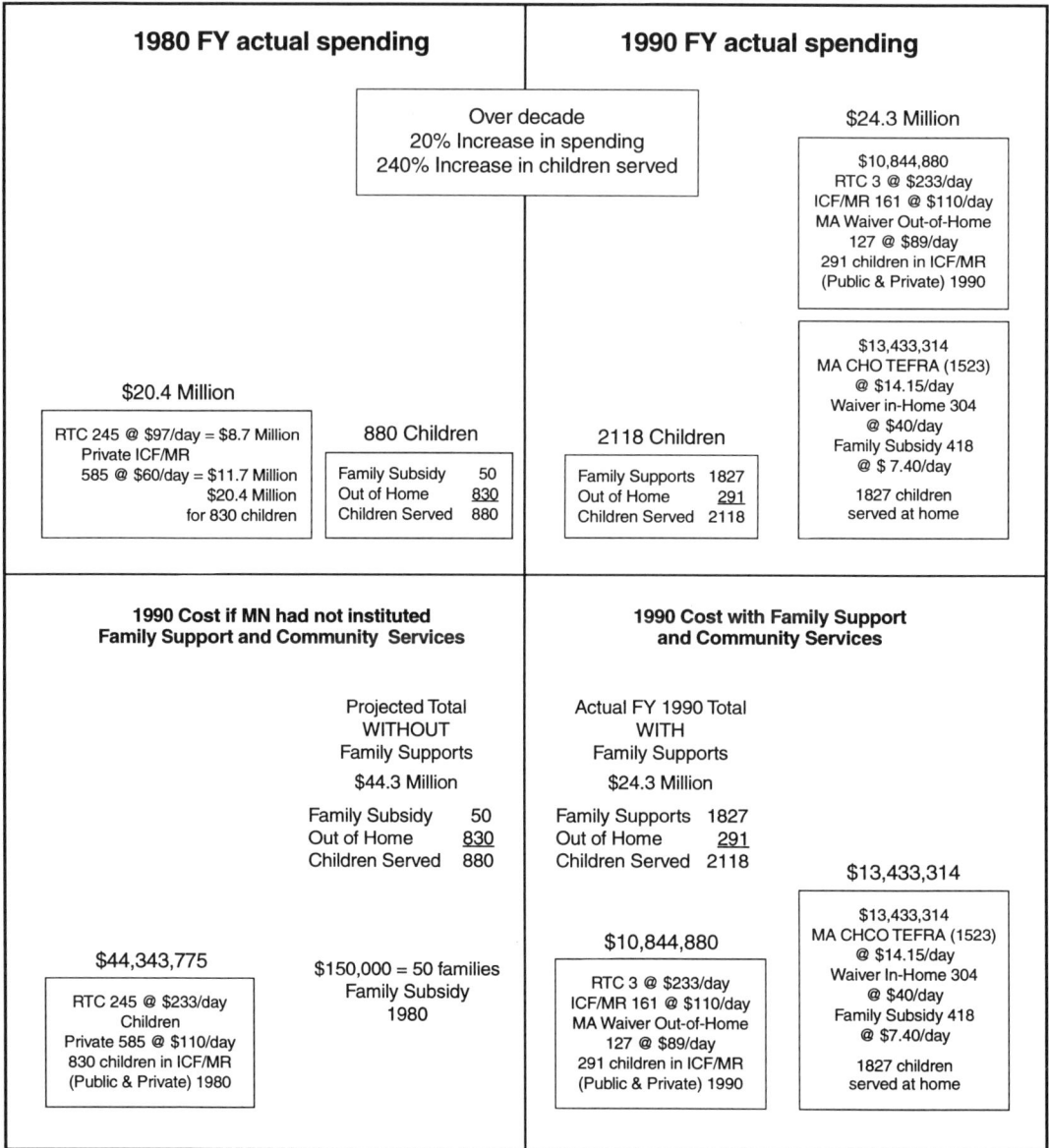

Figure 2.   A comparison of people served and dollars expended in Minnesota before and after downsizing state institutions to create family support services.

the usual income and asset limits for Medicaid, provided they are serving children at high risk of institutionalization.

The most important point illustrated by the Minnesota data is that when public policy changes from a focus on crisis intervention for children who have been placed out of home to a more preventive, proactive approach to build the capacity of families and communities to serve children, it is possible to actually serve larger numbers of people. Another point to note is if Minnesota had kept those same 830 children in institutions, the cost for them in 1994 dollars would have been $44 million dollars, instead of $24 million. The state saved money, expanded the numbers of children served, and served the children and their families in a more valued context through this policy shift.

Other states using a more family-centered service approach have also reported positive reactions to the change. In New York, "95% of the responding families indicated that the reimbursement services helped them, and 99% rated them as either 'good' or 'excellent' " (*Family Support Bulletin,* 1992–1993, p. 19). In West Virginia, the family support program has greatly reduced costs. The average institution costs for an individual, which can easily total $60,000 annually, are now leveraged to families caring for members with disabilities in the home and average only $1,000 annually. However, in 1992–1993, only 600 of the 10,000 families with members with disabilities were served. Still, of those 600 families, 99% report that their quality of life has improved as a result of the program, and 95% feel that they have an active role in decision making. One family member said, "This is the first time anyone has ever helped our family in any way" (*Family Support Bulletin,* 1992–1993, p. 15).

IMPLICATIONS FOR FUTURE PROGRAM DEVELOPMENT

A profile of the basic components necessary for a family support system has been developed, based upon the experience of the states that have been innovators in family support services. Table 8 lists these program elements. First is guiding legislation that establishes principles of family support. The values behind this policy innovation make an enormous difference; therefore, a clear statement of the guiding principles enacted into law is needed. These values include a recognition of the vital importance of families in the lives of people with disabilities, an attitude that respects the variety of family forms, a commitment to letting families determine their own needs, and a commitment from the community to assist families in caring for people with disabilities. In addition, the guiding legislation must create policy-making bodies that are dominated by people with disabilities and their family members. Control of the policy-making apparatus must be in the hands of the people who will be served. Furthermore, the guiding legislation must commit to providing flexible funds, as well as a basic core of services, for families. These core services include family support coordina-

Table 8.   Fourteen components of a comprehensive system of family support

1.   Legislative mandate
2.   Guiding principles
3.   Family focus
4.   Parental control
5.   Parent oversight
6.   Flexible funding
7.   Core services in place
8.   Service brokerage
9.   Interagency collaboration
10.   Inclusive eligibility
11.   Statewide
12.   Medicaid policy
13.   Community centered
14.   Active outreach

Source: Human Services Research Institute,
1990.

tion, respite care, special therapies, flexible funds, information and referral
services, and linkages to other families.

One of the recommended principles, based upon the experience in
these pioneering states, is that the family support legislation should have
inclusive cross-disability eligibility, rather than strict, narrowly targeted categorical eligibility. To date, most of the state models have focused on children with developmental disabilities, with an emphasis usually on children
with the most severe disabilities in this group, which leads to problems
with equity. In some states, families who have almost identical support
needs are not both eligible for support because of a categorical eligibility
requirement.

For example, the family support system in New Hampshire is primarily set up to serve children with mental retardation and other disabilities.
In the same town, the family of one child who uses a wheelchair and needs
a ramp to get into his house can qualify for help from a family support
coordinator who might organize a volunteer group to build the ramp and
use some flexible family support funds to pay for the wood. However,
another family of a child who also uses a wheelchair may not be eligible
for services because she does not experience cognitive disabilities. Too often
in the recent family support movement, entire groups of children and families have been excluded, including children with complex medical conditions, children with physical disabilities, and children with severe emotional
problems. For this reason, PL 103-382 defines disability broadly with the
intent that states will begin planning for all families of children with special
needs.

The new federal law represents 8 years of grass roots and national
leadership effort to convince legislators that federal policy should aim for
family support initiatives. The law begins with a statement of values: "It is
in the best interests of our nation to preserve, strengthen, and maintain the
family." Furthermore, it states that families are a great national resource in

the care of people with disabilities, seeking empowerment to better meet their concerns and those of their members with disabilities. Thus, the purpose of the law is to strengthen families by supporting their capacity to care for family members with disabilities by empowering them.

The legislation also states that many families now experience significant physical and emotional challenges in providing care at home for members with disabilities. These challenges include financial disincentives, an institutional bias in funding of services, and severely limited access to a family-centered service for information and coordination. Goals of the law include establishing family supports that will enable families to nurture and enjoy their children at home and make informed choices and decisions. After stating these basic values, the law encourages states to create planning entities that can improve or establish family supports.

This new federal law is a systems change act; that is, it is designed to encourage states to follow the lead of those pioneering states that have begun to set up community-based support systems for families. The law, when funded, will provide planning grants to states on a competitive basis. States need to create planning councils that will represent the different agencies that work with families but are still dominated by families. The law spells out the basic principles for these state planning entities and describes some of the characteristics of the service system that states should develop; some of these are listed in Table 9. However, it does not create a

Table 9.   The National Conference of State Legislatures (NCSL) task force on developmental disabilities recommendations for state legislatures

1. Create and fund family support programs for those families who provide care at home for their children with developmental disabilities, adhering to the following guiding principles:
    - The program should support the family rather than the service provider.
    - All children, regardless of disability, have the right to grow up with a family, biological or otherwise, and need enduring relationships with adults.
    - The role families play in providing care at home must be recognized and supported so that family members are enabled and empowered to make informed decisions.
    - Means for supporting family efforts should build on existing support networks and natural sources of support within the community and should be culturally sensitive.
2. Provide flexible programs to meet the needs of individual families, recognizing that their needs change over time.
3. Require coordination of all family support-related activities undertaken by state agencies, such as departments of developmental disabilities, education, human resources, public welfare, and mental health.
4. Use all public and private sector resources available to families, including government agencies, private employers, and private health insurers.
5. Ensure adequate training for people who provide family support.
6. Design all family support initiatives to promote the integration of people with disabilities into the community.
7. Monitor the quality and effectiveness of all service programs through systematic reviews, which should include input from consumer families.
8. Define family support as a benefit program that is not included as income for purposes of state taxation.
9. Provide independent living and work training to youth with disabilities to facilitate transition into adulthood and to promote independence.

Source: National Conference of State Legislature's Policy (1991).

new funding stream for family support services. As a result, states are going to have to learn to make use of existing funding streams, as well as generate new funds out of the state general funds.

The lack of new federal funds to accompany the Families of Children with Disabilities Support Act of 1994 need not deter states from moving ahead. One of the lessons to be learned from states like Minnesota, New Hampshire, New York, West Virginia, and Wisconsin is that family support services can be created by learning how to redirect public funds. By identifying the institutional biases in existing programs and making use of waivers, it is possible to redirect existing public funds in order to support families. As part of their planning efforts, states will need to closely examine how funds are allocated now. By giving primacy to the values and principles that underlie the new approach of community building in disability policy, there is a great potential for redirecting funds in ways that better open up inclusive communities for all children and their families.

Chapter Review

CHALLENGES

- From 1850 to the 1970s (Phase 1), policy emphasized removal and separation of people with disabilities; medical professionals dominated decisions about labeling, treatment, and care; and public funds were spent almost exclusively on large institutions.
- Also in Phase 1, children with disabilities were excluded from public school and adults with disabilities were excluded from work and community living.
- Although their populations have declined since the mid-1970s, institutions are very expensive and still use a major proportion of resources for people with disabilities.
- In the 1970s and 1980s (Phase 2), policy emphasized the creation of a continuum of community services. Funds were invested in building centers and congregate care programs in the community, rather than in individuals with disabilities.
- People with disabilities have been required to demonstrate certain skill levels before they could have access to typical community settings.

CHARACTERISTICS OF HELPFUL PROGRAMS

- Resources are put into providing whatever support is needed to allow people with disabilities to participate in typical, generic community settings and activities.
- The central role of the family is recognized and resources are channeled to families.
- There is an emphasis on flexibility and true individualization.
- Service providers seek active input from family members and people with disabilities; parents and family members are encouraged to envision desired lifestyles and outcomes for their relatives with disabilities—these dreams are used to shape individualized programs.
- People with disabilities are provided with education, supports, and accommodations that permit them to determine their own lifestyles.

POLICY IMPLICATIONS

- Family support is comprehensive, based on a philosophy of *do whatever it takes*.

- Services should accept the family's definition of family membership and accommodate all family forms and all social classes with widely inclusive eligibility rules.
- Services should bolster informal social support networks rather than supplant them.
- Families should be given maximum flexibility and control in determining how resources will be used and should help set policy for programs.
- Programs should conduct customer satisfaction surveys.

References

Boswell, J. (1988). *Kindness of strangers*. New York: Random House.

Center on Human Policy. (1987). *A statement in support of families and their children*. Syracuse, NY: Author.

Education for all Handicapped Children Act of 1975, PL 94-142. (August 23, 1977). Title 20, U.S.C. 1401 et seq: *U.S. Statutes at Large, 89*, 773–796.

Families of Children with Disabilities Support Act of 1994, PL 103-382. (October 20, 1994). Title 20, U.S.C. 1491 et seq: *U.S. Statutes at Large, 108*, 3937.

Family Support Bulletin. (1992–1993). *Winter*. Washington, DC: Human Services Research Institute, United Cerebral Palsy Associations, Inc.

Howe, S.G. (1866). *The nature of institutions*. Boston.

Human Services Research Institute. (1990). *Family support services in the United States: An end of decade status report*. Cambridge, MA: Author.

Individuals with Disabilities Education Act of 1990 (IDEA), PL 101-476. (October 30, 1990). Title 20, U.S.C. 1400 et seq: *U.S. Statutes at Large, 104*, 1103–1151.

Luckasson, R., Coulter, D.L., Polloway, E.A., Reiss, S., Schalock, R.L., Snell, M.E., Spitalnik, D.M., & Stark, J.A. (1992). *Mental retardation: Definition, classification, and systems of support workbook*. Washington, DC: American Association on Mental Retardation.

Minnesota Disability Law Center. (1992). *Residential services for children with developmental disabilities in Minnesota*, St. Paul, MN: Author.

National Conference of State Legislature's Policy. (1991). *Recommendations for state action*, Denver, CO: Author.

PARC v. Commonwealth of Pennsylvania. 334 F. Supp. 1257; 343 F. Supp. 279.

Seligman, M., & Darling, R.B. (Eds.). (1989). *Ordinary families, special children: A systems approach to childhood disability*. New York: Guilford Press.

Index